NEBRASKA

NORTH PLATTE R.

PLATTE R.

IOWA

INDIANA

MISSOURI R.

ILLINOIS

W9-ATH-523

Fort Leavenworth

Westport

KENTUCKY

SOUTH PLATTE R.

KANSAS R.

MISSOURI

OHIO R.

KANSAS

Pueblo

Bent's Fort

TENNESSEE

ARKANSAS R.

ARKANSAS

Fort Smith

OKLAHOMA

MISSISSIPPI R.

MEXICO

CLAIMED BY TEXAS

Fort Towson

RED R.

SABINE R.

Natchitoches

T E X A S

Nacogdoches

LOUISIANA

New Orleans

Austin

CLAIMED BY MEXICO

San Antonio

Presidio
del Río Grande

NUECES R.

CONCHOS R.

Corpus Christi

RIO GRANDE

Monclova

Palo Alto

× Resaca de la Palma

Fort Brown

Camargo

Matamoros

×
Saltillo × Monterrey

Parras

×

Buena Vista

GULF OF

MEXICO

Durango

Victoria

Mazatlán

Tampico

San Luis Potosí

PÁNUCO R.

Statute miles

0   300

palacios

Tuxpan

Chapultepec   Guadalupe
Molino del Rey   Hidalgo
Churubusco   ×× Mexico City
Padierna   ××

Jalapa   × Cerro Gordo
× Vera Cruz

Frontera

Puebla

By John Edward Weems

To Conquer a Peace (1974)
Dream of Empire (1971)
Men Without Countries (1969)
Peary: The Explorer and the Man (1967)
Race for the Pole (1960)
Fate of the *Maine* (1958)
A Weekend in September (1957)

Growing Up in Texas (CONTRIBUTOR, 1972)
The Schiwetz Legacy (CONTRIBUTOR, 1972)
A Vanishing America (CONTRIBUTOR, 1964)
U.S.S. *Ashtabula:* Her History
(CONTRIBUTOR AND EDITOR, 1946)

TO
Conquer
A
Peace

TO
Conquer
A
Peace

THE
WAR BETWEEN
THE UNITED STATES
AND MEXICO

John Edward Weems

1974
DOUBLEDAY & COMPANY, INC.
GARDEN CITY, NEW YORK

Quoted material from *Fifty Years in Camp and Field: Diary of Major-General Ethan Allen Hitchcock*, edited by W. A. Croffut, is used by permission of G. P. Putnam's Sons. Copyright 1909 by G. P. Putnam's Sons.

Quoted material from *Polk: The Diary of a President, 1845–1849*, edited by Allan Nevins (revised edition), is used by permission of David McKay Company, Inc. Copyright 1952 by Longmans, Green and Company, Inc.

Quoted material from *To Mexico with Scott: Letters of Captain E. Kirby Smith to His Wife*, prepared for the press by his daughter, Emma Jerome Blackwood, is used by permission of Harvard University Press. Copyright 1917 by Harvard University Press.

Photographs of Ulysses Grant, Robert E. Lee, and Winfield Scott from *Texas and the Mexican War*, by Nathaniel W. Stephenson (vol. 24, *Yale Chronicles of America*) are used by permission of United States Publishers Association, Inc.

For Jane

Some men in government during the administration of James K. Polk used a four-word maxim to describe the goal of the United States in the war against Mexico, which resulted from years of bickering and bitterness between the two nations. A paraphrase was used even by General Winfield Scott, a Whig and thus a political opponent of Democrat Polk. The words were

"to conquer a peace."

PREFACE

The text of this book represents not a catalogue of names, dates, and statistics of the war between the United States and Mexico but an attempt to tell the story of that conflict and to depict its color, drama, tragedy, and meaning mainly through the use of ten principal characters who participated in the war and who left behind written accounts.

Unfortunately, but for good and obvious reasons, first-person accounts from the Mexican side are scarce. Nevertheless, I have sought to show as well as I can how the war appeared to a Mexican.

The ten principal characters enter the story in this order:

Sam French, an artillery lieutenant and a recent graduate of the United States Military Academy.

Sam Grant, an infantry lieutenant who graduated from West Point with French and who became known later as General Ulysses S. Grant.

Ephraim Kirby Smith, an infantry captain and a brother of the Civil War general, Edmund Kirby Smith.

Antonio López de Santa Anna, the Mexican political and military leader.

James K. Polk, President of the United States from 1845 to 1849.

Ethan Allen Hitchcock, grandson of Ethan Allen and a lieutenant colonel in the United States Army.

John C. Frémont, captain in the Topographical Corps of the U. S. Army and an early traveler in California.

John T. Hughes, a Missouri cavalry volunteer—from his job as schoolteacher—for Stephen Kearny's Army of the West.

Joseph Warren Revere, grandson of Paul Revere, who participated in the California drama as a lieutenant aboard the U.S.S. *Portsmouth.*

Robert E. Lee, then a relatively unknown captain of engineers in the U. S. Army.

Among them, these ten individuals figured in most of the important events in every sector of the war theater, and in many unimportant happenings. Other persons enter the story, of necessity, but the focus is on these principal characters.

CONTENTS

xiii

PART III
War
FROM MAY 1846
TO SEPTEMBER 1846

PART IV
Changing Strategy
FROM SEPTEMBER 1846
TO MARCH 1847

PART V
An Elusive Peace
FROM APRIL 1847
TO JULY 4, 1848

ILLUSTRATIONS

MAPS

PLATES

following page 70

President Polk
Sarah Polk
Captain Robert E. Lee
Lieutenant Sam—Ulysses—Grant
Ethan Allen Hitchcock
Captain Ephraim Kirby Smith
General Winfield Scott
Antonio López de Santa Anna
View of the Capitol at Washington
Executive Mansion
Sutter's Fort
Monterey Bay, California

following page 166

Camp of the Army of Occupation at Corpus Christi
Battles of Palo Alto and Resaca de la Palma
Heights of Monterrey, Mexico
Riding a Donkey
Using a Lariat

xvii

Illustrations

following page 310

Tampico
General Taylor's Kitchen
A Camp Washing Day
Battle of Buena Vista
Landing on the Beach Near Vera Cruz

following page 406

U. S. Naval Battery at Vera Cruz
U.S.S. *Mississippi* Battling a Storm off Vera Cruz
General Scott's Entrance into Mexico City
Inauguration of General Zachary Taylor

PROLOGUE

Distant Cannon

Offshore, in predawn gloom, gentle swells raised every vessel of the anchored fleet in slow succession, then quietly lowered each craft into its own small trough away to seaward. Along the flat coastline other small swells spent themselves on the land, lapping it softly in a rhythmical series of sighs, while, nearby, most men of Zachary Taylor's tired army slept.

Inlets, lagoons, and bays of the Gulf of Mexico are shallow. From them the land rises gradually, and in times of poor visibility almost imperceptibly when viewed from a distance, especially along this stretch of Texas coast. In the early morning hours of May 3, 1846, water and earth would have seemed to blend, a quiet union of those two primeval elements.

Some distance inland, on the adjacent coastal plains, playful Gulf breezes skipped across fields of waist-high saw grass, creating more pleasant, peaceful sounds for any man who could hear: soft rustlings across the land—more sighs of nature. An army awaiting battle in the midst of this serenity seemed particularly out of harmony with the universe, but the tranquillity was deceptive. Along this same coastline a storm-whipped Gulf of Mexico could make any dreamer forget the gentle sighing sounds of surf and breeze and send him running for safety, if he could find any, from battering waves and shrieking winds that assailed the unprotected shore and left it a morass for miles inland. Usually such a phenomenon might be anticipated during the peak of hurricane season, toward the end of summer, but on the Gulf Coast catastrophic gales could blow any time of the year. Powerful north winds—"northers"—could sink vessels at sea and, near land, could pick up and throw enough sand to fill in a watery sea pass six feet deep and a hundred feet wide. Subject to these poundings, this Gulf shoreline changed in some places more than fifteen hundred feet during a hundred-year period of record-keeping.

Even those lush meadows of tall coastal grass, billowy in the Gulf breeze, deceived a man. Taylor's army had tramped through that area the day before, and his soldiers had found that the luxuriant growth sometimes concealed mud and pools of water through which men on foot had stumbled and sloshed while, from above, a bald sun had steamed them all into enervation. Even with solid ground underfoot the men had enjoyed little real relief, for in dry places, they suspected, rattlesnakes might be lurking. To one man, at least, the distance covered had seemed twice as long as it actually was.

The march of about thirty roundabout miles to their present location, Point Isabel, had begun in midafternoon of the first day of May—two days earlier—from Fort Texas, a spacious earthen fortification thrown up by craggy-faced General Taylor at a position on the north bank of the mud-colored Rio Grande opposite the Mexican town of Matamoros. Taylor had been ordered there by the President of the United States ostensibly to protect the former Mexican territory of Texas (and more recently the self-declared Republic of Texas) from invasion by the previous owners following its annexation as the twenty-eighth state in the North American union. In late March Taylor's engineers had begun constructing the sturdy, six-sided, bastioned fort, enclosed by walls built eventually to a height of nine feet and a thickness of fifteen feet at the base. Inside, more than two thousand men could be sheltered. For additional security a deep, dry moat surrounded the walls. Artillerymen had manned Taylor's promptly emplaced 18-pounder siege guns and had aimed them across the river at Matamoros.

Despite this activity, Taylor had sought to persuade the Mexican commander of the peacefulness of his mission, but the Mexican had answered with threats, not thanks. Some members of Taylor's patrols probing the Fort Texas side of the river had been fired upon, first by irregulars —*rancheros*—then by Mexican troops who had crossed the Rio Grande to launch their attack. Some of Taylor's men had been killed, and the general had sent off to Washington a messenger bearing details of these tragedies.

Next, Taylor had learned from his spy companies that Mexican troops had crossed the Rio Grande in force, apparently moving to threaten his base at Point Isabel, where his supplies arrived by sea from New Orleans, and to isolate Fort Texas, which already needed replenishment. Acting quickly, he had left as a garrison force at Fort Texas five hundred able troops, a number of laundry women who had accompanied the soldiers to their new station, and all the men on the sick list. With the remaining two thousand or so troops he had begun his hurried, grueling march northeastward away from the river: through rough, prickly chaparral country thick with dense mats of thorny bushes, across a few open prairies, and through those fields of tall coastal grass, to Point Isabel.

Surprisingly, Taylor had encountered no Mexican force on the way, but he had felt little relief from anxiety. After his officers had allowed the weary marchers a few hours' sleep sometime after midnight of May 1–2 on chilly, exposed ground where they had halted, the command had ordered all troops up again for a quick, cold breakfast without coffee and had prodded them once more toward Point Isabel, where the exhausted army had arrived about noon of the second.

General Taylor's lightly fortified supply depot there carried the grandiose name of Fort Polk, after the President of the United States. For defense it relied largely on some earthen breastworks quickly thrown up around the twenty-foot-high prominence of the point, the only elevated ground in the entire area. Because of Gulf shallowness none of Taylor's supply operations in the vicinity showed much efficiency, but locating the depot at Point Isabel had seemed to be the only choice possible.

A more logical selection might have been somewhere around the mouth of the Rio Grande—nine miles farther south and about twice that distance down the winding river from Fort Texas—but at that location a mud bar thrown up by the river as it swept into the Gulf obstructed navigation. Elsewhere in the immediate area access to the mainland by deep-draft vessels was blocked by long, narrow, sandy islands offshore— all of them subject to storm-tide inundations. Opposite Point Isabel, however, lay a shallow inlet separating two of those islands. The pass, named Brazos Santiago (from "Arms of St. James" in Spanish), afforded no safe entry for larger vessels, but these ships could stand outside the inlet and dispatch cargo by boat through the pass to the supply depot. This they could do with confidence, because Mexico had no naval force to offer a challenge.

At Point Isabel the men of Taylor's army had toiled during the afternoon of the day of their arrival, helping hired Mexican laborers to load scores of wagons with ammunition, cannon, slabs of bacon, barrels of flour, and other supplies for Fort Texas, which now monopolized the general's thoughts.

That night the troops were given a brief respite from their work. They slept, guarded by sentinels who had not made the wearisome march from Fort Texas. Few of the tired men would have needed those rhythmical sighs from the nearby shore to lull them into slumber, and in the early morning hours of May 3, 1846, few of them would have heard the sounds.

On bare earth stretched a sleeping second lieutenant three years out of West Point. Twenty-seven-year-old Sam French, a solemn-faced officer assigned to the 3rd Regiment of Artillery, had been forced to leave behind a newly acquired friend at Fort Texas when he burned his letters, packed his "traps," struck his tent, and departed for Point Isabel: a mockingbird that had serenaded him daily from a perch on the ridgepole of French's tent. The lieutenant, who was susceptible to soft emotions despite aptitude for and love of his hard profession, had admitted to a feeling of sadness as he departed Fort Texas and saw, for the last time, his avian friend perched this time on a railing, singing for him one more happy song.

French's non-military sensibilities might have been passed on to him by his forebears. One ancestor named Thomas French had fled England for the American colonies to escape persecution following his abandonment of the Church of England in favor of the Society of Friends—the Quakers. Even now many members of the family professed Quakerism, including Sam French's father—although the Society of Friends no longer regarded Samuel French, Sr., as an orthodox member because he married "out of meeting." Aunts and uncles remained orthodox, however, and young Sam French had said good-by to them with some uneasiness before leaving his native New Jersey for an education at the United States Military Academy.

Lieutenant French claimed militant ancestors, too: "The Frenches were Normans and went to England with William the Conqueror. In after days some of the family went with Strongbow, the Earl of Pembroke, when he invaded Ireland and 'laid waste the country, reducing everything to subjection,' whereby they gained great possessions."

Perhaps Sam French was a young man who could serve two masters.

He always spoke proudly of his heritage—of his forebears both pacific and warlike. He was a young man who could feel sadness at parting from a singing mockingbird, and he could despise profane men around him who "cursed their Creator," as he put it. But he could write, as he did once, "War is not barbarous, nor is it 'hell'; it is just what parties choose to make it. When confined to the enlisted troops [meaning that civilians thus would be spared] it is seldom cruel."

The poetry in Sam French's soul seemed to ebb and flow, like the tide that ruled the sea near him while he slept on the ground at Point Isabel. Upon arrival there at midday of the second he had been delighted to see the "old ocean" again. He always enjoyed being near the sea and hearing its surging sounds.

Not far away from French, in a tent near the shore, slept another second lieutenant three years out of West Point. The two young men, both still bachelors, had graduated in the same class (of 1843) and they were both called Sam by fellow officers, but they differed in many ways.

Lieutenant Sam Grant, an Ohioan, did not display much feeling of pride in the military profession. In fact, enrolling at West Point had not been his own idea at all (as it had been French's), but his father's. Sam Grant had disliked, even hated, much of the time spent at the Academy, especially the first year or two, and he had hoped to be able to find a position with some small college as teacher of mathematics, thus to be able to resign from the Army at an early date.

This desire did not indicate that Grant had been a good student at West Point, only that mathematics had been a strong and a favorite subject. Unlike Sam French, whose scholastic record had been much better than average, Grant had completed his education with a standing somewhere around the middle of the class and had given most instructors an impression of being a person absolutely incapable of pushing himself to high effort. French's record had won him assignment to the artillery, which ranked just below the engineers as the plum West Point graduates might pick, but Grant had been given a choice only between the cavalry and the lowly infantry, and despite his acknowledged skill with horses and his choice of the cavalry he had been assigned to the 4th Infantry, where he would eventually be further assigned, against his wishes, to the utterly inglorious job of regimental quartermaster and commissary, a duty that required seeing after transportation of supplies and equipment and the animals used in that work. But at this time, at Point Isabel, Grant remained an untarnished infantry officer, lowly though he was.

The differences between French and Grant extended even to hearing ability. Sam Grant, tone deaf, would not have shared French's enjoyment of a singing mockingbird; Grant had been almost incapable of marching to music at the Military Academy. But Grant showed some advantages over his former classmate, although military men might not have admitted one of them. Whereas plain-faced Sam French would not have attracted much attention in a crowd, young Sam Grant often did, especially as an army man, because of his appearance. His fair skin, wavy hair, soft blue eyes, and apparently delicate five-foot, eight-inch frame made him look like something of a doll, as he was once described. Complementing his appearance was a shyness that made his movements awkward, particularly in early West Point days. Only when Grant rode horseback could he make much of a favorable impression on military colleagues. But "man proposes and God disposes," as Sam—Ulysses S.—Grant borrowed and wrote years later in his *Memoirs*, and now, despite his early abhorrence of a military career, he lay sleeping in a tent at sandy Point Isabel with the rest of Zachary Taylor's army.

Another infantry officer sleeping on that same shore offered as great a contrast to Grant as Grant did to French. Captain Ephraim Kirby Smith of the 5th Infantry, thirty-nine years of age, looked and acted like a soldier—and he was a good one, of twenty years' experience now, from a family that had provided Regular Army officers over a period of three generations. Smith's grandfather, Ephraim Kirby, had fought the British around Bunker Hill and elsewhere during the Revolutionary War. Smith's father, Joseph Lee Smith, had fought the British in the War of 1812. Furthermore, his brother, Edmund Kirby Smith (also present at Point Isabel), later was to become a noted Confederate general.

Captain Ephraim Kirby Smith's appearance implied military command to the highest professional degree. His face suggested responsibility, confidence, integrity: solid masculine features, deep-set bright eyes and a prominent nose, long, thick sideburns cultivated toward clean-shaven, firm lips that rarely opened unnecessarily. Nevertheless, Smith showed a gentle side, too. Once he persuaded a fellow officer to free a trembling antelope captured on a prairie; and he continually thanked God for "a glorious world."

Smith knew the names of many flowers. He loved to pluck them, and occasionally he pressed one to send home in a letter to his family—a wife and three children. He reveled in the beauties of nature—in the sight of the sparkling sea and of the wind-blown coastal grass, and in the gentle sounds to be heard around Point Isabel after the men had settled down for the night.

About dawn of May 3, before reveille, another sound startled Smith: a rumbling noise like distant thunder. Smith listened carefully and professionally, and he realized that man made this sound, although for twenty years now Smith had "worn the sword" without facing an enemy.

The rumbling awakened Lieutenant Sam French, sleeping on the soil of Point Isabel. He stirred, raised his head, rested it on his arm, heard nothing more, and lay back. Then he felt the ground vibrate beneath him and heard "the boom! boom! of distant cannon." Other men heard it, too, and Fort Polk came awake.

From inside his tent Lieutenant Sam Grant realized the meaning of the low grumbles coming from the direction of Fort Texas, although he "had never heard a hostile gun before." Once more the cannon were calling men of intelligence, gentility, and sensitivity to kill—to forget the possibilities of "a glorious world" and to inflict destruction on one another the way nature sometimes did to itself in this very region. For a moment Grant (as he indicated later) wondered about the reactions of the men now astir around him—General Taylor and others. Would they "chafe to get into the fray?" Grant doubted that many men would, particularly those who talked most about it. As for himself, facing war from the present loneliness of an army tent, there was no escaping his own feeling.

Later he recorded it. "I felt sorry," he wrote, "that I had enlisted."

PART I

The Beginnings

FROM 1783
TO JUNE 1845

1.

Background for Conflict

A needless but inevitable war between the United States and Mexico had been coming for years. The conflict actually had been predestined when Anglo-Saxon colonists settled along the eastern coast of the North American continent and, after a time, began looking westward. But when war finally came it resulted directly from various aggressions, mistakes, and blunders committed by both sides. Sincere desire for peace by either the United States or Mexico might have prevented war, but the self-righteous aggressiveness of land-seeking North Americans aroused Mexican suspicion and hostility, which in turn spurred Latin pride beyond any possibility of peaceful discussion of problems—a development that some important and confident officials in the United States did not regret at all.

A common bond might have seemed to unite the two young nations: independence won after revolt against European monarchies. But the facts of history, together with cultural differences between the two countries, precluded the development of many bonds in those early years and provided only a background for conflict.

In a treaty of peace signed in 1783 Great Britain, beset by other difficulties nearer home, had acknowledged the independence of the former North American colonies, and the newly created United States of America had begun a noble experiment that reached far beyond the organization of a new national government: first, an assertion that all men are created equal, then a declaration that governments, which must function with the consent of the governed, have the responsibility of assuring citizens the rights of life, liberty, and the pursuit of happiness, or be subject to overthrow by their people if those rights are not made

3

secure—all this in an age when many men still acknowledged the divine right of kings to rule, and when a man born into any given station was almost certain to remain there for the rest of his life.

The great experiment also gave birth to some inconsistencies and hypocrisies. In the land where all men were created "equal" there existed slavery for many of the three million Negroes, with at least passive co-operation of the central government; the Indians native to the country rarely received any consideration other than the careful aim and blasts of various weapons; and women did not share in rights originally given the free-and-equal men. But the anarchy that some observers had predicted for the new nation governed by such liberal laws failed to develop. After some initial disagreement among themselves the Americans, who had been allowed much self-rule by an enlightened Britain even before independence, generally united in support of their central government, and their remarkable Constitution attracted interest and even admiration among thoughtful Europeans.

As time passed and experience increased, American confidence and faith grew. By 1845 many of the seventeen million white citizens of the United States had become political evangelists, believing it their duty to convert outsiders and to bring them, or at least their lands, into the republican heaven. Like professed followers of Christ, their human fallibility impeded their progress toward an ideal, whether or not they realized it, but this shortcoming did not diminish their youthful zeal.

More than politics came with the American evangelism. A quest for religious freedom had been a major reason for the settlement of the colonies, and in 1845 religion still loomed large in the minds of many United States citizens. Extremely influential had been New England's Puritanism, which related every earthly activity to God, heaven, and hell. Man lived his life on God's time, Puritans emphasized, and none of it could be wasted without an accounting being demanded later.

Ceaseless toil would be a passport to heaven. It would preclude waste of time, would automatically keep a man free from temptation, and, incidentally, might enable him to accumulate riches. Puritans exuded self-righteousness, flaunted strict but arbitrary morals that they sought to impose on others, and inevitably considered themselves God's chosen people. They saw themselves as children of Israel returned to life, with England the Egypt of Israelite bondage and North America the Promised Land, Canaan. They gave their children Hebrew names from the Bible: Adam,

4

Abraham, David, Isaac, Jacob, Jonathan, Joshua, Luke, Moses; Delilah, Rachel, Rahab, Rebecca, Ruth.

More than Puritanism, however, had contributed to the self-assuredness, energy, and toil of the Americans. After British rule had been thrown off thoughtful men had regarded as a challenge the freedom and equality handed out. In the absence of hereditary titles and the ensuing property rights common to Europe, money and political influence became the measure of an aristocracy in the United States. Most Americans could garner neither except through hard work, and competition became fierce. When an established order of society came into existence on the Atlantic Coast men began moving westward—westward into a forested wilderness, following some fewer numbers of bold adventurers who had preceded them there. Soon the trickle became a flow of such magnitude that settled Easterners sought to stop it, fearing that the result for their area would be irreparable economic damage and loss of influence nationally. But the westward movement continued—even increased. Men moved into the new land of plenty, chopped down trees and burned them to clear cultivable fields, gave the soil hard use for a few years, then moved on westward to repeat the performance—westward in a continual search for fortune. If Americans wasted little of God's time they did waste plenty of His earth.

Restlessness, curiosity, energy, and individuality characterized these Americans. They were the people who had forsaken Europe (including the British Isles) for the uncertainties of the New World, or they were the descendants of those people. Pioneering on the constantly receding western frontier taught them self-reliance, resourcefulness, and the need occasionally for common effort in solving problems too large for an individual. These pioneers wanted no ties with the past: no kings, no noblemen or other privileged classes, no standing armies—and only as much republican government as might be necessary to improve life, but certainly not to regulate it. Americans generally felt they had established such a government—indeed, one blessed by heaven itself. A fiery clergyman, Lyman Beecher, declared:

> The time has come when the experiment is to be made whether the world is to be emancipated and rendered happy, or whether the whole creation shall groan and travail together in pain. . . . If it had been the design of Heaven to establish a powerful nation in the full enjoyment of civil and religious liberty, where all the energies of

man might find full scope and excitement, on purpose to show the world by one great successful experiment of what man is capable . . . where should such an experiment have been made but in this country! . . . The light of such a hemisphere shall go up to Heaven; it will throw its beams beyond the waves; it will shine into the darkness there, and be comprehended—it will awaken desire, and hope, and effort, and produce revolutions and overturnings until the world is free . . .

Such sweeping statements logically led to a description of American democracy of that time as militant. Man stood tall under his Creator, and man's institutions were capable of heavenly perfection. The period was one of restless ferment and exciting new developments: urbanization and industrialization, especially on the settled East Coast; new and faster methods of communication and transportation; and social reforms conducted in that interest of perfecting man and his institutions. Desire for reform was represented by drives for temperance, for better education, and for feeding and otherwise caring for the needy. It was also represented by campaigns against brutalities practiced in prisons and in insane asylums, and (in some localities) by campaigns against slavery; and by exhortations in favor of universal peace, women's rights, and Christianity—especially the Protestant kind.

Americans wanted to accomplish everything quickly. They could not be patient, and they could not abide idleness. A visiting Englishman observed the popularity of whittling—in court, on street corners during casual conversation, and elsewhere—and remarked that it was a habit arising from a man's restlessness when not employed in this new country. If American ambition, self-centeredness, and self-esteem had become exorbitant, the United States Government nevertheless then offered more people greater liberty and better chance for happiness than did any other established nation.

In contrast stood the sovereign government of Mexico. There, in 1821, the Spanish Viceroy had been compelled by a superior force to recognize Mexican independence after Spain had been bloodily successful in suppressing earlier rebellions led by two insurgent priests, Miguel Hidalgo y Costilla and Jose María Morelos. But the Mexican who had commanded the victorious revolutionary army, Colonel Agustín de Iturbide, proved to be nothing more than a selfish, arrogant, onetime Spanish royalist who had taken advantage of unrest in Spain to play on

Mexican emotions for support in setting himself up as Emperor, a title he had been allowed to keep for about a year before disaffected Mexicans deposed him and eventually executed him.

Having thrown off the despotism of both Spain and Iturbide, Mexico might have seemed ready to take the highroad for a good life, some degree of liberty, and its own pursuit of happiness—and, in fact, that nation sought to use for this purpose an adaptation of the United States Constitution—but Anglo-Saxon democracy stood no chance of functioning in a land where individuality and liberty had been deliberately stifled from the first appearance of a central government, and where illiteracy, bureaucracy, corruption, and a rigid caste system—all inherited from the Spanish occupation—paralyzed the country. Whereas British rule in North America had allowed the development of liberal political thought (as had been the case also in Britain itself, where one king had been killed and the power of his successors limited), watchful Spanish viceroys had prohibited this vital step in Mexico.

In the waning days of Spanish authority, the early nineteenth century, power had been vested as before in the thousands of natives of Spain residing in Mexico—a group called *gachupines* by the Mexicans—and not even the million *criollos* (American-born Spaniards) had been allowed to share in it, although *criollos* could and did amass wealth. Given such scant responsibility, the *criollos* had become creatures of leisure, enjoying gambling, cockfighting, and love-making, and when independence from Spain and from the *gachupines* placed power in their hands they possessed neither the experience nor the desire to use it wisely. Those New World *criollos* reflected the image of Spaniards as depicted by Havelock Ellis in his book, *The Soul of Spain* (1909): lovers of idleness (as Ellis described the Spaniards) with little inclination for sustained, detailed labor, but a people inclined toward an aptitude for violent, bloody action.

Even less equipped to wield power were the two classes at the bottom of the social ladder: the two million *mestizos* (of Spanish and Indian ancestry), whose mixed blood and usually illegitimate birth following rape or concubinage made them outcasts and often forced them to beg, steal, or rob for a living, and the three or four million lowly Indians, who showed scant interest in anybody's politics immediately after independence.

Had numbers meant anything the Indians would have ruled Mexico

7

then, but they were illiterate, politically leaderless, largely divided into tribes each with its own language and customs, and frequently isolated in remote areas. Their political unconcern notwithstanding, these people had been the first victims of Spanish tyranny in Mexico. Conquered originally by gold-seeking Hernando Cortés and four hundred Spaniards supported by cannon and horses—awesome war equipment never seen before in this primitive region—the Indians had watched Spaniards destroy their temples, take their women, burn their kinsmen as troublesome heretics, and establish themselves as despotic rulers, although occasionally benevolent ones (in contrast to the situation in the British colonies of North America, where areas of white settlement were swept clean of the pesky natives). Spaniards took land from Indians, enslaved them, and gave virtually nothing in return—refusing them permission even to own horses, realizing what strong foes this mobility could make of them. All of the plunder the Spanish King or his appointed representatives eventually got.

The Indians had endured their ordeal with surprising placidity, exploding only infrequently throughout the centuries in bloody, sporadic, and futile uprisings. Such resignation evinced a side of Indian character still noticeable years later. The Mexican Indian was likely to be a stoical man content with whatever simple pleasures his surroundings might offer to relieve the pain of existence; a yielding man to whom life was cheap but certainly not easy; a silent, unaggressive, but quietly tenacious man whose long-smoldering stubbornness might be expected eventually to overcome his submissiveness, especially when encouraged by some energetic leader, and to propel him into violent uprisings against his oppressors.

Still another facet of Indian character manifested itself: a simplicity that precluded understanding abstractions such as forms of government or vague political ideas. Independence did not excite the Indian—or, in fact, benefit him at the time. A sovereign government located in the city of Mexico was an invisible something he could not comprehend. He gave his loyalty instead to visible entities: to his relatives and friends who resided in his immediate vicinity, where customs were the same as his own and where he was not a tense stranger. Members of higher social classes looked down the ladder at the Indian and considered him a lazy, stupid drunkard, which he indeed tended to be. Spanish authority had taught

8

him for centuries that any display of intelligence, industry, or individualism might only bring him trouble.

So the Indian had not taken over Mexico after independence; the *criollo* had. Eventually, however, power would pass to the *mestizo*, after political experience had been acquired by that caste while providing early opposition to the *criollo*. Because of his ancestry the *mestizo* exhibited some Indian traits, but the infusion of Spanish blood had fired him out of the Indian's submissiveness and had made him frequently volcanic and sometimes unstable—a man infuriated by the Spaniard's claim of superiority and more apt to fight against it. But Spanish blood affected the *mestizo* in other ways, too. He could be a polite, courteous man, even if his words might be short on sincerity. He could be impressed by elegant clothing, graceful manners, and fine conversation. He could be almost as devoted to an ideal as was the Spaniard, whose seven-hundred-year battle at home against the Mohammedan invader had produced a proud Catholic warrior ready to plunder and kill non-believers.

All four castes of Spanish Mexico combined to make the young nation what it was in 1845: a land of divided people separated socially as well as geographically—and frequently locked in conflict; a land of unhurried people who did not share the Anglo-Saxon's craving for wealth or his planning for the future, because the vicissitudes of life in Mexico made the arrival of tomorrow so uncertain; a land of sensuous people attracted by ostentations seen, heard, or read, with little thought of what deceptions might lie behind the display; and a land of floundering people still in the grip of certain Spanish legacies like militarism and a state church, yet without outstanding leaders of their own to fulfill wisely the duties and responsibilities of government.

2.

The Greatest Political Figure of Mexico

The most widely known Mexican leader of the time could be described as notorious on the basis of his performance to 1845. Antonio López de Santa Anna did not personify Mexico—no one man could have fit such a sweeping description—but he was an appropriate product of the age there, and his biography to 1845 illuminated that period of Mexican history.

Born in Jalapa in 1794 or 1795, he came from a family variously described as *criollo*, as Indian-"tainted," and as gypsy with a Portuguese origin. Whatever the true ancestry, Santa Anna's father managed to establish himself well as a lawyer and notary, and he hoped to interest his son in a business career. But young Santa Anna had been enchanted early by the color and pomp of Spanish army detachments in nearby Vera Cruz. "From my first years," he wrote near the end of his life, "I was inclined toward the glorious career of arms, feeling a true vocation for it." He persuaded his mother to speak in his behalf to his father, and in 1810 he won appointment as a cadet in the Royal Army of New Spain, while still in his early teens.

Some activities of the youth foretold the man he would become. Cadet Santa Anna showed himself to be an argumentative and a cocksure student, one who displayed courage and talent despite a dislike for the hard work of study and despite a virtual absence of social and literary training. His faults notwithstanding, he could be ingratiating, and he learned how to apply himself to improve this characteristic. In early campaigns against Indians Santa Anna won praise from his commander as a cadet "who had enough constancy to suffer the inconvenience of continuous marches, giving an example in this way to the troops." In those campaigns, including one in the Mexican state of Texas, young Santa Anna also learned the technique of inflicting exquisite brutalities on a foe to bring government forces victory. Abetting a growing desire for power over people, about this time he received a transfer to the cavalry, thus enabling him to feed a craving for duplicating the feats of early Spanish horsemen in spreading terror among humble men.

In time Santa Anna also proved himself unreliable to commanders. Once, after several years of service, he paid gambling debts by drawing on royal army funds, forging on official drafts the names of two superior officers. The regimental surgeon helped him to extricate himself from the ensuing difficulty by lending him money to make repayment.

Some years after that Santa Anna's unreliability blossomed into treachery. When Iturbide's revolt broke out Santa Anna led two hundred royalist troops from Vera Cruz in a successful, though minor, skirmish against a small rebel band. Santa Anna immediately reported a great victory to the Viceroy and requested promotion to lieutenant colonel, then heard of the presence nearby of two thousand rebel soldiers and rushed off to parley with them. Soon afterward he became a full colonel, then a brigadier, on Iturbide's side (a change apparently agreed upon earlier with Iturbide, to take place whenever a moment seemed appropriate).

Not long after Iturbide's triumph of securing independence Santa Anna displayed another talent for which he was to become famous later: a knack for writing bombastic proclamations that would appeal to Mexico's affinity for the ostentatious. "Let us . . . speed to proclaim the immortal Iturbide as Emperor, pledging ourselves as his most constant defenders even to laying down our lives; may the regiment which I command be the first to offer this irrefragable proof. . . . Let us multiply our voices full of jubilation, and let us cry out without ceasing, congratulating ourselves in repeating: 'Viva Agustín the First, Emperor of Mexico!' "

Obviously Santa Anna hoped those words might appeal to Iturbide, too, and persuade that great man to promote him further, even beyond the gold-braided commanding general of the province of Vera Cruz that Iturbide already had made him. For the sake of security, however, Santa Anna—a tall, slender, dark-haired but light-complexioned twenty-eight-year-old man with a flock of pretty, black-haired mistresses—began devoting amorous attention to Iturbide's sixty-year-old sister, Doña Nicolasa. Such an absurdity strengthened Iturbide's already aroused suspicions about

11

Santa Anna's integrity and eventually brought an order for the young brigadier's recall from Vera Cruz to the city of Mexico, where he would be nearer governmental eyes. Santa Anna asked for a few days' delay, probably consulted with other disaffected men of greater political wisdom than he, raised a cry of revolt against that despotic monster Iturbide, and helped to send the man into history in favor of elected presidents.

After that Antonio López de Santa Anna had become the greatest political figure of Mexico, although certainly not a consistent one. He was forever ruled by his self-interest and by his emotions, although he gave a much more stable appearance—with bright, restless, searching eyes, a clear voice, and fluent speaking ability. He praised the republican form of government and urged its adoption by Mexico (and later admitted he had not known at the time the actual meaning of the term "republican government"), became a hero among liberals, then turned on these political friends, declared Mexico unready for democracy, and assumed dictatorial powers. A general at an early age, he knew very little about the techniques of warfare. The head of an aspiring young nation, he knew virtually nothing about statesmanship. In and out of the presidential office (sometimes voluntarily in distressing times, when he chose to turn over the hard work of office to a Vice-President and to retire temporarily to the ease and comfort of his growing estate, Manga de Clavo, near Jalapa), he always managed to dupe the people somehow, to come back, and to resume his practice of ignoring the masses. Nevertheless, revolts often flared against him. Usually they were instigated by liberals, and particularly by Federalists opposed to a powerful central government.

Geography encouraged these rebellions and made them difficult to subdue, especially in regions far away from the city of Mexico, which was the perennial center of authority. Vast distances, jagged mountain ranges paralleling the Pacific and the Gulf coasts, baked northern deserts dried by centuries of sunburn, and steaming southern jungles awash with excessive rainfall confronted men in various sections of this expansive country. The high mountains and a lack of roads and navigable rivers slowed communications, made travel tedious and dangerous, and prevented much exercise of central authority in outlying areas. Only in the vicinity of Mexico City and the surrounding Valley of Mexico, a lush south-central region at an altitude of seven thousand feet located midway between the Pacific and Gulf coasts, could a central government be very certain of holding reins at any given time. There a temperate climate, fertile soil, adequate rainfall, abundant sunshine, and magnificent scenery distinguished by glittering snow-capped peaks to the south and by silvery lakes on the flat valley floor combined to make the land a pearl prized by many men—including that early conqueror, Cortés—and the unity of this area made it easier to govern than the distant isolated regions.

Whenever rebellions broke out Santa Anna preferred to take the field himself in command of the government forces. He still enjoyed military campaigns, especially when the scales of strength tipped in his favor, and because of previous successes he had begun to think of himself as another Napoleon, a personage he had come to admire through reading. In May of 1835 Santa Anna had led a large army against Federalist rebels in Zacatecas, had won a victory in two hours, then as a sort of reward had allowed his troops to rape and plunder the people there. More than two thousand Zacatecans died, and the intrepid editor of an opposition journal, El Crepúsculo, compared Santa Anna to a tiger, "which, sated with the flesh of its prey, reposes on what it does not wish to devour."

After that Santa Anna had focused on another troublesome spot, Texas, with an intention of disciplining its people in a similar manner. The population in Texas included some thirty thousand Anglo-Saxons, many of them originally encouraged by Spain, then by Mexico after independence, to settle in the area as an anticipated economic boon and as a hoped-for buffer against wild Indian tribes and other potential invaders. At first these colonists had been welcomed heartily and had been granted several privileges: duty-free imports, considerable self-rule, and a legal loophole allowing retention of slavery, although independent Mexico had abolished that institution. But as Mexican distrust of the growing numbers of Anglo-Saxons became ever greater, governmental restrictions in Texas increased—and the angered colonists finally rebelled. Nine months after the bloody triumph in Zacatecas Santa Anna led an army into Texas and wreaked on dissenters there the Alamo tragedy and a massacre at Goliad, where his orders resulted in the execution of 342 Texas captives. But then Santa Anna and his force of some 1,300 men blundered into the hands of 783 vengeful Texans led by General Sam Houston at the Battle of San Jacinto. Six hundred Mexicans died and the rest, including Santa Anna himself, fell prisoners—all this against a Texan casualty count of nine dead and thirty-four wounded.

No doubt Santa Anna foresaw his own speedy execution at the hands of his angry captors, but a few reasoning leaders persuaded Texans to spare the man's life for the sake of world opinion and for another purpose: Santa Anna humbly agreed to send withdrawal orders to Mexican Army commanders remaining in Texas and to sign a secret treaty promising that he would return to Mexico and would work for formal recognition there of Texas independence, with the national boundary to be the Rio Grande.

The battlefield disaster and the ensuing imprisonment, however, had lost for Santa Anna power and influence at home. After he had returned to Mexico by way of the city of Washington, where he had conferred with President Jackson, Santa Anna found himself largely discredited by the Texas fiasco and, worse, suspected by many of having engaged in self-seeking, treasonable activities while in Texas and the United States.

Santa Anna retired at once to Manga de Clavo to let other leaders make mistakes. For a year and a half he lazed in his verdant retreat scented with the perfume of myriads of flowers. Without important activity to occupy his interest he always could vegetate. This was such a time in his life, but he enjoyed it nevertheless. He reveled in the comfortable climate of Jalapa, enjoyed spectacular morning views of distant, snow-capped Orizaba, basked in the solicitous attentions of his modest, widely esteemed wife, and alibied for his Texas defeat whenever people would listen. Conveniently and characteristically he forgot the treaty promises.

Then Santa Anna returned to power with a sudden turn of luck as good as San Jacinto had been bad. In 1838 some unpaid damage claims against Mexico resulted in a punitive blockade by a French fleet, which one day opened fire on Vera Cruz. The sounds of the bombardment reverberated in the mountains near that port city, reached Manga de Clavo, and pricked the sensitive ears of Santa Anna, who forsook a cockfight in progress, mounted a favorite white horse, and galloped off toward the action. At Vera Cruz he was welcomed in this time of trouble by former army comrades, and soon he was given command again of Mexican troops. During a small fight against a French landing force already in the act of withdrawing, a cannon ball tore into Santa Anna's left leg, requiring surgery that left him without that limb. Subsequently Mexico settled the dispute with France by paying the claims, but nothing could quiet the pompous, wounded hero of Vera Cruz, who declared himself near death in another of his famous utterances, this one fifteen pages long:

> . . . On coming to my end, I cannot but manifest the satisfaction which accompanies me, of having seen the beginnings of reconcilia-

tion among the Mexicans. . . . I beg . . . the government of my country that my body may be buried in these very dunes [near Vera Cruz], so that all my companions in arms may know that this is the battle line I marked for them.

Santa Anna asked to be remembered in death as "The Good Mexican."

He recovered instead, and on February 17, 1839, he rode into the city of Mexico, into the presidency for a fifth time now, and temporarily into the hearts of thousands of hero-worshipers who greeted him with thunderous *vivas*. Later his severed left leg followed him to the capital. Santa Anna ordered it disinterred from its initial resting place at Manga de Clavo for removal to the city of Mexico and reburial there, with great ceremony, in a magnificent cenotaph.

Santa Anna's presidency became a dictatorship again. Appropriately, the general used an ornate chair designed for the late Agustín I. Santa Anna acquired a new estate, El Encero, near Manga de Clavo. He funded his government on forced loans inflicted on countrymen. He jailed or killed his opponents. But the usual violent ups and downs of Mexican politics continued to plague him: dissatisfaction, treachery, open revolt.

Then his wife died. An unpretentious woman, Doña Inés García de Santa Anna had shunned the glitter of the capital for the privacy of Manga de Clavo. Her seclusion and her known acts of charity had won the admiration of Mexicans—she was their idea of an ideal woman—and they mourned her death. When Santa Anna married by proxy an impetuous fifteen-year-old girl, Señorita María Dolores de Tosta, within a month of his first wife's death, then ordered the girl escorted from the capital to him at his new estate, his again sagging reputation waned further. By late 1844 many Mexicans once more decided they had endured enough from the vain, arrogant despot they had made President. Rebels wrecked a Santa Anna statue in the capital, ruined his magnificent cenotaph, dragged his grisly leg through the streets, and forced him out of office and out of the country. On December 6, 1844, José Joaquín de Herrera, a moderate man, became interim President. In June of the following year Santa Anna, his young wife, and other members of his family departed their homeland for Venezuela and a decreed exile of ten years.

Santa Anna published a parting proclamation heavy with self-pity and pleading:

> Mexicans! in my old age and mutilated, surrounded by a wife and innocent children, I am going into exile to seek a resting place

among strangers. Mercifully forgive the mistakes I made unintentionally; and believe me, in God's name, that I have labored sincerely that you should be independent, free, and happy. If I have not succeeded in fulfilling your desires blame only my lack of ability. In whatever strange place, wherever I may end my days, I shall raise my humble petitions to the Eternal for your success in any way that may be most suitable to your best interests, that you may raise your native land to such a degree of prosperity that it may be listed among the leaders and with the happiest of the nations of the earth.

While en route to Venezuela Santa Anna stopped over at Havana. Cuba attracted him, and he determined to make his residence in exile there. He saw another advantage. Nearer Mexico, he could watch events at home and stay in closer communication with supporters.

Oddly, Santa Anna still had some influential followers in Mexico. How this could have been possible after his years of misrule might have been indicated in two contemporary descriptions of him, one left to history by a well-educated, sophisticated woman and the other by a prewar United States minister to Mexico.

The woman, Fanny Calderón de la Barca, wife of the Spanish minister, once studied Santa Anna silently and observed a gentlemanly, handsome man, one who struck her immediately as the most interesting individual in a group of several persons. She wrote a detailed description: Santa Anna was quietly dressed, sallow-complexioned, and lacking that left leg (about which he spoke frequently), but his fine, dark eyes appeared soft and penetrating, and his manly, melancholy-tinged face appealed to her. Had she not known who the man was, she said, she would have assumed him to be a philosopher in dignified retirement—"one who had tried the world, and found that all was vanity."

The United States minister, Waddy Thompson, equally impressed with Santa Anna, declared, "I have seen no countenance except that of General [Andrew] Jackson, whose range of expression was so great, where there was so great a difference between the quiet expression of the face when at rest and in a gentle mood, and its terrible ferocity when highly excited." Inside Santa Anna, said the envoy, could be found the gentleness of a lamb and the fierceness of an enraged tiger—that split personality of Mexico. But by nature, Thompson added, Santa Anna was a kind and an affectionate man.

With a capacity for thus impressing two intelligent foreigners, Santa Anna assuredly possessed the magnetism to hold a hard-core group of political supporters. Even as he established his residence in Cuba during the summer of 1845 a small group of friends at home began plotting for his return to Mexico. The growing crisis involving the United States seemed to offer opportunity.

3.

An Advocate of National Expansion

While those die-hard *Santanistas* intrigued in Mexico in behalf of their leader, in the United States people greeted with varied reactions their eleventh President, a man who was almost as appropriate a product of his country and its age then as was Santa Anna in Mexico. James Knox Polk, forty-nine, at that time the youngest man ever to win the presidency, looked westward along with most of his countrymen. He had been elected as an advocate of national expansion in that direction.

Even his early life had reflected that disposition. With his family James Polk had moved west at the age of eleven. He had been born in North Carolina—in 1795, of Scottish and Irish parentage—but he had grown up on the other side of the Appalachian Mountains in the fertile, rolling farmland of central Tennessee, where his father had moved in search of new opportunity in 1806.

As a youth James Polk was somewhat out of place in his environment. He did not share his father's love of farming, and he was not a sturdy frontier boy. From a distance, however, his physical appearance struck an observer favorably enough. Slender though somewhat shorter than medium, he appeared to be well formed, and his dark hair, bright eyes, and sharp features made him a handsome youth. But he tired quickly, and he frequently suffered from various ailments. Closer observation showed him to be a boy too small for his age, one whose complexion appeared sickly and whose small-boned, delicate hands seemed to indicate frailty.

James, the oldest of ten children, had been born into family responsibility, but he hated the work expected of him: helping on the farm. He preferred to read or to listen to the political discussions of his elders.

At the age of fourteen he underwent an operation for gallstones—this in a day when the only anesthetic came from a whiskey bottle and when massive bleeding on the operating table or blood poisoning soon after vacating it greatly decreased chances for survival. But he recovered and showed more mental toughness because of his experience, although the operation did little for his health generally.

The elder Polk realized his boy's limitations and tried to interest him in merchandising, believing this more active role to be of greater benefit than that of a student, but James hated the work as much as he did farming. Eventually education provided the answer. His father allowed him to enroll in the University of North Carolina—after a year of pre-liminary study elsewhere—and he relished his bookish surroundings, devoted himself to reading, and graduated three years later (in June of 1818) with a reputation as an outstanding student. He chose the practice of law as his profession, and this proved to be a bridge to politics. He became a protégé of an attorney who was an intimate friend of Andrew Jackson, the Tennessean (transplanted there) whose controversial political career brought to the fore consideration for the "common man" and figured prominently in founding the modern Democratic Party. Polk's ability and political enthusiasm caught the eye of Jackson—"Old Hickory," Polk's senior by twenty-eight years—and Jackson offered support and advice to the extent that Polk eventually became known as "Young Hickory." Before Polk's inauguration as President he had won campaigns for the Tennessee legislature, the United States House of Representatives and the speakership of that body, and the governorship of his home state. Sometimes he had run at the specific suggestion of his mentor, and always with Jackson's support. But Polk had lost campaigns, too, because Jackson's strong will and some of his policies had made vehement enemies, in Tennessee as well as outside the state, and the enmity had fallen on Jackson's followers.

Some understanding of Andrew Jackson's turn of fortune and other events leading to Polk's election can help with an understanding of the war with Mexico.

Jackson's presidency, 1829–37, had represented the climax of a period of United States history known as the "awakening of democracy." The movement had been Western-inspired. New states there had entered the Union with constitutions allowing expanded political rights. This had forced the older states, faced with a loss of emigrating residents, to liberalize their own political structures. Such developments had been advantageous for Jackson the Democrat. But the longer Jackson retained political power, the more he had antagonized large groups of people—an inevitable occurrence. His administration also had brought about some sectionalizing of the still young nation, pitting poor against wealthy, laborer against industrialist, states' righters against federal government, young West against the older East.

Jackson's "common man" interest had caused much of the turmoil. He had contended that all men were wise, good, and equal, whatever their station, and that these individuals deserved greater consideration than property—a much more liberal attitude than an earlier one held by Thomas Jefferson and his followers, whose ideas of any man's worth and wisdom depended largely on the man's intelligence and education. Under Jackson free schools funded by public taxation had come in. Imprisonment for debt had become history. Wealthy Americans had regarded Jackson as a dangerous radical who ignored property rights.

Other issues had compounded the friction. Jackson, Carolina-born, nevertheless had opposed Southerners who declared that states possessed the right to nullify unwanted federal legislation, and he had threatened war to hold the Union together. His reputation as a fighter for individual rights notwithstanding, he had made his presidency so strong (in working for the common man, he said) that foes had labeled it autocratic and had founded the Whig Party in opposition. Whigs, largely representing manufacturing, commercial, and financial interests, believed ultimate power should rest in Congress as the people's representative, not in the executive branch of government, but Jackson had fought them mostly with success. At the close of his second term in 1837 he had been able to name his successor as President, crafty Martin Van Buren, a New Yorker whose political deftness had earned him the nickname "Little Magician."

Andrew Jackson had been the more able wizard of the two men, but not even Jackson risked great involvement in a developing storm regarding Mexico and the recently self-declared Republic of Texas. Beginning with independence in 1836, Texas had clamored for annexation to the United States. Mexico countered with refusals to recognize that independence and with threats of war to oppose any move toward annexation by the United States. American sentiment regarding suitable action became divided largely along a line that would later result in a deadly split. Antislavery Northerners wanted no annexed Texas, which would certainly become a slave state. Southerners tended to sympathize with Texas. Seeking to cool the smoldering slavery passions, chief executives in those days tried to avoid momentous issues involving that explosive question. Jackson, a Westerner, choked down his Texas partiality and risked only a formal recognition of the existence of the new republic—and that near the very end of his last term. Texas waited in vain for invitations to join the Union.

Under Van Buren the Democratic Party lost its hold temporarily. The "Little Magician" inherited from his predecessor a ruinous financial panic of 1837 and a resultant depression caused in part by Jackson's inflationary depositing in state banks of federal funds taken from the congressionally chartered Second Bank of the United States, which Jackson opposed as a dangerous monopoly, then (to check the inflation) Jackson's order to accept only gold or silver in payment for government lands. Along with the stifled economy that followed this action came a reversal of the usual roles. Whigs accused Van Buren, the common man's President, of luxurious living in the Executive Mansion in the midst of depression.

The magic was gone. In 1841 victorious Whigs installed their own men in Van Buren's old haunts: William Henry Harrison, President, and John Tyler, Vice-President. But then a bit of previous political strategy exploded on them. Tyler, a former Virginia Democrat nominated with the Southern vote in mind, became President a month after the inauguration, when Harrison died, and Tyler in turn became more of a Democrat than a Whig, to the dismay and disgust of his adopted party. That change enhanced the chances for Texas annexation.

Another development favored Texas. Some officials of the new republic, angered by earlier American rebuffs, sought friendship with France and Britain and planted hints in the city of Washington about the favorable progress of their endeavors. The possibility of a Texas alliance with Britain particularly concerned Washington, where some persons still remembered the War of 1812, and this aroused people elsewhere, too. In April of 1844 the Tyler administration drew up an annexation treaty and ordered military units to Louisiana, where they would be available to defend Texas against Mexican attack. Two months later the United States Senate rejected the treaty and left Texas still outside the Union, but the troops stayed in Louisiana. Disappointed Texas officials renewed their European overtures, with the usual talk of success.

In Tennessee retirement, Andrew Jackson heard the Texas rumors, and he remembered vividly the threat Britain could pose. At this time the old man still had hopes that his defeated favorite, Van Buren, might come back a winner in the 1844 election. But when Van Buren and the leading Whig candidate, facile Henry Clay, agreed to take Texas out of the next campaign by what amounted to a mutual rejection of annexation in advance Jackson began to look elsewhere for a suitable candidate on whom to bestow his still strong support.

He chose James K. Polk, although the man had never been considered presidential material and had himself only hoped for vice-presidential nomination at best. But Polk had once written in a letter an aggressive declaration about what United States policy to westward should be: annex Texas and assume sole ownership of the Oregon territory, which had been occupied jointly with Britain according to the terms of a treaty. This stand appealed to Jackson, who believed in leaving no cracks in North American doors for John Bull's foot, and who shared the Western sentiment for acquiring more land toward the sunset.

Jackson's Democratic Party met May 27–30, 1844, in Odd Fellows' Hall in Baltimore and quickly adopted a rule requiring two thirds of the vote for nomination—a move that effectively blocked Van Buren's already acquired lead over stolid Lewis Cass of Michigan and held it off through seven ballots. Until the eighth ballot Polk received no mention and no votes at all. Then, taking advantage of the deadlock, Polk supporters put his name before the convention as a compromise candidate, and on the ninth vote delegates stampeded to him, mostly with hopes of being the first to nominate a man who might soon be in a very important job and in an excellent position to return favors. Polk won unanimous nomination—the first time a "dark horse" candidate had been selected—and for the first time in history a telegraph crackled the news: from Baltimore to a room in the Capitol at Washington.

Chosen as Polk's running mate was George M. Dallas, a man whose Pennsylvania residence and high-tariff advocacy (in opposition to Polk's low-tariff desires) represented mostly an appeal to voters of that section of the country.

"Who is James K. Polk?" jeered the Whigs, whose great favorite Henry Clay seemed likely to swamp the Democratic nominee. But Clay had helped to defeat himself with his stand on Texas. Concern about British intentions, sympathy with blood kin, and desire for more land and economic opportunity finally outweighed the idealistic objections of anti-slavery people. Polk won, and outgoing President Tyler took the victory as a mandate for inviting Texas into the Union. Through a joint resolution of Congress he offered annexation to Texas, a choice its citizens would have to approve by vote later—but with little doubt at this time about the outcome. Thus the Texas decision had been made even before Polk's inauguration, but the history of it certainly had not been written. The Mexican minister angrily left Washington amid rumors and threats of war.

Polk had assumed his presidential duties before the envoy departed. With Sarah Polk, his wife of twenty-one years, and a group of relatives and friends the President-elect had boarded the steamboat *China* in late January 1845 at a wharf at the foot of Broad Street in Nashville to begin a slow, cold journey along the winding Cumberland to the Ohio, then up the icy expanse of that river to Wheeling, where they had arrived February 9. From Wheeling creaking, tossing horse-drawn coaches carried them up the National Road and over the mountains to Cumberland, Maryland; during this three-day trip Polk rode in a gilt-trimmed coach of polished olive wood. At Cumberland they transferred to a new transportation marvel, railroad "steam cars." Behind a coughing locomotive they sped past trees, houses, and barns that appeared and vanished through open car windows with such dazzling rapidity as to make eyes ache, while ashes and sparks drifted in and settled on faces, clothing, chairs—everything. Most of the railroad right of way remained unfenced, and cattle would have posed a hazard to the presidential express but for an ingenious device placed in front of the locomotive (and all others then in operation): a shovellike apparatus that could sweep up an animal and toss it off the tracks. Every hour or so the steam cars came to a grinding halt at a depot where passengers piled out and crowded into refreshment rooms. There they bought hard-boiled eggs, ham, pies, and custards and hoped to devour the food before a bell rang signaling imminent departure. Upon hearing that sound they rushed back on board—many passengers with hands and mouths still full.

Members of the presidential entourage had been jolted this way, with the ladies' faces swathed in veils, for the final two hundred miles into Washington—a stretch covered in the amazingly fast time of twelve hours. They had arrived in chilly darkness at 7:30 P.M., February 13, but despite this discomfort an enormous throng of welcomers carrying banners and torchlights had turned out to greet the Polks. As the locomotive chugged to a halt cannon roared a greeting, the Marine Band broke into a sprightly rendition of "Hail to the Chief," and men helped the President-elect and his wife to push through the crowd and into a carriage waiting to take them to Coleman's Hotel.

Some two weeks later a steady, chilling rain dampened the inauguration, but not Polk's expansionist fervor. From an open platform on the east steps of the Capitol Polk looked down on an expanse of upright umbrellas and spoke in a firm, distinct voice of the Texas annexation as a national enterprise and of the Oregon acquisition as a national duty. Chief Justice Roger Taney, a controversial Jacksonian, administered the oath of office; cannon thundered again; soaked spectators roared approval. Samuel F. B. Morse used his new telegraph from a position assigned him on the platform to tap out a description of the proceedings for Baltimore.

What kind of man was the new President? He was a man already detested by some political foes for his past loyalty to Andrew Jackson, particularly while Speaker of the House of Representatives during Jackson's administration.

Polk had been above all a Democratic Party man. Politics encompassed his whole life. At the time of his inauguration he belonged to no church, although his wife was a staunch Presbyterian, and the Polks had no children to demand attention. He devoted himself entirely to whatever office he held, and his wife devoted herself to furthering his ambition. For her, pride in his political success seemed to take the place of pride of motherhood.

To an observer Polk appeared robust enough now despite his sometimes sickly youth. Still slender and rather below middle size, he nevertheless impressed people with his scrupulousness in dress; with his firm, upright carriage of body; and with his well-formed, angular head distinguished by piercing gray eyes, by a serious, high-browed face, and by a patch of long, dark, but gray-streaked hair brushed straight back behind his ears. When he walked he strode uprightly and energetically—a man who knew where he was going and what he would do when he arrived. When Polk sat in a chair, an observer remarked, he usually looked as if he were in attendance at a formal dinner party. His entire appearance indicated dignity, urbanity, decision. As an orator he lagged behind eloquent speakers like the accomplished Henry Clay, but his firmness made up some of the deficit. Polk rarely straddled issues.

Closer examination, however, showed that flaws lay below the superficial. Polk also was an untraveled small-town lawyer whose intense school-book reading had not produced any sort of Renaissance man. Humorless, cold, narrow, plodding, secretive, and sly, he lacked imagination for the creation of new political concepts, although he excelled in the mechanics of pushing routine legislation through lawmaking bodies. Despite his church non-membership, he displayed much of the Puritan's self-righteous-ness and attitude toward ceaseless toil, and especially the Puritan's flaunt-ing of strict but arbitrary morals.

One historian described Polk this way: "[His type] is the leading citizen and schemer of the small town, who marches up the center aisle on public occasions with creaking shoes and a wooden smile, and takes his seat with a backward, all-embracing glance."

A phrenologist also described Polk once, either with remarkable general accuracy or with some prior knowledge of his subject:

> [Polk] is very quick of perception; when he enjoys, he enjoys remarkably well, and when he suffers, he suffers most intently. . . . His is a remarkably active mind, restless unless he has something of importance to do; cannot be idle for a moment, is by nature one of the most industrious of men; loves mental labour & hard study as he does daily food; . . . and is throughout a *positive* character. . . . He thinks well of himself; often asks advice, & does just as he pleases; is one of the firmest of men; slow in committing himself, but once committed does all in his power to carry through his measures . . . has many acquaintances, few bosom friends . . . has an astonishing command of *facts* and can call to mind with great precision what occurred long ago.

Polk's austere personality placed more pressure on his wife as First Lady, but in the past she had proved equal to similar tasks. Born Sarah Childress in 1803, she was the daughter of a prosperous Tennessee farmer. Refined and capable, she displayed sound sense and personal charm, al-though one portrait of her seemingly depicted a rather forbidding woman with dark hair parted in the middle and with a disapproving mouth curled downward in a slight frown. The picture must have been deceptive. Even Polk's bitter enemies often complimented his wife.

After the Polks had installed themselves in the Executive Mansion following the rainy inauguration the new President devoted part of that same night to planning for the next four years, instead of spending the entire evening in continuing celebration. Expansion naturally occupied his thoughts, and despite his lack of imagination Polk had a remarkable vision of the United States of the future. It would be a country that would fill out a continent.

Already the growth had been great. In Northeastern states manufacturing had boomed, spurred on by the War of 1812, when isolation from other sources forced Americans to develop their own industries rather than to rely on unavailable foreign imports. In the South plantation farming had grown ever larger, stimulated by Eli Whitney's gin, which had increased the output of cotton by providing mechanical means of separating the seed—and which had revived a dying slave economy at the same time. In the agrarian and independent West new lands had continued to open up for fresh opportunity.

Large chunks of earth had been added to the area of the original thirteen states: the Northwest Territory, more than a quarter million square miles of land north of the Ohio River, east of the Mississippi, south of the Great Lakes, and west of Pennsylvania, ceded by Britain in 1783; the Louisiana Purchase, nearly a million square miles of varied lands roughly west of the Mississippi River (but excluding Texas) and east of the Rocky Mountains, bought from France in 1803; the Florida Territory, ceded by Spain in 1821 for five million dollars; and smaller acquisitions. These additions already had persuaded some cautious Americans that their distinctive form of government would not be threatened (as had been feared earlier) by great expansion. They had seen new states added even from that giant Louisiana Purchase, and the federal system still stood as sturdily as ever.

Polk wanted more new territory. His first Secretary of the Navy, George Bancroft, recalled many years later that on inauguration night Polk indicated this in a discussion of his coming administration. Warm, dry, and confident beside a fire, Polk listed his main objectives: "There are four great measures which are to be the measures of my administration: one, a reduction of the tariff; another, the independent treasury; a third, the settlement of the Oregon boundary question; and lastly, the acquisition of California"—presumably referring to Upper California, not the lower peninsula. Polk slapped his thigh for emphasis, Bancroft said.

California actually belonged to Mexico, although jurisdiction had proved difficult to maintain in that region remote from the city of Mexico, and Mexican troops occasionally had been driven out of the country by the Californians. In Polk's United States comparatively little was known about the area, although a few leaders, including Andrew Jackson when President, already had sought unsuccessfully to buy it—a move that had opened suspicious Mexican eyes to United States designs. Some American explorers had written exciting reports about the land, and several trappers had passed around some colorful tales. Personnel from sailing vessels belonging to New England merchants also had brought back descriptions of a wonderful harbor and a beautiful land to the north—and rumors of foreign interest in the region.

Polk feared that Britain might be trying to acquire California, and he wanted to outrace John Bull for the prize. This would secure United States expansion all the way to the Pacific Ocean. To get the place he would have to deal with a nation that no narrow, small-town lawyer could understand, particularly one who would scarcely try.

4.

Orders

James K. Polk's election on the promise of adding Texas and Oregon to the Union, his ensuing inauguration, and the angry departure from Washington of the Mexican minister brought closer the fighting that would call men of intelligence, gentility, and sensitivity to kill—men like Ephraim Kirby Smith, that 5th Infantry captain who loved to pluck flowers and press them for sending home to his family; men like Sam French, the artillery lieutenant who could enjoy a mockingbird's cheerful song; and men like Sam Grant, the young infantry lieutenant whose early shyness had made such a mark at the Military Academy. Immediately after the new President's inauguration two wars, not just one, seemed to lie ahead for these men—one war with Great Britain over Oregon, and another with Mexico over Texas.

Soldiers at posts throughout the United States foresaw a drastic change looming, but for most of them the old routine of pleasant familiarity continued temporarily. For the lower ranks this meant roll call at reveille, as dawn broke, then a rush back inside barracks or tents to sweep, make beds, and otherwise set possessions in order for an inspection twenty-five minutes later. After breakfast each man cleaned his musket or rifle; polished his breastplate, cartridge box, and buttons; brushed his hat, pompon, and uniform; and lined up for nine o'clock parade: the raising of colors, playing of "The Star-Spangled Banner," marching of officers to the formation front for a ceremonial doffing of hats to the commander, then passing in review by the ranks. After dismissal each man not on guard duty changed into fatigue uniform for drill, drill, drill, and for work around the post: mowing grass, sawing lumber, repairing chimneys, shoeing horses, nailing boards, collecting trash. At one o'clock came dinner; at sunset, the roll call of retreat and the lowering of the colors, then supper. At nine o'clock—tattoo—came another roll call, followed thirty minutes later by taps sounded on a drum.

The moves and long marches being talked about proved disturbing to many men. They would have to leave the familiar for the unknown. But some army personnel already had been shifted because of the conflict that threatened.

At Fort Jesup, a U. S. Army post located in the mugginess of Louisiana's Red River Valley, a non-smiling lieutenant colonel who could be best described as a military iconoclast mused over the situation regarding Mexico and concluded with disgust that the leaders of his country had become involved in a plot to embroil the nation in a foreign war with the idea of breaking up the Union, for their own purposes, into North and South. Ethan Allen Hitchcock, a man of military bearing accentuated by a large, balding head and a face indicating firmness and often melancholy, had been ordered to Fort Jesup in April of 1844 with other officers and men of an "Army of Observation" whose duty had been to watch for trouble during President Tyler's first serious maneuvering toward Texas annexation. That treaty had been defeated in the United States Senate, of course, but the soldiers had stayed. Since their commander continued to be rough, countrified, tobacco-chewing Colonel Zachary Taylor, a brevetted brigadier general whose usual post uniform of baggy blue jeans, long linen duster, and crumpled straw hat resulted in the creation of many hilarious stories about mistaken identity, chances were the "Army of Observation" really was meant to go into battle someday. As Hitchcock and everyone else knew, old Colonel Taylor was a fighter, an inspirational leader in battle, not an observer or a possessor of much other military talent outside of the brawling ability for which he had become known.

Taylor looked the part, with his informality of dress and his tendency toward corpulence and his other heavy features: large nose, thick eyebrows underlining a broad, wrinkled forehead, too prominent mouth set wide above a double chin. He even lived the part, preferring quarters in a tent located in the shade of a tree to something finer. His chair there frequently consisted of a wood box cushioned with a blanket; for a dinner table he might push together two rough blue chests containing personal belongings.

Taylor had won his promotions slowly, mostly through years of

Indian fighting, without benefit of a West Point background and, in fact, without much education of any kind.

Ethan Allen Hitchcock—commander of the 3rd Infantry Regiment —was another kind of officer. He had been known as an excellent student and a model cadet at the Military Academy, where he had graduated in July 1817, but even before enrolling there he had acquired a reputation for scholarship. A letter of recommendation for admission to the Academy written by a brother-in-law who held the army title of assistant adjutant general described Hitchcock as a master of the English language and an able student of Latin who was well bred, correct in moral habits, and guided by strict ideas of honor and integrity.

The same writer observed also that Hitchcock was the grandson of Ethan Allen, a luminary of the American Revolution and a notably independent thinker. Allen, a native of Connecticut, had moved in 1769 to the present-day Bennington, Vermont, which then lay in an area known as the New Hampshire Grants, a region that became involved in a jurisdictional struggle between royal authorities of New York and New Hampshire. After New York representatives of the Crown had rejected an appeal that the territory later known as Vermont be established as a separate province Allen organized a group of volunteers called the Green Mountain Boys to fight against New York control. The royal governor of New York promptly labeled Allen an outlaw.

When the colonies revolted against Britain Allen and his volunteers joined the rebellion, and with a Connecticut soldier named Benedict Arnold they surprised and captured Fort Ticonderoga early on a May morning in 1775. Later Allen fell prisoner to the British, but after a three-year captivity he returned home, still working for Vermont—toward statehood in the new Union now—and still without success. Between 1780 and 1783 he negotiated with the governor of Canada for the establishment of Vermont as a Canadian province, an activity that later led to a United States charge of treason against him. But the allegation never was proved. Allen obviously had conducted the negotiation with an actual intention of forcing approval of statehood by the Continental Congress, and eventually he succeeded.

A worthy grandson of this strong-willed man was Hitchcock, born in Vermont in 1798 to a woman who was the last of Ethan Allen's children by his first wife. Hitchcock's mother, the former Lucy Allen, always thought her son the "living image" of Ethan Allen.

In the U. S. Army Hitchcock soon became recognized as quite a non-conformist himself. He proved to be an egotistical man with an active, probing, perceptive mind beyond control of those everlasting military reins that bound men of more yielding individualism. Hitchcock's extravagant self-confidence stemmed mostly from wide reading, remarkable recall, and quiet but hard meditation that enabled him to separate what he considered to be the wheat from the chaff. As a professional soldier he took pride in knowing military tactics and discipline as well as (or better than) any other officer around him—a knowledge that enabled him to survive in an atmosphere that would have destroyed ordinary nonconformists—but he also knew many other subjects. When off duty Hitchcock often fled the roistering of camp for the solitude of the nearby countryside, where he would sit for hours reading Shakespeare and Chaucer or Montesquieu, Hegel, Spinoza, Burke, or Tacitus. At other times he withdrew to the privacy of his own quarters to write or to play the flute. Always he sought to avoid fellow officers who devoted their leisure time to drinking, quarreling, boasting, and reciting the latest scandal, amorous conquest, or vulgar joke. Consequently Hitchcock spent much of his military life in solitude.

Some of his diary entries indicate his unusual thinking:

> I find so little to interest me in the military profession that I had rather study or read books of philosophy. I fear I am not in my proper vocation—that is, I have read and studied myself out of it. The study of philosophy and my general reading have subdued all spirit for action and induced a wish to retire from the world into some solitude.

> . . .

> My mind has undergone changes. I feel stronger than I did. What appeared great has diminished. Generals and great men are pygmies. Principles, laws of Nature, truth—these alone seem grand.

> . . .

> No man knows how little he knows unless he thinks a great deal and reads a good many books.

> . . .

> I have been much with Indians [in military campaigns against them] and look upon them as a part of the great human family, capable of being reasoned with and susceptible of passions and affections which, rightly touched, will secure moral results with almost mechanical certainty.

. . .

It is plain that Goethe was a pantheist, and I see that a pantheist may be a Christian, a Mohammedan, and a heathen at the same time. Pantheism ought to be regarded as the very reverse of atheism, being the admission of everything and the denial of nothing. He has the most accurate knowledge of God who has the most comprehensive knowledge of Nature . . . for these two are one.

Once Hitchcock wrote of his early-formed dislike of formal dining, "especially dinner parties, where a chief object seemed to be to bring out a dozen different kinds of wine, bottle by bottle, of each of which there must be a long account given, setting forth its history, the date of vintage, date of importation, date of bottling &c., &c. I used to get weary beyond description at such parties, and longed for the open air; and when free my desire to be learning something would come back upon me."

Here was a singular U. S. Army officer: a man who never hesitated to speak against superiors and even the United States Government itself when he felt they were wrong; a man who once invited and endured arrest for signing a protest, with some other officers attached to the Military Academy, contending that certain of Superintendent Sylvanus Thayer's actions lacked authority; a man who sympathized with the very Indians his army fought and who declared that a war conducted by the United States to disperse (and thus to "pacify") the Florida Indians was an outright injustice; and a man who often laughed at the nonsensical "show part" of military life while admitting its importance to army discipline.

Why did such an officer remain in the service? Perhaps Hitchcock felt he might improve things there, and certainly he felt secure in his knowledge of the profession. How had he been able to endure a career that seemed so disagreeable? His egoism had helped him, as had his carefully defined and staunchly followed rules of conduct. He had determined early to regard himself impersonally—"that is, as an impartial observer"—and to keep in mind a maxim, "True virtue sets a man above the hope of heaven and the fear of hell." Finally, Hitchcock's ability and integrity had won recognition from thoughtful superiors, although he frequently had antagonized them—having missed promotion at least once because of his outspokenness. On sheer ability Hitchcock had drawn some assignments of prestige, such as instructor at the Military Academy (where he had taught Edgar Allan Poe) and, later, commandant of the cadet corps there.

Despite his growing dislike of military life, Hitchcock always fulfilled his duties conscientiously. Indicative of this was his inability to sleep on the eve of some important activity. He would lie awake at night mulling over plans for the morrow.

But it was Hitchcock the impartial observer who watched events in Washington and in Texas from his vantage point with the "Army of Observation" in Louisiana. Already he had come to regard "the whole area of our proceedings in the Southwest as being wicked, so far as the United States were concerned," and he "felt averse to being made an instrument for such purposes." During his wait at Fort Jesup he turned for solace to an eight-volume translation of Tennemann's *Manual of the History of Philosophy*, to a translation of Spinoza's *Ethics*, and to Gabriele Rossetti's interpretation of the esoteric meaning of medieval writers.

When, in October 1844, Zachary Taylor (as Fort Jesup commander) had shown Hitchcock a confidential order from Washington to keep the troops in readiness to move in support of Texas in event of trouble during President Tyler's first (and unsuccessful) annexation maneuver, Hitchcock fumed and wrote in his diary, ". . . it is evident that President Tyler or his adviser, Mr. [John C.] Calhoun, is determined to embroil this country before going out of office and perhaps, as Colonel [Thomas Hart] Benton has charge[d] on the floor of the Senate, to prepare the way for separation of the Union. . . . These instructions are infamous."

Nevertheless, Hitchcock the professional soldier had helped Zachary Taylor the senior commander to keep the men ready for any move. In mid-October of 1844 they had expected further orders daily, but no instructions arrived. With the approach of the penetrating chill of another wet Louisiana winter Hitchcock's regiment began building huts to keep themselves snug, and Hitchcock devoted himself to supervising the work with his usual professionalism.

Then winter arrived, and still Taylor's army had not moved. Hitchcock drilled his men daily. His regiment became recognized as the best disciplined of any.

No orders arrived. In leisure time Hitchcock continued to read: *Pantheisticon*, Strauss's *Dogmatique*, Plutarch's *Isis* and *Osiris*, and twelve volumes of old plays.

By this time Hitchcock had heard of Tennessean James K. Polk's election as President, and he looked upon the event as only another step toward the annexation of Texas and the breakup of the Union.

33

On January 1, 1845, Hitchcock awoke clearheaded, unlike many fellow officers, and celebrated the arrival of another new year by riding his bay, named Jim, then by reading from the *Meditations* of Marcus Aurelius Antoninus. That evening he played his flute—"the opera of *Oberon* and one or two others"—and inventoried his books (761) and his music (60 volumes bound "and enough music in sheets for 20 volumes more").

Winter passed without orders to move. Hitchcock read accounts of President Polk's inauguration and of the inaugural address without being persuaded into any change of heart regarding Texas. In March the colonel took a short leave of absence for a steamboat excursion down the Red and Mississippi rivers to visit friends in New Orleans and, later, Mobile. A mishap marred the trip: the steamboat, named *De Soto*, plowed aground in the Red River, but Hitchcock had a book to read during the delay: *Vestiges of the Natural History of Creation.*

Then he returned to duty—and found no orders yet. In May and most of June he continued to read a great deal. In his diary for that period he devoted fewer than ten lines to military and social life and twenty-five pages to his reading.

For some men the camp hours dragged interminably, but not for Hitchcock, with his affinity for reading. Furthermore, his good friend Captain William W. S. Bliss was present in camp, on Zachary Taylor's staff, and this brilliant man (whose West Point nickname had been "Perfect" Bliss) happened to be one of the few officers anywhere who could match or perhaps excel Hitchcock in conversational ability. Hitchcock enjoyed talking with Bliss, and the two men spent satisfying hours together.

One balmy late June night this life of leisure suddenly changed. Hitchcock recorded it in his diary:

> Fort Jesup, La., June 30, 1845. Orders came last evening by express from Washington City directing General Taylor to move without any delay to some point on the coast near the Sabine or elsewhere, and as soon as he shall hear of the acceptance by the Texas convention of the annexation resolutions of our Congress he is immediately to proceed with his whole command to the extreme western border of Texas and take up a position on the banks of or near the Rio Grande, and he is to expel any armed force of Mexicans who may cross that river. Bliss read the orders to me last evening hastily at tattoo. I have scarcely slept a wink, thinking of

34

the needful preparations. I am now noting at reveille by candle-light and waiting the signal for muster. . . . Violence leads to violence, and if this movement of ours does not lead to others and to bloodshed, I am much mistaken.

5.

Momentous Moves

Most officials in the city of Washington did not share Colonel Hitchcock's grim assessment of the situation. At that time they might not have formed such portentous views even had they been inclined toward Hitchcock's melancholy, because 1845 Washington rested blissfully ignorant of split-second urgencies. Slowness of communication meant that days—maybe weeks—must elapse before receipt of any intelligence regarding a move by Taylor and Mexican reaction to it. True, Samuel Morse had his telegraph, but the wires essential for its use did not stretch southward toward Taylor's camp in Louisiana or toward Texas, and they would not for some time.

The Washington of this period was a sleepy, smelly, often muddy town built in an expansive "District of Columbia" designed to take care of a large metropolis. People liked to sneer at the place as a "City of Streets without Houses," as the "City of Magnificent Distances," and as the "Capital of Miserable Huts." An assortment of scattered houses, ugly business establishments, and unimposing government structures all leaned on two notable buildings for whatever favorable impression the community could make on an unprejudiced observer.

One of these two buildings was the Capitol, built of stone and located then as now on the hill named for it. But in 1845 the United States Capitol looked more like today's statehouse—or even courthouse. From a domed central section protruded two stubby north and south wings, each topped by a small dome. Construction of this edifice had been begun fifty-two years earlier—President Washington had laid the cornerstone—but because of architectural disputes work had proceeded slowly. Then during the War of 1812 British troops had set fire to the building (in August 1814), necessitating extensive repairs and restoration. By 1845 the Capitol and its grounds had been made grand enough to impress most people, even travelers from Europe, but the structure was small by comparison to today's building (which utilizes the old Capitol for its central section, but with the original domes removed and a much larger central one substituted). An English visitor of those days looked at the three-dome stateliness, then poked around Washington and remarked, "The Capitol lacks a city." The building reminded him of a general without an army, surrounded only by "a parcel of ragged, dirty boys"—the ugly, poorly built, scattered houses of the thirty thousand or so inhabitants.

Only one street had been paved—tree-lined Pennsylvania Avenue—but the macadam had not been maintained and had broken, rutted, and accumulated a layer of dirt that always left it slushy and slippery after a hard rain. Other streets, all of them as broad as the founders' visions, resembled bogs or deserts, depending on the weather, and they provided thoroughfares for neighborhood hogs, pigs, and cows that roamed at will, as well as for the luxurious four-horse carriages of foreign diplomats who were attended by servants dressed in bright livery. The diplomats and the other necessities of national government taxed the town's meager housing facilities severely, forcing many lower officials and even some senators and representatives into cramped quarters in boardinghouses and hotels, where they occasionally had to double up in rooms and to alternate as cooks for their respective messes.

In winter Washingtonians huddled around Franklin stoves and tried to keep warm. In summer they fled the mugginess, if possible—or if not possible they fanned away perspiration and suffered through the hot months overdressed as required by the fashion of those years and undercooled in the low, poorly ventilated buildings. In any season they had reason to exercise caution while outdoors at night. The dark streets, dimly lighted (and then only at long intervals) by oil lamps flickering from atop wooden poles, harbored young toughs who amused themselves by smashing windows and by other acts of vandalism. In any season, too, Washingtonians encountered still another barrier to happy life: raw sewage carried by a stream called the Tiber that meandered through the town and under a Pennsylvania Avenue bridge, where it deposited some of its filth in a stinking, stagnant pool.

Men chewed and spat. Dueling had been outlawed only recently.

The city of Washington did not stand as much of a monument to the great governmental experiment. The Englishman who had remarked, "The Capitol lacks a city," also commented on United States claims to superiority and high morality. "The Americans," he wrote, "are the happiest people in the world in their own delusions."

Nevertheless, Washington life could be pleasant, interesting, and even exciting at times, partly because of the political and social activity that went on in the other notable building in town: the Executive Mansion (linked with the Capitol by Pennsylvania Avenue), where James and Sarah Polk had recently installed themselves. Like the Capitol, the presidential residence in those days was small compared to what it eventually would become after much remodeling and expansion. But in 1845 Washington it was impressive enough: a white, two-story building stately in its simple dignity, surrounded by picturesque, landscaped grounds. The scene evoked admiration and sometimes callow comment regarding mansion grandeur amid all the squalor. Although a few attractive two-story red brick residences stood nearby—invariably brightened by green blinds and comfortably linked by red brick sidewalks—nearby also stood some huts through which winter winds cut with penetrating cold drafts. Furthermore, at no great distance southward from the Executive Mansion lay marshland where more sewage accumulated and spoiled the air.

Within half a mile or so west of the mansion lay pastures and fenced fields. The President was only a few years removed from having his residence completely open to any caller for any random purpose, with no questions asked, and even in Polk's day it seemed frequently that anyone could gain entrance. Martin Van Buren, when Andrew Jackson's successor, had installed the first "police force" at the mansion: a few men wearing star badges and carrying sticks to prevent hoodlums from making absolute bedlam of his levees. (But this bit of repression might have helped to keep Van Buren from re-election. That charge of expansive living in the mansion during hard times had contributed largely to his defeat.)

The 1845 occupant could have used more policemen. Their scarcity made the Washington spring that year an ordeal for Polk instead of a respite from winter discomforts. While the trees lining Pennsylvania Avenue burst into new life, while the Marine Band began playing lively twice-a-week concerts at the Capitol, and while Mrs. James Madison (widow of the late President) maintained her dignified presence in

Washington society for yet another year, attired for formal events in old-fashioned frilly dress and white turban, President Polk spent hours fending off hordes of office seekers who pestered him for salaried appointments to one government job or another. For a man like Polk who refused to accept any gift greater than an occasional book or cane the job seekers, whose patriotism consisted mostly of a desire to draw that government salary, constituted a public menace. The deluge of these people resulted from the spoils system of government, for which Andrew Jackson had become famous and of which Polk himself initially had approved. But Polk soon found himself despising the beggars after a somewhat tolerant beginning. "They are most importunate in their demands," he remarked once, "and I have learned that the only way to treat them is to be decided and stern."

For Polk sternness could come naturally—with all that innate austerity of his. By spring of 1845 the new President already had established himself as a firm and generally prudent man, one who would listen to advisers like cabinet members, then determine for himself a course of action. Although Polk continued to be narrow-minded, limited, and unimaginative (as a diary kept during his term showed), he became a Chief Executive who ruled his official family, and a remarkably strong President. Polk knew what he wanted, and he intended to get it. His cabinet members quickly became aware of this characteristic at their twice-weekly meetings, held at noon on Tuesdays and Saturdays.

Secretary of State was Pennsylvanian James Buchanan, whose pink plumpness seemed to indicate some lack of self-discipline—and apparently did: Buchanan showed himself to be changeable, fussy, obstinate, petulant, and insolent, yet all the while timid in moments of great responsibility. Buchanan's selection for the State Department represented another concession to Democrats of industrial states who favored a considerable protective tariff, but the concession at times proved instead to be a cross for Polk to bear. Buchanan yearned to be President himself, and he sought to please various sections of the country from time to time as opportunities arose, even if this sometimes meant altering previously stated beliefs. The man aroused a growing distrust in Polk, who once wrote in his diary this description: "Mr. Buchanan is an able man, but is in small matters without judgment and sometimes acts like an old maid."

Secretary of the Treasury was Robert J. Walker, a Pennsylvania-born planter and lawyer from Mississippi hated by Whigs and disliked even by some Democrats, who suspected his honesty. His short stature, bald head, and wheezy voice belied his jaunty conceit and his impetuosity. Walker fervently supported Polk's expansionism and worked at the Treasury desk in behalf of other presidential policies.

Attorney General was languid John Y. Mason, Secretary of the Navy in the preceding Tyler administration (a post to which he would eventually return under Polk). His looks indicated (as did Buchanan's) the man he was: a portly lover of creature comforts, and a man who seemed to work only as much as necessary to hold his job. Being a University of North Carolina college mate of Polk's helped to keep him in favor, but even that connection wore thin as Polk saw more of the man's inefficiency.

Secretary of War was another expansionist and the oldest and ablest member of the Cabinet: William L. Marcy, who would turn sixty in the early years of Polk's administration. Marcy's age enhanced rather than hindered his performance. His years and his experience had brought wisdom, ability, and tact that supplemented integrity and administrative talent. All this enabled him to deal firmly with vain generals without displaying the slightest lack of confidence. For Polk, Marcy's only drawback was a history of leading Democratic opposition to Martin Van Buren in New York, and his appointment thus embittered Van Buren's friends. But Marcy's assets easily outweighed this handicap.

Secretary of the Navy was George Bancroft, a Massachusetts Democrat who had helped secure the nomination for Polk and to whom Polk, on inauguration night, had confided those four main objectives of his administration. Bancroft believed in the greatness of American destiny, and he had long exhibited interest in California. But Bancroft, an author and a scholar, actually showed greater zeal for recording history than for making it, and after one notable accomplishment—founding the United States Naval Academy at Annapolis—he would leave his cabinet post (given him mostly as a reward for political support) for a more agreeable assignment as diplomatic representative.

Postmaster General was Polk's closest political friend, sagacious Cave Johnson from Tennessee, a practical, methodical man who not only improved mail service during his tenure but continued to counsel Polk on many other matters and always to work against large governmental appropriations—a stand that caused him to be called "the watchdog of the Treasury."

In the months following inauguration political writers inevitably focused their attention on these six cabinet members and on their probable influence with Polk. Earlier some observers had expressed surprise that Polk, the compromise candidate, had shown such independence in his cabinet selections. No one but Polk's intimate friends had known at that time of his determination to be President in fact as well as in name. Even much later, when the truth should have become apparent, some writers speculated that Polk's Cabinet, which they considered superior while they dismissed Polk as mediocre, would dominate the President. But from the very first day in office Polk worked from early morning until night six days a week (excepting Sunday unless absolutely impossible to do so), and eventually he would know various duties so well that he could take pride in possessing the ability to administer the entire executive branch of government without reliance on any member of the Cabinet.

A diary entry indicated the extent of Polk's concentration on his job. "No President who performs his duty faithfully and conscientiously can have any leisure. If he entrusts the details and smaller matters to subordinates constant errors will occur. I prefer to supervise the whole operations of the Government myself rather than entrust the public business to subordinates, and this makes my duties very great." Once Polk wagered Buchanan a basket of champagne that a formal letter the Secretary of State had prepared for presidential signature had not been drawn up in proper State Department form, and Polk won.

From Polk's first day in office he also devoted himself to following three continuing developments of vital interest. One was annexation activity in Texas, where the United States chargé d'affaires, energetic Andrew Jackson Donelson (nephew of the former President and a graduate of West Point), began working to encourage Texans' prompt acceptance of the offer of membership in the North American union in the face of an apparent intrigue by Britain and France to keep Texas a republic. Another was the Oregon question, which Polk determined to resolve as soon as possible, even though this could lead to war. Polk intended to terminate that treaty with Britain specifying joint Oregon occupation, to decide on a firm boundary separating holdings of the two countries there, and to establish sole jurisdiction in the land belonging to the United States. The third important development was the growing Mexican crisis.

The trouble with Mexico involved more than Texas. For years the

United States had been pressing for payment of various damages incurred by its citizens in Mexico, largely as a result of the disorder and violence that stemmed from governmental instability there. In 1841 a neutral claims commission accepted by both nations had awarded two million dollars in damages to American citizens. Mexico had acknowledged the debt and had paid three of twenty quarterly installments agreed upon. Then payments ceased. The always poor Mexican Government had exhausted its ready cash.

This non-payment had angered American officials and had reinforced their conception of Mexican irresponsibility and meanness. In most American eyes Mexico represented little more than a nest of poisonous reptiles. Americans saw those massacres of Anglo-Saxons during the recent Texas rebellion as proof. Furthermore, Mexicans were "blustering cowards" who used the safety of their own country to insult the United States flag, American diplomatic representatives, and plain citizens—and to confiscate their property. An adventuresome trader, Josiah Gregg, had described some aspects of the Mexican character in a recently published book (*Commerce of the Prairies,* 1844) that attracted attention in the United States.

Nothing could be left exposed in Mexico without fear of having it stolen, Gregg said, and people there were mostly on the side of the thief, especially if the property stolen belonged to an American or to another foreigner. Even if caught, Gregg added, the brigand might draw only a wink and no punishment from a magistrate.

Gregg provided more information about Mexicans. They loved gambling, drinking, smoking, midday siestas, and cockfighting on Sundays. Certainly they were not a people with whom many Americans could develop much empathy.

One activity described by Gregg proved especially repulsive to most readers. For sport Mexican men would tie the feet of a greased fowl to the limb of a tree, allowing the squawking thing to hang barely within reach of a man on horseback. Then each contestant, mounted, would race past at full speed and try to grab the bird. Usually it would slip from their hands and flap its wings weakly. When a man succeeded in tearing the victim loose he would spur his horse in an attempt to escape with his prize while other men followed in pursuit, hoping to wrest the fowl away. Often they would rip the bird into a bloody mess, but if it survived intact the man holding it invariably presented it to his mistress, who carried her trophy to the evening fandango as testimony to the prowess of her lover.

Now these people had alienated Americans further; they had reneged on their payments. Polk began to ponder ways of getting the rest of the money. Perhaps Mexico would be willing to settle the disputed Texas boundary, conceding it to be the Texas-claimed Rio Grande instead of the Mexican-claimed Nueces River farther east, if the United States Government would assume the lapsed payment of damages. Regardless of the outcome of any such negotiation, however, Polk intended to stand on the Rio Grande, as was indicated in a letter written June 6, 1845, to the former President of Texas, Sam Houston, soliciting support for annexation. "You may have no apprehensions in regard to your boundary," Polk declared. "Texas once a part of the Union & we will maintain all your rights of territory & will not suffer them to be sacrificed."

Polk's thinking simultaneously raced ahead to California, and, characteristically, he mulled over the use of money for a deal. Perhaps some kind of cash settlement might be worked out so that California could come under United States jurisdiction. Polk's lack of understanding of the Mexican character, however, precluded any mutually satisfactory solution of this and other matters. To a Mexican, money did not have exactly the same value that it had to a small-town Tennessee lawyer with puritanical instincts. Furthermore, many Mexicans had a pride that forbade selling off their country to foreigners. Finally, there was that basic problem regarding Texas. Mexico never had acknowledged its independence in the first place and had declared repeatedly that annexation by the United States would mean war. No Mexican leader could back away from a stand like that without making some very good explanations to his countrymen.

Most of this was lost on Polk—or was at least ignored by him. He continued to mull over Mexican problems and to bring them up for discussion occasionally at cabinet meetings. Of greater urgency in his first months as President, however, was Oregon. Polk had been elected with the help of a Democratic slogan, "Fifty-four Forty or Fight"—meaning the United States claimed Oregon all the way up to North Latitude 54 degrees 40 minutes, a line considerably north of present Edmonton, Alberta, Canada—and though he privately desired to compromise with Britain if a prompt settlement could be reached, he had no intention of avoiding the issue and the British threat that it portended. While some members of the Cabinet urged caution, Polk began to propel the United States toward a simultaneous showdown with both Britain and Mexico.

Of the three momentous matters—Texas, Mexico, and Oregon—the annexation of the Lone Star Republic was first to be resolved, although not without some last-minute anxiety in Polk's Washington. The concern stemmed from official silence in Texas regarding the offer of annexation sent by John Tyler shortly before he left office early in March. Toward the end of April Andrew Jackson Donelson arrived at Galveston in his job as United States chargé d'affaires to urge prompt action by Texas, but immediate action was not forthcoming—as he soon discovered. Weeks passed, then a month. Colorless, quiet Anson Jones, a medical doctor who had been elected President of the Republic of Texas, had made no statement regarding the annexation proposal, a neglect that infuriated many Texans who had yearned for statehood in the Union for a decade now.

Was Jones another Texas leader who had fallen victim to empire fever? Sam Houston and Mirabeau Lamar, previous Presidents, both had spoken at times of a Texas empire that might encompass lands as far away as those bordering the Pacific Ocean. Now Jones, too, seemed to be having dreams of empire. Or was he involved in some intrigue with Britain and France, as Sam Houston had been after the United States rebuffed Texas in earlier attempts to gain annexation? Whatever the reason, Jones quickly fell from Texans' favor in the spring of 1845. They burned him in effigy, assuming he intended to sabotage this chance of joining the Union. In Washington, Polk became anxious.

But all the time Jones had been working to give Texans a delightful choice: Mexican recognition of independence and the chance to establish a genuine republic, or annexation. British and French ministers, laboring urgently to prevent further expansion by the growing North American giant, had won Jones's agreement to delay action on annexation until they could persuade Mexico to recognize Texas' independence, with the stipulation that Texas stay out of the Union and remain a republic. By June 3, 1845, Jones had all the promises necessary to submit his proposal, and he presented it to the Texas Congress in its shacklike Capitol at Washington-on-the-Brazos, a ragged town of frame buildings strung out along a street still cluttered with stumps.

The Texas congressmen voted unanimously for annexation, then censured Jones for his delay. Still needed were approval of annexation and drafting of a state constitution by a convention called to meet July 4, then at-large voting on both matters, but everyone knew the outcome had been decided.

In Washington the Polk administration began making momentous moves without further consulting the United States Congress. That order went out to General Taylor in Louisiana "to move [as the disgusted Colonel Hitchcock recorded it] without any delay to some point on the coast near the Sabine or elsewhere, and as soon as [General Taylor] shall hear of the acceptance by the Texas convention of the annexation resolutions of our Congress he is immediately to proceed with his whole command to the extreme western border of Texas and take up a position on the banks of or near the Rio Grande. . . ."

Word of the death of Andrew Jackson, who died at the Hermitage June 8, had saddened Polk—but had not slowed him. Another order went out from Washington, but the date of ultimate arrival at its destination was extremely uncertain. On June 24 Polk's Navy Department started a dispatch on its slow, tortuous way to remote waters: to ancient, fussy Commodore John D. Sloat, ordering him to avoid aggression but to occupy California ports in the event of a war declaration by Mexico.

6.

Far Western Vastness

About this time a tanned, lithe thirty-two-year-old U. S. Army officer with dark hair and keen eyes was making final preparations in Washington for traveling toward California in command of a government-sponsored exploring party that would probe the central Rocky Mountains and the area around the Great Salt Lake, then examine raw mountain ranges west of the Rockies in Oregon and California with the intention of finding passes through them to be used by American emigrants. The United States would have its share of the Pacific Coast one way or another.

John Charles Frémont already had visited that far western vastness; this would be his third major expedition. He was one of the very few men in Washington who could talk first hand about experiences in California. This distinction gave him entree into many important households, including the Executive Mansion, and brought him invitations to countless parties.

Other assets also helped to make him attractive. Frémont had the looks and manners of an interesting, exciting man, and his pretty, lively, brown-eyed wife, Jessie, was the daughter of powerful Senator Thomas Hart Benton of Missouri.

Frémont's Gallic appearance and his place of birth—Savannah, Georgia—could be reconciled. His mother, a Virginia beauty, had been seventeen years old at the time of her marriage of convenience to a gouty but rich man old enough to be her grandfather. When a dashing refugee from the French Revolution, Charles Frémon, swept into Richmond, Virginia, where the incongruous couple made their home, the bored young wife was easily charmed into taking a stagecoach with the attractive stranger to a passionate new life. But Frémon died five years later, leaving her with John Charles and two other young children.

The family moved to Charleston, South Carolina, where John Charles Frémont—Charley—grew into a dark, handsome, agile youth who learned his Latin, Greek, and mathematics easily, but who also evinced restlessness and impetuosity. At times he forsook his books for the company of a pretty French Creole girl or for the outdoor companionship of her two brothers in delightful tramps through the dense woods near Charleston and in thrilling boat trips on spray-swept Atlantic coastal waters.

Only months before his scheduled graduation from Charleston College rashness again overcame practicality in Frémont, and he found himself dismissed from the school because of negligence. His ability in mathematics and his attractiveness remained, however, and he obtained a teaching job to support himself and his mother. Eventually this evolved into a United States Navy instructorship in mathematics aboard the U.S.S. *Natchez* (whose executive officer was David Farragut), but Frémont hated the tedium of shipboard confinement and was glad to return to land.

One of the many Charlestonians who had been charmed by Frémont's youthful good looks, intelligence, and high spirits helped to launch him on what proved to be his career. Urbane Joel Poinsett, an influential Democrat, a former minister to Mexico, and a member of a wealthy Huguenot family, saw promise in the son of that dashing Frenchman who had terminated so unhappy a marriage. Poinsett had, in fact, helped Frémont to get the naval appointment, although not enthusiastically. Poinsett did not believe this was really the course Frémont should take.

In 1838 Poinsett, while Secretary of War under Van Buren, arranged for Frémont a commission as second lieutenant in the Topographical Corps of the U. S. Army. The work seemed ideal for Frémont. He could use his mathematics in surveying, map making, and land navigation, and he could revel in nature. Frémont accompanied an expedition west of the Mississippi River and returned to Washington, where the Missouri senator, Thomas Hart Benton, inevitably invited him into his home for frequent and long discussions.

Benton the Westerner was, of course, an expansionist. Although he opposed Texas' annexation and the war he believed it would bring, he urged the acquisition of Oregon—but he wanted it effected through negotiation, not open conflict. Benton knew a great deal about the West, not because he had traveled extensively there, but because he had talked with men who had explored the area. Now the senator from Missouri interrogated this young second lieutenant, and both men enjoyed the discussions.

Frémont found no reason to share some common Washington objections to Benton. The senator was known as an opinionated, pompous, conceited man—a long-winded speaker who could empty his chamber in the north wing of the Capitol the minute he rose to deliver another of his interminable orations. But Benton also could be a good listener at times, especially when he had for company a young explorer like Frémont, and he was a man with broad knowledge and interest. Finally, he had a pretty daughter, Jessie, about to turn fifteen. Frémont began visiting the Benton home with regularity that became alarming. The senator and his wife could see clearly that Frémont's frequent appearances now were not primarily for the purpose of imparting more geographical information about the West. Senatorial influence that Frémont did not want got the explorer a commission to make a lengthy survey of the Des Moines River, in far-off Iowa Territory.

When Frémont returned to Washington he married Jessie in secret, in October of 1841. The angry Benton could only accept this arrangement, after an initial explosion, or in effect lose a daughter who was as strong-willed as he. Thereafter Benton became a staunch congressional supporter of Frémont and his Western explorations.

Much earlier the United States Government had sponsored expeditions toward the Pacific Coast. Meriwether Lewis and William Clark had been sent in 1804 by the ever curious Thomas Jefferson, then President, to determine exactly what kind of country the United States had acquired by the Louisiana Purchase. For two years the two explorers and their men had roamed the Western wilderness, mapping unknown country, making extensive observations, gathering specimens, wintering when howling blizzards made travel impossible. Along the Missouri and Columbia rivers they had crept—from St. Louis all the way to the Pacific Ocean, then back.

Zebulon Pike followed, in 1805–7, seeking the headwaters of the Mississippi, Arkansas, and Red rivers; discovering in the jagged Rockies the 14,109-foot-high peak later named for him; being apprehended by

Spanish troops for encroaching on Spanish territory. The wary Spaniards had realized where the United States was headed.

Now came Frémont, and if he was not to be a pathfinder like the earlier explorers, he certainly was to become a pathmarker—as his biographer, Allan Nevins, said. By 1845 Frémont had led two surveying expeditions along the Oregon Trail, already in use by growing numbers of American emigrants but badly in need of marking and mapping for their safety. Northwest from Independence, Missouri, the trail wound—at first along the dark expanse of the Missouri River for a short distance, then into present Kansas and Nebraska, to a point near Grand Island, and up the Platte Valley—comparatively smooth traveling, level land. Near the northeastern tip of present Colorado, however, the emigrants came upon hills, then mountains. Up the North Platte River to the Laramie their loaded wagons groaned and creaked and sometimes broke. Those able to continue rumbled slowly through broad South Pass, in the southwestern part of what is now Wyoming, then down the Green River Valley to Fort Bridger, an isolated trapping post near the southwestern tip of present Wyoming. From there they took a more northerly course—but also westward, always westward—through an awesome region across present Idaho toward Walla Walla, then almost due westward to the fertile green goal: the valleys of the Columbia and the Willamette.

Two thousand miles separated the western end of the Oregon Trail from the eastern beginning. By 1845 the long road had been cluttered in places with the bones of horses and oxen, with mounds that denoted human graves, with assorted possessions thrown out to lighten wagons, and with debris left from Indian attacks. More than five thousand American emigrants, however, had arrived in the distant land.

The United States Government sought to encourage more settlers and for that reason had sent Frémont and a party of men on those two earlier Oregon Trail expeditions to chart the way. The guide had been Kit Carson, a clear-eyed man who was, fortunately, as cool as Frémont was impetuous. In those two expeditions, during 1842–44, Frémont and his men had surveyed, mapped, and marked the Oregon Trail all the way to the mouth of the Columbia River on the Pacific Coast, then—in a display of Frémont's impetuosity—had made a foolhardy winter march toward California over unmapped Sierras blanketed by deep snow and swept by intermittent blizzards.

For a month they had struggled across "rock upon rock, snow upon

49

snow," eating their animals to avoid starvation, estimating the height of drifts to be from five to twenty feet, tying handkerchiefs over their eyes sometimes to avoid snow blindness, stumbling on. Finally they had reached the California paradise, and there Frémont had met a short, fat, blue-eyed Swiss adventurer, John Sutter, who instructed his servants to set before the starved men a feast of trout, salmon, venison, bear, beef, fresh vegetables and fruit, and Rhine wine. Then Sutter showed Frémont around his vast estate, founded on a Mexican grant of about fifty thousand acres around present Sacramento, and aroused in Frémont a deep love for this land.

Frémont became acquainted with California, its people, and its enchanting life. Virtually the entire country was devoted to ranching, an activity that did not require continual heavy labor, and the customs of the people reflected their easy existence. The fifteen thousand white residents of California (most of them Spanish-speaking) lived mostly on beef, readily available in unlimited quantity. They rode horseback everywhere and rarely walked anywhere. They relied on fine climate and soil and picturesque surroundings for a good life, and not on money. To obtain desired goods they could not provide for themselves they had long before acquired the habit of visiting Yankee trading vessels anchored offshore. There they would offer a trade of hides for manufactured articles marked up many times in price; life in California was too good to waste on worry about available cash. "If I must be cast in sickness or destitution on the care of a stranger," said an American visitor about this time, "let it be in California; but let it be before American avarice has hardened the heart and made a god of gold."

Not even the twenty thousand or so Indians (including four thousand domesticated) posed much of a problem. Nor did Mexican bureaucracy. Mexican troops had been driven out of the country, and California was enjoying at least a momentary independence similar to that of the Republic of Texas in 1836.

After his 1844 visit to California Frémont had returned to Washington, and to his wife Jessie, determined to go back to the land where Sutter had found comfort and happiness. At that time the young explorer probably did not realize how soon this would be—or under what circumstances. That spring of 1845, while Washington was awaiting word of the Texas action on annexation and while Polk was mulling over the problems involving Britain and Mexico, Frémont was preparing to carry out those new orders to explore the central Rocky Mountains and the area around the Great Salt Lake, then probe the mountains west of the Rockies—the Cascades in Oregon and the Sierras in California—for passes that might be used by American emigrants. This time he would have a strong force accompanying him, an unusually strong force for a party of explorers: sixty men—topographical engineers, Delaware Indian scouts, mountain men—all leathery and all to be well armed.

Frémont claimed later, correctly or not, that he had secret orders to use his men as a military expedition to secure California for the United States in the event of a Mexican declaration of war while his party roamed around the area. The eight hundred or so Americans already in California might help him in whatever military action seemed necessary, although in reality many of those settlers were undisciplined beachcombers, horse thieves, and deserters from ships.

Shortly before Frémont left on his third expedition he accompanied his beaming father-in-law, Senator Benton, to the Executive Mansion for a talk with President Polk. Frémont and Benton long before had reached enthusiastic agreement on the value of Oregon and California to the United States, and both men knew of Polk's desires in that direction. Instead of enjoying an inspirational visit, however, Frémont left dismayed and somewhat depressed. His emotional turnabout resulted from a display of Polk's narrow-mindedness.

Frémont gave Polk an account of his activities and observations in Oregon and California, spoke of their importance, and remarked on his countrymen's ignorance of both areas. For example, Frémont said, he had just examined a map in the Library of Congress that depicted the Great Salt Lake as being linked with the Pacific Ocean by three large rivers. One emptied into the Columbia, one into the Gulf of California, and one into San Francisco Bay. All were impossibilities, Frémont declared. He knew better from firsthand observation.

Polk was not a man to reject a map so quickly, even though the cartographer might not have been within a thousand miles of the area depicted. Long afterward Frémont recalled Polk's chilly reply: "He found me 'young,' [Frémont said] and [commented on] the 'impulsiveness of young men,' and was not at all satisfied in his own mind that these rivers were not running there as laid down."

By late August 1845 Frémont had gathered his exploring party at distant Bent's Fort, near present Las Animas, Colorado, and had summoned his noted guide, Kit Carson, from an agricultural retirement on the Little Cimarron River. Frémont and his sixty men, two hundred horses, and a supply of beef cattle on the hoof clattered away westward, ahead of the dust cloud they raised, bound for the Rockies, for the Great Salt Lake, and eventually for that golden land around John Sutter's fort.

"My path of life . . . led out from among the grand and lovely features of Nature, and its pure and wholesome air," Frémont would write years later in his *Memoirs*, "into the poisoned atmosphere . . . of conflict among men. . . ."

PART II

Toward a Collision

FROM EARLY JULY 1845
TO EARLY MAY 1846

7.

For the Protection of Texas

Zachary Taylor's "Army of Observation" also had been on the move westward. The Texas convention scheduled to meet at Austin July 4, 1845, had set it in motion. No one doubted that the assembly would approve annexation, and on the very day it did so (by a vote of 55 to 1) troops of the 4th Infantry Regiment, recently stationed near Fort Jesup at a camp named Salubrity, began disembarking from steamboats at New Orleans bound eventually for the protection of Texas, under those previously dispatched orders from Washington.

With the 4th Infantry was that shy, tone-deaf lieutenant, Sam Grant. But months earlier, while Grant had been stationed at expansive Jefferson Barracks, a scenic post composed of whitewashed buildings and isolated powder magazines located among sprawling Missouri hills and meadows that were cut by miles of bridle paths, the music of love had played upon his soul. He had thrown off most of whatever bashfulness might have plagued him in that situation to court the pretty sister of a West Point classmate.

The girl's name was Julia Dent. Her father, a leading citizen of the St. Louis area where Jefferson Barracks was located, happened to be an Andrew Jackson Democrat, a friend of that powerful Senator Thomas Hart Benton, and a slaveowner. None of this showed any affinity with Grant's past or present life. But Julia, four years younger than he, proved to be a powerful attraction soon after he first met her, and his visits to the rambling Dent home, White Haven, became frequent. Before Grant left Jefferson Barracks for Camp Salubrity and Army of Observation duty he had asked Julia to marry him, but he had been much too shy at first to speak to Colonel Dent about this. He settled for a quiet engagement, and typically he kept this secret from her father and even from his fellow officers. He had written Julia regularly from Louisiana, and just before moving on to New Orleans he had obtained leave of absence to visit her. At that time he had summoned the courage to talk with Julia's father, who had reluctantly agreed to their plans for the future.

Now, disembarking at New Orleans, Grant carried with him those soft memories. He also carried a resentment about his present assignment that resembled Colonel Hitchcock's, although as a very low junior officer Grant apparently refrained from expressing this to army companions and, in fact, might not have felt so strongly about it at that time as he did later. Long afterward he wrote about his feeling:

> Ostensibly we [of the "Army of Observation"] were intended to prevent filibustering into Texas, but really [we stood as] a menace to Mexico in case she appeared to contemplate war. Generally the officers of the army were indifferent whether the annexation was consummated or not; but not so all of them. For myself, I was bitterly opposed to the measure, and to this day regard the war, which resulted, as one of the most unjust ever waged by a stronger against a weaker nation. It was an instance of a republic following the bad example of European monarchies, in not considering justice in their desire to acquire additional territory.

Like Hitchcock, Grant believed the "occupation, separation, and annexation were, from the inception of the movement to its final consummation, a conspiracy to acquire territory out of which slave states might be formed for the American Union." Grant's and Hitchcock's views represented those of a great many military officers from Northern and Eastern states.

Nevertheless, they followed orders—and they apparently shared a pride of profession. Even in those ominous days of trouble with Britain and Mexico the United States Congress was debating whether to close West Point as a breeding place for a dangerous military clique that could in time engulf the grand New World republic with friction, faults, and fighting common to the European monarchies to which Grant referred. This action resulted in some closing of ranks by Military Academy graduates—even reluctant career men like Grant and (in time) Hitchcock, who certainly resented unfavorable implications regarding integrity and fitness.

Paradoxically, however, the civilian officials of government, not the military officers, had been foremost in taking the militant stand against

Mexico, and this continued to be the case. Army officers could only carry out orders, and many did so at this time with great effort, stifling their personal feelings—and in some cases expending themselves physically. In 1845 the U. S. Army had no retirement system, and numerous old, feeble senior officers had been long absent from the units to which they were attached. With a war looming, however, the most conscientious of them sought to show themselves as commanders in actuality as well as in name, and they rejoined their units. One such instance aroused that feeling of professional pride in young Lieutenant Grant.

His 4th Regiment had encamped at a post four miles below New Orleans, a city then in the simultaneous grip of deadly yellow fever and another sizzling summer. Those health hazards certainly should not have been ignored by Grant's decrepit regimental commander, Colonel J. H. Vose, but the old man determined to do the job expected of him. One torrid mid-July day, after his soldiers had established themselves in their temporary quarters, Vose took command at a battalion drill, gave two or three orders, then abruptly dismissed the unit. He began walking toward his quarters but dropped in a faint and died of an apparent heart attack—"not a man," Grant commented, "to discover infirmity in the presence of danger."

Nor was the commander of the 3rd Infantry Regiment a man to give way to weakness. Colonel Ethan Allen Hitchcock recorded in his diary that one officer of his regiment was "on sick leave from old age and its disabilities" and that he had been ill himself, with diarrhea. Nevertheless, Hitchcock accompanied his regiment during its move downriver in two steamboats to New Orleans. The men of the 3rd arrived there July 10 and went into stifling quarters at a large cotton press rented for one hundred dollars a day—"pretty costly," Hitchcock sniffed. "The United States Government, or the executive [Polk], rather, is evidently determined to send troops into Texas if the least color of a pretext can be found—the only object being to make a practical exhibition of annexation."

Hitchcock's superior, Zachary Taylor, had stayed behind at Fort Jesup directing the departure for Texas of Colonel David Twiggs's 2nd Regiment of Dragoons. The mounted soldiers clomped off southwestward toward San Antonio, their immediate destination, and Taylor rejoined his infantry regiments at New Orleans on July 15. Four days later a company of the 3rd Artillery commanded by arrogant Lieutenant Braxton Bragg arrived in the city from Charleston. The U. S. Army certainly appeared to be girding for battle, but its numbers at this time made Lieutenant Grant's subsequent statement about a war "waged by a stronger against a weaker nation" a temporary incongruity. The United States had, altogether, only eight thousand or so troops—many of the enlisted men foreign born, many of the soldiers still scattered around some hundred outposts. The Mexican Army was four times as large. Most American officers had never maneuvered a unit larger than a company, but their army, small and scattered though it was, had begun moving toward a concentration of force, and they would soon have a chance to exercise broader command.

The concentration was to be at a hamlet on the western shore of Corpus Christi Bay, in Texas. The movement would be supported by the U. S. Navy's Home Squadron, commanded by Commodore David Conner —battle-experienced in the War of 1812—who already had received orders to cruise the Gulf near the Mexican coast and to attack Tampico and the fortress San Juan de Ulúa at Vera Cruz in event of war.

Taylor himself had chosen Corpus Christi Bay as the assembly site rather than the mouth of the Rio Grande, which Washington kept mentioning. Advice from some Texans had persuaded him. Taylor himself knew little about the country, and Washington, equally ignorant, had been able to provide scant information. But knowledgeable Texans had declared the shallow mouth of the Rio Grande much too hazardous for navigation; so Taylor had determined to gather his men at Corpus Christi Bay, probably attracted also to that location by descriptions of its beauty and of the abundance of fish, oysters, and deer in the vicinity. From there he could, if necessary, march his army by land to the Rio Grande. Moreover, the reluctant Taylor must have reflected, choosing this more cautious site for the original encampment might not provoke a Mexican attack. At this time the general seemed anything but eager for a war against Mexico.

The movement from New Orleans to Corpus Christi Bay began early on July 22 with loading of 3rd Regiment baggage and supplies aboard the steamship *Alabama*, lying quietly alongside a pier that jutted into the turbid Mississippi. Luggage belonging to Taylor and four officers of his staff—including Hitchcock's brilliant friend, Captain Bliss—also went aboard. Then, at eleven o'clock that warm evening, the infantrymen of Hitchcock's 3rd Regiment formed in line outside the cotton press, wheeled into column, and marched to the music of the regimental band through moonlit streets to their waiting transport.

The music and the constant tramping awakened residents along the route. The people peered cautiously but curiously from behind half-opened doors and windows "to know what all the fuss could be about." They saw bayonets glistening in a mellow moonlight that also seemed to gild nearby domes and housetops. "The deep shadows on one side of the street, the bright moonlight upon the other, the solemn quiet of a sleeping city, disturbed so harshly by the martial music of the column, formed a scene . . . not easily . . . forgotten," one observer remarked.

At the *Alabama* the men clambered noisily up wooden gangways and crowded on board the ship. Already on board now were Hitchcock, Taylor, the four staff officers, and several manservants (allowed to accompany officers on campaigns in those days). For most of the passengers sleep on this exciting night was not possible, and many men lined the rail to watch the ensuing activity.

At three o'clock in morning darkness of July 23, 1845, the *Alabama* cast off lines and began the voyage to Texas: down the swiftly running Mississippi, in growing daylight; past the rickety, sun-splashed houses built on piles at the river's mouth; southwestward across the Gulf of Mexico—its waters left almost unruffled by a gentle breeze—in a losing race with the afternoon sun. A sloop of war mothered a flock of sailing vessels that straggled behind the ever churning *Alabama*.

Two days later the steamer made a Texas landfall off narrow Matagorda Island, which stretched for many miles along the coast. All afternoon of July 25 the *Alabama* chugged southwestward toward its destination, with Matagorda in sight to starboard: white sandy beaches, all lifeless, against a backdrop of rolling sand hills topped with summer greenery. The scene reminded one officer of Florida, but without the palmetto and the pine found there. By the following morning the setting had lost some of its charm. High winds and rough seas battered the lumbering steamer and posed a problem for landing the troops.

General Taylor wanted to get his men on land as quickly as possible, but neither weather nor shoreline appeared favorable. Gulf shallowness and an absence of reliable navigational charts precluded taking the *Alabama* to an anchorage anywhere near the selected camp site on Corpus Christi Bay. Taylor would have to transport his men by boat to St. Joseph's Island, which lay off a bay named Aransas that adjoined Corpus Christi Bay, then move them down that island and across Corpus Christi Bay by lighter, raft, or boat to the camp site.

On this tempestuous morning anxiety overcame Taylor's usual placidity, and his officers hastened to assuage his increasing impatience and grumpiness. Colonel Hitchcock ordered a lieutenant ashore "and he planted a small U.S. flag on a sandhill—the first stars and stripes ever raised in Texas by authority." Then Hitchcock sent three companies of infantry ashore with their mess chests. Shallowness of the water around the frequent sand bars forced them to leap overboard from their boats and to wade the last fifty yards or so to the island—overboard into a boiling surf, but "they made a real frolic of it." A few of the laundry women who inevitably accompanied the soldiers "took to the element as if they were born in it; while others, more delicately nerved, preferred a man's back, and rode on shore."

They found St. Joseph's to be a low island—an elongated pile of sand just high enough to poke its uneven topside out of the Gulf. But it was already providing a habitation for three or four families residing there, and, oddly, it afforded fresh water, although this tasted "most unpleasant." Some drinkable water could be found in ponds incredibly scattered among salty pools. More could be found by digging three or four feet in the sand.

By July 28 all of the 3rd Regiment had landed, delighted to have escaped the crowded, prisonlike atmosphere of the ship and pleased to find excellent fishing and hunting on the island. Men located oyster beds. In the surf they caught sheepshead, drum, mullet, and redfish. Venison and duck provided more variety for menus. Hunters stationed atop any of the numerous sand hills could see a deer half a mile away, and if feeding grounds or a pool of fresh water happened to be nearby the innocent animal might come close enough for a waiting hunter to blast away without much chance of missing his target. Around those same ponds flocked teal and mallard duck. St. Joseph's Island seemed more like an outdoorsman's paradise than a steppingstone to war.

Early on the morning of July 28 Colonel Hitchcock rode around St. Joseph's on a regimental inspection, then enjoyed a breakfast of fresh fish and oysters. His men had encamped along a three-mile stretch of shoreline. Enjoying plenty of room, drinkable water, and good fishing and hunting, they were in no mood to concern themselves about the good or bad aspects of the annexation of Texas. Hitchcock, too, believed the encampment a comfortable one and was himself in no hurry to remove his men to the selected site on Corpus Christi Bay. But General Taylor wanted to go on to the destination.

The next day Taylor ordered Hitchcock to load two of his infantry companies aboard the lighter *Undine*, which would transport them down Aransas Bay into Corpus Christi Bay and to the camp site.

> The difficulty was [wrote the disgusted Hitchcock] that the lighter drew more than 4 feet of water and it was reported that there were but 2½ feet on the flats [between the two bays]. The General changed his mind two or three times as to the expedience of trying it, but we finally got off before noon, and ran aground about 5 miles down the bay. There we stayed all day and all night; but we at last landed some men and provisions on a raft. Another night passed. It was still found impossible to cross the flats and General Taylor directed the quartermaster to hire all the fishing boats that had gathered around us from curiosity and transfer the men and cargo to them. He was quite beside himself with anxiety, fatigue, and passion. I undertook to tell him that the troops could be very comfortable on St. Joseph's Island till a high southwest wind should give us high water on the flats; but he would not listen to me and was exceedingly impatient to have the companies off.

The quartermaster hired seven small boats, and shortly before noon of July 31 Hitchcock and his stranded infantrymen transferred to them, crossed Corpus Christi Bay in a rough sea, and landed at sunset on the western side of the inlet, near a high bluff and not far from a village commonly known then as Kinney's Ranch. The hamlet—the most southerly settlement of the Texans—actually was nothing more than a commercial post established by a man named H. L. Kinney for dealings with traders and smugglers from Mexico.

"All comments agree that our safe arrival is little short of a miracle," Hitchcock remarked. The doubting colonel had been placed in temporary command of the operation on Corpus Christi Bay—General Taylor had stayed behind, on St. Joseph's—but Hitchcock expressed no joy in his assignment. He remained unconvinced of the legality or the morality of coming here in the first place, and in a diary entry he wrote, "Corpus Christi, 'Texas' "—taking pains to put the quotation marks around "Texas." Although the camp was far removed from the Rio Grande, it was west of the Nueces River, which Mexico still contended represented the Texas boundary.

Compounding all the unpleasantness, Hitchcock was ailing again with the diarrhea that had bothered him earlier. "I have been ill for the last two days," he wrote early in August, "but am better today. My sickness is per-

61

haps partly disgust at the state of things here—the haste and ignorance displayed in this movement. . . ."

Lieutenant Sam Grant arrived in Texas in mid-September. His 4th Regiment traveled across the Gulf in two vessels: the side-wheel steamboat *Dayton*, which carried most of the men, and a sailing ship Grant identified later (in his *Memoirs*) as *Suviah*, in which he and the remainder of the 4th were embarked. When Grant reached Texas he was shocked to see the *Dayton* lying wrecked offshore. The steamer had blown up on September 13, killing two lieutenants and four other members of the 4th Regiment. Grant had known the dead officers since West Point days.

Grant continued to echo Hitchcock's cynicism, although probably not publicly at this time. The fledgling soldier felt that he and the others had been sent to Texas to provoke a war—"but it was essential that Mexico should commence it. . . . Once initiated [Grant said] there were but few public men who would have the courage to oppose it. Experience proves that the man who obstructs a war in which his nation is engaged, no matter whether right or wrong, occupies no enviable place in life or history."

8.

War Will Not Be Our Fault

While Colonel Hitchcock and Lieutenant Grant suffered through mental and physical discomforts in Texas, residents in the city of Washington began looking forward to autumn to relieve the misery brought by another muggy summer.

The stifling weather had not turned President Polk aside from his usual arduous routine. Rising early, he began his work promptly—after shaving himself. Following an interruption for a light breakfast, he went back to work. He continued his labors until late at night in that exhausting six-day-a-week schedule of his. During his term to date Polk had not enjoyed even a brief vacation—but he probably could not have really enjoyed a respite from labor anyway. To him constant work and the accomplishment to be relished from it provided the only satisfaction in life.

In August, Oregon and Mexico nearly monopolized Polk's thoughts. Despite the militant tone of his inauguration speech and of some subsequent declarations, Polk did not want war—and did not expect it at this time. On July 28 he had written a letter in which he stated, "I do not . . . anticipate that Mexico will be mad enough to declare war. I think she would have done so but for the appearance of a strong naval force in the Gulf and our army moving in the direction of her frontier on land." Nor did he anticipate immediate war with Britain. He had made no move to ask for a larger standing army or for increased military appropriations.

So the President was no fanatical "Fifty-four Forty or Fight" man, as were many of his countrymen, but neither was he an entirely peaceful man. Should hostilities be "forced" on the United States by the obstinacy of Great Britain or Mexico, he indicated he would not tremble with fear

63

or indecision. He calculated that he could attain his goals through war if through no other way. Therefore, with remarkable inconsistency, Polk continually spoke of peace but thought of war, as shown by the wording in orders to Commodore Conner, commander of the Home Squadron: ". . . it being the determination of the President to preserve peace, if possible; and, if war comes, to recover peace by adopting the most prompt and energetic measures."

Polk's diary for August 1845 reflects this apparently incongruous attitude. A month earlier his Secretary of State, Buchanan, had offered Britain a compromise Oregon settlement along the forty-ninth parallel, but without the right of free navigation by the British of the Columbia River. A similar proposal had been made before Polk's presidency began; so the British minister in Washington, Richard Pakenham, rejected this latest offer insolently and without even referring it to his government—a blunder by Pakenham, because Britain (unknown to Polk and apparently to Pakenham, too) actually had no intention of provoking a fight with the United States over Orgeon, having encountered enough trouble nearer home. But the affront stiffened Polk's stand on Oregon, and in a cabinet meeting held near the end of August he stated the course he would follow. Buchanan would send a note to Pakenham reasserting United States right to all of Oregon, from 42° to that famous 54°40′ North Latitude, and withdrawing the offer to compromise at 49°. Polk instructed Buchanan to say that the rejected compromise had been proposed "first in deference to what had been done by our predecessors, and second, with an anxious desire to preserve peace between the two countries."

Now this offer was to be retracted, and there the matter would rest. If Britain wanted to make a counterproposal, the United States would listen. If Britain wanted to fight, the United States would oblige. "Let [Britain] take the one course or the other, the United States will stand right in the eyes of the whole civilized world, and if war was the consequence England would be in the wrong." These were militant words for the President of a nation that proclaimed a love for peace, but Polk had his formula for dealing with Britain: "The only way to treat John Bull is to look him straight in the eye."

Polk's Secretary of State did not share this assuredness. In a meeting of the Cabinet Buchanan said he agreed with Polk's retraction of the compromise offer and with his reassertion of the Oregon title, but the Secretary of State wanted to insert a paragraph soliciting a counterproposal from Britain.

Polk refused to consider this suggestion. The compromise at 49° already had been rejected by the British minister, the President pointed out, and any proposition less favorable to the United States certainly would be rejected by Polk himself. "Why then invite a proposition which cannot for a moment be entertained?" Polk asked.

Outdebated but not silenced, Buchanan warned that the result of his following Polk's instructions would be a war that most citizens would not support. Any fighting, Buchanan argued, should be for a better cause—and in any event for self-defense.

Most other members of the Cabinet remained silent during the discussion. Only Robert Walker, the wheezy-voiced Secretary of the Treasury, spoke out for Polk. But cabinet support—or any lack of it—did not matter. Polk already had made up his mind, and he believed popular sentiment would support him. Futhermore—and with rationalization peculiar to a man like him—he declared, "If we do have war it will not be our fault." At a special meeting of the Cabinet called for the following day Polk asked Buchanan to read the note to Pakenham as prepared to his specification, expressed the opinion that it was "an able and admirable paper," and heard his Cabinet voice approval too. That evening Secretary of the Navy Bancroft accompanied Polk on a horseback ride into the countryside around the Executive Mansion—about the only diversion Polk allowed himself— and expressed admiration of the President's firmness. "I will now go with you," Bancroft said. "I believe you are right."

Two days later Polk called still another special cabinet meeting, to discuss Mexico "and the threatened invasion of Texas." The Mexican situation had deteriorated further in recent months, even after Mexico had broken diplomatic relations with Washington in March following passage of the congressional resolution offering annexation to Texas. In June the Mexican Congress had authorized an increase of military forces to prevent annexation, and in July the Mexican President had recommended to his Congress a declaration of war upon receipt of information that the United States was moving to effect a take-over of Texas.

Polk's clash with Great Britain over Oregon at first encouraged the Mexicans in their stand. They foresaw a war between the United States and Britain, and when this occurred they believed Mexico would be the direct, or at least the indirect, recipient of military aid from that other enemy of the United States. But many Mexicans lacked no confidence in their own military capability. Their Regular Army, four times as large as that of the United States (32,000 to 8,500 troops then), appeared to be better tested and trained through years of quelling or assisting revolts. Some European military observers also assumed this to be true and predicted a quick Mexican victory in battle.

Facts differed considerably from assumptions. Later a Mexican officer, Manuel Balbontin, wrote (in *La Invasión Americana*, 1883) a description of the Mexican Army at this time. Although many commissioned officers (usually political appointees) could boast of having Spanish blood, he said, the ranks consisted mostly of Indians recruited from among a criminal element or impressed for service by tough military detachments that roamed city streets and countrysides. Few men ever volunteered to serve in the ranks, Balbontin said—either in militias or in the Regular Army.

Following such an induction, the recruits learned in and around the barracks the manual of arms and the routine of military life, taught under the stick of a stern corporal. Rarely, however, did the men go off the post for maneuvers with large bodies of troops. Mexican military tactics and regulations remained the same as those used by the Spaniards before their departure (a predictable development), but because of the frequent revolutions army discipline had sagged badly, and for this and a variety of other reasons large-scale maneuvering had been virtually abandoned.

Balbontin said that the best-looking uniforms and the most efficient equipment always were given to soldiers stationed in large-city garrisons—this in order to make that inevitable Mexican show. Elsewhere, troops frequently dressed out in ragged clothing and sometimes lacked even the most essential military apparel and equipment. Everywhere pay was short and sometimes unavailable for months. Soldiers were allowed to hire themselves out as laborers, a largess that kept some of them from starving, for food was almost as irregular and as scant as was pay. When in garrison, Balbontin said, troops generally bought their own provisions, but when on a march they could expect to be given rations collected from the countryside: meat, tortillas, corn. Mexican troops on the move usually lived off the land through which they traveled.

Balbontin continued his description of the Mexican Army of those days. Infantrymen carried smooth-bore flintlock muskets brought from England two decades earlier. Artillerymen fired antiquated guns mounted on rough, heavy carriages. Actually, no part of the Mexican Army could equal the U. S. Army in range, mobility, or accuracy. But the individual Mexican soldier still could be a hard man with whom to contend when he geared his mind to a task.

Those European military observers who predicted a quick Mexican victory based their guess on still another factor besides inaccurate information. At that time the United States never had really proved itself in a war. The North American Revolution had ended successfully for the colonists partly because Britain finally desired to disengage itself rather than to expend more money and men for a military victory, and the ensuing War of 1812 had ended with the signing of a treaty (at Ghent, Belgium) that did little more than terminate hostilities on behalf of mutually weary participants. Not even mentioned at Ghent were impressment, rights of neutrals, and other issues that had propelled the United States into the 1812 conflict. Therefore, in 1845 a showdown between the United States and Mexico did not appear universally as a match between respectively stronger and weaker nations. To some observers the roles were reversible.

Under those circumstances Polk's intrepidity was all the more astonishing. But Polk never was a man to quail, whatever his faults might have been. Still, he hoped to avoid war and thought he could, believing (as he reiterated) that "the appearance of our land and naval forces on the borders of Mexico and in the Gulf would probably deter and prevent Mexico from either declaring war or invading Texas."

Such use of force, however, virtually assured a war. No Mexican leader could afford the embarrassment of backing down under pressure after all the boasts and threats about Texas that the Mexican Government had shouted in recent years. The effect of all those declarations—many for political show only, some not—had been to solidify public opinion among Mexicans who mattered. Mexico would not retreat—would not sacrifice national honor.

Even Polk's non-military moves proved antagonizing to Mexicans— either because Polk actually planned it that way or, more likely, because he failed to recognize nuances that would ignite the Mexicans as being seemingly deliberate insults. Soon after Polk's inauguration his State Department had sent a confidential agent to Mexico with the hope of arranging future negotiations and thus avoiding war. The man, a sometime dentist named William S. Parrott, apparently had been chosen for the assignment because he had lived in Mexico for years and could speak Spanish fluently. But there his congeniality ended. He had been unpopular in Mexico, and he was one of those United States citizens who had demanded reimbursement for damages from the Mexican Government. A former United States minister to Mexico described Parrott's claim—for $690,000—as "exaggerated in a disgusting degree" and remarked, ". . . If [all these claims] were referred to me as a judge, I could not admit them, nay more, I cannot with a clear conscience assist them." Despite this, Parrott was the man selected for the peace mission, and he was under orders to say that, although the annexation of Texas was not negotiable, other disputes could be discussed and settled in a friendly manner.

At this time the interim President of Mexico happened to be the moderate leader who had succeeded Santa Anna. José Joaquín de Herrera was a temperate, honest man who actually seemed to desire peace, although public opinion and the weakness of his position apparently forced him to speak of a war over annexation. Earlier, in a peaceable attempt to forestall United States expansion, Herrera had made that offer through insistent British and French intermediaries to recognize Texas independence if the Texans would remain out of the North American Union.

Like most other Mexican presidents of this period, Herrera had come into office with a very uncertain future. The perennial problem of government finances plagued him, as did that inevitable Mexican threat of an aspiring leader waiting in the wings for a propitious moment to take over the stage by either force or trickery. This time the presidential adversary was Mariano Paredes y Arrillaga, a noisy, pretentious Mexican Army commander who had been among the men responsible for bringing Santa Anna into his most recent tenure, then responsible for driving him out. Now Paredes waited for Herrera to make a ruinous mistake, and Polk, whose self-declared efforts for peace would have been enhanced by sincere dealings with a moderate man like Herrera, helped to give Paredes his chance.

Whether or not Polk realized it, Herrera had weakened himself by his earlier soft stand on Texas. His government's promise to recognize Texas' independence providing Texas stay out of the Union had exhibited to Mexicans Herrera's willingness to make ignominious concessions, because most Mexicans felt that Texas still belonged to them. The Texans' rejection of that offer embarrassed him further. Now Herrera had to contend with the presence of Polk's agent in Mexico City, the unpopular W. S. Parrott.

Parrott found the country ablaze with anger over the moves in the United States and Texas toward annexation. Herrera, making his defen-

sive stand, could not afford to talk openly. He was instead making that
display of preparing for war, to satisfy his grumbling people. Herrera
moved to strengthen Mexico's northern frontier and ordered Paredes to
take his army there. But Paredes refused to move. He saw great troubles
about to overwhelm Herrera, and he, Paredes, would use his army command to take over the presidency at the right time.

Parrott reported all these maneuverings to Washington. He predicted
there would be no declaration of war against the United States and no
Mexican invasion of Texas, because the government had all it could do to
prevent revolution. But he also made a private observation that only "a
severe chastisement" of Mexico would secure Americans from future insults there.

In a later dispatch (dated August 28, 1845) Parrott reported that the
Mexican Government did seem willing at that time to receive a special
emissary from the United States in an attempt to solve at least some of its
problems. When this communication reached Polk in mid-September he
consulted the Cabinet, and the members agreed unanimously "that it was
expedient to reopen diplomatic relations with Mexico; but that it was to
be kept a profound secret that such a step was contemplated, for the reason mainly that if it was known in advance in the United States that a
Minister had been sent to Mexico, it would, of course, be known to the
British, French, and other foreign ministers at Washington, who might
take measures to thwart or defeat the objects of the mission."

Thus did Polk himself describe the situation. With characteristic lack
of imagination he apparently failed to see the need also for keeping such a
move secret from the Mexican public.

Polk and his advisers selected as the emissary John Slidell, a suave,
tactful lawyer from New Orleans and a man who spoke Spanish as fluently
as Parrott—but a man free of Parrott's taints. By the very next day, however, fresh rumors of war from Mexico had reached Polk through newly received New Orleans newspapers, which represented a primary source of
government intelligence about Mexico then. Polk called a special meeting
(on September 17) of the Cabinet and discussed the situation again.
Everyone agreed Slidell's departure should be delayed until the mood of
Mexico could be reascertained.

That same day Secretary of State Buchanan addressed a query to
the United States consul in Mexico City, John Black, who was acting in
the absence of a minister there. Would Mexico receive an envoy from the

United States, entrusted with full powers to adjust all questions in dispute between the two governments? Black in turn asked Foreign Relations Minister Manuel de la Peña y Peña, and a month later Buchanan read Black's reply: Mexico would indeed receive a "commissioner" if the United States would recall its naval force cruising off Vera Cruz in compliance with those earlier orders sent to Commodore Conner. Black quoted Peña y Peña's elaboration: "[The U. S. Navy's] presence would degrade Mexico, while she is receiving the commissioner, and would justly subject the United States to the imputation of contradicting by acts the vehement desire of conciliation, peace, and friendship, which is professed and asserted by words." (Three days earlier, a message from Commodore Conner himself had indicated this same Mexican willingness to negotiate.)

Thus reassured, Polk commissioned John Slidell as "Envoy Extraordinary and Minister Plenipotentiary" (not as "commissioner," as Peña y Peña had requested) and sent him on his way in November, apparently despite some warnings by Americans knowledgeable about Mexico that the government there would not dare to receive a man appointed as "minister." They said this would mean immediate re-establishment of diplomatic relations and thereby display a cowardly retraction of all those blatant threats against Texas' annexation.

Nevertheless, Polk believed (according to diary entries) that re-establishment of relations was the actual Mexican desire, and he instructed Slidell further in some detail. A primary object of the mission, Polk said, would be to agree on a permanent boundary between the United States and Mexico. Ideally this would be the Rio Grande from its mouth to "the Passo" (El Paso), then due west to the Pacific Ocean—"Mexico ceding to the United States all the country east and north of these lines." Polk thought this territory could be purchased for fifteen or twenty million dollars, but he expressed willingness to go as high as forty million for it.

Had Polk known Mexico better he would have been less optimistic. Mexican newspaper editors, hearing rumors of intrigue between the United States and Herrera, reacted immediately. One wrote:

> The vile [Herrera] government has been and is in correspondence with the usurpers. The Yankee Parrott and the American consul at Mexico [Black] are those who have agreed with the government for the loss of Texas, and this same Parrott has departed for the north to say to his government to send a commissioner to make with our government an ignominious treaty on the basis of the sur-

President Polk, photographed by Mathew Brady, February 14, 1849.

Sarah Polk, from an unflattering daguerreotype.

Captain Robert E. Lee during the war with Mexico.

Lieutenant Sam—Ulysses—Grant, whose young face has been described as prettier than this.

Ethan Allen Hitchcock after the Mexican War.

Captain Ephraim Kirby Smith—an old family photograph.

General Winfield Scott, whose genuine ability Polk never recognized.

Antonio López de Santa Anna, veteran of many magnificent failures.

During the days of the war with Mexico, Washington, D.C., had only two impressive government buildings: the Capitol (above), later redomed and enlarged into the present structure, and (below) the Executive Mansion, where occasionally was received a nauseous whiff of sewage from an infamous accumulation in Potomac marshland.

Faraway California attracted President Polk, who never had seen the place but nevertheless wanted it for the United States. It absolutely fascinated John C. Frémont and Joseph Warren Revere, visitors to that land. Two sights they saw: (top) Sutter's fabulous fort and (bottom) the blue bay of Monterey.

render of Texas and we know not what other part of the Republic. This is as certain as the existence of God in heaven.

Like the newspapers in Mexico, American publications mirrored their own national moods and reported accurately on some discussions that were taking place behind closed doors. This was especially true of opposition journals. Polk's expansionism had divided the country, particularly by inciting increasingly bitter criticism on the part of his political foes, the Whigs, who (correctly or not) warned of perils created by a man of Polk's ilk: probable war brought on solely and secretly by a President who did his own maneuvering without consulting or confiding in Congress, as required by the Constitution; territory-grabbing at the behest of the same President, who seemed willing to forget stated national ideals for the satisfaction of selfish interests; and expansion of slavery by this man—significantly, a Tennessean—who plotted to add Texas to the Union so that Southern states could enjoy compatible company and strengthen the hold of that "peculiar institution" that kept human beings in bondage.

The *National Intelligencer* expressed the Whig view in a article published August 7. Although the writer admitted that Polk might be justified by necessity in defending Texas, he said:

> . . . the President is quite indefensible, if, in exceeding the measure of the necessity, he keep not strictly on the defensive and within the *settled limits* of the land, whose proper population merely, and not its territorial pretensions, it is now necessary to defend. But it is apparent that Texas [has] claimed, and we fear it is equally apparent that the Executive has granted, the occupation of everything up to the Rio Grande, which occupation is nothing short . . . of an invasion of Mexico. It is *offensive war*, and *not* the necessary defense of Texas. And should it prove, as we think it will, that the President has gone this additional length, then the President will be MAKING WAR, in the full sense of the word, on his own authority, and beyond all plea of need, and even without any thought of asking legislative leave.

The Whigs' argument about the Texas boundary ignored one important point that in retrospect weakened their position, but not their voice, at this time. Mexico itself had not initially emphasized the Nueces River boundary claim (as the Whigs did here), maintaining instead that all Texas to the Louisiana dividing line—the Sabine River—belonged to Mexico and that an American movement into any part of it would be an invasion. Nevertheless, the Whig argument in its day proved increasingly effective and persuasive, and gave Polk great political pain.

Other Americans, like their President, thought of the vast new areas that could be open to them—and a diverse group these people were. Proslavery Southerners wanted Texas safely in the Union (but cared little about California or Oregon, where the land, climate, and potential crops seemed to make slavery unlikely). Dollar-seeking New England merchants wanted Pacific Coast ports like that talked-of San Francisco Harbor for vessels engaging in Californian or Asian trade (but generally opposed Texas' annexation and the war it seemed likely to bring). Opportunity-hungry Westerners wanted more land, always more land, to move onto in their continuing search for fortune and freedom (and resented certain Atlantic Coast attempts to restrict expansion).

Still other Americans fell in none of these broad categories, but wanted national expansion for various reasons. Religious evangelists yearned for a chance to bring heathen Indians and Catholic Mexicans into the Protestant fold. Political evangelists expressed that singular enthusiasm for bringing new territories into the republican heaven. Defense-minded citizens wanted to move quickly to prevent a grab of California or other lands by Britain or another foreign power. Examination of any 1845 map made this reasoning logical to thoughtful, wary Americans who lived in a day when some powerful nations still felt little constraint in taking undeveloped (if not uninhabited) lands for burgeoning empires. Suppose Britain should occupy the Pacific Coast—Oregon and California—and maybe even Texas, too? With those Western possessions and with the holdings in Canada to the north—and working in co-operation with Mexico on the south—Britain might catch the United States in a vise that could someday undo everything the Revolution had accomplished.

People with these various feelings would give Polk the support he needed to embark on his program. But their support would be splintered, controversial, and at times halting—while the political opposition would become increasingly tough and bitter. In the end it would be a spirit of "manifest destiny" that would provide the conclusive momentum.

This term describing United States expansion westward apparently was first used by editor John O'Sullivan in the *Democratic Review* of July-August 1845, when he wrote of ". . . our manifest destiny to overspread the continent allotted by Providence for the free development of our yearly multiplying millions." But the sentiment certainly had not originated with O'Sullivan. Other individuals had expressed it openly, and earlier that year the Democratic Washington *Union*, Polk's mouthpiece, had published similar statements in at least two editions.

> Let the great measure of annexation be accomplished, and with it the questions of boundary and claims. For who can arrest the torrent that will pour onward to the West? The road to California will be open to us. Who will stay the march of our western people?
>
> . . .
>
> A corps of properly organized volunteers . . . would invade, overrun, and occupy Mexico. They would enable us not only to take California, but to keep it.

Furthermore, United States occupation of the place would help the Californians themselves, many Americans declared. Mexico never would be able to extend its jurisdiction there, these people reasoned, and Upper California could only remain an undeveloped, anarchic land incapable of helping itself. The editor of the *American Review* spoke for them in a January 1846 issue:

> No one who cherishes a faith in the wisdom of an overruling Providence, and who sees, in the national movements which convulse the world, the silent operation of an invisible but omnipotent hand, can believe it to be for the interest of humanity, for the well-being of the world, that this vast and magnificent region should continue forever in its present state.

9.

Road to California

Late in November, while the vessel carrying Envoy Extraordinary and Minister Plenipotentiary John Slidell plowed across a gray-green Gulf of Mexico toward a Vera Cruz landfall, the explorer John C. Frémont paused on the shore of an expansive lake near the western boundary of present Nevada and contemplated that "road to California" mentioned by James Polk's Washington *Union*.

For Frémont the route would not be smooth. From the camp on Walker Lake Frémont could see looming to westward the white-topped Sierra Nevada range—those same towering mountains that had nearly frozen him and his men during that terrible winter march to John Sutter's fort. Now he intended to return to the golden plain where the genial Swiss adventurer had entertained him so lavishly twenty months earlier. An increasingly bitter chill that had begun to creep in with the nights told him he could not delay much longer.

Nevertheless, Frémont radiated optimism, as any explorer would, and his expedition until this time had been pleasant and rewarding. After the August departure from Bent's Fort onto hot, dry, windy plains of what is now southeastern Colorado he and his men had begun a slow ascent up the Arkansas River into a cooler, greener region that provided awesome scenery as the trip progressed: past the present site of Pueblo, on the Arkansas, and past the great canyon—Royal Gorge—with red granite walls rising above the river a thousand feet or more, almost perpendicularly. From there, only thirty miles away to the north, the snowy top of Pike's Peak reached its majestic height of more than two and a half miles.

This was the kind of life Frémont had relished from his youth. The coolness of late summer, the lushness of grass, the noonday shade afforded by aspen and pine, and the availability of clear water in swiftly flowing streams heightened his enjoyment.

If one assumes his routine resembled that of an earlier expedition as he described it, his days on the march were busy, carefully scheduled, and cautiously guarded against surprise Indian attacks. After traveling a distance depending on the terrain (about twenty-five miles over open prairie), Frémont found a camp site well before sunset and halted his men. Equipment like wagons and carts were wheeled into a close circle. Inside this, men pitched tents and started fires for roasting meat while, outside, others hobbled horses and mules and guarded the animals as they grazed.

Before sunset supper was finished. Campfires flickered weakly in late afternoon shade, smoldered, and died. Darkness brought greater precautions: No fires now to light up the scene. Animals driven in closer to camp and haltered. A guard posted at eight o'clock and changed every two hours throughout the night. By nine o'clock men not on watch were asleep, with the usual exception of Frémont.

At four-thirty next morning they woke to begin another long day. They freed the animals (except for hobbles) for more grazing, cooked breakfast, then began the day's march by six-thirty. A pause of an hour or two at noon allowed for astronomical observations by Frémont and for a brief rest for men and animals. Throughout the day Frémont carefully observed the country, and he recorded this information in his journal as soon as time allowed.

Northwestward they rode: across the mighty Colorado River snaking through this land at the bottom of deep canyons and red stone gorges; into the brown badlands of present eastern Utah, a dry region of mountainous walls and eroded plateaus; across the abundant Green River, main tributary of the Colorado; over the twelve-thousand-foot barrier of the Wasatch Mountain Range, bisecting the northern part of present Utah; down onto arid plains around the Great Salt Lake, a vast body of water (seventy-five miles long and fifty miles wide) so dense with salinity that a man could float on its surface without sinking.

Frémont's arrival at the Salt Lake meant the commencement of an announced major purpose of his expedition: exploration of the Great Basin, an area bounded on the west by the Sierra Nevadas and on the east by the Wasatch Range. In this region (as has become evident) no streams flow on to the sea but empty instead into lakes or vanish in alkali flats called sinks.

Frémont had arrived at the Great Salt Lake in September of 1845. There he stayed about two weeks, exploring, observing, sketching, hunting, and taking sights. Then he headed westward again, into a forbidding desert that no one he knew ever had crossed—not even the guide Kit Carson.

The Indians warned Frémont against going, saying that no water would be found there. Most men would have detoured hundreds of miles to avoid such a wasteland, but not the impulsive, impatient Frémont, who might also have been propelled by the desire for an earlier arrival in California. But beyond his impetuosity this time lay solid reasoning. Frémont could see on the western horizon—probably sixty miles away—a mountain, and he guessed that it would have water and vegetation. Because of the mountain's visibility at such a distance it seemed to have sufficient altitude to prove Frémont right, and if this were true he would have reasonable chances of finding still more water on the other side.

Early one evening Frémont sent Carson and two other men on horseback across the desert toward the distant elevation. With them went a mule carrying water and other supplies. This small party would press on under cool night skies. The rest of Frémont's men would follow at a slower pace, but they would go fast enough and far enough to be able to make out signal smoke from Carson on the mountain in the event that he found water there. If it became necessary the entire expedition could return to its starting point safely and seek another way west.

Daylight far out on the desert illuminated for Frémont the truth of the Indians' warnings. The level, sun-baked land certainly held no water in this vicinity, and the flat, barren, shimmering distance told Frémont that possibilities anywhere else could be no better.

But the mountain ahead apparently held life. The closer Frémont came to it the greener it grew. His advance party found water there, and two days after the separation the entire expedition had been reunited on a pleasant slope that offered water and grass and wood for cooking. (So Frémont *could* be a pathfinder as well as a pathmarker. Later, emigrant trains bound for California would use the short cut he had blazed across this same desert rather than make a far-north detour.)

Frémont rested his men and animals, then rode westward again— on into present northern Nevada, a dry land but nothing like the lifeless waste near the Great Salt Lake. Usually he could make his camp near water—a creek or a spring—found after diligent search by scouts during the day, and thus his men could allow their animals to graze. He crossed more mountain ranges, minor ones compared to the sprawling Rockies, and more valleys. Then he reached the banks of a river whose name, Ogden, Frémont changed to Humboldt, for the noted German geographer Friedrich Heinrich Alexander von Humboldt. He determined to learn more about the stream.

Like all Great Basin rivers, the Humboldt showed that peculiarity of terminating in a lake or a sink instead of flowing into an ocean. In this case the terminal point was a sink located some sixty miles northeast of present Reno—nearly four hundred meandering miles from the river's headwater. But details remained unknown, and Frémont sent most of his men off to follow the Humboldt's winding course. To lead this group he designated Edward M. Kern, a lively young Philadelphian originally chosen for the expedition because of his nature-sketching ability and his high spirits. After Kern's men reached the river's terminus they were to ride on westward toward the Sierra Nevada foothills, then to turn southward and proceed to Walker Lake, taking a route parallel to the mountains. At Walker Lake Frémont would meet them.

Meanwhile Frémont and ten carefully selected men (including Carson) would have conducted a second exploration, one focusing on the Great Basin itself. Frémont intended to leave the Humboldt River for a southwestwardly course that would take him across the heart of the Great Basin area, into what is now central Nevada, and eventually to the Walker Lake rendezvous with the other party. His trip would be the more hazardous, but he would have only himself, his own party, and his work to occupy his thoughts. Kern and his men, though less accomplished explorers, would have no difficulty following their own route: along a river and down a mountain range to a large lake.

Frémont's journey proved easy, too—and mostly uneventful, except for occasional encounters with Indians. One of these occurred at night in the light of a campfire, indicating that Frémont had gained more confidence since that earlier expedition when he had seen to it that all fires were out by dusk—or that Frémont was again merely displaying some of the brashness that characterized him throughout his life. Earlier, shortly before Frémont halted his men at a camp site near a spring, one of his Delaware Indian scouts had pointed out in the soil the footprints of a woman. But this had not caused alarm. They all knew they were in Indian country, and in fact they had already come upon one of the natives. The Delaware scouts had wanted to kill the man, but Frémont had restrained them and had sent the stranger away with a present.

Encamped now, Frémont and his men built a fire to warm themselves against the evening chill and to cook a newly killed antelope. They finished their meal, then sat around the still blazing fire talking, smoking, and relaxing, while night closed in around them. In the flickering firelight Frémont quietly studied his guide Carson and observed utter contentment. Carson, taking hard-earned ease after a long day's work, "was lying on his back with his pipe in his mouth, his hands under his head, and his feet to the fire."

Then Frémont saw Carson suddenly come alive and heard him shout. The man was pointing to the other side of the fire, and a surprised Frémont saw there the reason for his guide's uncharacteristic agitation:

> In the blaze of the fire, peering over . . . skinny, crooked hands . . . was standing an old woman apparently eighty years of age, her grizzled hair hanging down over her face and shoulders She had thought it a camp of her people, and had already begun to talk and gesticulate, when her open mouth was paralyzed with fright, as she saw the faces of the whites. She turned to escape, but the men had gathered about her and brought her around to the fire. Hunger and cold soon dispelled fear, and she made us understand that she had been left by her people at the spring to die, because she was very old and was no longer good for anything. She told us she had nothing to eat and was very hungry. We gave her immediately about a quarter of the antelope, thinking she would roast it by our fire, but no sooner did she get it . . . than she darted off into the darkness.

On November 24 Frémont and his men reached Walker Lake and found that the other group had not yet arrived. Frémont's speedy traversal of the Great Basin had turned up nothing that would prove truly startling back home, but he had made at least one surprising discovery.

In the past, the few people who had shown any interest at all in the area had assumed the entire Great Basin from the Salt Lake to the Sierras to be a dry, dead, sandy plain—none of it good for anything. Maps of the time depicted it that way. The Sierras (as is known now) tended to block movement inland of moisture-laden clouds rolling in from the Pacific and contributed to the aridity. During his trip, however, Frémont had seen that the land was not all bad. "Instead of a barren country [there were to be found] mountains . . . covered with grasses of the best quality, wooded with several variety of trees, and containing more deer and mountain sheep than we had seen in any previous part of our voyage." For years Frémont's findings in this mysterious region were to pass largely unnoticed by Americans, who would continue to follow established trails through the dreaded Great Basin to areas of known fertility farther west and to leave the feared region largely uninhabited.

Three days after Frémont reached Walker Lake, Kern's group arrived. With November fading into its final few days Frémont's anxiety to cross the Sierras into Sutter's blissful kingdom increased. A freezing chill had begun to come with the night air and apparently had sent many animals fleeing south toward warmth—or into dens for a long hibernation—because game was getting hard to find.

A snowfall powdered the hills at the foot of the Sierras. Despite the storm's brevity Frémont foresaw the high passes being clogged if he waited much longer. Again he divided his party, for convenience and for speed. He selected fifteen men to accompany him in a dash across the Sierras and sent the others southward along the mountains toward passes where snow rarely fell. The two groups would reunite later in California.

Up, up into the Sierras Frémont's party climbed, making the most of every hour, watching for stormy weather that could block them off from their destination. December was here now, and heavy snows certainly could be expected soon. Within four days Frémont had reached the vicinity of the coveted pass into California, and the weather continued to favor him. But his anxiety did not lessen. The summit still lay ahead, and beyond it more tortuous traveling. While encamped on the night of December 4 Frémont kept a watch of the night sky. If bad weather seemed imminent he would have his men up and struggling toward the crest. Memories of the bitter and nearly disastrous 1844 Sierra crossing were riding with him—and ever closer.

At the pass Frémont found clear ground, fair skies, a temperature only ten degrees below freezing, and snow confined to the higher areas around him. Elated, he began the descent at a pace that grew more leisurely as the snow threat vanished.

The scenery could not be surpassed. They rode through forests of giant pine trees rising to a height never seen back home; into a region where grew thick-trunked oaks rich with acorns; past fascinating villages of friendly Indians who ground the oak nuts into food; through an ever warmer paradise of bright flowers, green grass, and abundant game stretching out from the banks of the cool, clear American River. Five days after clearing the pass Frémont reached Sutter's Fort and received a warm greeting from the friendly folk who knew him from his earlier visit.

So Frémont was again in fabled Upper California, an area of geographical contrast, of political ferment, and of great potential. Frémont himself had fallen in love with the land, but many concerned officials of his government expressed more interest at this time in the strategic importance given the area by its juxtaposition with the Pacific Ocean, which rolled ashore along the length of the coastline in thundering cold breakers that from a distance sometimes sounded like the far-off roar of cannon. Focal point of interest was that giant, well-protected bay called San Francisco. It had been described by Charles Wilkes of the U. S. Navy after a Pacific exploration a few years earlier.

Approaching from the sea, Wilkes had come upon a lofty, tree-covered coast broken by a narrow entrance that led to an inlet. Once inside that, Wilkes observed a broad expanse of water stretching north and south, large enough (he estimated) to shelter all the world's navies. Along the shores of this bay (as he found later) lay many coves, forested hills, and green valleys. A few small settlements dotted the region. On the site of present San Francisco he found only a sleepy, ugly village named Yerba Buena, composed of adobe ruins, a few scattered frame buildings, and a poop cabin detached from a vessel that served as somebody's residence.

Knowledgeable Americans saw more than lethargy around Yerba Buena. Prevailing westerly winds happened to put San Francisco Bay along the sea routes linking teeming ports in faraway India, China, and Manila with Pacific harbors in South and Central America and in Mexico, and even the great-circle (shortest distance) route between these eastern and western points passed not far distant. Possession of San Francisco Bay certainly would be a key to a vast American trade in the Pacific—the only logical key.

No other significant harbor lay north of the bay for eight hundred miles—only forbidding cliffs that towered above a ribbon of sand and that were paralleled inland by mountain ranges for most of that distance. The next significant harbor to the north lay at Juan de Fuca Strait, a water passage through a broken land mass (at the northern tip of present

Washington State) that afforded navigation into an eighty-mile-long inland sea, Puget Sound.

South of San Francisco Bay the coastline continued to show a rugged appearance, but at Point Conception, where it made an abrupt turn eastward, the shore began to level out and to lose verdure. The only notable harbor to be found in Upper California south of San Francisco Bay was San Diego Bay—in a warm, dry area far removed from the high mountains—where two long arms of land reaching out toward a narrow sea passage provided protection for vessels engaged in hide trading. At this time San Diego Bay, too, remained mostly uninhabited. A scattering of ugly adobe huts built on the north side comprised the only village in the vicinity. Inland, only barren sand hills could be seen.

Other California harbors were in use at this time, but none of them afforded much protection. North of San Diego Bay, at exposed San Pedro, vessels trading in hides risked damage from shallow water and a rocky shore. Thirty miles inland from San Pedro, across a land barren of trees, lay casual, carefree Pueblo de los Angeles, a ranching and farming town of adobe buildings. Northward up the coast from San Pedro Bay lay another poorly protected harbor, Santa Barbara, and a village that most sailors considered a dull place indeed. And north of Santa Barbara—again in that area of rugged California coastline—lay Monterey, distinguished at that time as being the leading port of California. Monterey had beauty as well as life. White adobe buildings topped by red tile roofs overlooked a shimmering beach and the blue expanse of the Pacific. Inland, green hills covered with pine and oak rolled away eastward.

Frémont knew a great deal about Upper California through observation and conversation. He realized fully its value to the United States —from the majestic mountainous region of the forested north through a warm, dry central valley region to the southern deserts, all of these areas rimmed to westward by a picturesque coastline with a mild, stimulating climate.

Probably Frémont hurried on across the Sierras into California during that December of 1845 because he did realize its value to his country, and because he anticipated engaging in some military action that would bring it under United States jurisdiction. The exact orders under which he acted have never been clarified to everyone's satisfaction. But if he had not expected to assume the role of a military commander in Upper

California why had he not remained longer in the Great Basin, an area largely unknown, instead of hurrying through it to a region that was comparatively well mapped—if not thoroughly familiar to Americans? A closer examination of the mysterious country east of the Sierras would have been of greater scientific value. Instead of devoting himself to that work, however, Frémont had crossed the mountains in forced marches, playing tag with winter blizzards, to arrive in a foreign country of "poisoned atmosphere" (as he would write later) and impending "conflict among men."

10.

3,900 Men

Whatever military role John C. Frémont envisioned for himself in California, the actual concentration of U. S. Army forces lay more than fifteen hundred miles southeast of Sutter's Fort—on the southwestern shore of crescent-shaped Corpus Christi Bay, in Texas, near that trading post known as Kinney's Ranch. Although there was no mistaking their purpose—to fight Mexico for Texas if necessary—their numbers left room for many doubts. That winter of 1845–46 Zachary Taylor had available at Corpus Christi Bay not more than 3,900 men at any time. This total included one regiment of dragoons (David Twiggs's 2nd Regiment, which had completed the overland trip from Fort Jesup after three deaths and fifty desertions), five regiments of infantry, four batteries of field artillery, a few companies of Louisiana volunteers, and a detachment of Texas Rangers. The total also included all men on the sick list, which occasionally claimed 30 per cent of the entire army and kept the twenty-two medical officers swamped with work. An additional force of 150 dragoons operated mostly outside the area as a communications link with the Texas Government and with other U. S. Army units.

The men at Corpus Christi Bay had arrived from posts all over the United States. Lieutenant Sam French had come to Texas from coveted duty at Fort McHenry and the delightful society of Baltimore, where "the ladies . . . inherited beauty; and from their environments naturally acquired retiring manners, low and sweet voices, gentleness, [and] attractive grace." One girl in particular French remembered fondly: a young lady named Charlotte. From Texas he carried on a passionate correspondence with her. But the trouble with Mexico had changed whatever course French might have taken toward marriage.

In late summer of 1845 French had been ordered to Texas along with the other men, guns, and animals of a horse artillery unit commanded by Major Samuel Ringgold, a dedicated, imaginative Military Academy graduate whose inventiveness and training procedures had revised some cumbersome old methods of transporting and firing horse-drawn cannon, so that the detachment and a few others patterned after it had become known as "flying artillery." Down the Atlantic Coast and across the Gulf of Mexico French and his companions had sailed, in a chartered vessel named *Hermann* mastered by a man who would (as French observed with revulsion) "lie on his back and curse even his Creator" when becalmed. The *Hermann* had arrived at its Texas destination in mid-September, and French had left the vile ship joyfully after spending forty-six days aboard.

A much faster trip to Corpus Christi Bay had been made by Captain Ephraim Kirby Smith. Smith's group had left its Detroit post in mid-August, had traveled by canal to the Ohio River, had voyaged by steamboat down the Ohio and Mississippi to New Orleans, and had crossed the Gulf in the steamship *Alabama*. Smith had arrived at Corpus Christi Bay about the same time as French, but his trip (of twenty-five hundred miles) had taken only twenty-one days. Smith believed no war with Mexico would develop, only that "we shall remain in this neighborhood, perhaps march to the Rio Grande, until all difficulty is settled by negotiation between the two governments."

Lieutenant Sam Grant, who had arrived from New Orleans on the sailing ship *Suviah*, tried to pass part of the time hunting around Corpus Christi Bay, but he failed in this endeavor. Once he came upon a flock of wild turkeys that fascinated him so much he forgot to shoot. But he would not have relished a kill anyway, because (as he said) he could never "eat anything that goes on two legs." Even beef and venison gave him trouble. The meat had to be cooked well done, or he could not swallow it—a hangover from the days when, as a youngster, he had seen and smelled bloody skins stretched for drying in his father's tannery.

Grant passed up hunting, then, to concentrate on recreation that he thoroughly enjoyed: horseback riding, which also permitted him to make that favorable impression on military colleagues. On one occasion he mounted a fierce stallion—after blindfolding the animal long enough to leap on—and rode it into submission. On other occasions Grant enjoyed watching the horsemanship of the fabulous Texas Rangers. Some of those men could lean from their saddles—with horses going at full gallop—and grab silver dollars placed in rows on the ground.

Neither Grant nor Sam French mentioned it in later writing but, having been classmates at West Point, they would have used the collecting of forces at Corpus Christi Bay to renew their acquaintance and perhaps to laugh over an old cadet story that French always delighted in telling on Grant. The two young men had been in the same West Point section as it marched one day to a mathematics recitation. On the way to class another cadet had produced an old silver-cased watch, four inches in diameter, and had passed the curiosity along for each section member to examine.

The cadet proved to be a practical joker. He knew the watch would not be returned to him by his curious colleagues before the section entered the classroom, and he had set the alarm to go off within the hour.

> [The watch] chanced to be in Grant's hands as we reached the door of the recitation room [French would recall as he told the story], and he slipped it under his coat bosom and buttoned it up. The regular professor was absent, and Cadet Zealous B. Tower occupied his chair. [Tower] sent four cadets to the blackboards—Grant being one. Grant had solved his problem and [had] begun his demonstration, when all of a sudden the room was filled with a sound not unlike a Chinese gong. All looked amazed, and Tower, thinking the noise was in the hall, ordered the door closed, [but] that only made the matter worse. Grant, with a sober countenance, had the floor to demonstrate. When the racket ceased the recitation proceeded. Tower had no idea whence the noise came.

Along with Grant, French, Captain Smith, and Colonel Hitchcock, many other army regulars had assembled on Corpus Christi Bay, and General Taylor believed the gathering "fully adequate to meet any crisis which might arise." Certainly it was a larger force than had been collected in years, and its size proved confusing and even embarrassing to many officers who had never seen anything like it. Colonel Hitchcock studied their perplexities with his usual humorless scorn. "What a pretty figure we cut here! . . . Among the senior officers, neither General Taylor nor Colonel [William] Whistler [an inept alcoholic who had replaced the deceased Colonel J. H. Vose] . . . could form [the troops] into line! Even Colonel Twiggs could put the troops into line only 'after a fashion' of his own. As for [maneuvering], not one of them can move a step in it. Egotism or no egotism, I am the only field officer on the ground who [can] change a single position of the troops according to any but a militia code."

If Hitchcock seemed to radiate ownership of the post on Corpus Christi Bay perhaps he had some excuse. He had commanded it first, of course—during that period when General Taylor had remained behind on St. Joseph's Island. Under Hitchcock's supervision the first troops had assembled and encamped, and the work of entrenchment had begun. Now it had been mostly completed, and an impressive sight it made: neat rows of tents by the hundreds lying along sandy shoreline more than a mile in length. At this location the beach curved northward toward a distant inner bay—where the Nueces River had its mouth—and southward toward a long, low island named Padre that paralleled the coast for many miles on south. Fronting the expansive camp site was the bay, a shallow, gray-green lake usually white-capped by breezes that rarely died. Inland behind the camp, as a kind of backdrop, stretched a bluff that rose gently from the level shore to a height of one hundred feet.

From this bluff a U. S. Army officer studied the surroundings the morning after his arrival and pronounced the location "God's favored land—the Eden of America." The man saw a pastoral scene. Mesquite grass covered an inland plain sprinkled with clumps of black-green chaparral. Across the emerald landscape a herd of cattle lumbered, driven by two Mexicans mounted on swift mustangs. Beyond, scattered across distant hills, hundreds of sheep and goats grazed, tended by a shepherd and his dog. Far to westward lay a seemingly endless plain, and in fancy the officer saw its occupants—mustang and buffalo, the bold Comanche and the fierce Lipan. He thought the scene "magnificent," but apparently he had been carried away by momentary exhilaration. He had just completed a sea voyage and now was standing once again on solid earth —the only place for a soldier. He was seeing a strange land, always exciting adventure. And he was enjoying a soft, stimulating breeze that blew in from the Gulf of Mexico. In time his enthusiasm would subside, and he would decide this was not "exactly" the Eden of America.

Colonel Hitchcock never believed it was Eden, although some of the countryside impressed him favorably enough. He had not changed his mind about the lack of legality to excuse their presence here, and he believed most other military officers, being Whig opponents of President Polk's Democratic Party, agreed with him that United States troops did not belong west of the Nueces River—if only slightly west, as described their present location. In Hitchcock's opinion the claim to the Rio Grande remained absurd. "The United States of America, as a people, are undergoing changes in character, and the real status and principles for which our forefathers fought are fast being lost sight of. If I could by any decent means get a living in retirement, I would abandon a government which I think corrupted by both ambition and avarice to the last degree."

Many other matters troubled Hitchcock, as always seemed to be the case, and he filled pages in his diary with grumblings and reflections.

Rumors of war came frequently during that autumn and winter to upset the camp. Actually the reports had begun to drift in as early as the evening of August 14, while Hitchcock was in command of assembling and quartering troops on the bay. Mexico had declared war, he had heard then. General Taylor had sent him hurried instructions about building fortifications, and Hitchcock typically had doubted the logic of some of the general's advice. The war rumor had proved false, but Hitchcock had continued to fortify the camp.

Other excitement also flustered the troops. A violent storm struck, filling the countryside with crashing thunder that sounded from some distance exactly like a cannonade. Alarm, then calm: nature had created the entire disturbance. Next Hitchcock heard talk of the movement of large Mexican forces toward the Rio Grande, an act for which he, with his detached objectivity, could not hold them in disfavor: ". . . if the Mexicans are 'smart' they can give us trouble." Few of these rumors could be verified or disproved. General Taylor himself seemed entirely ignorant of the numbers and intentions of Mexican forces and unwilling to learn through any efficient kind of intelligence gathering. This neglect galled Hitchcock: "The General may have information which he keeps to himself, but I know him too well to believe he has any." Much of whatever information arrived in camp came from the lips of Mexican traders who continued to travel without restriction between Kinney's Ranch and the land south of the Rio Grande, as they had for years. When they returned to their own country they no doubt carried back word about the activities of the U. S. Army on Corpus Christi Bay.

Also irksome to Hitchcock was the community that had sprung up around the encampment. By the end of December two thousand civilians had moved in to grub for their share of a private's seven-dollar-a-month pay. They had built a town (present Corpus Christi) that showed hurried construction: tents and wood shanties for most occupants and their businesses, with the inclusion of a few scattered solid frame buildings. Most occupants were men. Hitchcock observed that the town had "no ladies and very few women." Virtually all businesses catered drinking, gambling, and girls. Possibly in an attempt to counteract these influences the Army constructed an eight-hundred-seat theater in which Sam Grant surprisingly played the part of Shakespeare's Desdemona. Colonel Hitchcock took part in "no one of the amusements or dissipations of the place," but instead wrote, read, or meditated in the privacy of his tent, or walked through town simply to observe. "I can read Spinoza's *Ethics* when nothing else instructs me," he remarked; but for further diversion about this time he carried on a correspondence with Henry Wadsworth Longfellow regarding the work of the Italian poet Gabriele Rossetti.

Another letter-writing endeavor put Hitchcock in direct opposition to the ranking general of the U. S. Army—the vain, tactless, but able Winfield Scott, who had used his position "to give precedence to brevet rank [as Hitchcock wrote] in violation of law and reason." Hitchcock prepared a letter of protest to send to Washington, obtained the signatures of 158 fellow officers, and persuaded President Polk to overrule his highest general.

This astonishing development came as a direct result of a dispute that had flared earlier on Corpus Christi Bay. The trouble had stemmed from the contentions of two of Taylor's colonels: David Twiggs—a white-haired, thick-necked, friendly bellower—and William Worth, a handsome, hot-tempered, impetuous (and sometimes erratic) veteran of brutal fighting against the Seminole Indians. For a long time Twiggs had outranked Worth as a colonel, but Worth had been brevetted a brigadier general after some action against Indians. This was a feat that Twiggs had not had a chance to duplicate, because Twiggs had not recently been on a battlefield—the only place for winning brevets (awards of temporary promotion roughly equal in value to today's battle decorations). The two men ranked directly below Taylor, but in what order? Each claimed precedence.

Taylor personally supported Twiggs, and he had designated the colonel to command at a review of troops until Worth's bitter complaints persuaded Taylor to call everything off. Taylor eventually referred the problem to Washington, where General Scott decided in favor of brevet rank. That action prompted Hitchcock's letter, which in turn led to President Polk's overruling Scott in favor of Twiggs. When Polk's decision reached the army in Texas Worth wrote out an angry resignation, but later he withdrew it.

Hitchcock's delight in his intellectual victory over Winfield Scott did not last long. The old trouble with diarrhea returned to plague him occasionally. He believed it essential to leave the devilish South Texas climate to recover his health, but his conscience refused to allow him to ask permission to go. Meanwhile, as autumn passed into winter, the unpredictable weather grew even worse. One day would be warm and sultry, even uncomfortably hot; the next (following the arrival of a "norther") would be blustery and cold, with drenching rain. Army tents provided little protection against freezing weather. A frigid wind seeped through them. Rain and sleet froze on the canvas outside, then cracked and shattered when winds slapped against the cloth. Water in pails turned into ice. For protection men heaped piles of brush on the north sides of their tents and reinforced these windbreaks with embankments of earth, but still the chilly wind whined through the fragile shelters.

Compounding the discomfort were other difficulties: a scarcity of wood for fuel, a siege of illness caused by General Taylor's lack of attention to sanitation and by drinking brackish water in the vicinity, and a general depression of spirits brought on by idleness and boredom.

All this Hitchcock observed and endured without asking for leave of absence. He even raised his hackles at this time in defense of the Army, which had been criticized recently in the House of Representatives by a South Carolina congressman, J. A. Black, himself a former soldier. Hitchcock might voice his own disapproval of the military service, but when an outsider did this the colonel usually reacted by showing a deep loyalty. Furthermore, his quarrel at this time really was not so much with the Army as with the civilians who controlled the government and who showed what he considered to be greed, dishonesty, or ignorance. In this case Hitchcock felt the display was one of ignorance.

Black had just completed a report to Congress on the state of the Army, and investigation had shown him that the condition was poor indeed, with many senior officers infirm or senile and younger ones "enervated by the ease and luxury of a peace establishment." Hitchcock read the congressman's report, snorted, and wrote a sarcastic reply, thanking Black for his fairness and declaring that the Army could rejoice in having such a well-informed champion. "It is consoling to know that our services and sacrifices are appreciated," he wrote, then added a reference to Black's own previous military service. "The facility with which you have drawn the picture can be explained only by supposing that you referred to your own experience and sat for the picture yourself." Hitchcock went on to describe hardships of the current winter and added, "This is a feeble testimony of the feeling so naturally excited by your laudable endeavors to do justice to an *entire class of men*, . . . exposed, as the army is, to defamation from demagogues, often so destitute of honor and honesty themselves as to hate all that is noble and virtuous in others."

In the weeks that followed Black read not only Hitchcock's original letter as addressed to him but also copies of the same letter that had been sent to and published in several journals. A year or so later Hitchcock heard from Secretary of War Marcy about what happened then, and he recorded it in his diary.

Furious, the congressman stormed over to Marcy's office and demanded Hitchcock's dismissal. But the wise old Secretary of War was not an easy man to pressure.

> Mr. Marcy lightly replied [Hitchcock wrote] that gentlemen in the army must be allowed to have their opinions. Black then, with great violence, denounced the letter as an insult to Congress and repeated his demand for my dismissal. Mr. Marcy said he could not see that Congress had been insulted: that the letter was addressed exclusively to Mr. B., and, in its tenor, was in the highest degree complimentary on the face of it, and he did not see how it could be the subject of a charge of disrespect to Congress. "However," Mr. Marcy concluded, "you can prepare and submit your charges and they will be considered; but, as the court for the trial of Colonel Hitchcock will have to be composed of officers, you may naturally conclude where their sympathies will tend."
> On reflection, Mr. Black . . . dropped the subject—and returned to obscurity.

Army life nevertheless continued to rankle Hitchcock, and especially at this time one facet of it: the still impending march to the Rio Grande. Zachary Taylor's gradual toleration of this imminent move aroused in Hitchcock renewed resentment of the general, a Whig who (as Hitchcock knew) had initially "denounced annexation as both injudicious in policy and wicked in fact." The colonel realized that Taylor could only follow the orders sent by Washington, but he also suspected that Taylor had begun to anticipate the glory to be won by a victorious commander in a war.

Once, after Taylor had visited Hitchcock's tent to talk about the move, Hitchcock recorded that "the General is instigated by ambition—or so it appears to me."

He seems quite to have lost all respect for Mexican rights and willing to be an instrument of Mr. Polk for pushing our boundary as far west as possible [Hitchcock continued]. When I told him that, if he suggested a movement (which he told me he intended), Mr. Polk would seize upon it and throw the responsibility on him, he at once said he would take it, and added that if the President instructed him to use his discretion, he would ask no orders, but would go upon the Rio Grande as soon as he could get transportation. I think the General wants an additional brevet, and would strain a point to get it.

11.

Judge the World in Righteousness

Chilly breezes of another Washington autumn rustled through the trees lining Pennsylvania Avenue and sent brown leaves fluttering toward the ground. Cold rain splashed from grim, gray skies, soaking bundled-up pedestrians and turning dirt streets into deep, squashy mud. Gloom sometimes seemed to pervade everything—the Executive Mansion included. That had been obvious on the President's birthday: November 2, 1845.

The day had fallen on a Sunday. Usually the President accompanied Mrs. Polk to her church, the Presbyterian, although his own preference was for the Methodist. But a steady downpour began falling early in the morning, and Mrs. Polk chose to stay home. The President and his private secretary attended services at the Methodist Church. Polk mused over the text (from Acts 17:31), "Because he hath appointed a day, in the which he will judge the world in righteousness, by *that* man whom he hath ordained. . . ." The text and a solemn sermon evoked somber thought. Polk had lived fifty years now, he reflected, and before another fifty years passed he "would be sleeping with the generations" that had gone before. He concluded he must put his house "in order."

Returning to the warmth of the Executive Mansion and to the dinner companionship of his family, he would have cast off these melancholy thoughts. Certainly the duties of the presidency did not allow him time to dwell on personal matters. Many problems kept him occupied during that autumn of 1845.

Fresh rumors of British and French activity in California gave him concern for the safety of the land that he hoped to add to the Union. The United States consul in Monterey, Thomas Larkin, had forwarded to him (in a letter dated July 10) reports of British activity. An agent of the Hudson's Bay Company had given Californians arms and money to help them in their successful attempt to expel Mexican troops from the area, Larkin declared, but now Britain was instigating a Mexican invasion. Larkin added the ominous information that, although Britain and France maintained consulates in California, neither office seemed to transact commercial business.

This word upset Polk, especially considering the sagacity of the person who had sent it. The President knew Larkin as a shrewd man. Mercantile business had drawn the Massachusetts-born trader to California, and to prosper there a man needed to be clever. Soon after receiving Larkin's letter the President instructed Secretary of State Buchanan to reply (in a dispatch prepared October 17) that the future of California was "a subject of anxious solicitude for the Government and people of the United States. Whilst the President will make no effort and use no influence to induce California to become one of the free and independent States of this Union, yet if the people should desire to unite their destiny with ours, they would be received as brethren, whenever this can be done without affording Mexico just cause of complaint. Their true policy for the present in regard to this question, is to let events take their course, unless an attempt should be made to transfer them without their consent either to Great Britain or France. This they ought to resist by all means in their power, as ruinous to their best interests and destructive of their freedom and independence."

Further, Larkin was to be made a confidential agent of the Department of State—while continuing to serve as consul—although the promotion and the ensuing secret work in behalf of the United States were to be effected quietly.

Such a communication had to be kept out of unfriendly hands. Polk decided to send it by a special secret courier, who would memorize the instruction and reproduce it upon arrival in distant California. Selected for the mission was U. S. Marine Corps Lieutenant Archibald H. Gillespie, who also would carry other verbal instructions and orders and some nonincriminating letters to Larkin, Commodore Sloat of the U. S. Pacific Squadron, and Captain Frémont of the Topographical Corps.

For the trip Lieutenant Gillespie would pose as a Massachusetts commercial agent traveling to Monterey, California, to look after business interests there. He would carry fake identification papers obtained from a Boston firm—Bryant, Sturgis, and Company—and would travel in civilian clothes, first to Vera Cruz, then overland across Mexico to Mazatlán, where he could expect to meet the Pacific Squadron, which often lay over in the port. From Mazatlán he would go on to Monterey.

Later that same month Polk received Lieutenant Gillespie at the Executive Mansion and talked with him. The President's diary entry for Thursday, October 30, recorded this event in an intriguing way. "I held a confidential conversation with Lieut. Gillespie of the Marine Corps, about eight o'clock P.M., on the subject of the secret mission on which he was about to go to California. His secret instructions and the letter to Mr. Larkin, United States consul at Monterey, in the Department of State, will explain the object of his mission." Polk was referring in part to Buchanan's October 17 letter to Larkin, but Gillespie's oral orders never have been fully documented to everyone's satisfaction.

While doubts about foreign intentions in California tortured Polk, Europeans voiced their own concerns about American designs on that same territory—an anxiety of which the President was unaware or was inclined to ignore. The New York *Herald* of September 21, 1845, quoted one European observer as saying, "California and Santa Fe are tempting baits, and Jonathan, by an instinctive love of interest, would stand pardoned, by his own reading of the moral code, in laying violent hands on them." In Paris, the editor of *Journal des Débats* foresaw United States conquest of all Mexico and predicted that this development could presage a dire situation indeed. "Between the autocracy of Russia on the East, and the democracy of America . . . on the West, Europe may find herself more compressed than she may one day think consistent with her independence and dignity."

As autumn waned Polk prepared his first annual message to Congress, which assembled then in December. In the speech, given December 2, 1845, the President announced what has since become known as the "Polk Doctrine"—an elaboration of the Monroe Doctrine, with emphasis on Oregon, Texas, and California. The United States, he said, "can not in silence permit any European interference on the North American continent, and should any such interference be attempted will be ready to resist it at any and all hazards." Later in the speech Polk added, ". . . it should be distinctly announced to the world as our settled policy that no future European colony or dominion shall with our consent be planted or established on any part of the North American continent. . . ."

The warnings obviously were aimed at Britain in regard to Oregon, and at Britain and France concerning possible moves in California or in support of Mexico—even upon Mexican request. With those warnings Polk broadened the Monroe Doctrine to forbid European *interference* in North American affairs and to prohibit territorial transfer even with *consent* of the inhabitants.

In his speech Polk reasserted the United States claim to all of Oregon and recommended that Congress give Britain the required one-year notice of termination of the Oregon treaty that provided for joint occupation. He also spoke of Texas annexation as having been fulfilled despite British and French interference, discussed Mexico's severance of diplomatic relations, and mentioned John Slidell's mission to Mexico hopefully. He expressed a desire for peaceful settlement of the claims against Mexico but indicated he had in mind strong measures if Slidell failed to obtain satisfaction. "Until that result is known," Polk said, "I forbear to recommend to Congress . . . ulterior measures of redress for the wrongs and injuries we have long borne. . . ."

Slidell carried with him to Mexico full authority to settle the boundary between the United States and that country. If Mexico would agree to a Texas border at the Rio Grande, Polk had told him, then the United States Government would assume the obligation of those still unpaid claims against Mexico, for which Americans had waited "long and patiently." If Mexico would throw in New Mexico and Upper California, Polk had said, the United States would pay up to forty million dollars for all this. In any event, Slidell had been told, Mexico was to be reminded of the old Monroe Doctrine, as re-emphasized now by Polk. The United States would not permit the establishment of new European colonies in North America. This was a warning calculated to caution that nation against a variety of agreements with foreign powers.

With the onset of the same winter weather that would lay a coating of ice over those army tents far to the south, Polk was devoting much attention to the prospects and progress of the mission to Mexico. Slidell arrived at Vera Cruz toward the end of November, two months earlier than expected by the Mexican Government. He found the moderate Herrera administration on the verge of collapse and again in no mood or position to negotiate. Word of his mission, carefully withheld at first from foreign representatives in Washington, had been heard in the worst possible place—in Mexico itself—and the political opposition there had erupted in anger, accusing Herrera of treachery. General Paredes, waiting

95

at San Luis Potosí with those seven thousand troops to take over the government at an appropriate time, sniffed opportunity. On December 14 he pronounced against Herrera for allowing Slidell to come to Mexico for the obvious purpose of slicing off chunks of Mexican territory.

When Herrera's Minister of Foreign Relations, Peña y Peña, heard that Slidell had come as a minister, not as the commissioner requested, he was astounded and sought to dissuade Slidell from even coming ashore. To accept the humiliation of thus renewing diplomatic relations with the United States would, he knew, knock over his tottering government. Nevertheless, Peña y Peña did offer to receive Slidell for confidential discussion of mutual problems if he would get his credentials changed to commissioner.

Slidell reacted in a manner characteristic of the President. He insisted on being received as minister, apparently failing to comprehend the disaster this would bring on Herrera. But perhaps he did know what would happen and did not mind, as indicated in a letter he wrote to Polk even while Herrera was trying to fend off Paredes' threat. Slidell said that he felt his main purpose now, after having been refused reception as minister, was not to seek a settlement but to put the blame for failure of negotiations on the Mexican Government. "This will place us upon the strongest possible ground & I have no doubt that if an appeal be made by you to the country, it will be met with a hearty & unanimous response."

The day after Slidell wrote his letter Paredes coincidentally won a majority following of the Army, always the decisive factor in Mexican politics of this period, and three days later the general rode into Mexico City as the new President. On January 4, 1846, he took the oath of office and in the heat of that moment declared his intention of defending Texas as Mexican territory all the way to the Sabine River. His refusal to accept the facts of history—of a Republic of Texas whose independence had been recognized by major European powers and whose citizens had now voted for annexation to the United States—apparently assured a war.

Information about events in Mexico reached the Executive Mansion in Washington many days—even weeks—after they had occurred. Not until January 12 did Polk hear definitely of Slidell's rejection in Mexico. After that, word arrived regarding the ascendancy of Paredes. Instructions went out to Slidell to submit his credentials to the new government—a remarkable move, considering Paredes' stand, but Polk's Secretary of State indicated one reason for it. Buchanan wrote Slidell to act with such prudence and firmness "that it may appear manifest to the people of the United States and to the world" that a break could not be avoided.

On January 13—the day after the report of Slidell's snub reached Washington—Polk had orders sent to General Taylor to move his army from Corpus Christi Bay to the north bank of the Rio Grande, and had orders sent to Commodore Conner's Home Squadron ordering the ships back to stations off Vera Cruz.

12.

Abuses to Uproot

At his sunny hacienda just outside Havana Antonio López de Santa Anna passed the time in exile training his fighting cocks and watching them in battle. The spectacle magnetized him. Each bird, armed with sharp steel spurs in place of natural equipment, had been taught to leap to an attack upon a foe. Fights did not last long. One bird or the other usually fell in a pool of blood after a few minutes, jerked convulsively, and died.

January brought no bitter weather to Cuba. Santa Anna could expect life to proceed at the same easy pace all year long, year after year. Furthermore, with typical foresight about such things he had endowed himself with funds sufficient to see him through in comfort. Such living could be vegetating, of course, but Santa Anna had shown himself capable of enjoying a similar existence on his estate in Mexico.

That had been *Mexico*, however, and this was Cuba. Santa Anna longed to return to his homeland and perhaps even to the power he had held there. He had maintained constant communication with friends back home, and with his sure knowledge of Mexico and Mexicans he had followed events with a strong intuition of what would—and could—unfold.

Herrera's loss to Paredes of the tenuously held presidency would have come as no surprise. Among Herrera's Federalist followers there had been much division of opinion on how to deal with problems facing Mexico, especially regarding relations with its burgeoning northern neighbor. Herrera and other moderate (*Moderado*) Federalists generally distrusted the masses, sought to rely on the middle classes for support, strove to avoid more of the internal conflict that had been plaguing Mexico for years, tried to placate the Army and the Church (both Centralist in sentiment), and feared that war with the United States would prove fatal. But in Mexico of the 1840s Herrera's moderation, especially in regard to the United States, looked more like weakness, even to many Federalists. Herrera had enjoyed less following than most other Mexican leaders holding interim office, and much of that support had been lost when he seemed to have begun seeking negotiations with the United States. Some influential Mexicans had wanted to bring Santa Anna back to power during Herrera's interim term.

Santa Anna realized that Centralist Paredes' days in power also would be numbered. Even after Herrera had left, political factionalism and personalism continued to nurture discord and distrust. Federalist rebellions flared occasionally. Some of Paredes' adherents suspected him of planning to solve Mexican problems by establishing a monarchy—including importing a foreign ruler. Not every Centralist favored that eventuality, although no other form of government had worked: native-son emperor, Federalist republic, Centralist republic, dictatorship.

Furthermore, the Mexican treasury was no richer than usual. Foreign credit had become ever harder to get, and the Army, which had supported Paredes in his grab of power, quickly showed signs of discontent. The Army supported a man only as long as he could meet the military payroll, and in 1846 Mexico that was becoming increasingly difficult. Army upkeep cost 21 million pesos. Revenue brought in only 12 million. The national debt approached 150 million.

Most Mexican difficulties of that period actually stemmed, of course, from the absence of leadership—and the lack of political training—that had become obvious after Spanish withdrawal. One Mexican political observer of the time perceived this and recorded during those dismal days a series of astute observations.

> Everything tends to prove a sad and shameful state of affairs: that we are trained neither in theory nor in practice, nor do we have the virtues or the personal character demanded by a well-regulated system of representative government. Weak men, who are impressed more by individuals than by events; indolent men who do not care to trouble themselves about thinking or working, and who vote without a conscience; these ought only to obey because they are unable to command.

. . .

These citizens of ours are nothing but a flock of sheep that need the lash. They are good for nothing except to maintain a few ambitious and ignorant demagogues in power.

. . .

[The Mexican people] are more worthy of pity than of censure, because no one can be expected to do what he has not been taught to do, nor to be different from what he is. Republican institutions, based on the system of representation, demand . . . a great pooling of individual knowledge . . . ; the system can thrive only if it is nourished by customs which themselves are the products of toil and industry, stimulated by institutions that have attained the power to develop as they have in the United States. We lack both these elements; but on the other hand, we have a people who have the least physical and spiritual requirements: in other words, a people who are the easiest to govern. As long as our institutions are not adapted to the people's character and general moral make-up with which the Creator has endowed them, we must avoid both the anarchy of halfhearted efforts and the dissension of military men, until Europe, tired of our vacillation, imposes upon us the yoke of a foreign monarchy. Our institutions will have a firm foundation only if they follow the dictum of Tacitus: Neither too much liberty nor too much servitude.

Santa Anna knew the Mexican character as well as did the author of those observations, and Santa Anna intended to put that knowledge to his own use—just as he had done in the past. Any means to attain the end would do. Santa Anna preyed on Federalists and Centralists alike.

This time, with Centralist Paredes in power for the moment, he began plotting seriously with the Federalists (after some overtures to Paredes himself) and particularly with an intense leader of a radical wing called the *Puros* (so named because they considered themselves the only pure Federalists), who had disagreed violently with that *Moderado*, Herrera, on how to deal with the United States. Valentín Gómez Farías, a physician from Guadalajara, wanted to return to the Federal Constitution of 1824, with an amendment deleting special privileges given the Army and the Church; wanted to break up the wealth and power of landowners and other higher classes in favor of an elevation of the masses and a recognition of their rights; wanted military reliance placed on state militias, to break up the power of the Army; and wanted separation of Church and State.

Farías and his *Puros* had fought Herrera particularly on dealings with the United States, contending that any agreement made for transfer of territory would appease Mexico's land-hungry neighbor for only a short time. Having annexed Texas, the growing northern giant now wanted Upper California and New Mexico. Given them, he probably would want more northern provinces—possibly all of Mexico. The way to deal with the United States, Farías had declared, was to refuse to negotiate and to prepare for war. If war came, Farías argued, Mexicans might unite sufficiently to hold off the Americans until they became weary of fighting and agreed to make peace.

So Herrera had been thrown out of Mexico City largely because of his soft attitude toward the United States. Now Paredes had taken over—Paredes, whose Centralists were generally wealthy, powerful men, either in civil life or in the Church or the Army; men who violently opposed Federalism as anarchic, particularly in Mexico; and men who had listed among their ranks until his recent downfall and exile the great Antonio López de Santa Anna.

Santa Anna reached Paredes' political enemy, Farías, through the mediation of a mutual friend, Manuel Crecencio Rejón, who was—like Farías—a *Puro* leader. Years earlier Rejón had been an admirer of the United States and its Constitution, but his admiration had turned to hate after he began to suspect the United States of scheming to take Mexican territory. To fend off that threat, Rejón had decided, Mexico needed a strong government—something like Santa Anna's Centralist government then in power. Although an advocate of Federalism, Rejón had accepted appointment by dictator Santa Anna as Minister of Foreign Relations. When Santa Anna's corrupt government had been toppled Rejón found political friendship with Farías because of their mutual hatred of the United States—this despite Rejón's tenure as a member of Santa Anna's despised government. Now, with Santa Anna gone, Herrera gone, and Paredes in power, Rejón still was linked amicably with both his recent chief, Santa Anna, who yearned to establish residence and influence again in his homeland, and with Farías, the *Puro* who hoped to oust Paredes. Ordinarily Santa Anna, who already had betrayed political liberals at least once, and Farías, an unyielding liberal, would have remained almost as far apart as the earth's poles, but these were not ordinary times.

Rejón thought over some odd possibilities—perhaps nudged into this by Santa Anna himself. The *Puros* wanted to take over the government. The government, with Paredes, was Centralist. The Army, concerned about a shriveled treasury and the possibility of cheerless paydays, had become restless. But the Army always had been Centralist in sentiment and always had suspected—even hated—Federalists in any form. Essential to an overthrow of government at this time, however, was the Mexican Army.

Rejón's thinking continued. One reason for Santa Anna's recent ouster had been a loss of Centralist support. But Santa Anna, a career military man, still enjoyed a strong following in the Army. Maybe Santa Anna, disgusted with the Centralists who had helped to force him out, could be persuaded quietly to take up the Federalist cause as commander of the Army, thus allaying suspicions there.

As history already had recorded, Santa Anna was ready, chameleon-like, to do anything to enhance his own well-being. But Rejón obviously believed in Santa Anna's sincerity. To Farías he wrote, "Santa Anna is firm in his decision not to return to rule the republic, and will gladly contribute to your splendid plans, acting as a soldier and helping with all the influence that he has, providing only that he be allowed to pass the rest of his days in the corner he selected some time ago to rest in his old age." Rejón added that Santa Anna now knew his real enemies: the Centralists, who had been responsible for his fall from power.

Finally, after much intermediation, Santa Anna himself wrote to his old foe Farías—about the same time that Farías addressed a friendly letter to the exiled dictator in Havana. Their communications apparently crossed in the mail.

Santa Anna's letter stated, ". . . we can bring about a real fusion between the people and the army. . . . I will give you the affection of the army, in which I have many good friends, and you will give me the affection of the masses over whom you have so much influence . . . there are so many abuses to uproot and so many interests to fight in order to establish on a solid footing the rule of a prudent democracy. . . ."

So Santa Anna the despot, the ostentatious author of bombastic proclamations that said rather than did, once again endorsed Federalism and awaited an opportunity to return to Mexico to do his part for the welfare of the masses—those people who, said the astute Mexican political observer, "are more worthy of pity than of censure, because no one can be expected . . . to be different from what he is."

13.

A Species of Death

Orders to move to the Rio Grande reached Brevet Brigadier General Zachary Taylor on February 3, 1846—three weeks after Polk had them sent. Still, they left the general some leeway. He was to go at his convenience. Since the winter at Corpus Christi Bay had been hard and unusually wet, and since the weather or Taylor's nonchalance had precluded gathering much reliable information about the route, the general took his time in complying. Nevertheless, "a considerable stir" was soon to take place, Colonel E. A. Hitchcock predicted, and the camp roused itself out of idleness to prepare for the march.

Taylor determined to establish his new supply base at Point Isabel, a mainland location accessible through the pass known as Brazos Santiago that lay between those two offshore islands. He would erect a fort some miles farther south—on the north bank of the Rio Grande opposite the Mexican town of Matamoros.

As departure time grew near Hitchcock was ailing again, but he refused to consider a doctor's suggestion that he stay behind. Elsewhere in camp, other officers also prepared for the move.

Lieutenant Sam Grant would carry with him all those soft memories of Julia Dent that had been etched in his mind now, but he would not take three fleet mustangs he had bought while encamped at Corpus Christi Bay. The animals had run away. They had been broken to the saddle and represented a twenty-dollar investment (this out of his sixty-five-dollar-a-month pay), but now they were gone. Grant prepared to walk to the Rio Grande, and since he served in the infantry he felt this would be only logical, after all.

Just before the movement commenced, however, Grant's company commander put him back astride a horse—infantry officers being allowed to ride on a march when this did not interfere with military duties. The company commander had two fine animals, one for himself and an extra one for his servant. He offered his lieutenant a loan of the extra horse, but Grant refused it, declaring that he would go on foot with the men. His commander, however, could not abide the thought of a commissioned officer walking while a servant rode, and he bought a mustang to salve his conscience. "There, Grant, is a horse for you," he declared firmly, and Sam Grant could only accept.

Sam French packed his tent and his possessions on March 7 and prepared to depart with the very first troops scheduled to leave. His battery of horse artillery was due to file out of camp immediately following Colonel Twiggs's regiment of dragoons that would begin the movement to the Rio Grande. After that three brigades of infantry would follow, each of them marching one day apart.

Captain Ephraim Kirby Smith packed his possessions, still believing there would be no war. But his prediction about "perhaps" marching to the Rio Grande was about to be fulfilled. Six months after his arrival in Texas the negotiated settlement that he had hoped for seemed farther away than ever.

At ten o'clock in the morning of March 8, a Sunday, the advance to the Rio Grande began, across country in the bloom of a South Texas spring. The mounted dragoons, 378 of them, clomped out first, followed by creaking supply wagons and by Ringgold's rumbling horse (or "flying") artillery and its young lieutenant, Sam French, who felt elated that his desire "to know the world by sight and not by books" was being satisfied further.

French's enthusiasm dimmed a little with every hour that passed. That evening his column encamped in beautiful country covered "with blue flowers like the hyacinth"—probably the Texas bluebonnet—but also infested with another Texas native—the deadly rattlesnake. As he halted he saw earlier arrivals standing beside their grazing animals and occasionally hitting at uncovered rattlers with long sticks cut for the purpose.

In the next few days sun and wind brought further discomfort, burning and chapping lips and noses. Many lips became so raw that men could not stand touching them to tin cups filled with hot coffee. Instead they waited until the drink had cooled.

French fared somewhat better. During the day he wore a huge Mexican sombrero, despite the warnings of fellow officers who predicted a stiff rebuke or even arrest by Taylor when the general saw it. But French's colleagues had overlooked Taylor's famous dislike for military attire. When the sombrero-shaded French happened upon Taylor he heard the general's greeting with much satisfaction: "Good morning, Lieutenant, good morning. Sensible man to wear a hat." French noticed that Taylor's nose was white with peeling skin and that his lips had become badly chapped.

The first of the infantry brigades left on the morning of March 9, led by Colonel (or Brevet Brigadier General) William Worth. The men tramped out in double-file order, bound on a course slightly north of west. Later they would turn southward toward the Rio Grande and Matamoros. In the rear followed more supply wagons (one for every ten soldiers) and artillerymen riding beside rumbling 6- and 12-pounder guns that gleamed in the bright sunlight.

On the following morning the second brigade departed, commanded by rough Lieutenant Colonel James McIntosh and accompanied by the usual supply wagons and a detachment of artillerymen, this time without cannon. With the brigade marched Captain Ephraim Kirby Smith, whose love of flowers enabled him to find a degree of satisfaction in a hike that quickly became exhausting in the day's heat. Around him trudging infantrymen almost smothered in their heavy blue uniforms. The knapsack, blanket, musket or rifle, and cartridge box that each man carried soon seemed twice as heavy.

Smith commenced the journey unmounted, too, but for him the scenery compensated. He walked across a grassy prairie sprinkled with chaparral and clumps of stunted timber; on to a view, to his right, of the Nueces River winding across a plain "like a blue ribbon . . . thrown on a green robe"; through fields of bright flowers that he identified as the spiderwort, phlox, lupin, primrose, and the Spanish bayonet—or yucca— in full bloom. "The day was hot though cloudy with a pleasant breeze." It reminded him of July at home.

After that, however, the march became grueling indeed. The first night in camp Smith drew guard duty and slept very little. He found that recent rains had bogged lowlands and had left them almost impassable for the baggage train. They shared camp sites sometimes with a variety of "varmints"; Smith once saw emerging from the same hole in the ground a rabbit, a rat, a rattlesnake, and a tarantula. Near his tent he killed another rattler six feet long.

Rains soaked the men. A fiercely tropical sun dried them and left them thirsting for water. Farther south desert dust coated them, and the sun continued to stream down "like living fire." Smith became ill and unable to sleep—even after long, exhausting marches. But then another officer lent him a horse, and his health and spirits improved.

The third brigade left on March 11, led by old Colonel Whistler and followed by another smart battery of flying artillery, this one commanded by Lieutenant Braxton Bragg. With the departure of this brigade the camp on Corpus Christi Bay assumed a forlorn look. Left behind were eight or nine hundred men—including Taylor's fourth (and last) battery of field artillery, a small garrison force, and hundreds of men on the sick list. Most of these soldiers, together with four large siege guns and additional supplies, eventually would be transported by sea to the new supply depot at Point Isabel.

Riding with the last brigade to leave the bay was Colonel E. A. Hitchcock, who had left a sickbed to make the trip. Continued weakness compelled him to accept makeshift hospital quarters on a hard pallet of ammunition boxes bunched together in a jolting ox wagon. As soon as he was able he transferred to his horse, but fatigue and debility left him scarcely able to ride.

Sam Grant rode with this brigade, too—on that mustang provided by his company commander. Grant learned that the animal had never been under saddle before, but this did not deter such a horseman as he. "I had . . . but little difficulty in breaking [the mustang], though for the first day there were frequent disagreements between us as to which way we should go, and sometimes whether we should go at all. At no time during the day could I choose exactly the part of the column I would march with."

A few days after departure Grant's brigade came upon an enormous herd of mustangs—the very group from which the horse he was riding had been captured only a few weeks earlier, Grant believed. From a rise on the prairie he observed the animals. They were scattered across the plain to his left and right as far as he could see. Probably all of Rhode Island or Delaware could not have held them, he reflected, without pasturage giving out in a single day.

Toward Matamoros marched the men of Taylor's army, numbering now only three thousand at most. They heard constant rumors of large Mexican forces in their front, ready to dispute their advance, although Taylor had sent ahead by Mexican traders proclamations seeking to calm residents. In those broadsides Taylor declared that personal safety would be assured, religious liberty guaranteed, all supplies purchased well paid for.

Ten miles a day the army averaged, across a country that gradually lost beauty as the troops entered a barren, dry land. From their starting point Matamoros had lain some two hundred winding miles away, across sun-baked soil, through suffocating dust, past occasional holes of brackish or salt water, through ankle-deep sand that burned like hot ashes, into areas of terrain capable of supporting a thin growth of grass, and across ugly black patches where Mexican guerrillas had burned even this light covering.

Nearer the Rio Grande the country began to change again. Sandy soil became black clay. Grass thickened. Trees and flowers reappeared. But Mexican patrols also came into view from time to time.

Near a wide, salty, steep-banked tidal stream named the Arroyo Colorado, lined on its far side with a forest of thorny brush, Taylor's army began collecting again. There the general halted his men and waited for engineers to prepare a ford.

From the wooded bank opposite came sounds of Mexican activity. A brightly uniformed officer appeared from behind the brush with a warning for Taylor: come no farther. Taylor replied that he intended to cross the arroyo and would open fire if opposed. Quickly he sent back messengers telling rear columns to close up and be ready to assist. He ordered four infantry companies to the arroyo, then instructed Ringgold to unlimber and load his guns. The long-anticipated war seemed certain to begin on this morning of March 20, 1846, at a location some thirty miles north of Matamoros.

Lieutenant Sam French, with Ringgold's waiting battery, saw and heard the excitement that followed. He stood behind his gun on a section of bank cut down by engineers for easy fording and looked across the stream. It was eighty yards wide, he guessed, and maybe four feet deep. From behind that brush on the other side he soon heard an "awful din" produced by Mexican bugles, drums, and fifes. Around French, artillery-men lighted their slow-burning matches; a short distance away American infantrymen waited for the command to advance.

Nearby, Lieutenant Sam Grant also heard the concealed buglers and thought that "if the troops were in proportion to the noise, they were sufficient to devour General Taylor and his army." To the right of the waiting infantrymen stood Captain E. K. Smith, certain that a fierce conflict was about to begin but ready for it now. Smith heard those awesome bugles sounding from many different locations up and down the opposite bank. The Mexicans obviously had assembled a powerful force.

At 10:30 A.M. French heard a shouted command, "Forward!" He saw blue-clad infantrymen plunge into the stream, holding muskets and cartridge boxes high above their heads. Near French, Smith waited in anxious silence for the Mexicans to open a deadly fire. Then he gradually relaxed. Around Smith, curses muttered as the infantry quietly neared the other bank told him that his troops had been as ready for battle as he. He saw the splashing column reach the opposite side, wade ashore, and form in order of battle. Then cheers broke the silence, and Taylor's military band struck up "Yankee Doodle." The Mexicans beyond had vanished toward Matamoros.

Once across the arroyo Taylor ordered a long halt to reassemble his army. Then he went on, moving in parallel columns across an open prairie, with his long baggage train close in at the rear and scouts out far ahead and on the flanks, examining every thicket.

Twelve miles beyond the arroyo the general and a detachment composed of a cavalry escort and teamsters driving a train of empty wagons left the main body of the little army temporarily. They made a quick detour to the left—to the site of the newly selected supply depot on Point Isabel, which had been only recently evacuated by a small Mexican force. There Taylor ordered the wagons loaded with supplies from a fleet of recently arrived vessels. Then he set men—most of them landed from ships—to constructing Fort Polk, on the Point, while he, his escort, and the supply wagons hurried back to rejoin the rest of the army waiting for him a few miles from the Rio Grande.

On the southern side of the Arroyo Colorado the men found richer soil, some fresh-water ponds, and more picturesque scenery, although chaparral still grabbed at their clothes. Ducks and plover flocked around the green-rimmed ponds. Rabbits abounded in the denser vegetation. Spirits improved, too. Well clad, well fed, and well armed, the men radiated success—no matter what vicissitudes might face them. Some who had expressed doubts earlier about the legality or logic of their move now fell silent, caught up in the excitement and enthusiasm of adventure. Many men still felt there would be no war, although others predicted a battle before reaching their destination. If a fight came, one rumor said, the probable site would be somewhere in a two-mile-wide belt of thick chaparral that reportedly lay parallel to the Rio Grande and several miles from it. Only one narrow road cut through that wilderness.

Late in the morning of March 28 Taylor's army neared its goal. No one barred the way through the chaparral belt. Once past it, the soldiers came upon a tidy area of cultivated fields fenced by tall hedges and sprinkled with thatched-roof hovels that had been hurriedly abandoned by occupants. Then the men saw, ahead, the mud-colored Rio Grande, running two hundred yards wide beneath steep banks that appeared to be perpendicular. Across the river lay Matamoros, a city of white houses set amid tropical gardens. The scene appeared "like a fairy vision" before enchanted American eyes.

Taylor's men, gaping, saw in the city residents standing atop the flat roofs and staring back at them as they commenced making camp in a singularly exposed location: on an expansive plot of plowed land that protruded southward because of a long curve of the river in that direction. Mexicans across the Rio Grande could look into Taylor's camp from east, south, and west, but the general ordered the construction of earthen Fort Texas at that point.

Soon after arrival Taylor sought to assure the Mexican commandant in Matamoros—young, swaggering Francisco Mejía—of his peacefulness, but Mejía declared through an aide that Mexico considered war commenced by the "invasion," and he would hold no conferences. Mexican soldiers reinforced the defenses of Matamoros, garrisoned already by several thousand troops, and Mexican officers and priests began soliciting desertions from Catholic members of Taylor's army—with success, especially among the foreign-born. Some peculiarities of American society then encouraged these desertions.

In recent years a sudden wave of immigration had engulfed the United States, causing anxiety among citizens already established in the country. More and more foreigners were seeking the liberty and opportunity afforded by the Constitution that Americans had spoken of so proudly. In 1830 only 1 per cent of the population had been foreign-born, but by 1850 the figure would jump to 10 per cent. This development was helping to encourage a native-American movement throughout the land—an anti-foreign attitude that had resulted in an outbreak of angry rioting in Philadelphia (in May 1844) and in other localities against all foreigners and against the Catholic Church, in which many of these people claimed membership. As jobs for immigrants had become increasingly scarce more of the men had sought refuge in the U. S. Army, whose lowest ranks stood open to almost anyone willing to accept the poor pay.

Now, at Fort Texas, foreign-born men made up nearly half of Taylor's army. Of all his troops 24 per cent were Irish, 10 per cent German, 6 per cent English, 3 per cent Scottish, and 4 per cent other nationalities. Mexican appeals for desertion attracted listeners among the Irish and among some other nationalities because of religion, and among Englishmen (to lesser degree) because of the long-standing antagonism between the United States and Britain, represented now particularly by the Oregon dispute. Mexico would welcome these deserters and pay their way to "the beautiful [national] capital." Later they could enlist in the Mexican Army and form their own battalion—and they did, naming their unit the San Patricio Battalion, evincing both Irish and Mexican influence.

So some of Taylor's soldiers began swimming the Rio Grande to yet another new life. The general posted sentries to shoot men seen making for the opposite bank. Guards hit a Frenchman first, then a Swiss native. But the exodus slowly continued despite these potshots and despite the occasional drowning in mid-river of a poor swimmer.

Taylor gritted his teeth, entrenched himself in Fort Texas, and aimed his siege guns at the Mexican city. In the evenings, however, bands on both sides serenaded foes lying across the river. Matamoros peddlers wandered freely about Taylor's camp selling food and souvenirs. The Americans watched happily as Mexican girls bathed in the nude and in all innocence, as had been their custom, in the Rio Grande—another attraction that would have encouraged desertion.

During following weeks the situation grew more tense. In April a new commandant replaced Mejía—stern, self-centered Pedro de Ampudia, not well liked even in Matamoros. Apparently the man's brutality had become known. In 1844 Ampudia had captured a troublesome Mexican general and fourteen aides and had ordered them shot and their heads boiled in oil so that their skulls could be displayed at once inside iron

cages. Now Ampudia brought two thousand additional troops to Matamoros, and he gave Taylor twenty-four hours to begin a withdrawal
toward the Nueces. Taylor answered by obtaining a U. S. Navy blockade
of the mouth of the Rio Grande, which had been used by the Mexicans
for transporting supplies to Matamoros after their abandonment of
Point Isabel.

Later in April a tall, muscular, dignified Mexican general—José Mariano Arista, a onetime resident of Cincinnati—took over command from
Ampudia with specific orders from Mexico City to begin action.

The Mexican attitude toward the United States had hardened. A
very few wealthy Mexicans selfishly and quietly half hoped that the
Americans might take over their country and ensure order and prosperity,
but Mexicans in overwhelming numbers hated their northern neighbor
more than ever now for a number of reasons. They believed the United
States Government had secretly plotted with and had aided Texans in
their rebellion with the aim of annexing the territory. They suspected that
the United States planned to try to take all of Mexico, piece by piece,
using Texas as a pattern—and that Americans would incite Indians to
violence if necessary to achieve their goal. They took American openness
of speech and action and the characteristic brusqueness of manner for
haughtiness. Privileged classes in Mexico feared the influence of American
democracy. The vigorous American Protestantism made Catholic clergy-
men in Mexico apprehensive.

Now these heretics had come to Mexico, and it was time to teach
them a lesson. Mexican officers at Matamoros studied their enemy and
(as was learned later) grew more confident. Seedy old Zachary Taylor
certainly could not be much of a general, they thought, and his troops
appeared to be equally inferior. Back to Mexico City went optimistic
reports: U. S. Army officers lacked zeal and harmony. Their men—many
of them foreigners—had become discontented and would not fight, or
they had engaged in such enormous dissipation at Corpus Christi Bay
that the march southward had left them enfeebled and virtually worthless.
American cavalrymen could not shoot accurately, ride well, or control
their horses. The Americans excelled in only one area, these reports said.
They all had mighty appetites and ate huge amounts of food.

So the Mexican Army at Matamoros, ordered to commence action,
did not quail. Scattered shooting already had resulted in American casualties, but apparently this violence had been inspired by guerrillas who

roamed the area—not by regular Mexican troops. On April 10 Taylor's quartermaster, Colonel Trueman Cross, had left the fort unescorted for a pleasure jaunt on horseback up the river, and he had failed to return before dark. Taylor had ordered cannon fire to guide the colonel back, but days had passed—then a week—with no word. One day Lieutenant Sam French, riding up the river with a group of officers, found a blue coat presumed to be Cross's. Then a search patrol led by popular Lieutenant Theodric Porter (brother of Admiral-to-be David D. Porter and son of a commodore who had, ironically, been employed as the first commander of the Republic of Mexico Navy) had drawn guerrilla fire that proved fatal to Porter and one of his men.

Eleven days after Cross's disappearance his body was found. His skull apparently had been shattered by a heavy blow, giving credence to a rumor circulated around camp that Cross had been stripped and killed while a prisoner of a guerrilla band.

Cross was buried late in the afternoon of April 24 at the base of the Fort Texas flagstaff. His body was carried there in a slow procession that could be seen by hundreds of Mexicans crowding rooftops, riverbanks, and other heights across the Rio Grande. Eight companies of infantry, marching to a solemn beat, led. Following them came a squadron of dragoons; then the flag-draped body, carried on a caisson drawn by six horses; a single mourner—the colonel's son, also a member of Taylor's army; a riderless horse led by two dragoons; and, finally, all off-duty officers. Beneath a half-masted flag a colonel read the service for the dead. Three rifle volleys cracked a final tribute. The colors raced back to the mast top, and the escort marched off to a lively tune, leaving the dead man to eternal repose. "Such is a military funeral," remarked one observer. "We have no time for grief."

The entire area seemed ready to erupt now. Reports of river crossings by Mexican regulars came in constantly to Fort Texas, and General Taylor sent out larger and more frequent patrols to investigate.

One patrol rode away late in the afternoon of the day following Cross's burial to investigate a report of an upriver crossing in force. Gaunt, daring Captain Seth Thornton with sixty-three dragoons and a hired Mexican guide named Chapita comprised the group.

The very next day Chapita returned to camp and reported a disaster. Thornton's patrol had been surrounded and attacked by Mexican soldiers, he said, on the north side of the Rio Grande. Sixteen men had died; others were wounded. All survivors had been captured.

Fort Texas throbbed with the latest excitement. General Taylor ordered his men to rush the work of fortification. Under evening darkness he sent to Point Isabel a messenger carrying two momentous communications: a request to be forwarded to the governors of Texas and Louisiana that they recruit and send him five thousand three-month volunteers (under authority given Taylor before his departure for Texas), and a dispatch addressed to President Polk in Washington: "Hostilities may now be considered as commenced."

Then concern for the supply base at Point Isabel prompted Taylor to return there with most of his army, leaving the security of Fort Texas to five hundred able men, a number of laundry women, and the men on the sick list—all under the command of Major Jacob Brown, a man not easily unnerved. Taylor and his men completed the hurried, grueling march to the Point in surprising peace, but at that location, before reveille on May 3, 1846, that "rumbling noise like distant thunder" startled Captain E. K. Smith; the "boom! boom! of distant cannon" caused the ground to vibrate beneath an awakened Lieutenant Sam French; and the sounds of hostile cannon evoked from Lieutenant Sam Grant the remark that he felt sorry he had enlisted.

Colonel E. A. Hitchcock missed hearing those sounds of cannon fire. On the same day (April 10) that Colonel Cross had left on his tragic pleasure jaunt Hitchcock had yielded to advice of doctors and to the urgings of fellow officers—including General Taylor himself—and had applied for a sixty-day leave of absence to recuperate in a better climate.

His illness had lingered. His bones had ached as if he were overfatigued. Never had he had fever—only recurrent diarrhea and constant debility that had become more acute. Despite his torpidity and his unfavorable assessment of this military movement he had felt continually humiliated by his physical inability to take his place at the head of his regiment. He had missed being with his men during the excitement on the Arroyo Colorado—had missed most of the labor of setting up Fort Texas. Instead he had languished in his tent.

His request for leave had come back signed by General Taylor an hour after he submitted it. On the very next day he had begun the trip to Point Isabel—and eventually to the United States—escorted on the first leg by ten dragoons. Leaving Fort Texas, he had ridden horseback, but later he had lain on a bed improvised in a baggage wagon. When those sounds of distant cannon eventually reached the ears of Taylor's army at Point Isabel that morning of May 3 Hitchcock was nearing St. Louis on the steamboat *Louisiana*, which he had boarded at New Orleans.

Not even his lassitude had caused him to waver in his opinion of the war that seemed to impend. While en route to the Rio Grande he had roused himself out of lethargy to write in his diary:

> . . . I have said from the first that the United States are the aggressors. We have outraged the Mexican government and people by an arrogance and presumption that deserve to be punished. . . . We have not one particle of right to be here. Our force is altogether too small for the accomplishment of its errand. It looks as if the government sent a small force on purpose to bring on a war, so as to have a pretext for taking California and as much of this country as it chooses; for, whatever becomes of this army, there is no doubt of a war between the United States and Mexico. . . . My heart is not in this business . . . but, as a military man, I am bound to execute orders.

For a week Hitchcock talked with doctors in St. Louis and met old friends there. Then word arrived about the death of Colonel Cross and the attack on Captain Thornton's patrol: sixteen men dead, the rest captured (but eventually released by the Mexicans). Saddened by the fatalities and by the outbreak of violence that he had predicted nearly one year earlier, Colonel Hitchcock nevertheless showed himself again a military man. Removed from the action by fifteen hundred miles and by his feeble health, Hitchcock reflected moodily, "My absence from my regiment at such a time as this is a species of death."

PART III

War

14.

Forbearance Exhausted

General Taylor's April 26 dispatch, "Hostilities may now be considered as commenced," required nearly two weeks for delivery from the Rio Grande to Washington.

During that time, paradoxically, President Polk was giving much attention to the other potential war—with Great Britain over Oregon. On April 23, after long debate, Congress finally had voted by an overwhelming majority to approve his suggestion about sending Britain formal notice of termination of the joint-occupation treaty. But the victory had left the President unhappy and even seething. He felt that notice should have been given much earlier—in December. He did not approve of the soft wording eventually adopted, believing this would make Britain more arrogant. And he was furious at some senators—especially Democrats—who sought in their speeches to pacify Britain with the obvious intention of avoiding a fight. "The truth is," Polk wrote, ". . . too many Democratic Senators have been more concerned about the Presidential election in '48 than they have been about settling Oregon either at 49° or 54° 40'. 'Forty-eight' has been with them the great question. . . ."

That was no way to look John Bull "in the eye." Polk believed such a tentative stance as Congress had taken might even encourage Britain to commence hostilities. "If war should be the result," he speculated, "these peace gentlemen and advocates of British pretensions over those of their own country will have done more to produce it than any others."

Polk need not have worried. The British Government, of course, wanted no war for such a remote territory. The Prime Minister, Lord Aberdeen, already had commenced a campaign to reconcile his countrymen to a peaceful settlement of Oregon, but Polk obviously was not aware of it.

At this time, then, the possibility of simultaneous wars had seemed more likely to Polk—even before the arrival of General Taylor's dispatch. John Slidell had received no invitation from the newest Mexican administration to discuss differences. President Paredes, like the man he had recently overthrown, realized the fatality in the first place of admitting a man with the designation of United States minister and anticipated the humiliating territorial demands Slidell would make if received. On March 21 the Paredes government sent Slidell a final rejection and asserted that any war would be the responsibility of the United States for insisting that a man called by the unacceptable title "minister" be recognized by Mexico before discussion of mutual problems could begin.

Polk's envoy had received prior instructions to cover such a climactic occurrence. Secretary of State Buchanan had written Slidell in January that he should demand his passports and return to Washington whenever the Mexicans gave him a final rejection. The President would then "submit the whole case to Congress and assert . . . just rights and avenge . . . injured honor." Declaration of war by the United States thus seemed to await Slidell's reappearance in Washington—no matter what Mexico might do—and Slidell himself favored the eventuality. After his last rejection he wrote Buchanan, "We can never get along well with [Mexico] until we have given them a good drubbing."

Slidell and Polk harmonized. Both men advocated the use of force. Both men harbored suspicions about British involvement in Mexico—for them that would explain the firm and confident tone of the Mexican rejection. Slidell reported that President Paredes had been calling on the British minister in secret, and Polk, who suspected British intrigue everywhere anyway, deduced from this that the British had been instrumental in Slidell's lack of success. Neither man knew the real attitude of the British Government. London wanted war over Mexico or California no more than over Oregon. But when Polk heard of his envoy's rejection he echoed the ominous statement that Buchanan had written to Slidell earlier: "My opinion was," Polk wrote in his diary, "that I should make a communication to Congress recommending that legislative measures be adopted, to take the remedy for the injuries and wrongs we had suffered into our own hands."

Nevertheless, about this time Polk was quietly pondering another chance, however slim, for obtaining peacefully most of what he wanted from Mexico. In February he had talked twice with a curious man who claimed to be on a mission from the deposed Antonio López de Santa Anna, still residing in Havana. Polk remembered that he had met the man, Alexander Atocha, once before—in June of the preceding year—in regard to claims against Mexico. Atocha, a native Spaniard and a naturalized United States citizen, had been a banker in Mexico where he had become an intimate friend of Santa Anna's. After Santa Anna's most recent fall from power Atocha had been expelled from the country, too.

At the first of the two February meetings—on the thirteenth—Polk listened in amazement while his visitor unfolded an intrigue. Atocha said he had recently visited Santa Anna and had learned that the former President was in constant communication with Mexican followers who wanted to return him to power. Atocha declared that Santa Anna had expressed himself as favoring a treaty with the United States, settling on the Rio Grande as the western boundary of Texas. Furthermore (as Polk recorded in his diary), Atocha quoted Santa Anna as saying that "the Colorado of the West down through the Bay of San Francisco to the sea should be the Mexican line on the north, and that Mexico should cede all east and north of these natural boundaries to the United States for a pecuniary consideration, and mentioned thirty millions of dollars as the sum." Santa Anna, experienced both in holding Mexico together and in seeing it break into pieces, knew how this money would have to be used by any government leader who hoped for permanence: to pay the Army and certain other groups, thus enabling the government to gain a firmer footing. All that would be Santa Anna's own plan, Atocha said, for settling differences with the United States.

Santa Anna's geography around San Francisco Bay, as Atocha quoted it, might have been confused, but this did not deter Polk. He knew what the man actually was proposing: selling all the Mexican territory that Polk wanted for thirty million dollars.

What did discourage the President was Atocha's apparent slipperiness. Polk, like most secretive men, always tended to distrust more than to trust, and for the small-town lawyer in Polk this suspicion would have been increased by the visitor's Spanish accent. "Col. Atocha is a person to whom I would not give my confidence," Polk wrote. "He is evidently a man of talents and education, but his whole manner and conversation impressed me with a belief that he was not reliable, and [that he] would betray any confidence reposed in him. . . . I therefore heard all he said but communicated nothing to him."

Polk talked with Atocha again during the afternoon of February 16—three days after the first visit—and Atocha elaborated on some suggestions from Santa Anna as further proof of the general's desire to work with the United States. Polk recorded the advice.

> . . . the United States should take strong measures before any settlement could be effected. He [Atocha, quoting Santa Anna] said our army should be marched at once from Corpus Christi to the Del Norte [Rio Grande], and a strong naval force assembled at Vera Cruz, that Mr. Slidell, the United States Minister, should withdraw from [Jalapa] and go on board one of our ships of war at Vera Cruz, and in that position demand the payment of the amount due our citizens; that it was well known the Mexican government was unable to pay in money, and that when they saw a strong force ready to strike on their coasts and border they would, he had no doubt, feel their danger and agree to the boundary suggested. . . . He said the last words which General Santa Anna said to him when he was leaving Havana a month ago [were], "When you see the President, tell him to take strong measures, and such a treaty can be made and I will sustain it."

Coincidentally, Polk already had ordered Taylor's army to the Rio Grande, of course, and had sent the Home Squadron to station off Vera Cruz. Furthermore, Polk's Secretary of State, Buchanan, had instructed Slidell to leave Mexico—as soon as his final rejection came—in a manner similar to that proposed by Santa Anna. But neither Polk nor Santa Anna could have had prior knowledge of the other's thoughts or actions, and the events were only a historical happenstance.

By May the Mexican situation had deteriorated so much in Washington that no intrigue devised by Santa Anna could have been carried out quickly enough to solve problems for Polk. Daily the President awaited the reappearance of John Slidell and the detailed information he would bring. Daily, too, Polk awaited word from Zachary Taylor on the Rio Grande. Late in the evening of May 6 Polk read dispatches from Taylor dated April 15. The President noted, "No actual collision [has] taken place, though the probabilities are that hostilities might take place soon."

Slidell arrived before the receipt of any other dispatches from Taylor. Polk welcomed him at the Executive Mansion on May 8, listened for about an hour as the envoy related his experiences, and agreed with him that the only course left "was to take the redress of the wrongs and injuries which we had so long borne from Mexico into our own hands, and to act with promptness and energy."

On the following day, a Saturday, the President brought up for discussion by the Cabinet a war declaration based on the claims still not paid by Mexico and on the rejection of Slidell as minister to negotiate differences. Numerous American journals had been urging action instead of negotiation, and many readers reflected this militant mood. With Congress near adjournment, the President informed leaders there of his intention to keep the lawmaking body in session until it could dispose of the Mexican problem. Now, at the May 9 cabinet meeting, the President addressed his listeners.

> I stated . . . that up to this time, as we knew, we had heard of no open act of aggression by the Mexican army, but that the danger was imminent that such acts would be committed. I said that in my opinion we had ample cause of war, and that it was impossible . . . that I could remain silent much longer; that I thought it was my duty to send a message to Congress very soon and recommend definite measures. I told them that I thought I ought to make such a message by Tuesday next [May 12], that the country was excited and impatient on the subject. . . .

Only one cabinet member disapproved of a war declaration. Secretary of the Navy Bancroft said he would favor this move only if the Mexicans attacked. Secretary of State Buchanan said he would prefer declaring war only after a Mexican attack, but he added that the United States already had endured enough provocation for a war and would support action by the President.

"It was agreed," Polk wrote, "that the [war] message should be prepared and submitted to the Cabinet in their meeting on Tuesday."

Polk realized, however, that he would have strong opposition. He had already discussed the situation with some congressional leaders, in fact, and had uncovered resistance. Missouri Senator Benton, the ardent expansionist, did not want war with Mexico and did not even want a war with Britain over his prized Oregon. Fiery Senator John C. Calhoun of South Carolina, a power among Southern Democrats, opposed war with Mexico, although he favored Texas annexation. Many Whigs would refuse to vote for war, Polk knew, for political reasons. Anti-slavery Northerners and Easterners would oppose it as having been brought on by a President from Tennessee apparently seeking to strengthen the hold of that peculiar Southern institution. Other citizens would believe simply that any war fought by the United States should be solely for the life-or-death defense of their country.

Nevertheless, Polk was ready to begin drafting a declaration of war against Mexico largely on the basis of those unpaid claims. His momentous cabinet meeting had been adjourned only a few hours when, about six o'clock that Saturday evening, Adjutant General Roger Jones of the Army appeared at the Executive Mansion with dispatches just received from General Taylor.

Polk read about the Mexican attack on Thornton's dragoons and saw Taylor's assessment: "Hostilities may now be considered as commenced." Immediately the President summoned the Cabinet back for a seven-thirty meeting at the Mansion, told them about Taylor's dispatch, and won unanimous agreement for submitting a war message to Congress on Monday. That second momentous May 9 meeting of the Cabinet adjourned at 10 P.M., and the President began drafting his message that same night.

Early Sunday morning Polk rose, told aides to admit no casual visitors, and continued working on the declaration. About 9:30 A.M. Secretary of the Navy Bancroft arrived to help with the writing. An hour and a half later the President stopped and took time off to attend church with Mrs. Polk. After a two o'clock family dinner in the Executive Mansion, with Bancroft a guest, Polk returned to his message. He completed a first draft, although excited senators and representatives called occasionally throughout the afternoon and evening.

By ten-thirty the last visitor had left. The President brought his diary up to date with a brief account of events and concluded, "It was a day of great anxiety to me, and I regretted the necessity . . . for me to spend the Sabbath in the manner I have." Then he retired for the night.

Monday morning Polk made revisions in his message. He sent it to Congress at noon. In the document he summarized events leading to the trouble: the Texas claim to a Rio Grande boundary, Texas annexation, General Taylor's moves to Corpus Christi Bay and on to the Rio Grande, Mexico's ensuing belligerence, and the attack on Thornton's dragoons reconnoitering the north bank of the river. He continued:

> The cup of forbearance had been exhausted even before the recent information from the frontier of the Del Norte [Rio Grande]. But now, after reiterated menaces, Mexico has passed the boundary

of the United States, has invaded our territory and shed American blood upon the American soil. She has proclaimed that hostilities have commenced, and that the two nations are now at war.

As war exists, notwithstanding all our efforts to avoid it, exists by the act of Mexico herself, we are called upon by every consideration of duty and patriotism to vindicate with decision the honor, the rights, and the interests of our country. . . .

Administration proponents in the Democrat-controlled House of Representatives rushed through passage of Polk's war bill so quickly that critics claimed ever afterward the measure never received fair discussion and debate.

Criticism was indeed virtually muzzled by the Speaker. He conveniently overlooked Whigs who rose to request permission to address the House; and a huge stack of documents sent by the Chief Executive in support of the war declaration lay on the Speaker's desk, unexamined and unexaminable. Excerpts from the papers were read aloud by the clerk of the House, but a Whig request for a one-day delay to allow study of the documents drew immediate rejection. Within a few hours of submission Polk's war bill passed the House (174–14, with 35 abstentions).

The Senate devoted a few more hours to its consideration, although no extra time was allowed for examination of those documents. Every Whig who spoke criticized the wording of the bill that declared American blood had been shed upon American soil, but in the end exigencies, Democratic pressure, and a patriotic stampede saw the bill through (42–2) on the day following House passage.

Polk affixed his signature at one o'clock in the afternoon of May 13, 1846. Congress had voted him ten million dollars for conducting the war and had given him authority to enlist fifty thousand soldiers. All would be volunteers; as was usual in those days, no American would serve in the armed forces against his will.

Actually, however, the war bill was anticlimactic. Polk already had used his power as President and Commander-in-Chief to deploy military units in such a way that congressional authority to declare war had diminished to the point of merely recognizing that a state of war existed.

Many persons continued to debate the ethic of a war declaration. Whig editors almost unanimously attacked the oncoming conflict as unjust. Senator Calhoun, the fiery Southern Democrat, voiced disapproval, too. He said that fewer than 10 per cent of the congressmen would have supported the war bill had they been given time to study the "supporting" documents, and he always contended that fighting could easily have been avoided. Later Calhoun voted for men and equipment to prosecute the war, but he had refrained from voting for the declaration itself, maintaining that all blame could not be placed on Mexico.

15.

Here They Come!

The rumble of cannon fire from isolated Fort Texas, opposite Matamoros, had not stopped that morning of May 3. At the supply base on Point Isabel the men of Taylor's army listened to the sounds with increasing concern for the fate of those left behind on the banks of the Rio Grande.

At midmorning Captain Ephraim Kirby Smith paused to write a letter. Perhaps it would be his last, although he did not dwell on the possibility. The Army had received orders to march for the relief of Fort Texas at one o'clock that afternoon.

"It is now ten in the morning," Smith wrote, "and we can still hear the cannon. What will be the result no one can conjecture, for in truth we know little in regard to the forces of the enemy, their numbers being variously reported from five to fifteen thousand. . . . We are about two thousand strong and may be interrupted in our march."

The hard facts not known in detail by Smith or by General Taylor, whose spy system until now had been best known for its blind spots, were that the Mexicans had indeed crossed the river in force, both above and below Fort Texas. Sixteen hundred Mexican cavalrymen led by General Anastasio Torrejón, a native of Pensacola, had crossed above the fort. This was the force Captain Thornton and his dragoons had been seeking when surrounded and attacked. Following that fight, Torrejón's cavalry had circled southeastward, crossing Taylor's vital supply road that linked Fort Texas with Point Isabel, then had continued on to a location on the river below Fort Texas. There they had deployed along the banks to cover five thousand more Mexican soldiers (commanded by General Arista) who were engaged in a giant movement northward. Arista hoped to be in position on the road between Fort Texas and Point Isabel before Taylor could make any move, but a shortage of boats delayed him.

While Arista's men were engaged in their river crossing Taylor had hurried his small army from Fort Texas to Point Isabel on that forced march to protect his supply line, prodded by reports of the Mexican threat. By the time Arista arrived at his destination he could see that Taylor already had rushed past. Arista halted his army astride the road to await Taylor's next move and detached a force under General Ampudia to besiege Fort Texas with cannon. Some Mexican officers were said to have believed Taylor's withdrawal represented a quick and shameful retreat.

At Point Isabel, Captain Smith finished his speculative letter while the distant artillery still grumbled. Soon he learned that the order to march had been canceled. Taylor's penchant for changing his mind had shown itself again.

The general had decided on more caution. Taylor put his men to work improving fortifications at Fort Polk and to loading every available wagon—more than two hundred of them—with supplies for Fort Texas. Then he dispatched a nerveless Texas Ranger captain and four volunteers to ascertain the situation at the beleaguered fort.

Samuel H. Walker, a slight, slouchy, blue-eyed man with an innocuous look that belied his reputation of rarely bringing in prisoners, was the Ranger captain, and he was a reason that Taylor's spy system was to become more effective—by relying more on Rangers like him. During the night of May 3–4 Walker and his four companions sneaked through country thick with chaparral and Mexican soldiers to the vicinity of Fort Texas. There they waited, hidden in a brush thicket, for sunrise. At dawn Walker left his companions, crept into the moat surrounding the fort, and called out to sentries, identifying himself. Fort Texas soldiers helped him crawl inside. Walker informed Major Brown that Taylor's army was safe at Point Isabel and was coming soon to the relief of the fort.

The Ranger spent the rest of that day within the high earthen walls of the isolated outpost. He learned that the bombardment had caused little damage. Effective return fire from Major Brown's guns had helped to encourage Mexican inaccuracy, and for further protection men inside Fort Texas had thrown up strong shelters of sandbags, dirt-filled barrels, and timber. Only one American had been killed during the first two days of bombardment. Even the animals had escaped heavy casualties.

Walker learned that Major Brown's 18-pounders had blasted two Mexican cannon out of action. Brown himself expressed no doubt of his ability to hold out further, but to conserve powder for repelling a possible infantry assault the major had virtually silenced his own guns by the time of Walker's visit. The Ranger noticed that men passed the time mostly by listening to the roar of enemy artillery, then hugging shelter whenever a splutter overhead warned them a shot had been well aimed.

That night Walker climbed back over the walls, and with his companions he returned to Point Isabel undetected. His arrival there—on the fifth—evoked wonder and acclaim from Captain Ephraim Kirby Smith and other regulars, and cheered them all when they learned that the distant cannon had caused so little damage.

All day of the sixth Smith and the rest of the little army made final preparations for departure: packing and loading, readying two cumbersome 18-pounder cannon for the long haul, digging and further entrenching Fort Polk for the garrison force that would stay behind. Sounds of that continuing cannonade spurred them on.

Taylor had ordered his officers to limit their baggage to absolute necessities—to make room for more supplies—but one literary lieutenant included a carton of books. Colonel William Whistler, the grizzled alcoholic, noticed the box and flew into a fury. "That will never do," he yelled to a nearby officer supervising the loading. "We can't encumber our train with such rubbish as books." The officer removed the carton and remarked apologetically that he had packed among his own possessions a small keg of whiskey. "Oh, that's all right," the colonel rasped, "anything in reason, but [the lieutenant] wanted to carry a case of books."

On the seventh two hundred undrilled recruits from Louisiana and five hundred sailors and marines from Commodore Conner's Home Squadron assumed the duty of protecting the supply base at Point Isabel. General Taylor, hearing the continued rumble of Mexican guns, was ready to move. With the grammatical help of his literate adjutant, "Perfect" Bliss, Taylor drafted a dispatch to the War Department announcing his intention: "If the enemy oppose my march, in whatever force, I shall fight him." Taylor also distributed for promulgation among his soldiers the following command:

> Headquarters, Army of Occupation,
> May 7, 1846.
> Order No. 58.
>
> The army will march to-day at 3 o'clock, in the direction of [Matamoros]. It is known the enemy has recently occupied the route in force. If [the enemy is] still in possession, the general will give him battle. The commanding general has every confidence in his officers and men. If his orders and instructions are carried out, he has no doubt of the result, let the enemy meet him in what numbers they may. He wishes to enjoin upon the battalions of Infantry that their main dependence must be in the bayonet.
>
> Signed,
> W. W. S. Bliss,
> Assistant Adjutant-general.

In midafternoon mugginess they moved out, not many more than two thousand men: cavalry, infantry, field artillery—all slowed by the lumbering, creaking supply train of two hundred loaded wagons and by the two clumsy 18-pounder cannon. A team of twenty straining oxen pulled each gun.

Many officers thought Taylor should have left the supplies and the artillery behind. They would have preferred to sally forth from Fort Polk, crush the Mexicans, and clear a way for later movement of guns and supplies. But Taylor was the general, and despite his frequent lack of imagination, his old-fashioned ways, and the occasional behind-the-back sneers of younger officers who boasted a West Point background while he did not, the old man inspired confidence among the lower ranks.

Furthermore, even now some officers believed the Mexicans would not oppose them. Look at that ridiculous performance on the Arroyo Colorado. Lieutenant Sam Grant, worried four days earlier by the first distant thunder of cannon, had since then almost convinced himself that there would be no fight, that the Mexicans were good only for paper wars. Captain Ephraim Kirby Smith also had shown a change of mind. He doubted now that the enemy would oppose the march. Time and familiarity had eased the anxiety brought on by the first sounds of the guns. Lieutenant Sam French, riding with Major Ringgold's flying artillery, recorded no thoughts of the moment, but observation had left him with small regard for Mexican military capability.

After traveling only five miles or so the men halted for the night and slept within reach of their weapons. Soon after sunrise they resumed the march, buoyed by a scouting report brought in by the meek-looking Ranger, Sam Walker. During the night Walker had crept up to a known camp site of Mexican troops and had found it deserted. So the Mexicans were not opposing their return to Fort Texas, after all.

The Mexican Army had spies, too—men as familiar with this kind of country as were Texas Rangers. Mexican scouts had become aware of Taylor's departure from Point Isabel with "an estimated three thousand soldiers" accompanied by "an abundance of artillery, and numerous wagons." The spies reported to General Arista that Taylor was returning now to his fort across the river from Matamoros, and Arista happily prepared to wreak on the invaders the havoc that he had missed earlier because of the boat shortage that had delayed his river crossing. He recalled General Ampudia's force of Fort Texas besiegers.

Arista chose to make his stand on a spacious grassy plain (spotted with a few fresh-water ponds) across which the Americans would have to advance as they moved down the road to the relief of Fort Texas. At midmorning of May 8, with Taylor's main body still miles distant and unknowing, Arista began forming his army for battle. He brought cavalry, artillery, and infantry in that order and positioned them, facing the plain, a short distance in front of a stand of trees. On his right, sheltered atop a wooded elevation of ground, he placed a light infantry regiment. In order farther left he positioned an artillery piece, a battalion of sappers, then his main force of infantry and artillery. Four hundred yards away to the left he stationed General Torrejón's cavalry, supported by two fieldpieces. Thus drawn up, the Mexicans waited to greet the foe. They numbered at least five thousand, although Mexican accounts later estimated the strength at three thousand—about equal to Taylor's force.

Time now for a nationalistic pride to surge through Mexican ranks. It tried. Here were Mexican soldiers facing an arrogant, heretical invader who had no right to be in this part of the world. God must help these troops throw the enemy back. "For the first time [the two armies] came to measure their strength," a Mexican wrote, "and to sustain the rights of their respective nations; these sons of two distinct races, now meeting to appear before a Supreme Being, destroying each other in the new continent as they had destroyed in the old. The one assumed the work of usurpation and treachery; the other defended a sacred cause in which it was true glory to die as a sacrifice."

The noble sons of Mexico surely would prevail. *Libertad o muerte!*

The morning of May 8 became searing as the sun rose higher. The Americans sweated and cursed this climate, but their march progressed with the steady swishing sounds of feet swinging through the gray-green coastal grass. In the rear, shouts and whip cracks could be heard urging on the struggling animals that pulled supply wagons and cannon. Five miles, six, then seven—still no opposing army appeared to block their way. Shortly before noon, however, word arrived of the presence of Mexicans ahead, shouted by advance scouts who had seen them and were riding back to report to Taylor. But the march continued.

The sun was blazing down from overhead when the Mexicans came into view. Two miles away, beyond a grassy plain, Taylor's men saw a long, dark line of soldiers stretching across the road leading to Matamoros. The Mexicans' right flank was anchored on the tree-covered rise east of the road, their left flank in a swampy thicket west of it.

Closer observation showed that Arista's men presented a front more than a mile long. Quick estimates of their numbers ranged as high as seven thousand. Even from a distance could be seen the glint of sunshine on bayonets along the Mexican line, the shimmer of brass cannon—apparently clean and ready—interspersed among the infantry (twelve guns in all, the largest two 8-pounders), and—on the Mexicans' left flank—the grim metallic gleam of hundreds of lances carried by General Torrejón's horsemen. Behind the Mexicans rose the stand of tall timber (this location would be known by its Spanish name, Palo Alto) that seemed to reinforce their superiority.

Lieutenant Sam Grant stared at the scene, hoping and expecting to see the foe vanish—as at the Arroyo Colorado. Grant and the others had by now received orders to halt, to allow the supply train to close up. Soon the idle men recognized this location. It was where they had waited for General Taylor to rejoin them after he had made his detour to Point Isabel six weeks earlier, during the initial move to the Rio Grande.

Taylor ordered his own deployment for battle. He placed his three artillery batteries between infantry regiments. On his right flank he put the 5th Infantry—with Captain E. K. Smith. Into position next to it swung Major Ringgold's battery of flying artillery—with Lieutenant Sam French. Then, in order farther left, came the 3rd Infantry, the two 18-pounder guns, the 4th Infantry—and Lieutenant Sam Grant, another battery of field artillery, commanded by zealous Captain James Duncan, and the 8th Infantry. A rear guard of dragoons stayed with the wagons.

Lieutenant French, the militant from a Quaker family, heard the long roll sounded with less enthusiasm than he had perhaps envisioned as a newly graduated West Point cadet: ". . . hearts beat, pulses kept time, and knees trembled and would not be still." But he and the rest of Ringgold's flying artillery immediately proved themselves. Operating with precision and swiftness and in rhythm with their animals, they had guns in position to fire in less than a minute.

After that French could take time to look at the rest of the army. He noticed the two 18-pounders being dragged into line by oxen. Shouts of "Haw, Buck! Haw, Brindle! Whoa, Brandy!" got the big guns moving slowly in a large semicircle, and eventually brought their muzzles pointing to the front. French thought how much grander the spectacle would have been—not to mention the time saved—had elephants been substituted for oxen.

Ready for battle now, Taylor nevertheless delayed a while longer, allowing each man a tepid drink to renew some of the vitality lost in the day's dripping humidity. From the ranks every other man was allowed to go to a fresh-water pond nearby to drink and to fill his canteen. Upon his return the other man went. During the pause Taylor slouched sideways on his favorite horse, Old Whitey, chewed tobacco, peered around, and casually replied to remarks of passers-by. If he had begun to harbor illusions of greatness, as Colonel Hitchcock had remarked, this did not seem to show through today.

Pomposity was a monopoly of the other side—that Mexican fondness for a big show.

"Immediately before commencing the action," said a Mexican Army man who was there, "the General-in-chief [Arista] reviewed the line, rectified the corps one by one, represented the glory that would ensue from a triumph, and the gratitude which they might anticipate from their countrymen."

Arista, on horseback, rode in front of his line inciting his soldiers.

He was a large, muscular man apparently out of place in the Mexican Army. His fair complexion set him apart. He had sandy hair and a face full of freckles. But he was firm and fiery, and his men responded to his exhortations with cheers.

". . . Banners floated to the wind," the eyewitness continued, "the soldiers stood to their arms, the horses pawed the ground, the bands [played] inspiring and beautiful music, and shouts . . . of 'Viva la Republica' [filled the air], as if bearing up to the throne of a just God, the cry of vengeance raised by an offended nation."

Lieutenant French, waiting astride his horse near Ringgold's cannon, shifted his thoughts from elephants pulling guns to the Mexican display. "Arista must have thought he had performed his whole duty when he barred the road with his troops. . . . He had been in line of battle all the morning awaiting our coming, yet he permitted us to deploy undisturbed." French saw next that Arista even allowed two horsemen to approach within a hundred yards of his line, to dismount, and to inspect his position through their glasses. They returned unhampered to Taylor with their report.

After the last American had returned from the fresh-water pond, about 2:30 P.M., the advance began—slowly, deliberately, and so quietly as to seem eerie—through sharp, prickly grass shoulder-high in places. Young Lieutenant Grant looked at the moving American line and reflected on the fearful responsibility General Taylor must be feeling, sending these men "so far away from friends" to attack an enemy extremely formidable in appearance.

The Mexicans opened fire first. Flame and smoke rose from their guns as they began lobbing cannon balls from a distance of seven hundred yards—beyond their range, as it developed. The balls slashed through tall grass ahead of the advancing Americans, who simply sidestepped each missile as it rolled past. But when Taylor's forward movement carried Ringgold's and Duncan's 6-pounders within range, those guns—eight altogether—commenced hurling destruction on Arista's force with both shot and shell. The battle that Taylor had expected to be decided with the bayonet became an artillery duel. The infantry halted out of musket range, ten or twenty yards to the rear of the thundering American batteries, and acted mostly as awed spectators when not dodging cannon balls.

Initially Sam French of the artillery was only a spectator himself. His commissioned rank had assigned him "the duty of sitting on [a] horse to look at the fight and watch the caissons" while around him guns roared and Mexican shot plummeted earthward. He happened to be staring at a man on horseback nearby when he saw a shot rip off the pommel of the saddle, tear through the man's body, and burst out with a crimson gush on the other side. Pieces of bone or metal tore into the horse's hip, split the lip and tongue and knocked teeth out of a second horse, and broke the jaw of a third.

French never had seen a man killed in battle before, and the sight apparently did not measure up to his cadet-conceived notions of the glories of war. Certainly this was no time to be sitting idly on the back of a horse. French dismounted, entrusted the animal to a holder, strode to a howitzer nearby, took command of the piece, and helped to fire it.

Taylor's deadly fieldpieces on both right and left, together with the two roaring 18-pounders in the center, were proving accurate. They were firing at concentrations of enemy troops, while the Mexican guns were firing mostly at Taylor's batteries. Lieutenant Grant, waiting with the infantrymen, could see that bursting shells (which the Mexicans did not have) "did a great deal of execution." He saw Taylor's artillery clear "a perfect road" through Mexican ranks. But other soldiers quickly closed the interval, Grant noticed, and Arista's line did not waver.

On the Mexican left General Torrejón even managed to mount a potent attack. Gathering a force of lancers and infantrymen and two cannon, he sought to sweep out of the swampy thicket and around Taylor's right flank, to get to the supply wagons in the rear.

Captain Ephraim Kirby Smith, waiting on that same flank with other men of the 5th Infantry, observed the activity. General Taylor saw it, too, and sent orders for the 5th to intercept. The regiment made a quick oblique march of about a quarter of a mile—forward and somewhat to the right. Then the awesome sight of a Mexican cavalry charge and frantic shouts of "Here they come!" stopped the movement. "We at once formed square . . . and stood firmly at a shoulder," Smith said. "They rode upon us eight hundred strong. When about a hundred feet from us they delivered their fire and continued their charge. A few of our men fell wounded. . . . At this moment the fire of our second front was delivered with as much precision as on drill, and with a most withering effect." Off to Smith's right appeared the ubiquitous Ranger Sam

Walker and twenty of his men. They poured another deadly volley into the surprised attackers.

Torrejón then determined to destroy the pesky infantry square with his two cannon. While the gunners readied their pieces Sam French and another artillery lieutenant, daredevil Randolph Ridgely (only five feet seven inches in height but tall in military esteem), wheeled into action with two of Ringgold's "flying" guns, unlimbered, loaded, and blasted away with grape and canister before the Mexicans could get off a shot.

Torrejón's artillerymen reeled backward under the shattering fire, but they retreated so slowly French was amazed—"perhaps it was Mexican pride." Other of Torrejón's attackers were faster in their withdrawal. They broke and ran. Taylor sent a force of dragoons in pursuit and pushed the Mexican's left flank farther back.

Still the battle raged. Captain E. K. Smith heard "some twenty pieces of artillery thundering [along the lines] from right to left [and] . . . the tramping of horses and the wild cheering of the men."

After an hour or so of fighting, a prairie fire brought a temporary halt. On Taylor's left a wad from Captain James Duncan's battery, which had been firing eight rounds a minute, had ignited the dry grass. A breeze whipped the flames into a conflagration that engulfed the plain between the two lines and carried billowing smoke into Mexican eyes. Under this cover Taylor advanced his right while, coincidentally, Arista withdrew his left and advanced his own right, too. When the air cleared an hour or so later Captain Duncan, still commanding the battery on Taylor's left, saw that the enemy line opposite him had advanced. He poured in shells that drove it back.

Guns from both sides continued their cannonade as dusk approached. Lieutenant Grant, waiting with the 4th Regiment, saw a ball crash into ranks nearby, tear a musket from one soldier's grasp and rip off the man's head, then dissect the face of a captain he knew. Hurtling wood splinters and pieces of bone injured several bystanders. Red-dripping flesh spattered on some of them. Grant stared in awe at the dying captain as he lay on the ground—his lower jaw "gone to the windpipe" and his tongue "hanging down upon the throat"—and realized for the first time that the fear he had felt gnawing at him upon hearing those distant cannon had returned.

After another charge by the Mexicans, however, fighting ceased. Some fifty of Taylor's men had fallen casualties during the day, including the artillery innovator, Major Ringgold—fatally wounded by a cannon ball that had ripped through the insides of both legs just above the knees. As many as five hundred Mexicans lay dead or wounded.

Night blanketed weary men who fell asleep where they dropped on the trampled prairie grass, while around them other prostrate men from both armies screamed and groaned in agony from wounds. By the eerie light of torches "the surgeon's saw was going the livelong night."

16.

Shouts and Screams

Morning of the second day of actual war would bring the first battle command to pretty-faced Lieutenant Sam Grant.

In faint light of predawn on May 9 dark groups of men—Arista's soldiers—could be seen emerging from distant chaparral and crowding onto that one road that led through the brush in the direction of Fort Texas and Matamoros. Probably the enemy intended to dig in again somewhere ahead and to make another attempt to stop Taylor's advance, the talk went, and this time he would no doubt choose terrain where artillery could not mangle him.

Slanting rays of the risen sun later illuminated a surprise. The Mexicans had vanished completely. Was this a trick, or did Arista really intend to flee across the river? At a hurriedly called council of war Taylor's ranking officers advised him to await reinforcements before trying any pursuit, but the general overruled them. This time, however, he would leave behind the two hundred supply wagons and the two cumbersome 18-pounders, to be guarded by a detachment whose numbers would deplete his own striking force to a total of seventeen hundred men.

Taylor sent his wounded and all the Mexican prisoners back to Point Isabel with a small escort. For reconnaissance he sent ahead a patrol of Texas Rangers led by Sam Walker. The general also ordered two infantry units to probe ahead. One of the groups was to be under the temporary leadership of Sam Grant's company commander. This left Grant in command of the company, an honor and responsibility he thought "very great"—no matter what had been his attitude about the war or his private fears stemming from it.

Stifling heat of another midday had arrived to torment the men before the general advance could begin. Near the plain where yesterday's battle had been fought lay many Mexican dead and wounded. Some of them, "in the agony of death . . . had caught at the rank grass, and died with their hands clinched firmly in it, looking defiance at the enemy." Taylor had ordered his men to bring in the dying and the dead, no matter what their uniform, for medication or for burial, but many had not been found.

Down the hot, dusty road toward the Rio Grande they traveled, passing between dense clumps of thorny bushes that grew on both sides. They were sweating and cursing as usual and wondering when, or if, they would meet Arista again. Fort Texas lay only ten miles away now, maybe less. Perhaps they would reach the beleaguered post without having to fight another battle.

In the van of the main body of troops marched the 5th Infantry and Captain E. K. Smith, with no fields of flowers for consolation now. On every side he saw only more chaparral country cut by deep ravines and—stretching on ahead—the narrow, all-important road toward the river.

Just behind the 5th came the men, horses, and guns of Major Ringgold's flying artillery battery, now commanded by Lieutenant Randolph Ridgely, with Lieutenant Sam French riding along, musing over General Taylor's change of attitude in regard to cannon. Guns had become so unwieldy that Taylor and most other generals (even in Europe, where Napoleon had developed field artillery) seemed almost to have given up the idea of using them in battle—Ringgold's experiments notwithstanding. But the artillery duel at Palo Alto had left Taylor obviously impressed. The general even seemed to have changed his attitude toward artillery officers, for whom (some said) he had previously developed an intense dislike.

Farther back, with the 4th Infantry, plodded the temporarily promoted company commander, Sam Grant, his thoughts alternating between the grim reality of his present situation and the vision of beauty, love, and hope that was Julia Dent, in faraway St. Louis. Now that war had commenced, Grant reflected, he intended to devote himself to ending it in victory—the only proper attitude for a military man. Julia would be impressed if she could see him now. Sam Grant, the veteran of one battle, could be a romantic about war, after all.

One scorching mile, then two. Three miles, all dry and dusty. Fort Texas must be only a few miles farther on, many men were thinking.

About three o'clock came the rattle of musketry from somewhere ahead. Time provided detailed information. The shots had been aimed from behind a dense thicket at the advance party led by Grant's company commander. Arista's men had dug in again across the road. This time the Mexicans were not exposed to fire from that deadly artillery, and (as discovered later) they had been reinforced by hundreds of fresh troops from Matamoros, more than enough to make up for yesterday's losses.

Taylor's scouts probed and saw that Arista had concealed his soldiers along the brush-covered banks of an old bed of the Rio Grande called Resaca de la Palma, which cut across the Matamoros road at a location directly ahead of Taylor's advance. The *resaca* made a very rough horseshoe turn in the vicinity, with the concave side of that turn facing the Americans as they traveled along the road into the horseshoe and on toward the *resaca* crossing.

The *resaca* afforded defenders good protection and strategic position. The banks of the old river bed dropped off nearly perpendicularly three or four feet, providing cover for the infantry, and the bed itself—two hundred feet wide—was matted with brush and small trees and spotted with sunken ponds. The Mexicans had concealed themselves further by throwing up in their front an accumulation of brush and felled trees. They could aim musket fire on the Americans moving along the road not only from ahead but also from the sides—from along the rim of the horseshoe—and they could use artillery, too. Arista had planted one gun directly in the Matamoros road and had positioned other cannon on his side of the *resaca*.

Taylor ordered Ridgely's battery of artillery to the front to destroy the Mexican guns. Captain E. K. Smith, with the still leading 5th Infantry, halted, stood aside with the rest, and watched the battery as it lumbered past down the road in the direction of the *resaca* crossing. Then Smith and his men deployed as skirmishers in dense chaparral to the left of the road while, on the right, Lieutenant Sam Grant's company and other infantrymen commenced a similar movement.

Guiding the battery was Ranger Sam Walker, who had previously looked over the thicketed terrain. He and Ridgely and Sam French rode along ahead of the guns and the other mounted men, leaving behind billows of powdery dust.

As French rode toward more action he reflected with a tinge of West Point superiority, tempered with anxiety, on what he believed to be a flaw in old General Taylor's plan. "Because the artillery rendered such signal service on the field yesterday [the general] was impressed with the idea that it was available for pursuit of cavalry in mountain passes, for storming entrenchments, or charging a line of battle. Here . . . was the singular [tactic] of a battery of horse artillery all alone, leaving the entire army behind, moving down the road through the woods without any support whatever."

They had traveled half a mile when a roar from the bushes ahead and a crash in a nearby thicket told them they had come under the fire of Mexican cannon. Ridgely shouted the command, "At a gallop, march!" and his men raced forward to a point where the road made a left turn. There they could get a battery front to the still unseen Mexican artillery —and there they halted, tugged their guns into place by hand in the absence of maneuvering room for the horses, and returned fire, aiming at telltale smoke rising above brush clumps four hundred yards away.

Sultriness and stillness of sweltering midafternoon compounded the heat of the guns, and the artillerymen stripped to their waists. Grapeshot showered around them. Mexican lancers charged up the road trying to spear them—but were themselves mangled by Ridgely's canister. In the thorny underbrush on either side of the road Taylor's infantry poked and probed for a passage to support the guns and to get at the Mexicans hidden along the *resaca*. The foot soldiers had to contend with slashing thorns of almost impenetrable thickets as well as with grape and canister thrown at them while they sought to gain position for an attack.

In the chaparral thickets to the left of the road Captain Smith had realized quickly the futility of fighting this battle by the usual tactics. Pockets of prickly brush had forced his men to creep forward singly or in small groups, and some of his soldiers had become mixed with men from other units. Balls from Mexican cannon crashed into the bushes around them.

Eventually Smith gained a narrow vantage point in the thorny jungle and examined the Mexican position. The *resaca* was deep, the crest opposite entrenched to protect infantry, and the entire area covered with more thickets. He realized then the necessity of charging the continually roaring guns on the other side, and he rounded up as many men as he could find.

Together they crept to their right, toward the road they had abandoned. They would have to use it for any assault on the cannon. At the side of the road they stopped and were joined soon by more men from the 5th.

By this time fierce hand-to-hand fighting was raging throughout the thickets lining the *resaca*. Other of Taylor's infantrymen had hacked their way to the enemy. Shouts and screams rent the chaparral as bayonets jabbed into flesh and bone and combined with musketry and cannonry to wreak agonizing deaths on men of both armies.

To the right of the road Sam Grant led his company slowly through an underbrush maze and came upon the Mexican line almost without knowing it. Musket balls began to whine over his head, thrashing the topmost branches of the thicket. Grant ordered his men to lie down—"an order that did not have to be enforced"—until he became certain that his company had not been the target of the fusillade. Then he and his men quietly withdrew to find ground better suited for an advance.

They discovered it in a clear space separating two stagnant ponds. Grant ordered a charge. His company advanced into the brush without resistance and captured several Mexicans, including a wounded colonel. Grant was detailing a guard to escort his prisoners to the rear when he saw emerging from woods ahead a blue-clad private helping a wounded American officer to safety. The lieutenant realized then that his own army had charged over this ground earlier. (Years later he would laugh at the experience: "My exploit was equal to that of the soldier who boasted that he had cut off the leg of one of the enemy. When asked why he did not cut off [the] head, he replied, 'Some one had done that before.'")

Off to Grant's left, General Taylor had waited long enough for Ridgely's—and Sam French's—fieldpieces to blast the Mexican cannon off the Matamoros road. The general ordered the battery to stand aside for a charge by a company of dragoons led by blustering Captain Charles May, whose abundant black beard was long enough to indicate prevailing wind. French watched as May and his horsemen, in column of fours, galloped toward the battery—May's beard streaming behind him—and French heard Ridgely yell, "Hold on, Charley, till I draw their fire!"

The guns roared once more. As soon as Mexican cannon replied, May and his dragoons bolted forward, swords ready, and raced down the road out of sight—and (as French learned later) entirely past the enemy cannon, whose gunners plunged into the underbrush for refuge. From those everlasting thickets bordering the road Mexican infantrymen poured destruction on the dragoons—killing or wounding nineteen men, killing eighteen horses—as May's company wheeled and sought to race back.

The effort had not been completely in vain. When May galloped back to American lines he brought as his prisoner a Mexican general, Rómolo Díaz de la Vega, who (as it developed) had been acting commander of all Mexican troops on the field. Journalistic accounts of the feat later won for May a two-brevet promotion—to the disgust of most enlisted men and many jealous officers who had heard that an infantry sergeant actually had captured the general.

Captain Smith, waiting alongside the road with other men of the 5th Infantry, had witnessed the beginning of May's dash. Almost simultaneously he and the others had heard an order—"Charge 5th!"—shouted from farther back on the road, where General Taylor would have been sitting astride Old Whitey. Smith and the rest of the regiment sprinted ahead in the dust of May's sweep—and into hand-to-hand combat with the Mexicans, who "fought like devils." More shouts and screams, more bayonets driven into flesh and bone. The men of Smith's regiment had one advantage: desperation. They fought in the belief that retreat would not be possible and that surrender would bring execution. They and the survivors of Taylor's seventeen-hundred-man force charged cannon in the very act of throwing shot in their faces, captured the guns, and fired the pieces at fleeing artillerymen. On the right, men found an unguarded pathway leading southward beyond the *resaca* and came upon the Mexican rear. On the left, constant pressure forced the Mexicans back.

Lieutenant French, with Ridgely's now advancing battery, noticed a Mexican hiding behind bushes near the road, walked warily toward him, and saw that the man was an officer of junior rank. "*¿Teniente o capitán* [Lieutenant or captain]?" French asked, in his best Spanish. The man immediately pulled a biscuit from a pocket and offered it to the amazed French, who concluded his question must have been misunderstood as "*¿Tiene usted pan* [Have you any bread]?" One of French's fellow officers observed the exchange with equal amazement and told the story for years afterward.

By five o'clock Arista's line along the *resaca* had broken completely and his soldiers were fleeing in panic toward the Rio Grande three or four miles away. Blazing guns of nearby Fort Texas hurried them along even faster.

Why had God deserted the Mexican soldier? His cause was just. The *norteamericano* was a heretic and an invader deserving of defeat and death. The Mexican soldier had meant to fight well—his cheers for Arista before the Palo Alto battle had attested to that—and indeed he had displayed courage. Look at the way he had closed ranks at Palo Alto when the American artillery plowed furrows of death through the Mexican lines. He closed ranks and died.

Something had happened. Something always did happen in those days to smother a Mexican's hopes. His guns would not fire, or they fired too high, or sometimes they even blew up in his face. An enemy always seemed to be blessed with better fortune.

This time the fault seemed to rest with the Mexican officer. He had been helpless to counter the American challenge. He had not even been aware of certain hazards—as had been the case with General Arista, who had insisted that what proved to be the Battle of Resaca de la Palma would amount to nothing more than a skirmish and had turned over the day's command to General Rómolo Díaz de la Vega, who had then been captured. The trouble was that a Mexican leader needed a leader himself. But that was too much vagueness for the Mexican soldier, who needed understandable blame for placement.

His officers, or at least a high officer, must have turned traitor. That would have been a logical reason for the initial disaster at Palo Alto. The rumors had started making their rounds soon after that defeat. They had been responsible for a waning desire to fight at Resaca de la Palma. Now, following that catastrophe, the gossip resulted in great confusion and panic as the Mexican soldier sought to escape to the familiarity of Matamoros. Whatever morale was left crumbled.

Mexicans fleeing toward the river plunged into briers, tearing clothes and flesh. They trampled over their own wounded and over each other. At the river they found only a few boats and rafts. These they packed beyond capacity and sank with them. Above the yells of wildly thrashing men could be heard more shouts—warnings this time. The enemy was approaching.

False rumor or not, both disorder and din increased. Men threw themselves into the dirty brown water and flailed for the opposite shore. Many disappeared after only a few minutes of thrashing. Those who succeeded in reaching Matamoros brought dismaying news. "Terrible and mournful was the impression which the defeat and dispersion produced in [the town] on the first arrival of some flying from the field, and confirmed by those who followed."

Matamoros had been ready to celebrate a great victory. What had happened to God? Mexican losses for the day numbered about 1,500, Taylor's around 120. Would the enemy come on across the river and take Matamoros, too?

French, Grant, Smith, and other members of the victorious American Army saw evidence of the hasty retreat. Arista's men had abandoned eight cannon, fifteen hundred muskets, hundreds of pack mules with supplies intact, and many loaded wagons. General Arista himself had abandoned all of his personal baggage and his papers. Mexican prisoners said he had been writing in his tent when the action commenced—and he had continued writing, insisting until too late that the fight would be only a skirmish. Arista had felt certain Taylor would not attack such a position so soon after yesterday's battle.

At Fort Texas Taylor's men received a joyful welcome from old comrades whose haggard appearance bespoke the strain of a bombardment that had lasted nearly a week now. They learned that Major Jacob Brown, left in command of the garrison, had died of wounds. In his memory the post later was named Fort Brown—and the town that sprang up nearby, Brownsville.

Taylor halted his men at Fort Texas. He could have crossed the river in pursuit of Arista only with great difficulty—and probably not at all. A pontoon bridge he had requested months earlier never had been shipped, and he had no more boats for ferrying his army than did the Mexicans. The absence of the pontoon bridge especially rankled him, but many other requests of his had not been filled by the quartermaster's department, either.

On the north bank of the Rio Grande Saturday night, May 9, proved to be an evening of blissful peace. Across the dark water lay Matamoros, a bedlam tonight but no longer a threat. That same evening, two thousand miles northeast, President Polk began drafting his war message. Noise, turmoil, and anxiety were somewhere else now. Taylor's men bedded down.

Martial spirit returned in force to Lieutenant Sam French, whose poetry always could flow and ebb. The two battles had given him confidence. He had fought well and had survived, and any more cannon balls that scrambled a man's intestines and tore them from his body would be fired on a nebulous tomorrow. That was nothing to worry about now. "The conduct of our troops . . . was courageous in the extreme," French wrote. "Banners were captured by gallant old officers from the hands of the enemy and held aloft in the front during the conflict. . . ." French's calling was indeed a glorious one.

Captain E. K. Smith, the man with every look of a professional soldier, thanked "a kind God who yet spares me" and expressed gratitude for another blessing. "It is a glorious fact for the army," he declared, "that there were no volunteers with us." Smith wondered what the critical Congressman Black (who had infuriated Smith as well as Colonel Hitchcock) would have to say now about career military men.

Lieutenant Sam Grant, the sometime military misfit, probably thought over events of the day: the company he had commanded temporarily—those men under fire who had not really needed any instruction to fall flat on the ground; the advance and withdrawal he had ordered; the colonel he had captured on that previously charged-over ground. All this left no doubt in his mind (as he remarked years later) that "the battle . . . would have been won, just as it was, if I had not been there."

17.

The Time Has Come

Saturday night, May 9, brought high excitement to John C. Frémont, now encamped with his men in Oregon wilderness two thousand miles northwest of where Taylor's tired soldiers lay sleeping. U. S. Marine Corps Lieutenant Archibald Gillespie, sent by the Polk administration to California with those letters and secret verbal instructions, finally had overtaken Frémont and had delivered the messages. By glimmering firelight Frémont mused over the information and tried to reach a decision about what to do, on the same night that the weary victors of Resaca de la Palma rested at Fort Texas. Anyone who knew Frémont would have known that his decision likely would involve impulsive action.

Frémont's impetuosity already had shown itself during the current expedition. Upon arriving at Sutter's Fort in December he had learned that John Sutter was absent on business in the San Francisco Bay area; so he had asked Sutter's superintendent for sixteen mules, six packsaddles, and provisions, explaining that he wanted to leave immediately to locate the rest of his party—those men who had taken the southern route into California. Sutter's assistant replied that he had no mules to spare —only some unbroken horses—but that he could provide packsaddles and supplies. Frémont exploded upon hearing this, believing that the man was lying out of fear of antagonizing Mexican officials. Not until John Sutter returned and greeted Frémont could the explorer be convinced that he was as welcome as ever at the fort and that mules really were not available.

After that Frémont (while awaiting the appearance of the southern group), made a trip to Monterey—that enchanting town of white, red-

145

roofed adobe buildings built on a breeze-cooled shore that lay like a bright ribbon separating blue Pacific waters from rolling green hills of tall pine. There he talked with United States Consul Thomas Larkin and with officials of the local government, to whom he emphasized without much success the scientific and peaceful purposes of his expedition. The Californians, wary and reluctant, nevertheless gave Frémont permission to buy supplies in town and to conduct explorations in the direction of the Colorado River.

Before Frémont could explore further, however, he had to find the rest of his men. By mid-February he had located them, and the entire expedition encamped to relax and recuperate at a site about fifteen miles south of San José Mission. At the end of the month Frémont and his armed force moved on—southward for some reason, toward the heart of settled California. At Monterey the commanding general, self-important José Castro, heard of Frémont's audacity and sent a blue-and-red-uniformed cavalry officer after him with an order: get out of California. The officer overtook Frémont at a camp twenty-five miles east of Monterey and delivered Castro's ultimatum.

Frémont then gave a second notable exhibition of impetuosity. He replied angrily that Castro had given him permission to explore, and he would stay in California as long as he desired. After Castro's officer had left to carry back the gist of this outburst Frémont ordered his men up to the wooded summit of nearby Hawk's Peak. There, amid plentiful timber, water, and grass, he built a log fort and prepared to fight in this foreign land. Someone erected a flagstaff of straight, stripped sapling, and Frémont had the United States colors run up, to the cheers of his men. This was early in March, weeks before any fighting had broken out in Texas.

From his Hawk's Peak eminence Frémont enjoyed a grand view of a green valley below. While he waited for a move by Castro he continued to spout fire for a while. In a dispatch to Consul Larkin he stated his determination to fight to the death if attacked and to leave vengeance for such injustice to his countrymen.

On the second day of his vigil he saw a cavalry force approaching from the valley. Then the horsemen withdrew, conferred among themselves, and departed.

After two days of sitting, watching, and thinking Frémont began to be troubled about his action. Perhaps he was not serving the best interests of the United States after all. His doubt grew when he read a message from Larkin urging caution—and no shooting. Finally, Frémont observed a large force gathering in the valley, and he saw that their weapons included cannon.

About this time the Hawk's Peak flagstaff happened to fall to the ground. Frémont used the event as an excuse to announce to his men that he considered it an omen telling him to move. In evening darkness of March 9 he and his men abandoned their fort and traveled to John Sutter's place—and eventually to Oregon, leaving turmoil behind them. Frémont's presumptuous conduct had tended to unite Spanish-speaking residents against the threat from the United States and had left American settlers excited and ready to join forces with him in a war against the native Californians.

For weeks Frémont made a show of exploring Oregon. In his *Memoirs* covering this period he wrote about the attraction of "going into unknown places—the unknown lands of which I had dreamed when I began this life of frontier travel." He admired "the winter beauty of the snowy range farther north, when at sunrise and at sunset . . . rose-colored peaks stood up out of the dark pine forests into the clear light of the sky."

For some reason, however, Frémont did not travel very far north—and nowhere near the Columbia River, where much exploring of considerable service to his country remained to be done. He tarried instead nearer the California border. On the evening of May 8, at a camp in deep forest, two settlers from California found him and announced that a Marine Corps officer named Gillespie had arrived at Sutter's Fort looking for him. Gillespie had continued on, but had asked the two men to hurry ahead, through an Indian-threatened region that they knew well, to find Frémont and to ask him to return southward.

Before sunrise on May 9 Frémont, on fire with curiosity, had his men up. By dawn they had begun their march. At sunset they counted forty-five miles traveled—while far away to the southeast a calm had just settled over the battlefield of Resaca de la Palma.

Frémont saw four white men—Gillespie and three companions—ride out from behind a clump of trees, and he heard their greeting. The explorer listened as Gillespie recited the secret instructions from Washington —whatever they were. Frémont eagerly read other messages—official communications and personal letters from his wife Jessie and from Senator

Benton. Certainly one of the items would have excited Frémont—the instruction to Consul Larkin at Monterey telling him to assist native Californians if they desired to re-enact the Texas drama: to break away from Mexico and join the great North American Union.

Frémont knew nothing of the declaration of war, of course, and nothing of the skirmishes that had led up to it. Until Gillespie's arrival, in fact, his knowledge of the situation had remained about where it was when he left on his expedition during the preceding summer.

Nor did Gillespie know of the skirmishes that had led to a war declaration. After leaving Washington in autumn of 1845 he had visited Mazatlán, on the Mexican Pacific Coast, were he had found Commodore Sloat and the Pacific Squadron. From there he had been forced to travel by way of the Sandwich Islands (now Hawaii) to Monterey, California, where he had arrived in mid-April on board the U.S.S. *Cyane*. Thus he had been far removed from the momentous occurrences along the Rio Grande.

But Gillespie did have information and rumors of a later date than those contained in the letters and oral instructions he had brought from the United States. War seemed imminent, he told Frémont, and whenever it came the Pacific Squadron had orders to take the offensive—to blockade or to take San Francisco Bay, Monterey, and other Pacific ports.

Later Frémont sat quietly and reread his letters by that glimmering firelight of night camp. Nearby, a brook made sounds like a tinkling bell.

Frémont thought he had some specific orders, particularly in a letter from his father-in-law. Senator Benton's letter—full of friendship and family details—also "contained passages and suggestions which, read by the light of many conversations and discussions with himself and others at Washington, clearly indicated to me that I was required by the government to find out any foreign schemes in relation to California, and so far as it might be in my power, to counteract them."

Frémont's thinking was flawed. Senator Benton was only a father-in-law and an influential politician—not a military commander empowered to send him orders. But Frémont had in mind action, glory, and fame—and whatever other instructions Gillespie might have brought. "I sat by the fire . . . going over again the home letters," Frémont wrote in his *Memoirs*. "These threw their own light upon the communication from Mr. Gillespie and made the expected signal. In substance their effect was: The time has come. England must not get a foothold. We must be the first. Act, discreetly, but positively."

Frémont must return to California. Such a plan could hardly be carried out discreetly, and it certainly would result in violence, considering the past trouble with Castro. But tonight was not for agonizing over qualms. Frémont lay down on a bed improvised under some low-hanging cedar branches and soon was asleep. Excitement of the moment had caused him to neglect posting a guard.

He awoke with a start at the sound of Kit Carson's voice calling, "What's wrong over there?" Frémont heard only a groan in reply to the question, then the shouts of Carson and another man: "Indians! Indians!"

Frémont leaped to his feet. Around him the camp came alive with men grabbing rifles and running for cover. Frémont saw by the dim firelight that the attackers were Klamath Indians, who had long inhabited this region. More shouts, then the whispering sounds of flying arrows and, in reply, the blasts of rifles. Still more cries, accompanied by thumping noises of a rifle butt battering a human head.

The Klamath chief fell, and his confused warriors vanished into the darkness surrounding the camp. For the rest of that night fighting flared at intervals, but at dawn the attackers withdrew for good.

Three of Frémont's men lay dead. An ax had split the skull of one of them. This noise had roused Carson.

The Klamath chief lay dead where he had fallen. Frémont saw Carson seize the Indian's own ax and use it to rain angry blows on the dead man's skull.

Later, en route southward to save California, Frémont and his men wreaked more vengeance. They attacked a Klamath village, killed fourteen braves, burned all the huts, and destroyed large quantities of fish the Indians had been drying for food.

18.

To the Colors

In the United States men rallied to the colors after Congress voted authorization for the President to accept as many as fifty thousand twelve-month volunteers. Only in the Northeastern states, where existed greater anti-slavery sentiment, much opposition to war by pacifists, and some innate antipathy toward national expansion, did recruiting problems seem likely to develop.

The President determined to call for volunteers from every state and territory, to give everyone a feeling of sharing in the war, but he chose to enlist for immediate service twenty thousand men from Western and Southwestern states—those nearest to the war theater and most likely to help: Texas, Arkansas, Illinois, Missouri, Ohio, Indiana, Kentucky, Tennessee, Alabama, Mississippi, and Georgia. These recruits would furnish their own clothes and, if necessary, horses and trappings. For this "use and risk" they would be given forty cents a day in addition to the pay of a regular soldier of equivalent rank.

Some Missouri volunteers happily contemplated immediate adventure. They were to join a force of regulars—the 1st Dragoons—to form an Army of the West with orders to take and to occupy Santa Fe— that celebrated town at the other end of a long trail linking Missouri with a million-dollar-a-year trade.

Among the volunteers was a young, intense bachelor schoolteacher from Liberty, a town thirty miles down the Missouri River from the austere frame buildings and blockhouses of rectangular-built Fort Leavenworth, where the Army of the West was gathering. John Taylor Hughes, twenty-eight, had the solemn look of a beginning teacher still on trial—

an oval face distinguished by an appearance of gravity; wide, blue-gray eyes that seemed silently inquiring; lips that curved neither frivolously upward nor morosely downward but lay inexpressive like a straight pencil mark. His carefully combed dark-brown hair, parted on the left, swept back from a high forehead and accentuated a ruddy complexion. Except for some strongly cut features, however, Hughes was not a very impressive man physically. His height was five feet eight inches; his weight, a hundred and sixty pounds.

It was Hughes's solemnness that struck everyone he met. "He was a serious man," said an intimate friend, "[but] he was a man whom all delighted to meet. He was a scholar, and it pleased him to illumine his conversation with rich thought. He seemed to know everything, especially on grave subjects."

How great a scholar Hughes really was might have been debatable. In that day a little education went a long way toward impressing the masses, and Hughes had graduated in 1844 from an institution of higher learning—Bonne Femme College six miles from Columbia, Missouri. The college was Baptist. Hughes was Baptist—even from his youthful days as the hard-working son of a farmer who had moved westward from Kentucky to Missouri, and to newly opened lands there.

Many other Missouri residents besides Hughes had been born in Kentucky and other states and had moved westward. Some intended to make Missouri their permanent home. Others planned to join the flow of emigrants moving on. Nearly everyone who undertook the tortuous overland journey to the Pacific slopes passed through Missouri—the gateway. In many respects the focal point of the westward movement lay here in Missouri, and its residents, like their Senator Benton, clamored for expansion. This was a good place for recruiting volunteers to fight Mexico—a nation that had already angered Missourians by inflicting some terrible massacres on Texans, with whom many Missourians had close ties.

Hughes was an enthusiastic volunteer for the war. "He took a lively interest in public affairs, and was a frequent contributor to the newspapers published in Missouri. . . ." When he heard about the declaration of war he was in the last days of another school year. As soon as his teaching duties ended he put his personal affairs in order and rode off to serve as a private in Company C of the 1st Regiment of Missouri Mounted Volunteers.

This was to be no mere adventure for Hughes. He had followed closely the events leading to the conflict, and he believed in the propriety of his country's actions. "Hughes was a firm believer in the righteousness of the American cause," said one man. Hughes proudly corroborated this remark. Later he wrote in a book of war experiences (by "John T. Hughes, A.B."), "Bigoted and insulting Mexico, always prompt to manifest her hostility towards this government, sought the earliest plausible pretext for declaring war against the United States."

His elaboration on the causes of the conflict reflected the thinking of President Polk himself and of a great many other Americans.

> The . . . indiscriminate murder of . . . Texans who unfortunately fell into Mexican hands; the repeated acts of cruelty and injustice perpetrated upon the persons and property of American citizens residing in the northern Mexican provinces; . . . the forcible detention of American citizens, sometimes in prison and at other times in free custody; . . . the repeated insults offered our national flag; the contemptuous, ill-treatment of our ministers, some of whom were spurned with their credentials; the supercilious and menacing air uniformly manifested toward this government, which with characteristic forbearance and courtesy, has endeavored to maintain a friendly understanding; . . . [the Mexican] army's unceremonious passage of the Rio Grande in strong force and with hostile intention; [Mexico's] refusal to pay indemnities; and a complication of less evils . . . are the causes which justify the war. . . . Or should we have forborne until the catalogue of offences was still deeper dyed with infamous crimes, and until the blood of our brothers, friends, and consanguinity, like that of the murdered Abel, should cry to us from the ground? Who that has the spirit, the feelings, and the pride of an American, would willingly see his country submit to such a complication of injury and insult?

In newly recruited Company C Hughes joined 119 other men from Clay County, where Liberty was located, and on June 4 they all commenced a two-day ride up the Missouri River to Fort Leavenworth. There they began military service with zest for an exciting new life—and in Hughes's case, at least, with strict adherence to a principle. Many of the men were acquainted—many besides Hughes had become well known among Clay Countians.

There was, for instance, Shakespeare-quoting Henry Ogden, a bright, educated man full of nervous energy that required continual activity for an outlet. In spare moments he turned to pranks. Once, among strangers, he pretended to be deaf and dumb, and he startled and embarrassed them all when they discovered the hoax.

There was also dead-eye William Beale, a native Virginian bound to get his share of the enemy. Beale could boast of killing two deer with one shot.

Company C contained still other Clay Countians famous for various reasons. Obadiah Sullivan, another native of Kentucky, previously had served as a regular soldier for five years, and he knew his way around the U. S. Army. Sullivan's presence came to be particularly desired by hungry men foraging for food. It was said that he could steal even from watchful commissaries. But devout Benjamin Everett, the son of a minister, hungered more after food for the soul. He read his Bible constantly while off duty, and apparently because of his sincerity the pranksters and gossipers treated him with solid respect. Giant Alexander Scott, also a native Kentuckian, earned renown because of physical characteristics. Age had whitened his hair and beard so that he had become known to everyone as "Frosty."

The most famous man of Company C, however, proved to be Private Alexander William Doniphan, an unpretentious but impressive man of large size—physically and mentally. Doniphan stood a massive six feet four inches. His looks appealed in a masculine way: sandy hair, high forehead, hazel eyes bright with perception, a fair complexion tending toward surprising delicateness. In Clay County Doniphan had been an eminent lawyer, and he had earned a military reputation by leading an 1838 campaign against the Mormons.

Now that renown as a warrior stood in his favor. On June 18, 1846, when the last recruits for the Missouri cavalry regiment were riding into Fort Leavenworth, the men voted for officers to lead them (as was then customary for volunteers) by lining up behind candidates of their choice. They elected Doniphan colonel of the regiment.

Doniphan's superior—the commander of the Army of the West—would be a colonel of the regulars, hard-driving Stephen Watts Kearny, a veteran of the War of 1812 with a reputation for discipline. Colonel Kearny came directly from the command of Fort Leavenworth's 1st Dragoons, who would also participate in the campaign.

Even before electing officers the Missouri volunteers had begun lengthy two-a-day cavalry drills—one in the morning and one in the afternoon—under the direction of men from the 1st Dragoons. On a nearby plain quickly nicknamed Campus Martius they went through their exercises, awkwardly at first, then gradually with more precision—march by sections of four, saber drill, and other cavalry tactics like charge and rally.

Private John T. Hughes, the former schoolteacher, observed the efficiency of the regular officers with admiration and thought them kind and gentlemanly in sharing their knowledge with raw recruits. Among volunteers of less devotion, however, military discipline soon began to pall. These recruits especially resented the rigidity of a man elected lieutenant colonel from the ranks of privates—Charles F. Ruff, a former regular officer who had resigned his commission in 1843, then had enlisted for the war against Mexico. Ruff's fellow volunteers delighted in making life as uncomfortable for him as he made it for them.

Their attacks began late at night, when they could use darkness as an ally. From one side of camp would come a yell: "Who is a scoundrel?" A shout from a different location would answer: "Ruff—he is a damned scoundrel!" Other questions and answers would follow, all concerning the personal qualities of Lieutenant Colonel Ruff. By the time investigators could penetrate the darkness in search of the anonymous voices silence would have returned and the nocturnal noisemakers would be snuggled inside their tents.

While the volunteers drilled, seethed, and played their jokes on Ruff, the assembling of men and supplies at Fort Leavenworth continued. Steamboats puffed and paddled daily up the broad Missouri River to unload more men and war cargoes at Leavenworth, where security was provided by the rectangular enclosure of frame buildings guarded by sentries watching from inside sturdy blockhouses constructed at each corner. By late June nearly seventeen hundred regulars and volunteers—most of them mounted—had gathered at the fort, and the services of fifty Delaware and Shawnee Indian scouts had been enlisted. The Army of the West also had collected sixteen horse-drawn field guns, thousands of head of cattle, horses, and oxen, and hundreds of wagons crammed with supplies. Still, it was not much of an assemblage of men and matériel for the mammoth job ahead.

Early in June, even before the arrival of most of the mounted volunteers, Colonel Kearny had ordered two companies of dragoons toward New Mexico to intercept and detain trading caravans already reported to be en route to Santa Fe. He had also sent on ahead of the main army a supply train of wagons and beef cattle accompanied by hunters hired to procure still more meat for the soldiers.

Toward mid-June orders arrived from Washington expanding Kearny's operations further. Not only was he to subdue and occupy Santa Fe and the rest of New Mexico; he was ordered also to march on to Upper California afterward and to join the Pacific Squadron and John Frémont's party of explorers in subduing and occupying that place. Kearny's orders designated him as commander of military forces in California upon his arrival there.

For this additional task Kearny received authorization to enlist five hundred more men from a Mormon colony waiting at Council Bluffs for a chance to move on to the Pacific Coast. The Mormons were to be assured of discharges from military service in California after completion of their assignment. They filled their quota quickly.

At Fort Leavenworth the June days grew hotter, the twice-daily drills more tiring. But the 1st Regiment of Missouri Mounted Volunteers began to look like a military unit, and its members prepared to take the trail southwestward toward Santa Fe. From many counties of northern Missouri wives, children, brothers, and sisters flocked to the fort for final visits. They arrived on the same steamboats that brought more war goods. Delegations of patriotic women also came, to deliver to the various companies handmade flags along with stirring exhortations about duty that seemed to the dedicated Private Hughes "to inspire every heart with courage, and [to] nerve every arm for the dangers of the campaign."

On June 23 a group of Clay County women appeared at the fort to present "the finest flag" of all to Hughes's Company C. The volunteers lined up to hear the ringing oratory of a Mrs. Cunningham, who delivered the homemade national ensign.

> "In presenting to you this token of our regard and esteem, we wish you to remember that some of us have sons, some brothers, and all of us either friends or relatives among you, and that we would rather hear of your falling in honorable warfare, than to see you return sullied with crime, or disgraced by cowardice We trust, then, that your conduct, in all circumstances, will be worthy [of] the noble, intelligent, and patriotic nation whose cause you have so generously volunteered to defend; your deportment will be such as will secure you the highest praise and the warmest gratitude of the American people—in a word . . . let your motto be: 'Death before dishonor.'"

Hughes's company commander, Captain O. P. Moss—a Baptist and thrice sheriff of Clay County during his lifetime—formally accepted the flag with modesty that Hughes thought becoming. Moss responded with a brief speech centered around the theme, "The love of country is the love of God." Hughes was enthralled by the fervent speechmaking, but he managed to record most of it. He also added a comment of his own that, viewed in context with Moss's theme, might have made the Almighty gasp: ". . . we are for our country, right or wrong."

Between June 26 and 29 the Missouri volunteers rode out "upon the boundless plains of the west." They left Fort Leavenworth in small, manageable detachments. By July 6 the last units of the Army of the West had departed—all bound southwestward, across unmarked prairies invitingly green at first, toward a juncture with the Santa Fe Trail seventy miles away. Hundreds of merchant wagons followed, heavily and hopefully laden with dry goods for the markets of Sante Fe and Chihuahua. The entire expedition was not visible to one person at any one time. It stretched across miles of Western wilderness.

The movement proceeded slowly. Loaded wagons broke down often. At ravines and steep-banked creeks sweating men were forced to carve a road with picks and shovels while the summer sun blistered them. Level prairie sometimes offered no relief. There the heavy wagons occasionally sank to axles in earth soaked by recent rains. Men helped the overworked teams of oxen drag the wagons out of the mire.

For Hughes potential glory overshadowed present hardship. He thought the daily spectacle a thrilling one: the long file of cavalrymen extending out of sight ahead across a green landscape; the white canvas of trailing covered wagons glistening in the rear like distant banks of snow; and, on every side, the emerald pasture land of the buffalo providing a carpet for the glorious movement.

The scene moved Hughes to write the editor of the Liberty *Tribune* a letter that was later published. His attitude reflected the thinking of many Americans.

> There is a novelty in this . . . invasion of Cols. Kearny and Doniphan. For the first time since the creation, the starred and striped banner of a free people is being borne over almost one thousand miles of trackless waste, and the principles of republicanism and civil liberty are about to be proclaimed to a [Mexico] fast sinking in slavery's arms; and fast closing her eyes upon the last expiring lights of religion, science, and liberty.

19.

A Coal of Fire

Long before the approach of that summer of 1846 James K. Polk had become the firm master of the Executive Mansion and had imparted his personality to it. But the demands he had made of himself as President had left him thinner, more nervous and tired, and grayer. With a third of his term almost completed Polk had allowed himself no vacation at all and only scant relaxation of any kind. Sometimes the pressing duties of office had forced him to forgo the two diversions in which he indulged with any regularity: brisk walks and refreshing horseback rides—usually taken daily around sunrise or sunset.

The Executive Mansion had been refurbished, from sheer necessity. Only once since the occupancy of President Monroe (1817–25) had the house been given a thorough revitalizing, and the ragged upholstery, worn carpets, and dreary drapes could serve no longer. Polk's predecessor, John Tyler, had sought funds for redecorating, but his Whig-to-Democrat switch while in office infuriated many lawmakers, and they vengefully refused his request.

Soon after James Polk's inauguration Congress had voted a generous appropriation for interior work in the Executive Mansion, but Polk, with typical frugality, declared that he would spend only half the sum.

Sarah Polk had supervised the refurbishing. It had brought restoration to a badly deteriorated interior, with fresh paint, new carpets (costing $1.50 a yard), bright velvet curtains, and tasteful reupholstering.

Left to his own choice, Polk would have been similarly sparing about entertaining. He preferred the companionship of a few friends or relatives who visited the Mansion occasionally or who lived there: pretty young Jo-anna Rucker, Sarah Polk's niece, and other young kin whom the childless Polks fostered. But formal entertaining was a presidential duty, and Polk fulfilled it with the same dedication that he gave to everything associated with the job.

Dinner décor was far removed from Polk's personal frugalities. The President and the First Lady seated their guests in chairs of carved rosewood luxuriously upholstered with purple velvet. Around the walls hung regal window drapes of purple and gold. Down the center of long dining tables lay vine-bordered mirrors that reflected the light of hundreds of candles flickering in chandeliers overhead. Placed on the mirrors at intervals and brightly reflected there, too, were silver candelabra and flower arrangements. Directly in front of each guest appeared exquisite settings commanded by a blue-crested, gold-banded plate and a blue cut-glass goblet. Glasses of wine added alternate colors: champagne pink, port red, Rhine pale green, sauterne yellow, sherry gold, Madeira amber.

The menu matched the physical splendor. For formal entertaining President and Mrs. Polk—perhaps aided by a knowledgeable chef—could be quite cosmopolitan. They favored dishes like canvasback duck, turkey, oyster pie, garnished ham, *croquettes poulet, pâté de foie gras, côtelettes de mouton*, peas, snowball potatoes, ices, oranges, prunes, and sweetmeats.

During congressional sessions Polk entertained groups of legislators at dinner every two or three weeks. As his term progressed and various animosities grew, he sought more and more to avoid all political talk at dinner parties, and he even tried to smooth some existing differences (without much success) by seating political foes next to each other. But the President's most notable attempts at amiability seemed to have been confined to Executive Mansion dinners. In his own everyday relationships Polk, although rarely rude and usually carefully polite, stood firm politically.

He recorded in his diary his share of anger, frustration, and prejudice. Much of his unhappiness evolved from his ideas about party loyalty. He believed any Democrat who opposed any part of his program to be a traitor to the party. This was the kind of loyalty Polk himself had given President Jackson. It followed naturally, then, that Polk found it almost impossible to trust any member of the Whig opposition. Unfortunately for him, most of the senior military officers were Whigs.

Difficulties with the generals had begun soon after congressional approval of the war declaration. Polk had asked the senior commander of the

U. S. Army, General Winfield Scott, for suggestions about the number and disposition of volunteers to be called, had thought Scott's ensuing reply incomplete, and had sent him back to his desk like a schoolboy to prepare a more formal report. Nevertheless, Polk had offered Scott—a Whig—command of the army to be raised, and Scott had accepted.

"Though I did not consider him in all respects suited to such an important command," Polk commented, "yet being commander-in-chief of the army, his position entitled him to it if he desired it."

At the same time Polk had begun formulating his own ideas about conducting the war—a responsibility that he would come to consider as belonging to himself. One evening soon after his command appointment of Scott, Polk conferred with the general and Secretary of War Marcy. The President stated his opinion that "the first movement should be to march a competent force into the northern provinces [including Upper California] and seize and hold them until peace was made." Scott and Marcy concurred, and the lengthy discussion ended toward midnight. After the two men had left the Mansion Polk opened his diary and wrote, "General Scott did not impress me favourably as a military man. He has had experience in his profession, but I thought was rather scientific and visionary in his views. I did not think that so many as 20,000 volunteers besides the regular army was necessary [as Scott had advised], but I did not express this opinion, not being willing to take the responsibility of any failure of the campaign by refusing to grant to General Scott all he asked."

Polk's opinion of Scott waned even more in following weeks. The general, an aging giant of a man with a habit of constant labor toward what he conceived to be perfection and with a lack of humor that resembled Polk's, assumed leadership of the new army by binding himself to his Washington desk for fourteen hours a day of preliminary planning that he considered essential to field command later. The President heard with dismay that Scott estimated this preparatory work would keep him occupied in Washington until September—four months away. At that time, said the general, he would be ready to move his headquarters to the Rio Grande and to assume personal command of the army collecting there.

Polk had a much different idea about the war. He thought it should be a simple operation—rapidly effected and brought to a quick end. Furthermore, the President felt (as he remarked in his diary) that peacetime garrison life had made the professional soldier soft and lazy. The army regular needed "a coal of fire" applied to his back to make him move.

About this time two incidents fanned Polk's smoldering anger. A caller at the Mansion showed him a letter written by Scott in which the general had criticized the President. "It proved to me [Polk remarked] that General Scott was not only hostile, but recklessly vindictive in his feelings towards my administration." Then Polk heard that a bill proposed by himself to authorize appointment of two additional major generals and four brigadier generals was being quietly lobbied against in Congress by Generals Scott, John E. Wool, and Roger Jones. "These officers are all Whigs and violent partisans," Polk fumed, "and not having the success of my administration at heart seem disposed to throw every obstacle in the way of my prosecuting the Mexican War successfully. An end must be speedily put to this state of things."

General Scott, deliberately or not, helped to put an end to his own proposed command. Pressed by Polk and Secretary of War Marcy to hurry on to the Rio Grande, Scott made an unfortunately candid reply in a letter containing a coincidental reference to "fire" that reminded a reader of the coal Polk advocated applying to officers of the Army.

> I am too old a soldier, and have had too much special experience, not to feel the infinite importance of securing myself against danger (ill-will or pre-condemnation), in my rear, before advancing upon the public enemy. My explicit meaning is, that I do not desire to place myself in the most perilous of all positions— *a fire upon my rear from Washington, and the fire in front from the Mexicans.*

Polk read the letter after Marcy had passed it on to him. The President agreed immediately with Scott that the general need not go on to the Rio Grande after all. Although Scott sought later to explain that he had not meant to say he feared the President's personal ill will, Polk retracted his offer of command and looked around for someone else on whom to bestow it.

At that time official information about Zachary Taylor's victories at Palo Alto and Resaca de la Palma still had not reached Washington. Four days after Scott had written his fateful letter dispatches finally arrived from Taylor with details of the triumphs, and Polk had a logical alternative. "I sent a message to the Senate today nominating General Zachary Taylor of the army a Major-General by brevet," Polk wrote on May 26, "for his gallant victories obtained over the Mexican forces on the Del Norte on the 8th and 9th days of this month."

Taylor would command the growing force on the Rio Grande. He was already on the spot anyway—and not tied down by a supposed necessity of fighting paper for four months before taking on any Mexican armies.

Unfortunately for Polk, Taylor (who was, of course, also a Whig) had begun to harbor his own doubts about the sincerity of this Democratic Administration. For one thing, requested supplies seemed extraordinarily slow in reaching him, and some of his pleas apparently had been entirely ignored. For another, Taylor felt that the President took a suspiciously long time in acknowledging word of the victories at Palo Alto and Resaca de la Palma. Polk, who had been mired in that General Scott mess as well as in other war planning, actually had meant no slight by the delay. Nevertheless, irreparable damage had been done to personal relationships.

On the Rio Grande a black mood engulfed Taylor, who wrote home on various occasions about this time: "I heartily wish the war was at an end"; ". . . our ambitious views of conquest & agrandisement at the expense of a weak power will only be restrained & circumscribed by our inability to carry out our view"; ". . . we will be fully as anxious [after six or eight months of war] to make peace as they are"; "for real & pretended rob[b]eries committed on our commerce" the President probably intended to claim Mexican territory, including Upper California, as war indemnity—and no land-grabbing scheme by Great Britain could have been "more outrageous." When Washington officials, ignorant of both the terrain and the situation, requested information and advice from Taylor, the general hedged. He did not intend to become a scapegoat any more than did Scott.

In the Executive Mansion Polk continued to work his long desk hours without realizing at this time the extent of Taylor's vexation, but painfully aware of Taylor's Whig affiliation and of the political possibilities that might ensue from his military successes. Polk himself had determined not to stand for re-election—he always declared he had made this decision before inauguration—but he was not happy about enhancing the chances of a Whig candidate. Possibly for this reason, as well as because his concept of the presidency meant close supervision of all matters, Polk had begun drawing those plans of his own for prosecuting the war.

As they unfolded they showed detailed thinking, good and bad. First came that project of invading the northern Mexican provinces and occupying them until a surrender had been forced. This, of course, included the invasion and occupation of Upper California, to be effected by General Kearny after he had taken Santa Fe.

The northern provinces, far removed from Mexico City, tended toward Federalist sentiment. They wanted no centralized government administered in a distant place. This might even make them amenable to United States occupation, some of Polk's people thought.

The President elaborated on the project after a cabinet meeting held Saturday, May 30. "I stated that if the war should be protracted for any considerable time, it would in my judgment be very important that the United States should hold military possession of California at the time peace was made, and I declared my purpose to be to acquire for the United States, California, New Mexico, and perhaps some others of the Northern Provinces. . . ."

Polk's planning even extended into a kind of psychological warfare and showed unusual imagination that might have been inspired by a suggestion from Secretary of State Buchanan. Polk invited Catholic Bishop John Hughes of New York to the Executive Mansion and asked for help in recruiting Spanish-speaking priests to serve with the U. S. Army in Mexico, to assure residents there that the United States did not intend to interfere with worship or to rob Catholic churches—where much wealth could be found. Bishop Hughes agreed to help, and priests later accompanied the Army for this purpose.

Another plan involved General Santa Anna and that fantastic scheme suggested by the mysterious Spaniard named Atocha. Although Polk had said he did not trust Atocha, the President continued to mull over the project Atocha had proposed. What if it worked? Polk certainly preferred to accomplish his continental expansion bloodlessly. Any man would. The more Polk mused, the likelier the prospects seemed.

In May Polk instructed Secretary of the Navy Bancroft to send a confidential note to Commodore Conner, whose naval squadron had begun blockading the Mexican coast: "If Santa Anna endeavors to enter the Mexican ports, you will allow him to pass freely." In June Polk sent a naval officer, Alexander Slidell Mackenzie (John Slidell's brother, who had taken an uncle's surname) to Havana to confer with Santa Anna confidentially. Polk later learned of the results with both satisfaction and annoyance.

Mackenzie, who as commanding officer of the U.S.S. *Somers* in 1842 had shown temerity in executing a problem son of the then Secretary of War in an alleged mutiny, exhibited rashness again in his dealing with Santa Anna. The President had given Mackenzie only oral instructions (as Polk was fond of doing), but Mackenzie had written them down on paper and had presented the document to Santa Anna as a formal message. In it the President was quoted as telling Santa Anna he might return freely to Mexico through the United States blockade, that upon the general's return to power in Mexico the United States Government would be happy to negotiate with him for a settlement of claims and boundaries, and that the United States would provide the cash necessary for Santa Anna to accomplish all this. These were indeed valid offers from the President, but Polk seethed when he heard that Mackenzie had recorded everything in writing. The more surreptitiously Polk could operate, the better he liked it.

Mackenzie's subsequent report mollified the President somewhat. Mackenzie said that Santa Anna agreed with the plan and that the general's sincerity seemed apparent. Santa Anna even sent some further advice for prosecuting the war against his homeland: invade and occupy the two important ports of Tampico and Vera Cruz.

Events suddenly seemed to be going in Polk's favor. The Oregon question, too, had taken a turn toward what appeared to be an impending peaceful solution. About this time Polk actually suffered greater vexation from Secretary of State Buchanan than from the British Government.

The trouble had commenced soon after the declaration of war against Mexico. At one cabinet meeting Polk listened impatiently as Buchanan proposed sending foreign governments—especially Britain and France—a statement of causes and aims of the conflict, together with a declaration that the United States had not gone to war with the intention of acquiring California, New Mexico, or any other Mexican territory. If Britain and France believed the United States had commenced the war for purposes of expansion, Buchanan said, both countries would join Mexico in the fight.

Such a suggestion angered Polk, whose desires regarding Upper California already had become well known to the Cabinet. Buchanan seemed to be taking more and more pleasure in antagonizing the President, who conducted foreign affairs entirely to suit himself, giving his Secretary of State scant latitude—just as the President operated in every other field. Polk recorded his reply.

. . . I told him that before I would make the pledge which he proposed I would meet the war which either England or France or all the Powers of Christendom might wage, and that I would stand and fight until the last man among us fell in the conflict. I told him that neither as a citizen nor as President would I permit or tolerate any intermeddling of any European Powers on this continent. . . . I told him there was no connection between the Oregon and Mexican questions, and that sooner than give the pledge he proposed that we would not if we could fairly and honorably acquire California or any other part of the Mexican Territory which we desired, I would let the war which he apprehended with England come and would take the whole responsibility. . . .

Polk apparently had a coal of fire ready to apply to everybody. Fortunately for him, however (but still unknown to him), the government in London remained firm in its desire to concentrate on problems other than a possible war with the United States. In June the British minister submitted a proposal for settling the Oregon question: "that the . . . territory shall be divided between the parties by the 49° parallel of latitude from the Rocky Mountains to the Straits of Fuca, thence through the main channel of such straits to the sea, the country south of this line to belong to the United States and that north of it to Great Britain."

When the proposal came up for discussion at a meeting of the Cabinet June 6 Polk was astounded to hear Buchanan hold out for a division along 54°40′—that magic line that had ignited the slogan, "Fifty-four Forty or Fight"—despite Buchanan's earlier advocacy of an Oregon compromise and despite his urgent desire to avoid war with Britain over Mexico. Polk concluded that the Secretary of State was seeking to avoid responsibility for compromising and thus alienating some Westerners who might in later years support him for the presidency.

Polk submitted the proposal to the Senate with the determination to let that body reach the decision. Senators voted in favor of the settlement (38–12), and on June 15 a new Oregon treaty was signed—about the same time that Mackenzie was leaving for his Havana conference with Santa Anna.

For Polk the pressure eased momentarily after that, but not the work load. He still had to devote himself to war plans. Furthermore, the small annoyances of office never let up. Early in July he received a large delegation of Indians, mostly Comanches, who had arrived in Washington "nearly in a naked state" and had been persuaded only after much difficulty to dress with more decorum for their visit to the Executive Mansion. Polk learned later that some Indians, "especially the squaws," had to be restrained from ripping off their clothes in his presence. If he was amused by this—or by the fact that many Indians discarded their shoes and walked barefoot across the grounds after leaving the Mansion—Polk gave no indication of it in his diary.

20.

Resplendent Star

Westward across the entire North American continent from the Executive Mansion lay San Francisco Bay. There, on a mid-June day, Lieutenant Joseph Warren Revere paced the sun-warmed wooden deck of the anchored sloop of war U.S.S. *Portsmouth* and, like the distant President, mused over the great value of California to his nation.

Unlike Polk, however, Revere had seen much of this country himself. The lieutenant knew that its beauty and its potential had not been exaggerated. He did not know that war had been declared and that President Polk already had commenced active operations to seize the place, but he did know that the U. S. Navy had orders to "protect United States interests" in California in event of an outbreak of fighting or an attempt by Britain to move in.

Revere, a Boston-born grandson of Paul Revere of Revolutionary War fame, was not a man easily impressed. He had seen much of life and of the world since entering the Navy in 1828 as a sixteen-year-old midshipman. Thirteen years later—in 1841—he had been promoted to his present rank. The rise had been slow and hard, because the Navy of Revere's youth was stagnated.

Congress had suspected the officer "caste" system of the Navy as well as that of the Army, and it had kept both service branches small—barely adequate to fill the least demands of a young nation that had anticipated peace, not war. Like the Army, the Navy had no retirement system, and as a result four grizzled sea dogs left over from the War of 1812 still held command of four major squadrons in the 1840s. As another result, only one officer had been promoted through the rank of commander into a

Battalion of Artillery — 8th Infantry; — 2nd Dragoons — 7th Inf — 5th Inf — Light Artillery — 3rd Inf — 4th Infantry — Inn.

1st Brigade; 2nd Brigade; 3rd Brigade

GENl WORTH   COL TWIGGS. Lt COL McINTOSH   COL WHISTLER

Mexico threatened war if the United States annexed Texas. When that event
occurred anyway, Polk sent Zachary Taylor and an Army of Occupation to Corpus
Christi Bay, pictured here, then later ordered Taylor to the Rio Grande, where
the pressured Mexicans finally attacked.

After some preliminary skirmishing two battles in southwestern Texas formally inaugurated the war with Mexico: (bottom) the Battle of Palo Alto on May 8, 1846, and (top) the Battle of Resaca de la Palma on the following day. Both sites were near present Brownsville, Texas.

General Taylor conquered Monterrey, Mexico (then spelled with one r), after sending General Worth's division westward around the city in a flanking movement toward the Saltillo road, shown here. In the background to left is Independence Hill, with the Bishop's Palace on a slope; in the background to right is Federation Hill. Obviously the movement was not so casual as depicted here.

Mexicans rode superbly, whether (top) mounted on a donkey at a position near the very stern, or (bottom) on a horse. Guerrillas riding fast mustangs could lasso a norteamericano caught alone in chaparral and make him pay for his carelessness with his life.

captaincy during the years 1816–26; and in the 1830s and 1840s navy rolls included midshipmen past the age of thirty. Drinking, fighting, and carousing that resulted from boredom and damaged egos were almost as common among junior officers as among enlisted men. It was a rough time when punishment still included flogging, finally banned with the help of a censorious book written by a former seaman named Herman Melville.

Another significant naval change had become evident before the outbreak of the war against Mexico: a gradual conversion to steam. This was not a popular development in the Navy, where life was uncomfortable and hazardous enough without having to shovel or to carry dirty, dusty coal that suffocated and to give up good, airy shipboard space to paddle wheels that could be easily crippled by enemy guns or to boilers that had a tendency to blow up and to scald to death the "black gang" who worked around them. But steam as a propellant was inevitable, whether or not reluctant sailors realized it, and Matthew C. Perry ("the cast-iron commodore" of the U. S. Navy) and a few other officers were using their influence to hasten the conversion.

At the outbreak of war they still had a long way to go. The U. S. Navy possessed some steamers, but many vessels still relied solely on those clean sails. Given this reprieve from inhaling coal dust, many seamen (despite the austerity of their existence) could find breezy happiness at times —especially during cruises to exotic lands. They sang a song that reflected their occasional ecstasy:

> *I lost my hat at Cape de Gat,*
> *And where do you think I found it?*
> *Behind a stone at Port Mahon,*
> *With three pretty girls around it.*

Revere had enjoyed his share of travel and the company of pretty girls. By June of 1846—aged thirty-four, married since 1842 to the former Rosanna Duncan but rarely at home—he had lived through more experiences than many men twice his age. He had visited South America, Europe, Africa, China, Russia, Ceylon, Sumatra, and many other places. For a year he had been on a ship engaged in hunting Caribbean pirates.

His appearance and actions gave quick indication of his character. Revere was a dark-complexioned, gregarious, educated man with one notable trait: an abiding curiosity in the world about him and in its people. The interest in people might have been a legacy from his father, John Revere, who had been a physician and a professor of medicine in the University of the City of New York.

Revere seemed to have had a particular fascination for interesting women in the various countries he visited, and apparently they were attracted to him, too. Despite his fondness for new faces and new landscapes, however, he believed in his own country and in its destiny.

In this and some other respects Revere typified a career naval officer. He loved the strict shipboard discipline that chafed men of less devotion —but helped to carry them and their vessels safely through the furies of Cape Horn, which Revere himself had rounded several times. The combination of discipline and work meant to him what it meant to a New England Puritan. Once he remarked on "anarchy and idleness, those master architects of ruin," after a visit to Peru, which had inspired the comment.

But Revere also showed some surprising deviations. He saw limits to the American system of government: "The republican system which works so admirably with us, seems to engender sloth, anarchy, and desolation, among the Spanish race." He viewed organized religion cynically: "Where there is no established religion, the people are in little danger from the sacerdotal authority, because the competition of the various sects for proselytes leads to a minute exposure of all the weak points, errors, and dangers of the rival systems. . . . But where a national religion . . . lies at the foundation of the civil government, and . . . forms the 'first article' of the political constitution, the 'drum ecclesiastic' beats no alarum to awaken the conscience and reason of the people, but keeps up an everlasting and monotonous tattoo, to lull suspicion, prevent inquiry, and preserve implicit faith and obedience."

Revere expressed impatience with "religious despotism," especially as exhibited in missionary work among natives, and with the "scare-teaching" of death and hell. He believed that the poor human race should at least be accorded refuge in a Being understanding and sympathetic—"all love," as he said. Natives and their mores unchanged by contact with representatives of "civilization" usually interested Revere the most, and he declared once, "New England manufacturers have many sins to answer for to Apollo and the Graces, for their innovations here [in this instance, Peru] as well as in almost every other country under the sun."

Furthermore, although Revere liked shipboard life and naval disci-

pline, he also loved the outdoors with a passion close to that of John Frémont, and he reveled in the personal freedom afforded by shore leave.
During these breaks in naval routine he enjoyed tramping around the
countryside—sight-seeing, hunting, and fishing. Until this cruise he had
never had a chance to explore Upper California, and he went ashore at
every opportunity.

Nearly a year had been required for Revere to reach his present station. His ship, initially the sloop of war *Cyane* (which later carried Polk's
messenger Archibald Gillespie from the Hawaiian Islands to Monterey,
California), had sailed from Norfolk in midsummer, 1845, with orders to
reinforce the U. S. Pacific Squadron during that prewar period of growing
tension.

The voyage had been long and arduous. Fifty-six monotonous days to
Rio de Janeiro—a long journey filled with watches, ceaseless drills with
sails and guns, and an encounter with a roaring storm. Fifty-three days to
Valparaiso—battling to round the Horn through heavy seas, being pum-
meled by storm winds that made nearby icebergs a menace and that
sometimes brought rain and snow and hail, and on one occasion discovering a shipboard fire that "man-of-war discipline" quickly extinguished.
Then more leisurely sailing northward—a lengthy stop at the Peruvian
port of Callao, a voyage on up the South American coast in pleasant
weather, a rendezvous with Commodore Sloat's five-ship Pacific Squadron
at a poorly protected anchorage off the then dirty Mexican town of Mazatlán.

At Mazatlán Revere had been transferred from the *Cyane* to the
Portsmouth, whose commanding officer, Commander John B. Montgom-
ery, received orders to proceed to Upper California to look after United
States interests and specifically to perform this service:

> . . . You will communicate frequently with our consul at [Monterey]
> and will ascertain as exactly as you can the nature of the designs of
> the English and French in that region, the temper of the inhabitants
> —their disposition toward the U. States and their relations toward
> the central Government of Mexico. You will do every thing that
> is proper to conciliate towards our country the most friendly regard
> of the people of California.
>
> When at [Monterey] and San Francisco you will distribute
> the accompanying constitutions of the State of Texas printed in
> Spanish.

169

The first sight of California had fascinated Revere: that high, forested coastline around Monterey, with a backdrop of magnificent mountains lost in a blue haze except for the peaks, which caught the last rays of the setting sun in a fiery farewell to the day. The scene had reminded him of the Maritime Alps.

At Monterey Revere and a group of other officers had obtained permission to go ashore on a horseback expedition for hunting and sightseeing. The countryside charmed Revere from the moment he left town: a ride through a dark pine forest to a level plain, where a swift, sparkling stream sang its way to the dark blue sea lying off to the right. On to the tottering tower and decaying adobe walls of old Carmel Mission, closed years earlier (along with other California missions) by the Mexican Government in a brief move toward breaking up Church holdings for private ownership. Up into a region of lofty green hills; through cool, fertile valleys; on to the scenic crest of coastal mountains; and, finally, down to a camp site near a clear stream that curved through a valley richly scented with nature's greenery. "Vegetation, like everything else, is on a vast scale in California, which will yet prove one of the brightest stars in the American galaxy," Revere commented.

In days following, the landscape continued to excite Revere as much as did the hunting for bear and deer, whose flesh the officers roasted on a spit over a crackling fire. Exhilarated, Revere mused over his surroundings.

> Who cares for the artificial world across the continent, when he can thus enjoy wild and uncontrolled independence? Who cares for the wealth of Wall street, when, dashing over the painted plains and far-surveying hills, he may exclaim with Goldsmith—
>
> "Creation's heir, the world, the world is mine!"

Every nation in that world would want California, Revere decided, and he jotted down a few suggestions about how the United States could secure "the resplendent Star of the West": by an increase of trade with the territory, by better communications (including a transcontinental magnetic telegraph), and by more rapid and safer transportation, like coast-to-coast rail service.

> . . . Asia . . . will be brought to our very doors. Population will flow into the fertile regions of California. The resources of the entire country traversed by the [railroad] will be developed, and discoveries of the greatest importance will be made. The public lands lying

along the route will be changed from deserts into gardens, and a large population will be settled [there]. . . .

Revere had heard of the presence in California of a man—John Frémont—whose purpose was to explore a route from the United States to the Pacific. After Revere had returned to the *Portsmouth* from his own informal explorations ashore he heard something else about Frémont. The captain was said to be in northern California, having gone there after incurring the wrath of Mexican authorities by that intrusion into settled areas farther south.

Revere's ship received orders to sail from Monterey for San Francisco Bay. One reason for the move was to be nearer Frémont.

The *Portsmouth* proceeded northward up the coast, keeping close in to shore. On a late spring day the ship sailed between the high, dark cliffs forming the entrance to San Francisco Bay, past Alcatraz (or Bird Island, as it was sometimes called), and toward the north shore. The ship anchored at Sausalito, a watering and provisioning place.

Days passed tranquilly there and merged into weeks. Revere had time for another horseback trip around the countryside: to Yerba Buena, that small cluster of huts on the south side of the bay entrance; to straggling San José village, "hardly worth describing"; to the old Santa Clara Mission, whose buildings appeared in better state of preservation than those of other secularized missions.

On June 14 Revere returned to the *Portsmouth*. That was the day he paced the sun-warmed deck and mused over what he had seen in this beautiful country that was of such obvious value to the United States.

By coincidence, on that same day a group of American settlers began a movement not far to the northward that was intended to bring California, like Texas, into the North American Union.

21.

Golden Gate

Thirty miles due north of the U.S.S. *Portsmouth* anchorage lay another of those dilapidated missions that had fallen into disuse after the secularization move years earlier. Mission San Francisco de Solano, at Sonoma, was the twenty-first, the northernmost, and the last of the string of California missions established by Spain and later maintained by Mexico to Christianize Indians and to ward off what had once looked like a Russian threat from the north. Russian fur traders seeking sea otter had established a settlement on Kodiak Island in Alaska as early as 1784, and in ensuing decades their successors had gradually moved southward into Upper California—as far as Rossiya (Fort Ross), one hundred miles from San Francisco. But by 1841 the fur trade had declined. The Russians sold Rossiya to John Sutter and went back to Alaska or to their homeland—all to the delight of the proper owners of California.

The buffer mission and a settlement at Sonoma remained, however, as did the officer who had served as commandant of the northern frontier during the last years of the Russian threat—Mariano Vallejo, an urbane man who contributed much to the early development of that part of California. His Sonoma residence overlooked an old plaza, now bone-strewed because of the many beeves slaughtered there in the past. Nearby, in other buildings facing the plaza, lived his brother Salvador, a pioneer in California wine making; a brother-in-law, Jacob Leese, who was cautiously helping Consul Larkin to conciliate the Californians; and some others. These human inhabitants found themselves greatly outnumbered by the enormous population of fleas that thrived in the otherwise listless village.

Many American settlers in northern California knew Mariano Vallejo as a friendly man. Vallejo, in fact, could visualize some advantages of being annexed to the United States—eventual stability and peace, greater economic activity and prosperity. But on the morning of June 14 a group of thirty or forty settlers sent by John Frémont surprised the town, captured it and the inhabitants, and took possession of all public property. After that—and still unaware of a declaration of war by the United States —the settlers proclaimed California a republic and hoisted a crudely made flag that displayed, among other things, a picture of a bear that some critics were to scoff at later as looking more like a pig.

The "Bear Flag Republic" had been born, but not spontaneously or accidentally. Some notable events had preceded the attack on Sonoma.

Although no one in California knew of the outbreak of war (or about the dispatch of the Army of the West under General Kearny to take California or about the now effective orders to Commodore Sloat to blockade and to take possession of California ports), war between the United States and Mexico had, of course, seemed imminent. Furthermore, Frémont's previous activities had left the area in ferment. Lieutenant Joseph Warren Revere apparently had not had a chance to observe the extent of friction during his leisurely horseback excursions across the countryside.

When Frémont returned with Lieutenant Gillespie from the Oregon woods and from those encounters with the Klamath Indians, the fiery captain rode in among a group of Anglo-American settlers excited by a series of rumors, correct or not: that General Castro intended to dispossess and to evict all American settlers who had not become California citizens (as required by law); that the Herrera-Paredes feud in Mexico City was having repercussions in California, where some government officials (including Governor Pío Pico, a political foe of military commander Castro) wanted to break completely away from troubled Mexico and to seek British protection; that the British were scheming to take Upper California on their own; that General Castro and other officials had conceived a plan, soon to be effected, to enlist Indians in a war on American settlers—to burn their crops, destroy their homes, and drive them from California.

Frémont listened sympathetically. He had seen for himself the results of some remarkable Indian atrocities: bodies of white men who had been skinned alive, and bodies of white women who had been impaled on sharp sticks until death slowly relieved their agony. Furthermore, he had shaped his own opinion of Mexican trustworthiness—and he probably had heard by now of a Yankee ship captain who had been attacked during the preceding October on the main street of Yerba Buena by residents wielding knives and clubs. The man had been left for a long time lying on the street in a bloody pool, but officials had taken no compensatory action—not even after formal complaints.

Some other outrages had equaled these. Frémont determined that he would use his men as appropriate and as necessary to protect his countrymen residing in California. But he also determined on broader activity. After musing over the verbal orders and letters that Lieutenant Gillespie had brought, Frémont had come to regard his expedition as a military force now—not just one for exploration. He said in his *Memoirs*, "I clearly saw that my proper course was to observe quietly the progress of affairs, and take advantage of any contingency which I could turn in favor of the United States, and, where uncertainties arose, to give my own country the benefit of my doubts by taking decided action." The plan sounded like a rather cautious, subtle one, but Frémont was a man incapable of much cautiousness or subtlety.

After returning from Oregon Frémont and his men encamped on the Sacramento River near Sutter's Fort. There he lingered, obviously waiting for something to happen—like the arrival of news of war. While he waited, numbers of Americans rode into his camp and volunteered to join his "army." These men comprised a motley crowd. Some were legal landowners and presumably responsible men. Many were squatters, hunters, and trappers. Some were troublemaking malcontents who were in California for various reasons—as deserters from ships or as escapees from judicial judgment following crimes committed in the United States. But they shared some common characteristics: hardihood, audacity, and a tendency to look down on the native Californians as lazy, worthless people whose Catholicism kept them in mental bondage and whose "racial traits" condemned them to perpetual inferiority.

Frémont's tough-minded volunteers clamored for war, but, surprisingly, Frémont held back. Perhaps last-minute contemplation again had brought him to reflect on the embarrassment he could cause his government by an effort—particularly an unsuccessful one—to throw established rule out of California in the continuing absence of a declaration of war. No doubt he knew of the experience four years earlier of a U. S. Navy officer, Commodore Thomas ap Catesby Jones, who had heard rumors of war with Mexico and, assuming them to be true, had taken his squadron into Monterey Bay and had occupied the town of Monterey. Jones had meant to thwart British occupation, which had been feared then, too. But then the commodore had learned to his great grief that no war existed. He quickly lowered a United States flag he had hoisted, raised in its place the colors of Mexico, and gave that sovereign republic a thundering, red-faced salute. Later he tried to apologize to the governor. But not even these amenities saved him. Jones's embarrassed government had no choice but to recall him and to hope that Mexico might forget this brief exposure of official United States thinking.

So Frémont stayed in the background for a time. He did lead a group of fifty rough volunteers against Indian villages located nearest the settlers, killing some of the natives, sending the rest fleeing for safety into the murkiness of adjacent woods, and (he felt certain) checkmating the rumored plot to loose Indians on the Americans before any protective move could be made. But against the Californians themselves Frémont chose not to commit himself further at this time.

His reluctance temporarily alienated numbers of militant American settlers. They generally shared the belief of a pioneer among them who typically went to the Scriptures for support of an attempt to possess California. "The Israelites took the promised land of the East by arms," the man pointed out, "and the Americans must take the promised land of the West in the same way." Some of those disgruntled settlers accused Frémont of urging them into an action that would call forth retaliation from the Californians. When that happened, they predicted, Frémont would bring his little army into the fighting and feel completely justified.

Another rumor and the reaction that it prompted brought open warfare one step closer to California. Castro sent one of his officers with a group of soldiers into country north of San Francisco Bay to round up branded horses belonging to the government. Excited speculation spread throughout the land. The horses were to be used by Castro, it was said and repeated, to mount an army for an attack on the American settlers.

Tall, impetuous Ezekiel Merritt, a hard man among rough men, mounted an attack of his own. He recruited a dozen fellow settlers from among Frémont's volunteers, surprised the Californians in a bivouac, herded all 170 horses back to Frémont's camp, and sent the soldiers on their sorrowful way to tell Castro about their lack of vigilance.

The daring raid elated many settlers, but some others who preferred peaceful settlement to military decision were not so joyful. John Sutter received the information with downright dismay.

Californians reacted with anger. To them it had all the appearances of horse stealing—not a crime to be condoned in a land where a mount meant so much to a man.

One of Frémont's own "soldiers" openly questioned the propriety of the raid, but the temperamental captain clapped the man in a "dungeon-like room"—as Frémont himself described it—full of fleas of "indiscriminate ferocity," and the man stopped voicing his doubts.

Frémont had not taken part directly in the raid, but he and the leader, Merritt, already had become devoted friends and mutual admirers. Ultimate responsibility did not really matter now, anyway, because open conflict had been assured.

Soon after the raid came another surprise American assault—this one definitely planned by Frémont, although again the captain refrained from taking an active role. He sent a force of some thirty men under the joint command of his friend Merritt and William B. Ide, a shrewd Vermonter, to attack Sonoma. There lived General Vallejo—now without an army, but still a commissioned Mexican officer. Frémont knew the man to be a friend of American settlers and possibly of the United States. He speculated that Vallejo might be used somehow to persuade his countrymen to accept annexation to the North American Union.

Some time later Frémont heard the full details of the action against Sonoma, the listless village that the attackers referred to as a "fortress."

The faint glimmer of predawn on June 14, a Sunday, outlined the silent residences built around that bone-cluttered plaza, but illuminated little else—no military activity, no tents sheltering sleeping soldiers, not even a single sentinel for a garrison force.

At daybreak Mariano Vallejo, that commandant once responsible for watching Russians, was awakened by a noise from somewhere near his house. He rose, peeked outside, and saw to his alarm a group of wild-looking men apparently surrounding the residence. Most of the men were "dressed in leather hunting shirts, many of them very greasy; taking the whole party together, they were about as rough a looking set of men as one could hope to imagine." Apparently all of them carried weapons.

Vallejo's frightened wife urged her husband to flee through a back door, but Vallejo considered such an exit too undignified for a onetime *comandante general*—and probably impossible anyway. He dressed hurriedly, ordered the front door opened, walked quickly into the living room, and there met a group of the strangers streaming in.

Vallejo demanded to know their business. After some ensuing language difficulty the Mexican officer was made to understand that he was a prisoner, but that he need not worry about his safety. Further discussion brought Vallejo to a realization that these men were acting under orders of John Frémont. This reassured him somewhat. He knew that his acknowledgment of the advantages of California annexation by the United States had become known among the Americans. An enforced arrest by a United States military officer would not be disagreeable. It would relieve Vallejo of the delicacy of his position as a commissioned officer of a government not at all sympathetic to annexation. So Vallejo submitted, surrendered keys to public property, and commenced negotiations with his captors for guaranteeing in writing the safety of civilian residents of Sonoma—the only ones there besides himself.

With California friendliness he produced bottles of *aguardiente*. Most of his guests accepted the hospitality eagerly, and some of them apparently drank too much. Quarrels erupted. When Mariano Vallejo, his brother Salvador, Jacob Leese, and fifteen other Sonoma citizens were herded off under the guard of Ezekiel Merritt and ten men to meet Frémont at Sutter's Fort much of Mariano Vallejo's anxiety had returned. He hoped Frémont would release them all on parole without delay.

Remaining behind at Sonoma were William Ide, the crafty Vermonter, and the rest of the settlers who had captured the place. They took possession of all guns and ammunition, and prepared to fortify the town for their own use. But they wanted to emphasize that this was no ordinary dissent. Their vision, possibly unbridled by Vallejo's stock of *aguardiente*, encompassed a great republic—another Texas, which could either remain independent or annex itself to the United States.

Urgently needed as a civilized symbol for such a noble enterprise was a flag. One of the rebelling Americans—William Todd, nephew of the Mary Todd who had married a striving lawyer named Abraham Lincoln a few years earlier—set about designing a banner for the insurgents. He decided to use a star and a stripe to suggest the United States ensign and —significantly—the Texas Lone Star, which was now added to the North American constellation. But a symbol representing California itself was desired, too, and someone mentioned a grizzly bear—common then in that area and well known for its strength and unyielding resistance.

For the flag Todd found a piece of unbleached cotton about three by five feet. Sewed to the bottom of this as a stripe—and cut to appropriate length—were some strips of red flannel about four inches wide. In the upper left-hand corner of the cotton cloth Todd painted a crude star. He outlined it first in ink, then colored its body red. To the right of the star, and facing it, he painted a crude bear. Below these two objects he inked in the words "CALIFORNIA REPUBLIC."

Citizens of the Bear Flag Republic, in a proclamation written by Ide, promised peace and security to all "law-abiding individuals," but they vowed to overthrow the California government that had shown itself (as they contended) to be selfish, oppressive, and incompetent. In a letter to Commander Montgomery of the *Portsmouth*—Lieutenant Revere's ship —Ide stated another objective: ". . . to embrace the first opportunity to unite our adopted and rescued country, to the country of our early home." Ide asked for food and ammunition, but Montgomery—still unaware of the war declaration—formally replied only with offers of sympathy and encouragement.

At Sutter's Fort, Frémont followed the miniature insurrection with interest and pleasure. Everything seemed to be falling right for him, but still he refrained from active participation.

When Mariano Vallejo and other Sonoma prisoners were delivered to Sutter's Fort, Frémont did not free them on parole. Instead, to assure their continued presence, he kept them as prisoners. John Sutter protested such use of his property, but Frémont cut him off by threatening to eject him from the fort and to take complete control of it himself. Sutter stayed, but Frémont and his men assumed virtual control anyway.

Then Frémont waited a while longer. He heard from Commander Montgomery, who sent him congratulations for the recent success at Sonoma. The attack on the town had been masterfully planned and executed, Montgomery remarked to Frémont, but it should have been followed "by a rush upon Santa Clara, where Castro might have been taken by thirty men."

Frémont sent Montgomery a request for ammunition, food, medicine, and other supplies, indicating to Montgomery that he intended to use the provisions during a forthcoming return journey to the United

States. Frémont soon received the requested goods. Unlike the Bear Flag revolutionists, he was an authorized person. But still Frémont made no firm plans to set out for the United States. Instead, he tarried longer. No doubt many of his supplies went to the revolutionists.

Next Frémont received some information concerning Castro himself. That man, infuriated by Sonoma events, was raising an "army" in the south—the only place where he had any troops available—to retake Sonoma. Six days after that, on June 23, Frémont heard from the Bear Flag men at Sonoma that Castro's army, numbering about fifty men under the command of a subordinate named Joaquin de la Torre—had been observed approaching Sonoma. They appealed to Frémont for help. But their own numbers had increased to forty or more men by this time, and they felt confident enough to march out of Sonoma to meet the advancing enemy.

This they did. While en route they found the bodies of two Americans who had been tortured to death. This added fire to their fury. In a small battle near San Rafael they met the Californians, killed two of them, wounded others, and sent the rest fleeing southward.

At Sutter's Fort Frémont heard of Sonoma's plight (but not the details of the fighting) and knew that the time had come for action. He became determined not "to leave events to mature under unfriendly, or mistaken, direction." He wrote out a resignation of his commission and enclosed it in a letter to Senator Benton with the comment that the Army could accept it should ensuing events prove embarrassing to the United States Government. Then he and a hundred or more men rode off to the relief of Sonoma.

There Frémont heard about the victory near San Rafael, took command of the Bear Flag settlers at their request, and hurried away southward after the remnant of De la Torre's retreating army. But the Californians were mounted on faster horses, and they escaped. They left Frémont in command of all the area north of San Francisco Bay.

The captain's plans were as expansive as the country he occupied. He would soon lead his Bear Flag men farther southward, he decided. He would challenge Castro. Frémont had no doubt about that outcome. Monterey, Santa Barbara, and other towns would fall to him. As a sort of preliminary move, Frémont led a group of men across San Francisco Bay to the site of an old fort, seized it, spiked two-centuries-old cannon that had been incapable of firing for forty years, captured supplies, and returned to Sonoma. During this expedition he passed just inside the high hills that reached out from north and south like giant arms cradling the bay. He stared in awe at nature's beauty and gave the bay entrance a name suitable to his recurrent poetic vein, to the grandeur of the scene, and to the glory of the moment. He named the sun-gilded entrance "Golden Gate."

Three days later, on July 4, Frémont was back at Sonoma. More American volunteers had come in to join his army. On that day, which was observed with a noisy Independence Day celebration, and on the fifth Frémont organized his men, 234 in all, into a four-company California Battalion. Next in command to Frémont was the Marine Corps messenger, Lieutenant Gillespie. Their troops—bearded, long-haired, sunburned, lean, and leathery—might have overwhelmed foes simply by appearing before them, by smell if not by sight. Most men wore large, battered hats, buckskin or flannel shirts, buckskin trousers, and moccasins—all grimy with dust, blood, grease, and gunpowder. Many of them displayed gleaming hunting knives and a brace of pistols fixed to leather straps encircling their waists.

Frémont was making plans to march his army south when a courier arrived from Commodore Sloat telling him about the declaration of war. Frémont learned that Sloat had heard of the outbreak of war early in June, while his flagship, U.S.S. *Savannah*, was anchored at Mazatlán.

Sloat had not stirred for a while. Long before that the commodore had received those orders to blockade and occupy California ports upon hearing of war, but Sloat was an old, mostly burned-out man—and never a very resolute one anyway. Furthermore, he certainly would have been musing over the misfortune of Thomas ap Catesby Jones in occupying Monterey too quickly during that time of peace. Sloat waited, hoping to get reliable confirmation about the war.

Finally Sloat had sailed for Upper California and had arrived in Monterey Bay July 2, joining the United States sloops *Cyane* and *Levant*, which had arrived earlier. But even then he delayed acting. He actually made the customary courtesy visits to Monterey authorities.

By July 7 Sloat had moved. He demanded and received the surrender of Monterey. At ten o'clock that delicious summer morning a landing party of 250 excited sailors and marines unfurled the Stars and Stripes from the top of the old Customs House. "Three hearty cheers" rent the silence, while from the direction of the bay guns of the American squadron rumbled a salute. A proclamation prepared by Sloat and Consul Larkin and read immediately following the flag-raising ceremony declared California a possession of the United States and promised freedom from high customs duties and from governmental interference with individual rights. The proclamation also contained a prophecy of "great increase in the value of real estate and the products of California."

Sloat published an order to his men warning of severe punishments for those who failed to act with dignity and responsibility ashore. Another order went to the *Portsmouth*, still in San Francisco Bay: take possession of Yerba Buena. Men from Lieutenant Revere's ship accomplished this with no difficulty on July 9.

Revere himself had received from Commander Montgomery of the *Portsmouth* other orders agreeable to his penchant for sight-seeing. Take a ship's boat, Revere was told, navigate up San Francisco Bay, and proceed to Sonoma, where he was to read the Sloat-Larkin proclamation to the Bear Flag men and to take over the fort in the name of the United States.

In two o'clock darkness of July 9 Revere left the *Portsmouth*, with little more than the swishing of water between his bobbing boat and the rolling ship to mark his historic departure. He arrived at Sonoma before noon, summoned the garrison force to the public square, read the proclamation, and raised the United States flag from a staff in front of the barracks. Again guns roared in salute.

Revere then had the proclamation translated into Spanish and posted in the bone-strewed plaza. He also sent copies of the document into surrounding areas—including Sutter's Fort, to which he also forwarded a United States flag for ceremonious hoisting.

The lieutenant wrote Commander Montgomery, on the *Portsmouth:*

> I am happy to report that great satisfaction appeared to prevail in the community of Sonoma, of all classes, and among both foreigners and natives, at the country having been taken possession of by the United States . . . more particularly after the general feeling of insecurity of life and property caused by the recent events of the revolution in this part of California.

Upper California finally seemed secure for the United States—and indeed the northern section of it was now. But a subsequent appeal by Sloat to General Castro and Governor Pico for co-operation drew their firm rejection. Frémont's activities and the Bear Flag rebellion had so angered both men that the two foes had buried differences and united forces—eight hundred men—for a defense of Los Angeles and the sovereignty of Mexico. About the same time, on July 16, a British warship named *Collingwood* arrived at Monterey Bay, and Sloat sent his men to quarters, ready for battle.

In ensuing days the excitement waned quickly, however, and eventually flickered out. The *Collingwood* sailed out of the blue bay on July 23, a week after arriving, without having made any threatening gestures at all. That same day a vigorous, ambitious Commodore Robert F. Stockton arrived in U.S.S. *Congress* to relieve the ailing indecisive Commodore Sloat, who was to sail for home and retirement in the *Levant*. Two days later Frémont brought his California Battalion, now formally in United States service, aboard *Cyane* at Monterey for a voyage to San Diego and possible action there. Commodore Stockton also weighed anchor for San Pedro with a naval landing force of 360 men that would have as its objective the capture of Los Angeles.

Some time later Stockton's sailors marched overland from San Pedro toward their objective and were joined by Frémont and eighty horsemen riding up from the south. Opposing forces evaporated before this combination. Los Angeles surrendered without a fight on August 12. The gate to California lay open to the United States, and as Lieutenant Revere and that other visionary, John Frémont, had suggested, the future there would prove golden indeed.

22.

Duty

At quiet Fort Hamilton, where silent guns had stood ready since the early 1830s to repel an enemy who never appeared in New York Bay, a capable junior engineer officer of the U. S. Army fought boredom and the mugginess of another New York mid-August, while far to the southwest military reputations were being made.

Captain Robert Edward Lee, aged thirty-nine, had been stationed at Fort Hamilton for five dreary years now. During much of that time he had been entrusted with the repair of crumbling sea walls and leaky casemates, and with the strengthening of gun positions at Hamilton and three other forts nearby.

Lee was a man who devoted himself fully to the job he had been assigned, including the paper work that went with it in detestable quantity. Nevertheless, the captain hated office work. The routineness of his present labors, combined with a slowness of promotion, made him acutely aware of encroaching middle age. Lee had graduated second in his class at the Military Academy in 1829, having acquired not a single demerit during cadetship. But now, seventeen years later, he was only a captain —a rank he had held for the past eight years.

Lee's professional plight was not unusual for a peacetime soldier, but continued duty at placid Fort Hamilton meant staying in the same rut. Promotions certainly would go to the engineers who distinguished themselves in the recently declared war. Lee reflected privately on all of this, but he did not complain publicly or slight his work. This stolid attitude evolved from training that had begun during his earliest years. His mother had made him committed to life as he found it.

Robert E. Lee was born at Stratford Hall, the family estate in Westmoreland County, Virginia, on a raw winter day that emphasized the decline of the Lee fortune. On that January 19, 1807, a cold wind cut inshore from the Potomac, rustling the dormant vegetation that in summer threatened to engulf the untended outbuildings and seeping into several unheated rooms in the decaying mansion. Warmth permeated the bedchamber where Robert E. Lee was born, however, and Lee as a youngster would rarely feel the cold.

He was the son of Anne Carter Lee, a brown-eyed woman whose serenity indicated inner strength, and Henry (Light Horse Harry) Lee, a handsome, ostentatious young man when a Revolutionary War luminary, but by the time of Robert's arrival a self-indulgent, impractical, adulation-spoiled old hero through whose hands family gold had sifted and scattered with the breeze. Henry Lee, aged fifty-three at Robert's birth, was seventeen years older than his wife.

When Robert was two his father was arrested and jailed for a time for non-payment of debt. When he was eleven his father died. Robert's mother determined that the children would not repeat their father's ruinous performance. She instilled integrity, self-discipline, and frugality in them—and most successfully in Robert, who soon exhibited his mother's serenity and a remarkable self-confidence without any trace of arrogance. Money became a perpetual problem, however, and some exigencies were forced on Anne Lee. Robert's brother, Smith Lee, went to sea for his education, on an 1820 midshipman's appointment from President Monroe. Five years later Robert received an appointment to the Military Academy, where he consistently stood near the top in every subject. When he graduated he had become a model in accomplishment and in appearance—and a legend maker in regard to that absence of demerits. Second Lieutenant Lee stood very tall for his five feet ten and a half inches, and his look appealed to both men and women: finely formed, clean-shaved face; brown eyes that occasionally seemed black; very dark, glossy hair with an abundant wave and an inclination to curl at the ends. Various people wrote detailed descriptions of him: "as fine-looking a man as one would wish to see, of perfect figure and strikingly handsome"; ". . . a man . . . in the vigor of youthful strength, with a noble and commanding presence, and an admirable, graceful, and athletic figure"; ". . . [a man with] a finished form, delicate hands; . . . graceful in person."

Even more remarkable were those mental qualities: the total acceptance of life and the determination to devote himself completely to duty, which he considered an assignment by God's will. His thinking about this resembled in some ways that of Sam—Ulysses—Grant, who had agreed with Thomas à Kempis that "man proposes, God disposes." Early in his career Lee committed himself to a program of doing a job as well as he could and leaving the rest to God. But soon after his graduation from West Point the woman who had taught him all this passed away. Robert was at his mother's bedside when she died, and he would carry the scene with him to his own grave.

After his mother's death Robert E. Lee married Mary Custis, the only child of George Washington Parke Custis—George Washington's adopted son. Site of the wedding was the Custis mansion at Arlington, overlooking from a high Virginia hill the Potomac River and, beyond that, the city of Washington and the Capitol.

Lee's bride, no beauty, had her own kind of charm. She was effervescent. Her dark eyes flashed with spirit. But Mary Custis Lee had been coddled by an indulgent father. During ensuing years she frequently left her husband and his austere garrison life for visits home to partake of the luxuries to be found there. She enjoyed being looked after.

During these same years Lee labored as he had been taught, and mostly without recognition until a tour of duty at St. Louis in the latter 1830s. There he succeeded in saving the town as a shipping center by using an ingeniously built dike and the force of the Mississippi current to wash away a growing accumulation of silt that had threatened to block the river front. The feat made him something of a hero in St. Louis and certainly a capable engineer in the eyes of his superior officers, but then he returned to a series of dull assignments.

By August of 1846—that fifth year of looking after coastal defenses around Fort Hamilton—Lee was moving into the middle age of which he had become acutely aware. Mary Custis Lee had given birth to their seventh child, a daughter, some months earlier and had, as usual, returned home to Arlington for the event. At the same time Lee remained at Fort Hamilton, on the southwestern edge of Long Island, watching in leisure moments from the porch of his two-story white frame house as steamships and sailing vessels negotiated The Narrows to and from upper New York Bay. The ships were bound somewhere while Lee was sitting silently on the porch, as if already in retirement.

He followed the war only by reading and hearing about it. In July Mexico formally declared war, in a final reply to President Polk's action of May 12. Even before that time, of course, thousands of volunteers had begun rallying around the Stars and Stripes, including twelve thousand militia recruits illegally enlisted for a period of six months by old, quarrelsome, and irresponsible General Edmund P. Gaines, commander of the Western Department with headquarters at New Orleans. By law militia volunteers could be required to serve only three months (longer periods needed congressional action) and Gaines's new troops either had to sign up for a longer term as part of the authorized volunteer force or return home. Most of them chose home. Later Gaines was removed from command for his mistake.

Lee had read about the battles of Palo Alto and Resaca de la Palma —and about what had followed. General Arista and his mauled army had withdrawn from Matamoros little more than a week later, and General Taylor had moved his men across the Rio Grande to occupy the town.

Then had come a long pause. Taylor, lacking adequate transportation, stayed at Matamoros for more than six weeks before advancing northward up the Rio Grande, bound eventually for Monterrey, in the Mexican state of Nuevo León. By July 14 his army had reached and occupied Camargo, on the river. There Taylor halted again, with Monterrey distant to the southwest some 140 miles.

August came to Lee at Fort Hamilton without any further word of an advance by Taylor and with no information at all about the momentous occurrences in far-off California, which remained mostly a blank spot. But some turmoil in Washington from the fourth to the tenth of the month held his attention. President Polk was seeking from Congress an appropriation of two million dollars to be used "for the purpose of defraying any extraordinary expenses which may be incurred in the intercourse between the United States and foreign nations." Actually Polk intended to use the money in an attempt to effect a peaceful settlement somehow with Mexico. Any negotiations certainly would depend on secrecy, however, and this forced Polk to couch his request in generalities. Many congressmen nevertheless anticipated the eventual destination of the cash, and they accused Polk of plotting bribery of Mexican officials to acquire more land that, they suspected, would eventually be opened to slavery. In the House of Representatives David Wilmot of Pennsylvania— a Democrat like Polk but also an ardent anti-slavery man—tacked onto the bill a proviso that no territory obtained from Mexico could become slaveholding. The appropriation bill then passed the House. In the Senate it encountered a fatal filibuster, however, leaving Polk no alternative (for the time) but to prosecute his war. The unsuccessful bill also resulted in another legacy: controversy of increasing bitterness dividing northern and southern sections of the United States.

Fort Hamilton was a fine place for reading, ship watching, desk work, and (when Lee's children were there) removing shoes and letting the youngsters tickle his feet while he read to them. But it was no place at this time for a West Point graduate like Lee, with his deep sense of commitment.

Ironically, however, Lee did not approve of war—did not believe civilization would advance until reason and humanity prevailed in settlement of disputes. Nor did he fervently approve of the Polk administration. Like most other military officers, Lee was a Whig. But above all else Lee was a professional soldier with a concern not only for promotion but also for duty, as he envisioned it.

At Fort Hamilton that August Lee mused over the war, family responsibilities, and age. He longed to leave with the soldiers embarking at Governor's Island for Mexico.

23.

Uncertain Destiny

Even bachelor schoolteachers were moving west with the military forces. John T. Hughes, A.B., graduate of Bonne Femme College, and former tutor of Liberty, Missouri, children, had marched with Colonel Kearny's Army of the West into a land increasingly mysterious and fascinating.

Not every American, of course, shared Hughes's enthusiasm for that movement. Daniel Webster of Massachusetts echoed many New Englanders when he addressed Congress:

> What do we want with this vast, worthless area? This region of savages and wild beasts, of deserts, of shifting sands and whirlwinds of dust, of cactus and prairie-dogs? To what use could we ever hope to put these great deserts, or those endless mountain ranges, impenetrable, and covered to their very base with eternal snow? What can we ever hope to do with the western coast, a coast of three thousand miles, rock-bound, cheerless, uninviting, and not a harbor on it? . . . I will never vote one cent from the public treasury to place the Pacific coast one inch nearer to Boston than it now is.

That particular speech made Daniel more of an orator than a prophet, but it was consistent with his views. Webster also had opposed Texas annexation and the war with Mexico.

None of these doubts bothered Hughes. Exhilaration and a feeling of importance flooded his soul as he joined the rest of Kearny's army on its march into history.

Before every dawn the sounds of reveille awoke him to his duties. Usually he and the other soldiers had breakfasted, saddled, mounted, and ridden out of their camp before the first dazzling rays of the early morning sun gave a glitter to the dew-covered grass. "As the troops moved off majestically over the green prairie," Hughes said, "they presented the most martial and animating sight. The long lines stretched over miles of level [country], or wound . . . over . . . beautifully undulating hills, with guns and sabres [glistening] in the sheen of the rising sun, while the American eagle seemed to spread his broad pinions, and westward bear the principles of republican government."

That description was of a landscape in present eastern Kansas, where substantial rainfall nurtured vegetation, where the first experiences of the march kept spirits high, and where the new camaraderie proved stimulating. Martial life at this early stage meant fun and excitement to Hughes, who remarked during these rousing July days, with the innocence of an unbloodied volunteer, "An army is always cheerful and frolicsome." With smooth traveling temporarily he had forgotten for a moment some difficulties that already had begun to plague the men—frequent wagon breakdowns, the occasional necessity to level roads for crossing steep-banked creeks and ravines, and at one camp site on a creek an encounter with an infestation of snakes of various kinds, including rattlers, that slithered through the tall grass and even occupied branches of trees.

In the joyous beginning the marches seemed much the same from day to day, but the grandeur of the scene and the importance of the assignment precluded boredom. Every day Hughes and his companions rode away from the sunrise across emerald prairies whose green seemed boundless, chasing a flat horizon where the distant plain merged with an empty summer sky. Sometimes the broad prairies became a succession of gentle hills, reminding Hughes of paintings he had seen of swells rolling across an ocean. Occasionally the men came upon streams that flowed along foothills. Near the water grew trees in shady groves and wild sunflowers with bright blossoms. From somewhere in the marching column a song could occasionally be heard. A witty remark would evoke laughter and be passed from group to group until it reached the end of the line.

About midday the heat generated by a raging sun smothered some enthusiasm, but cheer usually returned toward evening. Night fell on general contentment. Cooking fires burned down to a smolder. Men relaxed and prepared for sleep under the care of posted guards. Animals—oxen, beef cattle, horses—grazed inside corrals formed by wagons, or from tethers attached to iron pickets driven into the ground.

A man took care not to lose his horse. Such a loss forced him to pay dearly for the purchase of another mount from some soldier who had brought extras—or, more likely, it meant that he must continue the march on foot or as a teamster helping with the wagons. A horse was everything to a volunteer cavalryman—comfort, dignity, prestige, companionship, and fighting potential. "No wonder then that Alexander wept when Bucephalus died," remarked Private Hughes, A.B.

Few other worries troubled Hughes at this time. Nights on Kansas soil were not very dangerous even when standing guard duty; friends were always nearby in considerable numbers. Miles ahead of Hughes's unit lay encamped other detachments—groups of two or three hundred men each, formed small for greater convenience in traveling. Behind, another detachment rested. Accompanying it were Colonel Doniphan, the towering commander of these volunteers, and Major William Gilpin, a tall, spare Pennsylvanian whose move to and enthusiasm for the West had made him Senator Benton's good friend. Somewhere farther behind them lay encamped still another—and last—group, composed of artillerymen, engineers, and dragoons, and accompanied by the Army of the West commander, Stephen Kearny. In this region sentinel Hughes really had no Mexicans to look out for—only winking stars in a black sky to count, a fingernail moon to study, or intermittent flickers of a distant thunderstorm to watch.

Farther on, in central Kansas, a drought caused some discomfort. Thermometers registered 95 degrees, even when protected from direct sunlight. Summer sun had baked cracks in the soil and had parched the grass. In the shimmering distance nebulous lakes invited sweaty men to bathe, but the water slowly vanished as the distance to it decreased. At the silent, majestic Arkansas River—no mirage—Hughes gave his mount the reins, and horse and man splashed into the cool stream for refreshment.

On up the banks of the Arkansas they rode: near plains dark with buffalo; past Pawnee Rock, where one company paused to bury the blanket-wrapped body of a man who had died suddenly without ever having seen an enemy soldier; through a land where cloudbursts had produced flash floods and left streams roaring bank-full, requiring construction of improvised rafts or bridges before crossing; and gradually into a drier, harsher land where abounded snakes, chameleons and other lizards, horned frogs, dry-land turtles, prairie dogs, and swarms of grasshoppers.

Colonel Kearny sent an observer on ahead into still distant Santa Fe to ascertain feelings there. The man returned after a time and made his report, which Hughes and everyone else heard about. The common people seemed to favor peace and even annexation to the United States, but people of wealth and power did not. Worse, Mexican authorities had assembled more than two thousand men for the defense of Santa Fe and were collecting others at Taos. The members of Kearny's army thrilled with excitement.

Miles ahead of John Hughes's position in the line of march, an advance party of dragoons crossed the Arkansas River on July 22 and set up camp on the south bank, a few miles downstream from the remarkable outpost known as Bent's Fort, located on the north bank. The post commemorated the name of its venturesome trader-manager, William Bent, whose grandfather reputedly had helped to toss British tea into the harbor at the Boston Tea Party. During the preceding decade Bent had built his adobe castle—near present Las Animas, Colorado—for trading with fur trappers and merchants. The fort had become a wilderness crossroads, a center of information and rumor.

Five days after the advance guard had made camp Hughes's detachment crossed the Arkansas and halted there, too. At this site Kearny planned to allow the fatigued men and animals a rest and to assemble his army for the final movement against Santa Fe.

Near camp three Mexicans, presumably spies, were captured. Colonel Kearny ordered them taken around for a look at the guns, men, wagons, and animals, then released for return to Santa Fe. The colonel could guess what their wide-eyed report would be.

Hughes did some looking of his own—around Bent's Fort, which fascinated him. The high adobe walls, standing on a summer-scorched plain, could be seen for miles. Closer observation showed Hughes the immensity of William Bent's trading post, which had been built by scores of paid laborers brought in from Taos. No other construction of its size existed in the wilderness between the Mississippi River and the Pacific Ocean.

Giant exterior walls of sun-dried brick fourteen feet high and more than a yard thick enclosed a rectangular space of approximately sixty by forty-five yards. At the northwest and southeast corners circular towers eighteen feet tall allowed weaponry to sweep all walls in event of an assault.

Looking at the fort from the east, Hughes saw the entrance, which could be barred by closing a heavy iron and wood door six and a half feet wide and seven feet tall. Above the entrance stood a watchtower, atop the watchtower a belfry, and atop the belfry a flagstaff, with the Stars and Stripes flapping in a hot breeze. Inside the fort adobe cubicles, apartments, and storerooms provided compartmentalization.

While Hughes looked around and rested, Colonel Kearny prepared and sent to Santa Fe two dispatches with the hope of effecting a peaceful entry. The first, carried by a trader favorably known in the town, advised New Mexico citizens of the approach of the army "for the purpose of seeking Union with & ameliorating the conditions of its Inhabitants" and promising good treatment of persons who did not resist the march. In the second, to be taken to Governor Manuel Armijo by high-tempered Captain Philip St. George Cooke and an escort of dragoons, Kearny stated that he came "as a friend & with the disposition & intention to consider all Mexicans & others as friends who will remain quietly & peaceably at their homes & attend to their own affairs." But Kearny also pledged to take possession of the country for the United States, and he reminded Armijo that Texas as a republic had claimed the land years earlier.

Accompanying Cooke and his dragoons in the role of persuader was a wealthy American, James Magoffin, whose twenty-year experience in Santa Fe trade and marriage to a Chihuahuan woman had brought him favor and influence among the Mexican population. Magoffin—at this time a resident of Independence, Missouri—knew New Mexico and its people thoroughly.

On the second day of August the Army of the West marched out of camp, bound again for the fabled town at the end of the long trail. For an entire day the men followed the Arkansas River, then they struck off southwestward into a forbidding desert, following a salt-tainted stream called the Timpas.

A hot, dry wind threw sand in Hughes's face. During the intervals when he could open his eyes to scan the landscape he saw growing only "the prickly pear, the wild sage, the . . . screw bush, and a mimic arbor vitae." In the distance appeared more desolation. Heat and thirst almost overwhelmed him—and did kill many animals. Their carcasses attracted buzzards that ate greedily, then followed the army for seconds. Camps along the Timpas provided drinks of bitter, nauseating water.

By evening of August 5 the situation had improved: a halt on the green-fringed Purgatoire River—a cool stream providing better water for drinking and washing—and visible to the southwest the lofty grandeur of the Spanish Peaks.

August 6—magnificent scenery with more peaks visible, all looking like dark thunderheads in the distance. August 7—up a rough and rocky way to Raton Pass, the day's march a fatiguing one for both men and animals and damaging to the creaking wagons. August 8—more exhausting travel along arduous mountain trails, but—finally—the summit, nearly eight thousand feet above sea level, and a glorious panorama of New Mexico below. August 9—a Sunday, and a day of rest amid plentiful wood, water, and grass before plunging on; but also a day of grief, when dwindling supplies resulted in reduced rations and increasingly shriveled stomachs. August 10—a march of twenty-two miles, with gray mountaintops looming off to the right, an expansive valley sloping away to the left, and hunger all around. August 11—information from scouts and captured Mexicans: Armijo had gathered at least five thousand men, and was ready to receive the Army of the West with fire and fury—not friendliness.

Mid-August found Private Hughes, like Captain Robert E. Lee, harboring some doubts about the future, but for a different reason. Hughes's initial enthusiasm had been tempered by hard experience. He remarked, "An uncertain destiny [awaits] us. Some [anticipate] victory; others [apprehend] disaster."

24.

An Old Hero Returned

A blanket of stifling humidity lay over Havana and its environs, but at his hacienda sad-faced Santa Anna, the man with the look of a retired philosopher, planned activity. He might have been spurred on (if he needed any spurring) by his teen-age wife, who would have become petulant in such inglorious existence after having taken for a spouse a husband she had thought to be the greatest man in all Mexico.

Recent contacts with President Polk through Commander Alexander Slidell Mackenzie and Colonel A. J. Atocha, and with Valentín Gómez Farías through mutual friend Manuel Crecencio Rejón, had kept Santa Anna in motion. He and his friends also had been in communication with President Paredes, endeavoring to arrange a return to Mexico—and even to the government—with that Centralist leader.

From Polk the former dictator had received that assurance of safe entry into Mexico through the naval blockade, with the assumption that once back in power he would stop the fighting and would amicably settle border disputes and other disagreements with the United States. From Farías he had received that assurance of Mexican Army command under a *Puro* Federalist administration, with the assumption that he would be satisfied with the position and would not attempt to regain his supremacy in the government.

In Mexico recent events had unfolded that favored Santa Anna's return to at least a degree of his former power and prestige. Centrally involved in those events had been the Army.

Mexican civilians of many beliefs had come to share one common view: the peacetime Mexican Army had become a parasite living on the

194

nation's depressed economy. Even with a war now being fought, no thoughtful man wanted to serve in ranks filled by poor Indians who could earn no other living and by convicts released from prison. Even in wartime few intelligent, responsible citizens cared to contend for the available commissions, most of which had been grabbed by men who were dangerously ambitious, selfish, arrogant, and self-indulgent. The Army during either war or peace devoured the treasury, usually leaving untouched only the wealth of the Church—the one Mexican institution that enjoyed much of a surplus in those days. Furthermore, the Army had for years contributed to Mexican chaos by participating in, and often instigating, the frequent civil wars and revolts. But no one had yet proposed any workable solution to this problem. The military stood ready to defend itself as an integral part of Mexican society—and its potential for doing so was the one certainty of its effectiveness.

Puro Federalist Farías, who wanted to take the government away from Paredes and who wanted eventual annulment of military privileges, knew this as well as anyone. That confidential plan of Rejón's to utilize Santa Anna as an army commander in a take-over by the Federalists seemed ideal; so the once corrupt but now "regenerated" general at whom Farías had once scoffed as "the hero of San Jacinto" would come back to lead the Mexican Army against the United States, now that war had commenced, and at the same time lead it out of the clutches of suspicious officers who hated Federalists as much as they hated the invaders.

Paredes himself unknowingly helped the plan, with his apparent desire to establish a monarchy—complete with foreign prince—as a solution to domestic problems. The Army opposed this idea as being potentially as disastrous as annexation to the United States. With pay lagging anyway, military dissatisfaction with Paredes increased. Threatened with a revolution at home and with United States attacks on the borders, Paredes discreetly left Mexico City at the end of July to assume an active army command himself. Vice-President Nicolás Bravo remained in charge of the government.

Paredes' departure ignited a revolt. It began in the Army, with Farías and his men working confidentially to encourage it. On July 31 the disgruntled garrison at Vera Cruz, where Santa Anna had entered military service as a cadet years earlier, revolted and petitioned the general to

195

return from his Cuban exile and to assume command. Four days later jovial General Mariano Salas, governor and commander of the Department of Mexico, brought his forces into the struggle against Paredes. Salas happened to be one of the few Federalists in the officer corps, and he was acting for Farías, who had assigned him the job of holding supreme command pending Santa Anna's arrival from Havana.

Paredes acknowledged the inevitable. On August 6 he resigned, and Mexico City celebrated noisily. Cannon roared, bells pealed, and citizens shouted approval.

Salas moved into the National Palace temporarily as acting President and issued a call for the return of Santa Anna, "because his unquestionable prestige in the army was the best guarantee of the union of this worthy class with the people and because his decision to be among the earliest republicans makes him the greatest supporter of this system against the perfidious plans of the monarchical system."

At Havana Santa Anna heard of these events with much pleasure. On the muggy night of August 8 (while in Washington President Polk was trying to get congressional approval for that appropriation of two million dollars to buy peace and the northern Mexican provinces, perhaps through the aid of a restored Santa Anna) the once exiled dictator boarded a British steamer, *Arab*, bound for the United States naval blockade and eventually for Vera Cruz. Accompanying Santa Anna were A. J. Atocha, Manuel Crecencio Rejón, Santa Anna's young wife, and others. The general's old leg wound had been bothering him recently, and some friends had urged him to stay in Havana. Santa Anna refused, saying, ". . . I could not resist an invitation of this kind, nor forget that I was a Mexican soldier, and I determined to accept it."

Engine trouble delayed the voyage across the tepid Gulf of Mexico. Not until eight days later did the *Arab* steam within sight of the low, sun-seared harbor of Vera Cruz and give Santa Anna his first sight, in the hazy distance, of snow-capped Orizaba, which he remembered so well.

The *Arab* threaded a way through the naval blockade. Commodore Conner later sent to Washington a report.

> I have allowed [Santa Anna] to enter without molestation, or ever speaking to the vessel, as I was informed by the senior English naval officer here . . . she carried no cargo and would not be allowed to take any in return. I could easily have boarded the *Arab*, but I

deemed it most proper not to do so, allowing it to appear as if he had entered without my concurrence.

Santa Anna, his wife, and his friends stepped ashore on a Vera Cruz pier around noon of August 16 to a staged celebration. Local authorities, acting on a request from Mexico City, had paraded the 11th Infantry. Farías' three sons—Fermín, Casimiro, and Benito—received the general officially. While the infantrymen stood formed in two facing lines a slightly off-key military band tooted brassy, patriotic music. Youngsters happily exploded firecrackers supplied by city officials. Guns of San Juan de Ulúa blasted a salute. But as the fifty-two-year-old general (who was magnificently dressed in full uniform that covered his wooden leg) walked proudly between the files of soldiers he became aware of the complete absence of thousands of citizens cheering from a distance. A few steps ahead of him his seventeen-year-old wife, on the arm of an officer, also observed the lack of thundering *vivas* and pursed her pretty lips in a pout. Benito Gómez Farías wrote his father, without Santa Anna's knowledge, "[The Vera Cruz] city council was rather displeased and greatly distrustful of Santa Anna's return to the country"; and Fermín wrote that people in both Vera Cruz and Jalapa appeared to lack confidence in the great man.

Following the staged reception, Santa Anna's first notable activity was to publish a long proclamation—this one containing four thousand words. In it he affirmed his support of Mexican republicanism, condemned Herrera for willingness to negotiate with the United States, and denounced Paredes for his monarchical plan. He also called for a return to the Constitution of 1824 until a new one could be adopted, declared himself a "slave of public opinion . . . subjecting myself . . . entirely to the decisions of the constituent assembly, the organ of the sovereign will of the nation," then pleaded:

> Mexicans! There was once a day, and my heart dilates with the remembrance, when . . . you saluted me with the enviable title of soldier of the people. Allow me again to take it, never more to be given up, and to devote myself, until death, to the defense of the liberty and independence of the republic.

Santa Anna then retired with his wife to the estate at El Encero, in the cooler country above Vera Cruz. There the general denied the gossip that the U. S. Navy had allowed him to return to Mexico, claiming instead that the *Arab* had slipped in.

Santa Anna awaited further word from Farías. While he waited, the bombast of his most recent proclamation apparently captivated some of his countrymen. Suspicion waned to a degree, and more Mexicans began to consider Santa Anna an old hero returned.

25.

Your Governor

Through deep, dark gorges of the mountains of northern New Mexico, along flinty roads, the tired, hungry soldiers of the Army of the West plodded toward their meeting outside Santa Fe with the gathering forces of Manuel Armijo. Private John T. Hughes observed with sorrow the occasional, recently dug graves of soldiers who had died only hours earlier in the long column ahead.

Despite the hardships encountered in crossing the desert south of Bent's Fort, and despite the withering existence now on one-third rations, Hughes had not lost all of his romantic view of military life. He had seen hunger and had experienced exhaustion, but he had taken part in no fighting yet.

Nor had he lost his flair for rhetorical excess.

> Almost every day some dragoon or volunteer, trader, [or] team-ster . . . who had set out upon the expedition buoyant with life and flattered with hopes of future usefulness, actuated by a . . . desire to serve his country, found a grave. . . . To die in honorable warfare; to be struck down in the strife of battle; to perish on the field of honor; to sacrifice life for victory, is no hardship to the fallen brave; is no source of regret to surviving friends; for the remembrance of the noble deeds of the slain sweetens the cup of sorrow. But to see the gallant, the patriotic, the devoted soldier, sinking and wasting his energies under the slow, sure progress of disease . . . fills the heart with melancholy.

The hearts of many soldiers also filled with faster beats. The closer they came to Santa Fe, the nearer they came to battle.

In the vicinity of Santa Fe the first settlements appeared. They were located in lush valleys, amid neatly cultivated patches of corn and other crops. In distant glades Hughes saw only peaceful scenes: cattle, sheep, and goats grazing quietly. Farther beyond still, cedar- and pine-covered hills provided a quiet, cool, blue-green backdrop.

Amid this placidity a letter arrived from Governor Armijo, delivered to Colonel Kearny by a Mexican lieutenant and a detachment of lancers. It was a reply to Kearny's earlier communication carried to Armijo by Philip St. George Cooke.

Kearny could not understand the letter. Armijo promised to meet him, but whether "in council, or in conflict," the colonel could not determine because of Armijo's ambiguity.

Kearny's army was following a route that passed Santa Fe to the east before turning toward the town and coming upon it, through a mountain pass, from the southeast. After a hard twenty-five-mile march on August 14 the men—with ranks now closed up—encamped on a shady creek near Las Vegas, a village forty miles east of Santa Fe. Later that night two scouts went on to reconnoiter the blackness ahead, and when they returned at dawn of the fifteenth the camp awoke to excitement. The spies reported finding a Mexican force estimated at as many as two thousand men dug in at a pass several miles beyond Las Vegas.

Soon after receipt of that information there arrived, from the opposite direction, mail and official correspondence from Fort Leavenworth, brought by a group of hard riders. Among the dispatches was a promotion for Colonel Kearny to brigadier general, but the rest of the mail went unopened temporarily. In the excitement, Hughes said, "there was no time for reading letters and newspapers"—and possibly no desire, either.

The men formed in line of battle. Kearny placed at the front his dragoon regulars and a detachment of mounted volunteers from St. Louis. Next came the volunteer artillery, then Colonel Doniphan's regiment of mounted volunteers—including Hughes. The lumbering baggage and merchant wagons followed, escorted by a mounted rear guard. Deployed on each side of the line were two companies of volunteer infantry. The sun still lay low in the east, and the morning remained cool.

At Las Vegas Kearny halted briefly and assembled local officials and citizens. About eight o'clock that morning he climbed a rickety ladder to the top of a flat-roofed building overlooking a plaza and addressed the wondering villagers through an interpreter.

Mr. Alcalde, and the people of New Mexico: I have come amongst you by the orders of my Government, to take possession of your country, and extend over it the laws of the United States. We consider it, and have done so for some time, a part of the territory of the United States. We come amongst you as friends—not as enemies; as protectors—not as conquerors. We come among you for your benefit—not for your injury.

Henceforth I absolve you from all allegiance to the Mexican Government, and from all obedience to General Armijo. He is no longer your Governor; I am your Governor. I shall not expect you to take up arms and follow me; but I now tell you, that those who remain peaceably at home, attending to their crops and their herds, shall be protected by me, in their property, their persons, and their religion; and not a pepper, not an onion, shall be disturbed or taken by my troops, without pay, or [without] the consent of the owner. But listen! He who promises to be quiet and is found in arms against me, I will hang! . . .

Kearny also assured the people protection against marauding Indians. Then he administered to all of them an oath of allegiance to the United States, directing particular attention to the alcalde and to the two captains of local militia. To one officer who stared at the ground during the ceremony Kearny demanded, "Captain, look me in the face, while you repeat the oath. . . ." That completed, Kearny declared the alcalde and the two captains retained in their offices. The general descended the same rickety ladder and gave orders to move his men on toward the pass where the defending force had been reported.

Bugles sounded the advance. Men unfurled guidons and colors. Officers on horseback dashed along the lines, shouting commands and encouragement. Mounted troops urged their animals from walk to trot to gallop as they neared the pass, "nerved for the conflict." Into the gorge the horsemen thundered—and safely out of it, on the other side, without having seen any sign of an enemy. The defenders—if ever there had been any in the force estimated—had vanished hours earlier. Dust clouds raised by the charge settled on men and horses and, as the day became hotter, mixed with sweat to make a sticky coating.

About noon that same day General Kearny halted his army at the village of Tecolote and repeated the allegiance ceremony while his grimy men watched. That night, at an encampment within six miles of San Miguel, they found water for washing—and plenty of wood and grass.

The next day, August 16, Kearny continued his forced bestowal of citizenships at San Miguel, on the Pecos River. This time, however, he encountered some resistance, which Private Hughes observed and recorded.

> Gen. Kearny, assembling the citizens of the place . . . delivered to them a stern . . . speech, absolving them from any further allegiance to the Mexican government. When the general was about to compel them to swear fealty to our government on the sacred cross, the Alcalde and Priest objected. . . . They replied, that the oath he required them to take would . . . render them traitors to their country. . . . Gen. Kearny having promised protection to their persons and property, as to other citizens of the United States, and also having threatened to subvert the town unless they should submit, they were at length induced to take the oath.

Other citizens submitted more readily. Along the line of march appeared men, women, and children offering for sale a variety of foods: bread, milk, eggs, cheese, fruits, chickens, and vegetables. Most of the hungry soldiers spent what little money they had, or they traded for items, then marched on with empty pockets but with fuller stomachs.

Another patrol report excited the men. Scouts now said that Armijo and a large army were dug in ahead at *"el cañon"*—Apache Canyon, a long, narrow pass in the mountains near Santa Fe, on the road Kearny was traveling. The next few days seemed certain to be momentous ones.

August 16—Camp made on the Pecos River, with "bold springs of delicious water" gushing from nearby rocks. Later that night Kearny's picket guard captured three more Mexican spies.

August 17—Once again Kearny ordered the spies shown through camp, with emphasis on the area where the cannon lay waiting to be hitched to teams that would haul them farther toward Santa Fe. Then the general ordered the spies released, predicting that they, too, would exaggerate their estimates of his force—"a truly Mexican characteristic." After that a march of ten miles brought the army to a historic Pecos River Indian ruin, inhabited for centuries before wars and plagues finally forced the residents to move out—sometime during the preceding decade.

Beyond the ruin lay Apache Canyon and the awaited showdown with Armijo, but Kearny received word that the Mexican force, like the one that had "defended" the gorge near Las Vegas, had vanished into the landscape. A loud, fat local official astride a badly overworked mule rode up to the general, extended his hand in congratulation, and declared, "Armijo and his troops have gone to hell and the *cañon* is all clear."

August 18—Rain soaked clothing and made the rugged, rocky road toward Santa Fe slippery, but it did not dampen enthusiasm. Further intelligence had corroborated the Mexican official: the Army of the West apparently would enjoy an uncontested passage into the town. Internal disputes, the reports of those awed Mexican spies, or the persuasiveness of the old Santa Fe trader, James Magoffin—or a combination of the three—had subverted the defending army. Another possibility speculated on by many of Kearny's men was that Armijo never had wanted to fight anyway. Citizens reported that their once pompous governor had fled southward to safety, far from New Mexico and the allegiance-imposing Kearny.

Only the weakened condition of the animals and an awful road stood in the way of Kearny's quick entrance into Santa Fe, twenty-nine winding miles distant as the August 18 march began. About noon the advance, still ready for battle if it should develop, sloshed into Apache Canyon and proved the accuracy of the reports about Armijo's flight.

Riding through the gorge, Hughes looked over the site and wondered at the Mexicans' lack of steadfastness. Around a narrow chasm that led through a mountain ridge the Mexicans had chopped down trees and thrown up breastworks so that artillery could command any attack. Then they had disappeared ingloriously. Hughes scoffed that "an army of near seven thousand Mexicans, with six pieces of cannon, and vastly the advantage of the ground, permitted Gen. Kearny, with less than two thousand Americans, to pass through the narrow defile and march right on to the capital of the State."

Another soldier wrote, "It is a gateway, which, in the hands of a skilled engineer and one hundred resolute men, would have been perfectly impregnable."

Kearny pushed on, intending to occupy Santa Fe that same day, but debilitation and the condition of the road began to show. Men, animals, and wagons lagged farther and farther behind. Eventually the rear lay more than three hours behind the van, and some scattered wagons could be found lumbering on farther back than that.

A few miles outside Santa Fe two Mexican officials met Kearny and delivered a letter of welcome from the lieutenant governor, Juan Bautista Vigil y Aland. At three o'clock the advance entered town. Soon after that American soldiers hoisted a United States flag over the Palace of the Governors, a long building facing the public plaza, while Kearny's artillery roared a salute from a height overlooking the town. The clouds had broken—an "omen" that a patriot like Hughes would have noticed with satisfaction.

General Kearny, who in the next few days would administer his oath of allegiance to Santa Feans and commence organizing a government with himself at its head, that night enjoyed a dinner given by leading citizens for him and his staff. Meanwhile, in the darkness around town, Kearny's soldiers, "overcome by fatigue," dropped wearily to the wet ground and slept, most of them having eaten no hot food during the day. That night, along the road into Santa Fe, straggling wagons still creaked and groaned through the blackness. Some did not arrive until the following day.

". . . Near nine hundred miles in less than fifty days," Hughes wrote of the grueling march. General Kearny deserved his reputation as a hard driver. But pride and a sense of accomplishment governed Hughes's feelings. The schoolteacher turned soldier had helped to take "peaceable and undisputed possession of the country." The only cannon fired had been those saluting the bloodless victory—the takeover of Santa Fe and of all New Mexico.

26.

Opportunity

Late that summer of 1846 the war had been progressing favorably for the United States, but Americans at home did not know it. Communication delays left them unaware of the occupation of California, of the bloodless conquest of New Mexico, and of the date of an impending movement toward the Mexican interior by Zachary Taylor. The most recent word of any major military activity in the field concerned the battles of Palo Alto and Resaca de la Palma, and those had occurred months earler—in May. So, although no one at home knew it, Polk's plan to take and to occupy the northern provinces (as long as he could not buy a peace), then to use these conquests as a bargaining lever for negotiating the permanent acquisition of Upper California and New Mexico, already had made progress.

Another part of that same plan was to be an occupation of the city of Chihuahua by an army under the command of Brigadier General John E. Wool, a sixty-two-year-old martinet who was told to assemble his force at San Antonio, Texas, and to march it westward across a dry, prickly wasteland to its destination nearly five hundred straight-line miles away. No one in authority knew how or whether Wool could provide food and water for his army on its march into desolation, but Wool had orders to try. Polk and his planners in Washington operated mostly with any old books and maps of Mexico they could find.

Wool had not yet begun his march, however, and in the absence of other favorable war news people were becoming restless and critical—including many who had favored the war from the very first. In Washington congressional leaders of the Whig opposition turned the supposed stagnation further against the President, labeling the Mexican conflict "Polk's War" and blaming him for countless irresponsibilities and mistakes.

At Fort Hamilton, New York, Captain Robert E. Lee had grown restless along with everyone else, but not in the same way. By August 19 the war was officially three months and six days old, and Lee had received no indication of having been considered for a role in it.

One week earlier, on the far side of the continent, Commodore Stockton and his sailors, reinforced by Frémont and his men, had taken peaceful possession of Los Angeles (but without Lee's knowledge, of course). Three days earlier, at torrid Vera Cruz on the Gulf of Mexico, Santa Anna had landed, with Polk's help, ostensibly to assist the United States in making a war settlement. Only one day earlier, General Kearny's Army of the West had rumbled down that mountain pass into Santa Fe. And on that same August 19, nearly two thousand miles southwest of Fort Hamilton, Zachary Taylor began moving his army out of the Rio Grande town of Camargo toward the Mexican interior and the immediate target, Monterrey.

Polk's pincer had begun working indeed, whether or not people in the United States knew it, and apparently it would continue operation without the services of the dedicated captain of engineers who had compiled such a remarkable record at West Point.

At Fort Hamilton August 19 came in with another stint of dull work in store for Lee. Later in the day, however, he opened a letter from the army chief of engineers and saw to his delight a set of orders. Turn over the work at The Narrows to a designated officer, the orders read, and proceed via Washington to San Antonio, where he was to report to General Wool for service in Mexico.

Opportunity thus came to Robert E. Lee, the man whose integrity, honor, and ability already had been recognized by most persons who knew him. Lee's Whiggish tendencies and his opposition to war as a method of solving disputes would be forgotten in this call to duty. He wrote, regarding the Mexican conflict, "It is rather late . . . to discuss the origin of the war; that ought to have been understood before we engaged in it. It may have been produced by the act of either party or the force of circumstances. Let the pedants of diplomacy determine. . . ." So Lee joined many other officers of the U. S. Army—Colonel Ethan Allen Hitchcock and Lieutenant Sam Grant, to name only two—who felt impelled to fight, despite some prior judgments to the contrary. They all provided fuel for the wrath of Henry David Thoreau, already a bitter critic of the conflict, who had been jailed for failure to pay a tax that Thoreau contended would support an unjust war. Thoreau wrote in his classic essay *Civil Disobedience:*

> Law never made men a whit more just; and by means of their respect for it, even the well disposed are daily made the agents of injustice. A common and natural result of an undue respect for law is that you may see a file of soldiers—colonel, captain, corporal, privates, powder monkeys, and all—marching in admirable order over hill and dale to the wars, against their wills, ay, against their common sense and consciences, which makes very steep marching indeed, and produces a palpitation of the heart. They have no doubt that it is a damnable business in which they are concerned; they are all peaceably inclined. Now, what are they? Men at all? or small movable forts and magazines, at the service of some unscrupulous man in power? . . .

Captain Lee, unlike other officers, took no advantage of a delay that orders to new duty might allow. He turned over the work at Fort Hamilton to his designated relief, packed, and traveled to Washington. There he spent a few days with his family in the mansion overlooking the Potomac, made business visits into the capital, and drew up his will. From Washington he took passage on the first available steamer down Chesapeake Bay and around the Florida Keys to New Orleans, then traveled to Port Lavaca, Texas, where he disembarked and rode horseback to San Antonio. He reported to General Wool September 21—only a month and two days after having been detached from duty at Fort Hamilton.

At San Antonio Lee found a different world: a town of perhaps a thousand inhabitants, most of them Spanish-speaking, who lived in residences ranging from flat-roofed, thick-walled, grill-windowed rock or adobe houses that fended off a searing sun and kept interiors cool, to insignificant huts made of mesquite posts chinked with clay and topped with roofs of tule—a bulrush that thrived in marshy land nearby.

When Lee arrived the summer heat was intense enough to bake the bare earth of the plazas into a dry powder, but life in the town could be comfortable enough if one stayed out of the midday sun. San Antonio had been built along the banks of a river that rose from a cluster of cool, clear springs several miles above town and provided a more even flow of water than that available to most other Texas streams. The river nourished a gentle valley that lay green along its banks, and it had brought water to a string of missions established by Spaniards years earlier.

One of the missions was the crumbled Alamo, only ten years removed from its bloody fall to the soldiers of Santa Anna when Lee first saw it. Other sights of San Antonio would have impressed him—especially the *señoritas*, who spoke in that lilting Spanish tongue while their magnificent black eyes flashed. Lee always had a quick eye for attractive women, even if he only looked.

Lee's chief interest, however, would have been the Army. In San Antonio when he arrived there were gathered between three and four thousand soldiers, all excitedly preparing for their coming adventure in Mexico. They crowded the dusty streets and plazas, drank away afternoon boredom, and later sought the companionship of those women with the flashing black eyes.

Lee had work to do. General Wool assigned him and another engineer the job of collecting as many tools as they could find for use in road and bridge construction. The general's intention was to march his men southwestward from San Antonio, cross the Rio Grande two hundred or so miles north of Camargo, and head for Chihuahua while, to southward, Taylor struck at Monterrey. Wool would be operating under Taylor's orders in this campaign, but communication being what it was, success or failure would fall mostly on Wool.

Professional failure was something that had never yet befallen Lee, and the captain did not intend this to happen. Nevertheless, Lee never had been genuinely tested in those military tactics he had begun studying twenty-one years earlier. Nearing the age of forty, Lee was beginning his first campaign against an enemy. He would not command artillery or troops in battle, but he would prepare a road into the heart of Mexico. He hoped to make it passable.

27.

Miserable Men and Suffering Animals

On that road into Mexico, though not on Robert E. Lee's immediate route, lay Monterrey. On September 19—two days before Lee reported to General Wool at San Antonio—Zachary Taylor's army, more than six thousand strong, had come in sight of the city.

Monterrey was located in a fertile valley set among the foothills of the Sierra Madre Range, and on the north bank of a river called the Santa Catarina. The city and its twelve thousand inhabitants stood in the way of any advance on Saltillo, and in the way of any march by this route into the heartland of Mexico. Taylor's current plans, however, were simply to capture Monterrey and Saltillo, then to join with General Wool—after Wool had captured Chihuahua—in holding a line across northern Mexico.

Accompanying Taylor's army were those two young veterans of the battles of Palo Alto and Resaca de la Palma—Lieutenant Sam Grant of the infantry and Lieutenant Sam French of the artillery. Another veteran, Captain Ephraim Kirby Smith of the infantry, had obtained a sixty-day leave, in the supposed absence of forthcoming action, to visit relatives in the United States after learning of the sudden death of his father. And the veteran of Taylor's original landing on the Texas shore, Colonel Ethan Allen Hitchcock, had not returned from the United States, where he had gone to recover his health.

Taylor's movement toward Monterrey had been slow in developing. After the Mexicans evacuated Matamoros, following their defeats at Palo Alto and Resaca de la Palma, Taylor had moved his men across the Rio Grande and had occupied that town, in May. He had remained in the summer clamminess of Matamoros for nearly two months, collecting more men and supplies—the latter always sent in insufficient quantity—and allowing himself to pay increasing attention to presidential talk.

With the two recent victories Taylor had become the nation's first genuine military hero in years. Newspapers lauded him, and the clippings reached him in stacks, which he read through with delight. A delegation from Louisiana, where Taylor maintained residence, arrived to heap upon him honors and praise. At home, Taylor had attracted many Whigs as a possible candidate for 1848. The man whose unpretentiousness as a general had resulted in the creation of countless anecdotes now had begun to have some illusions about his future role. Zachary Taylor, who led his soldiers mostly by inspiration only and who knew nothing at all about the administration of government, had begun to see himself as President.

The power involved in that office happened to appeal to him particularly at this time. Taylor was receiving thousands of volunteer soldiers, but not enough supplies. He had come to believe that this, too, was a Washington plot to create inefficiency for which he could be blamed—thus extinguishing his political star. But Taylor could not realize the heavy demands then being placed on the army quartermaster general—no more than Washington could realize some of Taylor's problems in distant Mexico.

The volunteers themselves had become problem enough. They had flocked to Taylor's headquarters from many areas in the United States. Gaudily uniformed in red, green, yellow—in almost every color except the regulars' "sky blue"—and in many different styles, their behavior often became as wild as their dress. Many of these volunteers, like others in United States history, had enlisted for excitement and fun. Far away from home, they took advantage of their anonymity, and in the absence of fighting (as had been their lot while waiting at Matamoros) they turned to other diversions to pass the time. Matamoros catered to them happily, providing saloons, gambling halls, and brothels, and giving them an idea that all Mexico was there for revelry. Rape became a growing crime in Taylor's army. Of all the volunteers the Texans generally seemed to be the most vicious. They had suffered Mexican atrocities in the past and did not intend to turn their cheeks.

Word of the volunteers' behavior drifted back to Washington and brought harried General Taylor more trouble. He received orders to

discipline the soldiers. Taylor angrily replied: stop sending so many un-
trained volunteers. With all these frustrations in Mexico, then, Taylor
was beginning to see the advantage of being the high man in Washington.

The army regular was a more dependable soldier. Besides being better
trained for his job, he took his home with him wherever he went. For
the serious professional, service in Mexico was not much different from
service in the United States. If he wanted to keep the present as comfortable as possible and to keep the future bright, he would need to
keep his record in good order. When Taylor began his move against
Monterrey he had planned to take as many regulars as possible. Garrison
forces left behind would be composed mostly of volunteers—usually
to the grief of native residents.

Early in July Taylor had begun moving his army from Matamoros
to Camargo, a hundred miles or more up the Rio Grande. Some men
made the trip by boat, the rest in overland marches—with fife and drum
playing "The Girl I Left Behind Me" as they marched out of Matamoros.
Sam Grant and Sam French traveled by land, and both remembered the
journey as being hot and dry beyond description. The sunny afternoon
became so punishing that officers quickly decided to march their men by
moonlight and to rest them by day.

At Camargo had come another delay—a tragic one. The town, built
on the San Juan River about three miles from its confluence with the
Rio Grande, proved to be extremely unhealthful. Two months earlier
Camargo had suffered a great flood that had forced inhabitants to flee.
Now many of those people had returned. The stench from mire left by
the floodwater had almost vanished, but much sun-baked mud had disin-
tegrated into a powder that seeped into shoes, clothing, supplies—everything. Large rocks scattered around the camp site reflected the sun's rays;
this in turn compounded the heat. Any relief provided by cool Gulf
breezes or mountain heights lay many miles away.

Even worse for the men was the absence of sanitation. Their general
was himself a hardy survivor of years of rough military life, and he paid
scant attention to the few health precautions then known. Troops relied
on the San Juan River, which meandered alongside their strung-out
camp, for washing, bathing, and drinking. Diarrhea, dysentery, and other
illnesses claimed hundreds of lives; death estimates exceeded a thousand.
The grim "Dead March" played by sweating military bands en route to
burials in the sandy chaparral country outside camp echoed in survivors'

ears long afterward. Eventually the number of deaths forced abandonment of most funeral formalities.

But the troops had continued to flow into sickly Camargo. As many as fifteen thousand were quartered there. Among them were numerous illegally enlisted six-month volunteers, and something had to be done with them. Officers exhorted the men to re-enlist for twelve months, but most refused. When one large group returned to Matamoros for transportation home a disgusted regular officer remarked, "The government . . . lost the service of six hundred men, for whom they have incurred the expense of clothing, subsistence, and transportation and have not received one iota of service in return. Within one hundred and fifty miles of the enemy, where the great majority of the army expected battle, they took their discharge. . . . I thought the patriotism of the Americans was so strong, that in the face of the enemy they . . . would have enlisted for twelve months. Experience has proved their patriotism not equal to their self-interest."

After an agonizing month at Camargo everyone was eager to leave— in one direction or another. General Taylor had dispatched scouts to find the best route to Monterrey and had decided on one that lay near the Rio Grande for another thirty miles or so to the town of Mier, where the river made an abrupt northerly turn. At Mier the army would leave the Rio Grande and cut southwestward across a wasteland that separated them from their objective.

This desolation appeared so forbidding that Taylor decided to leave most of his heavy artillery at Camargo. He would take only a 10-inch mortar, two 24-pound howitzers, and light artillery. This would not be adequate for a siege, but at least the guns could make the trip. With Braxton Bragg's battery of light artillery would go Lieutenant Sam French.

Lieutenant Sam Grant figured in the solution of another of Taylor's logistical problems. With summer ending, the pressure for movement increasing, and Monterrey still lying safely ensconced in mountains across a desert, the general was eager to advance, but he did not have enough wagons—another lack he blamed on Washington. Rather than wait for delivery of more of the vehicles, he decided to use pack mules—nineteen hundred of them—managed by Mexican muleteers hired for twenty-five dollars a month. The animals appeared to be better suited to the terrain anyway.

The muleteers and their beasts needed official supervision, and someone remembered Sam Grant's knack with animals. Furthermore, he was known as the son of a businessman and presumably would be able to handle accounting, too. Grant, then, would be the logical choice for a new position to be known as regimental quartermaster—of his 4th Infantry Regiment. In addition to supervising the pack train he would be responsible for paying the men, purchasing supplies for their messes, and buying fodder for the animals. As supposed consolation for these ignominious duties Grant would be excused from fighting during any battles. He could stay in the rear, with the train. To a sensitive young West Pointer such a reward could only have meant further ignominy (although other Military Academy graduates besides Grant received similar assignments).

The reluctance Lieutenant Grant had once felt about fighting had been waning for months now, anyway. Experience in two battles had given him confidence. The very last reluctance would have vanished with this assignment—a commissioned officer given the task of feeding and paying men and nursing mules! Grant protested and asked to be left with his company, but his request was not granted. When Taylor began moving his army out of Camargo, Grant supervised the loading of stubborn pack mules for the 4th Infantry.

The movement had begun on August 19, with the units advancing at widely separated intervals—a customary practice in those days. Leading off were two divisions composed largely of regulars, the first one commanded by William Worth, now a brevet major general, the second by David Twiggs, recently brevetted a brigadier general. Their detachments included dragoons, infantry, and artillery. Following those two columns came a volunteer division led by Brevet Major General William O. Butler, a political appointee to command, with infantry, artillery, and (loosely attached) two regiments of mounted Texas Ranger volunteers—one commanded by Sam Walker, the man who had communicated with Major Jacob Brown at Fort Texas for General Taylor during the siege, and the other led by Jack Hays, a shy, undersized, boyish-looking officer with a sad, silent face on which no beard would grow. Also in Butler's division, as commander of the 1st Mississippi Regiment, was Colonel Jefferson Davis, a West Point graduate who had resigned his commission to become a cotton planter and a congressman—and who had subsequently resigned from Congress to return to the Army during the trouble with Mexico. Ten years earlier he had married Zachary Taylor's daughter, but soon after the wedding she had died, and Davis had remarried.

Not until early September—almost three weeks after commencement of the advance—did the last man depart Camargo for Monterrey. Because of the difficulty of transporting supplies Taylor had been forced to limit the size of his attacking army to between six and seven thousand men. He had included all those regulars, who made up about half of the total. Left behind as a garrison force at Camargo were several thousand embittered volunteers.

Word of the overthrow of the Paredes government in Mexico City and the return of Santa Anna reached the advancing Americans about this time. To some of the soldiers this had the appearance of prospective peace, but at least one man asked, "With whom are we to negotiate? The president of today is a prisoner tomorrow."

From Camargo to Mier—up the valley of the Rio Grande—they marched, then southwestward across monotonous dry plains toward Cerralvo. The sun brought out sweat early every day, leaving uniforms soaked and smelly. The primitive transportation—those mules—added to general frustration. Neither officers nor enlisted men were allowed to pack their tents or other gear; that responsibility was left to the "experts"—the Mexican muleteers. "I am perfectly disgusted with this . . . transportation," one officer wrote. ". . . The *arrieros* must have daylight to pack, and the result is, the command is forced to march during the heat of the day, or the train must be left behind, thereby running the risk of its being attacked and cut off." Only eight mules were needed to carry the equipment of an infantry company, but lucky was the company that could locate its mules promptly at the end of a day and retrieve articles necessary for camping.

Years later both Sam Grant and Sam French remembered vividly experiences with the pesky animals. Grant wrote:

> The troops would take up their march at an early hour each day. After they had started, the tents and cooking utensils had to be made into packages, so that they could be lashed to the backs of the mules. Sheet-iron kettles, tent-poles and mess chests were inconvenient articles to transport . . . that way. It took several hours to get ready to start each morning, and by the time we were ready some of the mules first loaded would be tired of standing so long with their loads on their backs. Sometimes one would start to run, bowing his back and kicking up until he scattered his load; others would lie down and try to disarrange their loads by attempting to get on . . . top of them by rolling [over]; others with tent-poles for part of their loads would manage to run a . . . pole on one side of a sapling

while they would take the other. I am not aware of ever having used a profane expletive in my life; but I would have the charity to excuse those who may have done so, if they were in charge of a train of Mexican pack mules at the time.

French, who as a proud young artillery officer was detailed one morning to help load the mule train, described this humiliating event.

> After the muleteers had packed the old trained mules and started them one after another on their way, there remained a number of wild mules. . . . One was lassoed and thrown and the pack saddle [attached]. Then, for his load, two barrels of crackers were securely put on. All being ready, the blind was removed from his eyes. He looked slowly around, showed the white of his eyes, took one step, humped himself, and kicked so high that the load overbalanced him and he fell on his back unable to rise, and brayed. . . . Soon a blind was removed from another; he surveyed the load from right to left with rolling eyes, squatted low, humped himself, sprang forward, stood on his forefeet and commenced high kicking, [exploding] the barrels of "hardtack" with his heels . . . and ran away with the empty barrels dangling behind, as badly scared as a dog with tin buckets tied to his tail. A third, when his blind was removed, stepped lightly to the front, but casting his eyes on either side, made a loud bray, closed down his tail, and disappeared through the chaparral [like] a jack rabbit, followed with loud Mexican denunciations.

Between Mier and Cerralvo a range of blue mountains came into view far to the west: the Sierra Madres, with their distant, jagged peaks silhouetted against the sky. But between the advancing army and the mountains lay miles of dreary chaparral country to be crossed and numerous villages with those flat-roofed adobe houses to be passed. Many of the hamlets lay deserted before Taylor's advance—a vanguard of mounted Texas Rangers having frightened the people away. At others, inhabitants ventured forth to sell fruit, milk, and tortillas. Sometimes detachments of Mexican cavalry appeared far ahead, but they always disappeared before real contact could be made. Behind the Mexican cavalry, in Monterrey, a force under the command of General Ampudia of Matamoros acquaintance was reported to be large in numbers, but General Taylor felt he would not face much resistance.

In the highlands of Nuevo Léon the sky became clearer, the air purer and more bracing, and the infirmities of Camargo mostly forgotten. Fresh streams gave good water. Cerralvo, a neat town located in a cultivated valley, straddled a swift stream that carried water by irrigation ditches into house yards.

Farther on—twenty-four miles northeast of Monterrey—lay Marin, a small town surrounded by mountains. As the men marched along its deserted streets during the evening of September 15 a deathlike silence greeted them. The inhabitants and a detachment of Mexican cavalry had fled at their approach, and now, in the empty town, one American officer mused over Napoleon's probable feelings while riding through the deserted streets of Moscow. When the army marched straight through town and began encamping on the other side of Marin, however, the people began returning, some leading pigs on leashes, others driving goats, some riding three deep on the backs of horses and mules. Numerous residents found their homes had been plundered by Mexican troops during all the confusion and "were loud in their denunciations of their own soldiers."

After a two-day delay to concentrate forces for the final advance on Monterrey the army moved again, on the morning of September 18. Up a gently rolling valley with a backdrop of mountain cliffs pinked by the rising sun, across swift streams that made wading uncomfortably cold so early in the day, past a large hacienda whose inhabitants had the temerity to come out and stare. Another encampment; then—during the approach to Monterrey—past large farms with luxuriant fields of corn and other grain and sugar cane.

In view ahead lay the sunlit city, looking like a sparkling miniature from this dazzling distance: white stone houses, flat-roofed as usual, built in irregular rectangles along narrow streets that led out from a large plaza and several smaller ones. In the center of town could be seen a large cathedral with two towers.

The city had been built on the north and west bank of the Santa Catarina River, another of those swiftly flowing mountain streams and a tributary of the San Juan, on which the army had encamped at Camargo. After flowing past Monterrey in a west-to-east direction the river made an abrupt northerly turn at the outskirts, so that it barred approaches from south and east. Beyond the river to the south and beyond the city to the west loomed more mountains—formidable ones—reflecting the light of the morning sun.

To the defenders and inhabitants of Monterrey Taylor's appearance came as no surprise. The invaders had been expected for weeks—even months.

Among the Mexican soldiers garrisoning the city were some veterans of the Palo Alto-Resaca de la Palma fighting who had been ordered to Monterrey soon after their evacuation from Matamoros. Those defeated men had been withdrawn first to Linares, not quite two hundred miles southwest of Matamoros and about half that distance southeast of Monterrey. At Linares their embarrassed general, José Mariano Arista, had been relieved of command in favor of Francisco Mejía, but not before Arista had sent a section of engineers and a battalion of sappers from his army (or what remained of it) on to Monterrey, with orders to help strengthen fortifications there.

Demoralization of the Palo Alto-Resaca de la Palma veterans remained at the level to which it had crumbled. Among the eighteen hundred officers and men left from that once large army there was much dissension and bitterness. Alibiing and blame-fixing following the defeats had split the officer corps into bitter little groups, and this rancor had pervaded enlisted ranks, too. The hasty change of command to Mejía, ordered by irate officials in Mexico City, only compounded the demoralization.

The dissension had moved with the soldiers into Monterrey. There they joined with other Mexican forces ready to contest what everyone knew would be the Americans' next attempt at conquest. More orders from Mexico City, however, had resulted in further resentment. General Pedro de Ampudia, the man who boiled decapitated heads in oil, had been named governor and general-in-chief, and he seemed to have been no more popular in Monterrey than in Matamoros.

Frantic preparations to receive the Americans with the storm of shot everyone thought they deserved had taken minds off dissensions for a time. Inspired by newly energetic officers, soldiers had thrown themselves into strengthening the many bastions that protected the city. Citizens had donated food, money, and encouragement.

Nevertheless, the Americans had continued their inexorable advance on Monterrey ("with their characteristic energy," a Mexican writer observed), and as information about their progress spread among the soldiers and the populace old doubts surfaced again. Ampudia seemed to have no real plan of operation. Antipathies between the general-in-chief and his senior officers destroyed confidence further and spread more uncertainty. Not even the blaring of military bands and a surge of patriotism on the evening of September 15 in commemoration of

Mexican independence made much difference. Taylor was closing in on Monterrey with an army that had already been victorious in two battles.

Some families abandoned their homes for safety elsewhere. A contemporary Mexican account described scenes of "grief, tenderness, and disinterested generosity." Youths helped aged relatives out of the city. Fathers carried infants in their arms. Tears of good-by flowed almost like the nearby Santa Catarina that gushed from out of the mountains to the west. Monterrey citizens were making their sacrifices in the continuing attempt to stop the despised Americans (the Mexican writer added), although they "owed so little to the opulent and disdainful Mexico [City]. They offered themselves as a sublime expiation for all our crimes, that the [United States] flag should not profane our capital. . . ."

By the morning of September 19 the Americans finally had reached a location just outside the entrance to the city. Mexican cavalry pickets engaged in a brief skirmish with the invaders, then galloped into Monterrey shouting alarms.

Drums rolled and bugles blared. Soldiers ran for their weapons and for their places in formation. Military bands commenced playing, but their music was almost drowned by thunderous, excited *vivas* and by the confused noise of an army forming to fight. Many male civilians remaining in Monterrey filled the streets, ready to defend their city with various antiquated weapons they now carried. Terrified women and children added their screams to the din. Maybe the welter of sounds could ward off the danger.

Monterrey was now ready for the combat certain to come. Only those who had experienced war could have appreciated its brutality.

Outside the city, the Americans continued to advance.

General Taylor sent a detachment of mounted Texans ahead toward the city to probe. In the distance smoke appeared in a small puff that billowed. A shot arced toward the horsemen, and an ominous rumble followed. Another cannon hurled a challenge, then another. Taylor's men crept forward for a better view, but officers ordered them back. Eventually the general put them all into camp (with orders to stay there for now), located in a magnificent grove of moss-curtained oak and pecan trees at a site that became known, erroneously, as Walnut Springs. But the water was indeed there. It gushed cool and clear from a nearby slope.

The site looked like one for a picnic, but Monterrey lay two or three miles distant to the south, and Taylor must now learn more about it.

Engineers and dragoons returned for another reconnaissance, captured a few Mexicans, and obtained detailed information. Soon after that every man of Taylor's force knew beyond any doubt that Monterrey had been well fortified and would be a formidable objective.

Along the city's northeastern rim—the section facing Walnut Springs —lay a series of forts and gun emplacements. These were made more difficult to reach by a frontal terrain of orchards and tall crops of corn, cotton, sugar cane, and grain that (despite offering some advantages for an attack) blocked visibility and threw up other natural obstacles for an assault over that ground. The forts, from right to left as they appeared from Walnut Springs (and as referred to by the Americans), were these:

The Citadel, built around a large unfinished church building now heavily fortified, standing two thousand yards from the encampment and in the way of further direct advance by Taylor. Weather had darkened the huge stone walls, and Taylor's men gave the bastion a nickname befitting its ominous appearance: Black Fort. Long protective earthworks twice as tall as a man surrounded the place. Outward from the earthworks lay a moat, unfinished, intended to be twelve feet deep. The Citadel mounted twelve guns that commanded a large area north of the city. Three of those guns had been the first to fire at Taylor's advance.

El Rincón del Diablo (or Devil's Corner), a three-gun redoubt garrisoned by 150 men, built in the northeastern part of town near the Santa Catarina River. In its front lay a deep ravine that cut west to east through the northern suburbs of Monterrey before entering the river here; so the approach to the post was protected on the east by the Santa Catarina and on the north (to some extent) by the ravine.

La Tenería, lying just outside the northeastern corner of the city six hundred yards northeast of El Rincón del Diablo—and on the north side of that ravine. Here a stone building formerly housing a tannery had been converted into a fort for two hundred men. Its four guns had not been emplaced until Taylor's appearance, when they were quickly hauled up and mounted atop piles of earth. La Tenería, too, occupied the west bank of the Santa Catarina; so its eastward approach had the protection of that river.

Smaller works also had been prepared at strategic locations throughout the northeastern part of the city—for instance, at the stone Purísima

Bridge, which represented the principal crossing of the ravine that cut through the northern suburbs. North of the bridge a 12-pounder cannon had been emplaced; east of it, two more guns—all with crews strongly supported by infantrymen.

The forts thus barred entrance into Monterrey from the north and east. To the east also was that river, running three feet deep and swiftly this September. To the south lay the same river, before making its abrupt turn; beyond the river, mountains; and probably interspersed somewhere in that direction, more forts as yet undiscovered. From which direction should the attack be launched?

Westward seemed to offer little possibility. In that direction loomed more mountains—and from that direction wound the fortified road from Saltillo, which lay along the north bank of the Santa Catarina as it tumbled noisily from out of the mountains toward Monterrey. Ampudia's supplies must come from Saltillo; the road was vital. The fortifications reflected that importance.

Located on each side of the road as it entered Monterrey—and roughly paralleling it—were two long, commanding heights: Independence Hill north of the road and Federation Hill south of it. Each height had been armed for defense. On a section of eight-hundred-foot-high Independence Hill that sloped toward the city stood thick-stoned Bishop's Palace (*El Obispado*), rebuilt long ago as a fort and reinforced now by a redoubt located east of it on the same hill. On Federation Hill, half as tall as Independence, a redoubt to the west and Fort Soldado to the east stood guard over the river and the road.

So a western approach seemed to be as impractical as any. Worse, first intelligence about military capabilities inside the city itself proved discouraging. Defending Monterrey, those reports said, were seven thousand regular troops supported by three thousand irregulars. Available to this force were more than forty cannon and plenty of ammunition, which had been stored for greatest safety in the large cathedral downtown. Among the defenders were Irish Catholic members of that "San Patricio Battalion" who earlier had been persuaded to desert Taylor's army for religious reasons. Now they prepared to hurl death on their former companions.

Intelligence further reported the city itself to be easily adapted to stout defense. Stone houses had been built with openings through which weapons could be aimed and fired. Parapets surrounded many of the

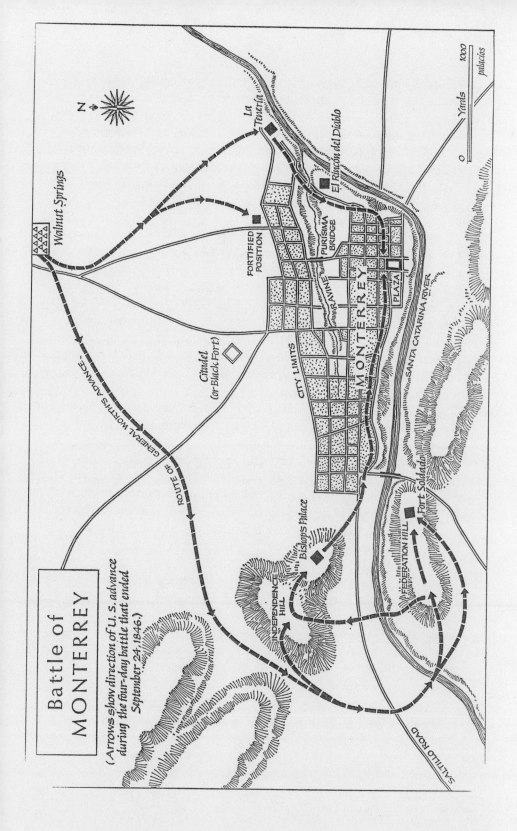

Battle of MONTERREY

(Arrows show direction of U. S. advance during the four-day battle that ended September 24, 1846.)

N

Walnut Springs

La Teneria

El Rincón del Diablo

FORTIFIED POSITION

PURISIMA BRIDGE

RAVINE

PLAZA

MONTERREY

CITY LIMITS

SANTA CATARINA RIVER

Citadel (or Black Fort)

GENERAL WORTH'S ADVANCE

ROUTE OF

Bishops Palace

INDEPENDENCE HILL

FEDERATION HILL

Fort Soldado

SALTILLO ROAD

0   Yards   1000

palacios

flat roofs, providing more opportunity for a defending force to take deadly aim. The narrow streets could be effectively barricaded.

". . . All is anxiety and excitement—storming parties—taking batteries —crossing ditches—all the subjects of conversation," an officer wrote. ". . . The city appears well fortified; and their heavy guns give them a great advantage over us, our small pieces being of no use in battering down their walls. All we have to do is to *take theirs*, and use them against themselves. . . . The general impression is, that the struggle will be fierce, but soon over."

Lieutenant French looked to his guns; they would be in use soon. Lieutenant Grant looked to his mules; if his job seemed inglorious it also had obvious importance. Supplies for an army that had marched this far into Mexico and now faced "a perfect Gibraltar" were as important as the army itself. Grant looked on as the muleteers rounded up their balky animals and unloaded them, then he settled down to stay for a while. He had been "ordered to remain in charge of camp and the public property at Walnut Springs." Around him, soldiers set up canvas tents in neat rows. Everyone wondered what General Taylor was planning to do.

Taylor now had the benefit of some fresh information. An officer of the engineers had discovered a way around those giant guns of the Citadel, so that American troops could safely reach foothills lying along the mountains to the west. The men could even get to the Saltillo road behind Independence Hill, the engineer believed, and thus could cut off Monterrey. The officer had studied that hill during his probe and thought an attack on it might be possible from the rear. The incline was steep, but no guns appeared to have been implanted on the summit immediately above. The Mexicans apparently believed that no attacker would be mad enough to try to scale those cliffs.

While French and Grant waited for something to happen, Taylor began musing over the best way to storm Monterrey. European military manuals would have told him that an attacker ideally needed a four-to-one advantage in manpower for a situation like this—certainly not inferior numbers as Taylor possessed—but this general was not an avid reader of European military manuals or of any other books. He had been commissioned before the U. S. Military Academy opened its doors to teach any tactics at all—had learned what tactics he knew through those experiences in the War of 1812 and in Indian fighting. Taylor preferred to feel his way through most battles—conducting them by hunch and crunch, climaxed by that final inspiration that he could ignite among his troops—and if he made mistakes, which he indeed did, he had been lucky or knowledgeable enough in the past to come out mostly victorious.

The battle for Monterrey would be conducted the same Taylor way. He determined to ignore further those odds greatly in favor of the besieged force by dividing his own army—small though it already was for the job at hand—and sending a large part of it around the Citadel southwestward, the way the engineer officer had suggested. Thus dividing his army deep in enemy territory violated another military rule, of course, but Taylor knew the Mexican penchant for fighting from behind barricades and walls. He did not expect them to come out and challenge. Furthermore, Taylor's observations of Mexican military ability thus far did not persuade him that the task of going after them would be an overwhelming one, despite all those fortifications.

Early in the afternoon of Sunday, September 20, Taylor started General Worth and his division of regulars, supplemented by light artillery and a detachment of mounted Texas Rangers, westward from Walnut Springs, away from the Citadel guns. Worth's force comprised little more than two thousand men—five hundred of them the mounted Rangers. Outside camp they encountered chaparral thickets and fields of dry cornstalks. Slowly they pushed through the parched vegetation, leaving behind crumpled stalks and bushes. At the deepest ditches and dry ravines engineers were forced to prepare makeshift bridges for the guns, slowing the advance further.

French and Grant watched the departure from different vantage points. The Texas Rangers rode ahead of the movement. They were heavily armed but wore no uniforms. Most of them had grown handlebar mustaches and flowing beards. They were daring young men astride fast, muscled ponies.

Inside the city and on Independence Hill to the west of it a burst of activity told Taylor's observers that the Mexicans had seen Worth's departure, too, and already had guessed its purpose. They had begun rushing reinforcements westward—and atop Independence, the hill with that unfortified cliff at the westernmost end, artillerymen hurried to emplace cannon that a more foresighted commander would have put there earlier. On Federation Hill, too, there was activity, but because of the greater height of intervening Independence, Taylor's men could not see it. On the western edge of Federation the Mexicans positioned a 9-pounder cannon.

All this activity worried Taylor. He ordered his remaining troops into view, to let General Ampudia know he still faced a strong threat from the northeast. Cannon from the Citadel roared at the display, but the random shots caused no damage. After dark the soldiers returned to Walnut Springs and slept on beds of Spanish moss—except for the men of Lieutenant Grant's 4th Infantry Regiment, who had been ordered to stand guard on a plain near the city while artillerymen used darkness to set up Taylor's few heavy cannon in a depression that seemed likely to afford some protection for gun crews. The pieces—including the old mortar that one man said looked like "some . . . witch's soup-pot," and the two 24-pound howitzers—would roar at the Citadel, fifteen hundred yards away, on the following morning.

But that night only the patter of a gentle rain disturbed the silence. Lieutenant Grant heard its melancholy music from inside his canvas shelter at Walnut Springs. He was not with the infantry guarding the cannon. Mules and supplies remained his responsibility.

Off to the southwest fires in Worth's camp had been visible earlier—soon after dusk—but now the darkness of the rainy night hid everything in that direction. From out of that blackness, however, word from Worth arrived at Walnut Springs, brought by a Texas Ranger who had ridden quietly through the wet shroud. Worth had scribbled his message by the light of cornhusk torches; it told Taylor that he had determined to assault the western defenses on the following morning, although his progress had been slower than expected—only five or six miles before being halted by nightfall. Worth asked for a diversionary attack in Taylor's sector to coincide with his own operation.

At Walnut Springs during the rest of that night some men slept fitfully, wondering what their first battle would be like. Sentinels watched for the approach of Mexican soldiers who never came. The slow rain continued to rustle leaves and to drop from soaked tufts of Spanish moss.

Grant and French awoke to excitement early on the morning of September 21, and to clear skies: "a fresh and balmy breeze played in the tree-tops, and the sun sent many a warm and kindly glance through the long aisles of the majestic grove."

Gunfire roared from Taylor's old mortar and the two howitzers, which were shooting ineffectively at the Black Fort. The Mexicans lost no time answering those pieces that had been so quietly emplaced during the night. Soon the rattle of small arms and the rumble of cannon from the southwest announced that Worth had begun his move.

Taylor hurried the rest of his diversion. Sometime after eight o'clock that morning he sent General Twiggs's division of regulars (temporarily commanded for Twiggs, who was ill, by Lieutenant Colonel John Garland) and Butler's division of volunteers against northeastern Monterrey. With the division now commanded by Garland went Sam French, attached to Braxton Bragg's light artillery, and Sam Grant's 4th Regiment—but not Grant. He watched his men march off to battle, then waited with the mules and the supplies in the delightfully shaded picnic spot known as Walnut Springs.

Garland, given the left flank of the attacking force, had orders to assault the extreme northeastern sector of Monterrey with sufficient strength to keep further Mexican reinforcements from flowing westward for use in the fight against Worth. An engineer who had scouted the area would lead Garland's troops into line, avoiding the fire of the forts.

Through more fields of tall, parched corn these attackers crept, leaving crushed stalks lying on the ground like dead soldiers. Over stone walls and through gardens they wriggled—toward the fort known as La Tenería, located at the northeastern tip of the city. They meant to stay well to the left of the Citadel and its murderous cannon.

But something went wrong. The advance veered too far right. Field-pieces emplaced in the city directly ahead and in El Rincón del Diablo, located beyond that ugly ravine, poured shot on them. La Tenería, to their left, added a deadly fire. Even the Citadel reached them from the right, raining grape and canister. Men broke, ran, and hid from the deadly storm, but Bragg's battery of light artillery pushed on into town to support the supposed assault, Sam French with it.

Bragg's cannon flashed and roared from time to time. French had no idea with what effect they sent their fire; poor visibility precluded making estimates. Houses lining the streets along which he and the others worked the guns "were mainly built of soft stone or adobe, and the shot from the [Mexican] batteries in town passed through the buildings, covering . . . men, horses, and guns with lime and dust, blinding us so that we could see nothing."

The fury of the cannonade excited Lieutenant Sam Grant, who had been watching over things in Walnut Springs. "Curiosity got the better of . . . judgment." He leaped on a horse and rode toward the front in search of his regiment.

Grant found his men just before he heard orders to charge shouted through the din. "Lacking the moral courage to return to camp—where I had been ordered to stay—I charged with the regiment," he said later. But the fate of the 4th Infantry was the same as the rest. The dreaded Black Fort poured screaming shot upon them, and as they advanced they walked into a shower of musketry and artillery fire from other positions. "About one-third of the men engaged in the charge were killed or wounded in the space of a few minutes."

The 4th fled in retreat—not backward, but eastward, away from the Black Fort. Grant, the only mounted man in his regiment, noticed a lieutenant badly fatigued by the action and gave the officer his horse. Soon afterward a shot killed the officer, who was regimental adjutant. Grant received orders soon after that to assume the dead man's duties.

The entire maneuver seemed badly managed, young Grant thought when he had time to reflect on it, and he blamed Garland for unnecessary deaths. Garland, had he wanted to, might have passed on the blame to the absent commander, General Twiggs. About this time Twiggs appeared and explained his tardy appearance to an officer: "I expected a battle today but didn't think it would come off so soon, and took a dose of medicine last night as I always do before a battle so as to loosen my bowels. A bullet striking the belly when the bowels are loose might pass through the intestines without cutting them."

Sam French had little time to think about blame, with the Monterrey maelstrom still swirling about him. He was helping to withdraw the battery to safety while, around him, grape, canister, and musket balls plopped into soft flesh and hard bone, leaving men and animals writhing on blood-soaked streets not far from La Tenería. Another officer came upon the scene and later described it. The battery seemed to him to be wrecked, with men and horses lying prostrate "in the same spot, making the ground about the guns slippery with their . . . foam and blood." Bragg himself was feverishly stripping harnesses from the dead and disabled animals, "determined that not a buckle or a strap should be lost."

But the battery was not completely wrecked. French and another officer and a group of enlisted men were seeking to get a caisson to safety when a shot smashed into the two wheel horses, killing both. French and the other men quickly unhitched the dead animals and continued their retreat, leaving the harness. Then they saw another shot rip into two horses pulling a gun. Again they freed the animals, but this time the horses had not been killed. French last saw them eating grass, with their entrails dragging along the ground.

Finally the survivors of Bragg's battery struggled out of the city, with Bragg fretting about the loss of that harness. He ordered French back to retrieve it, while the rest of the battery went on to Walnut Springs, where it had been ordered. Setting out on his hazardous errand, French met General Taylor, who asked his destination. French told the general about Bragg's order and heard the reply with delight. "That is nonsense," Taylor scoffed, and he sent French on to Walnut Springs.

Still the day's excitement had not ended for French. The nearest way to camp lay perilously close to the Citadel—and in open sight of it. "The gunners must have become quite vindictive"—they opened fire on the lone, and lonesome, horseman. But French put his artillery experience to use. He watched for every puff of cannon smoke, then stopped his horse and let each shot fall well ahead. Apparently the smoke prevented the gunners from seeing French's strategy, and he reached Walnut Springs safely.

In the city fighting continued, and with a bit more success for Taylor's men following the first confused attack. That success might have been due to "Taylor luck," as some observers have since termed several of his victories, but it was no less effective. A group of about one hundred men from various companies, thrown together during the battle with a captain as senior officer among them, raced across the ravine that cut through northern Monterrey and toward the safety of stone buildings on the other side of the ditch. Sheltered there—not far from La Tenería—and cut off from the rest of the army, they did not know the extent of casualties in Garland's division or of a subsequent order to retire. So they ventured to the rooftop of a house and there, protected by the usual parapet, discovered they could fire into La Tenería and into a redan and other fortifications on the opposite side. They sent carefully aimed shots into these positions and saw that amid the smoke, roar, and excitement of battle the Mexicans were failing to realize the reason for their suddenly dismaying losses.

Other men separated from their units joined the isolated force and peppered the defenders. When the Mexicans finally realized their enemy's location they panicked. Officers and men fled the redan and sprinted for the shelter of El Rincón del Diablo—some of them falling along the way from a fresh flurry of shots. The garrison in La Tenería, overwhelmed by the surprising turn of events, surrendered, giving up four cannon that the attackers now could use in their deadly work.

When Taylor realized that the old tannery had fallen he withdrew the command to retreat and ordered another attack—this one aimed at El Rincón del Diablo. Taylor himself accompanied his men, often doing the work of an ordinary soldier—breaking into doors with an ax while shot sprayed the street in which he stood. Furious resistance drove the Americans back, however, and dusk stopped the bloodletting.

During the day's "diversion" Taylor had lost nearly four hundred officers and enlisted men killed or wounded. Survivors brought casualties back to Walnut Springs, and again the army went into camp at the picnic spot while detachments remained behind to hold La Tenería and a few other captured posts. Some men sought to find wounded companions, using screams and groans for directions in the darkness. A slow, cold, melancholy rain began to fall again. The moisture had come too late to help the parched corn, but it succeeded admirably in making soldiers more miserable than they already were.

Another communication from General Worth arrived. Worth, west of town, had used the costly diversion well. A force of his men had waded the waist-deep Santa Catarina River, had stumbled across rocky, brushy terrain to the base of Federation Hill, had clambered up the steep slopes, and had carried the height, training captured guns on the defenders and sending them fleeing toward the city. Tomorrow at dawn, Worth said, he would attack the higher hill, Independence, which was protected at its western end by that almost perpendicular slope nearly a thousand feet high, and toward the east by stout Bishop's Palace.

Taylor ordered Worth's dispatch read to his wet, weary men. They received it with three cheers and improved spirits. Then they tried to sleep—cold and hungry, having eaten nothing since breakfast. Some tentless men flopped down for the night on wet ground, without the "warmth" of a single damp blanket.

September 22 provided a little relief for the bedraggled troops north of town. Taylor did not commit them again to such a diversion as the day before. On this day most of the work would be done by Worth's men to the west, and Lieutenant Sam French would observe its progress from afar.

French had been ordered with his battery into reserve on a plain north of the Citadel. In a depression there they waited for the new day to unfold. The terrain and a misty fog screened them from the guns of the Mexican fort, but Citadel cannoneers knew they were around there somewhere and sent occasional shots toward them.

Nevertheless, French lolled, relaxed, and looked around. These few shots were nothing like the terrible fire of yesterday, and the rain had let up again. He saw two horseback riders, long-haired Texans, clatter up from the rear, halt some distance away, and peer around. With the Citadel so near, French reflected, it seemed a poor place for sight-seeing. He recalled his own experience with Citadel gunners who had given him, a lone horseman, an expensive cannonade. Unlike most other artillerymen, these Mexicans did not rule out minute, unimportant targets.

From ahead a gun roared again. The ball whined over French and crashed into the earth between the two surprised Texans, who assumed the shot had been meant for the battery. One man wheeled his horse and galloped toward camp; the other rode down into the depression. "Them darned fool Mexicans shoot mighty wild," he exclaimed to the gunners. "They came near hitting me."

The morning ate into the mist and fog. Soon the improved visibility allowed French to see Independence Hill, to the southwest, with its bastion, Bishop's Palace, overlooking the countryside from the slope nearest town. Worth's men had attacked the position. Entranced, French watched the action, joining thousands of others in the area who had a view. He recorded a description.

> . . . The base of [the] hill was encircled in smoke, and almost simultaneously a wreath of smoke above it burst into view. The attack on the hill with infantry had begun. Our men could be seen climbing up from rock to rock, and the smoke from every musket indicated whether it was fired *up* or fired *down* the hill. Gradually the circles of smoke moved higher and nearer, as our men ascended, and when, near the top, they commingled into one the excitement was intense. Troops on both sides looked on in silence . . . now with hope . . . now with fear, as the line of battle advanced or receded. But soon it was seen that higher up the hill the combatants struggled, until with one wild shout and rush the lines closed, and the top smoked like a volcano. And then through the rifts of smoke we saw our men leaping over the parapets, and the Mexicans retreating down the slope. We clap our hands with joy, and wave our caps!

Now, the scene changes. From out the bishop's palace swarms of

[Mexicans] issue and rush up the hill to retake the fallen fort. They are met halfway. Our hearts [beat faster] as we look on. The enemy recede, break and run for the palace, where foe and friends [commingle] . . . and all is still. A heavy gun flashes, and a shell bursts *over* the city from a captured cannon. The [Mexican] flag descends, the stars and stripes go up and wave over the bishop's palace, and the battle is won . . . then [arises] a shout of joy so loud, so long, it [seems] to echo from the sky.

Later French learned some almost unbelievable details. The ascent of the steep slopes of Independence Hill had begun at three o'clock that morning, in chilly dampness. Five hundred men groped their way up the incline—clambering for handholds, struggling from ledge to ledge—while thunder and raindrops covered their noise. By daylight they still had not reached the top. Mexicans soldiers peering over the rim discovered them and sent down a fusillade—an almost harmless one: they fired their overloaded cartridges too high, a common Mexican error. The advance continued grimly but steadfastly and soon reached the summit with the shouts, shots, and smoke that French described. Later Worth's artillerymen took apart a 12-pounder cannon and hauled it piece by piece up the precipice, to use against Bishop's Palace. By sundown of September 22 American forces held the Saltillo road and those two commanding hills that had appeared so formidable. Monterrey, with its large defending force and once plentiful ammunition supply, was being squeezed by a smaller army, but one that did fantastic things and enjoyed amazing luck.

Fortune again figured to some extent in the fighting on September 23—and it was a bit more of the Taylor variety. Strangely, General Taylor had not communicated during the night with Worth, still on the other side of town, about what he planned for the next day. Taylor assumed Worth would press his attack on the city from the west, and he planned to send his own troops once more against the northeastern defenses. Worth in turn presumed Taylor must have sent orders that had somehow gone astray. On the morning of the twenty-third Taylor ordered his own attack and Worth, hearing the guns, guessed that he, too, should strike. Two daggers thus aimed at the heart of Monterrey.

Sam Grant, still acting as adjutant in place of the officer who had been killed while riding Grant's horse, fought into the city with the 4th Regiment. Before long the attackers realized that their foes had evacuated the outer fortifications to the north and east, except for that dreaded Black Fort. Ampudia, a general typical of his army at that time, had decided with complete lack of imagination to concentrate his forces for a last-gasp battle in the center of the city, around the plaza and the cathedral—and thus he admitted defeat, about as Taylor had foreseen.

Once in the streets leading toward the plaza, however, Taylor's soldiers met hard resistance. Snipers firing from behind parapeted roofs and loopholed walls picked off individual attackers. Mexican artillery hurled grape through embrasures in the solid masonry walls built to protect the guns. Only along streets not leading directly to the plaza did the fire fall off; the men found those places relatively safe. But when they crossed intersections with the plaza in view, speed and luck became essential to avoid being hit by the storm of metal, delivered "as if bushels of hickory nuts were [being thrown] at us."

The attackers found another way of coping, particularly on the west side of the city. There General Worth's men broke into houses lining the threatened streets and dug protected routes toward the plaza, tunneling through the thick walls separating the residences. On the northeast, Taylor himself joined in the work, "perfectly regardless of danger." One officer saw him crossing a shot-swept street and ran out to shout a warning, only to hear the general order coolly, "Take that ax and knock in that door."

Some men of Grant's 4th Regiment reached a position near the plaza before being stopped. There they lay under such cover as they could find, firing at human heads that appeared from time to time above sandbag parapets thrown up on nearby rooftops. The fierce fighting had cut into their ammunition supply, and Grant volunteered to ride back, report their position, and ask that more ammunition be rushed forward.

His mission required the horsemanship for which he had become famous. He mounted and galloped off, flirting at street crossings with the full fury of the Mexicans. At those exposed locations he put his horse between himself and the enemy, leaning over on the far side by hooking a foot to the cantle of the saddle and gripping the horse's neck with an arm. He usually crossed the intersections at such speeds that he "was past and under cover of the next block of houses before the enemy fired," and he delivered his message.

While the infantry pressed its attack Sam French and the rest of his battery remained inactive on the northeastern outskirts. About noon, however, he received orders to take a 12-pounder into Monterrey to clear one of the main streets that ran the length of the city.

Horses tugged at the gun. Off it went with a clatter down a stone street toward the center of town. French rode a pony into action. He had not yet realized how the Mexicans had arranged for their guns to sweep all streets leading toward the main plaza.

> I could see no troops in this street, except those on the house tops two or three squares in advance: so I moved on down until the musket balls began to clip and rattle along the stone pavement rather lively. To avoid this fire, I turned my gun to the left, into a street leading into the plaza. To my astonishment, one block distant was a stone barricade behind which were troops, and the houses on either side covered with armed men. They were evidently surprised, and did not fire at us. We were permitted to unlimber the gun, and move the horses back into the main street. . . . I shook my fist at [the men at the barricade], and gave the command to load. Instantly the muskets were leveled over the barricade and pointed down from the house tops, and a volley fired at us that rattled like hail on the stones. My pony received a ricochet musket ball that struck the shoulder blade, ran up over the withers, and was stopped by the girth on the other side. I dismounted, and turned back to the gun. The two men at the muzzle were shot. One poor fellow put his hands to his side . . . and tried to stop the flow of blood.

At that moment French was far removed from his Quaker ancestry. He had the gun run back into the protection of the street by which he had come; then he devised an ingenious method of aiming and firing. Soldiers secured two long ropes to the end of the trail and gave a group of men stationed on the lower side of the barricaded street one rope, another group on the opposite side the other one. "The gun . . . was loaded, and leveled in safety, then pushed out, and pulled by the ropes until it pointed at the barricade, and then fired. The recoil sent the gun back, and the rope brought it around the corner to be reloaded."

French worked the piece this way for two terrible hours, but still he lost four out of five gunners. Meanwhile, Taylor's infantrymen used the cover of his smoke to rush across the intersection and into houses on the other side. There they crept up to rooftops and opened fire— then battered their way into other houses and repeated the operation. "The infantry and riflemen . . . made good progress in gaining possession of the houses, and driving the enemy toward the plaza."

About midafternoon, however, Taylor ordered a withdrawal, probably because he expected Worth's soldiers to begin throwing shells on the city from the west. "It was a difficult matter to get the volunteers out," one regular officer said. "They were having their own fun." During the withdrawal Sam French and his battery commander, Braxton Bragg, had another brief encounter remindful of the go-get-the-harness order of two days earlier.

The men and guns, leaving the city under fire, became targets for a four-gun Mexican battery. One shot hurtled into the group and struck a mounted man in the elbow, ripping off his forearm, knocking him off his horse, and killing him with pain, shock, and loss of blood. Bragg ordered French to dismount and retrieve the man's sword. The lieutenant complied, then—remembering that order of September 21—searched through the man's pockets and took out a knife, thinking he might be sent back later if he did not save everything now. French handed the sword and the knife up to his commander, but Bragg declined the knife, declaring it was not "public property."

To the west Worth's troops continued their attack, and they succeeded in advancing far enough to shell the main plaza with the old mortar, which had been sent around to them. Ampudia's time had come.

In the darkness of the following morning an emissary from the Mexican commander arrived at Taylor's headquarters offering surrender of the city, but not the garrison. Taylor demanded complete surrender, and Ampudia eventually gave in. The American terms, however, proved to be generous; Taylor wanted no more casualties. His army had suffered a loss of five hundred men already. Furthermore (as he said later), he had heard about the peace proposed confidentially to Santa Anna, now back in Mexico, and he was concerned about developments there.

Taylor took Monterrey and all public property, but he allowed Ampudia's soldiers to keep their horses, their small arms, and one battery of six guns with twenty-one rounds of ammunition for each piece—provided they retired beyond a line forty miles or so south of the city marked by a pass named Rinconada. Taylor promised to keep his army from advancing beyond that point for at least eight weeks, "or until . . . orders . . . of the respective governments can be received."

Some of Taylor's soldiers howled at the terms. This was particularly true of the revenge-minded Texans. But Lieutenant Grant approved, because of the magnanimity shown. Another regular officer, Lieutenant George Meade, remarked, "It was no *military necessity* that induced

General Taylor to grant such liberal terms, but a higher and nobler motive." Lieutenant Sam French left no written comment; possibly his contribution to and survival of the bloody victory had brought out again the confident warrior in him.

Taylor's generosity evoked no *vivas* in Monterrey. A silent pall settled over the city, which had become "a vast cemetery," as one Mexican survivor described it. "The unburied bodies, the dead and putrid mules, the silence of the streets . . . gave a fearful aspect."

Again, many Mexicans had tried to defend their land, even though everyone in the city had realized in "silent fear" that another defeat was looming as soon as the Americans circled westward and cut communications with Saltillo. Nevertheless, when Ampudia had ordered that concentration around the plaza and the cathedral some soldiers reportedly had refused to leave the outer fortifications. Their ensuing actions, however, exhibited no heroism. Completely demoralized, they became uproariously and helplessly drunk, fired their weapons into the air, and fell quick victims to the invader on the morning of the twenty-third.

Other Mexicans had shown more resolution than that. A young beauty of Monterrey, Señorita María Josefa Zozaya, was said to have appeared on top of downtown *azoteas*—flat roofs—manned by Mexican musketeers and to have handed out food and ammunition during the fighting. She was a girl who ought to have been able to teach a man to despise danger and Americans, too.

But all of it had been in vain. "What barren sacrifices!" a Mexican commented. "What heroic burlesque! What safe and triumphant cowardice!" Not everyone in the city had sacrificed.

Monterrey had fallen. Many citizens who remained could not abide the thought of living with enemy occupiers, and they prepared to leave with the soldiers. In some cases they abandoned business establishments. They packed what few possessions they could carry, bundled up their children, and joined a sad exodus.

The recent rains had given way to bright sunshine when the Mexicans marched out of Monterrey after formal midday ceremonies on September 25. From a central flagstaff soldiers lowered the Mexican flag while a battery gave the defeated colors an eight-gun salute—an honor allowed the pride-conscious defenders by Taylor in the capitulation terms. Then the United States flag appeared. Guns at the Bishop's Palace greeted those colors with twenty-eight roaring salutes, one for each state in the Union. Taylor's men marched into the city while a band played "Yankee Doodle."

Later some of the soldiers laughed at the sight of Ampudia's bedraggled veterans marching out of Monterrey with the grubby civilians, and some hissed when they recognized among the defeated troops turncoats like Thomas Riley, a giant Irishman who had deserted to the Mexicans shortly before the declaration of war. But Sam Grant neither laughed nor hissed. He still had empathy for miserable men and suffering animals.

> My pity was aroused by the sight of the Mexican garrison of [Monterrey] marching out of town. . . . Many . . . were cavalry, armed with lances, and mounted on miserable little half-starved horses that did not look as if they could carry their riders out of town. The men looked in but little better condition. I thought how little interest the men before me had in the results of the war, and how little knowledge they had of "what it was all about."

The "little half-starved horses" carried the Mexicans far out of town. Ampudia, whose time would soon come for relief from command, did not halt permanently just beyond the truce line—or at Saltillo. On orders from Mexico City he eventually led his weary troops across a vast wasteland all the way to San Luis Potosí before terminating his march of withdrawal.

PART IV

Changing Strategy

FROM SEPTEMBER 1846
TO MARCH 1847

28.

Colossal Guardians of the Land

Neither leader of the two warring nations would likely have approved of this hiatus in the fighting, had they been asked about it beforehand. Not for many days, however, did word of the fall of Monterrey and the ensuing truce reach Mexico City, and not for weeks did this information arrive in Washington.

At El Encero, Antonio López de Santa Anna paused for almost a month after his tepid welcome. He did not journey on into Mexico City, nor did he plunge immediately into the military role he had promised himself and the Federalists. Instead he waited to watch developments, and he enjoyed his hacienda residence, built near that familiar grandeur of white-topped Orizaba and pine-forested Cofre de Perote. The peaks seemed like "colossal guardians of the land."

The scenery in the vicinity could scarcely be surpassed. The Spanish diplomat's wife, Fanny Calderón de la Barca, had written a description of it about seven years earlier. "The intervening mountains, the dark cliffs and fertile plains, the thick woods of lofty trees clothing the hills and valleys; a glimpse of the distant ocean; the surrounding lanes shaded by fruit trees: aloes, bananas, chirimoyos, mingled with the green liquid-ambar, the flowering myrtle, and hundreds of plants and shrubs and flowers of every colour and of delicious fragrance, all combine to form one of the most varied and beautiful scenes that the eye can behold."

At its zenith Santa Anna's El Encero was itself a show place—a luxurious cattle ranch of nearly ninety thousand acres. Improvements included a large residence, some tenant houses, a chapel, and pens that could hold two thousand calves, more than two thousand cows, and three thousand horses. The hacienda represented an investment of 140,000 pesos, its proud owner claimed. It was a fine experience seeing and smelling it again and being tickled by the cool breezes that blew in from the mountains. That awful Havana and Vera Cruz heat, which Santa Anna detested, became a forgotten discomfort.

But Santa Anna himself was now (like those peaks that rose around him) a guardian of the land—the savior of Mexico returned. He must bestir himself. If he had ever seriously considered acting in behalf of President Polk as he had indicated he would, he ignored the pledge now. The mood of Mexico favored fighting those selfish, arrogant heretics from the north, and Santa Anna knew better than to tamper with that mood —even if he ever had wanted to try.

About the middle of September, before General Taylor's army had come within sight of Monterrey, Santa Anna moved to take on the labors he had promised his countrymen. He traveled to Tacubaya—another pleasant place full of restaurants, gambling houses, and additional places of pleasure beckoning from amid scenic suburbs of Mexico City—and established quarters in the Archbishop's Palace, another favorite residence of his. Two days later he finally ventured into the capital, some two years after angry mobs had smashed his statue, exhumed and dragged his grisly leg through city streets, and sent him off in flight.

Santa Anna rode into Mexico City with Valentín Gómez Farías in the official state coach. An observer who witnessed the old hero's return wrote a description of it. The two men faced each other. Farías rode in a front seat, facing Santa Anna; the once deposed general reclined in a rear seat, facing forward. Santa Anna had dressed for the occasion in "democratic fashion." He wore a long traveling coat and white trousers, the witness said, and displayed absolutely no medals on his chest. He rode "sunk down among the cushions" of his plush seat, holding in his hand a copy of the venerated Constitution of 1824. From a staff to his right flapped a banner commemorating the same hallowed document. The observer thought that both Farías and Santa Anna looked more like victims than conquerors.

Vivas greeted Santa Anna in Mexico City. The new government had encouraged a festive welcome by distributing money for the purchase of *aguardiente* and other spirits. Santa Anna's name appeared again in places where it had been angrily erased two years earlier—among them the National Theater, named once again the Santa Anna Theater. Many people, however, still harbored suspicions about the man, believing him to be the greatest actor of them all, and his welcome to the city was something less than universal and spontaneous.

After his grand entry Santa Anna returned to Tacubaya. There he prepared to set out for San Luis Potosí and the collection of a great army that would march northward and exterminate Zachary Taylor and the invaders, while Farías remained in Mexico City as acting head of government. The Mexican treasury at this time held a total of less than two thousand pesos, however, and much more money would be needed to organize and to outfit the army Santa Anna envisioned. The general used his influence with Farías to suggest forcing contributions from the Church, then (probably realizing the storm this would provoke at home) marched away to San Luis Potosí, with a nucleus of three thousand troops, three days after General Ampudia and his defeated soldiers had left Monterrey, bound for the same ultimate destination.

At San Luis Potosí Santa Anna displayed the organizational ability for which he had become famous. His energy and bravado again attracted men, even in a region where he had once been hated for previous brutalities. He set up depots where supplies for his army could be donated —beans, corn, meat, lead, copper, and cash—and watched the coffers fill. But when these donations proved inadequate he confiscated silver bars at a nearby mint for his army's use and obtained loans from local merchants, putting up his own beloved El Encero and other property (it was said) as security. This time Santa Anna apparently meant business. "Every day that passes without fighting in the north," he exclaimed, "is a century of disgrace for Mexico!"

Santa Anna ordered the Tampico garrison to join him, recruited other men, and assumed command of Ampudia's troops when they arrived from Monterrey. Eventually Santa Anna gathered an army of twenty thousand soldiers to go after Taylor, but in his energetic bursts of recruiting and supplying them Santa Anna (who disliked details anyway) neglected to drill them thoroughly in military maneuvers.

His devotion and self-sacrifice did not go unrecognized in Mexico City. During his stay at San Luis Potosí the Mexican Congress once more elected him President, an office he again accepted, "reluctantly," because he said he felt Congress represented the will of the people. But Santa Anna did not take the oath of office at this time, and Farías remained in charge of the government and in charge of that controversial program to force money from the Church. Let Farías take the actual responsibility of being the guardian of this disturbed land for now.

Like Mexico, the United States had its own guardian of the land, but this one always operated on the theory of the more responsibility the better. In Washington, President Polk devoted himself more and more to running the war (this along with his strict supervision of the executive branch of government), and inevitably he began to consider the increased criticism of the conflict as disloyalty bordering on treachery.

The war had not progressed quickly enough for him. Early in September the country learned of Commodore Sloat's occupation of Monterey, California, but with November elections coming up Polk needed a faster finish to silence critics at home. The President had not yet heard of the victory at Monterrey, Mexico (or of the compromising truce), and he had been musing over some alternatives for hastening an end to the conflict.

One of these possibilities was soon eliminated. A query in Mexico City made after Paredes' downfall showed the new government there not the least disposed to talk about peace. Furthermore, it became evident in the Executive Mansion that Santa Anna had used his contact with the President merely to gain safe passage home, and that the man was going to do nothing for peace. This stiffened Polk's attitude.

Polk's impatience was reflected in a proposal brought up during a meeting of the Cabinet. What about a landing at the Mexican port of Tampico and an occupation of the state of Tamaulipas, which lay along the Gulf Coast below the Rio Grande? This idea inevitably broadened. If Tampico, why not also Vera Cruz, an even more strategic port? All this appealed to the President. At first Polk simply wanted Vera Cruz itself. Possession of the port city would help to isolate the Mexican capital from the rest of the world. At this time Polk did not envision sending an invading army into the mountains toward Mexico City.

The Tampico-Tamaulipas campaign became a more immediate concern. It fit that original strategy of occupying northern Mexican provinces, blockading the coasts, and forcing the encircled nation to ask for peace. General Kearny, with his Army of the West, would take care of the occupation of Santa Fe and New Mexico (word that he already had done so had not reached Washington in mid-September), and move on to California to ensure possession of that place, with help from the Mormon

Battalion, to follow later. General Wool would then occupy Chihuahua, with help from the Missouri Regiment of Mounted Volunteers (including Private John T. Hughes), who had been ordered to proceed there from Santa Fe. General Taylor would take care of Monterrey. The northern ring around Mexico, from west to east, would be completed by the occupation of Tamaulipas and Tampico, on the Gulf Coast.

But Polk and his Executive Mansion warriors continued to operate with a paucity of information about Mexico. The President, through Secretary of War Marcy, sought to get details from Zachary Taylor. That general, however, was becoming more and more unresponsive. Taylor did not intend for any intelligence he sent to Washington to be used against him in event of some failure evolving from its use. Furthermore, Taylor had been piqued by what he took to be those Washington slights and did not feel in a co-operative mood anyway. Finally, the intelligence-gathering arm of his organization, never its strongest limb, had not acquired much information about Mexico in the first place.

At meetings of the Cabinet Polk talked out details of his ideas for prosecuting the war, usually won approval (not that it mattered much), and complained about his generals—especially about Taylor, during that mid-September when the focus was on the Tamaulipas campaign. Polk grumbled:

> . . . Great embarrassment exists in directing the movements of our forces, for want of reliable information of the topography of the country, the character of the roads, the supplies which can probably be drawn from the country, and the facilities or obstructions which may exist in prosecuting the campaign into the interior of the country. General Taylor though in the country gives but little information on these points. He seems to act as a regular soldier, whose only duty it is to obey orders. He does not seem to possess the resources and grasp of mind suited to the responsibilities of his position. He seems disposed to avoid all responsibility of making any suggestions or giving any opinions.

Those irritating career generals would not be able to confuse the Tamaulipas campaign. Polk intended to give command to three political friends. The first was Robert Patterson, a Pennsylvania Democrat (with militia experience) who had been commissioned a brigadier general early in the war and who was now in charge of volunteer troops strung out along the Rio Grande. Patterson, promoted to major general, would have the highest command. Working with him would be Brigadier General James Shields, an Illinois Democrat, and Brigadier General Gideon Pillow, Polk's former law partner in Tennessee.

Still, Zachary Taylor was the senior commander in the area where the Tamaulipas campaign would be fought, and protocol dictated that he be brought into it. In September Secretary of War Marcy, acting for Polk, wrote Taylor a letter in which he told of the proposed invasion and occupation of Tampico and Tamaulipas, and requested recommendations and other information from Taylor.

The general never replied. He never even received the letter. It fell into Mexican hands—and apparently was one reason Santa Anna had ordered the Tampico garrison to join him at San Luis Potosí. Santa Anna was said to have believed Tampico indefensible against an attack by sea, and he did not want to fragment an army by leaving a garrison there or any other illogical place. Instead he continued to plan his strike against Taylor. This probably would serve to shatter the enemy's Tamaulipas plans anyway.

Toward the end of September Marcy sent Taylor another letter directing him to give General Patterson, then at Camargo, four thousand troops for the Tamaulipas operation. Marcy remarked that since Taylor had been complaining about too many volunteer troops having been sent to him this probably would be no hardship. The Secretary discreetly left the final decision to Taylor, but without much actual choice under the circumstances. Taylor had under his over-all command thirteen thousand men located along the line from Matamoros to Monterrey.

When the general opened this letter he received the first word of the proposed Tamaulipas operation, to occur in a sector that he supposedly commanded, and his reaction can be imagined. On the same day that Marcy wrote Taylor the Secretary also dispatched separate orders to Patterson to implement the campaign.

Such turmoil typified events of that September, October, and November. To some jaded Washington observers far removed from actual participation, the war (when they learned of these and other details) seemed to become almost a comedy of confusion. But President Polk, rarely amused by anything and certainly not by political embarrassments, became extremely grim—even before hearing of the Monterrey truce. He wrote in his diary:

The Secretary of War is overwhelmed with his labours and responsibilities, and is compelled to rely for the execution of many details of his department on his subordinate officers, some of whom I fear do not feel that they have any responsibility, and others seem to act as though they were indifferent about the success of our military operations. Several of these officers are politically opposed to the administration and there is reason to apprehend that they would be willing to see the government embarrassed. With these apprehensions I shall for the future give more attention than I have to their conduct.

But the absurdities continued.

Old General Winfield Scott, sniffing fresh activity in northern Mexico with the Tamaulipas talk, asked to be sent to command that area, declaring with logic unknowingly humorous that he believed his presence would be "neither unexpected nor undesired" by the "gallant" Taylor. Polk, however, mused over Scott's recent letter remarking on the danger of a "fire" upon his rear and was not persuaded by the nation's senior army officer. The President's diary about this time indicated he had indeed considered transferring Scott, but not necessarily to Mexico. "General Scott is no aid to the department," Polk wrote, "but his presence at Washington is constantly embarrassing to the Secretary of War. I will observe his course, and if necessary will order him to some other post."

Polk would have begun pondering some similar method of dealing with General Taylor when word of the Monterrey battle and truce arrived at the Executive Mansion after sunset on October 11, a Sunday. Secretary Marcy and the adjutant general accompanied the messenger, Captain Joseph Eaton, when Eaton delivered his dispatch to the Mansion.

Polk read Taylor's communication with increasing wonder and growing fury. "In agreeing to this armistice," he fumed, "General Taylor violated his express orders and I regret I cannot approve his course. He had the enemy in his power and should have taken them prisoners, deprived them of their arms, discharged them on their parole of honour, and preserved the advantage which he had obtained by pushing on without delay farther into the country, if the force at his command justified it."

Beyond that, the truce interfered with Polk's impending Tamaulipas project. The President and his Cabinet determined to answer Taylor immediately with a slap. They would congratulate the troops for their success at Monterrey, but not Taylor himself, and would order the general to terminate the truce at once. In that letter, when composed later, Marcy also mentioned the additionally proposed attack on Vera Cruz.

The absurdities extended to the U. S. Army in Mexico, as officials in Washington learned later. General Taylor, when fully cognizant of what Washington was planning about future campaigns and of his minor role in those projects, began making plans of his own. He would follow orders as they suited him, staying within certain bounds of discretion but using the long distance and the lack of communication between himself and Washington to act largely on his own. He did not intend to be sidetracked, militarily or politically. Admirers had persuaded him that he must indeed be President, and Polk's galling "neglect" provided the ultimate motivation.

Taylor determined to move forward fifty miles from Monterrey and to occupy Saltillo, then to leave General Worth's division there as a garrison force. After that Taylor, with the rest of the army, would march southward into Tamaulipas, too, aiming specifically at the capital city of Victoria and at Tampico. Taylor's troops would act in conjunction with Patterson's, who would launch their invasion from Matamoros, but Taylor—not Patterson—thus would be the senior commander on the spot and would be crowned with the victory laurel. Taylor knew that Santa Anna's gathering army in San Luis Potosí posed a threat to most of his plans and especially to Worth's division, which would be sitting at Saltillo, but about this time Taylor enjoyed some unexpected relief. The army of General Wool (accompanied by Captain Robert E. Lee) arrived in the area en route to Chihuahua from San Antonio.

Wool reported to Taylor by messenger-delivered dispatch and questioned the logic of going on to the original destination, which lay (as Wool now saw) far across a trackless desert and far from where future fighting seemed imminent.

Taylor agreed enthusiastically. The arrival of three thousand good troops to add to his own army elated him. Wool halted his men at Monclova—a hundred miles or so northwest of Monterrey—and later, on Taylor's orders, moved southwestward to occupy Parras—about the same distance west of Monterrey and Saltillo. They would be available to Taylor, who prepared now to march toward Tampico. Taylor did not know that the garrison there already had been removed by Santa Anna.

Developments in quick succession that November exploded Taylor's Tamaulipas plan. About the middle of the month he received a dispatch from Washington notifying him of a change of strategy. The initial target —those northern provinces—was to become a secondary consideration.

An incidental reason they had been chosen for exerting pressure in the first place was that possibility of rebellion there. Far removed from the seat of power in Mexico City, they had long sought more self-government. Federalist sentiment always had been strong in those provinces, but now a Federalist administration had returned to Mexico City. Currently even Santa Anna was their liberal friend. The northern provinces, then, had become less restive and more unified. Possibilities of winning sympathy for the United States there had dimmed.

Vera Cruz was to become the main target, Taylor learned. General Patterson would have charge of the operation. Troops would land above or below the city, surround it, and force its surrender. The strong fortress of San Juan de Ulúa would not be attacked—it need not be. The city would fall into American hands anyway. Taylor was to send Patterson two thousand additional troops for the campaign. This would cause no hardship, the orders indicated, because Taylor was told to maintain a holding line only and not to advance beyond Monterrey.

Next Taylor heard reports that the Mexican garrison had abandoned Tampico and had joined Santa Anna's army at San Luis Potosí, then that a U. S. Navy squadron had entered Tampico and had left an occupying force. All of this proved true indeed, but still Taylor did not intend to remain forgotten in Monterrey. He would advance on Victoria, the capital city of Tamaulipas.

The general was still thinking in terms of the original strategy of encircling northern Mexico, although he himself earlier had indifferently suggested something else to Washington in one of his rare recommendations: "to strike a decisive blow at Mexico . . . [a] force should land near Vera Cruz . . . and, after establishing a secure depot, march thence on the capital." This giant invasion would require twenty-five thousand troops, Taylor estimated, and in his own consideration the casualties that would ensue would outweigh the worth of such a campaign.

In Washington the idea of a Vera Cruz operation similar to that which Taylor so offhandedly suggested already had evolved from the original proposal to capture the vital port city. The northern-province strategy was simply too slow (and, unknown in Washington, had met reversal on the Pacific Coast, where in late September native Californians had risen against American forces, had retaken Los Angeles, and had formed their own government). As the war dragged on more Americans were becoming unhappy with it, and in the November elections they voted a Whig majority into the House of Representatives. There criticism of the conflict quickly became more frequent and more bitter.

One evening after the election Senator Thomas Hart Benton called at the Executive Mansion and extended the chain of ridiculous events. Polk received him cordially. The senator, once so opposed to the war, now declared himself ready to help the Administration in any way to bring the fighting to a finish. "He condemned the policy," Polk said, ". . . of holding the Mexican territory which we had acquired and not prosecuting the war further into the Mexican territory. He said the war would be much protracted by such a policy, and might not be ended for years."

Polk listened carefully; Benton was a formidable man. United States citizens are "a go-ahead people," Benton declared, and they would not settle for a stalemate. The senator proposed a campaign similar to what Taylor (and some others) already had suggested: take Vera Cruz, but follow it with a "rapid crushing movement" on Mexico City. Who would command such a giant operation? Patterson would be out of it. Polk voiced his doubt about the capacity of General Taylor, and Benton said he had no confidence in General Scott.

Benton volunteered himself. If Congress could be persuaded to create the rank of lieutenant general, an officer who would be general-in-chief of the Army, Benton said, he would accept the responsibility and would lead the troops into Mexico City.

The President, tired of dealing with Whig generals and of furthering their political aspirations, reacted favorably. "I remarked . . . that I would have confidence in him and would be pleased to see him at the head of the army in such an expedition." Later, however, Polk gave this some second thought, concluded that Congress probably would not agree to the appointment of a lieutenant general, and began looking for another possible commander.

Winfield Scott recently had submitted three thoughtful memoranda on a Vera Cruz expedition, but Polk continued to distrust him. The President suggested Major General Butler, a Democrat, who had commanded those volunteers serving with Taylor, but Secretary Marcy opposed his selection, and for a change a cabinet member had his way. Marcy believed Scott to be the only logical choice, despite the political disadvantages, and eventually Polk agreed. Besides, the President reportedly reflected with satisfaction, this would play Scott against Taylor.

Polk called Scott to the Executive Mansion and lectured him.

. . . I said to him that the capture of Vera Cruz was very important to secure peace. To this he assented. I then told him that it was important that the officer entrusted to command that expedition should have confidence in the government, and that the government should have confidence in him, and that without a cordial coöperation success could scarcely be expected. To this he agreed. I then intimated to him that if I was satisfied that he had the proper confidence in the administration and that he would cordially coöperate with it, that I was disposed to assign him to the command. He appeared to be much affected and said at once that he had the utmost confidence in the administration and in myself, and that he would cordially coöperate with me in carrying out my views in the prosecution of the war. . . . I then told him that I had at the commencement of the war given him my confidence and had tendered him the command, but that circumstances had occurred to change my determination. I was willing that bygones should be bygones and that he should take the command. . . . He was so grateful and so much affected that he almost shed tears. . . .

Scott was to maintain his new puppylike affection for Polk until just before sailing for the Vera Cruz campaign from New Orleans, when he would learn that the President had, after all, continued to mull over that surreptitious and eventually unsuccessful attempt of his to have Congress approve a lieutenant generalship to be given to Senator Benton.

In late autumn of 1846 the United States had new strategy, new hope, and a new commander for the war against Mexico. The nation also had a subcommander in Monterrey who had become increasingly angry, bitter, and resentful toward the Administration, and who had decided to do something definite about it. Zachary Taylor wrote his son-in-law that "if the good people were imprudent enough to elect me" he would probably serve as President.

Earlier Taylor had written another letter—to General Edmund Gaines, the same officer who had been relieved of command at New Orleans for enthusiastically but illegally enlisting six-month volunteers—giving his reasons for agreeing to the Monterrey armistice that had aroused Polk's ire and enumerating his complaints against Washington treatment of himself and his army. In the letter Taylor again referred to his suggestion about taking Vera Cruz, then marching on to Mexico City if "we are (in the language of Mr. Polk and General Scott) under the necessity of 'conquering a peace.' . . ." Taylor reiterated his belief, however, that "the amount of blood and treasure which must be expended in doing so" would not be compensated by the attainment.

Polk, the nation's guardian who liked to operate secretly whenever possible, certainly had been striving to keep the impending campaign against Vera Cruz and Mexico City confidential. But General Gaines (who happened to be a Whig, too) gave Taylor's letter to the New York *Morning Express* for publication, with the intention of bringing broad readership to his friend's grievances, and it was printed in entirety on January 22, 1847—then widely reprinted—with details of the very operation against Mexico that Polk had in mind.

Some administration friends could not believe that this remarkable letter was genuine, but Polk never doubted it. "It is a highly exceptional letter," he said, "assailing as it does the administration, uttering unfounded complaints, and giving publicity to the world of the plans of campaign contemplated by the government." The President summoned Secretary of War Marcy for a consultation on steps to be taken against the two troublesome generals.

Gaines, who contended that the letter contained no vital information, drew a formal reprimand. He was old and almost useless as a senior officer and further punishment seemed needless. (He would die two years later.)

The possibility of recalling Taylor was discussed, then abandoned, possibly to avoid creating a greater following for the general by allowing him a martyr's role. But Marcy wrote Taylor a stern rebuke, declaring, "Your letter will soon be in the hands of the enemy and should convey most valuable information to them." Marcy also called Taylor's attention to an army regulation prohibiting officers from writing for publication about impending campaigns. Punishment for offenders could be dismissal.

So Taylor fell further from favor with the Administration, but not with his admirers. The greatest effect of his published letter was to emphasize the division of American attitudes. Most Whigs approved publication; most ardent Democrats did not.

Some persons in those days of poor communication, however, remained entirely unaware of the letter. That autumn the unquestioning patriots among them joined pro-war Americans in singing a simple ditty that the general with those surprising pacific tendencies might not have approved of in entirety—but, for political reasons, probably would not have silenced, either.

> *Old Zack's at Monterrey—*
> *Bring on your Santa Anner.*
> *For every time we lift a gun*
> *Down goes a Mexicanner.*

29.

A Christmas Frolic

The Army of the West, never so large as its elevated name indicated, had been divided after the acquisition of Santa Fe and the rest of New Mexico. Its energetic commander, General Kearny, believed the occupation of a land taken so quickly and quietly would not require much of a garrison force, and he determined to use his troops as effectively as possible in bringing the war to a swift conclusion. By the end of September Kearny had supervised the preparation of a new code of laws for New Mexico, had appointed Charles Bent (of Bent's Fort attachment) governor, and had planned future moves. While Kearny and a force of dragoons marched on California, to be followed soon by that battalion of some five hundred Mormon volunteers under the command of Philip St. George Cooke (as called for in additional orders from Washington), Colonel Doniphan and his Missouri volunteers would invade Chihuahua from the north, and at the city of that name would link up with General Wool, who Kearny assumed (knowing Wool's previous instructions) would be there.

Another regiment of Missouri mounted volunteers, this one commanded by Colonel Stephen Price, arrived in late September to relieve Kearny for his California expedition. Without waiting for them, however, the impatient Kearny had taken three hundred dragoons and ridden westward into the jagged mountains and roadless deserts toward his destination on the Pacific. Two weeks out he had happened upon the scout Kit Carson riding eastward with a report from Frémont (sent before the recapture of Los Angeles by the Californians) describing the "complete conquest" of California. Kearny assumed he would not now need so large a force. He sent half the dragoons back to Santa Fe and went on with the rest of his men. He prevailed upon the reluctant Carson to accompany him, then arranged for someone else to take Frémont's message on to Washington.

Doniphan and his Missourians meanwhile had been dealing with the Navajo Indians, seeking (in accordance with Kearny's promise) to ensure safety for New Mexico residents before setting out for Chihuahua. Doniphan led his men into the broad wasteland between the Rio Grande and the Colorado River (where the Indians lived), recovered prisoners and stolen property, and eventually concluded a peace treaty. Then the Missourians turned their thoughts toward Chihuahua.

The expedition assembled in December at Valverde, the former site of a Mexican settlement that had been abandoned to the Indians, in the valley of the Rio Grande just below Socorro: 856 soldiers commanded by a giant colonel, and a merchant train of 315 wagons with accompanying traders and teamsters, all bound for the rich Chihuahua market.

The potential wealth of the trade caravan and the present straits of Doniphan's army contrasted. Neither Doniphan nor his soldiers had yet received one dollar of pay during their six months of service. Most men were forced to wear the same clothes—now badly frayed—in which they had begun the long march. And the dwindling food supply made hunger an ever present problem. One soldier recorded in his diary the death from starvation of one of the beef cattle, then subsequently added these entries regarding his own food: "Some Taos flour, coarsely ground in the little native mills on the Rio Grande, badly baked in the ashes, and some coffee without sugar, now comprise our only sustenance. Between meals, however, we parch some corn, which we now and then procure of the natives in exchange for buttons [cut from our clothing], needles, or any little matter we can spare. . . . A bull has just been killed, and the offals are being greedily devoured by our poor fellows." With December had come raw weather and winter desolation to compound the discomfort and the depression, forcing this same soldier to chop small limbs from a cottonwood tree to feed his horse.

John T. Hughes, the schoolteacher turned private, now saw the other side of military life. Not all of it was jolly companionship after all. Hughes endured some austere December days while waiting in camp for Doniphan's small army to move. Gales howled down from nearby mountains and sometimes brought cold rain that stung a man's face when it hit. "The 1st Regiment is much scattered, & a good many have died,"

Hughes wrote on December 7. Within a week he had fallen ill himself, with colic, and he scribbled suggestions of his misery on the twelfth and the thirteenth. "Very unwell—lonely & desolate to a sick man . . . dreary times." With increasing frequency he had been noting in his diary the deaths of friends, but Hughes himself began to mend, and returning health brought impatience to be going somewhere. The whole army was ready to move. Anywhere else must certainly be better than the present location.

Then, on December 14, Major William Gilpin and a detachment of three hundred men departed southward. Two days later Lieutenant Colonel Congreve Jackson and two hundred men followed. Colonel Doniphan and the rest left Valverde on December 19. A few more than 850 men would challenge the Mexicans deep in their own country. Between the detachments of volunteer soldiers traveled the merchant wagons, teamsters, and traders—all bound for potential wealth under the protection of these ragged, hungry troops.

Almost immediately upon leaving the encampment at Valverde, located on the east bank of the Rio Grande, Doniphan's army encountered an expanse of waterless desolation. Below Valverde the river curved westward for many miles before turning back to the east. To save time and miles Doniphan had determined that his men would follow the route of other travelers and would leave the river below Valverde, march almost due southward, and pick up the river again, after it had turned back eastward, at a settlement named Doña Ana, fifty miles or so northwest of El Paso. Between the two river points lay a stretch of sandy, seared land nearly one hundred miles long, and with only one water hole. Earlier travelers had given this region the name of Jornada del Muerto —meaning something like "Dead Man's March"—and they had preferred to cross it at night, halting during the killing heat of midday. But Doniphan's men would cross the area when piercing winter winds howled across the dry desolation.

When Hughes began the march across the dreadful desert he thought it well named. Water quickly gave out. No wood for fire could be found. Hughes and his companions rarely stopped. Instead, they rode or walked along the trail late into the night, everyone numb with cold, faint with hunger, and bone-weary. Sometimes in the darkness a man would come upon a bunch of parched grass and set fire to it, for warmth. The dry vegetation would burn like ignited gunpowder, but both blaze and warmth would soon vanish, leaving the man as cold as ever and the night as dark.

About midnight each detachment would halt, post weary guards, and try to rest. Supperless men flopped on the ground and sought to lose themselves in sleep, while stragglers trudged into camp throughout the rest of the night. At daylight reveille roused them all and they went on without formal breakfast. After more than three days of this ordeal they reached Doña Ana and found water, food, and forage.

After having been divided for the passage of the Jornada del Muerto Doniphan's army reassembled at Doña Ana and, on December 24, began moving again down the Rio Grande toward El Paso. The usual rumors spread quickly among the soldiers. El Paso would be defended by a force of two thousand men and four fieldpieces, it was said. But a Christmas Eve march of fifteen miles, in surprisingly pleasant weather, brought no Mexican challengers in sight. Despite the rumors and the location in enemy land, however, discipline became lax. That night animals were not tethered but were instead allowed to straggle off in search of grass.

Christmas Day broke brilliantly when the sun rose above mountains to eastward. At home schoolteacher Hughes would have enjoyed a holiday and probably a fine dinner on the farm where his parents lived, but all that was a life away now. Still, the atmosphere became festive—if a bit faked. This *was* Christmas.

Recently awakened men fired weapons—with the absolute abandon of celebrating volunteers—in honor of the occasion. They joined in singing songs, mostly of a patriotic nature—like "Yankee Doodle." Then they settled down to another day's routine.

Collecting loose animals that had strayed during the night delayed departure for a time. After that they marched eighteen miles to a location on the Rio Grande called El Brazito, or Little Arm. At El Brazito an island divided the flow of water. The smaller stream lay to eastward, washing against the bank on which Doniphan's men halted in mid-afternoon. They encamped on an open, level prairie bordered on the west by the Rio Grande, on the northeast by dry mountains, and on the southeast by chaparral. On the road behind them scattered units that had not yet made up for the delayed morning departure straggled along toward the camp site. On the road ahead a few mounted pickets took up stations to watch for an enemy's approach.

Hughes and other men attended to chores that had long since become

255

established procedure: bringing in water and wood for cooking, watering and staking out the animals for grazing. But a holiday mood continued to pervade the atmosphere. Men sang, joked, and laughed while they attended to the chores, some working as far as a mile away from camp. Colonel Doniphan and other officers began a card game.

Few men at first noticed a ballooning dust cloud in the direction of El Paso. Some who did see it (including Doniphan, it was said) presumed it to have been raised by the wind gusts with which they had become familiar in this devilish region. But the cloud grew nearer and larger, and within minutes a horseman dashed into camp shouting an alarm: Mexican dragoons by the hundreds and infantrymen in even greater numbers were bearing down on Doniphan's camp.

The colonel and his officer friends slammed down their cards and hurried off to rally their men. Bugles blared. More horsemen galloped up and down the road around camp, shouting word of the enemy's approach.

Some distance away, Hughes threw down his load and ran for his weapon, but other men sought to save the wood they had collected. They ran toward camp, slowed by their burdens, until an officer yelled at them, "Throw away your wood, and bring your horses into camp!"

For several harrowing minutes confusion engulfed the Missourians. Bugles continually sounded assembly. "The jingling and rattling of arms, the cries 'Fall into line!'—'Get your horses!'—'Fall in on foot here!' . . . drowned every other sound. . . ." When a man could not find his own weapon he seized someone else's and scampered off to defend the place. Most soldiers fell into line "under whatever [banner] was most convenient." But in a surprisingly short time Doniphan's Missouri volunteers had formed a front that stretched across the road.

Their enemy allowed them extra time. Instead of charging into the collecting army the Mexicans halted on a rise half a mile away—beyond a chaparral thicket, but visible above it—to form a battle line parallel to Doniphan's—and two miles long. Hughes could see the Mexicans clearly: a large force of as many as thirteen hundred men (opposed by some five hundred of Doniphan's soldiers then on hand). The Mexican dragoons, five hundred of them alone, especially impressed Hughes. They "were dressed [as Hughes wrote later and obviously after closer examination] in a uniform of blue pantaloons, green coats trimmed with scarlet, and tall caps plated in front with brass, on the tops of which . . . waved a plume of horse-hair, or buffalo's tail. Their bright lances and swords glittered in the . . . sun." They occupied the extreme right of the enemy line.

Soon Hughes observed other Mexican heraldry; this enemy seemed to him inclined more toward theatrics than to fighting. A horseman bearing a black flag left the Mexican ranks and galloped forward in the direction of the Americans. Fifty yards away he halted and waved the banner in a graceful salute.

The man proved to be a lieutenant sent by the Mexican commander. Hughes saw Doniphan and an interpreter advance a short distance, then halt. Doniphan sent his interpreter on to question the Mexican officer, whose black flag could be seen now, bearing on one side two white skulls and crossbones and on the other side the words, "Libertad o Muerte [Liberty or Death]."

Hughes recorded the ensuing conversation, as he or someone else translated it into stilted English.

"The Mexican general," said the messenger, "summons your commander to appear before him."

"If your general desires peace, let him come here," Doniphan's interpreter replied.

"Then we will break your ranks and take him there."

"Come then and take him."

"Curses be upon you—prepare . . . for a charge—we neither ask nor give quarter. . . ." The Mexican lieutenant galloped back to his own line, waving the black flag above his head. (Doniphan said later, in his battle report, that his final reply was "to charge and be d——d," but possibly the Baptist in Hughes precluded his committing these words to paper, even when bathed in the long dash.)

Hughes then heard the distant, brassy notes of a bugle. He saw the colorfully uniformed dragoons on the Mexican right spur forward in a charge—while, to the left of the dragoons, infantrymen and a sprinkling of cavalry joined in the attack. From a distance of more than four hundred yards the Mexicans opened fire—wildly and (as usual) shooting too high.

This was Hughes's first fight with the Mexicans, but he and his companions began acting coolly and with determination. Much of their inspiration must have come from their tall, leathery commander. Doniphan saw the enemy's wildness and allowed the first three volleys to go unanswered. He ordered his men instead to drop to the ground and to hold their fire until the attackers had come to a point within 150 yards —a maneuver that happened to yield an unexpected advantage of putting the Mexicans off guard. The sight of so many of Doniphan's men falling to the ground (not a commonplace battle tactic in those days) brought jubilant cries of *"Bueno! Bueno!"* from the advancing Mexicans.

Then Doniphan shouted his command to fire. Men who had apparently been hit earlier sprang up and loosed one deadly volley after another. On the Mexican left, infantrymen fled in confusion. On the right, the startled dragoons wheeled farther right and seemed about to threaten the supply wagons in the rear when fire from the teamsters and a scattering of soldiers still straggling behind the line sent them reeling away in disorder.

The Battle of El Brazito ended within half an hour, with nearly two hundred Mexican casualties against seven Americans wounded (all of whom recovered). It was "a Christmas frolic," Hughes wrote in his diary after it was all over, and he added with satisfaction, ". . . the men & officers all behaved gallantly."

On the following morning the Missouri volunteers commenced a march toward El Paso, twenty-five miles away. Doniphan and his men expected another battle, and their Christmas levity had given way to caution. But on December 27 they marched unopposed into El Paso (then located on what is now the Mexican side of the Rio Grande, at present Ciudad Juárez). The soldiers who had opposed them at El Brazito had scattered. Hundreds of them had simply vanished. Others had fled in groups toward the city of Chihuahua (where, of course, Doniphan was bound). Some had remained in El Paso, however, and there the Americans observed them walking the streets swathed in bloody bandages or hobbling about on crutches.

For a time the Missourians stayed in El Paso. The town lay in a lush valley of the Rio Grande. There, amid pleasant surroundings, they rested and waited for artillery that Doniphan had requested earlier from Santa Fe.

Private Hughes looked over the countryside with much favor. In the absence of Regular Army topographical engineers he assumed the responsibility of writing a letter directly to Secretary of War Marcy extolling the land—a naïve thing for a private to do, but Hughes was no ordinary soldier. He was a college graduate and a professional schoolteacher. He was also a dedicated political evangelist typical of his time.

If this valley were cultivated by an energetic American population, it would yield . . . ten times the quantity of wine and fruits at present produced. Were the wholesome influences and protection of our Republican Institutions extended to the Rio del Norte, an American population, possessing American feelings, and speaking the American language, would soon spring up here. . . . It would be an act of charity to rid these people of their present governors and throw around them the shield of American protection.

30.

The Goal of Their Hopes

While Doniphan and his men rested at El Paso before pressing on across another lifeless *jornada del muerto* to Chihuahua, John C. Frémont— newly promoted to lieutenant colonel—and an even smaller army paused at Santa Barbara, seventy miles up the Pacific Coast from Los Angeles, before continuing southeastward toward the California town that had fallen in September to inhabitants who had rebelled against United States occupation.

Before the fall of Los Angeles Frémont had been sent to the Sacramento Valley by Commodore Stockton to recruit more men for Frémont's California Battalion—and for Stockton's use, too. The ambitious naval officer, who had named himself governor of California, planned to leave Frémont in complete charge of the newly acquired area as soon as an adequate force had been raised. Then Stockton would sail away for operations farther south down the coast, around Acapulco, and perhaps launch from there an overland expedition against Mexico City. This would be a grand campaign that the commodore believed could bring him even greater glory.

With Los Angeles presumably secure after its original surrender, Stockton had left the marine officer Archibald Gillespie in command of a small American force there and had sailed to San Francisco Bay before departing southward for his grandiose operation. But Stockton had failed to realize the vulnerability of Los Angeles. Apparently the commodore was deceived by the ease with which the town had been taken and by placid conditions elsewhere in California. In the northern and central sections, where most of the American settlers resided, California authority had been more remote, and those areas had been easy to occupy. This did not prove to be true in the vicinity of Los Angeles, which lay closer to the homeland and was more heavily populated by people of Spanish and Mexican ancestry. While Stockton and his men and ships waited in San Francisco Bay the commodore heard that Los Angeles had fallen. Gillespie and his garrison force had been allowed to board a ship at San Pedro.

Other towns in the south also had fallen to the Californians, whose force was estimated now at more than four hundred men. Stockton dispatched against Los Angeles a naval landing party that went ashore at San Pedro, but the Californians sent the detachment reeling back. Stockton informed Frémont—still on his recruiting drive—of the loss of Los Angeles and ordered him south with whatever men he had been able to enlist. Then the commodore took his ships to San Diego, nearer the scene of rebellion.

Frémont had made some effort to comply with the orders. He had traveled with 170 men as far as Santa Barbara, where he learned that the Californians not only had defeated Stockton's earlier attempt to retake Los Angeles but also had taken measures to ascertain that subsequent invaders would not be able to obtain supplies. After that Frémont returned to Monterey, using as his excuse "discretionary authority" Stockton had given him. This action exasperated the commodore and in time left some observers perplexed by the unusual caution thus displayed by Frémont. But Frémont was a man who could recognize extremely unfavorable odds when they existed.

For a month thereafter Frémont had remained in the vicinity of Monterey, collecting supplies and recruits. By the end of November, with 430 men in his army, he was ready to challenge the Californians who had retaken Los Angeles.

Frémont and his men would have looked like formidable warriors indeed if summer descriptions of them left by two observers were still valid. One man who had expected to find Frémont a towering commander "looking blood, bullets, and grizzly bears" saw instead a slender, apparently sedate individual dressed in a blue flannel shirt open at the collar, a deerskin hunting jacket, blue cloth trousers, and moccasins. Around his head Frémont had tied a cotton handkerchief. But a closer look at his deeply tanned, bearded face showed fire burning in his eyes.

Another observer described Frémont's men: the dark Delaware Indians who acted as scouts and bodyguards, and the rest, especially the trappers, "many of them blacker than the Indians," who "rode two by two, the rifle held by one hand across the pommel of the saddle. . . ." Most of the trappers wore long, loose deerskin trousers. Many of them carried knives in scabbards slung at their hips.

As they rode down the Salinas Valley to San Luis Obispo the weather would have required more clothing than that mentioned in these descriptions. A rainy season accompanied by an uncomfortable chill had settled on central California, leaving roads boggy and men wet and shivering. The precious supplies carried by pack mules dwindled. Horses weakened and died from the extended journey and from the lack of grazing. Beef cattle were slaughtered at a rate that astounded one expedition member, who guessed that his companions must have eaten daily ten pounds of meat. On Christmas Day (while eight hundred miles to the southeast Doniphan was fighting the Battle of El Brazito in warm sunshine) Frémont and his men battled the elements during the descent of a ridge north of Santa Barbara.

Frémont had taken a mountain route from San Luis Obispo (which he had captured without firing a shot) to avoid being ambushed by the Californians. During his journey southward he and his men had sighted occasional armed horsemen. They had proceeded without meeting resistance, but now the wisdom of Frémont's wariness seemed debatable. A cold storm wind hurled stinging, blinding rain into the faces of men and animals. Water covered the trail and made slopes so slippery that even pack mules lost their footing and slid over precipices to their deaths or into flooded ravines, where they drowned. Not until well after midnight did Frémont and most of his men find themselves at the bottom of the descent and able to halt in safety—if not in comfort. Campfires proved impossible to keep lighted, and the earth had become a slush where sleep was possible only for men as exhausted as these. Some stragglers still on the mountain spent the rest of the night there, in such shelter as they could find.

For a week after that Frémont's army dried out and rested at Santa Barbara. Then they went on toward Los Angeles, riding and walking, following for a time the winding coastline, listening to the roar of the unplacid Pacific surf, and sometimes feeling the chill of the water as an occasional breaker washed far inland and died with a soft gasp beneath their tramping feet.

On January 11 Frémont met two excited Californians who bore surprising information: United States forces had retaken Los Angeles.

Frémont also learned some other details of interest. Toward the end of November General Kearny and his hundred or so dragoons had entered Upper California after enduring some terribly dry marches that had enfeebled men and animals, and there the Americans had discovered that much of the southern section had fallen to the Californians. Hearing that Stockton and his ships were in San Diego, Kearny sent word of his arrival to the commodore. In a few days a party of thirty-five men sent from San Diego intercepted Kearny with official messages and with word that a small army of Californians lay in wait on the road nine miles ahead. Kearny read the messages, then went on.

About sunrise of December 6, at the Indian village of San Pascual, forty miles from the Pacific Ocean, the Californians opened fire (the first hostile shots Kearny had heard since leaving Fort Leavenworth) and caused nearly forty casualties—including Kearny himself, wounded twice. But after only a brief battle the Californians withdrew. Kearny's men buried eighteen dead comrades under a large willow tree east of camp, "with no other accompaniment than the howling of the . . . wolves attracted by the smell," and pushed on for San Diego, weak and weary.

They carried the wounded on improvised, jolting ambulances: beds made of poles. The front end of each carrier was secured to a mule; the trailing end dragged along the ground. One of Kearny's officers described the expedition as "the most tattered and ill-fed detachment of men that ever the United States mustered under her colors. Our provisions were exhausted, our horses dead, our mules on their last legs, and our men . . . worn down by fatigue and emaciated." One man had been sent ahead to San Diego with a plea for help, but before any assistance could come more Californians blocked further progress of the little army. Near a ranch twenty-nine miles from San Diego they forced Kearny to halt and to dig in as well as he could, to fend off what looked like an impending attack. Hours passed—an entire night; no attack came. Neither did help. What had happened to the messenger?

On the following night, December 8, the scout Kit Carson and two more men volunteered to go to San Diego for assistance. They sneaked out of camp into the darkness and into an enemy country where huge clumps of cactus often afforded the only hiding places on a desolate landscape.

In Kearny's camp more painful waiting followed. The night of the ninth came and passed slowly, the hours seemingly darker than ever. Some wounded men died. Outside camp, not far away, Californians lurked. Once they sent a stampede of wild horses toward Kearny's position, but the maneuver only provided food for starved troops. The desperate men killed and ate several of the animals.

On the night of the tenth Kearny ordered a march for the following morning; he would take his chances in a fight rather than die penned up like this. Later that same night, however, one of his sentinels heard men speaking in English somewhere in the darkness beyond, shouted a challenge, and received a friendly reply. Commodore Stockton had sent 180 sailors and marines to Kearny's relief, in answer to the two requests.

On December 11 Kearny's fragmented Army of the West finally came in sight of the blue Pacific Ocean, and on the following day the men marched into San Diego. They saw a small village of adobe houses, abandoned mission buildings, and crude houses built for storing hides, and—in a quiet bay beyond—two ships riding at anchor. Both flew the United States flag: the U.S.S. *Congress*, Commodore Stockton's flagship, and the U.S.S. *Portsmouth*, the vessel to which Lieutenant Joseph Warren Revere was attached.

For seventeen days Kearny's weary men recuperated in San Diego. Then their driving commander had them moving again, toward Los Angeles—fifty-seven able-bodied dragoons, in company now with five hundred sailors, marines, and volunteer soldiers.

Kearny had urged Stockton to mount an attack on Los Angeles. The commodore approved it and put Kearny in direct charge of the movement while retaining for himself over-all command. Stockton accompanied the expedition. So did Joseph Warren Revere, although that naval lieutenant left behind few personal details of the operation. The attackers took with them six fieldpieces, one wagon, and ten oxcarts loaded with supplies.

On January 8—the anniversary of Andrew Jackson's 1815 victory in the Battle of New Orleans—the Stockton-Kearny army met California challengers at the San Gabriel River, twelve miles from Los Angeles. They charged, spurring themselves on with shouts of "New Orleans!" The

Californians fled, regrouped later, then after a skirmish on the ninth withdrew, retreating to a location in present Pasadena.

On January 10 the American force reoccupied Los Angeles, but absolute peace did not return to California. This time the adversaries were Stockton and Kearny, but the fault actually lay with the Polk administration, which seemed to have left the military forces in constant turmoil and confusion because of the President's distrust, prejudice, or ignorance. In this instance the blame could be placed on ignorance—or at least on carelessness.

Kearny had come to California under orders dated June 3, 1846, that declared, ". . . should you conquer and take possession of New Mexico and upper California, or considerable places in either, you will establish temporary civil governments therein." Two weeks later further orders authorized him to assume command over certain troops being sent by sea to the Pacific Coast, "and such as may be organized in California. . . ."

But Stockton was acting under similar orders. A dispatch from Washington dated July 22, 1846, had reiterated his duty of taking and occupying Upper California. "This will bring with it the necessity of a civil administration," the communication had stated. "Such a government should be established under your protection." Stockton had used those orders as authority for naming himself governor and for planning to hand that position over to Frémont when he left. Furthermore, Stockton had been senior officer during most of the actual occupation of Upper California, and he believed this gave him some prerogatives. Now here came an officer of the U. S. Army who, after an initial show of subjecting himself to a man presumably more knowledgeable about the situation, began to assert an authority that seemed to surpass Stockton's. The commodore must have reflected bitterly that had it not been for himself and his relief expedition of 180 sailors and marines Kearny probably would not have lived to see Los Angeles.

Friction increased in following days, but John C. Frémont, hearing of the fall of Los Angeles from the two Californians he had met south of Santa Barbara, would not know much of this dispute until later. Frémont listened to the men describe the conquest of the town on the preceding day—January 10, following the fight on the San Gabriel River and the subsequent skirmish—and he hurried on. Both Stockton and

Kearny had established headquarters in Los Angeles, but there still might be fighting in the area. Frémont wanted to be there for that.

On the following day Frémont and his men encountered a force of Californians near the mission of San Fernando, northwest of Los Angeles, but the Californians had lost all desire to fight. Instead they surrendered. Not surprisingly, Frémont assumed the responsibility and the glory of negotiating a treaty with them, ending all fighting in Upper California—while two superior officers sat not far away in ignorance of the action. On the condition that the Californians lay down their arms, return to their homes, and encourage their countrymen to submit to United States jurisdiction, Frémont granted liberal terms. The Californians would receive the same treatment as United States citizens, would be excused from military service or oath-taking, and would be allowed to leave the country at will. Despite Frémont's presumption in negotiating the treaty, Commodore Stockton did not disapprove it—and Frémont, with the generosity displayed in the surrender, finally made a genuine contribution toward peace in the area. "[The treaty] put an end to the war and to the feelings of war," Frémont remarked proudly. "It tranquilized the country, and gave safety to every American from the day of its conclusion." Not coincidentally, it also gave its sponsor greater claim to being the man who secured Upper California for the United States. The governorship of California that Stockton had promised him would brighten his star further.

On January 14 Frémont entered Los Angeles, feeling himself a hero and still relishing his recent triumph—all this exhilaration despite a steady, soaking rain that made mud puddles of the streets. Frémont, too, established headquarters in the town.

Soon he received a peremptory note from General Kearny: make no further changes or appointments in the California Battalion without Kearny's permission. Frémont learned that Stockton also had received an abrupt notice: stop all work in regard to organizing a civil government. Kearny said he would take over that duty. The commodore replied tersely that he already had organized a civil government, that it was functioning with himself as governor, and that he would forward Kearny's note to Washington with a request that the general be recalled.

Frémont also refused to obey Kearny's order. In an answer dated January 17 Frémont said, "I feel myself . . . with great deference to your professional and personal character, constrained to say that, until you and

266

Commodore Stockton adjust between yourselves the question of rank, where I respectfully think the difficulty belongs, I shall have to report and receive orders, as heretofore, from the Commodore."

That same day Frémont received from Stockton written appointment (dated January 16) as governor of California. The commodore, still anticipating greater glory, was planning to leave. Around Los Angeles Frémont immediately became recognized as governor, but Kearny's claim to superiority was acknowledged in some quarters—particularly among Regular Army personnel and among volunteers of the Mormon Battalion, under Philip St. George Cooke, who arrived at San Diego January 29 after completing a grueling march across southwestern desolation.

About this time Lieutenant William Tecumseh Sherman arrived in California after a voyage with other officers and enlisted men around Cape Horn. He saw the confusion, listened to arguments, and recorded a question many persons were asking: "Who the devil *is* the governor of California?"

Lieutenant Joseph Warren Revere, again aboard U.S.S. *Portsmouth*, harbored no doubt in this Army-Navy fuss about the governorship. Revere had seen and had helped ranking officers of the Navy secure California: first Commodore Sloat, then Commodore Stockton. The only U. S. Army representative in the area in those earlier days had been John Frémont. After the Navy planted the flag on the California shore Stockton had assumed the responsibilities of governor, under that authorization contained in his orders. Now, with Stockton preparing to sail for the lower Mexican coast in his flagship *Congress* (and with Revere's *Portsmouth* preparing to depart in company), Stockton had appointed Frémont governor. The legality of this appeared obvious to Revere. He was saddened by the friction that seemed to be increasing even on the day he sailed. The acquisition of California should have been an occasion for universal joy among his countrymen. His visit had doubly convinced him of that.

Months earlier, as military commander at Sonoma, Revere had fallen more deeply in love with this magnificent land. No wonder it held Frémont in a grip! Revere had traveled extensively through the northern section and had reveled in unsurpassed scenery and exquisite climate, with evenings that were bracingly cool no matter how warm the day had been. One night's camp he particularly remembered: "After joining my companions . . . in a comfortable drink of brandy and water . . . we all wrapped ourselves in . . . blankets; and stretched out upon the ground with our feet to the fire—while the silvery moon stole over the inland mountains and bathed us in serenist light. . . ." Several noisy Indians with the party had awakened him later, but he had silenced them and had quickly fallen asleep again.

Those Indians could be pesky, all right, but they were one reason Revere had been assigned the rapturous shore duty—so his patience rarely ran out. One of his major responsibilities at Sonoma had been to pacify the Indians and to protect them. In the past California *rancheros* had raided Indian settlements to obtain captives they later enslaved. That practice would stop now, as Revere had sought to emphasize in one address to tribal leaders gathered under a cluster of giant oaks near Clear Lake. Later he recalled that his speech went something like this:

> I have called you together to have a talk with you. The country you inhabit no longer belongs to Mexico, but to a mighty nation whose territory extends from the great ocean you have all seen or heard of, to another great ocean thousands of miles toward the rising sun. The country inhabited by that nation is called the United States, and its millions of people are called Americans. I am an officer of that great country, and to get here, have traversed both of those great oceans in a ship of war which, with a terrible noise, spits forth flames and hurls forth instruments of destruction, dealing death to all our enemies. Our armies are now in Mexico, and will soon conquer the whole country. But you have nothing to fear from us, if you do what is right. Our magnanimous government will protect you, and make you a happier and better people than you now are, if you are faithful to your new rulers. A stop will be put to the oppressions of the rancheros; for ours is a country of laws, and we do not suffer the crime of kidnapping to go unpunished. We shall do what we can to better your condition, and we shall expect you to do all you can to help yourselves. . . . We come to prepare this magnificent region for the use of other men, for the population of the world demands more room, and here is room enough for many millions, who will hereafter occupy and till the soil. But, in admitting others, we shall not displace you, if you act properly. . . . You can easily learn, but you are indolent. I hope you will alter your habits, and be industrious and frugal, and give up all the low vices which you practise; but if you are lazy and dissipated, you must, before many years, become extinct. We shall watch over you, and give you true liberty; but beware of sedition, lawlessness, and all other crimes, for the arm which shields can assuredly punish, and it will reach you in your most retired hiding places.

Hope for these people Revere did have, even if that hope proved in reality to have been dimmed by some attitudes of his time. Giving Indians full civil rights would be impractical, Revere added, singling out for emphasis voting privileges. The nation might as well allow children under ten to vote, he reasoned. But Revere favored giving Indians other equal rights: protection under "just statutes," the right of trial by jury, and the right to hold land "in limited quantities."

Musing over the future of California, Revere expressed another hope for humanity—this one not shared by most Americans. Perhaps it was the concerned physician's son in him that brought him to foresee a large influx of population from Asia: people seeking freedom and opportunity —a new, robust life. Was not that the dream, the purpose, of the United States? "Europe pours her thousands upon our Atlantic seaboard, and Asia will yet furnish her share of inhabitants for populating our possessions on the Pacific. The industrious and imitative Chinese will not make a bad cross with our restless and inventive Yankees."

But Revere's most confident hope regarding California probably was for the land, not the people. Unlike man, Nature could not be accused of fallibility, and at the time of Revere's visit Nature certainly seemed to have reached perfection in this luxuriant region.

> . . . The soil is of almost incredible fertility, the yield of wheat being as high as a hundred-fold, while corn and vegetables of all kinds, including the finest potatoes I ever saw, flourish most luxuriantly. The fruits of the temperate zone thrive here side by side with those of the tropics. Peaches, pears, apples, melons of all kinds, and rich luscious grapes, may be seen growing in the same garden with sugar cane, dates, figs, and bananas, leaving no room for doubt that all the other productions of tropical climates would, if introduced, flourish equally well. There is reason to believe that California will hereafter be dependent on no other country for the necessaries of life. . . . Indeed, it is difficult to name any product of the earth, whether it be to eat, drink, or wear, which California cannot yield, while her mineral wealth excites the astonishment of the world.

All this potential had been added to the young United States, and Revere had helped to acquire it, even if his role had been a minor one compared to Frémont's, Stockton's, and Kearny's.

The lieutenant's involvement had given him his paternal attitude toward the land and its people. He felt as strongly as did President Polk about keeping it. How could his country be most certain of not losing this jewel during these days of tenuous hold?

Build a road at once from east to west. "The first thing the Romans did on acquiring a distant province," Revere reflected (with some unintentional irony), "was to establish a *military road* running . . . from Rome to the capital of the conquered territory." Roman roads were fortified, and in event of distant rebellion Romans legions could use the highways offensively as well as defensively. But Revere contemplated a rather different road to California: one of iron rails, utilizing newly developed steam propulsion, ". . . to enable legions of toiling men to reach the goal of their hopes."

For Revere himself, the way would lead back home, slowly, after his contribution to the California conquest. Early in 1847 the *Portsmouth* sailed from Upper California with Stockton's *Congress* toward extended operations off the lower Mexican coast (but the commodore's grandiose invasion of Mexico never was to be launched). Revere left California to Frémont, whose gallantry and energy he admired; to Kearny, whose recently expounded contentions distressed him; and to the future. In a book later published Revere wrote:

> Perhaps a hundred years hence, some curious book-worm, while exploring a musty library, may alight upon this then forgotten volume, and will be tempted to find out what was said and predicted of California. . . . The poor Indians will then have passed away; the rancheros will be remembered only as the ancient proprietors of broad lands, which will have passed into the possession of the more enterprising race who are about to succeed them; the Grizzly Bear will live only in books and in tradition; the Elk will have become extinct; the wild horse will be seen no more; author, editor, publishers, readers, all will have passed away and mingled with the dust. . . .

Something did remain, however, and Revere can be commemorated for it by fellow Americans, if not by other men. The lieutenant himself wrote the memorial: "One of the most magnificent regions of the world is now incorporated with the United States."

31.

Fighting—But No Fighting

While an interservice spat flared in California, in Texas one intraservice feud was on the mend.

Colonel Ethan Allen Hitchcock, who at one time or another during his military career had antagonized virtually all of his seniors, had returned to the American base at Fort Polk, from where Zachary Taylor had departed for the relief of Fort Texas and the intervening battles of Palo Alto and Resaca de la Palma more than seven months earlier. After extended sick leave Hitchcock was en route to rejoin his regiment, now with General Taylor at Monterrey.

The supply base had mushroomed and had received a popular new name. Men stationed there or transported through it had begun to refer to the entire port area as "the Brazos"—an American corruption of Brazos Santiago. Through it at this time passed most men bound for the war against Mexico, and into it—on December 27, 1846, a day or so after Hitchcock's arrival—came the old giant, General Winfield Scott, and his staff, bound eventually for the invasion of Vera Cruz.

Scott—a furrow-faced, heavy-browed man standing six feet four inches and weighing more than two hundred and fifty pounds—had become well known for his strange mixtures of egotism and warmth, pettiness and professional ability, sensitive conceit and genuine bravery. His affinity for spit and polish had earned him the derisive nickname of "Old Fuss and Feathers" among his men—quite a contrast to the title, "Old Rough and Ready," that soldiers had bestowed upon Zachary Taylor. Scott busily established his temporary headquarters, then prepared to travel up

271

the Rio Grande to Camargo, where he planned to confer with Taylor early in January about a transfer of troops to the Vera Cruz expedition.

Winfield Scott already had written Taylor two letters about this. He planned to requisition nine thousand men from Taylor (whose total command in Monterrey and along the Rio Grande now numbered close to twenty thousand) and he knew Taylor would be bitter. The letters had been carefully worded, and they dripped with esteem.

Between General Scott and Colonel Hitchcock no esteem had existed for a long time. The colonel had on several occasions antagonized the senior general of the Army (most recently in the brevet dispute won by Hitchcock), and Scott had retaliated by overruling at least one good appointment for his antagonist. But in the meantime some act of Hitchcock's had evoked the admiration of Scott. Probably it had been that letter to Congressman Black defending the Army against the South Carolinian's charges of torpidity. Hitchcock never knew for certain.

On the morning of December 28—the day before Kearny and Stockton commenced their march against the Californians holding Los Angeles— Colonel Hitchcock was idling in the quartermaster's office, still waiting for transportation up the Rio Grande and on to his regiment at Monterrey, when General Scott's aide called him aside and said quietly, "The general will be pleased to see you."

"What?" Hitchcock asked, not believing the words he had heard.

"The general will be glad to see you. He desired me to say so."

"Indeed, you surprise me very much. Is it so?"

The aide repeated the message again, adding that Scott had seen a letter of Hitchcock's that had delighted him. Still surprised, Hitchcock tried to recall any letter of his "touching the general," but could not. The suddenly warmed relationship was "something like a miracle," Hitchcock concluded, and he called on Scott immediately.

The general rose, shook Hitchcock's hand, and offered him a seat. Then came more surprises. Hitchcock heard Scott declare that he knew of no officer of equivalent rank who could do more good for the Army and asked if he could accompany him the next day on a boat trip up the Rio Grande to Camargo, for the meeting with Taylor.

"With great pleasure," Hitchcock replied.

"Clever! Very clever! Right! Right! We start early."

"I will be ready, General."

Early the next morning Hitchcock departed with Scott and his staff for Matamoros. There they boarded the steamer *Corvette* for the voyage up the river.

During the trip Scott told Hitchcock of his recent interviews with President Polk. Although Hitchcock did not record details, Scott would still have been furious about Polk's recent attempt to have Senator Benton named general above him—this even after Polk had assured Scott he would have command of the Vera Cruz expedition. Congress had refused to approve the new generalship, but this action would not have silenced Scott—it never did. Years later, in his *Memoirs*, Scott would comment that "in the President I had an enemy more to be dreaded than Santa Anna and all his hosts. . . . Mr. Polk's mode of viewing the case seems to have been this: . . . 'Scott is a Whig; therefore his successes may be turned to the prejudice of the Democratic party. We must profit by his military experience, and, if successful, by the force of patronage and other helps, contrive to crown Benton with the victory and thus triumph both in the field and at the polls.' This bungling treachery was planned during the precise period of my friendly interview with Mr. Polk!"

Hitchcock would have listened sympathetically to the general. Hitchcock certainly had nothing good to say about Polk, either, and he had not changed his mind about the war—although he probably did not expound on this to Scott. Shortly before returning to Texas Hitchcock had written in his diary:

> 10th Nov. I am very much disgusted with this war in all of its features. I am in the position of the preacher who read Strauss's criticism of the *Gospel History of Christ*. Shall he preach his new convictions? Shall he preach what his audience believe? Shall he temporize? Shall he resign? Here the preacher has an advantage over the soldier, for, while the latter may be ordered into an unjust and unnecessary war, he cannot at that time abandon his profession. . . . In the present case, I not only think this Mexican war unnecessary and unjust as regards Mexico, but I also think it not only hostile to the principles of our government—a government of the people, securing to them liberty—but I think it a step and a great step towards a dissolution of our Union. And I doubt not that a dissolution of the Union will bring on wars between the separated parts.

> . . .

> New Orleans, Dec. 15, 1846. . . . My feeling towards the war is no better than at first. I still feel that it was unnecessarily brought on by President Polk, and, notwithstanding his disclaimers, I believe he expressly aimed to get possession of California and New

Mexico, which I see, by his message received here to-day, he considers accomplished. . . .

Nor had Hitchcock's old ailment improved a great deal. The extended leave of absence in a better climate had not remedied his diarrhea. It still plagued him occasionally, and during the boat trip he showed so much debility that General Scott treated him "as an invalid and advised as to . . . regimen with a view to . . . recovery." Scott also asked Hitchcock to take the job of inspector general of his army, and the colonel accepted, although in his diary he expressed a private preference for studying the Swedish philosopher Emanuel Swedenborg to being an instrument for carrying on "this abominable war."

During the trip Hitchcock came to be on even more intimate terms with the man he had once detested. Scott took him into his confidence on matters, including the orders under which he was operating—and their objective. Hitchcock carefully refrained from committing any of this to his diary, fearing that the book might be lost and fall into Mexican hands. Although he thus recorded little about the war, the situation in Mexico when Hitchcock made the boat trip with Scott was this (if not then entirely known to the colonel):

The Navy had occupied undefended Tampico; had made two attempts to take the port town of Alvarado, south of Vera Cruz, but had failed—largely because of weather and grounded vessels; then had taken the port of Frontera farther down the coast; and a small expedition had raided San Juan Bautista, capital of the province of Tabasco, seventy-five miles inland.

General Patterson, Polk's selection as leader of that proposed Tamaulipas invasion, had dispatched six regular artillery companies and a regiment of volunteers from his command to garrison Tampico. Patterson then sent word to Monterrey advising his superior, General Taylor, of this, and Taylor approved. Next, Patterson added more troops to the garrison force, and the War Department diverted some reinforcements originally meant for Taylor to Tampico for similar duty. Taylor was not notified until this had occurred, and he was furious. He had continued to plan that march on Victoria—the Tamaulipas capital—and had intended to "concentrate a respectable force" there to hold it. Taylor fired off more angry letters, to Patterson and to Washington. Then Taylor again devoted himself to his plans designed to avoid being relegated to a nonentity for the rest of the war—that fate he suspected the Polk administration of plotting for him.

Earlier Taylor had occupied Saltillo, as he had said he would, and had left General Worth and his men there. Now, in conjunction with General Patterson, Taylor began the movement against Victoria: a total of six thousand men marching from Matamoros (under Patterson) and Monterrey (under Taylor). Taylor had not received General Scott's letters about the January conference at Camargo and the impending troop requisitions.

The Victoria operation would be risky. It might even prove disastrous. What if, in the meantime, General Santa Anna struck with his army twenty thousand strong? The Mexicans could overwhelm the Saltillo garrison (twelve hundred men under Worth) and Monterrey (three regiments commanded by General Butler, whom Taylor had left in charge there)—or even the armies marching toward Victoria. Nevertheless, in mid-December the American movement began. Included in it was Sam French, the artillery lieutenant, happy to be headed out of Monterrey boredom and into new action.

Taylor had proceeded only sixty miles toward Victoria when word from Worth reached him—at Montmorelos—that an attack on Saltillo by Santa Anna seemed imminent. Taylor doubted the accuracy of the information, but he turned back toward Monterrey with a detachment of dragoons and infantrymen and sent the rest of his men on toward Victoria.

Other urgent messages from Worth brought General Wool and his army hurrying in a southward curve toward Saltillo from Parras, and started reinforcements marching from Monterrey. Then the excitement faded: Santa Anna was nowhere around. Taylor told Wool to keep his troops where they had halted after their forced march—at Agua Nueva, a village twenty miles south of Saltillo on the road to San Luis Potosí. He told Butler, at Monterrey, to move his headquarters to Saltillo and thus to rejoin the troops sent there earlier as reinforcements for Worth. Then Taylor set out again for Victoria, but he left behind him some nervous men. Fresh reports about an impending attack by Santa Anna continued to come in almost daily.

On December 24, while Taylor was still en route to Victoria, a dispatch bearer overtook him with the first of the two letters written by General Scott, this one dated November 25. Taylor then learned that

Scott was coming to command a Vera Cruz invasion, that Scott intended to take those thousands of men from him for the landing and to leave him strictly on the defensive in northern Mexico, and that Scott wanted a conference at Camargo during the first few days in January. Dismayed, Taylor read further in the letter. "This will be infinitely painful to you, and for that reason distressing to me. But I rely on your patriotism."

Taylor managed to contain himself and to write a polite reply. He would give Scott the troops, but it would be impossible for him to appear at Camargo as requested. Instead he must investigate a report of a gathering Mexican force south of Victoria.

Scott, with his guest Colonel Hitchcock, arrived at Camargo January 3 on board the *Corvette*. Hitchcock looked around the village where so many of Taylor's troops had died of disease earlier—"one of the most miserable places I ever saw, dirty and dilapidated and but little better than a Seminole village. . . . The people along the banks of the Rio Grande live very much as Indians in mud huts and look not unlike them in complexion, hair, and eyes. . . ."

Scott, meanwhile, was looking for Taylor, but not with success. Upon arriving at Camargo he was handed Taylor's reply to his first letter, and he read it with reaction unrecorded. Impatient to get on with the Vera Cruz campaign before the summer fevers struck, Scott wrote out an order that same day to General Butler for nine thousand men to be sent immediately from Taylor's area command. Scott had two copies of this dispatch forwarded to Taylor by different routes. Before sending the messages he showed them to Hitchcock, who read them and remembered later, "[General Scott said] at the close of his letter . . . that Providence may defeat him, but he thinks the Mexicans can not." After that the *Corvette* got up steam and churned back downriver, with Winfield Scott's far-famed wrath possibly standing up well even when compared to the boat's boiler pressure. After some delay caused by a norther the steamer arrived at the mouth of the Rio Grande, near the supply base named Fort Polk, on January 8.

In due course Hitchcock would hear of certain other events.

After having been delayed by the Santa Anna alarm, General Taylor arrived in Victoria January 4—the day after Scott had waited in vain on the *Corvette* at Camargo. General Patterson and his troops arrived at Victoria that day, too, bringing the personnel total there to six thousand. Then Taylor began to realize that the location had disadvantages for so large an army. Supplies would be difficult to bring in, and the country-side would not provide the subsistence required. Ten days after his arrival Taylor decided to order a complete withdrawal.

At this very time one copy of Scott's dispatch of January 3 requisitioning the nine thousand troops reached Taylor. Again old Zach exploded. Washington certainly was trying to finish him off as a national hero, and now even General Scott apparently was in on the plot. Lieutenant Sam French recorded a story that made the rounds of camp: the requisition so upset Taylor that he spooned mustard instead of sugar into his coffee. French, not a young man given to criticism of Polk (as were so many of his fellow officers), nevertheless concluded that "the administration, alarmed at [General Taylor's] growing popularity with the Whig party, hoping to divide . . . his fame with another, sent Gen. Scott with such an inadequate force that he was obliged to deprive Gen. Taylor of . . . troops. . . ."

Taylor fired off another furious letter, this time to Scott. But Taylor added that he would remain loyal and would send the troops Scott ordered, and he detached 4,700 men for an overland march to Tampico from Victoria. Then Taylor set out for Monterrey with some dragoons, infantrymen, and the battery of field artillery that included Lieutenant French.

Still other discouraging word reached Taylor. The second copy of Scott's dispatch had been captured by Mexican guerrillas who had lassoed the bearer, dragged him along the ground, and killed him—a favorite sport among the guerrillas. Learning of the loss of the dispatch, Taylor and other American officers assumed that Santa Anna would know the most intimate details of the Vera Cruz landing, and most of them predicted he would move his army against that new threat instead of challenging the troops around Saltillo and Monterrey. This would mean considerable relief for Taylor's withered force—if not for his political hopes—but on the other hand the Vera Cruz invaders would suffer.

While Taylor was marching back from Victoria in dejection many men of his garrison forces located in the Saltillo-Monterrey area already were streaming eastward toward the Rio Grande, Matamoros, and the Brazos—and toward the ultimate destination, Vera Cruz—on that requisition by Scott.

Among them was Captain Ephraim Kirby Smith, the veteran of Palo Alto and Resaca de la Palma, who had traveled home on leave after his father's death. Smith had rejoined his 5th Infantry Regiment after the Battle of Monterrey, and that unit later had moved as part of General Worth's division to the occupation of Saltillo. There the men of the 5th had been quartered in an old Franciscan monastery—Smith himself in the monastery apothecary shop, a room shared with another officer and with shelves, labeled boxes, fleas the size of "small crickets," and old smells of pills and rancid lard, all legacies of the previous resident. The two human occupants had made their bed on a counter left over from earlier days, and Smith was napping there after lunch on January 8 when a lieutenant of dragoons roused him.

"Up! You will be on the march in an hour."

The officer, a friend of his, had just reached Saltillo with that dispatch from General Scott at Camargo and would say no more, since the orders had been marked "private and confidential." But soon after the lieutenant had left, a major from Smith's regiment entered the room and announced, "Have your company ready to march in thirty minutes."

Despite such short notice, Smith—always a professional—was up and ready at the appointed time. Not until one o'clock the following afternoon, however, did he and his men begin the long journey—by foot to Camargo, then by boat down the Rio Grande—to join Scott's concentration of forces.

Smith left Saltillo sadly, despite the farewell to those giant fleas that had inhabited his quarters. He had made friends among the residents, and he commented on their own reaction to the departure: "The inhabitants had rapidly gained confidence in the regulars and were much alarmed when they found we were about leaving them to the mercy of the volunteers, of whom they have the utmost dread, and by whom they are generally treated with the utmost barbarity."

Lieutenant Sam Grant's 4th Infantry was quickly transferred to General Worth's command for the move to the Brazos—and, as it developed, for the duration of the war. Grant, too, received those hurried orders to pack. On January 11, when Worth's division, with Captain Smith, was passing through Monterrey two days after its departure from Saltillo, Grant and his 4th Regiment (and some other units stationed at Monterrey) fell in with the troops for the march.

In General Worth, Grant found a different commander from those under whom he had served previously—and a near opposite of the usually easygoing Taylor. Worth was "nervous, impatient, and restless on the march, or when important or responsible duty confronted him." On the way to Camargo (where the soldiers were to embark on boats for the trip downriver) he drove his men as if they were bound for the relief of a beleaguered garrison, Grant said, although "it was known that it would take weeks to assemble shipping enough [at the Brazos] to carry the army. . . ."

Near Saltillo, Captain Robert E. Lee, who was still with General Wool's army, was summoned to headquarters on the night of January 16. There Wool handed him a letter signed by General Scott and sent from the Brazos ten days earlier. "Of the officers of engineers, topographical engineers, and ordnance . . . under your command, I propose to take only Captain R. Lee, of the first named corps."

As he had shown earlier, Lee never was a man to waste time in reporting to a new assignment, and Scott's forthcoming operation required speed. The season of yellow fever—"black vomit"—would be on Vera Cruz with the coming of sizzling summer. Scott had to have his troops in there and out again, into the cool mountains toward Mexico City, before that time. Lee packed his belongings and the next day rode out of Wool's camp astride his mare Creole—no doubt in company with others who had been ordered to Scott. Lee made the 250-mile trip to the Brazos on horseback, and when he arrived at Scott's headquarters from Wool's subordinate command he walked through a door of opportunity.

Sam French of the artillery stayed behind, with the hapless Taylor. When French returned from the useless march to Victoria he went into camp with his battery at Walnut Springs, where the Monterrey operation had commenced so long before. Commander of his battery, arrogant Braxton Bragg, was so much disliked that enlisted men attached to the battery had made two attempts to kill him in retaliation for certain punishment.

Despite Bragg's overbearing and immediate presence, however, the stay at Walnut Springs was not all unpleasant for French. The scenery was delightful, and the poetic soul deep and sometimes hidden in the young warrior enabled him to appreciate it fully.

Nearly every morning a canopy of clouds would form around the breast of Saddle Mountain, extending overhead to a distance of five or six miles. Gradually, as the day advanced, the clouds from the outer edge would sail gently away one after the other, disrobing the mountain and exposing the beauty of its form to view.

279

Once I was on the mountain above the clouds, in the bright sunshine looking down upon this billowy sea. Beyond was the lofty ridge glowing in the sun; around, hiding the plain for miles distant, was an ocean of clouds white as snow, softer than carded wool, lighter than down, rolling and swelling as silent as the heavens above them. Then they floated slowly away . . . and left me to look down on the gross earth. . . .

In the skies above Monterrey were those billowy clouds, and heavenly peace. On the "gross earth" below was apparent peace—future fighting certainly seemed likelier elsewhere—but plenty of violence. The U. S. Army had occupied Monterrey and Saltillo and towns to the east all the way to Matamoros, along the supply and communications line, but the territory had not been entirely pacified, and some acts of American volunteers assured that it could not be.

Army regulars, especially the officers, were almost unanimous in condemning their tumultuous colleagues. Lieutenant George McClellan remarked, with some exaggeration, "You never hear of a Mexican being murdered by a regular or a regular by a Mexican." He added that the volunteers "think nothing" of robbing or killing the Mexicans. Lieutenant George C. Meade said that volunteers "made themselves so terrible by their previous outrages as to have inspired the Mexicans with a perfect horror of them."

It seemed that many volunteers had joined the Army for fun and frolic more than for fighting, and their revelry got out of hand. Their own officers were reluctant to discipline them for fear of reprisal later, upon return to civilian life; for all personnel in volunteer regiments came from the same localities. Soon after the capture of Monterrey the behavior of some Texas Rangers became so unruly that General Taylor sent them home at the expiration of their enlistment with this side comment: "We may look for a restoration of quiet and order . . . for I regret to report that some shameful atrocities have been perpetrated by them since the capitulation of the town."

Other riotous volunteers, however, took their places. A group of men apparently from a Kentucky regiment broke into a residence in the Monterrey suburbs, threw out the husband, and raped his wife. Soon after that a Kentuckian was found dead—his throat slashed. In following days other persons, both Mexicans and volunteers, were wounded or killed as a result of the initial crime. Victims included a twelve-year-old Mexican boy, who was shot in the leg.

Incidents like this one compounded the barbarism of Mexican guerrillas, who already had become famous for the horrors they could inflict out of hatred for the invaders. One soldier serving in northern Mexico at this time wrote of the dangers faced by any American who rode alone across the countryside on messenger duty or who straggled too far from his unit. "He [would be] lassoed, stripped naked, and dragged through clumps of cactus until his body was full of needle-like thorns; then, his privates cut off and crammed into his mouth, he [would be] left to die in the solitude of the chapperal [sic] or to be eaten alive by vultures and coyotes."

So, around Saltillo and Monterrey, plenty of fighting remained for individuals who sought it—but no fighting for an army. Reports of the approach of Santa Anna still seeped in from time to time, but the man and his large force did not appear.

This seemed fortunate. Taylor, after losing all those troops to Scott, was left holding a line in northern Mexico two hundred miles long with a manpower total that had fallen to between seven or eight thousand. Taylor's star seemed to have fallen even farther than his troop numbers.

Hundreds of miles away, around the Brazos, Colonel Hitchcock's own star continued its meteoric rise. General Scott had continued to be gracious and solicitous, usually preferring to address Hitchcock as "my dear Colonel." This politeness continued even after Hitchcock was ordered to court-martial duty late in January and at one juncture demanded successfully that the judge advocate "require" Scott to produce a document he previously had declined to give the court.

32.

Bugle Notes of Reveille

Nearly three hundred miles south of the Saltillo-Monterrey area, on a cool, dry plateau six thousand feet high, General Santa Anna, at San Luis Potosí, took a personal inventory.

Five months and more had passed since his return from exile. The Mexican Congress again had elected him President. He had accepted, of course, but had not taken the oath, thereby letting Valentín Gómez Farías remain in temporary custody of the government. Santa Anna's duty was to lead the army he had gathered against the invader, but the problem of finances still plagued him. Those voluntary contributions had been insufficient; so had the other means to which he had resorted. He demanded more money from Mexico City, and Farías, desperate to find new ways of funding the Army and the Mexican Government, resorted to a last-gasp effort. After a mild attempt to force loans from the Church had failed, Farías pressed for congressional passage of a bill that would confiscate for sale or mortgage Church properties to the value of fifteen million dollars.

Santa Anna originally supported the measure. The general, of course, had urged upon Farías the expediency of getting governmental hands on Church gold. After long debate the bill became law, but enforcement quickly proved to be impossible. On the very same day of passage Church officials issued a declaration threatening retaliation (including excommunication) for any mortal who thus seized or bought Church property. In the streets of Mexico City rioting flared—in favor of the Church.

At San Luis Potosí Santa Anna reacted immediately to these developments. He voiced his criticism of the new law—further embarrassing

Farías, whom Santa Anna himself had helped to place in this tenuous situation—and suggested congressional modification of the legislation. A virtual repeal soon followed.

This left Santa Anna still in need of money for his army, and he reiterated his demand that the government raise it somehow and send it soon.

That part of Santa Anna's personal inventory would have shown to his advantage, at least in his estimation. He had not antagonized the Church, certainly not the way Farías had. Santa Anna remained the elected President and could move into that office upon taking the oath. Finally, he still had his army, even if it was underfed, underclad, payless for long periods, and low in morale.

Other matters put Santa Anna on a shakier limb. Rumors of his disloyalty still floated around. How could he possibly have returned to Mexico through the American naval blockade, unless he had been allowed free passage for some secret purpose? Was he even now negotiating with the United States? Why had he evacuated the military garrison at Tampico, a vital port? Why did he linger at San Luis Potosí? Why was he making excuses for not fighting?

Santa Anna weighed all these things and knew he must act soon. His genuine eagerness to get at Zachary Taylor really was not lacking. Money actually had become a problem, as had the season of the year. Raw winter, plus miles and miles of desolation, now separated him from the area where Taylor had established his army.

That dispatch from General Scott containing information about the Vera Cruz landing and about the troop requisition might not have been delivered to Santa Anna by the guerrillas who captured it. Conclusive evidence that Santa Anna ever read it is absent. But he did not need it to know about Taylor's troop strength and position. Spies told him. Furthermore, two strong Mexican cavalry detachments operated in that vicinity and kept him informed of Taylor's movements. One force of several thousand men commanded by General Vicente Miñon roamed a large area south of Saltillo. Another detachment of fifteen hundred cavalrymen commanded by General José Urrea operated out of Tula, between Victoria and San Luis Potosí.

Finally, Santa Anna had the benefit of information wangled out of recently captured United States soldiers. Some eighty Americans had been captured inside a walled hacienda called La Encarnación, fifty-five miles south of Saltillo. The men, originally comprising two separate detachments, had been riding on mid-January patrols when a downpour drove them all inside the hacienda. They had neglected to post any guards (volunteers never were strict about military details), and they had awakened at dawn, following a good night's sleep, to the blaring of a bugle sounding charge. Then they had seen that General Miñon's cavalry stood encircling the place, and they had surrendered.

Later one man escaped and took word of the capture back to Saltillo —a Texan who had fallen prisoner to Mexicans once before, during the tumultuous days of the Lone Star Republic. He arrived too late, however, to halt the departure of another reconnaissance party of eighteen mounted men sent southward to locate the missing patrols. These riders happened to meet some apparently convivial Mexicans who invited all eighteen of them to a ranch, poured for them many drinks, then called in Miñon's cavalry for another easy capture.

So, with information acquired from several sources, Santa Anna knew Taylor's approximate troop strength and his position, even if he did not know about Scott's requisition and future plans. Now Santa Anna's challenge could wait no longer.

On January 26 he issued orders about equipment to be taken. Because of the large quantity of supplies that must be carried into the barren country, soldiers' baggage would be strictly limited: an extra shirt or two in addition to the one worn with the uniform, four rounds of ammunition for each man, and cooking equipment. Twenty-one wagons and 450 pack mules would carry more ammunition and other necessities. But the soldiers had very few possessions to be concerned about, anyway, and Santa Anna realized this. He sought to turn it to his own advantage in another of his ringing proclamations, this one addressed to his "companions in arms" and released on the day his army began its march. "Privations of all kinds await you; but when has want or penury weakened your spirit or debilitated your enthusiasm?" he asked, in an effort to instill some pride in his already dejected men. "The Mexican soldier is well known for his frugality and capability of sufferance."

Then he really spurred them on. "Today you commence your march, through thinly settled country, without supplies and without provisions; but you may be assured that very quickly you will be in possession of those of your enemy, and of his *riches*; and with them, all your wants will be superabundantly remedied."

The first group left on January 27: the artillery, with twenty guns ranging from 8-pounders to 24-pounders, and including one mortar. U. S. Army deserters—members now of the Mexican battalion named San Patricio—manned the heavier guns.

After that nearly twenty thousand men of the cavalry and the infantry left in sections one day apart. Many were accompanied by wives or sweethearts carrying wood and other supplies necessary for mobile housekeeping. On February 2 the headquarters group departed, making a display nearer to magnificence than any of the other units.

One of the Americans captured at La Encarnación saw this assemblage and later wrote a description of it. Santa Anna, dressed in a uniform heavy with gold braid, rode in a coach pulled by eight mules. Accompanying him were his colorfully uniformed, elegantly equipped staff, and a number of women. Behind trailed a line of pack mules carrying supplies and (the prisoner heard) many of Santa Anna's favorite fighting cocks in cages.

With the general's departure the entire army was on the road northward toward Saltillo, and General Miñon's cavalry (under orders sent by Santa Anna) already was riding to threaten Taylor's eastern flank and to stand by for a final assault on the *norteamericanos* from that direction when the enemy fled in retreat from this huge force.

Santa Anna left behind him a picturesque city of rose-tinted buildings and multicolored domes and towers—many covered with blue and white glazed tile—that glittered in the afternoon sun and gave some indication of the mining riches that had gone into the building of the place. The look of his army, however, reflected none of this wealth; and ahead the soldiers faced even grimmer days. They marched out upon a high plateau of increasing aridity and sterility. Across it they would travel on skimpy rations.

At the outset the weather alternated between too cold and too hot. A day's march mixed sweat with the dust that seeped through clothing and settled on skin, but soon after halting for the night a chill left the dampened soldiers and their women companions shivering. Many of them surely (if quietly) cursed the man who had led them into this realm of the damned—a man who provided for his own comfort: good, clean, warm clothes and ample food. Some soldiers vanished into the landscape, choosing to desert, even in this wilderness, rather than endure more marches. They risked death by starvation if successful in their attempt to escape and faced certain death as punishment if captured. Other men who chose to stay with the army sickened and died—agonizingly, because Santa Anna did not care much for medical assistance. The obvious lack of it, he believed, would help to convince his officers and men that death would be preferable to emerging wounded from battle.

On February 10 a sudden weather change attacked them almost with the ferocity of an enemy. Ahead, low on the northern horizon, lay the harbinger of this occurrence—a dark cloud that seemed to thicken and to draw nearer even as the people watched. Meanwhile, a south wind that had been playing through the ranks of the marchers weakened, then died. The slopes of the brown mountains nearby were more barren than ever, and with the absence of the slightest breeze, nature seemed for a while to have expired. Only the tramping sounds of men and horses heard in the vicinity of the moving column gave much indication of life in this trackless land.

The color of the horizon became dark blue—almost black. Ahead of this cloud mass a cool north wind of increasing chill began buffeting the advancing army. An icy rain commenced falling. Then came sleet. Shattering wind now carried the frozen droplets almost horizontally and flung them into thousands of faces.

A weather phenomenon peculiar to this part of the world had struck. Down narrow valleys, across lifeless plains, the winds of a "blue norther" howled, carrying rain, sleet, and snow in blinding sheets. The soldiers and their women gathered the skimpy garments they wore closer about them—and still they suffered. More sick persons died; others fell ill during the storm. Some simply vanished, having died or wandered away. Estimates of fatalities caused by the weather eventually numbered four hundred. Even after the savage norther had passed, dwindling food and water supplies and fresh torment caused by desert heat sent other people in flight from this dreadful march, and probably many of them died, too. "On this desert," said a Mexican eyewitness, "nothing was observed beyond sky and grass, save [occasionally] some distant rancheria, similar to the huts of savages and resembling an island on this terrestrial ocean." During the journey of more than two hundred miles Santa Anna lost as many as four thousand soldiers one way or another—nearly twenty men for each mile covered.

By February 20, however, the remainder of his army had collected at La Encarnación, where the eighty or so sleepy and foolish *norteameri-*

canos had been captured by General Miñon's cavalry. When Santa Anna's advance arrived there it encountered an enemy detachment that opened fire and caused some momentary concern, but the enemy rode off soon afterward—no doubt assuming the Mexicans to be more of Miñon's cavalry.

Even after taking such huge losses on the march Santa Anna boasted an army three times as large as Taylor's. At La Encarnación he lined up his men and reviewed them on horseback. His hardy soldiers still had enough spirit and enough air in their lungs to greet his appearance with cheers that resounded across the landscape. About eleven o'clock in the morning of the twenty-first they began moving on toward Agua Nueva, thirty-five miles farther north, where Santa Anna knew (from various reports) that most of Taylor's troops were now assembled.

For the last part of this march Santa Anna issued strict orders covering a variety of details. His troops would surprise Taylor early in the morning of February 22 with an immediate attack on enemy lines, while confusion about this sudden emergence of so large an army still prevailed. For that reason the last part of the march must be made cautiously. No fires were to be allowed that night—and certainly none on the morning of the attack. Troops would keep strict silence during the early morning of the twenty-second.

No water would be found in this final stretch; so Santa Anna ordered his men to drink well, to fill their canteens, and to water their horses carefully before leaving La Encarnación. The next chance for a drink would come at Agua Nueva, and Taylor's army would have to be defeated quickly to get it.

Food was another concern. Each soldier left La Encarnación carrying with him two rations. One contained a small piece of jerked meat, two biscuits, and a hard lump of brown sugar, to be eaten that night. The other ration would be eaten according to necessity. This would provide scant nourishment for men already on the verge of starvation, but Taylor's own supplies, when captured, would yield the vital supplements.

Across more barren wasteland Santa Anna's ragged column struggled —infantry, cannon, ammunition wagons, engineers, cavalry, more infantrymen and more cannon and wagons, then pack mules escorted by a rear guard of lancers. On this march the women were not allowed to accompany their men. They followed some distance behind.

The afternoon sun dropped low, then vanished, leaving behind it dimming daylight, increasing chill, and a mountain pass to be crossed in utter darkness. Men groped on, half frozen now despite their exertions, and engulfed by night.

Distant shots fired in the blackness ahead told them their advance had come upon another patrol of *norteamericanos*. Ensuing silence told them further there was nothing to worry about. Their advance units were strong. The enemy had been killed or, more likely, had been sent fleeing toward the main body of his army. Nor did General Santa Anna concern himself much about discovery. He knew that in the past General Miñon's cavalry had engaged in frequent skirmishes with the enemy. This would be considered just another one of those incidents.

A halt before dawn of the twenty-second, after the men had reached the summit and had begun descending the mountain, allowed some rest, but—in subfreezing temperature—not much sleep. "The cold was intense, beyond description," one member of Santa Anna's army wrote later in a Mexico City journal. ". . . The soldiers . . . were . . . half dead with cold, looking like an army of lifeless bodies." Subdued commands soon had the men up and marching again—quietly, as Santa Anna had ordered. Ahead lay Agua Nueva and Taylor's unsuspecting soldiers.

When Santa Anna's advance came in sight of the long-sought objective, however, no tents filled with sleeping troopers could be seen, and no emplaced guns half manned by relaxing artillerymen. Instead, visible in the distance was an empty, blazing, smoking camp site that must have been hurriedly evacuated before having been set afire. Word went back to the general, and Santa Anna hurried forward to see for himself. Inspection showed five U. S. Army wagons wrecked and abandoned in the vicinity, and piles of supplies that had gone up in flames. Hacienda buildings also were ablaze.

So Taylor had learned of Santa Anna's arrival after all, and had retreated! But Taylor had not simply withdrawn. The signs of panic were unmistakable. Agua Nueva ranch peons corroborated this. They said the Americans had left hurriedly. "They have fled! They have fled!" Santa Anna exclaimed, in his own tongue. The general was a man ruled by emotion in a time of excitement (despite that description of his philosophical appearance in peaceful interludes), and now he showed his agitation.

He would crush the enemy yet. His men were famished for water and nearly dead on their feet, but they had survived an awful 235-mile march through a dreadful land, and—being Mexican soldiers—they could go on a few more miles. Santa Anna drove them forward, on after the fleeing Taylor. A Mexican officer said later that the general refused to allow his men time to get a drink of water.

General Taylor really had not worried much about those reports of a large army gathering at San Luis Potosí under Santa Anna, because Taylor did not believe the Mexican troops could be marched across the forbidding country that lay between them and the Saltillo-Monterrey area. Although those false rumors of Santa Anna's approach had excited his men from time to time (and once, during Taylor's absence in Victoria, had even brought American civilians in Monterrey under arms to help repel the enemy), Taylor himself had remained unmoved. He believed in investigating reports, of course, but he felt sure that reconnaissance would show no attack by Santa Anna impending. The strongest enemy force in the area was General Miñon's cavalry.

While Taylor was on his useless march to Victoria still another report of Santa Anna's imminent appearance had caused General Butler, acting in Taylor's absence at Monterrey, to concentrate the dwindled American force more closely around Saltillo. Wool's division, which had stayed at Agua Nueva after the earlier scare and the ensuing forced march toward Saltillo, was moved nearer to that city, to a hacienda named Buena Vista—largely at the insistence of Wool himself, who argued that Agua Nueva lay on terrain too exposed for defense. At the same time men of a small garrison left behind at Monclova were ordered to join Wool at his new location. Outposts of cavalry responsible for reconnoitering areas to the south were brought in closer. American soldiers fortified Saltillo and barricaded city streets.

Taylor had returned to a headquarters thrown into fresh turmoil by still another report that Santa Anna was coming. On February 2—the day that the last units of the large Mexican army had indeed left San Luis Potosí—Taylor rode from Monterrey to Saltillo and, after conferences with subcommanders, decided on another change of position. He would establish a supply base southeast of Saltillo and move the body of his army to Agua Nueva, the place Wool had just abandoned. Taylor still did not expect to see Santa Anna's army, but if the Mexicans gathered at San Luis Potosí did try to attack him they would have to march northward through a dry land that offered a man no water for many miles until he reached Agua Nueva. By holding that place, Taylor declared, he could defeat Santa Anna's troops, who probably would arrive mad with thirst if they should ever come at all. But any attack would more likely be aimed at General Scott and his invasion of Vera Cruz, Taylor thought, especially now that (as he assumed) Santa Anna knew of the plans through that captured letter.

About the time that Taylor moved his army to Agua Nueva there arrived from General Scott a dispatch containing orders originally formulated in Washington. Taylor was told flatly to maintain a position at Monterrey and not to venture anywhere beyond that city.

Taylor refused to obey this order, declaring that Santa Anna must never be allowed to advance as far as Saltillo, where he would find plenty of water and other supplies for a famished army and could then mount an attack on Monterrey. But this was only another show of obstinacy from the recalcitrant general who believed that everyone in authority was against him now. Taylor still did not expect Santa Anna, of course, even though the Mexican general's march had commenced.

In accordance with Taylor's orders Lieutenant Sam French of the artillery moved with his battery from Walnut Springs to Saltillo early in February. He traveled that same westward road paralleling the Santa Catarina River that General Worth had reconnoitered more than four months earlier, before his attack.

The sixty-mile march provided fascinating scenery: past Bishop's Palace, stormed by Worth's soldiers during the battle that French had observed from a distance; along the base of mountains, with one notable peak lying eight miles off to the left but looking much nearer because of its height and the clear atmosphere; past more "lofty mountains, deep valleys, wild, narrow passes, beautiful green fields in cultivation," and—happily—across numerous streams of clear water. Still, the trip proved to be toilsome: always up, up, into more mountains, until French reached Saltillo, built on a slope.

Soon after that he and his battery were sent on to Agua Nueva with the rest of the main army. When they arrived they found the camp excited as usual by the latest report of Santa Anna's advance, said to have begun toward them from San Luis Potosí, with the huge army crossing the desert in detachments. Much of the fresh stir prevalent in camp would have been caused (as it often was) by the impressionable volunteers.

Except for two detachments of dragoons and two other field artillery batteries besides French's, Taylor's entire army now was composed of non-professionals, and only one regiment among these novices had been through any fighting at all.

French listened to the various rumors and on February 20 went on a leisurely hunting trip with another officer. But the brief outing became something less than a lark.

> . . . The day was warm; the winds were in their caves; an ominous silence pervaded all nature; the sun did not dazzle the eye, and was distinct in outline, like the full moon; the game was tame and stupid; [my companion] was heavy of heart and dreamy. There was something peculiar in this silence—like the desert—like the stillness that oft precedes the tempest and the earthquake. . . . The day left a lasting impression on my mind, it was so weirdlike and mystical.

Within hours after his return to camp that same day French had reason to become more concerned about the situation. The commander of the mounted detachment that had fired on the Mexican advance at La Encarnación before withdrawing had returned and reported the incident to Taylor. The officer added that he did not believe the Mexican troops he saw belonged to General Miñon, who was said to be operating east of Saltillo anyway.

Taylor listened to this officer. He was Ben McCulloch, one of those remarkable Texas Ranger leaders who, like Sam Walker and Jack Hays, had joined the U. S. Army for the war. McCulloch, a quiet, calm, blue-eyed Tennessean still in early middle age, was not known for making mistakes when they mattered. Like all other Ranger captains, McCulloch had acquired leadership in the first place by proving himself in Ranger ranks, and not by political appointment. Taylor himself had asked McCulloch to command his scouting detachments. The general recognized expertise when he saw it, even if he had been repelled by the actions of some other Rangers.

Taylor sent McCulloch and a few other men, all dressed like Mexicans, back to La Encarnación on February 20 for a closer look at the enemy. That same day Taylor also ordered Charles May, the officer who had made the disputed capture of a Mexican general at Resaca de la Palma, to take a strong force of dragoons eastward to see what General Miñon's cavalry was doing.

May returned early on the following morning with two grim reports.

He had lost an officer and an enlisted man, both captured by Miñon's soldiers after a bit of carelessness, and he had heard from a Mexican civilian that Santa Anna and a large army were encamped at La Encarnación—only thirty-five miles from Taylor.

In all the talk that ensued around camp Sam French heard something May did not. French's battery commander, ever critical Braxton Bragg, listened to the accounts of May's reconnaissance and his loss of two men and snorted to acquaintances ("in his usual sarcastic manner," French said), "I perceive that it is harder to *lose* one's reputation than to make it."

Later that same day, when Ben McCulloch returned from his own reconnaissance, General Taylor had information enough about Santa Anna's presence—and the entire camp marveled at another example of Texas Ranger daring.

McCulloch and his men had come upon the Mexican bivouac in darkness. About midnight they stole past the pickets, entered the Mexican lines, and rode around the camp. McCulloch realized its great size, and he sent all but one man back to General Taylor with this preliminary information. Then he and the other man climbed a hill inside Mexican lines and waited for daylight, for a better look.

Dawn brought the bugle notes of reveille, rousing the camp to life. McCulloch and his companion saw campfires beginning to blaze (this before Santa Anna's order forbidding them). The Mexicans were using green wood, McCulloch realized, and it eventually made a smoke that almost obscured his vision.

Still, McCulloch saw enough. He and the other man rode slowly out of camp between still unsuspecting pickets, then galloped away toward Agua Nueva with an estimate for Taylor, delivered in the afternoon of February 21—after Santa Anna had begun his final long march toward the attack. The Mexicans had twenty thousand men at La Encarnación, McCulloch said—and it was a good guess, considering the difficulties experienced in arriving at it. Taylor listened to the report and told McCulloch, "Very well, Major, that's all I wanted to know. I am glad they did not catch you."

Earlier, when McCulloch's men returned after their first glimpse of the darkened Mexican camp, Taylor had decided to abandon Agua Nueva as being untenable against so large a force as that gathered at La Encarnación—just as General Wool had said it was. Taylor now hurried his men fifteen miles northward to Buena Vista—to the same location Wool had chosen earlier. He ordered teamsters to load as many supplies as possible into the wagons, to take them to Buena Vista, and to return to Agua Nueva for new loads as rapidly as they could. To guard the supplies in the meantime he left behind a regiment of Arkansas cavalry—and farther up the road, to support a quick Arkansas withdrawal if needed, a Kentucky infantry regiment and some artillery pieces. Then Taylor went on with the rest of his army.

At Buena Vista he dropped off most of the troops, left General Wool in charge of them, and rode on with an escort to Saltillo, to take a look at defensive preparations there (especially around his supply depot southeast of the city) before returning to Buena Vista. Perhaps his supplies were to be the target of General Miñon's far-ranging cavalry.

The new ground chosen for a stand had excellent possibilities, particularly at a location just south of Buena Vista on the same Saltillo-San Luis Potosí road that Taylor had used for his withdrawal. (A direct Mexican attack from La Encarnación would have to come up that road.) The stand could be made at a point on the road called La Angostura— The Narrows. Certain peculiarities of the surrounding terrain combined to create a bottleneck there for a large body of men trying to march northward. To the west, between the road and some nearby hills, lay a deeply eroded area of ditches and gullies, some of them twenty feet deep. To the east lay steep ridges, seventy feet or more in height, and precipitous ravines that extended to a mountain some distance away farther east and provided protection for a plateau that lay behind the ridges. Sam French looked over the position and wrote his own description: "If the Hudson river, where it passes through the Catskill Mountains, were dry and wider, and its surface furrowed by deep ravines and water gullies crossing it, it would resemble the field of Buena Vista." Taylor remarked, "The features of the ground were such as nearly to paralyze the artillery and cavalry of the enemy, while his infantry could not derive all the advantages of its numerical superiority." Defenders' guns properly placed could command the road and stop any progress on it—or so the hope went as the small American force dug in to face overwhelming numbers.

General Wool had noticed the spot much earlier, during a ride through The Narrows, and had pointed out its advantage as a defensive position. Now, with Taylor gone to Saltillo, he had an opportunity to follow through with his own recommendations.

Night had come, but not for much sleep. Wool put men to work building breastworks and digging trenches at strategic places around The Narrows, and he formulated plans for emplacing cannon at first light of the following day.

Fifteen miles down the road, at Agua Nueva, teamsters were throwing another load of supplies on their wagons when, toward midnight, they heard firing in the distance to southward—the same shots, no doubt, that had been audible to the main body of Santa Anna's army before its halt, in darkness, in the mountains. Not long afterward mounted pickets galloped from out of the night into Agua Nueva and shouted to terrified teamsters and startled Arkansas cavalrymen that the enemy's advance units were not far off.

Teamsters leaped on half-filled wagons, cracked whips, yelled at animals, and raced off toward Buena Vista. In their rush they wrecked five wagons and left them abandoned beside the road. Cavalrymen carrying lighted torches hurried from one pile of supplies to another, making bonfires of them, and put their torches also to buildings, trees, and anything else of potential value to an enemy. Then they mounted their horses and galloped off toward Buena Vista, leaving Agua Nueva in flames that burned a little lower as the night wore on.

33.

The Soil of Buena Vista

The date—February 22, George Washington's birthday—would have meant nothing in particular to the exuberant Santa Anna as he hurried his men northward in pursuit of Taylor that morning. Santa Anna's own birthday celebration—certainly a subdued one if there had been any at all—would have come the previous day. But now Santa Anna had received, belatedly, a fine present. The five wrecked wagons at Agua Nueva offered convincing evidence that General Taylor's withdrawal had been not just an evacuation but a flight.

For this day of destiny Santa Anna—once more a democrat, self-proclaimed—was dressed in a most appropriate manner. He wore a very ordinary officer's uniform protected by a white duster and, perched atop his head, a straw hat—informality almost worthy of his unsophisticated adversary. During the advance from Agua Nueva, Santa Anna rode among his troops, urging them on, exhorting them to forget their hunger and weariness, calling for effort that would send the invader back where he had come from, back where he belonged. Several exhausted infantrymen collapsed and died. Their bodies lay stretched flat on the road. But the others went on.

The general's enthusiasm remained high for a while that morning. His weary men pressed on for five miles—six, seven; ten miles, to hacienda La Encantada. But then some cavalrymen galloped back from the van with surprising information: a strong enemy force had entrenched itself ahead on the Saltillo road, a mile or so south of the hacienda named Buena Vista, at a place where guns could shatter anything traveling along this route.

Santa Anna rode forward for a personal inspection. With his glass he swept the landscape, and he realized the strong defensive position Taylor's army had found and fortified. Further progress along the road would indeed be impossible, from the looks of things, and the deep gullies to the west made an attack there impractical. A glance to eastward showed possibilities there about the same.

For a general who only a short time earlier had been gloating over the enemy's panicky escape this was indeed an unpleasant surprise. Still, Santa Anna knew he had the Americans badly outnumbered—even if his own troops were virtually exhausted, having culminated their terrible journey from San Luis Potosí with a forced march of nearly fifty miles in less than twenty-four hours, with little food, water, or rest. Santa Anna knew also that General Miñón's cavalrymen were off to the east prepared to circle in and to pounce on Taylor from the rear. Victory would still come; it would only be slower and costlier. The fact that Santa Anna had brought so many men here in the first place was a triumph in itself. Probably no other Mexican general could have done it.

Subsequent inspection of the terrain gave Santa Anna more encouragement. Far to his right—to the east, along the foot of the mountain there—he saw a good chance for an assault. That route, not so rough, might give access to the plateau that lay beyond, toward the hacienda of Buena Vista. Furthermore, the diminished size of the army commanded by Taylor probably would preclude establishment of stout defensive positions along the entire line. The longer Santa Anna meditated, the more he felt that this path of Mexican advance would meet less resistance, although of course Taylor might shift his men as necessary to oppose an attack anywhere. The trick would be in not letting him see where the strike would come until the last minute.

Santa Anna commenced giving out orders that led to a bustle among the brightly uniformed troops around him. From this proximity their clothing would have shown the tatters of long and hard wear, but that would not be obvious to the *norteamericanos* staring from a distance. The brilliant colors of dress, the glittering lances, the radiant banners, and the noisy bugles characteristic of Mexican military show would make an awesome impression on the enemy, this self-styled Napoleon of the West no doubt thought as he began deployment. Certainly the pageantry and the band music that accompanied it would inspire his own troops.

Before commencing the battle, however, Santa Anna determined to offer Taylor a way out of it and (not incidentally) to gain for himself a little more time for last-minute details. He sent his surgeon general, a native German, and two other men, all mounted, under a white truce flag toward the American line. The surgeon general bore this written message from Santa Anna to Taylor:

> You are surrounded by twenty thousand men, and cannot, in any human probability, avoid suffering a rout, and being cut to pieces with your troops; but as you deserve consideration and particular esteem, I wish to save you from a catastrophe, and for that purpose give you notice, in order that you may surrender at discretion, under the assurance that you will be treated with the consideration belonging to the Mexican character; to which end you will be granted an hour's time to make up your mind, to commence from the moment when my flag of truce arrives in your camp. With this view, I assure you of my particular consideration.

The officer who proposed these liberal terms was the same man who had been responsible for the deaths of all of the 183 or so Texan defenders of the Alamo, for a Palm Sunday execution during the Texas rebellion of 342 Texan-American prisoners held at the small town of Goliad, and for an 1843 death lottery during which 17 of 176 Republic of Texas prisoners who had drawn black beans from a jar (containing 17 black and 159 white beans) were shot in punishment for an attempted mass escape—every tenth man among them thus executed. Santa Anna must have realized Taylor would know about these things, but Santa Anna was a man with the power of persuasion—as had been shown so often during his career. Furthermore, he really could be generous on occasion. Certainly he had Taylor in a bind now—and, he felt sure, doomed in any battle. Perhaps he had spoken the truth to Taylor about the generosity of his offer.

Sometime near 11 A.M. the communication was delivered to Taylor, who was standing with aides near eight guns lined up in The Narrows of the Saltillo road, facing southward. Commander of these pieces happened to be a Captain John M. Washington, although any coincidence ended there—the captain apparently was not related to the man of the same surname whose birthday on this date was being commemorated in the United States.

Eleven o'clock. Santa Anna had spoken. His deadline would fall, then, around noon.

Zachary Taylor did not share the Mexicans' love of pomp, and ringing proclamations, written or oral, meant little to him. Ostentations like these fell mostly on blind eyes and deaf ears as far as old Zach, the casual general, was concerned. A simple man, he believed in events as he saw them unfold, and not in words of promise, interpretation, or forecast.

Taylor listened to Santa Anna's message as it was being translated, then (according to one account) said angrily after its completion, "Tell Santa Anna to go to hell!" Taylor was a man capable of giving liberal terms himself—the Monterrey armistice had shown that. His generosity, however, did not extend to surrendering in the face of a challenge.

Taylor realized that even his terse seven-word reply needed translating; so he turned to his educated adjutant (and Colonel Hitchcock's erstwhile companion in conversation) and ordered, "Major Bliss, put that in Spanish, and send it back by this damned Dutchman."

Bliss had long before become expert at extensive revision of Taylor's official communications, correcting atrocious English and poor spelling, toning down curtness, and oiling Taylor's tactlessness. In the Army it was said that the literate Winfield Scott himself had sent Bliss to Taylor much earlier simply to get readable reports from the roughhewn general. So Bliss took this message, and—with Taylor's eventual approval—sent it back to Santa Anna in these words, in Spanish:

> Sir:—In reply to your note of this date, summoning me to surrender my force at discretion, I beg leave to say that I decline acceding to your request.

Knowing that no battlefield action would occur while the truce flag flew, Lieutenant Sam French had left his gun, located to the east of the road, and had ridden over to The Narrows, where Taylor and the group of other officers were chatting. French, too, heard Taylor's reply— "very forcible . . . toned down by Maj. Bliss"—but forgot the exact words and later regretted not writing them down. When the brief negotiations ended French returned to his gun, a 12-pounder, and waited for the fighting that was certain to begin soon. His piece and a 6-pounder commanded by Lieutenant George Thomas had been moved forward from their batteries, which were being held in reserve, and both guns now occupied positions alongside infantry units in the line of defense.

Taylor's army totaling 4,759 men (of whom more than 4,000 never had experienced battle) stood as ready as it ever would be to take on Santa Anna's 16,000 soldiers. The American troops had gone into position under General Wool's direction not long after daylight, before Taylor and his escort returned from Saltillo.

Captain Washington's battery of guns (the 4th Artillery) had been posted in that key position—directly in the road where it squeezed into the bottleneck known as The Narrows. Supporting the battery were troops of three regiments positioned nearby, on the crests of ridges: the 1st Illinois (commanded by Colonel John Hardin), the 2nd Illinois (Colonel William Bissell) with a group of Texas volunteers attached, and the 2nd Kentucky (Colonel William McKee). To the extreme left (or east) of the American line, near the base of the mountain there, were placed two cavalry regiments: an Arkansas regiment (Colonel Archibald Yell) and a Kentucky regiment (Colonel Humphrey Marshall). Held in reserve at various points behind the line, ready to move forward whenever and wherever needed, were the 2nd Indiana Regiment (Colonel William Bowles) and the 3rd Indiana (Colonel James Lane), both comprising the Indiana Brigade, whose commander was Brigadier General Joseph Lane; two light artillery batteries (commanded by Captain Thomas W. Sherman and Captain Braxton Bragg) of the 3rd Artillery (except for French's and Thomas' guns, already on the line); a regiment called the Mississippi Rifles (Colonel Jefferson Davis), and the squadrons of 1st Dragoons (Captain Enoch Steen) and 2nd Dragoons (Brevet Lieutenant Colonel Charles May). May's dragoons, Davis' Mississippi Rifles, and the batteries of Sherman and Bragg had accompanied Taylor during his trip to Saltillo for the quick look at defenses there, then had been ordered by the general to join the other units in reserve upon returning to Buena Vista earlier that morning, two hours before Santa Anna sent his surrender proposal under the truce flag. At that time Taylor also had ordered Sam French and George Thomas, with their guns, to leave their batteries and to take positions in the line.

Now, having returned to his 12-pounder after overhearing Santa Anna's message and Taylor's reply, French awaited the showdown. His gun had been emplaced to the left of the 2nd Illinois Regiment—with Thomas' 6-pounder to the right of the same unit. From this position, located east of the road on the plateau overlooking the ridges and ravines that cut through the land in front, French had a good view of what was about to become the Buena Vista battlefield. For another hour or so,

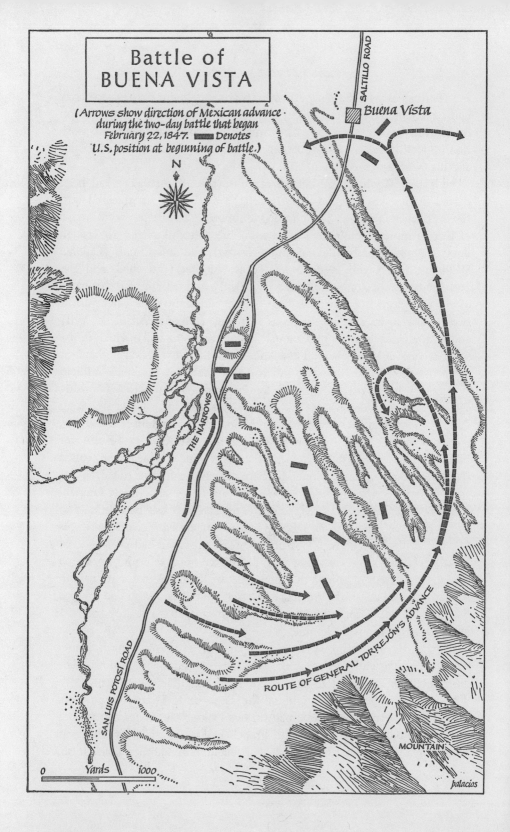

Battle of BUENA VISTA

(Arrows show direction of Mexican advance during the two-day battle that began February 22, 1847. ▬▬ Denotes U.S. position at beginning of battle.)

N

SALTILLO ROAD

Buena Vista

THE NARROWS

ROUTE OF GENERAL TORREJON'S ADVANCE

SAN LUIS POTOSI ROAD

MOUNTAIN

0   Yards   1000

palacios

however, no guns roared, no sounds of musketry shattered the strange calm as Santa Anna continued his deployment.

Far in the dust-clouded distance those colorfully uniformed Mexican soldiers continued to arrive on the scene, with banners waving, bands playing, and lances ominously flashing whenever they caught the sunlight. These were the rearmost troops in Santa Anna's long column. They moved into position even while French looked on. Watching also from nearby heights were other U. S. Army officers who relayed information to Taylor about Mexican movements—especially those in greatest strength —so that the general could dispatch reinforcements to counter enemy threats.

A concentration of Mexican troops to the west of the road brought the initial reaction from Taylor. Was Santa Anna thinking of trying an assault there, at the base of those hills, despite the deep gullies and ditches that extended from them? Taylor ordered the 2nd Kentucky and a section of artillery over to watch. The 3rd Indiana moved into the position thus vacated.

Nothing came of the threat—not even a skirmish—but the Kentuckians and their gun support remained. The move proved to be a feint by Santa Anna, who soon showed his true intention.

Sam French observed the maneuver. The enemy began ascending a ridge of the mountain to French's left, with the obvious aim of gaining a foothold at the top. Santa Anna had indeed decided to try that area to the east, at the base of the mountain, and he had ordered General Pedro de Ampudia, the former Monterrey commander, to move into it with his light infantry. The plan was, of course, to outflank Taylor and to strike him from the rear.

Colonel Marshall, waiting with his Kentucky cavalrymen, also saw the movement and sent his men, dismounted, up another slope of the same ridge, hoping to reach the summit before the enemy.

Taylor noticed the move, too, and sent three guns from Captain Washington's battery, supported by the 2nd Indiana, over to help. In command of the guns was a lieutenant named John Paul Jones O'Brien. The cannon soon roared, easily transcending the distant sounds of scattered small-arms fire.

Sam French continued to watch in fascination; the battle had not engaged him yet. The two slopes of the ridge that had become the site of so deadly a contest of speed "met at a point halfway up the mountain side; so the higher they went the nearer they approached each other."

Still others watched, too, and whenever the contest seemed to be going in favor of the Kentuckians a massive cheer rose from the plateau. Occasionally Mexican artillerymen sent random shots into Taylor's left flank, but without effect, and the skirmishing on the side of the mountain proved to be inconclusive, too. At one time the Kentuckians began a withdrawal, in mistaken compliance with an order never given, then had to recover lost ground. But Ampudia's troops climbed higher on the mountain and could look down on the Americans. The Mexicans' down-angled shots fired too high, however, and as usual caused few casualties.

Dusk came, and still French watched the fighting. Intermittent flashes of small-arms discharges dotted the mountainside. Soon after dusk the flashes ceased, but on the distant plateau campfires began to flicker. The enemy troops apparently were cooking and eating their rations—the last of them, as it developed. But Santa Anna gave them some additional food—for the soul—with another of his fiery exhortations, heard also by the Americans. He promised to appease their hunger on the following day with stores captured from Taylor. His soldiers gave him thunderous cheers: "*Viva Santa Anna! Viva la república! Libertad o muerte!*" Subdued sounds of distant military bands next reached the ears of the Americans. At least the Mexicans had that pageantry and a few fires to warm themselves.

General Taylor, feeling certain that no serious attack would be made before morning, returned to Saltillo with an escort of Mississippi Rifles, Charles May's 2nd Dragoons, and some troops he planned to leave behind as reinforcement for his supply depot. Taylor still felt concern for the security of his stores. He had heard that Miñon's cavalry had been seen near Saltillo during the day, and he suspected the enemy's aim might be to attack the town and his base of supplies—or possibly to fall upon the rear of his army.

On the field around Buena Vista Taylor's soldiers now began to fight a cold wind—mostly without the benefit of fires: not much flammable material could be found in the vicinity. French and two other officers—a major and another lieutenant—slept "bundled" for whatever warmth their collective bodies could provide. They placed one blanket on the ground, lay on it, and spread another blanket across themselves for cover. The major slept to windward, the other lieutenant to leeward, and French in the middle—but this did not help him much. "I cannot recall a night when I came so near perishing from cold," French said. To compound his misery a drizzle began to fall during the night.

Elsewhere around the silent battlefield an occasional alarm startled men. Pickets fired at various shadowy movements. Were the Mexicans planning something in the darkness? The shots roused chilled troops, but no action ensued.

At Saltillo, General Taylor enjoyed even less sleep than did French. He looked over his defenses and posted his reinforcements—in the city, four companies of Illinois volunteers and a detachment of artillerymen with two 24-pound howitzers, and at his supply depot, two companies of Mississippi riflemen and more artillerymen with another fieldpiece. Then he set out again for Buena Vista, taking with him the remaining escort, but action on the morning of the twenty-third had commenced before he returned.

Sam French rose stiffly from the freezing ground in early morning murkiness, unable to stop the chattering of his teeth. Nearby, some men had collected from somewhere sufficient parched vegetation to start a small fire, despite the dampness. French strode over to it and warmed his hands. The Mexicans allowed him time for such leisure for the moment; but better light brought him and his companions awareness of a renewed threat. During the night strong Mexican reinforcements had joined Ampudia's men on the steep mountain slope, and the enemy commanded the heights there—a good beginning for turning Taylor's left flank. A colonel ordered French to ride over to the base of the mountain to see if the enemy could bring his artillery across the rough terrain there. French made the trip without drawing fire, saw that the route was impassable, and returned with this report.

Not long after that Mexican divisions of infantry and cavalry commanded by Francisco Pacheco and Manuel Lombardini began moving toward French's sector, and they had the support of previously unobserved guns somehow emplaced during darkness on a high ridge that commanded the American artillery operating under John Paul Jones O'Brien.

The sputtering of small weapons first destroyed the morning silence. Then cannon added their reverberations to the din. More enemy guns opened on Washington's battery in The Narrows, and Mexican infantry units moved against that position in a strong diversion that served its purpose temporarily. The peace of Buena Vista—Good View—had been shattered once more.

General Wool, again commanding in the absence of Taylor, initially thought Washington's battery was the actual target. Then Wool recognized the threat to his left and sent reinforcements there: the 2nd Kentucky and the guns that had been moved westward (to the right of the line) the day before, when Santa Anna's feint indicated an attack in that direction.

Wool also ordered other units to shift eastward, to counter the pressure. Dismounted Arkansas cavalrymen climbed the steep slopes of the mountain to reinforce the Kentuckians. The morning had come in clear and sunny after the early drizzle, but soil and rocks remained damp, and footing on the mountain proved tricky for a time. Mexican fire made it even worse for the men who were seeking to ascend the slope.

Fighting engaged Sam French on the plateau. The Mexican commander Pacheco had managed to use for cover a deep ravine just in front of the 2nd Illinois to bring his division forward. French, standing at his gun, ordered fuses shortened in an attempt to burst shells over the heads of the hidden attackers, but apparently without much effect. Suddenly the Mexicans emerged almost in front of him—and about 150 yards away, French estimated. He heard the Illinois infantrymen positioned nearby open an intense fire; then he and George Thomas added showers of canister from their guns. But the enemy returned deadly volleys.

Farther off to French's left, Lombardini's troops joined with those of Pacheco in pressing the attack. To meet the thrust there the 2nd Indiana and the three guns commanded by John Paul Jones O'Brien rushed forward—into the left center of the American line. O'Brien unlimbered his guns and commenced shooting from his new position, but the Indiana infantrymen meant to accompany him were nowhere within supporting distance. Shattering enemy fire, along with an ill-timed regimental order to retreat, had propelled most of the troops into flight toward Buena Vista, two miles away. Colonel Bowles countermanded his order, but not in time to avert impending disaster. On the mountain, the Kentucky cavalrymen turned foot soldiers were pushed back and off the height. They ran for their horses, mounted them, and galloped off toward Buena Vista, too. Before nine o'clock that morning

General Taylor's left flank was folding—and Taylor himself was nowhere around. The enemy was clearing an eastward path to Buena Vista just as Santa Anna had planned, and by using it the Mexicans could outflank Taylor, attack him from the rear, and make good their general's boast to cut Taylor and his troops to pieces.

That very thing seemed to be happening, artillery officer O'Brien would have thought, but he kept blasting away until the Mexican advance had wreaked many casualties among his men and horses. Then he took two guns and withdrew, leaving the third piece behind because no soldiers or animals remained alive to move it.

Off to O'Brien's right, Sam French also was experiencing the disastrous effects of a crumbling flank. But he, too, continued to shoot at the enemy in front and to his left. He was placing his foot in a stirrup to mount his horse when he felt a blow on his right thigh—a sensation no more painful than "being struck with a club"—and realized he had been hit (by a small musket ball, as he learned later). Someone took time to help him on the horse, even with the battle raging nearby. Soon after that he received orders to bring his artillery piece back toward the road, to avoid being completely surrounded.

Sitting astride his mount and bleeding now, French had his gun limbered up and moved to a new position facing the enemy-infested mountain. There he opened fire again, "taking the [Mexicans] in flank and rear as they were crossing the plain." The position was not permanent, however, and French's gun moved again occasionally. At intervals the lieutenant searched for a surgeon to tend the wound, but all the doctors were occupied with more serious cases. Once French became so dizzy he had to be helped from his horse, but he did not remain dismounted for long. "I refused to be . . . put in a wagon," he explained, "knowing I would be 'lanced' by the Mexicans in case of disaster."

The morning wore on. French grew weary and weak from loss of blood through the wound that pained him constantly now. His leg had grown stiff. Still the battle flared around him: an inferno of roaring guns and cracking rifles and muskets, billowing, blinding smoke, yells and shouts, and distant screams of fleeing men who were being run down and lanced by cavalrymen.

The right side of the American line remained intact, but the left side had been bent back until it assumed a general north–south direction (rather than west–east) and lay facing that mountain to which the left flank once had been anchored—if not very firmly. This described the situation that existed when General Taylor finally arrived from Saltillo about 9 A.M. "The enemy was now pouring masses of infantry and cavalry along the base of the mountain on our left," Taylor said in his official report, "and gaining our rear in great force."

The time had come for Taylor to work his magic. The general, mounted as usual on Old Whitey, rode to a position in the center of the field where virtually every man of his small army could see him, and he began giving orders in his usual cool manner.

The first order had been given even before he assumed this deliberate posture. As soon as he had realized the seriousness of the situation he rushed his escorting Mississippi Rifles against the Mexican advance. The fiery Mississippians, led by Jefferson Davis, loosed a storm of metal that blunted the attack and even pushed the battered enemy back, to the cheers of relieved onlookers who witnessed that part of the fighting.

About this time Sam French assisted in repelling other attackers— a body of cavalrymen threatening the rear. Having left his fieldpiece in abler hands, French had ridden alone into the area, still searching for medical help, and he happened to be waiting there when another artillery lieutenant, John Reynolds, hurried by with his guns. French rode with him to lend a hand.

Reynolds took his artillery to a strategic location, quickly unlimbered, and fired as the Mexican cavalrymen mounted a charge. French remembered the scene long afterward: Reynolds himself standing at the caissons frantically preparing shells and cutting fuses while French, still stiffly mounted, directed fire. The shots sent the enemy reeling back beyond range of the guns. Then Reynolds moved on, looking for other targets, but French stayed behind. Soon French noticed another enemy threat and watched the skirmish it produced.

Weaker and wearier than ever, French had determined to ride to Buena Vista hacienda and to take himself out of the battle permanently when he saw, in the distance, a fight developing near the very place to which he was headed. Off to his right he noticed a large force of Mexican cavalry (under Anastasio Torrejón, the same general who had been operating around Fort Texas before the declaration of war) that had succeeded in passing along the base of the eastward mountain and in reaching the vicinity of the hacienda, which lay far in the rear. Even as French watched, the Mexicans were preparing to charge the hacienda—and the scattered, confused defenders were assembling assorted guns (including those of John Reynolds), horses, and men to make a stand. Among the men impressed for this job were some members of the 2nd Indiana who had fled earlier that day from the battered left flank.

French sat silently, entranced by the scene and apparently oblivious to the fate that would be determined in the next few minutes. He had never witnessed a cavalry duel before and, cadetlike still, he watched the action "with a great deal of interest."

The Arkansas and Kentucky cavalrymen who had commenced the Buena Vista battle by trying unsuccessfully to hold the left-flank mountain now sought to make a new stand. French saw them, all mounted, forming in line east of the hacienda to challenge the attackers, who French estimated "were over two to one of ours"—and probably considerably stronger than that.

"They came on in solid column," French said, "received the fire of our men without being checked at all, rode directly through our men, using their lances freely on every side." The Arkansas commander, Archibald Yell, was an early casualty—killed.

But the enemy column had been split. From Buena Vista rooftops other desperate Americans peppered the attackers with a furious fire. One part of the Mexican column wheeled back in retreat toward the east, the direction from which it had come, and the other group sped on westward, then southward, in its flight back to friendly lines—and thus "made the complete circuit" of Taylor's army, as the awed French saw.

Still the Mexicans pressed their attack, and helpless Sam French witnessed the next attempt, too. From the vicinity of the same mountain that already had brought near disaster to Taylor rode another strong force of enemy cavalrymen—lancers preparing to charge American infantrymen who occupied an area in the center of the battlefield just forward of Buena Vista: the Mississippi regiment, the 3rd Indiana, and men of the 2nd Indiana who had not fled—all with some artillery support. To receive the charge the Mississippians and Indianans hastily formed into a sort of V, with the open section facing the Mexicans.

French watched the ensuing action with near disbelief. Instead of making a headlong charge, the lancers wavered, slowed to a walk, and even seemed to halt as they neared the waiting infantrymen. At that moment the Americans opened upon their enemy from their V a deadly cross fire that killed or wounded scores of lancers in the van and sent the others galloping away in terror. Taylor's artillery poured shells on these men and on other Mexican units now in retreat along the base of the same mountain they had once used for their advance.

French saw no more of the battle, although bloody fighting continued. He finally rode on to Buena Vista—a safe place now—and into the courtyard of the main house there. Men helped him off his horse and carried him into a large room serving as a makeshift hospital. No surgeon was present—all doctors being employed still on the battlefield—but friendly hands helped him to lie back on the hard floor, which was covered with other wounded, and made him as comfortable as possible.

> . . . I was placed between two soldiers. One had both legs broken below the knee. The scene almost beggars description. The screams of agony from pain, the moans of the dying, the messages sent home by the despairing, the parting farewells of friends, the incoherent speech, the peculiar movements of the hands and fingers, silence, the spirit's flight—to where? And amidst all this some of the mean passions of humanity were displayed. Near me was a poor soldier hopelessly wounded. He was cold, and yet a wretch came and, against remonstrances, took the blanket off him, claiming that it was his.

Despite their presence in hell, not everyone at Buena Vista shared in the agony. French, peering around, saw hundreds of healthy men who apparently had fled the field for the safety of the hacienda or who had carried wounded comrades there and had stayed, comfortably out of firing range.

In the distance the fighting raged on, and French heard later how it went. The account described a scene of confusion and horror: continued withdrawal by the Mexicans along the base of the mountain; various bloody hand-to-hand encounters involving slashing knives and bayonets; a counterattack by Taylor, who suffered heavy losses in his attempt; a temporary truce of sorts, the real reason for which never has been explained; a storm accompanied by lightning and thunder that mingled with the roar of cannon and later sent down pelting rain that soaked the bodies of men and animals whether dead, wounded, or healthy; another desperate thrust by Santa Anna aimed at the center of Taylor's line.

The Mexicans nearly broke through again. Colonel John Hardin of the 1st Illinois and Colonel William McKee of the 2nd Kentucky, seeking to rally their men, fell dead in the battle. Another Kentucky officer, Lieutenant Colonel Henry Clay, son of Polk's opponent in the recent presidential race, was killed. His body and many other casualties of the fierce attack littered the soil of Buena Vista. John Paul Jones O'Brien, abandoned again by infantry support, fired his guns until his men had fallen. Then, with the charging Mexicans only yards away, he retreated on the run and left the pieces to the enemy.

Other cannon dammed the breach. They rumbled across the rough earth, unlimbered, and blasted away at the attackers, while infantry re-inforcements—those same Mississippians and Indianans who had stopped an earlier charge—hurried forward to send more deadly volleys tearing into Mexican ranks.

The attack faded; fighting waned. Guns fell silent. Dusk settled on cold ground covered with wounded and dead men wearing the uniforms of both armies. Neither side really had won, although Taylor had held his position—at a cost of 746 casualties, including 290 killed or missing. The battle actually had been a standoff, with the victor apparently to be decided on the following day.

Taylor's troops again suffered through a damp, freezing night, mostly without the benefit of fires. Men searched for the wounded, directed by those awful, now familiar cries, and carried them to mule-drawn wagons for creaking, jolting transportation to Saltillo, where casualties were to be assembled for such medical care as was available.

Some reinforcements reported in. They came from a nearby American outpost.

After dark Taylor visited the hacienda and talked with Sam French, shortly before the lieutenant was taken to Saltillo along with other wounded. Someone brought a wagon tail gate to serve as a stretcher, and some of French's fellow officers placed him on it. General Taylor, Charles May of the dragoons, a doctor, and several others then carried him outside the house and helped him into a wagon beside two other wounded officers—Colonel Jefferson Davis and an unnamed lieutenant of volunteers.

"I said to the General I hoped he would gain a complete victory on the morrow," French recalled later, "and his reply was: 'Yes, yes, if too many of my men do not give me the slip tonight.' I think he made this reply because he was mortified and pained to find so many men at the hacienda who had deserted the field, many of them by carrying off the wounded and not returning to their companies."

Then the wagon jerked, and French and his suffering companions commenced their jarring ride. At Saltillo French was helped into a tent, placed on frigid, damp earth, covered with the scant linen available, and left alone to suffer through another agonizing night—"The camp was silent, every one being away on or near the field of battle."

Hours passed without sleep for the young man who was so recently a cadet still under some degree of Quaker influence from his family. His battle experience now had broadened to include almost everything demanded of a career soldier, including an uncomplaining next-to-the-ultimate sacrifice, and he had come through it all in a thoroughly professional manner, despite his present pain.

"Success . . . is the measure of the greatness of a soldier," French remarked later. He was speaking of General Taylor, but—on a lower plane—he could have been referring also to himself.

Sam French's commission actually dated from his battle experience in the Mexican War. He would remain in the Army—would later fight for the Confederacy—and, despite memories of his own agony and of other mangled men wounded, dying, or dead, would be able to make that remarkable rationalization later in life, "War is not barbarous, nor is it 'hell;' it is just what parties choose to make it. When confined to the enlisted troops [and when civilians are thus spared] it is seldom cruel." The flickering flame of pacifism in Sam French had truly been extinguished, and his success at the bloody Battle of Buena Vista had helped to quench it.

In predawn light French heard someone walking near his tent. He called out, and a passing soldier peered inside. The man helped French to a crude, temporary hospital, where he began a slow recovery. Surgeons working without anesthetic cut the musket ball out of his thigh, and in time French returned home.

On the battlefield from which he had been taken a cold, dark, cheerless silence hung heavily over other weary, anxious men who expected the fight to resume, as usual, at sunrise.

Across lines veiled by night, in the chilly darkness far beyond those shadowy figures of U. S. Army pickets who kept watch for enemy move-

These two old sketches revive long-vanished scenes: (above) the port of Tampico, occupied by a U. S. Navy force November 14, 1846, and (below) General Taylor's kitchen, set up at Walnut Springs—just outside of Monterrey.

When camp had been made near water (not an invariable circumstance in an arid region) and when time permitted, most hot, dusty, aromatic soldiers reveled in the luxuries of washing and bathing.

At La Angostura, a narrow place in the San Luis Potosí road south of Saltillo, Santa Anna challenged Taylor in the Battle of Buena Vista. The fight proved to be mostly a standoff, but Taylor held his ground—and Santa Anna suffered heavy casualties before withdrawing.

March 9, 1847: Just as the sun sank below the 18,000-foot height of Orizaba, far inland, a signal gun sent troops of Winfield Scott's army ashore—unopposed—at Vera Cruz in the first "D-day" landing in United States military history.

ment, General Santa Anna brooded over his disappointment. Victory had been in his hands that February 23, but it had slipped away.

Santa Anna was no man to admit—or maybe even to realize—self-fault. In the blaze of battle General Taylor had committed the very last of his reserves; yet Santa Anna had not taken advantage of this by exerting pressure at some chosen point until the enemy line broke for good—as any first-class general with such numerical superiority would have done. But Santa Anna never expressed this afterthought—perhaps never had it in his mind. His reaction would have been to blame others for the mistakes, and to make himself look as good as possible under unfavorable circumstances. He began to concentrate on that effort now.

His losses had been enormous. As many as two thousand Mexican soldiers had been killed, wounded, or captured, and others had deserted during the battle. Many wounded and dead still lay on the darkened field; their cries and groans pierced the silence. Those with less serious wounds had been evacuated to a location two miles from the battlefield, where their injuries were attended to in the open air as well as the understaffed and underequipped surgeons could manage. These wounded would be evacuated—or at least as many of them as could be carried by the limited transportation system.

The able troops left to Santa Anna were almost useless, verging on starvation. Those promised enemy rations never had been captured—and morale was as low as the food supply. Mexican soldiers, hungry and thirsty and exhausted by their long marches, had fought well for the most part and had come close to driving the invader back, but they had spent themselves in the effort. Even those Mexican observers ordinarily critical of their countrymen's behavior gave the Army credit for a mighty attempt at Buena Vista. One man who saw the battle said, "Our soldiers had displayed a valor worthy of a better fate; they had rushed boldly upon the enemy, crossing barrancas, ascending hills, and throwing themselves on the American batteries, which swept their ranks. They had fallen killed or wounded, and with their last breath had shouted, 'Viva la república!'"

Now Santa Anna held a council of war with his senior officers and found all their fight gone—a reflection of his own mood. The only way out was to retreat—first to Agua Nueva, then across that awful wasteland to San Luis Potosí. The general ordered picket fires left burning to fool the foe, then quietly commenced his withdrawal in faint, icy moonlight, leaving many of those Mexican wounded on the field—"steeped in their blood, shivering in the cold, parched with thirst," a Mexican wrote.

For the retreat Santa Anna rode in the van of his army instead of in the rear. He took with him the guns captured from John Paul Jones O'Brien. This artillery he would exhibit, along with the American prisoners captured much earlier in the La Encarnación debacle, and would claim victory and the infliction of two thousand casualties upon the foe at Buena Vista.

Behind Santa Anna, in the eerie moonlight, his army straggled—pitiful men for whom death was "ringing in sounds about their heads" despite the absence of cannonade. Starvation, thirst, dysentery, and typhus stalked them, ready to thin their ranks further. Sick and wounded men dropped in their tracks and lay on rocky ground without assistance. "In sight already might be viewed the jackals and the dogs, who awaited . . . the moment when they might begin their frightful banquet." Still the gaunt, ghostly army trudged southward.

Their moving feet raised a column of powdery dust. Carried on a cold breeze, it could be smelled if not seen. Overhead, dimly visible in the moonlight, scattered clouds scurried across the night sky. In the distance ahead a prairie fire flickered—probably a belated result of Taylor's setting his Agua Nueva supplies ablaze.

The moon dimmed and set. Troops of the rear guard overtook and passed a convoy of wounded soldiers. More men deserted. It was another *noche triste*—sad night—but one with an ironic twist, one history-minded Mexican officer commented, harking back to the days of Cortés.

At Agua Nueva the Mexicans found the hacienda still ablaze, though the flames were burning much lower now. The flickering light illuminated a slimy pond lying beside the road. Into it plunged soldiers dying of thirst. Blood from their wounds mixed with scum on the surface and made the water "completely intolerable," but some men tried to gulp it down anyway at the risk of convulsions and death.

A man who was there described scene and sound. Dead bodies began strewing the ground; survivors walked and stumbled around and over them. Moans of the wounded and rattles of the dying mingled with curses of those still left on their feet. A woman sobbed over the lifeless body of her husband. On the road from Buena Vista stood idle carts and wagons, blocking further movement. Horses and mules as badly fatigued as humans could not be made to hobble out of the way. The entire

scene was appropriately lighted by a dim red glare from the slowly burning hacienda.

Some recently found provisions were distributed, but little cheer
went with the food. Many miles and more deaths lay between these
people and their destination. When Santa Anna's army finally returned
to San Luis Potosí it was less than half its original size.

Its commander did not wait to welcome the return. Santa Anna had
heard of a revolt in Mexico City, ignited largely by dissatisfaction with
Valentín Gómez Farías and his attempt to seize Church property. He
hurried there with his claims of victory and his captured cannon, and at
one town on his route he relished the sight of brightly dressed señoritas
scattering flowers in his heroic path.

In Mexico City Santa Anna succeeded in placating opponents, despite
some lingering distrust. He assumed the presidency, accepted an offer
from the Church for two million pesos in return for his support, secured
legislation that repudiated most of Farías' work, and won congressional
approval allowing himself as President to command Mexican armies in
the field while a Provisional President handled executive office work.
Farías, who had brought Santa Anna home from Cuba, himself left
Mexico in exile.

On the field of Buena Vista at dawn of February 24 Taylor's soldiers
searched for the next point of enemy attack and realized the Mexicans
had disappeared. The few men who first became aware of this cheered.
They were soon joined by others, as the word spread, until a mighty,
prolonged roar rose from the plateau. Near the headquarters tent those
two cool generals, Taylor and Wool, embraced ecstatically. Their soldiers
began carrying in enemy wounded.

In his official report Taylor remarked, "The great disparity of numbers and the exhaustion of our troops rendered it inexpedient and hazardous to attempt a pursuit." That would have been a sentence contributed by Taylor's erudite adjutant, Major Bliss. Old Zach could have
expressed his joy and his relief in much simpler words.

34.

Hard-won Position of Precariousness

For Taylor and Wool and the survivors of the Battle of Buena Vista, danger had passed—at least for the moment—on the fine morning of February 24. But for Colonel Alexander Doniphan and his Missouri volunteers, numbering fewer than a thousand, peril came closer that same day with every step forward toward the city of Chihuahua.

On February 24 Doniphan's small army was sixty or so miles from its destination, having marched from El Paso across more dry stretches of barren land as desolate as the Jornada del Muerto encountered in New Mexico. Isolated in enemy country, Doniphan had not received official word that General Wool would not be in Chihuahua to welcome him —and, in fact, would not appear there at all. People back home in Missouri, having read about Wool's presence in the Saltillo area, knew this, and they realized the danger faced by relatives and friends serving with the volunteer regiment that was now bound for Chihuahua.

Before leaving El Paso Doniphan himself had heard talk indicating that he would find no welcoming U. S. Army units at Chihuahua, which lay more than two hundred miles farther into Mexico, but the informality of this information forced him to classify it as rumor. Anyway, he had received orders, and he intended to follow them. His men were in almost unanimous agreement with this plan. Doniphan determined to go on, then, no matter what he might find around Chihuahua, and to join Wool wherever he might be in northern Mexico.

But those same rumors Doniphan had heard also spoke of large armies being collected for defense against the Missourians, and even of an impending attempt by the Mexicans to retake El Paso. He took on as spy, scout, and guide a man with a knowledge of the country: James Kirker, formerly employed by the state of Chihuahua as an exterminator of the universally feared Apache Indians. Aided by a group of Americans and by Indians from other tribes, Kirker and his men had sought to eradicate the Apaches for a promised bounty of forty dollars for every male scalp delivered and half that amount for the scalps of squaws and children. Chihuahua had not paid as promised, however, and Kirker had volunteered his services to Doniphan. The colonel did not exactly trust a man with a background like that, but he took him on anyway.

Doniphan had halted at El Paso for more than a month, waiting for the arrival of an artillery reinforcement requested long ago of Colonel Price in Santa Fe. Price had delayed sending the guns, because some ominous rumors were reaching his own ears: talk of an imminent uprising in northern New Mexico against United States authority. Finally Price sent six guns manned by more than one hundred men, all commanded by Major Meriwether Lewis Clark, son of explorer William Clark and namesake of his father's companion in adventure. This was not as many guns as Doniphan wanted, but it was enough to enable him to go on.

Following dispatch of the artillery, rebellion did indeed flare in northern New Mexico. Governor Charles Bent and other officials of the new government—native New Mexicans as well as Americans—were slain before Price could bring the disorder under control with his remaining force.

Men and guns of Clark's battery crossed that same torturous Jornada del Muerto that Doniphan's volunteers had become familiar with earlier. The effort weakened them to the point of exhaustion and starvation, and on the first day of February a messenger dispatched by the artillerymen arrived in El Paso with a request to send out provisions.

Men loaded supplies in a wagon. A detachment that included Private John Hughes escorted the stores to the famished soldiers. On the following day their guns were ferried across the Rio Grande, then were fired four times in a salute. After that they rumbled on toward town, to the joy of Doniphan's restless troops (for whom this meant the commencement of the Chihuahua campaign) and to the wonder of El Paso citizens who crowded rooftops and other high places for a glimpse of the monsters whose roar had disturbed them. The people saw four smaller guns—6-pounders—and two 12-pound howitzers.

One of Doniphan's men suggested returning the salute with an old

315

Mexican cannon captured at the recent Battle of El Brazito. Others noisily seconded the idea, with the unbridled enthusiasm of nineteenth-century American volunteers. But haste was necessary; Clark's battery even then was lumbering into town.

Men hurried away to render the honor. Some helped to get the powder and to stuff it into the cannon. One man took off his socks, wadded them, and rammed them down on the powder to make a blank charge, in the absence of any other material immediately available.

The gun roared. The socks flew out and hit the face of another soldier looking on. The victim did not join in the ensuing laughter, but instead bellowed in anger. He would rather have been hit by a solid ball, he swore, than by a pair of socks worn all the way from Fort Leavenworth to El Paso.

On February 8 Doniphan started his army toward Chihuahua—at the same time, far to the south, General Santa Anna was marching his troops from San Luis Potosí toward the Buena Vista encounter with General Taylor.

The beginning was pleasant enough: ". . . the whole army, the merchant, baggage, commissary, hospital, sutler, and ammunition trains, and all the stragglers, amateurs, and gentlemen of leisure, under flying colors, presenting the most martial aspect, set out with buoyant hopes . . . to reap undying fame,—to gain a glorious victory—or perish on the field of honor." Hughes the schoolteacher continued to be inordinately proud of his new profession.

For fifty miles or so the army followed the twisting, green-banked course of the Rio Grande. Then their route to the city of Chihuahua left the river westwardly and extended for sixty-five miles across that other *jornada del muerto*. Doniphan halted for a day before striking out across this desolation, which had been described for him earlier: a waterless desert of frequent deep sand.

On February 14, a Sunday that dawned fair and bright, he plunged into it, after burying on the banks of the Great River of the North two more of the numerous soldiers who had sickened and died during the long journey. Warned about the desert ahead, some men filled their saber sheaths with water. As they rode along, the naked blades dangling at their sides made soft jingling sounds whenever they struck the sheaths.

They struggled through deep sand that forced the quartermaster sergeant to double or quadruple teams of horses and mules to pull the wagons—and even then the cumbersome vehicles sometimes moved only with the additional help of scores of pushing, sweating, grunting men. "The mules were weak, and sunk up to their knees . . . the wagons stood buried almost to the hubs." Patches where the sand became lighter gave relief and even provided some grazing; but then the wagons would come upon more deep drifts.

The slow progress of that first day required a march into the night. Finally the men halted at ten o'clock, and they showed their resilience. "Jolly songs & merry glee went the rounds," Hughes wrote. This was the beginning, with hope still abounding. A surprising rain shower refreshed them further that night.

On into the sand, with a strong guard out front and rear. Then another pleasant surprise: a mounted artilleryman overtook them with mail forwarded from Santa Fe. After that the march continued and the sand grew worse. Hughes scribbled, ". . .—dying for water—horse & man parched with thirst. . . .—5000 lbs flour thrown out of commissary Trains & a vast quantity of salt. . . . Teams much worn out—Army & Trains scattered for 20 miles."

Finally, joyous discovery of the first water—little more than a muddy hole. Hughes said that "horse, mule & man vied with each other in drinking out of the same puddles," and he gulped down his own share. Later, when arrival at the shore of a fresh-water lake provided abundant refreshment and signaled completion of the desert crossing, one man, a recent bridegroom, drank so much that he died.

On February 20 Doniphan sent his newly employed scout, James Kirker, and sixteen men forward to reconnoiter two reported Mexican positions. One was said to have been established near a salt lake ahead, and the other farther on, around a river named Sacramento. Both positions lay on the other side of another lifeless expanse of desert. Before moving out upon it Doniphan halted his army for a few midday hours near a large, warm spring—Ojo Caliente—that flowed from the foot of a rocky hill. Private Hughes and others used the halt for bathing in the crystal, "blood-warm" water of the spring—a large one: forty yards long, twenty yards wide, four feet deep.

A distant dust cloud rising from the desert expanse later shattered this tranquillity. Horsemen were approaching—maybe Mexicans. The men formed for battle, but the mysterious riders proved to be friends—a scouting party returning. Colonel Doniphan, still anxious about the exact location and strength of the enemy and expecting battle at the salt lake ahead, dispatched another reconnaissance party of twelve volunteers led by a captain. Then he moved his army on toward the city of Chihuahua, across a land entirely barren of wood, water, and grass.

Not even camp halts provided comfort. On the twenty-second the night was so cold and the region so lifeless that Hughes and his companions simply "tethered their animals, and wrapping themselves up in their blankets, lay down on the earth without taking supper." At the same time, four hundred miles or so southeast, American troops shivered through a damp night following the first day of fighting at Buena Vista.

Two days later Doniphan's scouts returned with a report that some seven hundred Mexicans supported by artillery lay ahead, entrenched at a hacienda on the shore of the salt lake now only a few miles distant. On the following morning Doniphan again formed his men for battle and moved forward, but he discovered that the Mexicans had withdrawn —toward the river named Sacramento, he was told, where they would reinforce the large body of soldiers already waiting there.

At the lake Doniphan ordered another halt to allow his men a brief rest. But the relaxation proved costly: a campfire spread to some dry grass nearby and, fanned by a strong breeze, quickly threatened the entire area. Doniphan ordered his men to move on in an attempt to outrun the danger, but the wind happened to be blowing in the same direction he was headed. Shouting, sweating artillerymen whipped their teams, saw the fire gaining on them with the speed of an ocean wave, and ran their guns into the lake. Some ammunition wagons escaped the same way. Other loaded vehicles lumbered to various places of refuge while men desperately set backfires and sought to clear fire lanes. The conflagration roared on—across a plain, over a mountain. "The men spent the night on the bare and blackened earth," John Hughes said, "and the animals stood to their tethers without forage." Surprisingly, almost all of the other damage had been confined to the interrupted rest period.

On the following morning the men remained encamped in the vicinity. A high wind filled the air with sand and ashes, and made breathing difficult. The next day, formed for battle in case of surprise attack, they made an eight-mile march that brought them near the Sacramento. Chihuahua was little more than twenty miles away.

That afternoon Hughes accompanied three officers and two other enlisted men on a voluntary reconnaissance. Leaving the column, they rode ahead, climbed a rocky peak, and studied the Mexican position through powerful glasses. The enemy fortifications, clearly illuminated by a setting sun, lay along the river a few miles distant. Hughes studied the scene with fascination and probably with some concern about what tomorrow would bring. The line of defense appeared to be a strong one.

He saw that the road they were traveling—the only route southward toward the city of Chihuahua—stretched on for some distance, dropped down into a crossing of a dry arroyo, rose again to traverse a piece of elevated land, then descended for the river crossing. This last low point was commanded by adjacent heights that the enemy had fortified.

Further observation showed that the Mexicans had erected strong defenses, emplaced artillery, and stationed troops at several other strategic locations along the road—from a position just south of the arroyo to the south bank of the Sacramento. Mountain ranges to east and west precluded a detour around the river crossing, which was defended by men whose numbers Hughes and his companions estimated at three thousand.

Observations and estimate completed, Hughes and the others rode back to Doniphan (who had about one third the strength of the enemy for launching his attack). That night the colonel and his officers planned for the action that would certainly occur on the following day.

Farther on south, in the Mexican camp, other men also planned for tomorrow. They did not intend to give their enemy the city of Chihuahua.

After hearing of the loss of El Paso, Chihuahuans had redoubled their already commenced efforts to raise, equip, and provision an army that would keep them from the clutches of the greedy Americans. A local foundry had cast cannon. Arms had been repaired and readied. Men had been enrolled for service. Clothing had been provided for them. The people expected their army not only to provide protection but also to drive the invaders completely out of the state and to rescue the conquered New Mexicans.

"The good Chihuahuans looked with pride upon this result of their labors," said a contemporary Mexican account, "and in every piece of artillery, every musket, in every object which presented itself to their sight, they recognized the fruit of their personal exertions. Of this nothing [had] existed three months before."

On the night of the twenty-seventh the men of this confident new

319

army gathered for conversation centered around what they would do to the advancing Americans now not far distant—and to Americans generally.

> In every tent, in every friendly group, cheerful toasts were drunk to the liberty of the country, the young men abandoning themselves to the . . . delirium of expected triumph, and thinking more of their expedition to New Mexico, to assist their brethren, and to cast off the American yoke, than of the approaching encounter, which they looked upon as less important than it was.

The best stock of Chihuahua seemed to have been collected here, all under the command of General José Heredia. Overlooked was the fact that few of the soldiers ever had been engaged in combat.

Early Sunday morning, the twenty-eighth, Doniphan formed his army for its march toward battle. The day came in clear and bright, and seemed to Hughes to be an "auspicious" one—a feeling soon augmented by the appearance of a soaring eagle that followed the Americans. This the soldiers regarded as a good omen, disregarding the fact that Mexico claimed the eagle as a symbol, too.

Forward they moved, slowly, the four hundred or so merchant and military wagons lumbering along in four parallel files spaced thirty feet apart. In the center space between the wagons Doniphan had placed his artillery; in the two spaces on either side of that, infantry battalions. Cavalry detachments comprised the vanguard.

The day, already warm, grew hot as the sun rose overhead. For ten miles and more the army moved along, across more waterless land. By noon the two armies were in sight of each other. The Mexicans waited behind their fortifications; the Americans, closed up, proceeded slowly across the plain toward an assault. Hughes jotted a notation in his diary later that day: "It was now evident the battle must be fought before we could rest—every heart beat with hope—every arm was nerved for the conflict."

A short distance north of the arroyo Doniphan halted his men, then made a simple maneuver that apparently fooled General Heredia completely. When Doniphan moved again it was to the right—to westward— away from the road, up the north bank of the arroyo, away from the emplaced Mexican cannon. General Heredia, apparently assuming with remarkable lack of imagination that Doniphan would do as he himself would have done and would use the road for his attack, looked on but did nothing for a time. When the Americans reached a point out of range of Mexican artillery they turned left—southward—and crossed the arroyo far to the west of the Mexicans. Teams and wagons plunged down the banks, paused, and made it up the other slope, with animals straining and teamsters shouting and lashing. The entire army, now formed for battle, somehow gained the south bank while the foe did little more than observe quietly from a distance. Also looking on were hundreds of civilians lining the summits of nearby hills, watching with fascination and expectation.

In the van of Doniphan's army now were cavalry, infantry, and artillery. Wagons followed in the rear. Across the plateau they lumbered, apparently toward the Sacramento ahead, but then they turned left— eastward, paralleling the river—to face the enemy from an entirely new front. Finally they saw the Mexicans preparing to attack with a strong cavalry force.

John Hughes looked on. Romanticism again welled in his breast. Once more he was making history, not teaching it: "Nothing could exceed in point of solemnity and grandeur the rumbling of the artillery, the firm moving of the caravan, the dashing to and fro of horsemen, and the waving of banners and gay fluttering guidons, as both armies advanced to the attack on the rocky plain."

Doniphan's artillery opened on the charging cavalry, cutting down both men and animals in "fearful execution." The attackers fell back, leaving the battle temporarily to the answering fire of a battery of Mexican guns. For nearly an hour a furious cannonade rocked the countryside. Doniphan's gunners fired twenty-four rounds a minute, but still they could not silence the enemy artillery, which sent balls slicing through the ranks of the Missourians, killing some horses and crashing into a few wagons—but inflicting surprisingly few human casualties. Another man named Hughes, a dragoon sergeant not related to John, had both legs shattered by a cannon ball.

Doniphan ordered an attack on the center of the Mexican line, which was now spread out along the west side of the road just abandoned by the Americans. Three cavalry companies, including John Hughes's, were told to storm a central gun battery.

Buglers blared the advance. Hoofs thundered. Hughes's unit, commanded by Captain John Reid, plunged forward into gunfire. Missiles whispered through the air around Hughes, but he realized that the Mexicans were making that common mistake of theirs. Firing downward from a slight elevation, they were overshooting again. The roar of the guns, the whining shots, and the shouts and curses of excited men belied the light casualties that were being suffered by the Americans.

Orders came to the three cavalry companies to halt. Two stopped, but Captain Reid either did not hear or did not understand the instruction. Hughes saw his company commander, riding in front, stand in his stirrups, raise his sword, and shout, "Will my men follow me?" The Mexican battery lay four hundred yards ahead.

Hughes and other members of the company spurred their horses and raced after their captain. They galloped up a hill, scattered the gunners, carried the battery, and for a time silenced the guns. But their numbers were too few to retain possession. A counterattack beat them back. Some fell casualties—including Hughes, but with only a slight wound.

Help arrived. Doniphan's guns hurled grape and canister on the Mexicans from a distance of only fifty yards. Another American charge poured over entrenchments and into redoubts: shouts and screams and flowing blood—torn flesh, gaping wounds, all a red mess, no matter what color the uniform. Virtually all of the casualties, however, were Mexican.

The defenders fled—some down the Sacramento toward Chihuahua, others across the river into the fortifications on the south bank.

American guns now aimed their destruction at those positions, and a charge by cavalry and infantry followed. Before sunset—three hours after the fighting had begun—the last of the Mexicans were fleeing from the Sacramento battlefield, leaving behind three hundred dead and more than that number wounded. Only one American, a major, had been killed. Eleven men had suffered wounds; two of them died soon afterward.

In the city of Chihuahua residents had heard the sound of cannon without alarm. It meant to them that the Americans were getting what they deserved. People began preparing for a victory celebration. Their military endeavor had been their salvation.

Then came the first word otherwise, received with disbelief. The Chihuahuans' army had broken and was running. More eyewitnesses rushed into town with the same information. Frightened soldiers appeared, then vanished. Providence once more had treated Mexicans badly.

The Americans had won an astounding victory and were encamped just outside the city. They could enter at their pleasure.

Entire families rushed from their homes into Chihuahua streets. Women and children screamed their fear of facing a victorious army of foreigners. What would those beasts do?

Darkness engulfed the terrified city. Outside it, at the site of the recent battle, Mexican wounded abandoned by companions lay groaning near the bodies of Mexican dead, awaiting whatever help the few American surgeons might be able to give them.

The next day an American detachment of 150 men sent by Doniphan entered the city. On March 2 the rest of the army followed. They found that the last Mexican soldier had fled the area.

Their own position, however, remained a ticklish one. Here they were deep in Mexico, cut off from help, and ignorant of the exact location of the army they had been ordered to join. They had marched from Fort Leavenworth to Santa Fe to El Paso to Chihuahua in the tattered clothes they wore now, and most of them had ridden the animals still with them. Since entering the Army at Leavenworth they had received no pay at all— a poverty period extending from June 1846 to March 1847.

Three more months and their enlistments would expire. But where would they go? Where could they go? They might never be able to extricate themselves from their hard-won position of precariousness.

35.

The Lamp of a Sepulcher

Nearly seven hundred miles southeast of Chihuahua, at an anchorage down the Mexican coast from the American-occupied port of Tampico, that same March 2 dawned as another day of waiting for Captain Ephraim Kirby Smith of the regular infantry. While Colonel Doniphan, far inland, cautiously set up isolated headquarters in the city he had marched so far to conquer, Smith sought to pass more time as pleasantly as possible.

This would not be easy. For almost two weeks Smith had been a passenger aboard an overcrowded sailing vessel named *Huron*, engaged to transport him and other members of his regiment to a landing at Vera Cruz and into the subsequent invasion with which President Polk planned to squeeze Mexico into surrendering.

The ships had brought most of Winfield Scott's army to this rendez-vous—off a small, green Gulf island named Lobos. Lieutenant Sam Grant and other members of his 4th Infantry Regiment were packed aboard another sailing vessel nearby. Colonel Ethan Allen Hitchcock and Cap-tain Robert E. Lee were berthed with the rest of General Scott's staff aboard the steamer *Massachusetts*, where Lee shared a stateroom with an old friend, Captain Joseph E. Johnston. Other vessels swinging to anchors not far away carried more troops. On the island could be seen rows of white canvas tents lining the beach: quarters for volunteer soldiers who had been exposed to smallpox aboard one ship and were now waiting through quarantine before embarking again for the operation.

Winfield Scott had been plagued by the same problems that had frustrated Zachary Taylor earlier. All of them centered around a shortage of supplies and equipment. Scott had designed his own craft for the land-

324

ing on the Mexican coast, but not all of the boats had arrived. Furthermore, he still lacked adequate sea transportation for all of his troops, and he even lacked the troops in numbers promised. Ordnance had not been given him in quantities equal to his requests. Like Taylor, he fired off complaints: "perhaps no expedition was ever so unaccountably delayed— by no want of foresight, arrangement, or energy on my part. . . ." Scott and his troops needed to be in and out of Vera Cruz before that summer onset of yellow fever, but Washington seemed to be deliberately slowing him down. Nevertheless, by March 2 he felt he had almost enough men and equipment on hand to commence the effort, and navy officers had assured him they could provide firepower sufficient to eliminate opposition to the landing.

That March 2 was a day that Captain E. K. Smith decided to devote to fishing, despite a threat of rain. An infantryman like Smith might have been expected to seek his pleasure on land—to stretch his legs on the solidity of Lobos Island while searching for flowers to press. But the place was quarantined, and—anyway—Smith was something of a seaman as well as an infantryman. During the tossing voyage to Lobos, while his fellow officers had been incapacitated by extended periods of seasickness, Smith had passed much of the time reading on deck or studying the sea from the top of a mast, a place to which he liked to climb to escape the sickness and confusion that prevailed below. He wrote letters home proudly describing his affinity for ocean travel: "I am by hours the last at night to leave the deck; seated alone on the taffrail I gaze upon the beautiful moon and stars or down into the sparkling sea." And another time: "I climbed to the masthead with the captain. . . . I am the only [army] officer on board enough of a *sailor* to undertake this feat. . . . We lay over the fore top-gallant yard more than an hour, nearly one hundred feet from the deck, while the good ship was flying over the sea urged by half a gale. . . ."

At daylight on that morning of March 2 Smith collected his fishing gear and embarked in a small boat with the captain of the *Huron* and a lieutenant. A rain shower dampened them, but the squall passed on after sunrise, leaving behind a brightening blue sky. They rowed to a reef off the island, dropped anchor, and prepared their lines. Nearby, on the island, the blossoms of orange, lemon, and lime trees interspersed among the thriving caoutchoucs—rubber trees—sent a sweet scent seaward, toward them.

But the anchorage proved to be a poor choice, and they decided to move. They tried to raise the anchor, discovered it had been caught fast in coral, and finally broke the cable by their continued exertions. Disappointed, they rowed back to the *Huron* and breakfasted.

With the long day still ahead of him, Smith stepped out on deck for a look around and saw that the *Massachusetts*, anchored nearby, was displaying a signal flag from its mainmast. The cloth fluttered limply in a light wind. It summoned to the ship an officer from every vessel present. A short time after that Smith learned that Winfield Scott had concluded to move on at once toward Vera Cruz.

The day's calm did not delay the *Massachusetts*. With steam up, the ship churned a passage through the anchored vessels. The hulking figure of General Scott, pacing the deck, drew cheers from admiring onlookers. Other steamers paddled away, too—all of them standing to the southeast in the wake of the *Massachusetts*. The fleet would rendezvous at Antón Lizardo, a harbor just south of Vera Cruz already in use as an anchorage by ships of Commodore Conner's squadron. From there the vessels would proceed to a position off Sacrificios Island, a few miles from Vera Cruz, where landing parties would be transferred (out of range of San Juan de Ulúa guns) to their boats for the final assault.

The absence of wind delayed departure of the sailing vessels. Morning waned with only a slight breeze from dead ahead skipping across decks. But by early afternoon the wind rose; "as if by magic this large fleet spread . . . sails to the breeze and stood away close hauled upon the wind . . ."—sixty ships under billowing canvas, bound for the first major sea invasion in United States military history.

Captain Smith climbed to the masthead of the *Huron* to observe the spectacle, "one which few men ever see, [and] such as I never expect to look upon again." Noble sailing ships skimming along under sheets of brilliant white seemed to cover the sea. Thirty-six hours later, early in the morning of March 4, the wind shifted to the north, "blowing a cracking breeze." The *Huron*, crowding sail, passed most of the other ships and that afternoon came in sight of the mountains northwest of Vera Cruz. Then the tricky wind died, leaving the vessel becalmed for hours. Not until nine o'clock the following morning did Smith catch his first glimpse of a common landfall here: the distant peak of Orizaba (more than fifty miles inland)—three miles high, and "looking like a point of burnished silver in the sky."

326

I went to the head of the foremast, and lay over the fore topsail yard until in the dim distance the castle of San Juan [de Ulúa] and the city could be seen. Some shipping, probably English and French men-of-war, are lying at anchor in the roadstead of Sacrificios. It is eleven in the morning and before night we shall be at anchor at Antón Lizardo. We are near the scene of our struggle and 'tis strange that all doubt and misgiving [seem] to leave my mind as the place and time [come] near, and though I am as likely to be killed in the coming conflict as any other—it does not so seem to me. A celebrated author says: "All men think all men mortal but themselves, themselves immortal."

Later, closing distance and closer observation showed three men-of-war, including one steamer, maintaining a blockade of the fortress San Juan de Ulúa, and showed also many other vessels crowding the vicinity of the port—more than sixty, according to Smith's count. Some of them were bringing troops for the invasion, like his own ship. Eventually the fleet numbered some one hundred vessels of all types and sizes, all there for the purpose of putting Scott's 12,603 soldiers and their equipment on shore safely.

About four o'clock that same afternoon the *Huron* dropped anchor just inside a reef that helped to comprise the harbor of Antón Lizardo, but the location proved to be wrong. A steamer came alongside to tow the vessel to the correct anchorage, and during the maneuver one of its officers passed across some interesting information: General Santa Anna's official report of the Battle of Buena Vista, as received in Vera Cruz. Santa Anna told of having engaged Taylor's army for two days and of having inflicted two thousand casualties against half that many Mexicans killed and wounded. Santa Anna claimed victory. He had been forced to retreat, he said, only because of a shortage of supplies and because of the necessity of aiding his wounded.

Smith read the account and scoffed, like most other Americans aboard ships off Vera Cruz. "[Santa Anna] admits enough to show that he has been well whipped," Smith remarked, "though he claims a victory, and strangely enough says he is about to retreat. . . ." About the same time came word of the uprising against Farías in Mexico City, but few men of Scott's army gave this information much attention. Mexican revolutions meant little to them.

Comfort came in the knowledge that Santa Anna would not be leading an army opposing the invasion (although Winfield Scott said years later in his *Memoirs* that he assumed the crafty Mexican general would be standing against him). Nevertheless, Smith and the infantrymen who would storm ashore soon did not really know what to expect. "We shall probably have no difficulty taking the place," Smith wrote home on March 6. From the deck of the *Huron,* however, he often saw Mexican dragoons riding along the beach three miles away—although at that distance they did not appear "very warlike."

Aboard the *Massachusetts* Colonel E. A. Hitchcock had devoted time to studying the land, too, but mostly out of curiosity. As inspector general on Winfield Scott's staff (and thus responsible for seeing that men and equipment were in a constant state of readiness) Hitchcock would be going ashore with Scott, not in one of those early infantry landings. But the danger might be no less.

On the afternoon of March 6, the day when Smith wrote his letter about the probable ease of taking Vera Cruz, Hitchcock received a summons from Scott to accompany him on a boat trip for reconnaissance of the vicinity. Commodore Conner had invited Scott and all of his generals aboard a captured Mexican steamer named *Petrita* for this purpose, and all the generals brought their staffs. With Scott's aides came also Captain Robert E. Lee. Every American officer of senior rank eventually embarked on the steamer.

From the anchorage at Antón Lizardo the *Petrita* churned past Sacrificios. Most officers on board scanned that island and, opposite it, the mainland shore, soon to be the scene of the projected landing. When the *Petrita* had approached to within a mile and a half of the feared San Juan de Ulúa officers turned their glasses on the fortress. One colonel examining the scene remarked that the Mexicans were manning their batteries. Another officer verified this. "They are using their sponges," he said. "We shall have a shot presently."

Hitchcock, standing nearby, heard both remarks and waited for the projectile. Then he saw a puff of smoke appear above a distant gun. A shell arced toward them but fell short. Another one followed—short. The next shell burst high above them, and pieces fell around the *Petrita.* The fourth shot whined overhead and splashed into the water a hundred yards astern.

Hitchcock, the perpetual critic of blind generals, snorted at this lack of foresight. Here they were, he wrote later, "in danger with no adequate object, without means of defence, with all of our officers of rank on board. If a chance shot had struck our engines we should have cut a pretty figure!" But the *Petrita* extricated herself and took her passengers back to Antón Lizardo, where final preparations for the landing followed. It would commence at sunrise on March 8.

In predawn gloom Hitchcock, back on board the *Massachusetts*, wrote by fluttering candlelight a diary entry that could (as he reflected) be his last. It was long and thoughtful. It contained admonitions about the handling of his property and about caring for his brother's family, a compilation of his own reviews of favorite books, a statement of satisfaction regarding his long-held views of religion, and this memorandum: "As an accident may happen to me, I note that I owe my servant $36 to the 1st inst." The entry was a careful one by a meticulous, methodical man putting his affairs in order. But then Hitchcock learned that the landing had been postponed because of the threat of a strong norther. The storm failed to strike with the intensity feared, and twenty-four hours later the operation began again. General Scott had become increasingly "impatient to get ashore."

The original plan (drawn up in a carefully prepared, technical operation order ahead of its time) had been modified somewhat. To avoid confusion and to speed completion of the landing, troops would be transferred to fourteen naval vessels and five military steamers at Antón Lizardo, then proceed to Sacrificios for embarkation in the landing boats—thus avoiding a larger clutter of transports in the final staging area.

Captain Smith's infantry company, which was to form part of the initial assault wave, received orders to move from the *Huron* to the flagship *Raritan*, a frigate that would transport 2,500 troops to the embarkation point. Each man who was to participate in the landing carried a greatcoat, a haversack with rations for four days, a canteen of water, and arms and ammunition. "Now, hurrah for San Juan [de Ulúa] and a brevet!" Smith wrote home.

At daylight on March 9—a calm, clear day that left a glaze on the water—the movement began. Smith and his company were transferred to the *Raritan* in a surfboat that would later be used in the landing. Ten thousand other troops also boarded vessels that would take them the short distance to Sacrificios, which lay out of cannon range three miles south of the city and the fortress—and about twelve hundred yards offshore.

329

By eleven o'clock that sunny morning the invasion fleet was under way. Troops crowded decks. Landing boats, strung out in tow behind, tossed gently in ships' wakes. Still other naval vessels stood off the invasion site, providing a protective line between the mainland shore and the final embarkation point and preparing to commence a grapeshot bombardment at the proper time to clear the beach of any defenders. But the only people to be seen ashore in great numbers were in the city. When the inhabitants of Vera Cruz became aware of the naval movement they crowded onto high places for a better view. Now they looked on from walls, roofs, and church domes.

Slowly and without error the giant operation proceeded. Ships anchored off Sacrificios. Surfboats came alongside in an order previously assigned. These long, pointed boats had been built in three sizes—the largest forty feet long, twelve feet wide, four feet deep; the other two sizes successively smaller, just enough to allow the boats shipment to the scene in nests of three, to save cargo space. Not even half of the 141 boats ordered had arrived, but Winfield Scott would wait no longer. His troops crowded into the craft—forty or fifty to a boat, which in turn was manned by eight, seven, or six naval oarsmen, depending on the size. After loading, each boat moved to a previously assigned position and waited for a gun signal from the *Massachusetts* before heading shoreward.

Also waiting aboard the largest ships were several bands. When the landing began the musicians would strike up the inevitable "Yankee Doodle," "The Star-Spangled Banner," and other patriotic airs. In the distance the silvery peak of Orizaba, crowned by a late afternoon sun, emerged from haze that had hidden it earlier.

Captain E. K. Smith peered at the shore, not the mountain. The time was about five-thirty.

> We could see a few Mexican soldiers . . . but no evidence of any large force to oppose our landing, though we did not know but there might be batteries and troops behind the sand hills. . . . This was an interesting moment, and must have been a grand spectacle from the yards and tops of the shipping. Soon a cannon was fired . . . [aboard] the . . . "Massachusetts," and with loud cheers we pushed for the beach, each hardy sailor using his utmost exertion to be the first to land. The entire division reached the shore in good order, every one leaping from the boats as . . . keels grated on the sand, wading the short distance that remained. We were at once formed in order of battle and advanced over the sand hills. We met with no opposi-

tion, not a single gun being fired. As we gained the crest of the hill, we could see a few Mexicans, but they were far off and not in force.

Somewhere nearby Lieutenant Sam Grant also splashed ashore in that first wave, sharing Captain Smith's experiences. The sun set on this scene and, figuratively, on all of Mexico. Oarsmen rowed the surfboats back to anchored ships to bring in the second assault line, then the third. Well before midnight ten thousand American troops and their supplies and equipment had been put ashore without any loss, at the approximate site of Hernando Cortés' landing more than three centuries earlier.

Captain Smith and his men spent part of that first night dozing in deep sand near where they had landed. Along the beach alternate infantry companies remained awake to prevent surprise, but Smith's unit escaped that chore temporarily.

Two hours after midnight, however, a shout of "To arms" and a rattle of musketry from somewhere in the darkness roused Smith's company. Orders sent Smith and his men out toward the disturbance for picket duty; they crept forward four hundred yards across rough ground and through prickly thickets, then halted. The captain peered into the night and listened carefully, but a black silence prevailed until sunrise, when the company was recalled.

General Scott now addressed himself to the task of encircling and forcing Vera Cruz into surrender, but without directly attacking the old fortress of San Juan de Ulúa. Scott wanted to shed no American blood in storming the city; he wanted no more than one hundred casualties in taking it.

The task seemed formidable. A high wall enclosed the landward side of the city, and nine forts constructed at strategic intervals guarded approaches there. To seaward stood that massive fortress of San Juan de Ulúa.

Subsequent inspection of the walled area showed some grim improvements made especially to counter the American threat. Thick clusters of prickly pear had been set out around the forts. Outside the walls deep holes had been dug, fitted with sharpened sticks pointing upward, then covered. Any man who fell into such a trap would be impaled. Inside the walls, Scott heard, the Mexicans had available two hundred guns, four thousand troops, and a hoard of ammunition. Also haunting Scott was that specter of yellow fever, which the passing days would bring into existence. Yellow fever would topple his soldiers more effectively than would a thousand cannon.

Late on March 10, the day after the initial landing, Scott and his staff moved ashore. His troops already had begun the encirclement, flushing out small groups of Mexicans in areas outside the city walls and suffering an occasional casualty in the process. The general received many offers from ambitious officers who wanted to lead storming parties, which might have hastened the fall of the city. At meetings of his "little cabinet"—a group of staff officers that included Colonel Hitchcock and Captain Lee—he discussed various ways of conquering the city, but he never approved proposals that would greatly increase American casualties, despite the approaching threat of inevitable epidemic and despite the widespread public demand back home for what the men called a "butcher's bill" in corroboration of great victory. "The applicants [for storming parties] were thanked and applauded," Scott wrote in his *Memoirs*, "—nothing more."

This general preferred to use "headwork, the slow, scientific process," in taking the city. He was a thinking man, a planner—not a feel-as-you-go leader like Zachary Taylor. He would complete the encirclement of the city, then, with large guns brought ashore for the siege, he would demand surrender—all without a costly storming of those fortifications.

But then the weather went against him. A strong norther made it impossible to transfer the large guns to be borrowed from warships onto smaller craft for landing ashore. The storm caused even greater frustration. For days it completely isolated the army from the vessels offshore. It flung sand from a multitude of dunes into the faces of soldiers trying to attend to their various duties. Colonel Hitchcock rode out on March 12 to inspect Scott's extending investment line and breathed so much sand that he called the excursion "the most severe ride I ever performed." Nevertheless, on the following day Scott's army—working despite a bombardment from guns in the city and at the fort—completed its encirclement of Vera Cruz from the shore north to the shore south and shut off aqueduct water that supplied most of the inhabitants' needs. That same day one or two heavy guns were tugged ashore. More followed later.

Captain Robert E. Lee and other engineers had the job of emplacing the cannon. Lee helped to locate batteries and to build gun platforms. From the beach landing the pieces had to be dragged through deep sand to assigned positions—toil that required ingenuity and patience along with muscle. For a "naval battery" emplaced under Lee's supervision, six guns—all weighing more than three tons each and all borrowed from the fleet—had to be transported three miles across sand dunes and through a long lagoon two feet deep. These ponderous guns, when fixed in a position strongly protected by sandbags, gave Scott much greater firepower; at the last minute he had begun to fear that his own smaller pieces would not be sufficient for the siege. Lee emplaced the naval battery only seven hundred yards from the Mexicans, but without their knowledge of its presence until the guns opened fire later.

The north wind renewed its fury at intervals. It seemed to be in alliance with the Mexicans. An occasional rain squall joined in the conspiracy, soaking and chilling troops without settling for long the sand, which was much too plentiful to be rendered inert by a few scattered showers. Food and water were poor in quality and short in quantity. An epidemic of diarrhea broke out. But for most soldiers the worst discomfort came from the myriads of sand fleas that thrived around Vera Cruz. They made such an impression on young Lieutenant Dabney H. Maury, fresh from West Point, that he remembered them for the rest of his life. He wrote, "If one were to stand ten minutes in the sand, the fleas would fall upon him in hundreds. How they live in that dry sand, no one knows. They don't live very high, for they are ever ready for a change of diet. The engineer officers, [Gustavus] . . . Smith and [George B.] McClellan, slept in canvas bags drawn tight about their necks, having previously greased themselves all over with salt pork."

Not even the random shots lobbed from Mexican guns at soldiers employed in erecting artillery positions proved as disturbing as those fleas. The same George McClellan who fled into pork grease to escape the tiny pests could smirk at those enemy gunners. Colonel Hitchcock mentioned one such instance in his diary entry for March 16.

> . . . Cold, rainy day. Wind still from north but not strong. Surf higher. No business. Occasional guns, as usual, from city and castle. Yesterday two shells came near head-quarters. One passed over and burst in sand-bank. Lieut. George B. McClellan came in this evening with a working party. His clothes were very much torn, and he said laughingly that the Mexicans had been firing at his party nearly all day without hitting a man. . . . There has been considerable musketry firing.

During the siege Hitchcock recorded other bits of information that provided insight into the personalities of two fellow officers—Robert E. Lee, not widely known outside the Army then, and General Scott.

On the nineteenth Lee ("an admirable officer," the critical Hitchcock commented) was returning with Lieutenant P. G. T. Beauregard from work on gun positions when a nervous American sentry sprang out of dense chaparral and shouted a challenge: "Who comes there?"

"Friends!" Lee answered.

"Officers!" Beauregard replied, almost simultaneously.

The soldier, fearing Mexicans were upon him, paid no attention to the replies. Instead he pointed a pistol at Lee and fired. The ball passed between Lee's arm and his body, scorching his uniform. When word of the incident reached headquarters Scott demanded some minor punishment for the reckless sentinel and was not persuaded otherwise by Lee's intercession in behalf of the man.

The other diary entry by Hitchcock provided a portrait of Scott—the punctilious, demanding leader who sometimes acted old-maidish.

> . . . A funny scene occurred last evening [March 18] that would require a Dickens or a Lever to describe. The General called for his letter-book to show me a letter from himself to Commodore [Conner]. It had been copied by an interpreter, Colonel Edmonson. An error was discovered, and the General broke out: "Colonel Edmonson! Colonel Edmonson! (in rapid succession) "did you copy this?"
>
> "Yes, sir."
>
> "My dear Colonel! That is not right; that interlineation should be *there*" (pointing with his finger) "and not *there*, don't you see? The sense requires it. I never wrote it so! It is not sense! You make me write nonsense! You will kill me! I'll commit suicide, if you don't follow me. Follow *me*, no matter where I go—follow me, if out of a third-story window. . . . What? Send that nonsense to the government? My dear Colonel! Don't you attempt to correct me! And here again—over here—there should be a period and not a semicolon. The capital letter shows it. How *could* you make it a semicolon? Correct that on your life."
>
> "I'll correct it immediately!" exclaims the Colonel.
>
> "And *there* you've left a space at the beginning of the line! That shows a new sentence; but there was none—it was all one sentence in the original! *Never* leave a space at the beginning of a line except when beginning a new sentence. There! You've put a "g" in Colonel Hardin's name—I'll bet a thousand—ten thousand dollars to one farthing there was no "g" in the original. Follow me—follow me, if out of a third-story window. . . . I'll die before I send such a copy to the government! What would be said of me? That I write nonsense and don't know how to spell Colonel Hardin's name! Hardin—d-i-n—there is no "g" in it, and never was! No matter how strange the spelling—follow *me*! Don't you attempt to correct my spelling!"

This is about a fourth part of what he said of the same sort, and, what made it more funny, it was when time pressed; important orders were in progress to open the trenches. The work has now begun.

The siege progressed slowly. Morale zoomed within a week after the initial landing, when authentic information arrived about Zachary Taylor's success at Buena Vista. But scattered expressions of jealousy from regulars about the role of volunteers in that victory antagonized some of Scott's citizen-soldiers.

The siege continued. The Americans waited for emplacement of the last gun and for Scott's demand for surrender that would ensue. "I think when our batteries are established we shall make short work of it," Captain E. K. Smith wrote home.

Smith eagerly anticipated the armistice. By March 22 he had drawn picket-guard duty six nights out of eleven. His attitude toward the Army recently had undergone some pronounced changes, but his most immediate criticism presently centered around heavy demands made on himself and his men.

The sand insects and want of rest must soon break us down in this climate unless the duty becomes lighter. The enemy are using their heavy batteries incessantly, throwing . . . hundreds of solid shot and shells at us every day, yet but one man in our brigade has been struck, a marine, who was killed yesterday morning by a shot striking the wall of [a] cemetery behind which he was sitting. We owe our safety to the peculiar nature of the ground, all the distance from our camp to the trenches being a succession of high sand hills with valleys filled with chaparral in which we are entirely safe from all but vertical shot, the fragments of shells which burst in the air, and the chances are that not one in a thousand of them will be effective.

Night before last [March 20] I spent in advance of the trenches not far from the town. It was blowing a gale from the north, the fine sand pricking our faces like needles and nearly putting out our eyes. Being the advance post, and very near the enemy, great watchfulness was necessary to prevent surprise. I was up all the previous night and day, and yesterday at noon when I returned to camp I was completely exhausted. A good night's rest, however, has restored me and I am ready for the trenches again.

On the same day that Captain Smith expressed himself ready again— March 22—General Scott felt he had enough batteries in position to demand surrender. Scott's army had been before the city thirteen days now without firing a single artillery piece—having been engaged only in some minor skirmishes—while the Mexicans had thrown shot and shell by the thousands. "During the last three days," Colonel Hitchcock wrote on that March 22, "they have been constantly firing at our working parties in the trenches, which have been within 600 yards of the city walls, but they have not touched a single man in the trenches and only one out of them"—the marine whose death Captain Smith had recorded.

Hitchcock found a good vantage point to observe Scott's surrender ultimatum—atop a sand hill on the beach between the recent landing site and the city. From this rise he could see the ships riding at anchor off Sacrificios Island and—in the opposite direction—the walled city and the rambling fortress of San Juan de Ulúa, with its black guns facing seaward. Sitting there, Hitchcock watched as General Scott and a group of other officers, all mounted, rode out under a truce flag to give the city that choice of surrendering or facing bombardment. The colonel saw the officers halt after proceeding some distance. The bearer of the flag rode on to take the message to Vera Cruz authorities.

After a delay Hitchcock saw the flag-bearer return and deliver a letter to Scott. The general handed the paper to someone else—an interpreter, Hitchcock surmised—then the entire group began riding back toward headquarters. Hitchcock rose, dusted sand from his trousers, and commenced walking toward headquarters to learn the Mexicans' answer. Before he arrived he heard once more the constant booming of Vera Cruz guns and needed no more information.

Still free from duties temporarily, he joined other of Scott's officers who were watching the artillery duel from atop another sand hill. Hitchcock saw American mortars, firing rapidly, leave puffs of white smoke hovering over their positions. The mortars caused little damage to city walls, but their effect inside Vera Cruz would not be so slight. To seaward, U. S. Navy vessels crept up to stations near the fortress and sent shots into it and into the city. Mexican guns roared in continual reply.

Grimly fascinated by the scene, Hitchcock watched until nearly midnight. Flashes from the cannon cut through the darkness. The man-made thunder and lightning that killed and maimed by the scores convinced him "how very absurd is the whole tragical farce of war."

Inside Vera Cruz the bombardment seemed much more serious than "absurd" and "tragical farce" could describe. Those were words to be used by an observer looking on from a distance.

The Americans' first bombshell had burst in the Plaza de Armas, doing little damage. The next one hit the post office. After that bombs burst all over the city, hitting buildings indiscriminately. A Mexican account described the terror.

> The surgical hospital, which was situated in the Convent of Santo Domingo, suffered from the fire, and several of the inmates were killed by fragments of bombs bursting at that point. While an operation was [being performed] on a wounded man, the explosion of a shell extinguished the lights, and when [other illumination was] brought, the patient was found torn in pieces, and many others dead and wounded. . . . In the Convent of Santo Domingo itself the shells caused a fire, which was extinguished by the exertions of the engineers, the Ayuntamiento, the police, and troops; but flames soon burst out in another place, and then in another, and shells were thrown in greater numbers at those places. . . .

The same writer penned a plea that seemed more like an epitaph: "God save the Republic."

On the twenty-fourth Captain Lee had that naval battery ready, and Scott could add its awesome power to other artillery already blasting away at the city. Those navy guns, manned by officers and seamen from the fleet, could shatter the wall that had proved to be immune to destruction by smaller artillery.

About ten o'clock in the morning the naval battery commenced firing. It made an awful noise as it sent shells crashing into the wall and opening holes, and it completely surprised the defenders. After a time every artillery piece in the city opened upon these cannon, attesting to their effectiveness.

Captain Lee stood behind sandbags near the battery, helping to direct the fire and experiencing his first combat action. In command of one of the guns, a giant 64-pounder, was his brother from the Navy, Sidney Smith Lee—the gun and its commander and crew all having been landed from the *Mississippi*.

Robert's eyes followed his brother anxiously throughout the bombardment. He almost expected to see Smith cut down before him. But he saw instead that Smith Lee went about his bloody business with no apparent concern, with no noticeable loss of his usual cheerfulness, and with "his white teeth [visible] through all the smoke and din of the fire."

Robert E. Lee also felt anxiety about what the terrible cannonade

337

must be doing inside Vera Cruz. He observed that "the shells thrown from our battery were constant and regular discharges, so beautiful in their flight and so destructive in their fall. It was awful! My heart bled for the inhabitants. The soldiers I did not care so much for, but it was terrible to think of the women and children."

The Mexican defenders were making the vicinity of the naval battery a hazardous area, too. They threw back their share of shot and shell, but Lee apparently felt little concern—or at least did not mention it in letters home. Around him, an occasional hit struck down a man, but the sand-bags were providing good protection for men and guns. The naval battery continued firing until four o'clock that afternoon, when a shortage of ammunition enforced silence.

The damage sustained in Vera Cruz from this terrible new weapon brought an appeal to Scott from foreign consuls for a temporary truce, to permit foreigners and all women and children to leave. But Scott sent back a refusal, reminding the consuls that he had warned Vera Cruz what to expect. Only a surrender by the Mexican commander, he added, would allow anyone to leave the city—thereby deliberately exposing that officer to pressures greater than those he must already have been experiencing.

The naval battery eventually forced capitulation. Within two days after commencing fire the sailors had thrown thirteen hundred shells at Vera Cruz, making a rubble of the wall for a distance of fifty feet, and still the shells hurtled forth, screaming their warning to the terrified city.

At this time the military commander of Vera Cruz, General Juan Morales, suddenly fell ill, no doubt to avoid being the man forced into surrender. The foreign consuls took their pleas to the acting commander, General José Juan de Landero, the officer now burdened with admitting defeat. Landero asked Scott for terms. On the twenty-sixth firing ceased, under a truce, and two days later—following conferences of commissioners from both sides—terms of capitulation were signed providing for release on parole of Mexican soldiers with their promise not to fight again unless actually exchanged, and guaranteeing among other things freedom of worship.

Captain Robert E. Lee used the peace for a quiet ride around city walls to observe the effect of the bombardment. He noticed that many Mexican batteries had been destroyed, and he examined the huge breach blasted out by the naval battery. One sight inside the city he would not have seen until later was a ruined church, penetrated by a shell that had exploded among women and children who had sought safety there—the same people his heart had "bled for" during the bombardment. For them peace had come too late.

A Mexican writer could have described the city for Lee:

> . . . The condition of the place was frightful. From the gate of La Merced to the Parish, not a single house was uninjured. The greater part . . . was destroyed, and the streets were impassable from the rubbish. From the Parish to the Caleta . . . all the houses were damaged. There was no light, and there was no passing by the sidewalks, for fear that the balconies would fall. The storerooms of some commercial houses were occupied by families of whose habitations had been ruined; and that of the Consul of Spain, D. Telesfora Gonzalez de Escalante, was filled with . . . men, women, and children to whom he gave an asylum, and even generously supplied with food.

Captain E. K. Smith returned to Vera Cruz just in time to witness the surrender ceremony on the morning of March 29. He had completed three days of picket duty six miles inland, where he had been delighted to go—"into the green country away from the sand hills". Familiarity with war still had not blunted his affection for flowers. None could be found in that awful sand, of course, but he noted, "Wherever there is shade and soil here, there are many beautiful wild flowers in blossom. I shall send one in this letter. . . ."

Nor had familiarity with bloodshed created any cruel streak in Smith. His warlike spirit of "hurrah for San Juan [de Ulúa] and a brevet" had in fact subsided. After he had heard about the truce and the damage to Vera Cruz he had written home, from that temporary location on picket duty, "We hear the distress in the city has been dreadful, some hundreds of women and children having been killed by our shells. This is horrible!" Smith's reaction contrasted remarkably with that of many American civilians (including some contemporary war historians), who defended the bombardment of the city—civilians and all—against criticism by Mexicans, Europeans, and other Americans, who called the action inhumane.

On the morning of March 29 survivors of the shelling left Vera Cruz by the Merced gate for formal surrender on a sunny plain just south of the city. Scott ordered his men to remain silent while the Mexican soldiers marched out to stack arms. There would be no jeering, no insulting remarks. Lieutenant Sam Grant, waiting at the scene with the 4th Infantry, would have approved of Scott's order—judging by those remarks Grant had made after the Monterrey surrender.

Grant and other members of units representing the U. S. Army and Navy formed at eight o'clock in two long, polished lines facing each other. At ten o'clock, as arranged earlier, the Mexicans marched out to the music of drum and fife and passed between the facing lines. The paraded Americans saw some of the beaten defenders cast glances back at the battered city and wave emotional good-bys. Alongside many of the soldiers walked women and children—with some ". . . small children strapped upon their mothers' backs." The waiting Americans followed Scott's order. No one laughed or jeered. Possibly no one wanted to. Even a Mexican observer recorded, "Not . . . a look was given [the refugees] by the enemy's soldiers which could be interpreted into an insult." After the Mexicans' departure the Americans marched into the city to the music of "Yankee Doodle."

Colonel E. A. Hitchcock had seen the surrender ceremony, or at least as much of it as he had taken time to look at. The colonel had been a busy man during most of the proceedings. His responsibility had been to attend to paroling Mexican soldiers after they had marched out and stacked arms. Four men had been assigned to help him.

"These Mexicans are the devil for rank," Hitchcock thought. "'Tis said there are here 5 generals, 18 colonels, 37 lieutenant-colonels . . . 90 captains, 180 lieutenants." Only the rank of major seemed anywhere near proportional by American standards, with just five present.

After the surrender Hitchcock looked around the city and saw desolation: blackened walls poking out of rubble, roofs shattered by falling shells, street pavement ripped up as if by a giant earthquake. Few people remained, and they were "as miserable-looking wretches" as Hitchcock had ever seen. Mexican casualties, military and civilian, were counted by the hundreds, despite later figures revised downward by some American apologists. Scott's losses totaled sixty-seven.

The stench in the heart of the city sickened Hitchcock. He moved his tent to a location in the suburbs. There he escaped much of the foul odor, but not the memories of the destruction he had seen: "I shall never forget the horrible fire of our mortars . . . going with dreadful certainty and bursting with sepulchral tones often in the centre of private dwellings —it was awful. I shudder to think of it."

A Mexican editor published a more succinct and dramatic comment. After hearing of the surrender of Vera Cruz and San Juan de Ulúa he observed, "The sun of this day was but the lamp of a sepulcher."

PART V

An Elusive Peace

FROM APRIL 1847
TO JULY 4, 1848

36.

Stress, Frustration, and Anger

The pressure of war and presidential work had continued to erode James Polk's health. Unlike the victims of Vera Cruz, critics might have remarked, the Chief Executive had not been bloodied by any part of the war he had espoused. But the strain had been constant and real, nevertheless, and Polk showed the effects of it. His slenderness had withered away to a look of emaciation. Hard wrinkles cut deeply into his finely featured (but now ashy) face where no furrows had been visible before. Lately the President had been seen walking with the aid of a cane. Some of his debility could be traced to recent illness, but some of it was due to the stress of office, especially as occasioned by the Mexican conflict.

The war had further divided the nation, badly. Many Americans criticized Polk's actions for a variety of reasons, but the major opposition came, of course, from Northerners opposed to the extension of slavery, which they foresaw as making gains with the addition of any Mexican territory.

Their condemnations were loud and bitter but mostly non-violent. These people, being reformers and idealists, opposed fighting in the first place; their climactic wrath, exemplified by abolitionist John Brown's raids in Kansas and Virginia, would not boil over until later. Nevertheless, their outspoken opposition to the war seemed to border on treason—considering that crime solely by its legal definition—and this would have put some of those wrinkles in Polk's face.

The President never tolerated the abolitionists' affinity for linking slavery expansion with the Mexican conflict. "The slavery question is assuming a fearful . . . aspect," he wrote early in 1847. ". . . [It] will be attended with terrible consequences to the country, and cannot fail to destroy the Democratic party, if it does not ultimately threaten the Union itself. Slavery was one of the questions adjusted in the compromises of the Constitution. It has . . . no legitimate connection with the war with Mexico, or the terms of a peace which may be concluded with that country."

The anti-slavery people, however, continued to condemn Polk and "his" war. The President refrained from ordering large-scale legal action against them, possibly because he did not want to stir up more dissension and hatred, or possibly because he realized Northern jurors would be likely to sympathize with the accused. So the attacks went on—even increased in fury—in pulpits, lecture halls, and periodicals.

"War is an utter violation of Christianity," said New England minister Theodore Parker. "If war be right, then Christianity is wrong. . . . We can refuse to take any part in it; we can encourage others to do the same; we can aid men, if need be, who suffer because they refuse. Men will call us traitors; what then? That hurt nobody in '76. We are a rebellious nation. . . . Let God only be a master to control our conscience."

James Russell Lowell added his denunciation, through Hosea Biglow in the *Biglow Papers*.

> *Ez fer war, I call it murder—*
> *There you hev it plain an' flat;*
> *I don't want to go no furder*
> *Than my Testyment fer that. . . .*

Henry Thoreau was jailed for that refusal to pay taxes to a United States "that condoned slavery and war," and later he declared (in *Civil Disobedience*) that even a liberal government "becomes tyranny when it denies the right of the individual to be responsible for his intellectual and moral integrity."

The Massachusetts legislature resolved, "That the present war with Mexico had its primary origin in the unconstitutional annexation to the United States of the foreign State of Texas; that it was unconstitutionally commenced by the order of the President, to General Taylor, to take military possession of territory in dispute between the United States and Mexico, and in the occupation of Mexico . . . for the dismemberment of Mexico . . . with the . . . object of extending slavery." The legislators asked that citizens demand an end to the war and to slavery itself.

About this same time the Virginia legislature voiced the Southern stand: that the slavery question be left to each individual state and that the United States Government had no control, "directly or indirectly," over it. The more heated and widespread the arguments became, the more the Administration suffered.

In Washington Polk lost friends because of the war. Most Whigs had been critical of him for months now, but lately members of his own party had been sniping at him.

Senator Benton, always imperious, had grown even more demanding, especially in regard to some appointments he desired for relatives and friends. Another area of conflict with Benton loomed in the controversial role of the senator's son-in-law, John Frémont, in California—the extent of which would soon become known in Washington. Frémont had made that move of refusing to obey the orders of Polk's appointed commander, Kearny, and the infuriated general would demand a court-martial for his subordinate—thus angering Benton and embarrassing Polk, who believed Kearny right but who also would have preferred to smooth over the matter.

Another noted Democrat, John C. Calhoun, a man driven into seeming inconsistencies by ambition, had proved himself entirely untrustworthy, in Polk's opinion. Now the President heard a rumor that Calhoun favored the election of Whig Zachary Taylor for the next presidential term. The rumor proved to be false, but the President's low regard for Calhoun was indicated by a diary entry in which Polk gave the talk credence and remarked, "I cannot express the contempt I feel for Mr. Calhoun for such profligate political inconsistency."

Pennsylvania Democrat David Wilmot already had sabotaged Polk by attaching that proviso to the special two-million-dollar war appropriation (before its eventual death in the Senate) declaring that no money thus spent, and no land acquired from Mexico as a result of the appropriation, could be used for the expansion of slavery or involuntary servitude "except for crime, whereof the party shall first be duly convicted." This caused an uproar in Congress, where many men on both sides still sought (like Polk) to avoid slavery debate out of fear of wrecking the Union.

Even Polk's old friend Sam Houston, a Democratic senator from

Texas now and a sharer with the President of a close relationship with the late Andrew Jackson, cooled toward him—apparently because the President had not proposed him for important army command and because Polk had not catered to Houston's own presidential ambition.

The actions of other Washington Democrats, in and out of Congress, rankled Polk. Job seekers continued to stream into his office—as did ordinary well-wishers and visitors with no other motivation than a desire to stare at the Chief Executive. Polk's term came in a day when the Executive Mansion remained mostly open to the people—a holdover from the earliest days of the Republic—but when the President's job had become so demanding, the doors should have been closed to individuals who had no important business there. Polk the Jacksonian Democrat continued to strive earnestly to satisfy both demands—for an open door and for devotion to duty, an impossible combination—and he suffered from it.

For a politician to whom party loyalty was paramount, however, the worst torment no doubt came as a result of Democrats who defied and even vilified him. Polk came to consider these Democrats even more treacherous than his Whig foes. At least he expected the worst from the Whigs.

"Treacherous" was indeed the word on Polk's tongue. He regarded fellow Democrats who disputed his policies as traitors to the party, and he considered anyone—Democrat or Whig—who voiced that growing opposition to the war with Mexico to be a traitor to his nation. Most contemporary criticism of his Administration, however, continued to be centered around the conflict that political opponents referred to almost unanimously now as "Mr. Polk's war."

Congressional criticism, like that in areas outside Washington, had become more vicious the longer the war continued. One day early in 1847 Polk heard with amazement and no doubt with fury that Thomas Corwin of Ohio, a Whig who had voted in favor of the war declaration, had risen in the Senate to condemn the war and his countrymen's desire for more land with a statement that, were he a Mexican, he would say to the invaders from the United States: "Have you not room in your own country to bury your dead men? If you come into mine, we will greet you with bloody hands and welcome you to hospitable graves."

Corwin's speech represented an inflammatory height, but other Whigs opposed the war just as strongly. Later, Abraham Lincoln of Illinois (elected after the original war declaration and thus not on voting record in regard to it) would argue in the House of Representatives against the war and against Polk. Lincoln would contend that the President had begun the war unnecessarily and unconstitutionally, and he would demand to know the exact site "on American soil" where the first blood had been shed.

Nevertheless, Lincoln voted consistently for war appropriations and supplies—as did many other Whigs—and in a noted speech he sought to explain why.

> . . . When the war began, it was my opinion that all those who, because of knowing too *little*, or because of knowing too *much*, could not conscientiously approve the conduct of the President, in the beginning of it, should, nevertheless, as good citizens and patriots, remain silent on that point, at least till the war should be ended. Some leading democrats, including Ex President Van Buren, have taken this same view, as I understand them; and I adhered to it, and acted upon it, until since I took my seat here; and I think I should still adhere to it, were it not that the President and his friends will not allow it to be so.

Lincoln then charged that Polk had used "every silent vote given for supplies" as an endorsement of the justice and wisdom of the war—but Lincoln had voted for the supplies only because of that desire to "remain silent . . . till the war should be ended" and because of concern for countrymen committed to the war by military service.

In the same speech Lincoln declared that Polk had never proved the boundary between Texas and Mexico to have been the Rio Grande, despite the President's statement that war existed "by the act of Mexico," whose troops "invaded our territory and shed American blood upon American soil." Polk's claim had been based on the claim of Texas, Lincoln emphasized—and only recently had Texas itself claimed the Rio Grande as a boundary. Furthermore, this represented mere claim against claim, the congressman argued, since Mexico insisted the boundary lay along the Nueces River.

> I am now through the whole of the President's evidence [Lincoln said], and it is a singular fact, that if any one should declare the President sent the army into the midst of a settlement of Mexican people, who had never submit[t]ed, by consent or by force, to the authority of Texas, or of the United States, and that *there*, and *thereby*, the first blood of the war was shed, there is not one word in all the

President has said, which would either admit or deny the declaration. . . .

. . .

. . . [The President] knows not where he is. He is a bewildered, confounded, and miserably perplexed man. God grant he may be able to show, there is not something about his conscience, more painful than all his mental perplexity!

Despite Lincoln's accusation, the President knew exactly where he was (except for a date when peace might be expected), and Lincoln himself indicated at one point in his speech he believed this to be true. After his discussion regarding the absence in Polk's war declaration of any statement about the fact that American blood had been first shed "in the midst of a settlement of Mexican people," Lincoln said, "This strange omission, it does seem to me, could not have occurred but by design." (In the *Congressional Globe Appendix* Lincoln altered that sentence so that it read, "In this strange omission chiefly consists the deception of the President's evidence—an omission which, it does seem to me, could scarcely have occurred but by design.")

If ever a man knew where he was and what he wanted, Polk did. His countrymen might have argued (as they still do) about his mediocrity, but no one who knew him doubted his resolution. The President held the reins of his Administration, and he conducted his own war—as the two Whig generals, Scott and Taylor, realized fully by now. And by this time Polk, through his usual diligence, had become something of an authority on running the war, just as he had become expert in the duties of each cabinet member through intense observation and reflection.

An intense study of the problems had put Polk ahead of General Taylor in regard to transportation requirements in Mexico—a country the President had, of course, never seen. Polk learned from the quartermaster general that thousands of wagons had been requisitioned for U. S. Army use in Mexico, and the President believed this to be foolish. Polk noted in his diary, "I told [the quartermaster general] that I would issue no positive order on the subject, but expressed the opinion that long trains of miles of wagons in such a country as Mexico, in which, in all the wars which had ever occurred in that country, they had never been used, could only have the effect of retarding the movements of the army and rendering it inefficient in its operations. I expressed the opinion that packmules should be chiefly employed for the transportation of the army. . . ."

Polk also wondered why field commanders insisted on requesting shipments of horses and mules from the United States when they surely must have been available in unlimited numbers in Mexico. The native animals, Polk thought, would be better acclimated, probably could be purchased for one fourth the price, and would not require transportation. "The truth is," Polk concluded, "that the old army officers have become so in the habit of enjoying their ease, sitting in parlours and on carpeted floors, that most of them have no energy, and are content to jog on in a regular routine without knowing whether they are taking care of public interest or not."

Polk's cross that early spring of 1847 was a heavy one: abuses to be endured, job seekers and other visitors to be met and dismissed as quickly but politely as possible, work to be done personally without entrusting it to anyone else.

The President was, of course, incapable of much trust anyway. After making his diary entry about the pack mules and the unnecessary purchase of horses and mules in the United States he added, "I shall find it to be necessary to give more of my attention to these matters of detail than I have heretofore had it in my power to do." About the same time he remarked, "I am almost ready at some times to conclude that all men are selfish, and that there is no reliance to be placed in any of the human race."

Still another worry as spring of 1847 came in stemmed from Zachary Taylor's disobedience in advancing beyond Monterrey. Polk knew that Taylor had gone forward to Saltillo and Agua Nueva despite the depletion of his army by Scott's requisition and despite orders to the contrary, but Polk had not yet learned about the Battle of Buena Vista. The President's personal dislike of Taylor dissolved into concern for him and his men. Polk hoped to send reinforcements to Taylor, but their arrival would take much time, and meanwhile he and other Washington officials could only "wait in painful suspense."

On the first day of April Polk finally received definite word about the fighting at Buena Vista and, coincidentally, of the successful landing at Vera Cruz.

> By the Southern mail of this evening official despatches were received from General Taylor giving a detailed account of the battle of the 22d and 23d ultimo. It was a severe battle. Many valuable officers and men fell, and among them my old esteemed friend, Col. Archibald Yell of the Arkansas Mounted Regiment. I deeply de-

plore his loss. He was a brave and a good man, and among the best friends I had on earth, and had been so for twenty-five years. His eldest, and perhaps his only son, is now at college at Georgetown, and as my impression is that Col. Yell died poor, I will in that event educate the boy, and shall take great interest in him.

A despatch from Commodore Conner was received tonight communicating the information that General Scott's forces had landed near Vera Cruz on the 7th instant [actually the ninth] without serious resistance.

Had General Taylor obeyed his orders, and occupied Monter[r]ey and the passes beyond it, the severe loss of our army . . . would have been avoided. It was great rashness to take the position he did in advance of Saltillo. Having done so, he is indebted not to his own good generalship, but to the indomitable and intrepid bravery of the officers and men under his command for his success. He exposed them to an opposing army of three or four times their number. . . . General Taylor is a hard fighter, but has none of the other qualities of a great general. From the beginning of the existing war with Mexico he has been constantly blundering into difficulties, but has fought out of them, but with very severe loss. . . . I rejoice that our brave army have been successful in this battle, but deeply lament the severe loss they have sustained.

Ten days later Polk heard about the surrender of Vera Cruz, and he determined to send "a commissioner vested with plenipotentiary powers, who should attend the headquarters of the army ready to take advantage of circumstances as they might arise to negotiate for peace." The harried President was ready indeed for the war to end—but not without the final acquisition of those Western lands.

Polk discussed the matter of a commissioner with his Cabinet. He said he preferred James Buchanan for the job, then added that he could not spare the Secretary of State for such an indefinite period.

Buchanan suggested the chief clerk of the State Department: Nicholas P. Trist, an experienced man thoroughly familiar with the Spanish language and character—but also a man sometimes too impractical and egotistical for effective diplomacy. Polk approved the suggestion, then emphasized the need for secrecy in regard to Trist's journey. "Had his mission and the object of it been proclaimed in advance at Washington I have no doubt there are persons [here] . . . who would have been ready and willing to have despatched a courier to Mexico to discourage the government of that weak and distracted country from entering upon any negotiations for peace. This they would do rather than suffer my administration to have the credit of concluding a just and honourable peace."

The President instructed Trist to negotiate a Texas-Mexico boundary at the Rio Grande from its mouth to its intersection with the southern boundary of New Mexico—"the whole of the province of New Mexico and Upper and Lower California to be ceded to the United States." He also wanted right of passage from the Gulf of Mexico and the Pacific Ocean across the Isthmus of Tehuantepec. For all of this Polk proposed to pay Mexico fifteen million dollars, in installments of three million annually, in addition to settling the claims previously made against Mexico by United States citizens. He offered to go higher if necessary to conclude negotiations.

On April 16 Trist left Washington on his secret mission. Five days later Polk heard with consternation that the New York *Herald* had reported "with remarkable accuracy . . . the fact of the departure" of his envoy.

Stress, frustration, and anger gripped Polk again.

> I have not been more vexed or excited since I have been President. . . . The success of Mr. Trist's mission I knew in the beginning must depend mainly on keeping it a secret from that portion of the . . . press and leading men in the country who, since the commencement of the war with Mexico, have been giving "aid and comfort" to the enemy by their course. . . . I do not doubt that Mexico has been and will be discouraged from making peace, in the hope that their friends in the United States will come into power at the next Presidential election.

37.

Suspense and Agony

While Polk brooded about political foes who might be seeking to sabotage his negotiation efforts, in Mexico Santa Anna enjoyed success in unifying dissident factions. The rebellion against Valentín Gómez Farías had made it easier for Santa Anna, upon his return to Mexico City, to assert his claim of victory at Buena Vista and had supported his reinstatement as a national hero. The latest upheaval represented another example (as a Mexican historian once observed) of how "petty passions" could wreak continual havoc in a country where "everything is done for persons and nothing for principles."

Ostentation had made Santa Anna a person to whom Mexicans would look, and they did this now. Upon his return from Buena Vista he had paused outside the revolt-torn capital and refused to enter until the violence stopped. This show of reluctance had brought about the desired effect. A delegation of officials came to him and urged that he lead the nation again.

The hero of the fighting against the French now became, temporarily at least, the hero of Buena Vista. The Mexican Congress gave him almost unlimited power. Santa Anna quickly and successfully re-established functioning government and refinanced the treasury, with the aid of the Church. Certainly no other Mexican leader could have accomplished this as efficiently at that momentous time.

Before Santa Anna left the capital to lead troops against the American invaders now threatening Mexico City from the east he issued another ringing proclamation.

My duty is to sacrifice myself, and I will know how to fulfill it! Perhaps the American hosts may proudly tread the imperial capital of the Aztecs. I will never witness such opprobrium, for I am decided first to die fighting! Mexicans! You have a religion—protect it! You have honor—then free yourselves from infamy! You love your wives, your children—then liberate them from American brutality! But it must be action—not vain entreaty or barren desires—with which the enemy must be opposed. Mexicans! Your fate is the fate of the nation! Not the Americans but you will decide her destiny! Vera Cruz calls for vengeance—follow me, and wash out the stain of her dishonor!

In the afternoon of April 3 Santa Anna left the capital, after choosing as Provisional President to act in his absence Pedro María Anaya. Crowds swarmed around Santa Anna's coach, shouting *vivas* and *bravos*. The general spoke to them emotionally: "Union, Mexicans, union, union!" Then followed a clatter of hoofs and the rumble of coach wheels over rough pavement, and Santa Anna vanished down the road en route to his latest destiny. On the way, at Perote, he met large numbers of soldiers recently paroled by Scott from the Vera Cruz garrison and succeeded in adding them to his new army.

The nucleus of his reorganized force had preceded him eastward, on his orders. It consisted of several thousand veterans of the Battle of Buena Vista, gritty men who now had completed a thousand-mile march of incredible severity since departing from San Luis Potosí to attack Zachary Taylor so long ago.

Two days after leaving the capital Santa Anna arrived at his hacienda, El Encero, where he established headquarters and began working tirelessly to gather more men and supplies, just as he had done at San Luis Potosí. To feed his troops he slaughtered beeves from his own herds. He began planning a defense centered around a strategic height that lay to the east of the road running from Vera Cruz to Mexico City. The hill was called Cerro Gordo.

Santa Anna ordered the main body of his army into bivouac at the rear of the defensive position he had selected. The encampment lay on both sides of the road that led on northwestward to Jalapa. As would be expected of a planner with Santa Anna's blind confidence and love of comfort, the camp had some of the permanence and all of the bustle of a busy city, as a Mexican writer described it.

355

Large cabins, with palm-leaf roofs, situated at distances on each side of the road, were the habitations of the President-General, his [aides] and staff and all the principal chiefs and officers who were not in the line. In the intervals the reserve corps were encamped in the open air . . . the 1st, 2nd, 3rd, and 4th light battalions, with 1,700 men, and the 4th and 11th of the line, with 780 men. The pieces of artillery not yet placed, the carriages of the park, some tents, the hospital wagons, and a few eating-houses formed a wide street, in which were constantly moving soldiers and officers of all grades, and that multitude of adventurers who always accompany an army. But provisions for the troops were very scarce. The few sutlers to be found instantly sold all their bad provisions, without satisfying the hunger of those who reached their eating-shops at a later moment; the water, brought in barrels on mules from the bottom of the barranca, was obtained with much difficulty; and the reverberating sun, in that climate, excited a debilitating thirst, which the soldiers sometimes relieved by chewing the prickly leaves of maguey, that produced severe sickness. Finally, the multitude of insects, almost imperceptible, kept the blood in a continual irritation, and even lacerated the bodies of those on whom they fed.

Nevertheless, the position had distinct military advantages. Santa Anna harbored no doubt about his ability to stop the invaders at this very location. Some of his staff officers were said later to have expressed doubt, but none of them dared voice this or to give their chief the benefit of any suggestions. "[Santa Anna] required the humiliation of those who surrounded him," said a Mexican who should have known, "and was inaccessible to reason and truth."

While waiting at Cerro Gordo for the despised Americans Santa Anna frequently would mount his horse at sunrise, review his troops ("paying particular attention to the dismounted men and the construction of barracks for the troops"), and return to headquarters about noon. After a siesta he would ride again on inspections until sunset. Then he and a group of favorite officers would retire to dine, while a military band serenaded them with chosen selections.

This time Santa Anna, not the Americans, would be dug in at a strong place. The enemy would have to make the attack, and because Cerro Gordo lay at a low altitude in the mountains, at no great distance from Vera Cruz, the foe would be in country where the *vómito* soon would inflict on him execution—if Santa Anna, working from behind his fortifications, did not cut him down entirely.

At Vera Cruz Winfield Scott re-established order. He allowed the Mexicans to govern themselves under their own designated magistrates. He brought the Americans under strict martial law, as specified in a general order. He regulated food prices in the city for the benefit of the inhabitants, distributed rations to the poor, and paid native laborers to clear away debris left by his mammoth bombardment. He encountered the usual disciplinary problems with his troops, but he dealt more firmly with them than did Zachary Taylor. Scott ordered a rapist hanged—"a dreadful scene" (as Colonel Hitchcock remarked) that was reported in detail by the *American Eagle*, an English-language newspaper newly established for the soldiers at Vera Cruz.

Through it all, Scott never forgot the necessity of getting his army out of the low coastal area and into the mountains by mid-April. He would take with him ten thousand troops, leaving behind only a garrison for the protection of a supply base, and a number of men on the sick list.

Scott learned that he needed many more horses and mules. Not enough animals had been sent from the United States, and some of these had been lost aboard storm-wrecked ships during the sea voyage. Unknowingly complying with President Polk's suggestion as expressed to the quartermaster general, Scott determined to procure Mexican animals for the journey. The general and Commodore Matthew C. Perry, Conner's recent replacement as naval commander, planned to co-operate in a joint Army-Navy campaign to get the horses and mules. This Perry (younger brother of Oliver Hazard Perry of Lake Erie fame) was the same "cast-iron commodore" who, along with a few other officers, had been pressing for the Navy transfer to steam and who would, in time, command a naval expedition that would open Japan to the West.

The joint venture was aimed at the valley of the Alvarado River southeast of Vera Cruz. There the animals that Scott wanted were known to be available in large numbers, and fresh water that naval vessels needed could be obtained in quantity from the river. To ensure this water supply the Navy would occupy the town of Alvarado, situated on the coast near the mouth of the river (and, incidentally, thus make up for previous failures to take the place). Commodore Perry would hold off his sea attack, however, until a brigade under General John A. Quitman could complete a forty-mile march from Vera Cruz to a position inland from Alvarado, where he would lie in wait to prevent the Mexicans from running the animals into the interior, away from American use, when they realized the object of the expedition.

By the evening of April 1, while Santa Anna was preparing to leave Mexico City for his stand against Scott, Quitman's troops were approaching Alvarado after their overland trek. A naval messenger riding out from town found the general and handed him a scrawled note. It said that a small, one-gun naval steamer named the *Scourge,* commanded by a lieutenant and manned by a crew of forty men, already had captured Alvarado. The vessel, sent ahead of the fleet to reconnoiter, had lobbed a casual shot or two toward the Alvarado fort during the mission. The lieutenant in command of the ship, Charles Hunter, had been amazed by the reaction of the Mexican commander. The man offered to surrender immediately, having learned what had been the fate of the much more formidable San Juan de Ulúa. Hunter took possession of the fort and the town, left a garrison force of five men commanded by a midshipman, steamed on up the river, and captured the town of Tlacotalpan. Meanwhile, however, the inhabitants had driven those horses and mules beyond the grasp of the Americans. Hunter received no thanks from the commodore but a court-martial instead, thus making the lieutenant a national hero when people back home heard about his martyrdom.

Several days later Perry captured the port of Tuxpán, north of Vera Cruz, but this still did not give Scott his needed animals.

Captain Ephraim Kirby Smith was aware of this shortage (as developments showed) on the night of April 7, when he sat in his tent writing a letter home. A messenger summoned him to the quarters of Major Martin Scott. There Smith found other officers of the 5th Infantry assembled. All of them wondered about the nocturnal summons.

Major Scott, an officer whose importance impressed himself more than most other persons, addressed the group.

"Are you all here?" Scott held in his hand a sheet of paper, and he began reading from it: "Major Scott, Sir: You . . ." Then he stopped. The paper obviously held a written order.

"Where is Captain Ruggles?" Scott inquired. "Gentlemen, pay attention. We shall catch it before tomorrow night!"

"What?" Captain Smith asked. "The yellow fever?" For Smith, the Army had indeed begun to rankle.

"We are to go on desperate service," Scott replied. He commenced reading the order again, stopped, and began again. Finally he finished the reading. General Scott's subordinate, General William Worth, had ordered the major to have the regiment ready for unspecified duty early the next morning. Each man was to have with him a haversack with five days' rations.

Smith asked the major if he knew their destination. Scott answered that he thought he did and declared once more that the duty would consist of "desperate service," for which they probably had been chosen after careful consideration of their qualifications. Smith mused over this pompous reply, decided Scott had no idea what the job would be or where they would be going, and guessed that because of the major's "peculiar fitness" the duty probably would entail rounding up horses and mules and bringing them to Vera Cruz.

Time proved Smith right. On the following morning the 5th Infantry embarked on a steamer named the *McKim* for a voyage up the green banks of the Alvarado River—a deep, clear stream. At Tlacotalpan, the same inland town captured by Lieutenant Hunter, the men disembarked. While the quartermaster collected horses—spreading the word that he would pay for them, as General Winfield Scott had intended from the first—the 5th Regiment went into quarters in a filthy old building ordinarily used for storing cotton. The only comfort it offered was an opportunity to stretch out in the shade—"absolutely necessary in this hot climate."

The drabness of his present duty, the ridiculous pretensions of Major Scott, and a growing awareness of the pettiness of army politics had combined by now to disenchant Captain Smith, whose professionalism had centered around an idea of doing a job quietly and competently with the assumption that good performance would be rewarded. Smith had seen this was not always true. The louder and more boastful a man could be about an accomplishment, the further he went in the Army. But Smith was a quiet officer who told his wife, in one letter, "*Not a word I write must get into the papers*"—an uncommon request, it seemed, from a soldier in the field during this war, which was the first American conflict covered by newspaper correspondents accompanying the Army and was even more thoroughly reported in letters home that were published in various periodicals.

Smith and other members of the 5th Regiment remained at Tlacotalpan for nearly five broiling days, with no change of uniform available. On the evening of April 13 they marched for Vera Cruz, herding the animals that had been collected. This proved to be no easy task, because many of the horses were wild mustangs. "The march . . . was most horrible,—the men without bread, and had to be up all night watching the horses."

Smith arrived at Vera Cruz "worn out" and there learned of the issuance of the latest order of promotions and brevets. Not one man from the 5th Regiment was mentioned. "I am utterly disgusted with the service," he wrote his wife, "and were it not for you and the dear children would resign at once, but for your sakes I must continue to endure."

The captain returned to a camp bustling with activity. Using animals already available, General Scott had begun moving his army westward toward Mexico City, 260 miles distant, on April 8—the same day the 5th Infantry had left to shepherd in those additional horses.

Scott's immediate destination was Jalapa. A column led by impatient General Twiggs had moved out first, across hills of sand that seemed to stretch almost as far as a man could see. Twiggs rode horseback at the head of his struggling troops, who began falling behind his fast pace early in the day because of the debilitating heat, the deep sand through which they had to march, and the diarrhea from which many men suffered. As the midday temperature rose Twiggs's soldiers began discarding equipment—haversacks, coats, extra shoes. Some even gave up the march temporarily, flopping in the shade of occasional palmetto bushes and lying there, helpless, while their companions tramped on through the burning sand in the wake of their wild-eyed general.

As the miles passed, the road improved. General Scott's soldiers were indeed following in the footsteps of Cortés. The road (paved in this higher region) had been built three centuries earlier along the route that the Spanish explorer took during his own march on the Valley of Mexico and Montezuma's gold. By 1847 the highway had cracked and crumbled, but it still afforded an army comparatively easy passage into the mountains.

Weather improved much more slowly than did footing. Fifteen miles out of Vera Cruz the sun still poured its fire on the plodding soldiers. At that juncture they struck the southeastern edge of Santa Anna's estate, which (they were told) extended nearly to Jalapa, some fifty miles away, and held sixty thousand head of cattle, in addition to countless sheep and horses.

On they marched, hot and sweaty and almost suffocating in a calm that became "breathless" in midday heat. They progressed into a hilly country where shrubs, flowers, and trees made a gradual, welcome appearance. Past Manga de Clavo, Santa Anna's old home. Across the majestic, stone-arched National Bridge that spanned the swiftly flowing Antigua River, near a pass that "a few brave men" could have defended against an army larger than this one. Up toward lofty mountains looming higher now. On toward another gushing mountain stream, El Rio del Plan, and across it, then over another—smaller—arched stone bridge; and into a village called El Plan del Rio.

Beyond the town Twiggs's advance units of dragoons came upon a group of waiting Mexican lancers. After exchanging a few random shots the Mexicans leaped upon their horses and fled. The weary dragoons gave up any idea of a chase; the tiring march had exhausted their animals.

Shortly after noon of April 11 Twiggs halted his men in a large meadow near the scene of the skirmish, not caring to venture on with his entire division so tired. Three hot, hard days had passed since their departure from Vera Cruz. Even hotter and harder times seemed to lie ahead. Mexican troops numbering anywhere from six thousand to twelve thousand—or even more—were said to be entrenched five miles beyond, at a place where the road passed between mountains that towered above it on either side.

Subsequent reconnoitering showed the strength of this position. The Mexican line extended across the National Road for a distance of two miles. Its right was anchored on steep bluffs overlooking El Rio del Plan— terrain that precluded any outflanking there. Between the river and the road lay three ridges that Santa Anna had chosen for emplacement of artillery that could sweep the Americans' route of advance. On the other side of the road (on the left of the Mexican line) lay two hills bristling with more guns: the seven-hundred-foot conical height of Cerro Gordo (sometimes called El Telégrafo because of its early use in a visual communication system linking Mexico City and Vera Cruz) and, farther on, a slightly smaller hill, La Atalaya (appropriately: the Watchtower), where the Mexicans had anchored their extreme left. Beyond La Atalaya lay rugged, rocky, wooded land that Santa Anna believed (as became known later) impassable even for a rabbit. On the road in the rear of this defensive line lay the Mexican camp, where large numbers of troops waited in reserve for action against the Americans, whom they expected to advance up that road thoroughly commanded by Mexican cannon.

On the day after his arrival at El Plan del Rio, Twiggs sent out a strong reconnaissance. It reported the Mexicans dug in well around Cerro Gordo. Nevertheless, the ambitious general planned to launch an assault at four o'clock in the morning of April 13, without waiting for the reinforcements (commanded by generals who outranked him) that he knew must be strung out along the road behind. A volunteer division commanded by General Patterson had been scheduled to depart Vera Cruz after Twiggs's troops, then another division commanded by General Worth. Both groups had been forced to wait for the horses brought in by Captain Smith and the 5th Regiment.

The waiting men encamped at El Plan del Rio heard the order to prepare for early morning attack with scant enthusiasm, and they were delighted when reinforcements arrived late in the evening of the twelfth to delay action. The newcomers would have to be included in the assault, but their wearisome march required a twenty-four-hour rest before they would be ready to participate.

Then came another delay. General Patterson, who outranked Twiggs, arrived at the American bivouac and assumed command. Patterson ordered the attack postponed pending the appearance of General Scott, who had left Vera Cruz just ahead of Worth's division when he learned of the presence at Cerro Gordo of Santa Anna and a large army.

With Scott traveled staff members Colonel Hitchcock and Captain Lee. The trip had forced Hitchcock to put aside temporarily his latest intellectual endeavor, the study of Spanish. While at Vera Cruz the colonel had begun carefully recording in his diary many Spanish words and phrases, together with their English translations. But on the evening of the twelfth Scott had received a dispatch from Twiggs about Santa Anna's presence and had ordered his aides to move forward with him (after having first put them on twenty minutes' notice for doing so a day or two earlier). Hitchcock closed his diary entirely for a time.

Lee, before leaving, had enjoyed a final visit with his brother aboard the *Mississippi*, having anticipated orders to move. Then he, too, rode with Scott: ten miles across the same sands that had plagued Twiggs's troops, to a point where the disintegrating National Road commenced and provided better footing, then on toward Cerro Gordo and the mountains. As Scott's entourage crossed the bridge that spanned El Rio del Plan and entered the camp located in that meadow beyond, Lee heard the waiting soldiers send up a cheer for the general.

Scott ordered his own reconnaissance of the area ahead. Any advance •

up the road obviously would be suicidal, with all those Mexican guns ready to destroy anything or anyone that moved along it. A group of junior officers first scouted the area and returned with the information that a passage might be found off to the right of the road—the same area Santa Anna thought impassable even for a rabbit. Scott sent Robert E. Lee and another man into this rugged wilderness for a closer examination.

Lee and his companion left camp early on the fifteenth and vanished into a harsh land of deep ravines and thick brush. They picked their way carefully. Not only was the terrain rough, but they might come upon Mexican pickets, even here, at any moment.

Lee crept forward until he estimated his position to be behind the Mexicans' left flank. His progress had been slow and difficult, but obviously not impossible. With engineers to improve the route, he mused, a narrow path for an army and its equipment could be hacked out. He and the other man paused and relaxed near a spring of water.

Distant voices of men speaking in Spanish startled them. Then Lee saw a group of Mexican soldiers approaching, no doubt heading for a cool drink at this very spring. Lee hid in undergrowth that covered one side of a giant log lying near the water, while his companion slipped into another hiding place nearby.

The soldiers drank, chatted, and idled, while Lee lay behind the log in increasing suspense and agony. Crawling things crept over his body, but shaking them off was out of the question. Some soldiers plopped down on the log, their backs to Lee. One meandering Mexican barely missed stepping on him. More soldiers came to refresh themselves and to pass the time.

Hours passed. Still the crowd did not disperse. Afternoon waned; shadows reached out to claim new ground. With darkness approaching the crowd finally began to thin. Then the last man left. Lee waited in silence for a while and struggled to his feet, aching and unsteady.

With his companion he groped through darkness toward the American camp. Locating it would not be easy. Unseen trees, rocks, and ravines lay waiting to cause stumbles and falls. Eventually, however, Lee reached General Scott with his report: a path possibly could be cut through the area. Lee was not yet certain.

On the sixteenth Lee returned for another look, so ordered by Scott. This time the captain had with him a detachment of soldiers whose job would be to hack out a passage through the wilderness.

By nightfall a way had been made barely passable for troops and equipment. Some uncertainty, however, still bothered Lee. He had gone farther than the stopping point of his previous reconnaissance, but he had not come upon the National Road stretching on toward Jalapa from the rear of the Mexican line. Still, Lee believed that it lay near the limit of this probe. To isolate the enemy and to cut off his retreat it would be necessary for General Scott to control the road.

Scott could delay a decision no longer, with yellow fever creeping up on his army each day now. He determined to risk the by-pass around the Mexican left. On the seventeenth he ordered Lee to guide Twiggs's division along the rugged trail and to be in position to attack the enemy on the eighteenth—when General Worth would have arrived with his men, who could be used in the assault, too. Diversionary frontal attacks would be made that day, Scott announced, but the major strike would be the surprise one—Twiggs's.

Some distance away toward Vera Cruz, accompanying Worth on his march from that port city, rode mule tender Sam Grant. The lieutenant's recently displayed competence at getting his wagons through the sands outside Vera Cruz and his general efficiency in supply duties had just earned him the job of permanent—not conditional—regimental quartermaster. Grant did not record his reaction to this "promotion," but after arriving at Scott's camp he did leave a description of the difficulties faced by Robert E. Lee, an officer with whom he would one day have a historic meeting, in leading Twiggs's men to the new position from which they would seek to surprise the enemy.

> . . . Under the supervision of the engineers, roadways had been opened over chasms to [our] right where the walls were so steep that men could barely climb them. Animals could not. These had been opened under cover of night, without attracting the notice of the enemy. The engineers . . . led the way and the troops followed. Artillery was let down the steep slopes by hand, the men engaged attaching a strong rope to the rear axle and letting the guns down, a piece at a time, while the men at the ropes kept their ground on top, paying out gradually, while a few at the front directed the course of the piece. In a like manner the guns were drawn by hand up the opposite slopes. In this way Scott's troops reached their assigned position in rear of most of the intrenchments of the enemy, unobserved.

They maneuvered unseen until midday of the seventeenth, as another observer, Colonel Hitchcock, learned. Hitchcock returned to his tent on the

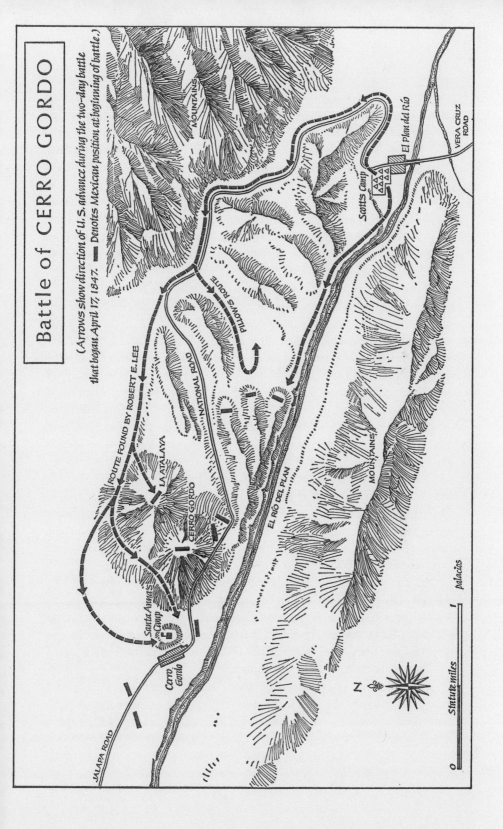

Battle of CERRO GORDO

(Arrows show direction of U.S. advance during the two-day battle
that began April 17, 1847. ▬ Denotes Mexican position at beginning of battle.)

MOUNTAINS

El Plan del Río

Scott's Camp

VERA CRUZ
ROAD

PILLOW'S ROUTE

NATIONAL ROAD

ROUTE FOUND BY ROBERT E. LEE

LA ATALAYA

CERRO GORDO

Santa Anna's Camp

Cerro Gordo

JALAPA ROAD

EL RÍO DEL PLAN

MOUNTAINS

N

palacios

Statute miles

0   1

plain after watching Twiggs's men commence the toil that Grant described. About noon the colonel heard firing—"evidently from the enemy." He jotted a note in his diary: "Very important events must occur within the next twenty-four hours."

They had begun to happen already, as Hitchcock soon realized. Mexican troops on the hill named La Atalaya had observed Twiggs's movement and had begun shooting. American infantrymen sent to take the top of the hill captured it after a skirmish, then pushed on toward Cerro Gordo and occupied its slopes. Night ended the fighting, and most troops withdrew from Cerro Gordo and La Atalaya. The surprise had been lost from the attack expected to be launched on the following day, but Scott had gained some ground.

That night many of Twiggs's weary troops slept on the earth they had taken, while reinforcements moved forward to help in the morning. Lee, as tired as anyone, enjoyed no sleep at all. Instead he spent the night directing the emplacement of artillery atop La Atalaya. He supervised men who tugged the heavy guns up steep slopes, then he saw that the cannon were made ready to fire at daybreak. That task completed, he joined an infantry force, ready to guide it (as ordered) to the supposed location of the Jalapa road in Santa Anna's rear as soon as fighting commenced on the eighteenth. This force would cut off retreat by the Mexicans, who would be attacked along their front and at their bent left flank as soon as daylight permitted.

Sunrise heralded the action. Scott threw his small army against Santa Anna's strong position. The La Atalaya guns emplaced by Lee roared at the enemy. Assaulting infantrymen clambered back up the Cerro Gordo slopes after the Mexicans who, firing downward, made that mistake of aiming too high. Lee and his infantry column moved forward toward the hoped-for road.

In the Mexican front, other of Scott's troops crept forward and charged. On the enemy right, around those ridges bristling with Santa Anna's cannon, the Americans suffered many casualties and eventually withdrew. Elsewhere on the field, however, the pressure resulted in forcing the Mexicans back. They left many dead and wounded after brisk fighting, but large numbers succeeded in escaping.

At a location near the Jalapa road Captain Lee happened upon a scene that moved him deeply even in the excitement of battle and remained in his memory for the rest of his life. A Mexican boy with a badly wounded arm lay prostrate under the weight of a dying soldier. Nearby, a Mexican girl looked on in terror, helpless to aid the boy but crying for him. Lee studied the girl, no doubt thought of his own children (as he usually did at such a time), and described what he saw: "Her large black eyes were streaming with tears, her hands crossed over her breast; her hair in one long plait behind reached her waist, her shoulders and arms bare, and without stockings or shoes."

Lee carefully lifted the fatally wounded soldier off the boy and saw that both individuals were taken to U. S. Army doctors. The girl thanked him, in Spanish, profusely but plaintively—and Lee remarked later that her tone "still lingers in my ear." Cerro Gordo provided Lee with his first view of a genuine battlefield and though his actions won him Scott's acclaim and, later, a brevet as major, Lee thought it "a horrible sight."

Well before noon that day the Battle of Cerro Gordo had ended. General Santa Anna had fled the scene early, leaving behind one of his wooden legs, his baggage, and one of his coin chests containing fifty thousand pesos. The human cost of Santa Anna's stand never was calculated, except that the Mexicans lost nearly half their army, dead, wounded, or captured. Scott lost four hundred men, including sixty-three killed.

On the following day Colonel Hitchcock rode with General Scott and several other staff members to Santa Anna's estate at El Encero. There they spent the night—at "a princely place. The country is quite elevated and continues to rise to the west, with mountains in the distance. The buildings are of soft limestone. . . ."

Hitchcock unconsciously wrote in his diary a reason for the present tribulations of Mexico, a nation left leaderless and adrift—orphaned, actually—by the Spaniards who had deliberately sought to eradicate every native quality during their rule.

"Santa Anna's property here was put under the protection of a guard," Hitchcock wrote, ". . . and nothing has been injured. [The hacienda] is full of very rich prints hanging on the walls of nearly all the rooms; but everything is foreign—nothing shows the genius of the Mexicans—no works of art or evidences of science."

38.

Rough, Ragged, and Ready

Still isolated in distant Chihuahua, Colonel Alexander Doniphan and his Missouri volunteers knew nothing of the momentous occurrences far to the southeast: Winfield Scott's expedition that aimed at the Mexican interior, and the recently fought Cerro Gordo battle. A short time earlier, however, Doniphan and his men had heard vague talk from natives about some fighting around Buena Vista, from which the Mexican troops were said to have emerged victorious. The Americans doubted the latter part of this rumor. They guessed that Zachary Taylor had prevailed.

Doniphan's resoluteness had by now proved itself present in proportion to his imposing physical size. But the colonel also was a realist, and the responsibility of command had made him acutely aware of the danger of his situation. Soon after occupying Chihuahua—and before he had heard the rumors of the Buena Vista fighting—Doniphan had written a friend in Missouri a letter to be mailed whenever an opportunity came.

> My orders are to report to Gen. Wool; but I now learn, that instead of taking the city of Chihuahua, he is shut up at Saltillo, by Santa Anna. Our position will be ticklish, if Santa Anna should compel Taylor and Wool even to fall back. All Durango, Zacatecas, and Chihuahua will be down upon my little army. We are out of the reach of help, and it would be as unsafe to go backward as forward. High spirits and a bold front, is perhaps the best and safest policy. My men are rough, ragged, and ready, having one more of the R's than General Taylor himself. We have been in service nine months, and my men, after marching two thousand miles, over mountains and deserts, have not received one dollar of their pay. . . . Half rations, hard marches, and no clothes! but they are still game to the last,

and curse and praise their country by turns, but fight for her all the time.

Eleven days after he had finished that letter Doniphan heard the talk about the Buena Vista battle. Still not absolutely certain of the outcome, he nevertheless determined to try to communicate with General Wool, who might or might not be beleaguered still by Santa Anna at Wool's reported location at Saltillo. To deliver his dispatches Doniphan sent an experienced trader-interpreter-soldier, J. L. Collins, a man who knew the country, and an escort of thirteen men—including Private John Hughes. Doniphan sent Wool his official report of the Battle of Sacramento and wrote the general a letter in which he reiterated the statement about his ticklish situation.

My position here is exceedingly embarrassing. In the first place, most of the men under my command have been in service since the 1st of June, have never received one cent of pay. Their marches have been hard, especially in the Navajo country, and no forage; so that they are literally without horses, clothes, or money, having nothing but arms and a disposition to use them. They are all volunteers, officers and men, and although ready for any hardships or danger, are wholly unfit to garrison a town or city. . . . Having performed a march of more than two thousand miles, and their term of service rapidly expiring, they are restless to join the army under your command. . . .

Collins, Hughes, and the other twelve men left Chihuahua March 20 on their perilous journey. They took a southeasterly course across the Mexican wilderness, riding at night to avoid detachments of enemy troops, averaging fifty miles a march "over stupendous mountains clad with horrible *cactus* and the *maguey*, and through vallies of mezquite."

Sixty miles out of Chihuahua—near a town named Saucillo, located on the banks of the cool, clear Rio Conchos—they sought to veer to their left, to take a more easterly course across a lonesome section of dry plains to Monclova (the town Wool once had occupied, before Buena Vista), and from there drop down to Saltillo—a more direct route. For two days and nights they traveled over deserts and across barren mountains, seeking water holes but finding none, their tongues feeling as thick and as dry as cotton bolls in their mouths.

Desperate to find water, Hughes, Collins, and two other men rode to a mountain for a better look around, while their companions remained behind. From the height they saw, five or six miles away, a green-shored lake with its blue surface ruffled by whitecaps blown before a breeze. Down the mountain they came, and with their companions they hurried toward the lake: one mile, two, then three. Four miles. The lake receded as they progressed. They "were pursuing a phantom." Eventually they did arrive at a beach of glassy sand, but no refreshing water lapped upon it.

Nearly perishing now of thirst and suffering from the stifling late afternoon heat, they commenced a race with death back to the river named Conchos. All night they rode, and at sunrise they reached the stream. "Great God! What a blessing to man hast thou made this one element," Hughes exclaimed, "and how poorly does he appreciate it. . . ."

From Saucillo they kept to a more southerly course this time: along the Conchos for a short distance to La Cruz and beyond, then southeasterly again through a region "majestically barren—[with] a grandeur in the very desolation around you. The eternal mountains with the cactus bristling on their sides shut out the horizon, the rising and setting sun, and lift their bald rocky summits high in the . . . heaven." But the land was not completely dry like the desert they had sought to cross, and thus it had human occupants—not a pleasant prospect. Three officials rode out from one village and asked their business. The Americans persuaded these challengers that they were only passing through the country peacefully, and they went on without interference.

The threat of being apprehended, however, became a greater concern. In the security of a mountain gorge they halted and burned all letters and papers they carried, with the exception of Doniphan's dispatches to General Wool, to avoid betrayal as expressmen in event of capture. Then they sewed Doniphan's official letters in a saddle pad and continued.

On they rode, past the sleeping town of Mapimí (in the state of Durango)—an unseen village over there somewhere, lost in midnight obscurity, then, in daylight of the twenty-ninth, into a brightly illuminated scare. Ahead they saw a dust cloud raised by columns of animals. These could only be companies of cavalry, they concluded, and they changed course toward distant mountains that might offer refuge. But the "cavalrymen" later proved to be traders with a caravan of pack mules carrying a cargo of caked sugar.

About dusk that same day they stopped near San Sebastian to brew coffee. A large group of Mexicans appeared, led by a man who identified himself as Don Ignacio Jimenez, a citizen of local influence. Jimenez said he had orders from Durango officials to arrest this party of Americans traveling across the country. Hughes listened and recorded the ensuing conversation.

"Well, what are you going to do about it?" Collins asked.

"I shall put the order into execution."

"I am going," Collins announced, "and you can use your pleasure about stopping us."

"Have you and your men passports?"

"Yes, sir, we have."

"Let me see them."

"These are our passports, sir, and we think they are sufficient." Collins held up his rifle in one hand and his revolver in the other.

The Americans buckled on pistols and knives, grabbed their rifles, and left without further challenge. They rode all that night and all the next day until they had left Durango and entered Coahuila. About sundown, dead tired and ravenous, they stopped near the base of a high mountain to try once more to brew coffee and to allow their weary animals to graze.

The Mexican Jimenez once more appeared, ruining their relaxation. Hughes saw that he and his companions were surrounded by a group of about seventy-five frowning men. Apparently Jimenez and most of his original force had been following them all that time, without their knowledge.

The Americans seized their weapons and formed a sort of battle line. Collins shouted to Jimenez in Spanish: "Here we are! If you want us come and take us!"

For an hour or so Jimenez and his men maneuvered around, alternately seeking to creep in, then pausing. Eventually the Mexicans withdrew, apparently concluding these soldiers were "a stubborn set to deal with," as Hughes guessed. And according to Hughes, the Americans could have been much more stubborn. He said later that he and his companions had determined to die fighting rather than to risk capture, torture, and execution—as they felt would have been their fate.

At sunset on April 2, nearly two weeks after leaving Chihuahua, they arrived at Saltillo, happily found American soldiers there, and delivered Doniphan's messages. The dispatches were sent on to Wool's senior, Taylor, who had returned to Walnut Springs—the camp near Monterrey.

During the next few days Hughes and others visited the battlefield of

Buena Vista, where they passed hours in "awful melancholy" examining the site of Taylor's bloody stand. General Wool's senior engineer officer pointed out the area where Santa Anna had marshaled his forces for the attack. Hughes, who had some of the imagination found in any writer, could almost see "a bristling forest of glittering steel" and "costly trappings of the officers and the men's bright bayonets [glistening] in the sheen of the sun." Hughes visited and talked with General Wool, in Wool's tent—a singular achievement (especially for a private) that was due to Hughes's membership in a remarkable volunteer unit whose arduous experiences fascinated even generals, and to Hughes's role as chronicler of that unit.

For a week Hughes looked around the Saltillo area while he and his thirteen companions awaited a reply to Doniphan from General Taylor. On the ninth the dispatch arrived from Walnut Springs, and the same fourteen men who had completed the hazardous journey from Chihuahua were told to carry the answer back to Doniphan. For this trip, however, they would have additional protection: an escort of twenty-six Arkansas cavalrymen commanded by Captain Albert Pike, and the company of a noted guide, Josiah Gregg, author of *Commerce of the Prairies*. Forty-two men in all—with fresh horses—would comprise the return party.

The trip back proved less exciting but not much faster. Two weeks after leaving Saltillo they came in sight of Chihuahua, on April 23, and there felt the first moment of real concern during the return journey. They saw in the distance a group of horsemen leaving the city and heading directly toward them. Above the riders blossomed a giant dust cloud that always heralded such movement in this dry region. Were they Doniphan's own pickets about to attack them in the mistaken belief they were the enemy?

Hughes and his companions halted, on Captain Pike's orders, and Pike studied the prospect. But the threat quickly vanished. The ominous riders proved to be Missouri friends who had galloped out of Chihuahua with fresh horses for their use.

The reunion was a joyful one indeed. Doniphan had heard on three different occasions that his fourteen expressmen had been killed or captured and that the captives had been taken to the city of Durango, where they were being tortured.

They all rode on into Chihuahua, then, and into an even greater welcome. Church bells clanged (operated by Americans, of course), artillery boomed in salute, other friends slapped their backs and wrung their hands. Everyone asked about the orders, and after Taylor's dispatch had been delivered to Doniphan the colonel told his men they were all "to march forthwith to Saltillo."

This was a move already planned tentatively. Doniphan had decided to leave Chihuahua and to proceed in that direction after hearing that his expressmen had been killed. Had that information been accurate his communication to Wool would have been intercepted, and speed would have been essential in an evacuation. Now, following Doniphan's announcement, Hughes prepared to make the journey a third time.

Five days later, on the morning of the twenty-eighth, Doniphan delivered to Chihuahua authorities the Mexican prisoners still remaining in his custody from the Battle of Sacramento and, with the last of his troops, left the city. Along with the army traveled a number of señoritas who had secretly dressed themselves as soldiers and were accompanying their recently acquired American lovers. But they went only as far as the point reached where Doniphan first heard about the subterfuge and turned them back.

At San Sebastian the troops foraged happily on the estate of Don Ignacio Jimenez, having heard about the man's successful challenge of their expressmen, and hoped Jimenez would return to face *these* odds. Don Ignacio, however, had fled upon learning of their approach.

By May 22 the Missouri volunteers, more tired and tattered than ever, had encamped near an Arkansas cavalry unit at La Encantada, not far from the battlefield of Buena Vista. That day they drew full rations, the first time they had been able to do so during all of their military service to date. They received so many items they could not carry everything. After they had filled pockets, bags, skillets, and kettles with supplies they left some articles behind—including all the soap issue—as they returned to their quarters.

A commissary officer called after a group of Missourians. "Here, you fellows, you are leaving your soap. Come back and get it!"

"Soap!" one soldier replied. "What do we want with soap? We have no clothes to wash!"

That same May 22 Hughes and the other survivors of Doniphan's hardy mounted regiment formed for a review by General Wool, who was one hour late arriving. Lines that never had been made very smart in the first place sagged as time passed, but Doniphan sought to hold his volunteers as well as he could. Finally Wool appeared, and the general, a martinet feared among the regulars, stared at the scene. Another man who was present left a description.

> It was an odd-looking line, for no two [men] were dressed alike. Most of them were in buckskin hunting-shirts and trowsers, and many had their trowsers' legs torn. Some were mounted on donkeys, some on mustang ponies, and others on mules. One officer on Colonel Doniphan's staff had on [a] cap ornamented with feathers and horns taken from [an] Indian chief; Colonel Doniphan had the left sleeve nearly torn off his coat. The drill of the regiment compared very favorably with its uniform—as they had not the least idea of precision in any of their movements, or of the silence which is expected of regular troops. The general and staff were dressed handsomely. [General Wool] pulled his feather-adorned chapeau over his eyes, and turned away his head, smiling. Then a salute to the general was fired by the flying artillery. . . . The general pronounced the troops the healthiest looking men he had seen in all Mexico. . . .

Later that day a group of curious Missourians gathered around Wool's tent. They saw that their own commander was chatting with the general, and they entered into the conversation zestfully. Some Missourians addressed their leader as "Colonel," some "Doniphan," and others—no doubt neighbors back home—"Bill."

A weathered volunteer peered at General Wool. "Old man," he said, using a then common form of address, "I heard you had a purty damned tight fight down yonder."

Wool's adjutant, standing nearby, interceded. "Please address him as 'General,'" the adjutant demanded. "That is his title."

"Wal," said the Missourian, staring back at the aide, "He *is* an old man. I reckon he can't deny that."

Doniphan's volunteers may not have been Wool's type on the parade ground, but they had proved their intrepidity beyond any doubt, and officers sought to recruit them for future service.

The Missourians, however, unanimously refused to extend their enlistments. They received orders to march to the Rio Grande and down that river to its mouth, where transportation would carry them to New Orleans and to discharge in the United States.

For John T. Hughes this would mean getting to work immediately on his story of the expedition, as soon as he returned to civilian life. He packed his notes carefully and looked forward to writing the history that he had helped to make. Following completion of the book, his schoolteaching career would be left behind for a more active life. After riding with Doniphan throughout the southwestern United States and a large part of northern Mexico a man could hardly return to a seat behind a schoolroom desk and be satisfied there. The expedition had amounted to very little as far as the war was concerned, but it had exhibited some incredible fortitude on the part of participants like Hughes.

One last duty remained: to turn in all cannon and ammunition and other public property at Walnut Springs, where the troops would be reviewed for the last time—by the senior commander himself, Zachary Taylor.

It was on May 27 that the gaunt volunteers sat on their donkeys, mules, and horses at Walnut Springs—"under the delusion," said the same observer who had witnessed Wool's review, "that they were drawn up in line." Zachary Taylor, riding along the ragged formation, pulled out a handkerchief and held it to his face—to hide a smile, some persons thought.

Halfway down the line an awkward giant of a man astride a donkey spoke to Taylor. "Well, old man, what do you think of this crowd?"

The general gave up trying to maintain his composure. He roared with laughter. Finally he answered, "You look as though you had seen hard times."

The extent of the humor was lost on the ragged volunteer sitting astride the donkey. It was not recorded that he laughed at all when he replied, "You bet."

39.

Movable Forts

As soon as General Santa Anna had realized that the tide of the Cerro Gordo battle was about to overwhelm him that April 18 he left the scene, probably never even remembering the resounding promise given to countrymen in his recent proclamation: "My duty is to sacrifice myself. . . . I am decided . . . to die fighting!" Scott's soldiers later found copies of the proclamation scattered about the deserted battlefield.

"Cerro Gordo was lost!" The misfortune was incredible. "Mexico was open to the iniquity of the invader."

With staff aides and other officers for companions Santa Anna fled on horseback toward El Encero, hoping to find some troop support left at his former headquarters there. He found instead a force of American cavalrymen in swift pursuit behind him; so he and his companions rode on, away from his beloved hacienda—one day before General Scott, Colonel Hitchcock, and other U. S. Army officers arrived at the "princely place."

Santa Anna traveled southward with his party, taking the road to the town of Orizaba. Exhausted physically and mentally, he rode in silence, with a perpetual frown souring his face. An evening chill from the mountains seemed to seep into his aching bones.

The general's companions appeared to be as miserable, and for good reason. Here they were in the presence of the "first chief" of Mexico, a man who only hours earlier had shown himself erect and proud and "possessed of power which he exercised." Now he was humble and confused, "seeking among the wretched a refuge to flee to." To the Mexican officers accompanying Santa Anna everything represented "a lively picture of the fall of our country, of the debasement of our name, of the anathema pronounced against our race."

Occasionally the general stopped and, with the help of his companions, dismounted to rest on a portable bench provided by an aide. There he would sit, motionless—not venturing to take a single step in a night that grew colder as the black hours passed. At one village he asked a curate for a fresh horse. The churchman refused his request. The ignominy of this depressed the spirits of the party further, but they went on. About sunrise the next morning they halted at the hacienda of Tuzamápan.

An hour before midnight the hacienda overseer appeared with alarming news: an American detachment was close by. Soon a series of shots coming from somewhere in the surrounding darkness apparently corroborated him. Fellow officers helped Santa Anna onto his horse, and with a hacienda Indian as guide they all vanished into the obscurity of a little-used mountain trail. No enemy appeared.

Eventually the general's entourage reached the town of Orizaba. There some "ill-judging flatterer" or a man with a sarcastic bent broke out with a shout of "*vivas* to the illustrious General Santa Anna, the hero of Tampico, and the deliverer of Mexico!" Santa Anna's officers could only have heard the remarks in embarrassed silence.

Nevertheless, the general was on the verge of making another amazing rebound. At Orizaba he found a Mexican Army detachment. His depression gradually lifted, and he began planning further defense of the homeland. Soon he had the nucleus of another army: three thousand soldiers. These men were not at all eager to fight, however, and not even Santa Anna's bombast could inspire them much.

This did not dissuade the general. From Orizaba he moved to Puebla—a town through which Scott's army must pass as it marched on Mexico City—and sought to enlist more men for a stand there. Distrust of Santa Anna, however, outweighed any desire of the populace to hurl back the invader.

Santa Anna gave up on Puebla. He decided to leave the defense of that area to guerrilla fighters.

Next he went to Mexico City, where he always had enjoyed more success with his ostentations. On May 22 he reclaimed the presidency from Anaya. Then he issued proclamations declaring that the capital never would be surrendered—that he would die first. He ordered all citizens to

377

deliver to the government weapons in their possession. Again he solicited contributions. Some of these "gifts" he forced, as usual.

But Santa Anna had lost much of his magic. More and more of his countrymen again were denouncing him as a coward and a traitor. The Mexican Congress recently had reiterated some belief in him, reapproving for him domestic power. But, significantly, that body forbade any communication between Santa Anna (or any other Mexican) and representatives of the United States, and branded as a traitor to Mexico anyone who would treat with the invader.

On the streets a few citizens laughed publicly at the old hero. Referring to the limb he had lost, they called him the "Immortal Three-fourths."

The day after their victory at Cerro Gordo the first American troops marched into Jalapa and into a natural paradise that made at least one observer think of the Garden of Eden.

Springtime had preceded the soldiers, giving the countryside a green lushness and bringing out myriads of flowers in colorful bursts. In the distance loomed high mountains. Behind the city towered the Cofre de Perote. Thirty miles away to the south, but seemingly closer, snow-capped Orizaba poked its height heavenward. In the direction from which the American advance had come—eastward—the Gulf of Mexico could be seen on a clear day, a distant expanse of blue-green. The altitude of Jalapa, more than four thousand feet, assured a moderate April climate. One soldier observed that neither a jacket nor mere shirt sleeves proved uncomfortable attire during an entire day.

On April 20, the day after the first American troops reached the place, General Scott and his staff arrived and set up headquarters. Some army units were not destined to stay long at Jalapa. They would instead proceed along the National Road in slow, careful marches, guarding against possible ambush, toward Perote and Puebla. On the twenty-second this advance, commanded by General Worth, occupied an abandoned fortress at Perote, forty miles beyond Jalapa and past an eight-thousand-foot summit that gave access to the Mexican plateau. But headquarters would remain at Jalapa for more than a month, as it developed. As always in this war, saloons and shops owned by American camp followers sprang up to vie with Mexicans for a share of soldiers' pay. An English-language newspaper commenced publication.

Colonel Hitchcock stayed with Scott during that time. "The Mexicans are confounded—lost in wonder and despair," he wrote of the reaction to their surprising defeat at Cerro Gordo. ". . . Grass grows in many of the streets of Jalapa."

As Hitchcock observed in following weeks, however, confusion was not limited to one side. Scott sought to rush supplies from Vera Cruz before yellow fever cut him off from his base, but his transportation facilities remained inadequate. Even then, the vehicles available were subject to attack and looting by guerrillas along the way. Scott needed more troops to force his way into Mexico City, but enlistments of three thousand twelve-month volunteers were verging on expiration. Not many of these men could be persuaded to re-enlist, and rather than risk their lives by sending them to Vera Cruz for transportation home at the peak of the yellow-fever menace Scott ordered them returned early. Their departure meant that he would have remaining about four thousand able-bodied troops.

For these soldiers—as well as for those departing—paydays had become erratic. Coins were the only medium of exchange universally accepted in this foreign country, and enough of this cash could not be provided to meet payrolls regularly—especially when coins were also required for purchases of forage and food from the native populace. General Scott had received from the President a suggestion designed to alleviate this problem and to pass on occupation costs to Mexico: levy contributions on the people—force them to provide army necessities. But Scott ignored the advice, realizing that the Mexicans would destroy their crops and cattle rather than give them up without compensation to his soldiers. Such a development would leave his army in a situation even more precarious than the present one.

While at Jalapa, Hitchcock heard Scott expound on these and other problems nearly every night. The general was fond of assembling his aides around the dinner table at 8:30 P.M. and discussing "public business" for two or three hours. As the talk became more and more serious, the difficulties of sustaining an army in the Mexican interior weighed more heavily on Hitchcock. The colonel never could sleep soundly when problems occupied his mind, and his nights at this time were frequently restless ones.

"[Half] past 2 A.M.," he wrote once. "Awakened by a band serenading the General, but I do not enjoy the music, for I cannot conceal from

379

myself that this army is in a critical situation." (Unknown to Hitchcock, a military observer in England agreed with his dismal estimate. The Duke of Wellington had been following with fascination the progress of the invading army as reports arrived, and shortly after this time he declared, "Scott is lost. He has been carried away by success. He can't take [Mexico City], and he can't fall back on his base.")

The ultimate vexation for Scott and his staff came after dark on May 7, when a group of cavalrymen rode up to the Jalapa headquarters to deliver a letter from Nicholas Trist, Polk's recently appointed commissioner. Trist had reached Vera Cruz the day before, but instead of venturing out along the guerrilla-infested mountain road to meet Scott personally and at once—as Trist had been told to do by his Washington superiors—he chose to remain at Vera Cruz temporarily.

Trist's dispatch gave inadequate and misleading explanation of his duties and powers to Scott, who had not been informed earlier of the man's impending arrival. With his own note Trist enclosed a sealed letter addressed to the Minister of Foreign Relations in Mexico City and a communication from Secretary of War Marcy to Scott saying that Trist had come to Mexico empowered to negotiate a suspension of hostilities with that government and that Scott should send the sealed letter on to the addressee in the Mexican capital.

Scott's wrath boiled over after he had finished reading all of this. Washington had sent the chief clerk of the Department of State to give him orders! A truce could be called at the discretion of a stupid civilian! Not only was this an extraordinary snub for the senior U. S. Army commander to endure; it risked soldiers' lives on the command of an unknowledgeable man.

The general refused to accept this. He wrote Trist a hot rejection of supervision by any government clerk and sent a copy of his letter to Marcy. He refused to forward the sealed letter to Mexico City and acidly informed both Trist and Marcy that he doubted it would be welcomed there anyway, since the Mexican Congress had just passed a law denouncing as a traitor anyone who would deal with the United States Government.

Even after Trist's arrival at headquarters Scott refused to talk with him—a humiliation that the egotistical Trist would return in kind. For more than six weeks the two men would ignore each other. In time, when the British minister in Mexico City began acting as intermediary in an effort to effect a truce, the representative he sent to Scott's headquarters would have to give the same briefing to both men separately. Scott and Trist refused to sit together in the same room even to listen to the man.

On the same day that Scott received the initial communication from Trist, President Polk, in Washington, first heard about the victory at Cerro Gordo. He was talking with several visitors in his Executive Mansion office when an aide handed him a telegram sent from Fredericksburg, Virginia, "in advance of the Southern mail." He read the text with satisfaction, then told his visitors about the success.

Polk had been expecting to hear about this battle for days now, having developed an acute sense regarding events in Mexico. Exactly one week earlier—on Friday, April 30—he had received word that Santa Anna "was reported to be in front of the American army [this on April 14] with 15,000 troops to resist their passage from Vera Cruz to Jalapa," and he guessed at that time a battle would be fought on the sixteenth or seventeenth. "I shall await the result with much anxiety," he had written in his diary, "but have no fears of it. Our forces are the best troops in the world, and would gain victories over superior forces of the enemy, if there was not an officer among them." So much for Polk's esteem of Whig commanders.

After that the President had waited seven days in expectation of receiving further word, but he had also occupied himself in his usual ceaseless way: rising early and shaving himself, as customary; working awhile before breakfast; meeting with members of the Cabinet, individually and in a group; laying the cornerstone for the building that would house the Smithsonian Institution; having a light lunch; receiving callers, including the usual detested job seekers; listening to Secretary of War Marcy read a dispatch from Colonel Doniphan describing his victory at the Sacramento ("one of the most . . . brilliant achievements of the war," Polk thought); dining late—and most enjoyably, of course, in the company of only family and perhaps a few friends; dutifully mingling with guests at Executive Mansion receptions, which one evening during this period included the granddaughter of his political enemy John Quincy Adams—"the first [actual visit] that has been made by any [member] of the family," Polk said.

After the President had received word of Scott's victory he anticipated a new concern, one that was even then weighing more and more heavily on the general himself in faraway Mexico. Its obviousness should have been apparent to everyone, but in Washington—with its poor communications and its bevy of fuzzy thinkers—many requirements of a distant invading force were being overlooked. "I brought to the notice of the Cabinet and particularly of the Secretary of War," Polk said, "the importance of re-inforcing . . . General Scott. . . . I informed the Cabinet that I was of the opinion that all our available force should be ordered without delay to join [his] column."

From May 28 to June 5 Polk made one of his rare trips out of Washington—to his alma mater, the University of North Carolina, where he attended graduation ceremonies held on the Chapel Hill campus. After that pleasant interlude he returned to the confinement of the Executive Mansion and to new distress.

On the first working day after his trip—a Monday, June 7—Jessie Benton Frémont called at the Mansion in the company of her husband's noted guide, Kit Carson. Polk was interested in meeting Carson, but the real purpose of Jessie Frémont's visit left him less enthusiastic.

> Mr. Carson delivered to me a long letter from Col. Frémont which had been addressed to [Senator] Benton. It related in part to the recent unfortunate collision between General Kearny and Col. Frémont in California. Mrs. Frémont seemed anxious to elicit from me some expression of approbation of her husband's conduct, but I evaded making any. In truth I consider that Col. Frémont was greatly in the wrong when he refused to obey the orders issued to him by General Kearny. I think General Kearny was right also in his controversy with Commodore Stockton. It was unnecessary, however, that I should say so to Col. Frémont's wife, and I evaded giving her an answer. My desire is, that the error being corrected, the matter shall pass over quietly without the necessity of . . . court-martial.

Polk did not admit, speculate, or probably even realize that much of the Stockton-Kearny-Frémont trouble stemmed from the vagueness of his own orders. Lack of care and clarity by the Administration also had contributed to the Scott-Trist feud, which the President learned about five days after Jessie Frémont's visit. On June 12 Scott's first angry dispatches about Trist and his mission reached Washington. Polk reacted as expected.

> . . . It is clear from this despatch, as well as one . . . enclosing a letter from General Scott to Mr. Trist, that [Scott] would not coöperate with Mr. Trist in accomplishing the object of his mission, the conclusion of an honourable peace. His . . . despatches are not only insubordinate, but insulting to Mr. Trist and the Government.

I gave my views on the subject, in which the Cabinet unanimously concurred. In accordance with them I directed the Secretary of War to prepare a despatch for General Scott rebuking him for his insubordinate course, and repeating the order in a peremptory manner to him to carry the despatch borne to him by Mr. Trist addressed to the Mexican Government to that Government, and requiring an immediate answer, to be returned by the bearer of the despatch, whether he had obeyed or intended to obey the . . . order of the Secretary of War. [Scott] deserves for his conduct in this matter to be removed from the command.

For days after that the Frémont and the Scott-Trist problems bobbed up again to rankle the President—as if he did not have enough other frustrations to endure. Jessie Frémont called on Polk again in behalf of her husband. More angry dispatches from Scott arrived (eventually the general would ask to be recalled as soon as he had affairs in order)—and in the same mail some volcanic messages came from Trist, too. At this distance the President could do little more than brood over his troubles, sigh, and write (on July 9) of the feud in Mexico: "[It] exhibited a wretched state of things. So far from harmony prevailing between these two officers, they are engaged in a violent personal correspondence. It does not as yet appear that they have had any personal interview. . . ."

By the time the harried President made his remark, however, Scott and Trist had settled their squabble and were well on the way toward the formation of warm companionship. What brought about such affability never became clear. Perhaps the mediation of mutual friends helped, or perhaps the continuing efforts of the British minister in Mexico City to assist in a peaceful settlement shamed the two countrymen into working together. On June 25, after the latest visit by a British representative who briefed Scott and Trist separately—as usual—on truce possibilities in Mexico City, Trist finally sent Scott a copy of his commission, along with a brief note. The general replied in a formal manner, but some days later, when he heard that Trist was ill, Scott sent him a portion of guava marmalade from his own mess for his "sick companion" to sample during recovery.

Trist acknowledged the gift with thanks. Soon after that each man was writing Washington to say that his earlier idea of the other had been poorly conceived and that he hoped his previous correspondence would be taken from the files.

Scott's primary concern always had been the advance toward Mexico City. As reinforcements and supplies trickled in from Vera Cruz he ordered more marches—first to Puebla, a picturesque place that General Worth's men had occupied on May 15, only hours after Santa Anna had given up his attempt to inspire a stand there. For weeks after that the American advance remained at Puebla. Reports of impending attack by large Mexican forces frequently disturbed the troops waiting there.

Worth, a nervous commander, had brought trouble, unintentionally, for his friend Scott by granting more liberal capitulation terms than Scott wanted, then later—during the occupation—by unsettling his men through the distribution of a printed circular (based on inaccurate information) that Pueblans were plotting to sell the Americans poisoned food. Scott overruled Worth's capitulation terms by instating the same martial law promulgated for Vera Cruz. As for the demoralizing circular, Scott ordered Worth to recall all copies. Worth angrily asked for a court of inquiry into his actions, got it, and received censure. Scott sought to smooth over the difficulty by ignoring the finding as much as he was officially able, but Worth had been alienated. After that Scott heard from Worth only about official matters.

These and other troubles plaguing Scott's army waiting deep in Mexico continued to interfere with Colonel Hitchcock's sleep. Diary entries at Puebla attested to his worry: "Air full of rumors of menacing movements. An army of 20,000 men said to be within one day's march. . . . The air is full of rumors every day. Reinforcements coming to us; enemy concentrating in front; our wagon train cut off with half a million of money. . . . Everything now shows that we are to have a fight before reaching the capital."

One night as Hitchcock lay sleepless in his bed, his mind occupied with forebodings, he determined to try his hand at alleviation rather than to give in again to dark meditation. The philosopher sprang into action.

He rose, lighted a candle, and began writing—"a sort of address to the Mexican people" that covered five sheets of paper by the time he had finished. Whether Hitchcock had deliberately studied those ostentatious Mexican proclamations or realized what appealed to the inhabitants, he wrote an address worthy of the pen of Santa Anna—but one written from an opposing viewpoint. The next morning he showed the piece to General Scott, who remarked on its "cleverness." Scott ordered the piece translated into Spanish and printed for general distribution.

The English-language newspaper *American Star*, recently founded in Puebla, printed the text of Hitchcock's "proclamation" in both Spanish and English.

The article would have been more impressive in its Spanish version. The printers, using Spanish-language type, could find no *w* or *k* in the fonts. Their *k* they fashioned roughly from an *h*; for a *w* they used two *v*'s together. Hitchcock's address, in English, thus read:

"I vvil begin and vvil end vvith nothing but facts vvel vvorth your attention."

Not a promising beginning for American readers, but for the Mexicans Hitchcock had the right touch. Frequently he began sentences with words calculated to attract their attention: "Mexicans, be not deceived; . . . Now listen! . . . Hear this, for it is the truth." Santa Anna himself would have done little better.

To Mexicans Hitchcock pointed out that the U. S. Army in Mexico had not come as robbers or rapists. Law and order prevailed with General Scott. Hitchcock wrote, ". . . we have not a particle of ill-will towards you—we treat you with all civility—we are not in fact your enemies; we do not plunder your people or insult your women or your religion . . . we are here for no earthly purpose except the hope of obtaining a peace."

The theme of Hitchcock's address was, for him, strange indeed: that the United States was right in this war, that Mexico was wrong, and that all reasonable Mexicans would acknowledge that fact. If Hitchcock, the old anti-war philosopher, thus seemed to fit Henry David Thoreau's description of "small movable forts and magazines, at the service of some unscrupulous man in power," it should be remembered that Hitchcock was first of all a soldier—and a good one, as conceded even by the superiors he had antagonized. His address was printed and distributed by tens of thousands. The exact degree of its influence on Mexicans could not be determined, but many citizens reportedly were swayed by it, and Hitchcock had made his own peculiar contribution toward ending the war he had so long disliked.

40.

Of Physical and Moral Courage

Following his latest defeat, Antonio López de Santa Anna tapped what seemed to be the last resource of wiliness to stay in power. Even then a powerful rival might have dumped him, but no man of universal appeal, real strength, and deep commitment appeared on the Mexican scene to pose a grave threat. Being at the head of the Mexican Government at this particular time did not have so powerful an attraction as it once had.

Still, the sad-faced man with that look of a retired philosopher wanted to keep the reins. His make-up included undying belief in himself. Probably he never doubted that he, and no one else, could serve his country best at this momentous time, and if his actions happened to serve Santa Anna personally—as they surely would—this represented only a prerogative of power. What was best for Santa Anna also was best for Mexico.

Only such self-belief could have given Santa Anna the ambition and the energy to come back from discouragements and defeats many times in his life. His resources went deep indeed, even if his final effectiveness proved to be limited by some superficialities relating to mental ability, integrity, and morality. For many Mexicans his showy appeal could overshadow his shortcomings.

Now, however, many of his countrymen again had turned on him in anger, with those accusations of cowardice and treachery. Santa Anna countered with a barrage of proclamations and with arrests of political foes. Neither his resounding words of patriotism nor the fear he sought to instill by his arrests swayed people much; so he tried something else.

On May 28 he tendered his resignation as President in a widely distributed letter that oozed sentiment and self-pity. Santa Anna would sacrifice himself again, he said—this time to ward off the threat of revolution at home in the face of General Winfield Scott's advance on the capital. "I this day terminate forever my public career," Santa Anna announced. Then he waited to be besieged by urgent pleas from the multitude imploring him to stay in office.

No pleas reached his eager ears. Not even his offer to resign seemed to have swayed anyone to his support. The Mexican Congress, in fact, appeared disposed to accept his generous offer. Therefore, four days after Santa Anna had submitted his resignation he abruptly withdrew it, explaining that many citizens had urged him not to abdicate his responsibilities. Congress stood by helplessly during Santa Anna's about-face, not having power to remove him. The lawmakers could only look on as the man again assumed what amounted to dictatorial authority.

Once more Santa Anna threw himself into the task of preparing a defense against the invader, and again he succeeded in establishing and manning some formidable fortifications, despite the hostility he faced at home. By the time that Winfield Scott and Nicholas Trist, waiting to eastward, had patched up their feud in July, Santa Anna had collected twenty-five thousand men to defend Mexico City. Among these troops, however, were the usual numbers of convicts released from prison for military service.

The soldiers were divided among three forces: an Army of the North, recently moved from San Luis Potosí to Guadalupe Hidalgo, just north of the capital; an Army of the South, located a few miles south of the city; and an Army of the East, located in Mexico City itself.

Geography had made the capital easier to defend. Lakes and extensive marshlands surrounded the city. Causeways across these water barriers afforded the only access to Mexico City, which was further protected at every entry point by fortified gates.

North and east of the city lay Lake Texcoco and miles of marshes. Entrance from the north must come by way of Guadalupe Hidalgo, where one of those three armies lay waiting behind newly strengthened positions. Southeast of the city lay more miles of impassable marshland and two more large lakes, Chalco and Xochimilco. The National Road from Vera Cruz, Perote, and Puebla—the road Scott's army would be traveling—entered Mexico City from the east, over a causeway erected along the southern shore of Lake Texcoco. Just south of that road, atop a large hill named El Peñon that rose above the marsh to a height of three hundred feet, Santa Anna emplaced some thirty cannon and posted thousands of troops. He believed Scott would have to attempt to force his way into Mexico City along this road, and he meant to defeat him at El Peñon.

Another road led into Mexico City from the south. But Santa Anna would be ready for Scott there, too. At Mexicalcingo, a strategic town on that road, the Mexican general placed more artillery and troops.

Scott, marching from eastward, surely would have to attack one of these three bastions, Santa Anna mused, and the most direct and most logical entry route would bring him against the bristling guns and waiting soldiers at El Peñon.

About this time Santa Anna might also have reflected on his "impossible" defeat at Cerro Gordo—or perhaps he was, as usual, looking into every alternative that seemed open. Despite the congressional prohibition against treating with the enemy, Santa Anna began talking peace with Scott and Trist, through emissaries like the British envoy. But to bring about an armistice in a country like Mexico, Santa Anna emphasized, money would be needed. About mid-July the American leaders at Puebla sent him ten thousand dollars in cash to cover "expenses," and indications were that they later sent much more than that.

Still, Santa Anna was unable to make himself influential for peace —if he ever really tried. His Congress disliked him, even with the invader just outside the door, but thought no better of an armistice. Ostensibly to soften their attitude, Santa Anna suggested confidentially to Scott that the U. S. Army be brought forward to the outskirts of Mexico City. Then perhaps the truculent congressmen might be more disposed to listen to peace terms, which would, after all, be in the national interest, as Santa Anna knew.

For his countrymen, however, Santa Anna had another suggestion. With the enemy aiming for the capital itself he issued more bombast. "War without pity unto death!" he exhorted.

Captain Ephraim Kirby Smith, now at Puebla with General Worth's troops, had been plagued by growing forebodings. His dissatisfaction with the Army and its handling of promotions, first expressed at Vera Cruz, had given way to thoughts of increasing gloom. Atmospheres always seemed to affect his moods, and lately he had been exposed to a number of dismal influences. At Perote he had been quartered in the vast old castlelike fortress, once used as a dungeon for prisoners political and criminal, where the outside din of evening downpours had combined with the inside aura of ghostliness to impart to him an "extremely sad and lonesome" feeling. "Every sound echoes through [the] vast halls and interminable galleries," he wrote home, "and although there are so many of us in it, it is so capacious that it scarcely appears to be occupied."

Later, reports of impending attacks had sent him and his men running for weapons to repel each threat, urged on sometimes by the dreadful sound of the "long roll"—"a call which always thrills to the very marrow of a soldier, as it never beats on light occasions and is the usual prelude to a battle."

At Puebla other alarms disturbed him and his companions. Stabbings resulted in the wounding of several soldiers, so that the men received orders not to venture out on the streets alone or unarmed. Once, on the night of Smith's arrival at Puebla, a young woman suffered fatal stab wounds inflicted directly in front of his quarters. Her body lay undiscovered until the following morning. The ghastliness of the crime, which was traced to a Mexican, settled on Smith's mind.

Two weeks later Smith developed a painful touch of rheumatism in one foot, and during the following week he fell victim to "chills and fever"—malaria, no doubt. He seemed alternately to freeze and to burn, and during much of that time he was also tortured by pounding headaches. Doctors dosed him with quinine, and he eventually returned to normal.

Worst of all, however, were the times when he felt sure he would never again see his family. Letters home, and (later) a journal kept for eventual mailing to his wife, poignantly reflected this feeling and made evident his dissatisfaction now with his military career and with the war.

> May 9 [1847]. This is the anniversary of the battle of Resaca. How differently I feel now with regard to the war from what I did then! *Then* vague visions of glory and a speedy peace floated through my brain. *Now* I have learned in common with many other poor fellows that it is not he who patiently does his duty, or who in the hour of danger is in the front of the battle, who gains the laurel or the more vulgar reward of government patronage. It is too frequently the sycophant who flatters the foibles of his commanding officer, he who has political family influence, or whom some accident makes conspicuous, who reaps all the benefits of the exposure and labors

of others. . . . How tired and sick I am of a war to which I can see no probable termination! How readily would I exchange my profession for any honest, mechanical employment, were it possible to do so! How instantly would I resign if I saw any certainty of supporting my family in tolerable comfort or even decency in civil life!

· · ·

It appears certain . . . that [the Mexicans] are assembling a large force—twenty thousand it is said—in and about the Capital. . . . If we advance they will probably make a stand a few leagues this side of the City of Mexico. . . . We [are now] over *eight thousand strong.* What an immense army to invade a populous country and conquer a nation! We may, in fact, be considered *a forlorn hope!* . . .

· · ·

. . . It will be well hereafter not to draw any pay until you hear that I am in the land of the living at the close of the month for which you draw. . . .

· · ·

June 17. My birthday—I am forty years old. . . . An American can scarcely appreciate the glorious freedom and blessings on his native land unless he has been banished as I have for months where everything is stamped by ignorance, vice, and misery. . . .

· · ·

How sad and dreary the hours pass! . . . One thing is certain,—there will in future be no more comfort in army life. Peace cannot bring back to us those pleasant western stations—they are lost to us forever. On our widely extended southern and western frontier will be many isolated posts—far, far from civilization—there it is to be feared our days will be passed in dreary banishment.

· · ·

. . . Alas, the chance is I shall never see you again!

· · ·

. . . I hardly think you will ever see these pages,—or the hand which guides the pen may be cold in death before they reach you. . . .

Early in August General Scott determined to continue the advance on Mexico City, seventy-five miles west of Puebla, just as Santa Anna himself had suggested. Negotiations with the enemy had proved useless, despite the cash given Santa Anna to help him buy peace. Furthermore, Scott estimated he now had received men and supplies enough to attempt the climactic move. The reinforcements and replenishments had traveled up the mountain road from Vera Cruz, and in many instances had been forced to fight off attacks by guerrillas.

Scott's ten thousand or so soldiers, collected again into four divisions, were ordered to march out of Puebla one day apart in the following order: General Twiggs's division, then General Quitman's, General Worth's, and finally, General Gideon Pillow's.

Captain Smith, with Worth's division, hurriedly collected his belongings and prepared for the hazardous days ahead. No longer was he searching for flowers to press and to send home in his letters. "[Lately] I have been too busy to think and I am glad it is so," he wrote his wife, "as I almost despair when I reflect upon the destitute situation in which you will be left, with the three children dependent upon you, should I fall in the coming battle. . . . I believe we shall have a severe, a desperate fight."

General Scott's effective army numbered exactly 10,738 soldiers now. With these men he was setting out to capture and to occupy a foreign capital inhabited by more than two hundred thousand people and well defended by geography, by strong fortifications, and by armies whose totals outnumbered Scott's own force by as much as three to one.

In predawn darkness on August 9 reveille roused Captain Smith and the other members of Worth's division to a hurried breakfast. Then the men loaded wagons and at six o'clock commenced the march, with Smith's infantry battalion following a company of dragoons and a battery of light artillery that comprised the advance. Their course was northwest across the extensive Puebla valley, not far from the towering white peak of Popocatepetl—nearly eighteen thousand feet high. The cold morning gave way to midday warmth as the sun rose above them, but the heat did not become oppressive at this altitude.

The day's march took them past cornfields in various stages of growth. Some fields of tall stalks, green and billowy in a gentle breeze, seemed ready for harvesting. Other fields, brown but touched with green, held shoots only a few inches tall. Distant white blotches marked the locations of haciendas scattered across the valley, while farther away mountain summits shone sparkling white, buried under their blankets of perpetual snow and ice. Off to the left Smith could see the giant form of an ancient pyramid, one built at Cholula by the Toltecan people for their feathered-serpent deity, Quetzalcoatl. An earlier traveler across this plain, Cortés, also had gazed upon that pyramid.

Subsequent marches brought them into a more densely populated region, where inhabitants ventured forth to sell fruits, vegetables, and meats; through chilly forests of cedar and pine; then upon a mountain summit dwarfed by lofty, cloud-veiled peaks towering above it. From this location the road plunged downward, and an hour or so later (on August 12) Smith suddenly saw, half a mile below his vantage point, the great Valley of Mexico and, twenty miles westward, the capital—"a most glorious spectacle, which we beheld from the same point where [Cortés] first gazed upon it. Far to the right scarcely perceptible was the great city, and all over the vast plain spread out before us like a map were lakes, towns, haciendas, and large cultivated fields."

The steep, winding road—hazardous for wagons—led into the valley below. Worth's army rumbled down it. After his awed pause to study the distant scene Captain Smith wrote, "We go to victory or death,—we can only be defeated by annihilation."

One day before Captain Smith looked upon the Valley of Mexico the leading American division—Twiggs's column—had gone into camp at a town named Ayotla, located on the valley floor just north of Lake Chalco, and on the National Road leading toward fortified El Peñon and Mexico City.

The first appearance of the Americans in the Valley of Mexico had occasioned great excitement in the capital, still fifteen miles removed from the advance of the hated enemy. Every resident had known that the Americans were on their way, and when Mexican sentinels first observed Twiggs's soldiers descending that steep, winding highway into their beloved valley they raised an alarm that spread quickly.

In Mexico City a prearranged signal told the populace that the enemy now had come into view: the roar of alarm guns, fired at two o'clock in the afternoon of August 9. Soldiers and citizens poured into the Plaza de la Constitución, the soldiers to assemble with their units and the citizens to seek and exchange all sorts of rumors and reports. Military bands broke out in brassy music, then left the beat entirely to the drum sections as detachments of soldiers marched off to their respective stations. The civilians, roused out of whatever lethargy might have remained to grip them in the wake of Santa Anna's latest fiascoes, greeted the display with their thunderous *vivas* and "felt in their breasts . . . symptoms of enthusiasm."

Through Mexico City streets men marched off to combat as if bound

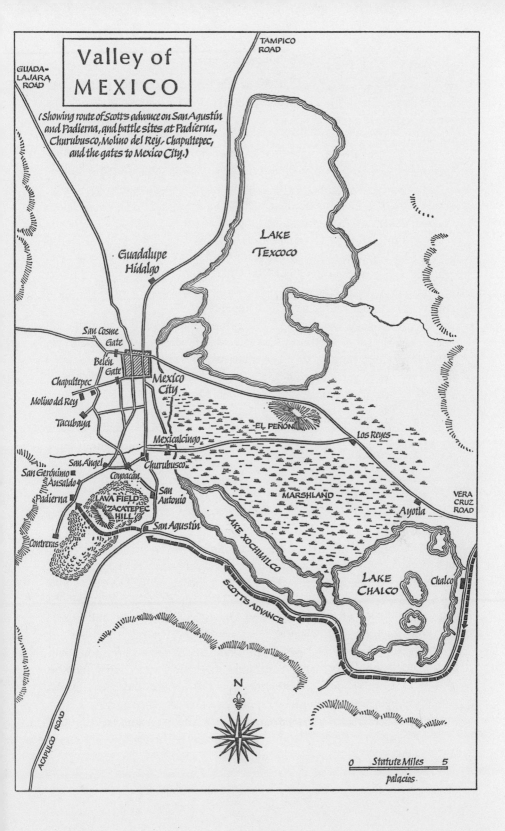

Valley of MEXICO

(Showing route of Scott's advance on San Agustín and Padierna, and battle sites at Padierna, Churubusco, Molino del Rey, Chapultepec, and the gates to Mexico City.)

GUADA-
LAJARA
ROAD

TAMPICO
ROAD

LAKE TEXCOCO

Guadalupe Hidalgo

San Cosme Gate

Belén Gate

Chapultepec

Mexico City

Molino del Rey

Tacubaya

EL PEÑÓN

Los Reyes

Mexicalcingo

San Ángel

San Gerónimo

Ausaldo

Padierna

Coyoacán

Churubusco

MARSHLAND

San Antonio

LAVA FIELD
ZACATEPEC
HILL

San Agustín

Ayotla

VERA
CRUZ
ROAD

Contreras

LAKE XOCHIMILCO

SCOTT'S ADVANCE

LAKE CHALCO

Chalco

N

ACAPULCO ROAD

0   Statute Miles   5

palacios

for a festival—to "victory or death," as Captain E. K. Smith was saying; to *"libertad o muerte,"* as the Mexican soldier would have declared.

After Twiggs had made his bivouac at Ayotla each subsequently arriving American division went into camp in nearby villages. Worth's column halted at Chalco, an eastern-shore village that Captain Smith described as "a dirty place nearly surrounded by marsh and mud." Scott himself set up his headquarters at Ayotla.

The American Army now paused again to allow engineers to do their work: finding the most feasible route into the city. For several months the engineers had been compiling maps of this very region, utilizing various sources of information, but now they would be expected to make the wise, momentous choice of the path of least resistance—when every route seemed either well defended or impassable.

Reconnaissance soon showed them that Santa Anna had anticipated their alternatives. Those three possible routes of progress toward Mexico City had become immediately evident to Scott's engineers: (1) a forty-mile detour northward around the lakes and marshland, followed by a turn westward, then southward, to enter the city from the north—a maneuver that would entail a long and laborious journey and would still bring the Americans into a confrontation at Guadalupe Hidalgo with the Mexican Army of the North, which would by that time no doubt have been reinforced by other units after Santa Anna had observed Scott's movement; (2) the direct way, along the National Road, past heavily fortified El Peñon into the city—an apparently suicidal approach; (3) a route along a causeway that branched left (westward) from the National Road before it reached El Peñon, then led across marshland to the village of Mexicalcingo, from where Scott's army might turn north toward the city. But this was another possibility that Santa Anna had anticipated; for he had left Mexicalcingo bristling with fieldpieces and the bayonets of many troops. Furthermore, the men and armament of El Peñon also might be brought to bear on such a maneuver, unless that hill were attacked simultaneously.

Robert E. Lee, a hero among his companions after that daring and ingenious reconnaissance at Cerro Gordo, was one of the engineers who performed scouting duty at Mexico City. His probe of defenses at El Peñon, along with other reports, quickly convinced General Scott that the most direct route into the capital, and the one Santa Anna had guessed the invaders would take, should be avoided, although Scott still felt that he could crash through there if he were willing to take heavy casualties. A week or so after the reconnaissance Lee penned a description of the formidabilities of El Peñon in a letter to a friend in the United States.

> . . . The hill . . . is about 300 feet high, having three plateaus, of different elevations. It stands in the waters of Lake Tezcuco [sic]. Its base is surrounded by a dry trench, and its sides arranged with breastworks from its base to its crest. It was armed with thirty pieces of cannon, and defended by 7000 men under Santa Anna in person. The causeway passed directly by its base; the waters of the lake washing each side of the causeway for two miles in front, and the whole distance, seven miles, to the city. There was a battery on the causeway, and four hundred yards in advance of the Peñon; another by its side; a third a mile in front of the entrance to the city, and a fourth at the entrance. About two miles in front of the Peñon a road branched off to the left, and crossed the outlet of Lake [Xochimilco], at the village of Mexicalcingo, six miles from the main road. This village, surrounded by a marsh, was enveloped in batteries, and only approached over a paved causeway, a mile in length; beyond, the causeway continued through the marsh for two miles further, and opened upon terra firma at the village of Churubusco.

Scott tentatively decided on a feint against El Peñon and an assault by way of Mexicalcingo. Because of the distance and delay involved the general apparently never seriously considered attacking by the northern route, although young Lieutenant Sam Grant believed this would have been the most logical road into the capital.

Grant, like Captain Smith a member of Worth's division, had set up his tent on the eastern shore of Lake Chalco. Once, after his duties to teams and wagons had been fulfilled, he asked Worth's permission to accompany a group of men sent to reconnoiter Mexican defenses. Worth neither approved nor disapproved the request, and Grant, taking this for approval, ventured out with the scouts to flounder through various "lagoons and quagmires."

After making the muddy trek, and after studying a map of the region, Grant felt sufficiently confident to give senior officers a suggestion through the chain of command that the army march northward, leaving Lake Texcoco to the west, then turn westward around that lake at a marsh-free point well above it and attack Mexico City from the north. This would mean confronting that enemy army waiting at Guadalupe Hidalgo, but the move, Grant reasoned, would at least have the decided advantage of keeping the American Army on solid ground "instead of floundering through morass and ditches and fighting . . . over elevated roads, flanked by water where it is generally impossible to deploy forces." Hard experience, even that gained by tending mules and supplies, had caused the lieutenant to lose shyness.

Grant, however, was almost two decades away from making major decisions. He was a mere junior officer, one still in charge of those animals and wagons and supplies. His suggestion apparently was not seriously considered, and probably never even reached General Scott.

Before the major attack was launched upon Mexicalcingo Scott changed his mind. For some time he and other officers had entertained slim hopes of being able to move westward along the shores of the lakes Chalco and Xochimilco, leaving them to the north, and to approach Mexico City from a direction nearly due south. Thus they could avoid both El Peñon and Mexicalcingo—as well as most of the morass. But that route certainly was questionable. The southern-shore waters of both lakes washed upon rough land—the base of mountains—and Santa Anna himself obviously had believed such a route impracticable, since he had not erected defenses against it.

At the last minute, however, a reconnaissance party sent by General Worth and led by artillery officer James Duncan, now a lieutenant colonel, examined much of the terrain and found that the route, although rough, was not impassable for guns and wagons, and certainly not for troops. Duncan reported his discovery to Worth, who informed Scott.

On August 15, following Scott's changed decision, the troops began a slow march southwestward, skirting Lake Chalco. Worth's division led off, followed closely by the columns commanded by Pillow and Quitman. Twiggs's division remained at Ayotla as a screen for one day, then began moving southwestward on August 16.

By the eighteenth, after only light skirmishing, Scott had all of his men, guns, and wagons assembled at the town of San Agustín (or Tlalpan, its Aztec name), located "on terra firma" nine miles south of Mexico City along the road to Cuernavaca and Acapulco. No Mexican force had massed to challenge him at San Agustín, as Scott had rather anticipated. Instead, blocking further progress westward was a huge lava field—*pedregal*—with a rough, jagged surface that one American officer said appeared to be a storm-tossed ocean instantly transformed into stone. Its southern extremity reached the rough foothill region along which Scott's army had been marching.

Now the general sent out more reconnoitering parties to gather detailed information. Their ensuing reports described the situation.

From San Agustín the road north to Mexico City led through a town called San Antonio, about three miles away. San Antonio had been heavily fortified when Santa Anna first observed Scott's surprise movement around the lakes. American engineers probing southern approaches to the town found that it could be entered only by the road, which in that area became nothing more than a narrow causeway. To the right (east) of the causeway lay marshland; to the left, the awful expanse of that seemingly impassable lava field. (During one reconnaissance of San Antonio an artillery shot killed Captain Seth Thornton, whose capture near Fort Texas a year and a half earlier had helped to bring on this war. Thornton had been released soon afterward by the Mexicans.)

From San Antonio the road to the capital led on northward for two miles to Churubusco, a town built on a canalized river of the same name. There the Mexicans had fortified a position at the bridge. Nearby, at a thick-walled convent-church named San Mateo (but called San Pablo by most of the Americans), Santa Anna had established a headquarters garrisoned by a strong force and protected by many guns.

From San Antonio another road forked northwestward, around the northern extremity of the lava field and into the town of Coyoacán, which lay off to the left of the main highway leading to the capital. The defenses of Coyoacán, too, had been heavily strengthened. Santa Anna had moved a large part of the El Peñon garrison there.

This defensive system seemed as formidable as the rest. Scott eventually chose not to attack San Antonio. He ordered Worth to keep his division in front of the town, to pose as a threat to it, and he looked elsewhere for a possible route.

"Elsewhere" meant on the other side of the lava field. Scott had come this far thanks largely to the ability and ingenuity of engineers like Robert E. Lee, who had found or had hacked out paths in rugged Mexican terrain that even knowledgeable natives like Santa Anna believed impassable.

On the other side of the *pedregal* lay a road leading northeastward toward Mexico City. From the town of Contreras, near the southern

397

terminus, the road passed the villages of Padierna, Ansaldo, San Gerónimo, and San Angel before crossing the Rio Churubusco at a point well west of the town of that same name and west of the fortified bridge there. This route also passed west of the garrisoned town of Coyoacán, although another road forked from it to the right and entered Coyoacán. Most advantageous of all, the road on the other side of the *pedregal* by-passed San Antonio and afforded a way of turning the strong Mexican position there.

But the route had disadvantages, too, as scouts soon discovered. The powerful Army of the North, commanded by General Gabriel Valencia, had moved down from Guadalupe Hidalgo into position first at San Angel, then (by the time of Scott's arrival at San Agustín) near Padierna, a ranch headquarters. Santa Anna thus had as many as twenty-five thousand troops assembled in the vicinity, and Scott's long detour seemed to have given him little advantage—actually not even the "terra firma" he had sought, unless he could somehow move men and equipment on westward across the lava field.

Colonel Hitchcock, who had been at Scott's side during the marches, remarked, "We begin to see that, while we move over the arc of a circle surrounding the city, the enemy moves over a chord, and can concentrate at any point before we can reach it. The only advantage we can expect is that the artificial defences are less complete south and west of the city."

The general again called on Lee to find a way, this time across that forbidding *pedregal*. The captain and a strong escort of infantrymen and dragoons set out across the jagged wilderness—one, then two miles of slow, rough going across steep, sharp inclines and deep chasms. They had proceeded three miles by Lee's estimate when they met a Mexican patrol that fired on them from a position near a rocky height known as Zacatepec. The Mexicans then fled westward.

That told Lee enough. Obviously the *pedregal* could be crossed— and even by artillery, he believed, provided some rough places were made smoother. He guessed that at this point the *pedregal* stretched on ahead for two more miles.

Before returning to headquarters Lee clambered up the volcanic hill named Zacatepec and swept the western landscape with glasses. He could make out some objects in the distance. Others he guessed at. Ahead, beyond the western edge of the lava field, lay Padierna (mistakenly referred to as Contreras in most American accounts), built on a gentle incline that led down to a deep ravine with a swift stream running at the bottom of it. Beyond the ravine lay the road leading northeastward to San Angel and Mexico City. A short distance beyond the road a hill rose from the land. Lee could see that on the eastern slope of this rise, facing the *pedregal*, Valencia's Army of the North had entrenched itself with artillery support.

Not until later, however, did Lee learn some interesting details concerning Valencia and his men. The Army of the North had moved down from Guadalupe Hidalgo to San Angel the previous day, but Valencia believed this new position untenable. He had asked Santa Anna for reinforcements or for permission to withdraw toward the capital. The Mexican commander at first had refused, approving a retreat only if Scott's army were seen advancing upon San Angel. Valencia, an ambitious as well as a cautious man, had then moved forward—to the hill near Padierna, a position in which he felt more secure and at the same time more potent. Santa Anna had ordered him back from there to a location closer to the rest of the Mexican forces, but by that time Valencia's patrol had encountered Lee and his escort crossing the *pedregal*. This was the place to be, Valencia concluded, and he refused to obey Santa Anna's order. The Mexican commander, apparently striving to avoid further internal conflict, merely replied that Valencia would be held responsible for the result of his action—a development Valencia did not mind at all. If there was a threat to Santa Anna's dictatorship in Mexico at this time it was in the person of Gabriel Valencia.

Lee made his way down from Zacatepec Hill, picked up his escort, and returned through the jumbled lava to Scott's headquarters. That night he told the general the army could advance through the *pedregal*, with the prior expenditure of some labor in cutting a road. Another officer who heard Lee's report to Scott remarked, ". . . [Lee] examined, counselled, and advised with a judgment, tact, and discretion worthy of all praise. His talent for topography was peculiar, and he seemed to receive impressions intuitively, which it cost other men much labor to acquire."

Scott accepted Lee's advice. On August 19 the general ordered Pillow's division, accompanied by engineers, into the lava field to begin the work of road-cutting. Twiggs's division would advance with it, to provide support in case of attack. Quitman's division was to stay at San Agustín to guard wagons and supplies. Worth's division would remain in front of San Antonio.

By one o'clock that afternoon a road had been hacked out to a point within sight and range of Valencia's artillerymen, who were looking on from that eastern slope of their hill near Padierna (or Contreras, as the Americans erroneously supposed). The enemy opened fire and put a stop to further work.

The Americans hurriedly brought forward light artillery and replied, but the range kept their shots mostly ineffective. In the battle thus suddenly developing American commanders ordered an infantry force of three thousand men to move off to the right—across the last part of the *pedregal* and onto good soil—to occupy the village of San Gerónimo, north of Padierna. This force would be in position to attack Valencia's position from the flank or rear, or even to cut off his retreat when the rest of Scott's army stormed the hill from the front, as some confident officers expected to do. The maneuver appeared destined for possible disaster, however, when in late afternoon thousands of Mexican reinforcements appeared to the north of San Gerónimo. Santa Anna himself commanded these men (as learned later), and he commenced a bombardment of the exposed American infantry force, now caught between two large Mexican armies.

The isolated Americans, more confident than frightened, prepared an attack on the Mexicans to the north. But after a short time, with night approaching, Santa Anna and his men withdrew northeastward, in the direction of Churubusco, and for some strange reason forsook this opportunity to inflict irretrievable damage on Scott (who, for his part, never worried greatly about the situation, not having much respect for Mexican fighting ability). Night dropped a curtain on the battlefield, and a heavy rain began falling.

On the fortified hill near Padierna, General Valencia sought shelter from the downpour in a barranca utilized as a gun emplacement. His hopes remained high. At this time he was not persuaded that Santa Anna and that large army of his had indeed disappeared for good. Valencia expected them back to help him sometime after daylight.

In the soaked surroundings Valencia's miserable soldiers endured the night as well as they could. They had not eaten. Not a piece of edible bread or a splinter of dry wood to provide warmth was available. Most of them had only cold mud for a bed.

About nine o'clock two officers sent by Santa Anna arrived at the hill, soaked and tired. In the darkness they identified themselves to Mexican sentinels and asked to be taken to Valencia. They informed the general that Santa Anna would not be leading his army to assist in a fight —that, in fact, Santa Anna was again ordering Valencia to withdraw his men from their position. That now beleaguered general answered with curses, all directed at Santa Anna, that everyone nearby heard. Valencia concluded his outburst by refusing to retreat. This message Santa Anna's officers carried back with them.

Word of Santa Anna's decision spread quickly from the dark, damp area where a group of Valencia's soldiers had first overheard it. In a very short time troops all over the rain-soaked hill knew about their misfortune. They were to be abandoned, and their general would not order them out. Morale fell faster than the huge raindrops that continued to splash down upon them.

At two o'clock that sleepless night one of Santa Anna's officers returned and, on behalf of the general-in-chief, ordered Valencia to spike his guns, destroy what equipment he could not carry, and withdraw. Valencia again refused, declaring that the Americans' positions made the cowardice of retreat almost impossible anyway. The officer left.

Two hours later Valencia mounted his horse, sought out some of his senior officers elsewhere on the hill, and asked for their opinions. They agreed with him to make a stand. Perhaps this would force Santa Anna to bring his army back to their assistance.

At San Gerónimo those American infantrymen isolated from the rest of the army had no shelter and virtually no firewood, either, but they did have two valuable possessions: recently acquired knowledge of an undefended ravine leading southwestward to a position behind Valencia's fortified hill, and the presence of Captain Robert E. Lee, who had crossed the lava field during the day and had arrived at San Gerónimo on a mission from General Scott. Early that same rainy night, at a conference of officers in the church of San Gerónimo, General Persifor Smith (acting as senior commander west of the San Angel road) outlined a plan: at 3 A.M. officers would have their men ready to march along the ravine to the rear of the fortified hill, where at the hour of daylight they would launch a surprise attack. Some men, however, would remain behind at San Gerónimo to man various small fires and to mask the maneuver in other ways.

Such a movement still would need a diversion in Valencia's front. Lee volunteered to carry a request back through the black, rain-swept expanse of the lava field to Scott's headquarters, which he presumed to be on Zacatepec Hill, where the general had arrived that afternoon.

Lee and a few men acting as escort left San Gerónimo about 8 P.M. They felt their way through the storm toward the San Angel road, where Mexican pickets could be lurking even in this weather. Thunder crashed around them. Rain soaked them. But the storm proved helpful in one way. The occasional ghostly flashes of lightning gave enough illumination for Lee to find his way. They also helped him to identify an advancing infantry unit as American troops ordered (so he learned) to reinforce General Smith's men at San Gerónimo. Lee detached one of his escorting soldiers to guide the men to their destination; then he groped on ahead into the black, slippery, chaotic *pedregal*.

From time to time lightning flashes provided faint silhouettes of Zacatepec Hill, now looming in the dark distance ahead. Lee and his companions climbed steep ridges, leaped across chasms when they could, and skirted others, all the while wary about encountering pickets from their own army who might open fire, assuming them to be Mexicans. On this night Lee would have been having flickers of recollection of his close call with the sentry at Vera Cruz.

When Lee and his men reached Zacatepec Hill they learned that Scott had returned to San Agustín. They could only follow, through rain that never slackened, across an abysmal wilderness that the Devil himself might have created. Three torturous hours after leaving San Gerónimo they arrived at Scott's headquarters, and Lee made his report. The general gave orders for the diversion, but the troops for this operation had to come from among those already in the *pedregal*.

Only Lee knew that terrain well enough to find the men and to see that the orders reached them in time for compliance. Back into the lava field he plunged, accompanied this time by General Twiggs and other of Scott's officers and aided somewhat by improving weather. At dawn, when Lee had been going about these exhausting duties for twenty-four hours with virtually no rest, the diversionary frontal attack commenced.

The firing did not last long. A pause in the Mexican cannonade told

Lee that Valencia's soldiers had discovered the presence of those American infantrymen preparing to assault the rear of their hill. Later Lee learned that seventeen minutes after the attack commenced in an outburst of shots and a swirl of bayonets the battle had ended. Fifteen hundred Mexican soldiers had been killed, wounded, or captured and the others sent off in flight. The Americans captured a hoard of supplies and ammunition—and twenty-two fieldpieces, including the two guns captured at Buena Vista by Santa Anna. In accomplishing all this they suffered sixty casualties.

The day had only begun. With a road open behind those southeastern defenses of Mexico City, Scott and his commanders sent their men on northward. They were aiming at San Angel and Coyoacán, located in the rear of Santa Anna's once formidable stronghold of San Antonio, and at the fortified convent of San Mateo, in Churubusco. They would have been wiser to halt for further reconnaissance, which would have told them that there were—to the west—easier roads to take into the capital. But there was no delaying this pell-mell advance. Furthermore, taking the other route seemingly would have meant leaving Santa Anna's army on their flank—and, worse, between themselves and Worth's men still lying in front of San Antonio.

Worth's division, however, soon joined in the forward movement. From it a strong detachment plunged into the northernmost section of the lava field—off to Worth's left—under orders to find a way around the town and to circle in for another one of those vicious American attacks from the rear.

They might as well have waited. San Antonio was being evacuated on orders of Santa Anna, who had (as learned later) also given instructions that General Valencia be shot on sight after word of the Padierna (or "Contreras") collapse arrived. Santa Anna seemed to have made some attempt to go to Valencia's aid before word of the disaster reached him. Now the general-in-chief was seeking to pull his forces back into positions around the convent of San Mateo and the bridge across the Rio Churubusco.

Among the men groping through the *pedregal* in an attempt to by-pass San Antonio was Captain Ephraim Kirby Smith. Once behind the city, he would see marching northward along the road many enemy soldiers—evacuees of San Antonio heading for Churubusco. For some time the two forces proceeded on courses nearly parallel, just out of range of each other. Then, shortly before noon, Worth's men pressed in from the lava field for an assault. Captain Smith described the ensuing fight in an account that vivified the confusion and the horror of battle as seen by one participant who had no knowledge of over-all events of that momentous day.

> . . . The point where our troops pierced the retreating column of the enemy was on the road from San Antonio to Mexico [City] near a hacienda. . . . Our battalion when the firing began must have been near a half mile to the rear. The "double quick" was sounded and the whole advanced at a run. We soon reached the road . . . a broad, stone causeway with corn fields and pastures on each side of it, divided by broad ditches filled with water from three to six feet deep,—the corn tall and very thick. It was soon seen as we rushed along the road [in pursuit] that the enemy were only retreating to a fortified position. . . .
> . . . We had advanced on the road less than a mile when we were ordered into the fields to assault . . . the enemy's position. . . . We soon formed line in an open field behind the thick corn in our advance. The escopet balls were whistling over our heads . . . and occasionally a cannon ball sang through the corn as it tore its path along in our front.
> . . . Immediately in front of us, at perhaps five hundred yards, the roll of the Mexican fire exceeded anything I have ever heard. The din was most horrible, the roar of cannon and musketry, the screams of the wounded, the awful cry of terrified horses and mules, and the yells of the fierce combatants all combined in a sound as hellish as can be conceived. We had not from our battalion as yet fired a gun, but now rapidly advanced, all apparently eager to bring the contest to a hand to hand combat in which we knew our superiority.

As Smith's battalion made its way forward the men were exposed to a storm of grape and musketry that swept the fields and left them littered with more dead and dying men. Directly ahead of Captain Smith and the battered American troops around him was the bridge of Churubusco.

The Mexicans fighting there were not in a mood to surrender the passage into their capital city. A Mexican observer reported seeing the Americans advance to a position near the bridge parapets, then Mexican artillery and infantry "with a hailstorm of balls cut them up and made them falter."

Two ammunition wagons had been abandoned some distance in

front of the Mexican battery that protected the southern entrance to the bridge. An intrepid Mexican artilleryman crept out of the battery position, set fire to the vehicles, and scurried back to shelter. The wagons exploded in the faces of the advancing Americans. Fragments tore through soldiers and caused "a frightful carnage."

Still the enemy came. A Mexican colonel shouted to bandsmen crouching nearby to strike up some piece of inspirational music—at a time like this a patriotic air might incite a Mexican soldier to still greater effort, if he could hear it. The music commenced (however reluctant the bandsmen might have been to play) just as a shot plowed into the colonel and sent him sprawling on the ground.

The Mexican defenders could see that the action off to their right was every bit as fast. "The convent of [San Mateo] appeared like a castle, with its . . . side and front illumined with lurid flashes." But not everyone was giving his best. Elsewhere along the defensive line a Mexican cavalry force, ordered up as reinforcement, started forward after considerable urging and cursing from the senior officer. "They [soon] encountered a small ditch, which they declared an obstacle," a Mexican witness recorded, "and with this pretext countermarched."

From that restricted vantage point in front of the bridge Smith could not even make out what lay ahead—a fort, some breastworks, or an enemy simply positioned behind hedges or ditches. Nor did he know immediately that many of the American troops who had destroyed Valencia's army earlier that morning also were now engaged in this same battle. These men were fighting off to the left (west), having reached positions there after their hurried march up the road from San Angel and Coyoacán.

Robert E. Lee, still on his feet and reconnoitering after nearly thirty-six hours without sleep, knew the embattled terrain as well as anyone. The Churubusco River, looking more like a canal, ran almost due east across the land. Under its protected banks lay Mexican infantrymen ready to send a crashing fire into attackers. On the south bank of the river, at the location where the Cuernavaca road crossed the stream over a bridge, Santa Anna had developed that fortification with emplacements for six or more guns and good protection for troops there.

About a quarter of a mile southwest of the bridge stood the fortified San Mateo convent-church, surrounded by a thick adobe wall twelve feet high. The defenders had dug in front of the wall a deep trench for additional protection and for gun emplacements. Behind the wall they had erected platforms from which infantrymen now were firing their weapons in relative safety. Manning the artillery were those desperate U. S. Army deserters who comprised the San Patricio Battalion. They knew what to expect if Scott won.

Men were engaged in bloody, confused, unco-ordinated fighting all along that front. On the American right, Worth's troops (including Captain Smith) sought to smash into the bridge. Farther left, Scott's veterans of the Padierna battle struggled to move forward through a deadly storm of projectiles in an area between the bridge and the convent and (still farther left) in an area to the front and the western flank of the convent. A strong force sent by Scott also crossed the Churubusco to the west of this battleground, then turned east, hoping to cut off a Mexican retreat when the defensive line gave way. Lee led this force across the river, although he had little knowledge of the land in that vicinity.

For three terrible hours the battle raged around Churubusco. The assault by American troops was slowed and stopped for a time by frantic defenders—especially by the San Patricio deserters, who occasionally tore down white flags raised by their less strongly motivated Mexican colleagues. On the right, Captain Smith at one time found himself and his men caught in a cross fire between two Mexican positions. "Many had fallen and the battalion was much scattered and broken. The grape round shot and musketry were sweeping over the ground in a storm which strewed it with the dead or dying. I found it extremely difficult to make the men stand or form, but finally succeeded. . . . Now as the whole army shouted and rushed to the assault, the enemy gave way, retreating as best they could to Mexico [City]." Some American dragoons chased Mexicans all the way to a heavily defended city gate, but Scott did not order a general pursuit for at least two reasons. He had suffered heavy casualties at Churubusco, and he feared that an assault on the capital would disperse government officials necessary for effecting a peace.

Those fields around Churubusco were now covered with thousands of human casualties and with mangled bodies of horses and mules that blocked roads and filled ditches. Four thousand Mexicans lay dead or wounded; three thousand others had been captured (including sixty-nine U. S. Army deserters, who required the protection of Scott's officers to escape execution at the hands of their former comrades). But Scott's cas-

Captain Robert E. Lee helped to emplace guns from naval vessels in a powerful "naval battery" that quickly shattered Vera Cruz walls. His brother, navy Lieutenant Smith Lee, commanded the third gun from the right, a 68-pounder off the U.S.S. Mississippi.

Storm-swept Vera Cruz proved to be hard on ships. Here the U.S.S. Mississippi battles the waves during a rescue mission. Aboard the vessel then was Matthew C. Perry, known later for opening Japan to Western nations.

September 14, 1847: General Scott, his staff, and U.S. Army detachments march triumphantly into Mexico City and to the National Palace following heavy fighting in the Valley of Mexico. Later, after months of negotiating, Mexico formally gave up the war and in February 1848 agreed to the Treaty of Guadalupe Hidalgo.

A reaction in the United States against the war with Mexico and against Democrat Polk ironically helped to bring the inauguration in 1849 of a hero of that war as President—Zachary Taylor, a Whig.

ualty list was immense, too, considering the fact that he had marched on Mexico City initially with only ten thousand troops. At Churubusco the Americans lost nearly one thousand men killed, wounded, or missing.

Sadness pervaded the entire area. In Mexico City residents had heard the distant thunder of battle for hours, then realized the sound was gradually diminishing. Tattered, bloody survivors began flocking through city gates, along with some men who appeared not to have done much fighting.

They brought word of new defeats.

The evening was growing gray, and nature seemed in harmony with the catastrophe. The horizon was obscured by . . . showers. . . . The night enveloped as a black pall . . . the unfortunate capital of the most unfortunate Republic. The measured tread of the . . . silent soldiers was heard in the midst of the storm . . . [retiring] to their quarters . . . leaving in the *garita* [fortified gate] only a small garrison.

By 9 P.M. Mexico City had fallen deathly silent. The quiet was broken only occasionally by the clatter of hoofs of a galloping horse carrying an adjutant somewhere with military orders or by the voice of a sentinel crying out in the darkness an ironic "*alerta*."

The next day an emissary requesting an armistice and negotiations for peace rode out from Mexico City. American spirits soared. Surely the war was over.

Scott moved his headquarters to the capital suburb of Tacubaya, about a mile south of fortified Chapultepec Hill. His divisions encamped there and in the surrounding area. At Tacubaya Scott waited for results, along with his new friend, Nicholas Trist.

Others also settled down to wait for a formal peace.

Colonel Hitchcock, who had inevitably been made a more dedicated soldier by the excitement, drama, and uncertainty of the Mexican campaign, now could look upon the victories at Padierna and Churubusco with the detachment of a field commander filing a battle report. "On the whole, the events of the day have been—as the phrase is—'*glorious*' in the highest degree. We have lost very few men, considering the nature of the works attacked and the desperate defence made in the afternoon. . . . General Scott was slightly wounded during the battle, but said nothing of it at the moment. I only heard the balls whistle."

Hitchcock was not a boaster about action. He had been busy overseeing army preparedness to comply with orders, ascertaining that those orders were carried out, and fulfilling other duties assigned by Scott.

Captain Smith thanked God for his escape, as he wrote in his journal (in an entry begun on August 22 at Tacubaya). He had been "in the thickest of the fight for more than an hour" and had survived—this despite his earlier premonitions about never again seeing wife and children. A few days later he even enjoyed hearing from Colonel Hitchcock some Mexican comments on the fighting, contained in letters captured before the armistice. Hitchcock translated while Smith sat in the colonel's quarters listening with fascination.

"God will pity our misery," one Mexican wrote after the August 20 disaster. Others remarked: "This must be a curse of heaven. . . . The temples were full of Mexicans praying for a triumph of our arms. . . . His Divine Majesty has sent these devils to punish us for our sins. . . . They say Santa Anna has been bribed! . . . All is lost, God has forsaken us, the sentence of Belshazzar is written upon our walls."

Young Sam Grant, who had as usual left his teams and wagons to take part in the fighting at the peak of battle, apparently never brooded over his ignored advice to attack from the north, although he still felt this strategy would have avoided some bloody fighting. Years later he commented in his *Memoirs*, "Both the strategy and tactics displayed by General Scott in these various engagements of the 20th of August, 1847, were faultless as I look upon them now."

After making that statement Grant paid a compliment, if only an indirect one, to Robert E. Lee: ". . . the work of the engineer officers who made the reconnaissances and led the different commands to their destinations, was so perfect that the chief was able to give his orders to his various subordinates with all the precision he could use on an ordinary march."

The battles and those rainy-night struggles across the *pedregal*, so far removed from the peaceful repose of Fort Hamilton, brought Robert E. Lee wide acclaim and started him on his way up the promotional ladder. He was brevetted a lieutenant colonel effective August 20, 1847.

General Scott called his journeys across the lava field "the greatest feat of physical and moral courage performed by any individual, in my knowledge, pending the campaign." Every other general Lee had assisted at Padierna and Churubusco had praise for him. Even Scott's censorious inspector general, Colonel Hitchcock, referred to Lee in his diary entry for August 20 as "the" engineer. (In his own reports Lee, too, was generous with praise when he believed the situation warranted. He even singled out "Lieutenant Grant, regimental quartermaster, who was usefully employed in his appropriate duties.")

Lee continued to serve Scott in Mexico, but his most spectacular achievement occurred in the *pedregal*. His ability had been displayed for all to acknowledge. Less than fourteen years later he would be offered top command of the U. S. Army, a position he would decline in order to fight for Virginia and for the South in the Civil War and, as fate would have it, to meet at Appomattox a victorious Sam Grant, the former muleteer whose one piece of tactical advice in Mexico had gone nowhere. At Appomattox the two officers would exchange brief reminiscences of the war against Mexico before the formal surrender of Lee's Confederate Army.

41.

Such Victories

"What a glorious scene lies before us!"

Captain Ephraim Kirby Smith's mood had changed. He had survived bloody Churubusco. Had *that* fight been the one great battle he had foreseen before entering Mexico City? Now peace was being discussed. The armistice, which had become effective August 24 (subject to termination on forty-eight hours' notice from either side), had brought a halt to all fighting. Neither army was to strengthen positions. Scott's wagons could enter Mexico City to get supplies. The end of the war seemed imminent indeed.

Captain Smith and the rest of General Worth's division had encamped at Tacubaya, where Winfield Scott had set up headquarters in a splendid mansion—the Archbishop's Palace, Santa Anna's old favorite—located atop a hill that afforded an unsurpassed view of the Mexican capital sprawling across the valley two and a half miles to the northeast.

General Pillow's division had encamped at Mixcoac, two miles south; Twiggs's at San Angel, three miles beyond Mixcoac; and Quitman's at San Agustín, ten miles southeast of Tacubaya. Casualties and illness had cut Scott's able-bodied total to little more than eight thousand men, but the effectiveness of these Americans had been demonstrated. Santa Anna and all Mexico surely must decide for peace now. Nicholas Trist's opportunity had at last arrived. He was holding daily conferences with Mexican commissioners.

Captain Smith listened eagerly to rumors and reports of the results of each meeting, hoped Trist did not have "more cloth cut out than he can make up in his shop," and prayed that God would "prosper and speed their consultations."

Smith's entire attitude seemed to have changed. He could foresee a real future now—not death in battle. In his journal he wrote a note to his wife (for whom the record was meant) that he would not mail any part of his daily narrative until he could be certain of its safe arrival at Vera Cruz, from where it would be shipped on home, "for rude as these memoranda are, they will interest you, and be a valuable reference for me. . . ."

Smith even expressed some anticipation about a change of fortune in the Army. He heard that he had been favorably mentioned in the official battle report, that he was being spoken of in high terms at head-quarters, and that he would now get the brevet he had earned "long ago." Everything called for words of qualification, however, because he had been disappointed before. "This, of course, is for you alone," Smith re-marked to his wife. "I have not much influence to aid me and would not resort to it if I had."

He reveled in the scenery. Tacubaya had been built on the crest and the slope of a hill. The climate seemed to be one of eternal spring, and it had bestowed upon the land a luxuriant growth: fruits, flowers, vines, and trees. In one orchard Smith saw "growing side by side, their branches com-mingling . . . apples, pears, quinces, figs, oranges, pomegranates, peaches, grapes, and other fruits, all growing in the space of half an acre of ground —all bearing. . . . Beneath, bordering . . . winding walks, are beds of strawberries, the ripe fruit looking most tempting."

The hill afforded a grand view of the valley below.

> . . . In the centre of the valley is the reedy lake of Chalco, its waters shining through the long lines of the arbor vitae, ash, cypress, and other trees which border causeways that cross its bosom in various directions, while around it and around us rise on every side the white haciendas of the wealthy owners of the soil, looking like lordly castles—and all appears fair, rich, happy, and most beautiful. En-circling all this rise the lofty mountains, a frame to this most glorious picture, the shining summit of old Popocatepetl forming the gilded ball at the top!

Smith looked more closely at the picturesqueness, however, and saw Mexico's peculiar problem during those early years of the nation's in-dependence—the same as had Colonel Hitchcock at Santa Anna's estate,

El Encero, where Hitchcock had observed that "everything is foreign—nothing shows the genius of the Mexicans—no works of art or evidences of science." Smith now added to his description of the glorious valley:

"'Tis distance lends enchantment to the view." Let us descend and examine more closely. Alas, how decay and neglect are stamped on everything around! The fields abandoned and uncultivated; the stone walls broken and scattered; the hedges torn, untrimmed, and in many places uprooted and gone for rods; the long aqueducts and vast stone reservoirs broken and dry, or filled with green, slimy, aquatic plants and all manner of reptiles; while the white, aristocratic-looking haciendas are in ruins and uninhabited, the monuments of a more prosperous age. Sad evidences that with the monarchy departed the glory, wealth, and happiness of this fair domain.

Smith realized that Mexico at that time was an orphan—one in the hands of a foster parent like Antonio López de Santa Anna, who seemed more and more to be using the armistice in a variety of ways while Captain Smith waited to go home: to wangle concessions and probably more money from the Americans, to persuade other Mexican officials of the necessity for peace, to strengthen Mexico City defenses, and simply to stall for time. Santa Anna always wanted to leave doors wide open as long as possible.

An unnamed city resident with whom Captain Smith had developed an acquaintance told Smith about Santa Anna's duplicity in regard to the armistice agreement. The man said that inside the capital work on defenses was proceeding. Smith passed the information on to General Scott in a formal letter. Scott did nothing about it, and Smith could only fret. Some of his earlier depression began to return.

Subsequent events, however, convinced both Scott and Trist that the Mexicans were not seriously negotiating for peace, that they were only stalling for time. An unarmed wagon train entering Mexico City to load supplies, as authorized by the armistice, was attacked by an angry mob that called for "death to the Yankees" and fatally stoned one teamster. Santa Anna sent an apology for this, and later wagon trains that entered the capital under cover of night returned without trouble and with the supplies, but Scott's suspicions grew.

In the daily meetings Trist observed the Mexican commissioners becoming more and more antagonistic. They demanded a Texas boundary at the Nueces River instead of the Rio Grande, insisted that the United

States pay Mexico for war damages, and specified other claims that gave them the look of victors, not losers. Finally the Mexicans submitted a treaty of their own (instead of the treaty President Polk and James Buchanan had proposed through Trist) with an implied ultimatum that it be agreed upon within three days. With that the talks promptly ended, although Scott later laid the reason to violations of the armistice agreement by Santa Anna. On the following day, September 7, American forces at Tacubaya prepared for yet another drive on the capital.

The delay had worked against Scott. Many of his soldiers who had survived previous fighting unscathed had fallen ill. His supplies had dwindled constantly, despite occasional replenishment from Mexico City. Santa Anna had again somehow collected a large army for battle, and he had strengthened his fortifications during the armistice—as Captain Smith's informant had said.

Smith himself wrote a good description of their predicament.

> . . . We are now no more advanced than we were previous to the battle of the twentieth last. In the sixteen days during which [Santa Anna] has been flattering us with the hopes of peace he has been actively collecting his scattered forces, and with all his energies preparing to renew the combat. He has now twenty-two thousand men under arms and the Capital placed in such a state of defence that the enemy loudly boasts we cannot take it. Fatal credulity! How awful are its consequences to us! By it, the fruits of our glorious and incomparable victory are entirely thrown away. In the sixteen days our provisions and forage have been almost entirely exhausted; eight hundred of our men are sick, which added to about the same number put *hors de combat* by death and wounds leaves us nearly two thousand weaker than we were on the morning of the twentieth ultimo, and now, alas, we have all our fighting to do over again.
>
> In my opinion a much bloodier battle is to be fought than any which have preceded it. . . .

From a window of his room in the Archbishop's Palace, Scott's hilltop headquarters at Tacubaya, Colonel Hitchcock could see one of the obstacles standing in the way of any attack on city gates: Chapultepec Hill, about a mile away, once the summer home of the Montezumas and the viceroys, but now the majestic site of a military school functioning around a formidable, fortified castle bristling with guns clearly visible through field glasses. For the present, however, they were silent guns.

Lying a little to the right of Chapultepec, Hitchcock could see, out the same window, Mexico City.

The setting and the momentary peacefulness entranced him. Under this very window grew fruits and vegetables. For his table he had fresh apples, peaches, bananas, green peas, corn. "What a country to dream in!" Hitchcock thought.

Dreaming was indeed what the American command had been doing in regard to a negotiated settlement, and it had been only a sleeping interlude. Now, upon awakening, the Americans faced that artillery atop Chapultepec.

Some other strong barriers stood in their way. The area around Chapultepec had been walled and, in some areas, ditched. Not quite a mile west of the castle, and well within range of its guns, stood some thick stone buildings of a supposed foundry, Molino del Rey (King's Mill), that stretched more than a quarter of a mile from north to south and comprised the western wall around Chapultepec. Another quarter of a mile west beyond Molino del Rey lay another strong outpost, this one consisting of trenches and gun emplacements encircling another large stone building called Casa Mata. Soon after disruption of peace negotiations Santa Anna ordered infantry-supported artillery and strong cavalry detachments into positions between Molino del Rey and Casa Mata, and in a confined area around the latter position.

Hitchcock, who moved out of the exposed Archbishop's Palace with the rest of Scott's staff, saw with regret the approach of renewed fighting. "I never was in favor of this war," he said, "and have hoped, within a few days, that the end of it was near. I have not relied much on it, though. The pride of this people is very great, and that pride has been wounded: this will probably go further to continue the war than any injustice of which they complain."

When the armistice expired at noon on September 7 Hitchcock expected to hear the roar of guns atop Chapultepec and to see shot and shell hurtling into the American positions around Tacubaya. After breakfast that morning he had ridden around the hillside with General Scott, studying Chapultepec and its surroundings. The two officers had watched Mexican reinforcements stream into positions around Molino del Rey and Casa Mata, and Hitchcock had guessed the enemy's intention—"of striking [our] division on its left flank, while Chapultepec [opened] its batteries on our front." But noon came and passed, and the guns still remained silent.

The calm seemed ominous. There *had* been those additional troops marching into the Chapultepec area. Furthermore, Scott had received information that convinced him Molino del Rey was even at that moment being used to cast new cannon from old church bells.

The Mexicans must not have the benefit of this additional artillery. Scott determined to send General Worth's division to destroy Molino del Rey. He would let Worth handle detailed planning, but the assault would commence at daylight on September 8. Scott did not anticipate a major battle, but Captain E. K. Smith, who would be a participant, thought differently.

For the sunrise attack Captain Smith received orders to lead a light battalion regularly commanded by Lieutenant Colonel Charles F. Smith (no relation), who had been taken ill. Smith's own company would be taken over in his absence by Lieutenant Fred Dent, brother of Sam Grant's fiancée, Julia Dent.

The major task of the morning, however, supposedly would fall on an elite five-hundred-man group picked from among the best soldiers of the various regiments. This unit would be directly responsible for assaulting Molino del Rey and destroying it. The men would be supported by Captain Smith's and Lieutenant Dent's commands and by all other 2,600 available troops of Worth's division. Nine pieces of artillery were to bombard Mexican positions before the infantry charge.

The evening before the attack Captain Smith wrote in his journal.

. . . This morning a heavy column of the enemy were seen marching from the city by Chapultepec. Their right was established at a large building [Molino del Rey], said to be a foundry, something more than a mile from Chapultepec, and their left resting on that strong fortification [Chapultepec itself. Actually, however, their right proved to have been established at Casa Mata]. Their line is along an aqueduct and a deep ditch covered by bushes and trees bordering an extensive pasture and grain field—an extremely strong position.

I have just learned that the plan of attack is arranged. A forlorn hope of five hundred men commanded by Major [George] Wright is to carry the foundry and blow it up. At the same time an attack from our artillery . . . [and infantry] . . . is to be made upon their line. . . . This operation is to commence at three in the morning.

Tomorrow will be a day of slaughter. I firmly trust and pray that victory may crown our efforts though the odds are immense.

I am thankful that you do not know the peril we are in. Good night.

Captain Smith closed his journal then and slept as well as he could.

The ghostly movement began on schedule at 3 A.M. The assaulting columns moved briskly and neatly into positon. The spectral forms of men in motion could be seen even in the dim light of predawn. By five o'clock the grim stone walls of Molino del Rey had become visible, phantomlike, in the distance.

The American bombardment began. A gun roared, then another. Each burst created a bright flash in the early morning grayness. After a series of blasts firing ceased: time now for the chosen five hundred to launch their attack.

Was this really the time, however, or had General Worth become impatient to get on with the battle? The cannonade had been surprisingly brief. Worth was known as an especially impatient and ambitious general. Most of Scott's senior officers had become recognized as aspiring men who wanted to be first every time, who were willing to make bloody sacrifices to achieve, and who often resented credit given elsewhere. The Army recognized Worth as outstanding in this respect, and some observers accused him now of curtailing the bombardment to hasten the victory. Perhaps the man even envisioned assaulting the strategic hill of Chapultepec after overrunning Molino del Rey and becoming *the* hero of the war, although Scott had instructed him to limit the day's attack to the immediate objective.

Major George Wright and the chosen five hundred men charged the foundry where those enemy guns were being cast. Captain E. K. Smith, waiting in reserve with his light battalion, would have seen them rush forward, shouting and screaming again, directly into a strong position that erupted with thundering artillery and spluttering musketry.

Within five minutes Major Wright's attackers had been mauled. They reeled back, pursued for a time by bayonet-wielding Mexican infantrymen. Only three of fourteen officers escaped becoming casualties—and fewer than half of the men in the ranks.

Captain Smith and his light battalion and a regiment also being held in reserve were ordered in now to press the attack on the foundry that Wright's men had striven to make. To the left and right of Smith other infantrymen sprinted forward, on Worth's orders, to assault Casa Mata and to strike the Mexican left, which was especially well covered by those Chapultepec guns.

Captain Smith would have seen Lieutenant Fred Dent dash into the front of the latest charge, leading Smith's company. Smith himself, probably showing his age, followed in Dent's footsteps. Smith led men into a Mexican artillery position in front of Molino del Rey, then—after subduing it with rifle and pistol fire and the coup de grâce of the bayonet—took them through an opening between two buildings of the foundry.

From there Smith and Dent separated, each leading groups of men into vicious hand-to-hand fights where slashing bayonets and butts of weapons used as clubs cleared a way. Dent and two of his men survived a storm of musket balls fired from nearby roofs and captured another gun; Smith might have seen this. Then Dent felt a slap on his thigh and became aware of blood flowing down his leg. Dizzy and weak, he nevertheless remembered later that Captain Smith and a group of men ran past the captured gun in a charge of their own. Dent was one of the last men to see his captain before a musket ball struck Smith in the face and sent him sprawling on the ground.

Other men pressed the attack and forced the Mexicans out of Molino del Rey. One of them was Lieutenant Sam Grant, whose 4th Regiment charged immediately after Smith's light battalion—and in the same vicinity. Grant noticed on a nearby rooftop numbers of Mexicans apparently preparing to send potshots into the Americans below.

Not seeing any stairway or ladder reaching to the top of the building, I took a few soldiers, and had a cart that happened to be standing near brought up, and, placing the shafts against the wall and choking the wheels so that the cart could not back, used the shafts as a sort of ladder extending to within three or four feet of the top. By this I climbed to the roof of the building, followed by a few men, but found [an American] private soldier had preceded me by some other way. There were still quite a number of Mexicans on the roof, among them a major and five or six officers of lower grades, who had not succeeded in getting away before our troops occupied the building. They still had their arms, while the soldier before mentioned was walking as sentry, guarding the prisoners he had *surrounded*, all by himself. I halted the sentinel, received the swords from the commissioned officers, and proceeded, with the assistance of the soldiers now with me, to disable the muskets by striking them against the edge of the wall. . . .

Later Grant came upon Julia Dent's brother Fred, examined his bloody thigh, concluded the wounded man could wait until surgeons arrived, and hurried on after the enemy.

Elsewhere Worth's division was taking heavy losses, especially at Casa Mata. One regiment charged that bastion, met a murderous fire, and staggered back looking more like a company than a regiment. After an effective bombardment and with the support of another regiment the survivors rushed the position again and carried it.

By seven o'clock that morning fighting had ended. Mexican losses numbered nearly three thousand, including prisoners, and Casa Mata and Molino del Rey had fallen. Worth lost as dead, wounded, or missing every fourth man who had participated in the attack.

Neither side had anything to rejoice about, although Mexican defenders had performed valiantly. At the peak of fighting, said a Mexican, "the roar of artillery and musketry resembled the explosion of a volcano, and smoke enveloped the combatants."

But in the end Mexico had lost another battle. The same observer remarked, "The greatest eulogium that can be made on this . . . is by referring to the reports of the enemy, in which they assert that out of 14 officers who led [Major Wright's] column of attack 11 were strewed upon the field."

Where had Santa Anna been during the fighting? The general-in-chief would have had a good alibi, but critics among his countrymen accused him of having retired to the National Palace for a good night's sleep after all the stress and strain he had been enduring. When Santa Anna had first heard about the battle he ordered up a light regiment for escort and departed for the scene, but before he arrived the Mexican defenders had been routed. "The action . . . of . . . Molino del Rey wanted a General-in-chief," one Mexican critic contended, "and it was reduced to isolated efforts on the part of those who had sufficient honor and patriotism to do their duty. . . ."

That evening of September 8 Colonel Hitchcock went to bed early—at eight o'clock. He had seen most of the fighting. Weary and sorrowful, he quickly found escape in deep sleep. Three hours later he awoke. Restless, he rose, lighted a candle, and began writing in his diary.

". . . There is general grief in the army, both for the loss of so many valuable men and because of the manner of it. . . . It is considered that General Worth made the assault blindly. . . . On Sept. 8th, we [are] like Pyrrhus after the fight with Fabricius—a few more such victories and this army would be destroyed."

A U. S. Marine Corps lieutenant attached to Worth's staff, Raphael Semmes, blamed Scott for the bloodiness. "He had originated it in error," Semmes said, "and caused it to be fought, with inadequate forces, for an object that had no existence."

Captain Ephraim Kirby Smith, carried mangled and unconscious from the field, lay in a makeshift hospital after the battle. Surgeons could have held no hope for a man struck squarely in the face by a musket ball.

Smith remained in a coma for three days until he died. His journal that had declared, in the last paragraph, "I am thankful that you do not know the peril we are in," later was sent to his family—the wife and three children Smith had yearned to support. The captain who had come to despise military politics and the promotions earned so often at the expense of other men, who had then reacquired some hope in regard to his profession, had been fatally wounded while under orders of an ambitious general to capture a cannon-casting foundry that was not there. Molino del Rey, after its fall, was found to have contained nothing more than many enemy troops and their deadly weapons.

The Americans withdrew from Molino del Rey and Casa Mata. Mexicans still held the strategic height, Chapultepec.

42.

Long-sought Destination

After all the maneuvering and fighting to avoid the necessity of an eastern causeway assault on El Peñon or Mexicalcingo, the way into Mexico City from Scott's present position still lay along two causeways. One entered the city from the west at a fortified gate named San Cosme, the other from the southwest at another strong gate known as Belén. The roads leading to both gates passed near Chapultepec Hill before making their final approach on the capital. Chapultepec guns could sweep either route.

Again Scott sent out his engineers to investigate other possibilities, but their reports persuaded him the final attack on Mexico City probably should be made from the west or southwest. This meant those Chapultepec guns must be silenced first.

An infantry assault on Chapultepec appeared to be a formidable task, possibly as bloody as—or bloodier than—the useless attack on Molino del Rey. The hill rose two hundred feet from the surrounding plain. The highest and steepest point faced the city, which lay to the northeast. Atop this rocky summit had been constructed a series of sturdy buildings that the Americans referred to as a castle—actually an old summer palace of the viceroys and now the site of that Mexican military academy, which was garrisoned by a thousand soldiers and cadets commanded by General Nicolás Bravo and further defended by thirteen cannon and (as learned later) a series of mine fields.

Terrain made Chapultepec unassailable from north and east. Only from the south and west did a somewhat more gradual ascent allow any possibility of infantry attack. To the west lay that infamous Molino del

Rey and, at the bottom of Chapultepec Hill, a grove of huge, centuries-old cypress trees.

The view of looming Chapultepec, combined with recollections of recent depressing events, put Colonel Ethan Allen Hitchcock in a gloomy mood. In the first place, he still sorrowed over the Churubusco deaths. Then the military necessity of hanging twenty U. S. Army deserters of the San Patricio Battalion (on September 9 and 10) lowered his spirits further. Twelve other deserters who had switched sides before the outbreak of war escaped with punishments of flogging and cheek-branding (with a "D"); some thirty more deserters remained to be chastised. Finally, General Scott had gone sour—not merely toward Hitchcock, but toward everyone around him.

The colonel knew what that meant. Scott foresaw bad days ahead. "When prosperous [Scott] is pleasant and good-humored, extremely kind and civil, but when his affairs seem unpromising he is rather harsh upon those around him, especially his young *aides de camp*. He is then apt to be abrupt and cuts off persons in the midst of what they are saying—indeed, his uncomfortability diffuses itself all around him."

The days following Churubusco were depressing ones indeed for Hitchcock. The U. S. Army appeared to be anything but victorious. Here it was at the gates of Mexico City with its effective troop total cut now to seven thousand men—and time could only decrease that number further. Hitchcock realized the need for quick action. He knew that Scott recognized this necessity. Every knowledgeable man would have had similar thoughts.

On September 11 Scott rode around for a last look at defenses south of Mexico City. An alternative still remained there: an advance up the causeways from almost due south. But the Mexicans had vastly strengthened southern defenses near the city. Chapultepec and the two gates farther on still appeared to be the most logical points of attack. Scott ordered Twiggs to take his division to Piedad, south of the capital, to pose as a threat from that direction, while other units launched the assault upon Chapultepec Hill.

This time a giant bombardment would precede the attack. No more of Worth's impatient half-attempts at softening an entrenched enemy before sending in troops to a slaughter. Perhaps cannonade alone could conquer Chapultepec, and an infantry assault would not even be necessary.

On the evening of the eleventh animals and men tugged big guns into positions south and southwest of the hill. Night hid them from enemy observation. In the early morning hours of the twelfth some of Scott's men reoccupied the empty buildings of Molino del Rey and Casa Mata. Later they emplaced more cannon near Molino del Rey and aimed the guns at Chapultepec.

Hitchcock rose early on the twelfth—a Sunday, but this was not to be a day of rest. He dressed and made his way to General Scott's quarters, ready for whatever duties the day and the general's demands might impose on him. Before 5 A.M. he presented himself, but an aide told him that Scott was still asleep in an adjoining room. Hitchcock waited.

Shortly before daybreak Scott rose, dressed, and stepped outside the building into the light of a young dawn. Soon afterward the guns opened fire and maintained a steady bombardment for fourteen hours, but Colonel Hitchcock at first could see no great damage inflicted.

The buildings standing atop Chapultepec Hill indeed suffered only little harm initially, but that was before the American artillerymen had an opportunity to correct their aim. In time the Chapultepec garrison of soldiers and cadets began to endure a remarkable bombardment. Shells crashed through walls and roofs and killed men who never had a chance to raise a musket. Mexican artillery never ceased replying, but still the enemy shells screamed in. By midmorning Chapultepec engineers were swamped with the work of trying to effect makeshift repairs on damage done by the American guns.

The duel continued all day. It even brought Santa Anna and a force of reserves out of Mexico City to see if Chapultepec could be assisted, but after a brief reconnaissance he ordered his men to withdraw. Later, after overseeing some work of fortification at a city gate, he returned to the National Palace for the evening. He refused General Bravo's pleas for reinforcements, apparently for two reasons: the threat from the south posed by Twiggs's division, and a disinclination to expose more soldiers to such an unnerving bombardment. So Bravo and his thousand or so men and boys stood alone.

Santa Anna and the Americans had left Chapultepec a shambles. "In the corridor, converted into a surgical hospital, were found mixed up the putrid bodies, the wounded breathing mournful groans, and the young boys of the college. . . ."

That night after firing had ceased engineers hurried to repair damage, to replace blinds, and to strengthen fortifications. Chapultepec still had hope. Perhaps reinforcements might yet be on the way from somewhere.

During the day's duel the Mexican artillery had proved virtually ineffective. Although the enemy had hurled his shot toward Scott's batteries in impressive amounts, American artillerymen suffered very few casualties.

Nevertheless, the Mexicans' own stand under that continued heavy bombardment convinced General Scott of the necessity for an infantry assault. On the evening of the twelfth, after darkness had silenced the guns, Hitchcock listened as Scott outlined his plans at a meeting of senior officers. The cannonade would be resumed at daylight on the following day and would continue for an hour or so. When the guns fell silent, sometime around 8 A.M., the assaulting troops were to charge Chapultepec —General Pillow's division from the west, assisted by a storming party composed of 250 seasoned regulars from General Worth's command, and General Quitman's division from the southeast, aided by a storming party of 250 men from Twiggs's command. The remainder of Worth's division would be held in reserve to support Pillow, and part of Twiggs's division would serve the same purpose for Quitman. Men participating in the assault would carry ladders, crowbars, and pickaxes as well as weapons. Storming rugged Chapultepec would require something like mountain-climbing ability as well as fighting prowess, and victory would hinge on annihilating or expelling the thousand or so troops sheltered there.

Hitchcock listened grimly to all these plans. "If we carry Chapultepec, well; if we fail or suffer great loss, there is no telling the consequences. . . . I confess that I am not without anxiety about the result of the enterprise on foot."

General Worth expressed even greater pessimism when he left the conference room. Before walking out he said to Hitchcock, "We shall be defeated." After everyone else had gone Hitchcock heard General Scott voice his own doubt. "I have my misgivings," Scott remarked to his inspector general. Sleep would not have come easily that night for Colonel Hitchcock.

The guns commenced their familiar thunder at six o'clock on the following morning. One hour later General Scott appeared on a rooftop of a Tacubaya house to observe the firing and to give the order for the infantry assault. Hitchcock stood nearby, possibly thinking over the dismal statements Worth and Scott had made to him the night before.

For two hours the bombardment continued without interruption. About eight o'clock Scott ordered a halt in the firing. The storming parties took this signal and charged on the run. Many of the men carried those ladders, pickaxes, and crowbars in addition to weapons, and they were heavily burdened.

As the assault commenced Scott turned to Hitchcock and told him to carry an order to the commander of a dragoon force waiting some distance away to westward. Scott's instruction called for the dragoons to ride forward and to circle northward of Chapultepec in support of the attack.

When Hitchcock reached the dragoon leader with this information he could see, off to his right, the battle raging on the western slope of Chapultepec Hill—the sector under attack by Worth's 250-man storming party and by troops of Pillow's division. From the buildings of Molino del Rey and along the high walls surrounding Chapultepec to the north and south the American troops pressed forward. The center of this assault wave quickly encountered some natural barriers—marshland dotted with boulders, and those giant cypress trees at the foot of the western slope—but the troops pressed on. They fired from behind the huge cypress trunks, then sprinted forward to the safety of others. The Americans carried the lower works of Chapultepec in such a rush that the Mexicans were unable to explode their mines beneath the attackers.

Hitchcock continued to stare, entranced by the "sight never to be forgotten." He saw the distant colors advance—saw the bearer shot down. Someone else seized the red, white, and blue banner and clambered on up the rugged slope for some distance. (This man proved to be Lieutenant George Pickett, just out of West Point, who would lead a tragic Civil War charge years later.)

Then Hitchcock saw the entire advance halt, and he learned later the reason for the delay. The attacking troops had reached a large ditch at the base of a retaining wall that supported the buildings standing on the rocky summit of the hill—and the men had no scaling ladders. Much equipment had been dropped and left behind in the cypress grove by bearers who had concentrated instead on returning the Mexican fire. Other ladder-bearers had fallen behind in the rush. The delayed attackers in the van of the assault now leaped for any cover they could find—boulders, trees, ravines—to escape the fire pouring down from windows and rooftops of the palace above them. Soon they sent up an effective reply.

When scaling ladders finally arrived the impatient Americans jumped into the ditch and hastily emplaced the ladders against the wall. Some men died; some fell wounded. Others took their places and clambered up the ladders, trying to reach firm footing at the top before the ladders could be pushed away from the wall or before Mexican musket balls found a mark. Again the first few fell, but again others took their places. Finally they secured a foothold on the crest of Chapultepec. Hitchcock, still looking on from the distance, rejoiced.

But the colonel could not see the battle on the southeastern slope. Quitman's men made slower progress over worse terrain and into the face of an enemy who stood even firmer than the force battling the charge up the other side of the hill. In Quitman's sector yells and shouts gave way to cries and groans. The rattle of small-arms fire subsided. The sound was replaced by the soft swishes of bayonets and swords cutting into flesh and by the thuds of rifles being used as clubs. The furious defenders slowed Quitman's advance, but they could not contain it.

Inside the palace a legend was being made. Many details of the Mexican defense never could be documented, but oral accounts from both sides later attested to the bravery of a group of Mexican cadets who had refused to obey prior orders to abandon the place because of their age and who stayed to fight alongside the Mexican soldiers.

Of the fifty cadets the youngest was said to have been thirteen, the oldest nineteen. Together with the regular troops they had endured the bombardment of the day before, and on the day of the assault they sought to repel the attack.

During the battle for Chapultepec six cadets died "fighting like demons"—as an American war correspondent said. Witnesses later told of a thirteen-year-old who saw a group of attackers running toward him, shouted a command to halt, tried to cock his rifle to fire, but died first with a bayonet through his body. Three other cadets were killed fighting inside palace walls. Another youth, aged fifteen, died on the school grounds outside. After the battle someone found him sprawled there with his rifle by his side.

Some Mexican accounts say that a seventeen-year-old cadet fought to the last from a position on the palace roof, near the flagstaff where the Mexican colors still waved in a gentle breeze. Below him, on school grounds and inside buildings, the battle swirled, sending up its usual din of shots, shouts, grunts, cries, and screams.

As resistance weakened, the noise waned. The cadet, aware of the imminent fall of Chapultepec, ran to the flagstaff, hauled down the Mexican banner, and sprinted across the roof toward a stairway. At least the invaders would not have the pleasure of lowering his flag. But before the youth reached the stairway a shot struck him and sent him reeling onto rocks far below. When his body was found later his hands still clutched the flag.

Some American accounts had it that Major Thomas H. Seymour of the U. S. Army fought his way to the roof with a group of men, ran to the flagstaff, and cut down the Mexican colors. Some versions credited Lieutenant George Pickett, who had seized the falling Stars and Stripes during the battle on the slopes, with raising the United States flag on the palace roof. Whatever actually happened, the bitter battle for Chapultepec lasted an hour and a half after the American storming parties attacked it. Scott lost five hundred more men from his dwindling army, and virtually every member of the Chapultepec garrison became a casualty—dead, wounded, or captured.

When the Stars and Stripes appeared fluttering from that disputed flagstaff atop the palace it signaled not only the fall of Mexico but the moment of death for about thirty remaining U. S. Army deserters of that San Patricio Battalion.

Having been tried and convicted and sentenced to be hanged, they had been prepared for execution in the plaza of Mixcoac, two miles from Chapultepec and well within sight of the place.

They had been brought to the plaza early that morning, during the preliminary bombardment of the hill and the palace, and had been placed on scaffolds erected atop U. S. Army wagons. There they were told they would wait—standing, with their hands and feet bound and with ropes fastened around their necks—and witness the assault until the American flag appeared victoriously unfurled on the Chapultepec staff. Then they would die.

When the colors suddenly flashed upon the distant pole the waiting teamsters and guards cheered, but the condemned men (for whatever reason) cheered loudest of all, as one witness remembered later. Drivers shouted to their teams, the wagons creaked, and the last members of the San Patricio Battalion died, dangling in Mexican sunshine.

One event the flag raising atop Chapultepec did not signal was the end of hostilities. This time Scott did not halt his men after their victory but sent them instead toward the gates of the capital.

They advanced along the two causeways selected earlier. Worth's division (with Scott and his staff eventually in company) pushed ahead northeastward up Verónica Causeway, a road divided by an elevated, arched aqueduct built in its center. At a point about two miles from Chapultepec this road intersected Tacuba Causeway, which entered the city from a direction almost due west, through that gate named San Cosme. Quitman's division took a more direct route, but one more strongly defended: along another causeway—also split by an arched aqueduct—that entered the city from the southwest through Belén Gate.

Quitman's soldiers reached their destination first. Sprinting from behind one arch to the safety of the next, enough of them avoided the frantic Mexican fire to advance up the road and to capture Belén Gate shortly after noon. But when they sought to fight their way on into the city a desperate counterattack drove them back, and for a time they battled desperately simply to hold their position.

Worth's men made slower progress, but by four o'clock that afternoon they were approaching San Cosme Gate, which blocked the causeway at a location not quite a mile west of the city proper. Along this same elevated road Cortés had retreated during the *noche triste*, and for a time the situation looked almost as bleak to Worth.

Mexican artillery and small-arms fire sprayed the causeway, but Worth thought he saw a safe route. Lining the north side of the causeway were some adobe buildings. Worth set his men to digging through them, burrowing a protected path from the side wall of one building into the side wall of the next—as his troops had done at Monterrey. Once in the rear of the San Cosme defenses, the Americans could spread panic.

Young Sam Grant contributed to this victory. Long ago he had learned to tend mules. Now he had learned leadership of men.

Grant had missed most of the fighting on Chapultepec Hill. He had seen it from a distance—with other members of Colonel John Garland's brigade, which had been ordered to the north of Chapultepec during the battle to assist in cutting that position off from reinforcements or retreat. After the fall of Chapultepec the brigade had hurried on toward the Verónica Causeway and San Cosme. A group of soldiers led by Grant were among the first to reach the vicinity of the gate—and they arrived without the loss of a man, due largely to the ingenuity of Grant in getting them safely from one shelter to the next.

Grant (as did Worth) saw that Mexican artillery commanded the road immediately in front of the gate. The lieutenant then looked over the rest of the landscape to see what damage he might inflict on the enemy elsewhere.

> . . . I found a church off to the south of the road [that] looked to me as if the belfry would command the ground back of . . . San Cosme. I got an officer of the voltigeurs, with a mountain howitzer and men to work it. . . . The road being in possession of the enemy, we had to take the field to the south to reach the church. This took us over several ditches breast deep in water and grown up with water plants. These ditches, however, were not over eight or ten feet in width. The howitzer was taken to pieces and carried by the men to its destination. When I knocked for admission a priest came to the door . . . [but] declined to admit us. With the little Spanish then at my command, I explained to him that he might save property by opening the door. . . . He began to see his duty in the same light that I did, and opened the door. . . . The gun was carried to the belfry and put together. We were not more than two or three hundred yards from San Cosme. The shots from our little gun dropped in upon the enemy and created great confusion.

General Worth, looking on from a distance, noticed the gunfire and was so elated that he sent an aide across the marshland to express his pleasure to whoever it was who had been so ingenious. The messenger carrying Worth's congratulations happened to be Lieutenant John Pemberton, who would one day command the doomed defenses of Vicksburg against a Union siege led by this same Sam Grant.

Grant's miniature bombardment and the panic created by the troops who had dug through those adobe walls to the rear of San Cosme Gate helped to bring an end to the defense of the Mexico City perimeter. By 6 P.M. of September 13 both gates, San Cosme and Belén, were in possession of the U. S. Army.

Scott's future nevertheless appeared to be bleak. His troop total had decreased further in the causeway fights. Supplies of ammunition and other necessities were dangerously low. Yet a city of two hundred thousand residents still remained to be entered and occupied.

The Mexicans themselves solved the general's problem. Santa Anna decided the capital could not be defended, and he took his remaining troops northward to Guadalupe Hidalgo. Early in the morning of September 14 a delegation of citizens surrendered Mexico City to the Americans.

Scott's troops preceded the general and his staff into the city. Some men were sent to guard against uprising, some to prepare for a military parade that Scott himself would lead to the National Palace. At 8 A.M. on September 14 the general and his staff rode up to take their places in front of the procession, and the column marched to the music of a band playing "Yankee Doodle" along the Street of the Silversmiths and the present Avenida Francisco I. Madero toward their long-sought destination.

Colonel Hitchcock would have ridden proudly with the general. Criticism of the war had virtually disappeared from Hitchcock's diary entries—although not criticism of President Polk. Hitchcock remarked once that he still disapproved of the war, but (though he did not say this) as a soldier he would long since have become resigned to the necessity of winning it.

Furthermore, the efficiency and valor displayed by his countrymen had aroused his admiration. Hitchcock probably esteemed competence (which implied other traits he admired) more than any other human quality. On the evening of the climactic victory he wrote:

> Tacubaya, Monday, Sept. 13, 10 P.M., and to-day we have taken Chapultepec, and entered the city of Mexico on two routes, our troops rushing over a multitude of batteries erected with infinite labor and even skill by the Mexicans.
>
> I had my misgivings last night—even the General had; but to-day the troops have outdone all former achievements—immeasurably so. I thought the fight of the 20th ult. unsurpassable, but to-day the troops have done more and in even finer style. . . . To-day [the Mexicans] have had a demonstration of skill, valor, perseverance, etc., on the part of our troops, which must affect them with astonishment. . . .

The war made a soldier of Sam Grant, the young second lieutenant whose first reaction upon hearing the distant boom of those hostile guns so long ago had been to regret entering military service.

Grant never had craved a military career, and for the rest of his life he believed the war against Mexico to have been "immoral," but once in the profession and in this war his pride would have compelled him to achieve. Later he would leave the Army temporarily, but the experiences and observations acquired during battles in Texas and Mexico made a real officer of him.

This development apparently was not noticed at the time by many of his colleagues. Years later Grant recalled, "I had gone into the battle of Palo Alto in May, 1846, a second lieutenant, and I entered the city of Mexico sixteen months later with the same rank, after having been in all the engagements possible for any one man and in a regiment that lost more officers during the war than it ever had present at any one engagement. . . ."

43.

Superlative Climaxes

Santa Anna's career seemed to be filled with superlative climaxes that culminated in tragedies so complete as to provide a theme for either poet or dramatist, as a biographer once remarked. In September of 1847 the great actor prepared to bring his present role to another inexorably disastrous conclusion, having been so directed by that lack of moral and intellectual training to support his genuine natural ability.

The attitude of General Gabriel Valencia, whom Santa Anna had ordered to be shot on sight after the defeat at Padierna, spoke for much of Mexico. Valencia called for revolt. He exhorted his countrymen to execute Santa Anna and to annihilate the American invaders. Many Mexicans still did not want peace at the cost of surrendering to a despised enemy, particularly when a negotiated settlement surely would mean giving up large chunks of territory. But by this time they hated their own leader almost as much as they did the foreign invader. They had heard fresh rumors of Santa Anna's duplicity—of his earlier communications with Scott and Trist and of his wangling an unknown amount of cash out of them, while (at the same time) he had been urging his fellow citizens to fight to the death in defense of their capital. Neither they nor anyone else ever knew for certain Santa Anna's sincere desire, if he had one. Was it for peace or for continued resistance? From time to time he gave strong indications of believing that a negotiated peace would be best for his country, as did a few other officials of the Mexican Government, but (like them) he dared not challenge inflamed public opinion.

During Scott's pause at Puebla Nicholas Trist had written to Secretary of State Buchanan (on July 23) that Santa Anna had promised him in confidence Scott could bring his army without challenge to El Peñon, the fortified place outside Mexico City. Then Santa Anna would arrange for a peaceful settlement. But those negotiations, if ever serious on Santa Anna's part, had failed.

As Scott's army pressed ever closer to the capital following victories over numerically superior Mexican forces, Santa Anna had alibied louder and louder for his defeats. Always the fault lay elsewhere. The Padierna fiasco had been General Valencia's responsibility, not Santa Anna's—although Santa Anna had missed that opportunity of destroying a considerable part of Scott's force as it waited at San Gerónimo. Instead of attacking the Americans isolated there Santa Anna had ordered that withdrawal of his large army after making only a brief appearance.

Following the Padierna defeat, Santa Anna had not even appeared on the field as a genuine battle commander, although he had freely criticized other Mexican officers who had striven to halt the American advance. He singled out the general in charge of the Belen Gate defense for especially ignominious punishment. He slapped the man's face, ripped off his military insignia, and placed him under arrest. Santa Anna even censured the Chapultepec cadets—*los niños héroes*—for an alleged lack of enthusiasm in holding the palace.

This time, however, General Santa Anna's pretense and pomposity truly fell flat. After he had withdrawn his army to Guadalupe Hidalgo from the capital most residents of Mexico City openly branded him as the traitor they had always suspected him of being, and they organized guerrilla resistance to Scott's occupying troops that caused much violence and bloodshed before Scott eliminated most of it by using a combination of wisdom and some fierce police action.

"Everybody, including the troops themselves, believed that Santa Anna . . . betrayed us," said a Mexican historian who lived through those days so tragic for his country. He added a condemnation of Mexican militarism as it existed then, calling most generals "cowards, ignoramuses, and men wholly devoid of even one spark of personal honor. Judged by their ability, they scarcely would make good sergeants. Judged by their character, they are what one of our . . . poets has said of them: Tortoises in the country, Vultures in the city. Select just one per cent of them to make an exception. . . ." One exception, the same historian added, was Gabriel Valencia.

Even after evacuating Mexico City, however, Santa Anna did not abdicate his role as the potential savior of his country. To free himself for further fighting he resigned the presidency on September 16, making known this event in another proclamation.

> With the most poignant and profound grief do I announce to you that it was after repeated and extraordinary efforts, and after fifteen hours' incessant fighting, I saw myself under the necessity of abandoning the capital, with my ranks considerably thinned by the projectiles of the enemy, which penetrated our nearest lines, strewing the way with their bodies and with those of the noble Mexicans who so gloriously defended, inch by inch, the rights and honour of their country.
>
> You have been witnesses that I have created resources at a time when there were none; that I laboured day and night. . . .
>
> The insubordination of one general subverted my entire plan of operations—a thing you already know. . . . I have anxiously sought death in all parts, because a loss so great has occasioned me the most profound despair. In Chapultepec I received a contusion, in Belen my clothes were pierced by the balls of the enemy. . . .
>
> I . . . announce to you that I have spontaneously resigned the Presidency of the Republic . . . because I feel it incumbent on me ever to place myself in that quarter in which there is the most peril. . . .
>
> Mexicans! Thirty years have passed over since you proclaimed your independence amid perils and privations. Sustain it forever!

Santa Anna named Manuel de la Peña y Peña as his successor. (That reluctant man finally agreed ten days later to accept the office—not because Santa Anna had chosen him, but because friends in the capital urged him to fulfill the duties in the interest of Mexico.) Then Santa Anna led a remnant of his army against the American garrison at Puebla, still hoping to break Scott's link with Vera Cruz and (not incidentally) to regain prestige among his countrymen. But he failed again—miserably. On October 16 he received a dispatch from Peña y Peña, acting for the Mexican Government, relieving him from all military command and informing him that his conduct of the war would be investigated.

Even after such implied censure Santa Anna produced another proclamation. It ended, "Soldiers! be faithful servants of your country! . . . Perhaps the moment is not far distant when conducted by another more fortunate chieftain, fortune will be propitious to you."

Peña y Peña's communication informed Santa Anna that he could reside anywhere in Mexico while awaiting the official inquiry—an obvious civility on the part of Peña y Peña, who was a considerate man. Santa Anna certainly could not leave Mexico. American forces held Vera Cruz and other ports, and the possibility of flight to Guatemala never went beyond a wishing stage. An appeal for asylum in the state of Oaxaca, on the way to Guatemala, received prompt rejection from Governor Benito Juárez, a liberal and Santa Anna's unswerving political and personal enemy.

Thereafter Santa Anna played virtually no part in the war, although violence continued. Guerrilla fighters attacked U. S. Army wagon trains and their accompanying escorts of soldiers traveling along the Vera Cruz –Mexico City highway and made life uncomfortable and uncertain for them. A Texas volunteer who arrived at Vera Cruz weeks after the fall of the capital wrote of his impending march with three thousand other soldiers to Mexico City, "We expect to fight the guerrillas every day till we reach . . . [Mexico City]. . . . I am fearful that some of us will die. . . ."

Occasionally guerrillas struck elsewhere, too. Some of this fighting came as a legacy from Santa Anna, who had helped to organize the guerrillas and whose disbanded troops had reinforced them. But Santa Anna himself could hope now for little more than survival—something made extremely difficult for him because of the presence in Mexico of another group of Texas Rangers attached to the U. S. Army. The Rangers saw their present situation as an opportunity to repay Santa Anna in kind for some of the atrocities he had inflicted upon Texans during their recent rebellion against Mexican rule.

The story of Antonio López de Santa Anna's last sad days in Mexico after the cessation of major fighting can best be told from the viewpoint of one of those Texas Rangers, John Salmon (Rip) Ford, whose memoirs lay unpublished in the Archives Collection of the University of Texas for sixty-six years after Ford's death in 1897. Santa Anna himself did not dwell on these details.

The narrative should begin when Ford and other members of a Texas Ranger regiment led by Colonel Jack Hays (the same officer who had commanded an earlier Ranger group under Zachary Taylor at Monterrey) entered Mexico City nearly three months after the city's surrender, to assist General Scott with his occupation of the capital. Guerrilla fighting still flared from time to time, and those Rangers could prove useful as policemen, Scott thought.

The general's staff officer, Colonel Hitchcock, thought so too. On December 6 Hitchcock watched the Texans ride into the capital and wrote, "Hays's rangers have come—their appearance never to be forgotten. Not in any sort of uniform, but well mounted and doubly well armed: each man has one or two Colt's revolvers besides ordinary pistols, a sword, and every man his rifle. All sorts of coats, blankets, and headgear, but they are strong athletic fellows. The Mexicans are terribly afraid of them." Most of the Rangers wore long beards, which contributed to a savage appearance.

Ford, regimental adjutant, added his own description of the respect paid him and his colleagues by the populace. "Our entrance into the City of Mexico produced a sensation among the inhabitants. They thronged the streets along which we passed. The greatest curiosity prevailed to get a sight [of] *los diablos Tejanos*—the Texas devils."

But the guerrilla activity continued, and it even bloodied these much-feared Rangers. Earlier, Sam Walker, the Ranger who had picked his way through Mexican lines to communicate with besieged Fort Texas for Zachary Taylor, had been killed in a skirmish outside the capital. Then one afternoon a Texan wandering alone in a section of Mexico City referred to by the Rangers as "Cutthroat" found himself surrounded by an angry mob. "He was assailed . . . and almost literally cut to pieces," Ford said. "Those who saw him said his heart was visible, and its pulsations were plainly perceptible. His horse brought him out. He lived eight hours in that dreadful condition."

Perhaps Ford had exaggerated his account of the wound, because during the man's eight extra hours of life he was able to give fellow Rangers a description of some of his attackers. That night, without the knowledge of Colonel Hays, some of the dead man's comrades re-entered "Cutthroat" and began shooting. By breakfast hour of the following morning Mexican police had collected fifty-three bodies, using a single wooden litter that was their standard equipment, and they reported that eighty more corpses lay in the morgue. Eventually Winfield Scott called Colonel Hays to answer for his men's actions, but Hays, instead of apologizing, enumerated other guerrilla attacks made on members of his regiment and declared, "The Texas Rangers are not in the habit of being insulted without resenting it." Scott passed all this off, but the general soon found duties elsewhere for the Rangers—chasing guerrillas across the Mexican countryside.

It was those duties that eventually brought the Rangers into the proximity of General Santa Anna, with an anticipation on their part and a dismay on Santa Anna's that can be imagined, considering the Rangers' work in "Cutthroat."

The Texans heard rumors that Santa Anna was hiding in Tehuacán, southeast of Puebla, possibly with a guerrilla force. Away rode Hays's men (along with a cavalry unit that included William Polk, the President's brother), eager to investigate and especially eager to look the old enemy of Texas in the eye. They rode all night and arrived at Tehuacán at four o'clock the following morning—only to discover that Santa Anna had been warned and had fled two hours earlier. In Ford's memoirs is preserved another man's description of that visit.

> . . . No noise was heard but the thunder of our horses' hoofs on the stone pavement, and the rattling clang of scabbards. All was silent. Not a living thing was in sight. Men and animals had disappeared, or were in deep sleep.
>
> We entered [Santa Anna's] deserted apartments. . . . There was a long table in a very long room. The cloth was still laid, and candles were burning. It was not yet daylight. The writer went into a long room off the dining-hall. A candle had been turned over burning, and had gone out, leaving a line of melted wax across the green covering of the writing desk. An ink-stand of crystal, with a silver top by its side, had been upset over a white satin mat, tied with pink ribbons, leaving a broad black stain across its middle, not yet dry. . . . Everything betokened the haste and hurry of flight. Seventeen packed trunks were left in a room adjoining the patio. . . .
>
> And now began the sack of the trunks. They contained everything, from a tiny slipper from the tiny foot of [Doña] Santa Anna to full court toilette; dresses by the hundreds [which were eventually returned to her]. . . . A coat of Santa Anna's, by actual test, weighed fifteen pounds, so much was it embroidered and embossed with solid gold. This was given to the State of Texas. There was a resplendent gold bullion sash of immense proportions and weight. This was sent to some other state. . . .
>
> But marvel of all, a Texas lieutenant, and . . . some privates, drew from the bottom of the trunk a long, tapering, green velvet-covered case. This was quickly opened, and from its satin cushions was taken a cane. . . . Its staff was of polished iron. Its pedestal was of gold, tipped with steel. Its head was an eagle blazing with diamonds,

436

rubies, sapphires, emeralds—an immense diamond in the eagle's beak, jewels in his claws, diamonds everywhere. The cane was a marvel of beauty.

The Texans cried out with one accord:"Give it to Colonel Jack!"

Though Hays accepted the cane, Major William H. Polk, brother of the President, expressed the desire to send it to his brother. Hays gave it to him, telling him to say that it was from the Texans.

The man who had expressed willingness to sacrifice himself for Mexico took to the road again with his entourage, willing indeed to sacrifice treasures in such an emergency, but hoping to escape the wrath of *los diablos Tejanos*. Later, after the Mexican Government had banished him from the country as punishment for his poor part in the lost war, he asked American officials for safe-conduct to go into exile in Jamaica. The same authorities who had let him enter Mexico under the assumption that he would help them now let him leave.

But Santa Anna encountered the Texas Rangers one last time before his final departure. Again, Rip Ford preserved an account of this.

Ford and other members of Hays's regiment were encamped near Jalapa when they heard that Santa Anna would be traveling down the National Road, which passed near their camp, on his way to the coast and embarkation aboard a ship.

Adjutant Ford and a major from Hays's regiment rode into Jalapa to observe Santa Anna's reception there. The two officers were still waiting when two Rangers from camp appeared and implored them to return. Colonel Hays and other officers were absent, the Rangers said, and trouble was imminent. "The men say they are going to kill General Santa Anna when he reaches there," one Ranger declared.

Ford and the major mounted immediately and rode back to camp, where they found the men heatedly discussing their plans.

> Revenge was the . . . passion of the hour [Ford wrote]. We knew the men we had to deal with. No attempts to exercise the authority of officers were made—no threats of punishment were let fall. We appealed to reason and to honor. What was said may be summed up in this [way]. The men said Gen. Santa Anna had waged an inhuman . . . war upon the people of Texas—had murdered prisoners of war in cold blood. We knew many in the crowd around us had lost relatives in the Alamo, Goliad, and elsewhere. To this [I] replied, "Yes, that is admitted, but did not the world condemn Gen. Santa

Anna for his cruel butchery of prisoners? . . . He is in his own country, and is travelling under a safe-conduct granted by our commanding general; to take his life would be an act the civilized world would brand as assassination. You would dishonor Texas! . . ."

Ford's speech persuaded the Rangers not to kill Santa Anna, but they still wanted a chance to confront their old enemy and if possible to talk with him.

Ford and other officers rejected this request, probably realizing what that talk would lead to. They told the men they would have an opportunity to look at the general as he traveled the National Road toward the coast, but they added that everyone was to maintain absolute silence.

> [A] line was formed on each side of the road [Ford said]. A courier came down . . . at a brisk gallop, and informed us that Gen. Santa Anna was nearby. Every eye was in the direction [from which he would come]. He [and] his wife . . . were in a carriage, which appeared to be an open one. All had a fair view. [I] was of the opinion that the old warrior's face blanched a little at the sight of his enemies of long standing. He might have thought of the bitter recollections these bronze and fearless men had garnered up from the past, and how easy it would be for them to strike for . . . retribution. He sat erect, not a muscle of his face moved—if his hour had come he seemed resolved to meet it as a soldier should. His wife was pretty. She bowed frequently, and a smile played upon her countenance. . . .
>
> The "ununiformed" representatives of Texas stood motionless and silent—not even a whisper disturbed the air. . . . The carriage passed on—the Mexican guard of honor marched by in good order. There were no salutations, no ungraceful remarks. . . . The Texans broke ranks and returned to camp.

Regardless of his true intentions, whatever they were, Santa Anna had left his country in a deplorable state: bankrupt, defeated, anarchic. What little government remained had moved out of the capital to Querétaro. Some Mexican liberals who viewed the apparent hopelessness even spoke of the benefits of annexation to the United States. At least they would enjoy stability and probably a fair amount of liberty—certainly more than that allowed under a countryman like the general who was now sailing for Jamaica exile.

The real tragedy of Santa Anna went far beyond his own misfortune; he brought disaster upon his whole nation. For many years Mexicans paid for Santa Anna's selfishness, egotism, and denseness. But, incredibly, they had not yet outgrown him and his ostentatious ways. Within a few years conservative leaders would be scheming to bring him back to power.

Santa Anna did not discourage such activity. Experience seemed never to teach him anything.

44.

The Perfect Tool

Except for his now wan appearance, James K. Polk was the same man who had been inaugurated: the President who controlled his Cabinet, who knew his objectives and kept after them. He continued to work as secretively as possible, without trusting many people, and those few to no great degree. Still lacking in humor and having no desire for any activity but work, he had made no new close friends—had, in fact, lost those old ones—and he devoted himself day after day to the usual drudgery.

Polk's unceasing toil had brought results and notable frustrations. Most remarkable of the frustrations continued to be those repeated intrusions of the curious and the office seekers. Polk had begun closing his office door for longer hours, but sometimes not even this device stopped the flow of humanity.

Once after he had told his porter to admit no one else a man who had evaded notice sneaked into the President's office and gave a spiel for some wine he hoped to sell Polk. Then the stranger sought to persuade the President to employ a friend of his in government work. Another time a man applied for a job and after polite questioning expressed an opinion "that he thought he would be a good hand at making treaties, and that as he understood there were some to be made soon he would like to be a minister abroad."

Polk continually fumed about the time lost listening to "voracious and often unprincipled persons who seek office" and vowed to write a book about them and their demands if time and health permitted following his retirement from office. "It is most disgusting to be compelled to spend hour after hour almost every day in hearing the applications for office made

440

by loafers who congregate in Washington, and by members of Congress in their behalf, and yet I am compelled to submit to it or offend or insult the applicants and their friends."

Meanwhile the war with Mexico dragged on, at a cost now of twenty-two million dollars annually, and four problems in particular developed there to whiten Polk's hair further. First came a new surge of anti-war sentiment in the Thirtieth Congress, which convened in December 1847. Then occurred an outbreak of peevishness and pouting among U. S. Army generals in Mexico following Scott's entry into the capital. Soon after that came the long-awaited court-martial of John C. Frémont, and it created for Polk enemies on both sides of the fuss. Finally, and extending throughout all of these difficulties, came the treaty negotiations with Mexico, which required Polk's continual attention. The negotiations became difficult, drawn-out, patience-exhausting work for several reasons. It was no wonder, then, that Polk's diary entries became more and more concerned with the end of his term and occasionally with death, although he and Sarah Polk were planning a Tennessee home for their retirement.

Pure politics became the focus of the Thirtieth Congress early in December. Whigs rallied almost unanimously against "Mr. Polk's war." The Democrats split. Whigs ranted against everything concerning the war except for the conduct of the troops and the generals, and they succeeded in getting House passage of a declaration asserting that President Polk had begun the war "unnecessarily and unconstitutionally." This actually had no vital effect, but it compounded the President's discomfort. Outside Congress, individualists like Henry Thoreau denounced the war ever more forcefully. The nation seemed to be breaking into pieces.

More splits within the Democratic Party developed to hound Polk. With the fighting obviously drawing to a close—but with no peace immediately in prospect—some Democratic congressmen now wanted to annex all of Mexico. Some wanted little or no land at all. Others wanted laws to keep slavery out of territories annexed. Still others wanted slavery to expand wherever it could. Polk's own Secretary of State, James Buchanan (that presidential aspirant known for his about-faces in behalf of potential vote-getting), advised the President to take more territory than he had planned originally—this despite Buchanan's initial desire to take from Mexico no land at all. Polk had needed a short war to avoid administration catastrophe, and this conflict verged on lasting entirely too long.

On October 20 the President had heard of Scott's entry into Mexico City. Considering the grim circumstances at home, this was good news indeed, especially after Polk had brooded over the earlier armistice (of which he had never approved, correctly believing that Santa Anna intended to use it for strengthening defenses). In the two months and ten days that followed the fall of Mexico City, however, Polk heard nothing of a peaceful settlement. Instead he received dismaying news about the antics of some of his generals in Mexico. All of the trouble apparently began with wording in official battle reports, and it involved petty jealousies.

General Scott had dispatched to General Pillow a few criticisms of Pillow's reports of the battles of "Contreras"—Padierna—and Chapultepec. Scott felt that Pillow had understated (as indeed he had) the part played by the commanding general—Scott—at "Contreras," and had sought to leave the senior commander entirely out of the Chapultepec battle. Pillow revised his reports, but two weeks later the feud boiled over again with an accusation by Scott that Pillow had taken as souvenirs of Chapultepec two small fieldpieces. A court of inquiry requested by the furious Pillow found that the general had not taken the guns himself, but because of laxness on his part someone had made off with the cannon for a time, until Scott ordered them returned. Pillow refused to accept this finding as accurate.

While Scott and Pillow glowered at each other there arrived from the United States editions of newspapers containing a series of anonymous letters describing military operations prior to the surrender of Mexico City and in each case belittling General Scott's role in the battles. In the New Orleans *Picayune* of September 16, 1847, appeared a letter (signed "Leonidas") that declared Pillow had been in sole command during the "Contreras" battle, where he had evinced "that masterly military genius and profound knowledge of the science of war, which has astonished so much the mere martinets of the profession." Soon after that copies of another newspaper—this one published in Tampico—created another uproar by carrying a letter (which originally appeared in the Pittsburgh *Post*) that declared the march southward around Lake Chalco had been the sole idea of General Worth—not Scott.

This time Scott issued an angry order calling attention to the army regulation prohibiting writing letters for publication. He concluded his instruction with an implied accusation that Pillow and Worth themselves had written the letters. This put the dispute beyond any hope of local solution. Later the officer who had originally reconnoitered the Lake Chalco area, Lieutenant Colonel James Duncan, admitted writing the letter about Worth, but Scott ordered all three officers—Duncan, Pillow, and Worth—relieved of duties and placed under arrest for a variety of easy-to-find reasons centering around insubordination.

The long-suffering President heard the details of all this on December 30. Characteristically, he blamed a Whig, Scott, for the difficulties, although Scott himself had suffered long and often unfairly at the hands of this very Democratic Administration. Scott had just completed a remarkable campaign into the heart of an enemy country, having under his command comparatively few troops and facing formidable obstacles and odds, to give Polk his chance to negotiate a peace. Throughout the campaign Scott had been burdened by having to rely on political officers like this same General Pillow, former law partner of the President, who had scant knowledge of military tactics but who also had great ambition for command, and by envious officers like General Worth, who was professional enough but who also harbored jealousy of Scott's seniority. But Scott himself could be petty about small things, too, as everyone knew. Now Polk blamed the entire problem on this trait.

"I deplore the unfortunate collisions which have arisen between the general officers in Mexico, as they must prove highly prejudicial to the public service," Polk wrote a few hours after he had first learned of Scott's action. "They must have been produced, as I have every reason to believe, more by the vanity and tyrannical temper of General Scott, and his want of prudence and common sense, than from any other cause."

Polk concluded that Scott himself should be relieved of command and the general's own conduct examined by a military court. The President appointed General William O. Butler, a Democrat, to succeed Scott in Mexico—an action that would antagonize most of the Regular Army personnel there.

(None of the charges ruined any military careers, as it developed. Those against Worth and Duncan eventually were dropped. A court of inquiry decided that Pillow had claimed a larger degree of participation at "Contreras" than facts warranted, but that general received no punishment. Scott returned to the United States a hero to too many Americans, and the charges against him were dropped.)

Another court-martial made Polk more enemies. John C. Frémont was tried on charges of mutiny, disobedience of orders, and conduct prejudicial to the public service during his California feud with General Kearny. Some of Frémont's trouble certainly had stemmed from the ambiguity of the President's own orders, but Polk (who rarely admitted failings and perhaps recognized them even less often) commented, "I regretted the whole affair but had no agency in producing the difficulty."

The trial dragged on for three months. When it ended on the last day of January 1848, Frémont was found guilty on all three counts and was sentenced to dismissal from the service. But the court added a recommendation for executive clemency.

Senator Thomas Hart Benton, who had helped to defend his son-in-law, erupted in anger that did not vanish with the passage of time. Nor did the President's attempt to lessen the severity of the findings placate the senator. Polk, with the concurrence of the Cabinet, approved the sentence except for mutiny (which seemed to him not to have been proved), then remitted the penalty and ordered Frémont restored to duty.

But the forever impetuous Frémont resigned from the Army, and Benton resigned as chairman of the Senate Military Affairs Committee, a position he had held for twenty years, to make his own war on the U. S. Army and on Polk.

"The decision in this case has been a painful and a responsible duty," the President remarked after it was over. "I have performed it with the best lights before me, and am satisfied with what I have done."

Benton never appreciated Polk's soul searching. Three months later the President noted in his diary, "I meet Col. Benton almost every Sabbath at church, but he never speaks to me as he was in the habit of doing before the trial of Col. Frémont."

The greatest test of presidential patience, however, came from Mexican peace negotiations. Polk could only follow this activity from afar, and only after a delay of weeks in receiving communications.

For a time after the fall of the capital Mexico had no government with which the United States could negotiate. Peña y Peña acted as President, but he lacked power to treat with American peace commissioners. Until November no quorum appeared at the temporary capital of Querétaro to enable the Mexican Congress to operate. Even when a quorum assembled the members became badly split between those favoring peace and those who wanted to continue the war: Mexico divided, as always.

Finally, on the eleventh of that month, the Mexican Congress elected

Pedro María Anaya President ad interim. Anaya showed himself to be inclined toward peace. He named Peña y Peña Minister of Foreign Relations and on November 22 appointed commissioners to talk with Nicholas Trist.

In Washington, Polk knew nothing of these events as they happened. Before hearing of the surrender of Mexico City he had determined to recall Trist, for several reasons. The man had not followed instructions, and he seemed to the distrustful President to have been acting too closely in conjunction with General Scott. But the main reason Polk gave for Trist's recall was that Mexico had not taken advantage of his presence to negotiate seriously. "Mr. Trist is recalled because his remaining longer with the army could not, probably, accomplish the objects of his mission, and because his remaining longer might, and probably would, impress the Mexican Government with the belief that the United States were so anxious for peace that they would ultimately conclude one upon the Mexican terms. Mexico must now first sue for peace, and when she does we will hear her propositions."

Polk did not change his mind after learning of the surrender of Mexico City. On the day after that, October 21, his anger even soared to new heights when he received dispatches indicating that his commissioner had been entertaining some idea in the recently interrupted peace discussions of setting a Texas boundary at the Nueces River.

Now the President had a new scapegoat for attack in diary entries. "Mr. Trist has managed the negotiation very bunglingly and with no ability." Probably Trist had sought the counsel of that villainous Whig general down there, Polk reflected, and the two of them had conspired to embarrass the Administration.

Unknown to the seething President, the order to return to Washington (dated October 6) reached Trist about the time President Anaya expressed willingness to negotiate. Nevertheless, Trist at first began to make plans to depart, and he so informed the Mexican Government.

While Trist waited for transportation to Vera Cruz the Mexicans pleaded with him to stay. The commissioner saw his duty in a new light. He determined to ignore the summons from Washington. He would remain where he was and would negotiate that treaty. Otherwise the possibility for peace might be lost for a long, long time.

Polk heard (on January 4, 1848) of Trist's decision with astonishment. "Mr. Trist has acknowledged the receipt of his letter of recall, and he possesses no diplomatic powers. . . . He has become the perfect tool of Scott. He is, in this measure, defying the authority of his Government. He may, I fear, greatly embarrass the Government."

On January 15 Polk read with more rage a letter some sixty pages long from the daring former commissioner to Secretary of State Buchanan explaining in some forceful language his reasons for staying and what he hoped to accomplish.

> It was dated on the 6th of December last [Polk said] and is the most extraordinary document I have ever heard from a diplomatic representative. Though [Trist] had in a previous despatch acknowledged the receipt of his letter of recall from the Secretary of State, he announced that he had re-opened negotiations with the Mexican authorities and had resolved to conclude a treaty with them. His despatch is arrogant, impudent, and very insulting to his government, and even personally offensive to the President. He admits he is acting without authority and in violation of the positive order recalling him. . . . I have never in my life felt so indignant, and the whole Cabinet expressed themselves as I felt. I told Mr. Buchanan that the paper was so insulting and contemptibly base, that it required no lengthy answer, but that it did require a short, but stern and decided rebuke, and directed him to prepare such a reply. I directed the Secretary of War to write at once to Major-General Butler, directing him, if Mr. Trist was still with the Headquarters of the army, to order him off, and to inform the authorities of Mexico that he had no authority to treat. . . . He has acted worse than any man in the public employ whom I have ever known. His despatch proves that he is destitute of honour or principle, and that he has proved himself to be a very base man. . . .

Little more than one month later a formal treaty of peace negotiated by Nicholas Trist and signed by Mexican commissioners at Guadalupe Hidalgo on February 2, 1848, arrived in Washington. James Freaner, a war correspondent for the New Orleans *Delta*, delivered the document at Trist's request to Secretary of State Buchanan when Freaner arrived in the capital from Mexico late Saturday evening, February 19.

Buchanan hurried over to the Executive Mansion with the astonishing paper. Its terms followed almost exactly those outlined by Polk when he ordered Trist to Mexico months earlier. Most importantly, it delineated a boundary the President had sought. For this the United States would give Mexico $15 million and would assume responsibility for paying those claims of American citizens up to a total of $3.25 million—a figure sufficient to spare Mexico any expense there.

The treaty covered other agreements: American troops were to be withdrawn in a specified time, and Mexicans living in lands acquired by the United States were to become eligible for American citizenship. But the momentous part of the treaty was the fifth article.

> . . . The boundary line between the two republics shall commence in the Gulf of Mexico, three leagues from land, opposite the mouth of the Rio Grande, otherwise called Rio Bravo del Norte, or opposite the mouth of its deepest branch, if it should have more than one branch emptying directly into the sea; from thence up the middle of that river, following the deepest channel, where it has more than one, to the point where it strikes the southern boundary of New Mexico; thence, westwardly, along the whole southern boundary of New Mexico (which runs north of the town called *Paso*) to its western termination; thence northward along the western line of New Mexico, until it intersects the first branch of the river Gila; (or if it should not intersect any branch of that river, then to the point on the said line nearest to such branch, and thence in a direct line to the same;) thence down the middle of the said branch and of the said river, until it empties into the Rio Colorado; thence across the Rio Colorado, following the division line between Upper and Lower California, to the Pacific Ocean.

Thus Polk not only had secured Texas, but he had also acquired the vast expanse of land between that new state and the Pacific Coast—including what would become the states of New Mexico, Arizona, California, Nevada, and Utah, and significant parts of Wyoming and Colorado. Mexico lost half of its territory, and with the later sale of land through the Gadsden Purchase the United States-Mexico boundary would be fixed as it stands today.

Some cabinet members called to an extraordinary meeting on the day (a Sunday) following receipt of the treaty favored rejecting any agreement tainted by Trist's hand. But Polk sent it to the Senate for a decision, and immediately thereafter he began to voice anxiety about its reception. "Extremes sometimes meet and act effectively for negative purposes," Polk remarked, "but never for affirmative purposes. They have done so in this instance. Mr. [Daniel] Webster is for *no* territory and Mr. [Edward] Hannigan is for *all* Mexico, and for opposite reasons both will oppose the treaty." At least one senator, Benton, opposed it largely out of hatred for the President. But the Senate passed the treaty on March 10 by a 38–14 vote, making only minor changes, and returned it to Mexico, where ratification there soon followed.

On July 4, 1848, President Polk planned to attend ceremonies that would accompany the laying of the cornerstone of the Washington Monument. His health had slipped again recently, but he felt compelled by duty to make an appearance.

At ten o'clock the Cabinet assembled at the Executive Mansion to accompany him. Polk recorded the historic event.

> . . . escorted by . . . the United States marshall of the District of Columbia, and his deputies, and by a troop of horse commanded by Col. [Charles] May [the questionable hero of Resaca de la Palma] . . . we were conducted in carriages to the City Hall, where the procession was formed and moved to the site of the Washington Monument on the banks of the Potomac and south of the President's Mansion. I witnessed the ceremony of laying the cornerstone, and heard an address delivered by Mr. Speaker [Robert] Winthrop of the House of Representatives.

Polk returned to the Executive Mansion, reviewed (at the request of General John A. Quitman of Mexican War fame) another troop of horse drawn up in Pennsylvania Avenue, and soon after that received from a messenger just arrived from Mexico the United States Government copy of the Treaty of Guadalupe Hidalgo.

Polk—a strong President, no matter what might be said about mediocrity—now had reached all the previously set goals of his Administration, although his ethics had been questioned by many persons. The only result of this criticism, and even of the House declaration that the war was unconstitutional, had been to add more lines in Polk's withering face, perhaps to take a few years off his life, and to leave many Americans wondering about the openness and honesty of their President. The condemnation never caused Polk to change his course or to loosen his hold on presidential power. Only impeachment could have pried that power loose, and Congress never ventured to try it.

A quick-tongued Whig from Georgia, Alexander Stephens, spoke for many Americans when he remarked after the war, "Why, if a man were ambitious of acquiring a reputation for duplicity and equivocation, he could not select a better example in all history than to follow in the footsteps of our President. He did not know any better fitting appellation in after times, than Polk the mendacious!"

Call him anything—Polk had come through as he had said he would and always intended. But those political battles, frustrations, enmities, and declining health permitted him scant rejoicing. For months his diary had been reflecting a somber mood, and the tone remained.

> *Tuesday, 2nd November, 1847.*—I am fifty-two years old today, this being my birthday. I have now passed through two-thirds of my Presidential term, and most heartily wish that the remaining third was over, for I am sincerely desirous to have the enjoyment of retirement in private life.
>
> . . .
>
> *Monday, 14 August, 1848.*—I am heartily rejoiced that the session of Congress is over. My long confinement and great labour has exceedingly exhausted me, and I feel the absolute necessity of having some rest. I have not been three miles from the President's mansion since my return from my tour through the Eastern States in June and July, 1847, a period of more than thirteen months. . . .
>
> . . .
>
> *Thursday, 2nd November, 1848.*—This is my birthday . . . fifty-three years old. It will be twenty-one years on tomorrow since my father died. My mother is still living. Upon each recurrence of my birthday I am solemnly impressed with the vanity and emptiness of worldly honours and worldly enjoyments, and of the wisdom of preparing for a future estate. In four months I shall retire from public life forever. I have lived three-fourths of the period ordinarily allotted to man on earth. I have been highly honoured by my fellow-men and have filled the highest station on earth, but I will soon go the way of all earth. I pray God to prepare me to meet the great event.
>
> . . .
>
> *Tuesday, 13th February, 1849.*—It is four years ago this day since I arrived in Washington, preparatory to entering on my duties as President of the United States on the 4th of March following. They have been four years of incessant labour and anxiety and of great responsibility. I am heartily rejoiced that my term is so near its close. I will soon cease to be a servant and will become a sovereign. . . .

That July 4, 1848, when President Polk witnessed the laying of the Washington Monument cornerstone he also witnessed, with the arrival of that treaty-bearing messenger from Mexico, the laying of a foundation of a great continental nation—one that would extend from Atlantic to

Pacific and, with that subsequent Gadsden Purchase addition, would encompass the famous "forty-eight states," as they were to become known.

It was President Polk's work, although he never received any outburst of acclaim for it. American moralists continued to denounce the acquisition of Mexican territory, although numbers of them later sought to find fortunes there. Anti-slavery people continued to regard Polk as a Southerner whose main hope had been to extend the limits of that "peculiar institution," although Polk knew (and cared not) that slavery never would be feasible in the Far West. Some members of his own party looked upon him as softheaded for not taking all of Mexico when he had the chance. A movement toward annexing all of Mexico actually had been gaining strength among impatient expansionists when Trist's treaty arrived, and one newspaper editor had declared, "Like the Sabine virgins, [Mexico] will soon learn to love her ravishers."

It had all been Polk's work, and if the thanks of his countrymen tended toward stinginess for a variety of reasons, at least Polk had his own compensation. When he left the Executive Mansion to the occupancy of that Whig general, Zachary Taylor (who had been elected, ironically, with the help of a wave of reaction against the Mexican War), Polk was as glad to see the last of the President's office as his critics were glad to see him go.

EPILOGUE

The Mournful War

Mexican citizens lamented the loss of their land that resulted from the war with the United States. They developed an increased distrust and dislike of Americans—feelings that lingered through the years and are still evident occasionally today. Still, many thoughtful Mexicans also blamed themselves, their countrymen, and contemporary Mexican society for at least part of the tragedy.

A Mexican veteran of the conflict remarked, "To contemplate the state of degradation and ruin to which the mournful war with the United States has reduced the Republic, is painful. . . . It is to be hoped that the hard lesson which we have received will teach us to reform our conduct. . . . There [remains] in our hearts a feeling of sadness for the evils that [the war] . . . produced, and in our minds a fruitful lesson of how difficult it is when disorder, asperity, and anarchy prevail, to uphold the defence and salvation of a people."

Few Mexicans disagreed with that observer's theory of the real cause of the war—"the insatiable ambition of the United States, favored by our weakness. . . . They desired from the beginning to extend their dominion in such a manner as to become the absolute owners of almost all this continent."

Not even President Polk could have disputed that statement, although his Secretary of State, James Buchanan, declared euphemistically at the very beginning of fighting (on May 14, 1846): "We go to War with Mexico solely for the purpose of conquering an honorable and just peace. Whilst we intend to prosecute the War with vigor . . . we shall

451

bear the olive branch in one hand, and the sword in the other; and whenever she will accept the former, we shall sheath the latter."

Although the war left the Mexican Government a shambles, the conflict resulted also in a perceptible (if at first barely noticeable) stir of genuine Mexican nationalism—a concern for the country. Monterrey residents (as that quoted Mexican writer had observed) rose to defend not only their city but the nation against Zachary Taylor's invasion, although (as the same writer added) they owed so little to Mexico City. In California, where revolt against Mexican rule previously had occurred, Castro and Pico eventually pooled their resources to battle the Americans (even if unsuccessfully) in behalf of the homeland. And at Chapultepec the legend of heroic defense by *los niños héroes* came into being and is still commemorated today. Many more years, pronouncements, and coups would take place before stable and responsible government could emerge in Mexico, but experience gained and attitudes developed in the war helped some, and—ironically—the loss to the United States of Upper California and other outlying areas, lands always difficult to govern because of their remoteness, resolved a few problems of administration.

Some 120 years after the end of the war the President of Mexico would be known to many persons as a dynamic, concerned official who visited every section of his sprawling country looking into domestic problems and who devoted himself with the same energy to improving Mexican foreign relations. The "time-worn stereotype of the lethargic Mexican, slouched at the base of a great cactus . . . [and] sleeping in the shade of his own sombrero" had been largely shattered.

That lazy image of the Latin American, however, was slow to fade from the minds of United States citizens, who continued to display feelings of racial and religious superiority long after the war with Mexico. Their attitudes, backed up whenever necessary for international purposes by the Monroe and Polk doctrines, made their country into the guiding adult of the Western Hemisphere and the nations of Latin America the children. Whenever the children became unruly they were spanked—by United States marines or other American military forces, who occupied the countries concerned until the youngsters there learned to behave themselves.

General John J. Pershing, commanding the U. S. Army in a 1916 chase across the Mexican countryside of Pancho Villa with the reluctant permission of a weak Mexican Government (after Villa's raid into New Mexico), sought settlement remindful of 1846–48 thinking. Unable to catch Villa, Pershing decided that the best method of bringing stability and peace to the southwestern border of the United States was to conquer the entire Mexican Republic—from where the troublemakers always came—and he suggested this to Washington. "Any assemblage of Mexicans . . . would be without intelligent leadership or organization, and their easy defeat by this command would be certain," Pershing advised. "Any army they can muster would be nothing but a mob without training or discipline and with little courage and not to be feared in the slightest."

Calmer minds prevailed. In Washington, President Wilson never considered the plan, calling the 1846–48 war with Mexico a blot on American honor that should not be repeated and declaring that all people—Mexicans included—have the right to do as they please with their own affairs. Nevertheless, Pershing spoke openly for many privately thinking Americans; and the fact that he was in Mexico in the first place with Woodrow Wilson's approval showed something else about the President's own attitude.

Today, after many other well-known disputes subsequent to the war have flared, a spirit of governmental co-operation has largely replaced the old antagonisms. The United States and Mexico work together officially in many areas—like flood control on the Rio Grande and the use of water there. And in a 1968 ceremony the United States even returned some land to Mexico—token acreage only, and it did not change the boundary as settled by the Treaty of Guadalupe Hidalgo and the 1853 Gadsden Purchase (of thirty thousand square miles in present Arizona and New Mexico for ten million dollars), but it served to soothe Mexican pride.

The surrendered land lay in an area near El Paso known as El Chamizal, which in 1864 had been transferred from the Mexican to the United States side of the border when the Rio Grande changed course permanently after a flood. Following a century of bickering, the two countries signed a Chamizal Convention (in December 1963), providing for the return of the 630 disputed acres to Mexico, for the building of a concrete channel to keep the Rio Grande where it should have been since 1864, and for the erection of three highway bridges and two railroad spans across the river. Total cost of the construction projects would amount to $78 million (more than five times what the United States had paid for

453

Upper California and all that other territory in 1848). Each nation would pay half the cost. The two Presidents signed the agreement— Lyndon Johnson for the United States and Adolfo López Mateos for Mexico.

Five years later, when the channel was officially opened, President Johnson (whose own war was elsewhere) remarked at the ceremony:

"The international boundary of Mexico and the United States was changed without a shot being fired, without the massing of troops on frontiers, without an exchange of threats through respective embassies.

"The finest thing I know to say about both countries, both Presidents, and both peoples is that we have no armies patrolling our borders. We have confidence in each other and peace with one another."

Gustavo Díaz Ordaz, then President of Mexico, responded. "It is my hope that the children of today [both Mexican and American] . . . will be able to get together at any point on our border and speak of the friendship that exists between them."

El Chamizal, however, included only 630 acres of land. The United States still retained its southwestern domain, and that acquisition had left many permanent marks on the country.

Americans, who were known for their mobility even at an earlier time, became more mobile. In a book (*Notes on a Journey in America*) published in London in 1818 an English observer had written, "[Americans] are . . . a migratory people and even when in prosperous circumstances can contemplate a change of situation which, under our old establishment and fixed habits, none but the most enterprising would venture upon when urged by adversity." With the continent now opened all the way to the Pacific Coast, Americans possessed broader spaces to roam, and since all that land had fallen under the jurisdiction of their own government they would encounter no political boundaries to slow or block their way.

The territorial acquisition compounded the American tendency to waste resources. Consider what happened to the buffalo in those new lands, which seemed for many decades to be so expansive and (in many places) so productive they would last forever. Under those sublime conditions thoughts of conservation never intruded.

Similarly, the expansion compounded American materialism. The story of the 1848 discovery of gold on John Sutter's land in California and of its effects is well known. And in ensuing years there were other riches besides gold to be found in the new territory.

The end of the war brought a large population of Spanish-speaking people into the United States. In time Los Angeles would become known as second only to Mexico City in numbers of residents of Mexican ancestry. By the latter part of the twentieth century Spanish-speaking citizens of the United States would number fifteen million; and 15 per cent of the nation's businesses would be owned by persons of Spanish origin. But many others of that ancestry would live in poverty that required answers to many problems.

The war with Mexico resulted in the first real flexing of American muscles. The United States emerged as a country on its way to becoming a genuine world power—and history shows that any nation that has power uses it. Possessing a long coastline on the Pacific as well as the Atlantic, the United States began looking more closely at Asian developments, with the results that history already has recorded.

The most immediate notable effect on the United States of the war with Mexico, however, was the inexorable advancement of the Civil War. Until President Polk's term most politicians had sought to avoid inflaming the slavery issue. Polk himself, of course, tried to avoid clashes, too. Toward the end of his presidency (on December 22, 1848) he wrote in his diary:

> The agitation of the slavery question is mischievous and wicked, and proceeds from no patriotic motive by its authors. It is a mere political question on which demagogues and ambitious politicians hope to promote their own prospects for political promotion. And this they seem willing to do even at the hazard of disturbing the harmony if not dissolving the Union itself. Such agitation with such objects deserves the reprobation of all the lovers of the Union and of their country. . . .

But the issue could not be ignored. The argument over the Wilmot Proviso and the other distrust and disputes that stemmed from the war with Mexico increased the tensions and eventually broke all reins. Polk would have served his own generation, and the following one, better by devoting himself to the slavery question; but he did not do so. The four Presidents who followed (before Lincoln's inauguration) could not ignore the question, but time was running out. Zachary Taylor (elected for the 1849–53 term) proved to be an ordinary President, a man propelled into a position (to which he brought little aptitude and experience) by ambition ignited by admirers of his military career. When Taylor died in 1850 Vice-President Millard Fillmore succeeded him, ineptly. Franklin Pierce (1853–57), a Democrat and a former general in the war with Mexico, defeated Whig Winfield Scott for the presidency and made an unsuccessful attempt to resolve the slavery crisis. Democrat James Buchanan (1857–61), Polk's frustrating Secretary of State, defeated Republican John C. Frémont for the office and sought to pacify the South, which was becoming increasingly secession-minded, but he satisfied no one in the controversy that had been heated by those flames from the Mexican War. It might be said, then, that the American blood which flowed so plentifully within two decades of the signing of the Treaty of Guadalupe Hidalgo served to pay for the lands that Mexican soldiers could not defend.

The individuals used as major characters for telling this story of the war lived out their lives this way:

Sam French, the artillery lieutenant wounded at Buena Vista, resigned from the U. S. Army in 1856. Although he was a New Jersey native, he moved to the South and he believed the Southern contention about the right to secede from the Union. Later he served as a general in the Confederate Army. Toward the end of his life (in 1895, at the age of seventy-seven) he wrote his memoirs, mostly for the benefit of children and grandchildren. The recollections were published in book form in 1901.

Sam Grant became known, of course, as General Ulysses Grant and acquired something of a reputation in the Civil War for willingness to take heavy casualties—in contrast to that Mexican War plan of his to save American blood at Mexico City. As Republican President (1869–77) he directed an Administration famous (or infamous) for corruption, although Grant himself escaped with his personal reputation intact. Four days before his death in 1885 he finished writing his memoirs; these were later published by Mark Twain.

Ephraim Kirby Smith fell mortally wounded in the Mexican War, and his death has been narrated.

Antonio López de Santa Anna received yet another call from certain of his countrymen to return from exile to the administration of Mexican Government. On April 20, 1853, he became President for the eleventh (and last) time. He sold the United States all that territory specified in the Gadsden Purchase, and this, with his other usual indiscretions, angered Mexicans again and propelled him out of office. After further periods of exile he was allowed to return home to live his last days. He died—penniless, alone, ridiculed in his old age by the Mexican press—on June 20, 1876, at the age of eighty-one. No national monuments sprang up in memory of the man.

James K. Polk, after leaving the Executive Mansion, looked forward to years of retirement in Tennessee with his wife Sarah. But the presidency had ruined his health, and sickness felled him. He died in Nashville on June 15, 1849, three months after leaving Washington.

Ethan Allen Hitchcock could have had a U. S. Army field command during the Civil War—probably the one that eventually went to Ulysses Grant—but poor health continued to plague him, and his wartime service was limited to advising President Lincoln and Secretary of War Stanton on military matters. Later Hitchcock moved to Sparta, Georgia, when advised by doctors to find a warm climate, and he died there August 5, 1870. He was buried at the United States Military Academy.

John C. Frémont returned to California after resigning from the Army and became a wealthy man—and one of the state's first senators, before losing the 1856 presidential race as the first nominee of the new Republican Party. During the Civil War he was commissioned again in the U. S. Army, but not successfully. Impetuous decisions as commander of the Western Department at St. Louis helped to bring about his removal there, and later failures in Virginia against Stonewall Jackson caused him to resign again in 1862. After that he devoted most of his time to developing his California holdings, until his death on July 13, 1890.

John T. Hughes, the schoolteacher who volunteered to serve with the Missouri regiment commanded by Colonel Doniphan, returned to Liberty, Missouri, after the Mexican War and married Mary Lucinda Carpenter there in August 1848. After a period of government employment and work as a Missouri legislator (elected as a Whig) he served as colonel with a Confederate force during the Civil War and was killed in fighting August 11, 1862, at the age of forty-six.

Joseph Warren Revere resigned from the Navy in 1850 because of slow promotions and began ranching near Sonoma, California. During the Civil War he volunteered for service, stating a preference for the Navy. The Army took him instead and gave him a commission as brigadier general. As senior officer of a division at Chancellorsville during severe fighting on May 3, 1863, he learned that his men were short of ammunition and lacked rations altogether. Without orders he moved them three miles to the rear, until General Sickles ordered the division back and relieved Revere of command. Later Revere received a court-martial and dismissal, but President Lincoln revoked the sentence and instead accepted his resignation. Revere died at Busche's Hotel, Hoboken, New Jersey, on April 20, 1880.

Robert E. Lee refused appointment as commander of the U. S. Army to work for a Southern victory in the Civil War. After surrender he became president of Washington College in Lexington, Virginia (now Washington and Lee), and urged Southern acceptance of defeat and restoration of the Union. He died October 12, 1870.

These and other individuals, both Mexican and American, who fought the war vanished from the earth long ago. But the spirit of war remains and is likely to linger indefinitely unless something miraculous reshapes human nature.

In 1972 a group of Texas farmers who owned land near the Mexican border strung barbed wire and planted sections of telephone poles at strategic locations to block off access to the proposed site of a music festival calculated to attract thousands of mostly unwanted visitors who would no doubt trespass on adjoining land. In their eagerness to erect barricades the farmers also cut off access to a neighborhood church (with the permission of that church, as later reports had it).

A newspaper reporter asked one farmer how church members would be able to enter the building for Sunday worship. The man's reply indicated the selfishness and the lack of empathy of too many human beings the world over—faults that have resulted in wars since man first inhabited the earth.

"Oh well," he replied, "it's just a Mexican church."

CHRONOLOGY
OF IMPORTANT EVENTS

1845

July
4 Texas accepts United States annexation proposal.
25 Zachary Taylor takes army to Corpus Christi; U.S. fleet cruises off Mexican ports awaiting war.

August
16 John C. Frémont, Kit Carson, and exploring party leave Bent's Fort for Pacific Coast.

October
15 Herrera government in Mexico offers to receive a United States "commissioner" to discuss differences, provided U.S. fleet is withdrawn.
17 U. S. Consul Thomas Larkin in California told to oppose any attempt by a foreign power to take over the country; U. S. Pacific Squadron already operates under orders to occupy California ports in event of war.

November
30 John Slidell arrives Vera Cruz on peace mission as "minister."

December
9 Frémont and his exploring party reach Sutter's Fort in California.
16 Herrera government refuses to receive Slidell as "minister"—only as "commissioner."
29 Texas formally becomes twenty-eighth state in the Union.
31 Herrera deposed as President of Mexico.

1846

January

4 Mariano Paredes becomes President of Mexico with vow to defend Texas to the Sabine River.

12 Polk hears of Slidell's rejection as "minister."

13 Washington orders Taylor to advance to the Rio Grande; U.S. fleet ordered back to stations off Mexican ports.

March

4 Frémont and his men dig in atop Hawk's Peak in California, having been ordered out of the country by Don José Castro.

9 Frémont retires northward from Hawk's Peak, eventually reaching Oregon.

21 Slidell receives final and firm rejection and returns to the United States.

28 Taylor arrives on the Rio Grande.

April

17 Marine Lieutenant Gillespie arrives Monterey, California, with instructions for Consul Larkin and Frémont.

23 U. S. Congress votes to terminate joint occupation (with Britain) of Oregon.

25 Mexican cavalry attacks U.S. force under Captain Thornton on north side of Rio Grande.

May

8 Battle of Palo Alto.

9 Battle of Resaca de la Palma. In Oregon, Gillespie overtakes Frémont, who turns back toward California.

11 Polk sends war message to Congress; Houses passes war bill.

12 Senate passes war bill.

13 Polk signs bill declaring war on Mexico.

15 General Stephen W. Kearny ordered to command Army of the West into New Mexico and California.

17 General Mariano Arista begins two-day evacuation of Matamoros; Taylor occupies city.

June

5 Kearny's Army of the West begins leaving Fort Leavenworth—immediate destination, Santa Fe.

14 Bear Flag revolt by American settlers in California.
15 British offer for ending Oregon dispute accepted by United States.

July
 1 Mexico formally declares war on United States.
 5 Commander Mackenzie visits exiled General Santa Anna in Havana.
 6 General Taylor begins advance up the Rio Grande from Matamoros.
 7 Commodore Sloat occupies Monterey, California.
14 Taylor occupies Camargo.
23 Commodore Stockton relieves Sloat as commander of U. S. Pacific Squadron.

August
 6 Salas becomes acting President of Mexico after Paredes deposed.
10 Bill appropriating two million dollars in quest for peace dies in U. S. Senate as congressional session ends; Wilmot Proviso had been attached.
12 Commodore Stockton occupies Los Angeles.
16 Santa Anna lands at Vera Cruz, ending exile.
18 Army of the West under Kearny occupies Santa Fe.
19 Taylor commences advance on Monterrey from Camargo.

September
14 Santa Anna enters Mexico City, returns to military command.
22 Californians rebel against U.S. occupation.
24 U.S. forces under Taylor take Monterrey after four-day battle.
25 General Wool leaves San Antonio for Chihuahua; General Kearny and dragoons leave New Mexico for California.
30 U.S. garrison at Los Angeles surrenders.

October
 8 Santa Anna arrives at San Luis Potosí on way to challenge General Taylor.
29 General Wool's army occupies Monclova.

November
14 Commodore Conner occupies Tampico.
16 General Taylor occupies Saltillo.
18 Winfield Scott appointed commander of the projected Vera Cruz invasion.

December
 5 General Wool occupies Parras, having given up march on Chihuahua.
 6 Mexican Congress names Santa Anna President, Farías Vice-President. In California, Battle of San Pascual is loss for General Kearny.

461

12 Kearny reaches San Diego with the assistance of Stockton. In New Mexico, Doniphan commences march on Chihuahua.
21 Wool's army arrives at Saltillo, joins Taylor.
25 Doniphan wins Battle of El Brazito.
27 Doniphan occupies El Paso; on the Gulf Coast, General Scott arrives at the Brazos.

1847

January
3 Scott seeks unsuccessfully to meet Taylor at Camargo, requisitions troops from him.
4 Taylor enters Victoria.
8 Californians lose Battle of San Gabriel.
10 Commodore Stockton reoccupies Los Angeles.
13 Frémont and Californians agree on treaty ending rebellion against U.S. occupation.
14 Taylor abandons Victoria, sends requisitioned troops to Scott at Tampico, and himself returns to Monterrey.
28 Santa Anna and his army leave San Luis Potosí to challenge Taylor.

February
5 Taylor moves his army beyond Saltillo, to Agua Nueva.
8 Doniphan marches on Chihuahua from El Paso.
15 Scott leaves Texas coast for Vera Cruz invasion.
21 Taylor moves back to Buena Vista from Agua Nueva.
22 Two-day Battle of Buena Vista begins.
27 Revolt against Farías erupts in Mexico City.
28 Doniphan wins Battle of the Sacramento.

March
1 Doniphan occupies Chihuahua.
9 U.S. forces land below Vera Cruz.
21 Santa Anna, again in Mexico City, takes oath as President.
29 Vera Cruz surrenders.

April
1 Anaya becomes President ad interim of Mexico while Santa Anna again engages in military duties.
8 Scott begins moving army inland from Vera Cruz.
15 Nicholas Trist appointed commissioner to seek peace with Mexico.
18 Battle of Cerro Gordo.

20 Mexican Congress prohibits treating with the U.S., although it grants Santa Anna power almost unlimited otherwise.

22 General Worth's army occupies Perote, on the way to Mexico City.

28 Doniphan's men leave Chihuahua for Saltillo, Monterrey, and transportation to the United States for discharge.

May

4 Scott returns twelve-month volunteers to Vera Cruz early for transportation home and discharge.

7 Beginning of Scott-Trist feud.

15 Worth occupies Puebla, farther along the road to Mexico City.

22 Santa Anna again takes up duties of President.

28 Scott moves headquarters to Puebla.

June

25 Scott and Trist end their feud.

August

7 U.S. forces march on Mexico City from Puebla.

19 Two days of fighting commence around Padierna, mistakenly called "Battle of Contreras" in U.S. accounts.

20 Battle of Churubusco.

24 Armistice proclaimed at Tacubaya for peace negotiations.

September

6 Tacubaya armistice ends in failure.

8 Battle of Molino del Rey.

13 Chapultepec stormed and captured by U.S. forces; two fortified gates into Mexico City also taken.

14 Scott's army commences occupation of Mexico City.

16 Santa Anna quits as President.

26 Peña y Peña becomes Acting President.

October

6 Polk issues order recalling Nicholas Trist.

7 Santa Anna ordered by Mexican Government to give up military command.

16 Santa Anna receives order relieving him of military command.

November

11 Anaya elected President ad interim by Mexican Congress.

16 Trist receives recall order from Washington.

22 Anaya appoints peace commissioners to talk with Trist.

25 Zachary Taylor relieved as commander in northern Mexico by General John Wool; Taylor returns home to campaign for presidency.

December
4 Trist decides to remain in Mexico for peace discussions.
6 Congress convenes in Washington.

1848

January
2 Negotiations begin in Mexico.
8 Anaya's ad interim as President of Mexico ends; Peña y Peña again becomes Acting President.
13 Polk sends orders relieving Scott of command.

February
2 Treaty of Guadalupe Hidalgo signed in Mexico.
18 Scott receives Polk's dismissal, hands over command in Mexico to General William O. Butler.
23 Polk sends Mexican treaty to U. S. Senate for approval.

March
10 Mexican treaty ratified by U. S. Senate with only minor changes.

May
25 Mexican Congress approves peace treaty as modified by U. S. Senate.

July
4 Polk, after attending laying of Washington Monument cornerstone, receives U.S. copy of the signed Treaty of Guadalupe Hidalgo.

NOTES
ON THE TEXT

No direct quotations have been composed by the author of this book. All quoted material appears as taken from old records. If the quotation is sufficiently identified in the text no further reference to it appears in these notes.

In some cases punctuation and style have been changed and misspellings have been corrected for clarity, but for the most part the quotations appear as given in the original sources. In any event the words appearing in quoted material have not been tampered with.

PROLOGUE: *Distant Cannon*

The description of the Gulf of Mexico is based on the author's personal observations of the area and on various eyewitness accounts mentioned below. For example, in a letter written home soon afterward—published later in the Chicago *Tribune* August 14, 1885, and quoted in *Captain Sam Grant*, by Lloyd Lewis (Boston: Little, Brown, 1950)—Ulysses Grant described the tall coastal grass and recorded the details of that grueling march from Fort Texas to Point Isabel. He was the man (mentioned in the text) to whom the distance covered seemed twice as long as it actually was.

Closing of the sea pass by blowing sand and the change in the Gulf shore are mentioned in a compilation of facts about the area in an introductory section of *The Lower Rio Grande Valley of Texas*, by J. Lee Stambaugh and Lillian J. Stambaugh (San Antonio: Naylor, 1954). Records of the sinking of vessels by "northers" are numerous, especially during the days of the Republic of Texas (1836–45), when many unseaworthy vessels were assigned to transport immigrants to Texas.

A more detailed description of Fort Texas may be found in *Climax at Buena Vista*, by David Lavender (Philadelphia: Lippincott, 1966).

Personal information on the three main characters introduced here— Sam French, Sam Grant, and Ephraim Kirby Smith—came from their eyewitness accounts: *Two Wars: An Autobiography of Gen. Samuel G. French*

(Nashville: Confederate Veteran, 1901); *Personal Memoirs of U. S. Grant* (2 vols.; New York: Webster, 1885–86); and *To Mexico with Scott: Letters of Captain E. Kirby Smith to His Wife,* prepared for the press by his daughter, Emma Jerome Blackwood (Cambridge: Harvard University Press, 1917). Some general information utilized here also came from another first-person account: *Campaign Sketches of the War with Mexico,* by Captain W. S. Henry (New York: Harper, 1847).

The invasion of Ireland to which French referred occurred in the year 1170; it was led by Richard de Clare ("Strongbow").

PART I: *The Beginnings*

1. *Background for Conflict*

For a detailed account of the evolvement of the United States from the early North American colonies (a narrative supplemented by many illustrations) see *Life in America,* by Marshall B. Davidson (2 vols.; Boston: Houghton Mifflin, 1951).

The quotation from Lyman Beecher has appeared in *Freedom's Ferment* (New York: Harper & Row, 1962) and elsewhere. The Englishman who observed the popularity of whittling in America was Frederick Marryat, whose *A Diary in America* has been edited by Sydney Jackman (New York: Knopf, 1962).

Two concise histories of Mexico used as references here are *A History of Mexico,* by Henry Bamford Parkes (Boston: Houghton Mifflin, 1970), and *Many Mexicos,* by Lesley Byrd Simpson (Berkeley: University of California Press, 1967).

2. *The Greatest Political Figure of Mexico*

For detailed information about Santa Anna see the acknowledged standard biography: *Santa Anna,* by Wilfred Hardy Callcott (Norman: University of Oklahoma Press, 1936). A more popularly written biography is *Santa Anna,* by Frank C. Hanighen (New York: Coward-McCann, 1934). See "A Selected Bibliography" herein for other sources of information about the man.

Santa Anna's statement regarding his early interest in a military career is from his autobiography. An English translation, *The Eagle,* has been edited by Ann Fears Crawford (Austin: Pemberton, 1967). Cadet Santa Anna's commendation (by Colonel Joaquín Arredondo on June 3, 1811) appeared in "The Career of General Antonio López de Santa Anna," a thesis by Walter Edgar Hancock in the University of Texas Library. Santa Anna's proclamation in favor of Iturbide has been quoted in *Men of Mexico,* by James A. Magner (Milwaukee: Bruce, 1943). Date of the *El Crepúsculo* edition comparing Santa Anna to a tiger was May 16, 1835. Santa Anna's proclamation following the loss of his leg at Vera Cruz has been quoted by Magner and others.

Callcott used Santa Anna's "parting proclamation," which was dated May 26, 1845, at Perote. Fanny Calderón de la Barca's description of Santa Anna is from her *Life in Mexico*, letters edited by Howard T. Fisher and Marion Hall Fisher (Garden City: Doubleday, 1970); Waddy Thompson's description is from his *Recollections of Mexico* (New York: Wiley and Putnam, 1846).

3. *An Advocate of National Expansion*

One of the few personal biographies of James K. Polk to be found is *Young Hickory*, by Martha McBride Morrel (New York: Dutton, 1949). It is fictionalized and is highly favorable to Polk, but it represents considerable research. For political background on Polk consult the other books about him listed in "A Selected Bibliography."

The historian who described Polk as "the leading citizen and schemer" was Justin Smith, author of the two-volume *The War with Mexico* (New York: Macmillan, 1919). The phrenologist's description was quoted in *James K. Polk: A Political Biography*, by Eugene Irving McCormac (Berkeley: University of California Press, 1922). George Bancroft used his recollection of Polk's inauguration-night statement about acquiring California in his entry, "Polk, James K.," in the fifth volume of *Cyclopedia of American Biography*, edited by James Grant Wilson and James Fiske (8 vols.; New York: Appleton, 1894–1900).

4. *Orders*

With the two exceptions listed below, this section has been based on Ethan Allen Hitchcock's diary, *Fifty Years in Camp and Field*, edited by W. A. Croffut (New York: Putnam's, 1909).

The description of army life has been prepared from material contained in *The History of the United States Army*, by William A. Ganoe (New York: Appleton, 1924). Source of the remark by E. A. Hitchcock's mother was *Ethan Allen*, by Stewart H. Holbrook (New York: Macmillan, 1940).

5. *Momentous Moves*

Marryat (see notes on Chapter 1) was the Englishman who visited Washington and described it. Other vivid descriptions of the Washington of this time can be found elsewhere—for example, in *Rehearsal for Conflict*, by Alfred Hoyt Bill (New York: Knopf, 1947).

As "A Selected Bibliography" shows, two sources have been listed for the Polk diary. One is the four-volume version edited by Milo Milton Quaife (Chicago: McClurg, 1910). Another is the one-volume version edited by Allan Nevins (New York: Longmans, Green, 1952). Nevins based his own (excerpted) work on the Quaife edition, but he made minor editing changes (in spelling, style, and punctuation) for easier reading. Therefore, virtually every quotation from the Polk diary used in this book is from the Nevins version (with the permission of David McKay Company, Inc., present owners of the rights). This is true of Polk's quotation regarding "importunate" job seekers—from the President's diary for January 9, 1846.

Dates of other diary entries used here include the following: on Buchanan's judgment, February 27, 1849; on Polk's concentration on his job, December 29, 1848. A copy of Polk's letter to Sam Houston was kept in the Polk Papers, and it has been quoted by McCormac. Polk won the champagne from Buchanan on July 24, 1847.

McCormac and Nevins (in an introduction to his version of the diary) discuss Polk's Cabinet in some detail.

Source of information on Texas annexation maneuvering was *Dream of Empire,* by John Edward Weems (New York: Simon and Schuster, 1971).

6. *Far Western Vastness*

Frémont: Pathmarker of the West, by Allan Nevins (New York: Longmans, Green, 1939), was the major reference here. For other sources see "A Selected Bibliography." Some of the description of California when Frémont first visited it has been based on *Three Years in California,* by Walter Colton (New York: Barnes, 1850), an excerpt from which appears in *California: A Literary Chronicle,* edited by W. Storrs Lee (New York: Funk and Wagnalls, 1968). Colton was the man who remarked about California hospitality "in sickness or destitution."

PART II: *Toward a Collision*

7. *For the Protection of Texas*

An account of Sam Grant's romance with Julia Dent has appeared in *Captain Sam Grant* (and elsewhere). Referred to in describing New Orleans at the time of Grant's visit there were his *Memoirs* and *Campaign Sketches of the War with Mexico.*

The account of Hitchcock's experiences and his quotations are based entirely on the diary. Supplementary information about the voyage to Corpus Christi Bay and the landing there came from *Campaign Sketches* and House Executive Document No. 60, a voluminous compilation of material relating to the Mexican War.

8. *War Will Not Be Our Fault*

McCormac's book and *James K. Polk: Continentalist,* by Charles Sellers (Princeton: Princeton University Press, 1966) discuss in detail Polk's problems at this time.

The President's July 28 letter (to A. O. P. Nicholson) was quoted by McCormac, from the Polk Papers. The orders to Commodore Conner (prepared by Secretary of the Navy Bancroft) were dated July 11, 1845, and appeared in House Executive Document No. 60.

Quotations from Polk's diary: "the United States will stand right," August 26, 1845; use of "our land and naval forces," September 1, 1845; "expedient to reopen diplomatic relations with Mexico," September 16, 1845; the suggested boundary, September 16, 1845. In his diary Polk himself recorded Bancroft's reply, "I will now go with you."

Other sources for quotations in this section: Parrott's claim against Mexico exaggerated (the man who said this was Waddy Thompson), *Claims as a Cause of the Mexican War*, by Clayton Charles Kohl (New York: New York University Press, 1914); Mexico would receive a "commissioner," House Executive Document No. 60, reprinting Peña y Peña to Black, October 15, 1845; "The vile [Herrera] government," quoted in *Texas and the Mexican War*, by Nathaniel W. Stephenson (New Haven: Yale University Press, 1921). The dates of the two editions of the Washington *Union* were June 2 and June 6, 1845, both quoted by Sellers.

9. *Road to California*

Pathmarker of the West and Frémont's *Memoirs* were the main sources. Charles Wilkes's description of San Francisco Bay appeared in his *Narrative of the United States Exploring Expedition During the Years 1838, 1839, 1840, 1841, 1842*, published in Philadelphia in 1845. Parts of it are included in *Empire on the Pacific*, by Norman A. Graebner (New York: Ronald, 1955), which also discusses other advantages of California's location beside the sea.

Frémont's description of the aged Indian woman is from his *Memoirs*.

10. *3,900 Men*

Except as noted below, narration involving French, Smith, Grant, and Hitchcock has been based on their recollections (*Two Wars, To Mexico with Scott, Memoirs*, and *Fifty Years in Camp and Field*). Some supplementary general description has been based on material in *Campaign Sketches* and House Executive Document No. 60.

Bruce Catton, in *U. S. Grant and the American Military Tradition* (Boston: Little, Brown, 1954), told the story about Grant's not shooting the wild turkeys.

Captain Henry (author of *Campaign Sketches*) was the officer who at first thought the area "Eden."

11. *Judge the World in Righteousness*

Polk's diary was the basis for all this except as follows:

Manifest Destiny and Mission, by Frederick Merk (New York: Vintage, 1963), details sending Lieutenant Gillespie to California, based on the George Bancroft Papers.

Buchanan's October 17, 1845, letter to Larkin about Californians being "received as brethren" appeared in Buchanan's *Works* (Vol. 6), edited by John Bassett Moore (New York: Antiquarian, 1960).

The communication from Peña y Peña to Slidell (dated December 20, 1845) appeared in *Diplomatic Correspondence of the United States: Inter-American Affairs, 1831–1860*, by William R. Manning (Washington: Carnegie Endowment, 1932–39).

Sellers, in *James K. Polk: Continentalist*, discusses the Slidell mission in detail. He quotes the letter from Slidell to Polk (dated December 29, 1845), "This will place us upon the strongest possible ground." Sellers also quotes Buchanan's subsequent instructions to Slidell (to act with prudence and firmness) from Buchanan's *Works*, and he quotes certain other material already cited for this section.

(Incidentally, Polk made a mistake in recording chapter and verse of the November 2 sermon text. He wrote it down as *Acts* 15:31, but 17:31 is correct.)

12. *Abuses to Uproot*

Two references were Callcott and Hanighen.

The Mexican "political observer" with "astute observations" was José Fernando Ramirez, whose *Mexico During the War with the United States* (where the quotations appear) was translated by Elliott B. Scherr and edited by Walter V. Scholes (Columbia: University of Missouri Press, 1950).

For a detailed discussion of the Farías-Santa Anna maneuverings see "Valentín Gómez Farías and the Movement for the Return of General Santa Anna to Mexico in 1846," by C. Alan Hutchinson, in *Essays in Mexican History*, edited by Thomas E. Cotner and Carlos E. Castañeda (Austin: University of Texas Press, 1958). Letters referred to toward the end of this section are mentioned in that essay. They are all to be found (along with other documents) in the Farías Papers, held in the University of Texas Archives.

Date of Rejón's letter to Farías ("Santa Anna is firm . . .") was July 7, 1845 (from Havana)—an earlier date than this chronological placement but still pertinent. Santa Anna's letter to Farías ("a real fusion") was dated April 25, 1846.

13. *A Species of Death*

Again, the narrative as it pertains to Hitchcock, Grant, French, and Smith was based on their respective recollections, already referred to, supplemented by *Campaign Sketches*.

Frederick Jackson Turner, in *The United States, 1830–1850* (New York: Norton, 1935), gave the figures about foreign-born population of the United States. Bill, in *Rehearsal for Conflict*, discussed the riots. Edward J. Nichols, in *Zach Taylor's Little Army* (Garden City: Doubleday, 1963) provided statistics on foreigners in General Taylor's force. The Mexican appeal for deserters is from a broadside by Pedro de Ampudia dated at Matamoros April 2, 1846, and quoted (along with many other war documents from both sides) in A *Complete History of the Mexican War,* by N. C. Brooks (Philadelphia: Grigg, Elliot, 1849). Justin Smith discussed the hardened Mexican attitude toward the United States in his history of the war.

PART III: *War*

14. *Forbearance Exhausted*

Polk's numerous quotations are from the Nevins-edited diary, all entered during the late winter and spring of 1846. (In his diary Polk recorded the House vote in favor of war as 173 to 14.)

A supplementary reference here is *James K. Polk: Continentalist.*

Slidell's letter to Buchanan, ". . . give [Mexico] a good drubbing," appears in Manning, *Diplomatic Correspondence* (Vol. 8).

Merk, in *Manifest Destiny and Mission,* mentions the congressional difficulties in examining documents in support of the war.

15. *Here They Come!*

Smith's letters (obviously) provided the material used to narrate his experiences. House Executive Document No. 60 contains information about Sam Walker and other details regarding the Palo Alto battle; Henry's *Campaign Sketches* also was used (in it was reproduced Taylor's order to march). Lewis, in *Captain Sam Grant,* told the story of the books and the whiskey loaded on U. S. Army wagons; the anecdote originally appeared in *The Development of Chicago, 1674–1914,* compiled by Milo Milton Quaife and published in Chicago in 1916. Bases for narrating Grant's experiences were his *Memoirs* and *Captain Sam Grant;* for French's, *Two Wars.* In some Grant-French sections Henry's book (*Campaign Sketches*) was referred to, to fill in details of which both Grant and French surely would have been aware—a plan followed in similar manner throughout this narrative.

The glimpse from the Mexican side came through utilization of *Apuntes para la Historia de la Guerra entre México y los Estados Unidos,* by Ramón Alcaraz and others (Mexico: Payno, 1848)—translated into English by Albert C. Ramsey under the title *The Other Side; or, Notes for the History of the War Between Mexico and the United States* and published in New York by Wiley in 1850. This book, the most important Mexican record of personal participation in the war, was compiled by Alcaraz and twelve other veterans of the conflict in 1847. Unfortunately, the account is written impersonally; so that it is impossible to tell which man participated in what battles. Other than showing some obvious errors in favor of Mexico, however, the book is accurate—and is an invaluable source for information in Mexican military activity.

16. Shouts and Screams

Source material for the Resaca de la Palma battle was virtually the same as that given for Palo Alto (Chapter 15).

Grant's company commander was Captain George McCall, later a Union general. Leader of the other infantry group sent to "probe ahead" was Captain Charles F. Smith, also a Union general later.

17. The Time Has Come

Primary source was Frémont's *Memoirs,* supplemented by *Pathmarker of the West* and Bancroft's *History of California* (see "A Selected Bibliography" for details).

18. To the Colors

Any standard history of the war listed in "A Selected Bibliography" will provide further information on volunteer service against Mexico.

The rest of this section has been based on *Doniphan's Expedition and the Conquest of New Mexico and California,* by William Elsey Connelley (Topeka: Published by the author, 1907). That volume contains a reprint of Hughes's own book, *Doniphan's Expedition* (Cincinnati: James, 1848) and the text of Hughes's diary.

19. A Coal of Fire

Sellers, in his book, detailed the appropriation for refurbishing the Executive Mansion. Morrel described a typical formal dinner. McCormac quoted Taylor on his "black mood" indicated in letters—to R. C. Wood (his son-in-law) dated May 19, July 14, August 4, and August 23, 1846. Otherwise, the Nevins version of Polk's diary is the source here (all entries quoted having been made in the spring and early summer of 1846).

20. Resplendent Star

Major source for information was *A Tour of Duty in California,* by Joseph Warren Revere, edited by Joseph N. Balestier (New York: Francis, 1849). The book also contains many engravings made from drawings by Revere. Some personal information on the man came from the eighth volume of *Dictionary of American Biography,* edited by Dumas Malone (New York: Scribner's, 1935).

The brief discussion of naval history was prepared after reading *The Compact History of the United States Navy,* by Fletcher Pratt, revised by Hartley E. Howe (New York: Hawthorn, 1967). The orders (by Commodore Sloat) to Commander Montgomery to distribute in California Spanish-language copies of the Texas constitution (and so on) were quoted by Merk. They were dated April 1, 1846, and are kept now in the Naval Records Group of the National Archives.

21. *Golden Gate*

Major sources included the following: *Pathmarker*, Frémont's *Memoirs*, Bancroft's *History of California* (for the attack on Sonoma), and House Executive Document No. 4 (for Revere's letter to Montgomery, the text of which does not appear in Revere's book).

The name of the "Yankee ship captain" attacked at Yerba Buena was Elliot Libbey, of the bark *Tasso* (see *Pathmarker*).

22. *Duty*

Chief reference was the first volume of the standard biography, *R. E. Lee*, by Douglas Southall Freeman (New York: Scribner's, 1934), supplemented by a more recent book that has some additional information, *Lee*, by Clifford Dowdey (Boston: Little, Brown, 1965).

The favorable descriptions of Lee as a young man ("fine-looking") appeared in *Lee the American*, by Gamaliel Bradford (Boston: Houghton Mifflin, 1929). They were given by three generals in this order: General Hunt (originally from another book, *Robert E. Lee and the Southern Confederacy*, by H. A. White), General Meigs (from the same book), and General Preston (from *Popular Life of General Robert E. Lee*, by E. V. Mason).

23. *Uncertain Destiny*

Connelley's and Hughes's books on the Doniphan expedition were the main sources, with one exception. (Even Daniel Webster's speech, widely quoted, appeared in Connelley's book, as a footnote.)

The exception concerns Bent's Fort. Hughes gave measurements that differ from these. This description of the fort uses as reference *Bent's Fort*, by David Lavender (Garden City: Doubleday, 1954). In it Lavender, in turn, relied on Bent's Fort data recorded by another member of the Army of the West, Lieutenant J. W. Abert, and reproduced in an article in the July 1953 issue of *Colorado* magazine.

24. *An Old Hero Returned*

For detailed information see Cotner, Callcott, and a brief biography, *Santa Anna*, by Oakah L. Jones, Jr. (New York: Twayne, 1968). The call by Salas for the return of Santa Anna was quoted by Jones.

Farías scoffed at Santa Anna as "the hero of San Jacinto" in a letter to José María Luis Mora (from New Orleans to Paris) dated April 23, 1844, in the Farías Papers.

In House Executive Document No. 60 can be found the texts of Commodore Conner's report of Santa Anna's entry into Mexico and of Santa Anna's proclamation in support of republicanism. Santa Anna's return to Vera Cruz, widely repeated, first appeared in a book published in London in 1847: *Adventures in Mexico and the Rocky Mountains*, by George F. Ruxton.

Dates of the Farías letters concerning the antipathy of Vera Cruz and Jalapa citizens to Santa Anna's return: August 14, 1846 (Benito), and August 15, 1846 (Fermín).

25. *Your Governor*

This was based almost entirely on Hughes's first-person account of the Doniphan expedition. An exception was the text of Kearny's speech at Las Vegas, which was recorded by another eyewitness, Lieutenant William H. Emory, in his *Notes of a Military Reconnaissance from Fort Leavenworth, in Missouri, to San Diego, in California,* and quoted by Connelley. Emory's notes also appear in Senate Executive Document No. 7.

26. *Opportunity*

Lee's quoted observation on the origin of the war appeared in *Life and Letters of Robert Edward Lee,* by William J. Jones (New York: Neale, 1906).

A good description of San Antonio two years or so before Lee's visit may be found in *Castro-ville and Henry Castro,* by Julia Nott Waugh (San Antonio: Standard Printing, 1934).

For details of this period of Lee's life see the Freeman biography.

27. *Miserable Men and Suffering Animals*

(NOTE: Monterrey, Mexico, then was spelled with one *r*. It has been spelled with two *r*'s here, as at present is correct, to distinguish it from Monterey, California.)

Grant's and French's published reminiscences are the basis for narrating their experiences (and for using their quotations). This information has been supplemented by *Campaign Sketches* (Captain W. S. Henry described Camargo, the loss of six hundred volunteers who insisted on returning home, the march through Marin, the anxiety before Monterrey, and the other volunteers having "their own fun") and by numerous general war histories listed in the bibliography, notably Brooks, Robert Selph Henry, and Rives. Walter Prescott Webb's *The Texas Rangers* (Boston: Houghton Mifflin, 1935) details Ranger activities at Monterrey.

A participant, Luther Giddings, described Bragg and his battery in the fighting, quoted in *Captain Sam Grant.* John Reese Kenley mentioned Twiggs's taking a "dose of medicine" before the battle, in *Memoirs of a Maryland Volunteer* (Philadelphia: Lippincott, 1873). Captain Henry described General Taylor's work as an ordinary soldier. House Executive Document No. 60 contains information about Monterrey truce terms, and House Executive Document No. 4 contains official battle reports. Lieutenant Meade's commendation of Taylor's terms appeared in his book, *The Life and Letters of George Gordon Meade* (New York: Scribner's, 1913).

The Mexican view of Monterrey and the battle came entirely from *The Other Side.*

PART IV: *Changing Strategy*

28. *Colossal Guardians of the Land*

Callcott, Hanighen, Jones, and Magner cover Santa Anna's life at this time in greater detail than is possible in this limited space. Ramirez, in *Mexico During the War with the United States*, described the entry of Farías and Santa Anna into Mexico City.

Polk's quotations are from his diary of this period (September, October, November, 1846). House Executive Document No. 60 carries information about Winfield Scott's desire to go to Mexico and his belief that Taylor would welcome him, and plans for the Vera Cruz campaign. Taylor's letter to his son-in-law (R. C. Wood) about the presidency was dated December 10, 1846, and appears in Taylor's *Letters . . . from the Battlefields of the Mexican War*, edited by William H. Samson (Rochester: Genessee, 1908). Taylor's letter to General Gaines was dated November 9, 1846. Marcy's rebuke to Taylor about publication of the Gaines letter was dated January 27, 1847, and was quoted by Robert Selph Henry. The ditty at the end of this section appeared in Hanighen's *Santa Anna*.

29. *A Christmas Frolic*

With the exceptions listed below, this narrative was based on material contained in Hughes's diary, later used in preparing the book, and on the book itself.

In the *Journal of William H. Richardson* (Baltimore: 1847) appeared the notation about one of the beef cattle dying (October 31, 1846), the "badly baked" Taos flour (November 2, 1846), and the bull's offals being eaten (November 17, 1846). Richardson was a private with Doniphan.

The Battle of El Brazito has been based on the combined accounts of Hughes and Richardson and these other participants: George R. Gibson and James Peacock, quoted by Connelley; and Marcellus Ball Edwards, whose 1846–47 journal was published in the fourth volume of the twelve-volume *Southwest Historical Series*, edited by Ralph Bieber (Glendale: Clark, 1931–45).

Hughes's letter to Secretary of War Marcy (reprinted in his book) was dated January 25, 1847.

30. *The Goal of Their Hopes*

Revere's and Frémont's published reminiscences served as primary sources.

The descriptions of Frémont and his men were by William D. Phelps, in the New York *Tribune* of August 14, 1856, and Lieutenant Frederick Walpole of the British warship *Collingwood*. Both descriptions appeared in *Pathmarker*.

What I Saw in California, by Edwin Bryant (Palo Alto: Osborne, 1967, but first published in 1848) provides a good account of Frémont's march to San Luis Obispo and beyond.

General Kearny's experiences en route to San Diego are detailed in his official report, dated December 13, 1846, at San Diego, and by Lieutenant Emory, one of Kearny's officers (Senate Executive Document No. 7). See also House Executive Document No. 1 for a description of San Diego and of Kearny's arrival there. Kearny's official report covering the march from San Diego to Los Angeles was dated January 12, 1847, at Los Angeles.

Nevins, in *Pathmarker of the West,* quoted the conflicting orders sent to Kearny and Stockton. They appeared in Senate Executive Document No. 33. Nevins also quoted the text of Frémont's January 17, 1847, letter to Kearny and William Tecumseh Sherman's remark (the latter appeared originally in Sherman's *Memoirs*).

31. *Fighting—But No Fighting*

Hitchcock, Smith, and French recorded their experiences, and these quotations.

House Executive Document No. 60 carried the text of Scott's troop requisition.

Some accounts dated Scott's arrival at Camargo January 2. Hitchcock (who was usually careful about details) recorded the date in his diary as the third, and this was used.

Freeman said no evidence existed that Scott specifically asked for Lee to join him. Dowdey, writing later, quoted the text of Scott's request. If the letter was written and signed at the Brazos on January 6 (as stated), however, there has to be an explanation not immediately obvious—and this is assumed here—because Scott was at Camargo on that date. The explanation would have been lost in the mists of time.

House Executive Document No. 60 discussed atrocities, and particularly Taylor's reaction to the Texas Ranger kind.

McClellan's and Meade's remarks appeared in their respective books.

Sam Chamberlain, in *My Confession* (New York: Harper, 1956), described how the guerrillas treated American stragglers.

32. *Bugle Notes of Reveille*

The Mexican viewpoint here has been based largely on a wealth of information in *The Other Side.* Used as references for the narrative as it related specifically to Santa Anna were Callcott, Hanighen, and Jones. James Henry Carleton, *The Battle of Buena Vista* (New York: Harper, 1848), included some narration of Mexican activity; Lavender's book on Buena Vista was a comprehensive, twentieth-century wrap-up of both Mexican and American maneuvering.

The Texan who had "fallen prisoner to Mexicans once before" was Daniel Drake Henrie, a veteran of the Republic of Texas "Mier Expedition."

Santa Anna's proclamation promising capture of the "riches" of the enemy appeared in Senate Executive Document No. 1 (and has been quoted by Lavender and others).

The La Encarnación prisoner who saw Santa Anna en route to Buena Vista never was named, but he wrote a book, *Encarnación Prisoners* (Louisville: Prentice and Weissenger, 1848) in which he described the Mexican general.

The Mexican who said Santa Anna refused to allow his men to stop for a drink was Manuel Balbontin, in *La Invasión Americana* (Mexico: Esteva, 1883).

French's *Two Wars* was the reference for all activity relating to that lieutenant.

See Webb, *The Texas Rangers*, for details about Ben McCulloch. (French retold McCulloch's experiences, but he did it from poor secondhand accounts and made mistakes, eliminated here.)

33. *The Soil of Buena Vista*

For the Mexican view: *The Other Side*. For Santa Anna specifics: Callcott, Hanighen, Jones, Magner. (Santa Anna's autobiography is full of self-serving errors and has been relied on only occasionally throughout this book, and then only when the inaccuracies and pleadings are made obvious.) Balbontin provided a vivid description of the Mexican retreat from Buena Vista; he was the officer who remarked on the *noche triste* aspect.

When possible, French's activities were followed, based on his *Two Wars*. Santa Anna's message summoning Taylor to surrender appears as printed in George C. Furber's *The Twelve Months Volunteer* (Cincinnati: James, 1848). It may be found in other sources, too. Sam Chamberlain was the authority for the "Tell Santa Anna to go to hell" anecdote. Senate Executive Document No. 1 included official reports.

David Lavender has written a vivid, detailed account of the battle for modern readers, in *Climax at Buena Vista*. Of the older books, Carleton's is the most informative.

Some inconsistencies have been resolved (here and elsewhere in this book) by using the most logical account when details differ. For example, *The Other Side* declared that no fires were permitted in the Mexican camp on the night of February 22, but American eyewitnesses, in various records, reported seeing occasional fires. There would have been little reason for not having them; by then everyone knew the Mexican soldiers were there, and in large numbers.

34. *Hard-won Position of Precariousness*

Major reference for the American side was Hughes's account of the Doniphan expedition; for the Mexican view, *The Other Side*.

For Kirker's bounty payments (information in Connelley's book relied on here) Paul Wellman, in *The House Divides* (Garden City: Doubleday, 1966), gave different figures—one hundred dollars for a brave's scalp, fifty dollars for a squaw's, twenty-five dollars for a child's.

35. *The Lamp of a Sepulcher*

Two obvious sources here are E. K. Smith's letters and E. A. Hitchcock's diary. For references to Grant and Lee see "A Selected Bibliography"— Freeman, especially, for Lee.

House Executive Document No. 60 contained information on the siege (as it did for many other events) including Scott's complaint about lack of supplies. Scott's *Autobiography* had appropriate material, too.

Maury's statement about sand fleas appeared in his *Recollections of a Virginian in the Mexican, Indian, and Civil Wars* (New York: Scribner's, 1894). Lewis and other writers have quoted it.

J. Jacob Oswandel, in *Notes of the Mexican War* (Philadelphia: published by the author, 1885), described the Vera Cruz surrender ceremony, but Grant participated and would have seen it this way.

Again, the Mexican view is based on information in *The Other Side*. The closing statement by the Mexican editor ("lamp of a sepulcher") was reprinted in *Niles' National Register*, May 8, 1847. There, the final word was spelled "sepulchre"—changed here for modern usage.

PART V: *An Elusive Peace*

36. *Stress, Frustration, and Anger*

Polk's diary (primarily) and general histories have been the references. Morrel has detailed the decline of Polk's health.

See also *Manifest Destiny and Mission* and *Freedom's Ferment* for lengthy discussion of American division at this time. The legislative resolutions of Massachusetts and Virginia were reproduced in *A History of the United States*, edited by Hugh T. Lefler (New York: Meridian, 1960). Lincoln's speech has been reprinted in (among other publications) the first volume of *The Collected Works of Abraham Lincoln*, edited by Roy P. Basler (New Brunswick: Rutgers University Press, 1953). The speech (made January 12, 1848) is out of chronological order here, but it fits the text logically.

37. *Suspense and Agony*

The historian who commented on Mexican "petty passions" was Ramirez, in *Mexico During the War with the United States*.

Senate Executive Document No. 1 reprinted Santa Anna's proclamation about sacrificing himself. Major references for the rest of the Mexican view: *The Other Side*, and Callcott's biography of Santa Anna.

Smith's letters provided information about his activities. Hitchcock's diary obviously served as another major reference here. House Executive Document No. 60 included some appropriate detail. Freeman and Dowdey, on Lee, were references. Grant's *Memoirs* were utilized—and quoted in regard to the work of the engineers.

38. *Rough, Ragged, and Ready*

The books by Hughes and Connelley on Doniphan's expedition provided virtually all of the source material (including direct quotations). The exception: James Hobbs witnessed the reviews by Wool and Taylor and described them in *Wild Life in the Far West* (Hartford: Wiley, Waterman & Eaton, 1873). He was also the source of the "old man" anecdote about Wool.

39. *Movable Forts*

The Other Side has the story, in detail, of Santa Anna's sad journey. Another reference here was Callcott, but he relied extensively on *The Other Side* for material, too.

The references to Hitchcock's and Polk's diaries in this section are obvious.

The Smithsonian Institution cornerstone was laid May 1, 1847. The granddaughter of John Quincy Adams visited the Executive Mansion during the evening of April 30, 1847.

Hitchcock, in his diary, made no mention of his curious change of attitude (about the cause of the war) as displayed in his address to the Mexican people.

40. *Of Physical and Moral Courage*

Otis Singletary, in *The Mexican War* (Chicago: University of Chicago Press, 1960), has discussed in detail Santa Anna's maneuvering in regard to his May 28, 1847, resignation.

For an account of Santa Anna's dickering with American officials see "Relations of General Scott with Santa Anna," by Carlos E. Castañeda, in *Hispanic American Historical Review*, November 1949.

Other narration relating to the Mexican view has been based on *The Other Side*.

The references to Smith's letters and journal, to Grant's *Memoirs* (supplemented by *Captain Sam Grant*, which detailed Grant's plan to circle north of Mexico City), and to Hitchcock's diary are obvious. For a complete account of Lee's activities in this period see Freeman's and Dowdey's biographies and Robert Selph Henry's history of the war. Various executive documents also record his different activities and reports.

Lee's letter describing El Peñon was addressed to Mrs. Joseph Totten (dated August 22, 1847) and was quoted by Freeman.

Raphael Semmes described the *pedregal* as a storm-tossed ocean instantly transformed into stone in his book, *Service Afloat and Ashore in the Mexican War* (Cincinnati: Moore, 1851).

Extracts from the Mexican letters written after "the August 20 disaster" are based on translated quotations presented by both Smith and Hitchcock, in their writings.

41. *Such Victories*

Again, the utilization of Smith's journal, Hitchcock's diary, and Grant's *Memoirs* (in which appeared the account of his climb to the rooftop) are obvious. Lewis, in *Captain Sam Grant*, mentioned Fred Dent's experiences (at Molino del Rey) while leading Smith's company. The details of Smith's death appeared in *To Mexico with Scott*.

Semmes's quotation blaming General Scott appeared in his book.

The Mexican view was based, of course, on *The Other Side*. That narrative has many obvious inaccuracies regarding this period, however, and was of very little use here.

42. *Long-sought Destination*

The narrative centers around Hitchcock and Grant, and their recollections were used as the basis for this section.

The Other Side provided the Mexican reference. The real story of *los niños héroes* (much of it word-of-mouth history handed down from those days) cannot be documented, but even American sources (as well as Mexican) agree that some cadets fought very well at Chapultepec.

43. *Superlative Climaxes*

Callcott was the biographer who remarked on Santa Anna's career. Lucas Alamán, who wrote a five-volume *Historia de Méjico* (Mexico: Lara, 1849–52), was the source for adding the observation regarding Santa Anna's lack of moral or intellectual training.

For detailed discussion of this period see *Mexico During the War with the United States*.

The text of Trist's July 23 letter to James Buchanan was reproduced in the eighth volume of Manning's *Diplomatic Correspondence*. The text of Santa Anna's proclamation ending, "Soldiers!" appeared in *Niles' National Register* December 4, 1847, and was quoted by Callcott. Santa Anna's proclamation upon resigning the presidency September 16 has been quoted by Brooks. The remark of the Texan about his expectation of fighting guerrillas was contained in a letter, F. S. Breeding to his brother John, dated at Vera Cruz October 29, 1847. A photostat of this and other material was provided by Seth Breeding of Austin, Texas.

The last part of this section has been based on John Salmon (Rip) Ford's memoirs, kept in the University of Texas Archives. Much of this material (but not all) was published in *Rip Ford's Texas*, edited by Stephen B. Oates (Austin: University of Texas Press, 1963). Ford saved many recollections besides his own, and his archival memoirs include items that did not come from his own firsthand observation. Virtually all of these items were eliminated from the published book.

The name of the Texan slain in "Cutthroat," according to Ford, was Adam Allsens. The story of entering Santa Anna's deserted apartments (an example of Ford's accumulation of other reminiscences in his memoirs) was written by Dr. David Wooster of San Francisco. Oates did not include it in his book, but Walter Prescott Webb used it, in *The Texas Rangers*.

44. *The Perfect Tool*

The references to Polk's diary here are obvious.

See Singletary's book for a detailed discussion of the Whig generals and Polk's relationship with them.

Brooks (and many others) quoted the treaty terms regarding the boundary line. Merk (and many others) provided a discussion of the dubious constitutionality of the war—and Merk quoted Georgian Alexander Stephens. John Douglas Pitts Fuller devoted an entire volume to a discussion of *The Movement for the Acquisition of All Mexico* (Baltimore: Johns Hopkins Press, 1936) and quoted the statement about "the Sabine virgins."

EPILOGUE: *The Mournful War*

The quotation about "the state of degradation" (and material immediately following) was found in *The Other Side*.

The description of the President of Mexico some 120 years later as "dynamic, concerned" has been based on a feature article on President Echeverria by William Giandoni (of the Copley News Service) that appeared in numerous North American newspapers of June 14, 1972. (The quotation that follows is his, too.)

See *Guerrilla Warrior: The Early Life of John J. Pershing*, by Donald Smythe (New York: Scribner's, 1973), for further information regarding the Pancho Villa chase.

The New York *Times* of December 14, 1968, reported on El Chamizal in a story by Neil Sheehan, "Johnson and Diaz Ordaz Shift Rio Grande into a Concrete-lined Channel."

Information about the later lives of the major characters came from their own writings referred to elsewhere (all included in "A Selected Bibliography") and from these supplementary references:

Sam Grant—*Webster's Guide to American History*.
Antonio López de Santa Anna—*Men of Mexico*.
James K. Polk—*Webster's Guide*.
John C. Frémont—*Webster's Guide*.
Joseph Warren Revere—*Dictionary of American Biography* (Vol. 8).
Robert E. Lee—*Webster's Guide*.

The quotation, "It's just a Mexican church," appeared in an Associated Press story datelined Harlingen, Texas, and used in numerous newspapers of April 1, 1972.

ACKNOWLEDGMENTS
AND PICTURE CREDITS

My particular appreciation goes to Dayton Kelley, then curator of the Texas Collection at Baylor University, Waco, Texas, for locating virtually every old book I asked for. Especial appreciation also goes to Victor Jeffress, librarian at McLennan Community College, Waco, for arranging photographic duplication of those books. Many are unavailable today even from rare-book dealers. Finally, particular appreciation goes to Carl Brandt of New York for stimulating my interest in this subject in the first place, and to Walter Bradbury of Doubleday for thoughtful editing from the very beginning.

Other persons helped. Seth Breeding of Austin, Texas, provided photographic copies of old family documents relating to the war. Jo Ann Johnson of Doubleday conducted some research in the New York Public Library when I could not be there, and Kathryn Tebbel of Doubleday gave some good advice about the manuscript. Bibliographic suggestions came from Santiago Sanz of Compañía General de Ediciones, Mexico City. Jones Ramsey wandered far afield from his regular employment as sports information director of the University of Texas (but on his own time) to look for urgently needed material in Austin libraries when I could not do so personally. Joe Mack Hight of Nashville made a similar contribution in the Tennessee State Library.

Still other individuals helped. My further appreciation goes to Mr. and Mrs. William Ming and to Laura Simmons of the Baylor University Texas Collection; to Ron Tester of the McLennan Community College Library; to Jerry Kearns of the Prints and Photographs Division of the Library of Congress; to Mary Washington Frazer and Ellen D. Ross of the Tennessee State Library and Archives; to Reba Ann Orman of the Memphis Public Library; to Paul R. Coppock, historical columnist for the Memphis *Commercial Appeal*; to Grace A. Briggs and Susan C. Metzger of the Harvard University Press; to Arthur H. Brook II of the United States Publishers Association, Inc.; to Barbara Hirshkowitz of David McKay Co., Inc.; to Edith Menard of G. P. Putnam's Sons; to O. R. Scott of Temple, Texas; to Mr. and Mrs. J. Eddie Weems, Sr., of Temple, Texas (my father and mother), for some financial assistance at a very momentous time; and to numerous individuals on the staffs of the Waco Public

Library and the Texas Collection and the Latin American Library of the University of Texas.

Picture credits are as follows:

President Polk: Library of Congress. Photograph of a daguerreotype by Mathew Brady, 1849.

Sarah Polk: Library of Congress. Lithograph by N. Currier, 1846, after a daguerreotype by Plumbe.

Captain Robert E. Lee: Appeared in *Texas and the Mexican War*, by Nathaniel W. Stephenson (New Haven: Yale University Press, 1921), with a note, "Engraving from a daguerreotype. In the collection of H. P. Cook, Richmond, Virginia." Used here by permission of United States Publishers Association, Inc.

Lieutenant Sam—Ulysses—Grant: Appeared also in *Texas and the Mexican War*, with this note, "Drawing from an engraving after a daguerreotype, published in Grant's *Memoirs*." Used here by permission of United States Publishers Association, Inc.

Ethan Allen Hitchcock: Appeared in *Fifty Years in Camp and Field* (Hitchcock's diary edited by W. A. Croffut) (New York: G. P. Putnam's Sons, 1909).

Captain Ephraim Kirby Smith: Appeared in *To Mexico with Scott* (Smith's letters prepared for the press by his daughter, Emma Jerome Blackwood) (Cambridge: Harvard University Press, 1917).

General Winfield Scott: Appeared in *Texas and the Mexican War* (see information for Captain Robert E. Lee illustration), with this note, "Engraved after a daguerreotype taken at the time of the Mexican War. In the Print Department of the New York Public Library." Used here by permission of the United States Publishers Association, Inc.

Antonio López de Santa Anna: University of Texas Archives.

View of the Capitol at Washington: Library of Congress. Engraving by C. J. Bentley after W. H. Barlett and first printed in 1840.

Executive Mansion: Library of Congress. Lithograph (north front) by Deroy, 1848, after Aug. Köllner—during Polk's occupancy.

Sutter's Fort: Appeared in *A Tour of Duty in California*, by Joseph Warren Revere, New York: Francis, 1849. After a sketch by Revere.

Monterey Bay, California: Appeared also in *A Tour of Duty in California*. Again, after a sketch by Revere.

Camp of the Army of Occupation at Corpus Christi: Library of Congress. Lithograph printed in color by G. & W. Endicott, New York, in 1847 after a drawing made on the spot by Captain D. P. Whiting, 7th Infantry.

Battles of Palo Alto and Resaca de la Palma: Library of Congress. Lithograph by Klauprech & Menzel after drawings made on the day of the battles by Ange Paldi, 5th Infantry.

Heights of Monterrey, Mexico: Library of Congress. Lithograph by G. & W. Endicott, 1847, after a drawing by Captain Whiting.

Riding a Donkey: Appeared in *Campaign Sketches of the War with Mexico*, by W. S. Henry (New York: Harper, 1847).

Using a Lariat: Appeared in *Anecdotes and Letters of Zachary Taylor*, by T. B. Thorpe (New York: Appleton, 1848).

Tampico: Appeared also in *Anecdotes and Letters of Zachary Taylor*.

General Taylor's Kitchen: Appeared also in *Anecdotes and Letters of Zachary Taylor*.

A Camp Washing Day: Library of Congress. Reproduction of a wood engraving in *The Journal of William H. Richardson* (a soldier with Doniphan) (Baltimore: Robinson, 1848).

Battle of Buena Vista: Library of Congress. Lithograph by Henry R. Robinson, 1847, after a drawing made on the spot by Major Eaton, aide-de-camp to General Taylor.

Landing on the Beach Near Vera Cruz: Library of Congress. Lithograph by S. Duval, 1847, after a drawing made on the spot by navy Lieutenant Charles C. Barton.

U. S. Naval Battery at Vera Cruz: Library of Congress. Lithograph by Sarony & Major, 1848, after a drawing by navy Lieutenant H. Walke.

U.S.S. *Mississippi* Battling a Storm off Vera Cruz: Library of Congress. Lithograph by Sarony & Major, 1847, after a drawing by Lieutenant Walke.

General Scott's Entrance into Mexico City: Library of Congress. Reproduction of a lithograph in *The War Between the United States and Mexico*, by George Wilkins Kendall (New York: Appleton, 1851).

Inauguration of General Zachary Taylor: Library of Congress. Wood engraving by Brightly & Keyser, 1849, after a drawing made on the spot by William Croome.

A SELECTED
BIBLIOGRAPHY

Many more books than those listed below have been published on the subject of the war between the United States and Mexico and on the most important characters through whom I have told the story. Titles listed here represent major references for this particular narrative and suggested supplementary reading for interested persons.

In the "Notes on the Text" section may be found references to other books, articles, and documents used less often and not listed again here.

Many Spanish-language books on the war also are available (although not many narrating first-person experiences), but this bibliography is limited to English translations of greatest interest to a general reader.

About the Major Characters

JOHN C. FRÉMONT
Bancroft, Hubert Howe. *The Works of Hubert Howe Bancroft: History of California*, Vol. 5. San Francisco: History, 1886.
Frémont, John C. *Exploring Expedition of the Rocky Mountains, Oregon and California*. Buffalo: Derby, Orton and Mulligan, 1853.
———. *Memoirs of My Life*. Chicago: Belford, Clarke, 1887.
Nevins, Allan. *Frémont: Pathmarker of the West*. New York: Longmans, Green, 1939.
———. *Frémont: The West's Greatest Adventurer*, Vol. 1. New York: Harper, 1928.

SAMUEL G. FRENCH
French, Samuel G. *Two Wars: An Autobiography*. Nashville: Confederate Veteran, 1901.

A Selected Bibliography

ULYSSES S. GRANT

Catton, Bruce. *U. S. Grant and the American Military Tradition.* Boston: Little, Brown, 1954.

Grant, U. S. *Personal Memoirs,* Vol. 1. New York: Webster, 1885.

Lewis, Lloyd. *Captain Sam Grant.* Boston: Little, Brown, 1950.

ETHAN ALLEN HITCHCOCK

Hitchcock, Ethan Allen. *Fifty Years in Camp and Field: Diary* . . . (edited by W. A. Croffut). New York: Putnam's, 1909.

JOHN T. HUGHES

Connelley, William Elsey. *Doniphan's Expedition and the Conquest of New Mexico and California.* Topeka: Published by the author, 1907.

Hughes, John T. *Doniphan's Expedition.* Cincinnati: James, 1848. (Reprinted in W. E. Connelley's book, listed above, along with Hughes's diary of the expedition.

ROBERT E. LEE

Dowdey, Clifford. *Lee.* Boston: Little, Brown, 1965.

Freeman, Douglas Southall. *R. E. Lee,* Vol. 1. New York: Scribner's, 1934.

Jones, William J. *Life and Letters of Robert Edward Lee.* New York: Neale, 1906.

Lee, Robert E., Jr. *Recollections and Letters of Gen. Robert E. Lee* (by his son). New York: Doubleday, 1904.

JAMES K. POLK

McCormac, Eugene Irving. *James K. Polk: A Political Biography.* Berkeley: University of California Press, 1922.

McCoy, Charles A. *Polk and the Presidency.* Austin: University of Texas Press, 1960.

Morrel, Martha McBride. *Young Hickory.* New York: Dutton, 1949. (Partly fictionalized and laudatory, but one of the few personal biographies of Polk.)

Polk, James K. *Polk: The Diary of a President* (edited by Allen Nevins). New York: Longmans, Green, 1952. (Extracts, with some style changes, from the edition listed below.)

————. *The Diary of James K. Polk During His Presidency* (edited by Milo Milton Quaife), 4 vols. Chicago: McClurg, 1910.

Sellers, Charles. *James K. Polk: Continentalist.* Princeton: Princeton University Press, 1966.

JOSEPH WARREN REVERE

Bancroft, Hubert Howe. *History of California.* (See entry under John C. Frémont.)

Revere, Joseph Warren. *A Tour of Duty in California* (edited by Joseph N. Balestier). New York: Francis, 1849.

ANTONIO LÓPEZ DE SANTA ANNA

Callcott, Wilfred Hardy. *Santa Anna.* Norman: University of Oklahoma Press, 1936.

Hanighen, Frank C. *Santa Anna.* New York: Coward-McCann, 1934.

Jones, Oakah L., Jr. *Santa Anna.* New York: Twayne, 1968.

Magner, James A. *Men of Mexico,* 2nd ed. Milwaukee: Bruce, 1943.

Santa Anna, Antonio López de. *The Eagle: The Autobiography of Santa Anna* (edited by Ann Fears Crawford). Austin: Pemberton, 1967. (English translation of Santa Anna's memoirs.)

EPHRAIM KIRBY SMITH

Smith, E. Kirby. *To Mexico with Scott: Letters of Captain E. Kirby Smith to His Wife* (prepared for the press by his daughter, Emma Jerome Blackwood). Cambridge: Harvard University Press, 1917.

About the War

Alcaraz, Ramón [and others]. *The Other Side* (translated by Albert C. Ramsey). New York: Wiley, 1850. (First published in Mexico in 1848.)

Bancroft, Hubert Howe. *The Works of Hubert Howe Bancroft: History of Mexico,* Vol. 5. San Francisco: History, 1887.

Bill, Alfred Hoyt. *Rehearsal for Conflict.* New York: Knopf, 1947.

Brooks, N. C. *A Complete History of the Mexican War.* Philadelphia: Grigg, Elliot, 1849.

Bryant, Edwin. *What I Saw in California.* Palo Alto: Osborne, 1967. (First published in 1848.)

Carleton, James Henry. *The Battle of Buena Vista.* New York: Harper, 1848.

Chamberlain, Samuel E. *My Confession.* New York: Harper, 1956.

Connor, Seymour V., and Faulk, Odie B. *North America Divided.* New York: Oxford, 1971.

DeVoto, Bernard. *The Year of Decision: 1846.* Boston: Little, Brown, 1943.

Dufour, Charles L. *The Mexican War.* New York: Hawthorn, 1968.

Executive Documents:

Executive Document No. 4, House of Representatives, 29th Congress, 2nd session.

Executive Document No. 1, Senate, 30th Congress, 1st Session.

Executive Document No. 7, Senate, 30th Congress, 1st Session.

Executive Document No. 33, Senate, 30th Congress, 1st Session.

Executive Document No. 41, House of Representatives, 30th Congress, 1st Session.

Executive Document No. 50, House of Representatives, 30th Congress, 1st Session.

Executive Document No. 52, Senate, 30th Congress, 1st Session.

Executive Document No. 56, House of Representatives, 30th Congress, 1st Session.

Executive Document No. 60, House of Representatives, 30th Congress, 1st Session.

Executive Document No. 65, Senate, 30th Congress, 1st Session.

Executive Document No. 69, House of Representatives, 30th Congress, 1st Session.

Executive Document No. 70, House of Representatives, 30th Congress, 1st Session.

Executive Document No. 1, House of Representatives, 30th Congress, 2nd Session.

Ford, John Salmon. *Rip Ford's Texas* (edited by Stephen B. Oates). Austin: University of Texas Press, 1963.

Fuller, John Douglas Pitts. *The Movement for the Acquisition of All Mexico, 1846–1848.* Baltimore: Johns Hopkins Press, 1936.

Furber, George C. *The Twelve Months Volunteer.* Cincinnati: James, 1848.

Henry, Robert Selph. *The Story of the Mexican War.* Indianapolis: Bobbs-Merrill, 1950.

Henry, W. S. *Campaign Sketches of the War with Mexico.* New York: Harper, 1847.

Hobbs, James. *Wild Life in the Far West.* Hartford: Wiley, Waterman & Eaton, 1873.

Lavender, David. *Climax at Buena Vista.* Philadelphia: Lippincott, 1966.

Merk, Frederick. *Manifest Destiny and Mission.* New York: Vintage, 1963.

Mexican War, The (edited by Archie McDonald). Lexington, Mass.: Heath, 1969.

Mexican War, The (edited by Ramón Eduardo Ruiz). New York: Holt, Rinehart and Winston, 1963.

Nichols, Edward J. *Zach Taylor's Little Army.* Garden City: Doubleday, 1963.

Price, Glenn W. *Origins of the War with Mexico.* Austin: University of Texas Press, 1967.

Ramirez, José Fernando. *Mexico During the War with the United States* (translated by Elliott B. Scherr; edited by Walter V. Scholes). Columbia: University of Missouri Press, 1950.

Ripley, Roswell Sabine. *The War with Mexico,* 2 vols. New York: Harper, 1849.

Rippy, James Fred. *The United States and Mexico,* rev. ed. New York: Crofts, 1931.

Rives, George Lockhart. *The United States and Mexico, 1821–1848*, Vol. 2. New York: Scribner's, 1913.

Scott, Winfield. *Memoirs.* New York: Sheldon, 1864.

Singletary, Otis A. *The Mexican War.* Chicago: University of Chicago Press, 1960.

Smith, Justin H. *The War with Mexico*, 2 vols. New York: Macmillan, 1919.

Stephenson, Nathaniel W. *Texas and the Mexican War.* New Haven: Yale University Press, 1921.

Taylor, Zachary. *Letters . . . from the Battlefields of the Mexican War* (edited by William H. Samson). Rochester: Genessee, 1908.

Webb, Walter Prescott. *The Texas Rangers.* Boston: Houghton Mifflin, 1935.

Wilcox, Cadmus M. *History of the Mexican War.* Washington: Church News, 1892.

General Information

Alba, Frederick A. *The Mexicans: The Making of a Nation.* New York: Praeger, 1967.

American Secretaries of State and Their Diplomacy, The (edited by Samuel Flagg Bemis), Vol. 5. New York: Knopf, 1928.

Annals of America. Chicago: Encyclopedia Britannica, 1968.

Branch, E. Douglas. *The Sentimental Years: 1836–1860.* New York: Appleton-Century, 1934.

Calderón de la Barca, Fanny. *Life in Mexico: The Letters of Fanny Calderón de la Barca* (edited by Howard T. Fisher and Marion Hall Fisher). Garden City: Doubleday, 1970.

California: A Literary Chronicle (edited by W. Storrs Lee). New York: Funk & Wagnalls, 1968.

Cline, Howard F. *The United States and Mexico.* Cambridge: Harvard University Press, 1965.

Documents of American History (edited by Henry Steele Commager), 7th ed. New York: Appleton-Century-Crofts, 1963.

Encyclopedia of American Facts and Dates (edited by Gorton Carruth and Associates), 4th ed. New York: Crowell, 1966.

Essays in Mexican History (edited by Thomas E. Cotner and Carlos E. Castañeda). Austin: University of Texas Press, 1958.

Freedom's Ferment: Phases of American Social History from the Colonial Period to the Outbreak of the Civil War. New York: Harper & Row, 1962. (First published in 1944.)

Ganoe, William Addleman. *The History of the United States Army.* New York: Appleton, 1924.

Graebner, Norman A. *Empire on the Pacific.* New York: Ronald, 1955.

Gregg, Josiah. *Commerce of the Prairies*, 2 vols. New York: Langley, 1844.

Kane, Joseph Nathan. *Facts About the Presidents,* 2nd ed. New York: Wilson, 1968.

Lincoln, Abraham. *The Collected Works of Abraham Lincoln* (edited by Roy P. Basler), Vol. 1. New Brunswick: Rutgers University Press, 1953.

Marryat, Frederick. *A Diary in America* (edited by Sydney Jackman). New York: Knopf, 1962.

Parkes, Henry Bamford. *A History of Mexico.* Boston: Houghton Mifflin, 1970.

Pratt, Fletcher. *The Compact History of the United States Navy* (revised by Hartley E. Howe). New York: Hawthorn, 1967.

Presidents of the United States, 4th ed. rev. New York: Horizon, 1969.

Record of American Diplomacy, The (edited by Ruhl J. Bartlett), 4th ed. New York: Knopf, 1964.

Simpson, Lesley Byrd. *Many Mexicos.* Berkeley: University of California Press, 1967.

Turner, Frederick Jackson. *The United States, 1830–1850.* New York: Norton, 1935.

United States and Latin America, The (edited by Herbert L. Matthews), 2nd ed. Englewood Cliffs: Prentice-Hall, 1963.

Webster's Guide to American History. Springfield: Merriam, 1971.

Wellman, Paul I. *The House Divides.* Garden City: Doubleday, 1966.

INDEX

Index

Index

Index

national debt (1846), 99; political factionalism,
98–102; Roman Catholic Church, 9, 100, 101,
110, 111, 195, 241, 242, 282–83, 313, 354; Spanish rule of, 6, 7

Mexico City, 12, 68–70, 111, 162, 197, 214, 217,
235, 239–42, 247, 248, 250, 260, 279, 282, 327,
355, 361, 377, 380–81, 383, 452, 455

Mexico City campaign, 386–430; casualties, 397,
403, 406–7, 416, 418, 421, 422, 426; at Chapultepec Hill, 420–30, 432, 442, 452; at Churubusco,
403–7, 409, 410; diversionary frontal attack,
403; El Penon hill, 388, 394, 395, 397, 420, 432;
end of, 429–30; first peace talks, 388; Lee's
advice on, 399–400; at Molino del Ray, 414–19,
420, 421; Padierna "Contreras" battle, 398–
99, 400, 403, 406, 407, 409, 431–32, 442, 443; at
the *pedregal*, 396–400, 402, 403, 408, 409; reconnaissance missions, 394, 397; Tacubaya armistice, 410–14; troop strength (U.S.), 421

Mier, 214, 215

Miñon, General Vicente, 283–85, 287–89, 291–93,
296, 302

Mission San Francisco de Solano, 172

Mississippi (ship), 337, 362

Mississippi Rifles, 299, 302, 306

Missouri Mounted Volunteers, 150–56, 243, 252–
59, 368–75

Missouri River, 48, 49, 150, 152, 154

Mixcoac, 410

Moderado Federalists, 98–99

Molino del Rey, 414, 422

Molino del Rey, Battle of, 414–19, 420, 421; beginning of, 416; casualties, 416, 418

Monclova, 289, 369

Monroe, James, 157, 184

Monroe Doctrine, 94, 95, 452

Monterey (California), 81, 92, 94, 145–46, 148,
169–71, 179, 180–82, 261; American occupation
of, 242

Monterey Bay, 175, 182

Monterrey (Mexico), 240–43, 244, 246, 249, 289,
290, 351, 371, 427; civilian evacuation of, 218;
northern suburbs of, 219; surrender of, 180–81;
U.S. occupation of, 175, 280

Monterrey, Battle of, 209–35, 242, 245, 278, 340;
American advance to, 209–19; armistice terms,
298; beginning of, 224–25; at Bishop's Palace,
220, 228, 229, 230, 235, 290; casualties, 226,
228; at the Citadel, 219, 222, 223–25, 227, 229;
city fortifications, 217–22, 227; El Ríncon del
Diablo, 219, 225, 228; end of, 233–34; Federation Hill, 220, 223–24, 228; Independence Hill,
220, 222, 223, 228, 229; La Tenería garrison,
219, 225, 226, 227, 228; map of, 221; reconnaissance missions, 219–22; Saltillo road and,
209, 220, 222, 230, 234, 235; street resistance,
231

Montesquieu, Baron de, 31

Montezuma, Emperor, 360

Montgomery, Commander John B., 169, 178–79,
181

Montmorelos, 275

Morales, General Juan, 338

Morelos, Jose María, 6

Mormon Battalion, 242–43, 267

Mormons, 153, 155, 242–43, 252

Morse, Samuel F. B., 24, 36

Moss, Captain O. P., 155–56

Napoleon I, 13, 137, 216, 296

Natchez (ship), 47

National Bridge, 361

National Intelligence (newspaper), 71

National Road, 23, 364, 378, 387, 392, 394, 437,
438

Native-American movement, 110

Navajo Indians, 253

Nebraska, 49

Nevada, 74, 76–77

Nevins, Allan, 49

New Hampshire Grants, 30

New Mexico, 95, 101, 162, 163, 190–93, 199–
204, 205, 314, 315, 319, 447; American takeover
of, 199–204, 242, 252; boundary of, 353; Villa's
raid into, 453

New Orleans, Louisiana, 84, 186, 374

New Orleans, Battle of, 264

New Orleans *Delta*, 446

New Orleans *Picayune*, 442

New York *Herald*, 94, 353

New York *Morning Express*, 250

North Platte River, 49

Northwest Territory, 26

Notes on a Journey in America, 454

Nueces River, 43, 61, 71–72, 86, 105, 349–50, 412,
445

Nuevo León, 186, 215

Oberon (opera), 34

O'Brien, Lieutenant John Paul Jones, 301, 303,
305, 312

Ogden, Henry, 152–53

Ogden, Utah, 77

Ojo Caliente, 317

Ordaz, Gustavo Díaz, 454

Oregon, 22, 24, 26, 28, 46, 48, 51, 63, 72, 145;
Columbia River navigation proposal, 64; Frémont and, 145–47, 173, 174; Great Britain and,
28, 41, 43–44, 64–65, 94–95, 110, 117–18, 121,
149, 161, 163, 164; Polk Doctrine on, 94, 95;
termination of joint-occupation treaty, 17

Oregon Trail, 49

Orizaba, 376, 377

Orizaba Peak, 326, 330, 378

Osiris (Plutarch), 33

O'Sullivan, John, 72–73

Pacheco, Francisco, 303, 304

Pacific Squadron (U. S. Navy), 93, 148, 155,
169

Padierna, 398–99, 400

Padierna "Contreras" Battle, 398–99, 400, 403,
406, 407, 409, 431–32, 442, 443

Padre Island, 86

Pakenham, Richard, 64, 65

496

Index

Sierra Nevadas, 75, 77, 78, 79, 81

Slavery, 4, 56, 268, 345–46, 347, 455, 456; cotton economy and, 26; Texas, 13, 20–21

Slidell, John, 69–70, 74, 95–97, 118, 120–21, 162

Sloat, Commodore John D., 45, 93, 148, 169, 173, 180, 181, 182, 242, 267

Smith, Lieutenant Colonel Charles F., 415–16

Smith, General Edmund Kirby, xi, xxiv

Smith, Captain Ephraim Kirby, xi, xxiv–xxv, 28, 105, 125–27, 128, 209, 277; Cerro Gordo battle, 358, 359–60, 362; Churubusco battle, 404, 406, 410; death of, 419, 456; Mexico City campaign, 388–92, 395, 403–4, 406, 410–11, 413, 415–17, 419; Palo Alto battle, 131, 133, 134, 137, 138, 141, 143, 144, 277; at Puebla, 388–91; Saltillo-Monterrey area, 277–78; in Texas, 84, 85, 104, 105–6, 108, 113; Vera Cruz battle, 324–26, 329–31, 335, 336, 339

Smith, Gustavas, 333

Smith, Joseph Lee, xxiv

Smith, General Persifor, 401–2

Social reform movement, 6

Socorro, 253

Somers (ship), 162–63

Sonoma, 172–73, 180, 181, 267; attack on, 172–73, 176–77, 178, 179

Soul of Spain, The (Ellis), 7

Spain, 6, 7, 26, 172

Spanish Peaks, 193

Spinoza, Baruch, 31, 33, 88

Spoils system, 39

Stanton, Edwin, 457

Steen, Captain Enoch, 299

Stephens, Alexander, 448–49

Stockton, Commodore Robert F., 182, 206, 260–70, 272, 382

Strauss, 33

Strongbow, Earl of Pembroke, xxii

Sullivan, Obadiah, 153

Sutter, John, 50, 52, 74, 79, 145, 172, 176, 178, 454–55

Sutter's Fort, 80, 83, 145, 147, 174, 178, 179, 181

Suviah (steamboat), 62, 84

Swedenborg, Emanuel, 274

Tabasco, 274

Tacitus, 31

Tacuba Causeway, 427, 428

Tacubaya, 240, 241

Tacubaya armistice, 410–14

Tamaulipas, 242, 246, 247, 274

Tampico, 58, 163, 242, 246, 274, 277; Mexican garrison at, 241, 244, 283

Tampico-Tamaulipas campaign, 242–47; Taylor's plan for, 246–47

Taney, Roger, 24

Taylor, Zachary, xix–xxv, 117, 186, 206, 208, 324, 325, 332, 346, 350, 355, 368, 373, 375, 452; Agua Nueva withdrawal, 288–89, 295; army promotions, 29–30, 160; Buena Vista battle, 295–313, 314, 316, 327, 335, 351, 372; at Corpus Christi, 83, 85, 87–91, 97, 103, 122; election of,

450; at Fort Jesup, 29, 33–35, 36, 45, 55; at Fort Texas, 110–13; Mexico City occupation, 434–35; Monterrey battle, 209–35; movement to Rio Grande, 91, 97, 103–14; nickname for, 271; occupation of Matamoros, 209–10; Palo Alto battle, 125–44, 160, 161, 205, 271; physical appearance, 29; popularity of, 277; as President, 455–56; Saltillo-Agua Nueva-Buena Vista operations, 283–94, 295; Saltillo-Monterrey area, 271–81; Tamaulipas plan, 246–47; Victoria operation, 275–77, 279; westward move to Texas, 55–62, 83, 87–91, 120, 122

Tecolote, 201

Tehuacán, 436–37

Temperance movement, 6

Tennemann, 33

Texas, 11, 55–62; Anglo-Saxon settlers, 13; annexation controversy, 20–23, 24, 41, 43–45, 47–48, 72, 188; boundary, 61, 119, 122, 349, 353, 412–13, 445; France and, 21, 41, 44, 68; Great Britain and, 21, 22, 41, 44, 68; music festival of 1972, 458; Polk Doctrine on, 94, 95; slavery, 13, 20–21; statehood convention, 55. *See also* Rio Grande

Texas, Republic of, xx, 20, 28, 43, 44, 50, 96, 177, 271, 297, 346, 447

Texas Rangers, 83, 85, 126, 129, 136, 213, 215, 223, 224, 280, 291, 292, 434–39

Thayer, Sylvanus, 3

3rd U. S. Artillery, 299

3rd U. S. Battalion, 356

3rd Indiana Regiment, 299, 301, 307

3rd U. S. Infantry, 30, 57, 58–59, 60, 131

Thirtieth Congress, 441

Thomas, Lieutenant George, 298

Thompson, Waddy, 16

Thoreau, Henry David, 207, 346, 385, 441

Thornton, Captain Seth, 112–13, 114, 122, 397

Timpas, the, 192

Tlacotalpan, 358, 359

Todd, William, 177–78

Topographical Corps (U. S. Army), 47

Torre, Joaquin de la, 179

Torrejón, General Anastasio, 125, 129, 130, 133, 134

Tosta, María Dolores de, 15

Tower, Zealous B., 85

Trist, Nicholas P., 388, 407, 410–12, 431–32, 445–46, 447, 450; appointed peace commissioner, 352–53; feud with Scott, 380–83

Tula, 283

Tuxpán, 358

Tuzamápan (hacienda), 377

Twiggs, Brigadier General David, 57, 83, 86, 88–89, 104, 213; Cerro Gordo battle, 360–66; Mexico City campaign, 391, 392, 394, 399, 402, 410, 421, 423; at Monterrey, 225, 226

Tyler, John, 21, 23, 29, 40, 44, 157

Undine (lighter), 61

United States Constitution, 4, 7, 71, 109, 346

499